COLLECTIBLES

HANDBOOK & PRICE GUIDE

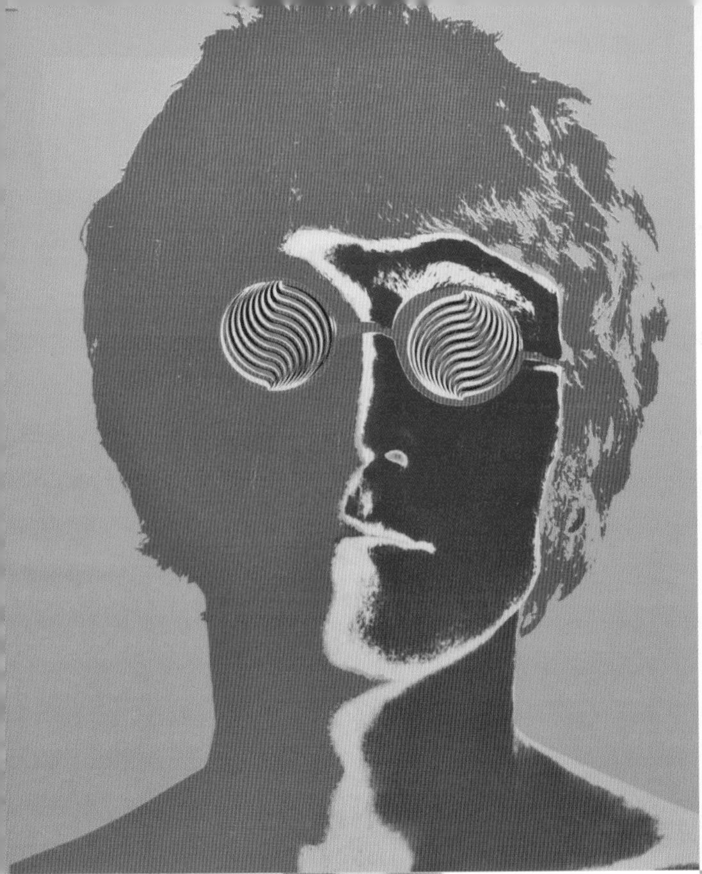

COLLECTIBLES
HANDBOOK & PRICE GUIDE

Judith Miller

MILLER'S

Miller's Collectibles & Antiques Handbook & Price Guide 2021-2022
By Judith Miller

First published in Great Britain in 2021 by Miller's, a division of Mitchell Beazley,
imprints of Octopus Publishing Group Ltd., Carmelite House,
50 Victoria Embankment, London, EC4Y 0DZ
www.octopusbooks.co.uk

An Hachette UK Company
www.hachette.co.uk

Distributed in the USA by Hachette Book Group
1290 Avenue of the Americas, 4th and 5th Floors, New York, NY 10104

Distributed in Canada by Canadian Manda Group
664 Annette St., Toronto, Ontario, Canada, M6S 2C8

ISBN 978 1 78472 670 6

A CIP catalogue record for this book is available from the British Library.

Printed and bound in China

1 3 5 7 9 10 8 6 4 2

Publisher Alison Starling
Editorial Co-ordinator Kathryn Allen
Proofreader John Wainwright
Indexer Hilary Bird
Design Ali Scrivens, TJ Graphics
Assistant Production Controller Serena Savini

Photographs of Judith Miller, by Chris Terry

CONTENTS

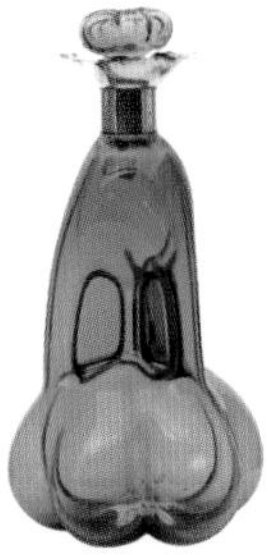

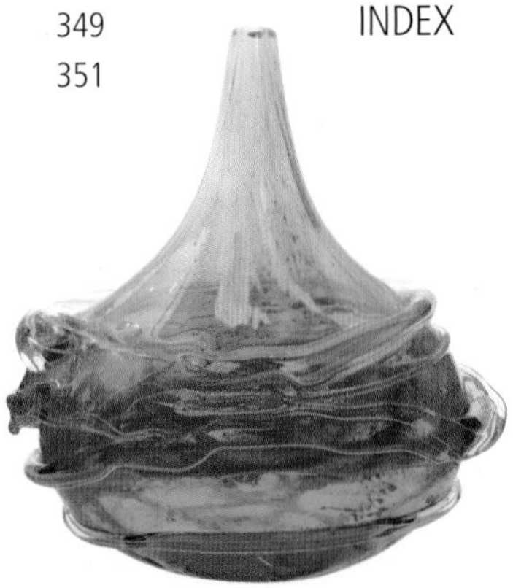

LIST OF CONSULTANTS

CERAMICS

Will Farmer
Fieldings Auctioneers
www.fieldingsauctioneers.co.uk

Wayne Chapman
Lynways
www.lynways.com

Michael G. Lines
John Newton Antiques
www.johnnewtonantiques.com

David Rago
Rago Arts, USA
www.ragoarts.com

COSTUME JEWELRY

Gemma Redmond
www.gemmaredmondvintage.co.uk

FASHION

Sophie Higgs
Fellows Auctioneers
www.fellows.co.uk

GLASS

Will Farmer
Fieldings Auctioneers
www.fieldingsauctioneers.co.uk

Mike & Debby Moir
M&D Moir, www.manddmoir.co.uk

Wayne Chapman
Lynways, www.lynways.com

SPORTING

Graham Budd
Graham Budd Auctions
www.grahambuddauctions.co.uk

We'd also like to thank our friends and colleagues who have helped and supported us in many ways with this book including: Laura Dove from Adam Partridge, James Street from Aldridges of Bath, Keith Butler from Arthur Johnson & Sons, Karolina Wegrzyn from Aston's, Ian Jackson from Bearnes Hampton & Littlewood, Amelia Randle from Bellmans, Sarah Jones from Brightwells, Caroline Hodges from Boldon Auction Galleries, Jackie from British Toy Auctions, David Parker from The Canterbury Auction Galleries, Sarah Flynn from Cheffins, Sarah Beer from Chorley's, Glen Chapman from C&T, Mark Hill and Aubrey Dawson from Dawson's, Lynn Strover from Duke's, Andrew Ewbank from Ewbank's, Alexandra Whittaker and Liam Bolland from Fellows, June Emery from Fieldings, Kevin Mullins from Fonsie Mealy, Andrew Lubas from Freeman's, Mark Gilding from Gildings, Michael Duce from Graham Budd, Simon Turner from G.W. Railwayana Auctions, Jill Gallone from Hansons, Emma from Hartleys, Emilie Ferraud from Ivoire France, Tom Warren and James Welch from John Nicholson's, Geoff Shepherd from Kingham & Orme, Helen Robson and Rachel Coomber from Lacy Scott & Knight, Rachael Salter from Lawrences, Michal Kosakowski from Leitz Photographica Auction, Chris Elmy from Lockdales, Sally Ellis from Locke & England, Cathy Marsden and Alex Dove from Lyon & Turnbull, Andy Ebbage from M&M Auctions, Nigel Kirk from Mellors & Kirk, Sarah Stoltzfus from Morphy Auctions, Deirdre Pook Magarelli from Pook & Pook, Kathy from Potteries Auctions, Anthony Barnes from Rago Arts, Peigi Mackillop from Roseberys, Hugo Marsh from SAS, Kelsie Jankowski from Swann Galleries, Diane Baynes from Sworders, Chris Markwick from Tayler & Fletcher, Max Sobolevskij from Tennants, Travis Hammond from Theriaults, Louise Harker at Vectis, Tim Brophy from W&H Peacock, John Macdonald from Waddington's, James from Wallis and Wallis, and Clare Durham from Woolley & Wallis.

HOW TO USE THIS BOOK

The object The collectibles are shown in full color. This is a vital aid to identification and valuation. With many objects, a slight color variation can signify a large price differential.

Source code Every item has been specially photographed at an auction house, a dealer, an antiques market, or a private collection. These are credited by a code at the end of each caption, and can be checked against the Key to Illustrations (see p. 418).

Quick reference Gives key facts about the factory, maker, or style, along with stylistic identification points, value tips, and advice on fakes.

The price guide These price ranges give a ballpark figure for what you should pay for a similar item. The great joy of collectibles is that there is not a recommended retail price. The price ranges in this book are based on actual prices, either what a dealer will take or the full auction price.

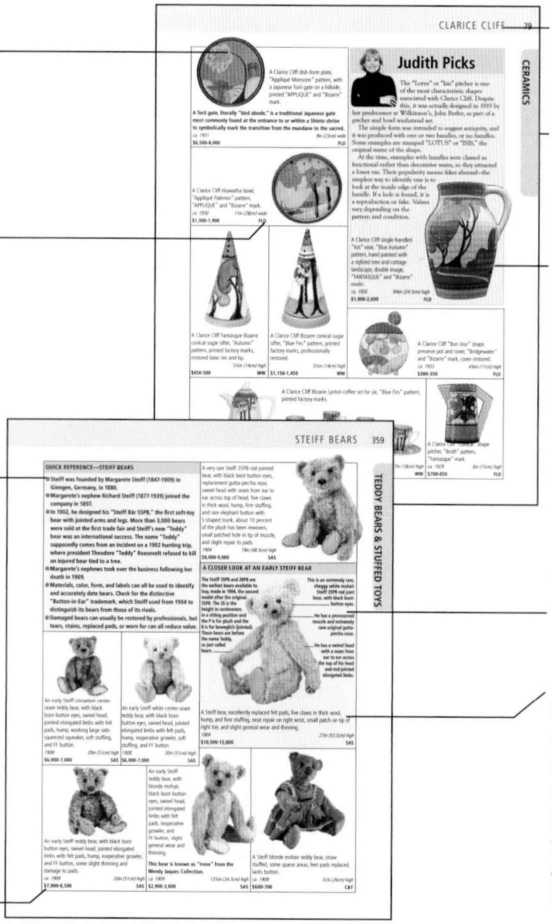

Subcategory heading Indicates the subcategory of the main heading.

Page tab This appears on every page and identifies the main category heading as identified in the Table of Contents on pages 5-6.

Judith Picks Items chosen specifically by Judith, either because they are important or interesting, or they might be a good investment.

Closer Look Does exactly that. Here, we show identifying aspects of a factory or maker, point out rare colors or shapes, and explain why a particular piece is so desirable.

Caption The description of the item illustrated, including when relevant, the period, the maker or factory, medium, the year it was made, dimensions, and condition. Many captions have **footnotes** that explain terminology or give identification or valuation information.

INTRODUCTION

Welcome to the new *Miller's Collectibles & Antiques Handbook & Price Guide*, in which I am proud to present more than 4,000 completely new, specially selected photographed collectibles. Representative of the domestic and international market, they range from advertising to automobilia, ceramics to clocks, glass to guitars, metalware to militaria, paperweights to posters, teddy bears to tribal art. All collecting fields, tastes, and passions are catered for.

Preceded by a table of contents, and a user-friendly explanation of how to use this book, every collectible depicted has a descriptive caption and a price guide. Many are also accompanied by detailed footnotes that highlight interesting aspects of the item.

You will also find additional information in the "Closer Look" and "Judith Picks" features, as well as in the "Quick Reference" boxes, which provide helpful introductions to particular collecting areas, designers, or makers. At the back of the book, the practical aspects of collecting—buying and selling—are supported by directories of auction houses, specialists, fairs, and societies.

A Royal Copenhagen tiger and two cubs, printed backstamp, numbered "4687" verso. 6in (15cm) high $650-800 LSK

So, what has happened to the collectibles market since our last guide? As always, some areas have strengthened, some have weakened. Ceramics have continued to be a particularly popular area. Clarice Cliff remains desirable, particularly rare patterns and interesting shapes. Lladró, Lenci, Royal Copenhagen, and Moorcroft continue to have devoted followers. One area that reflects the whole market is Doulton. The 19thC Doulton Lambeth stoneware has had a quiet time, except for pieces by George Tinworth, whose charming mice and frogs have continued to fetch record prices. The figurines and character pitchers have to be early and rare to get top prices. Flambé animals continue to excite collectors.

A Kosta "Winter" glass vase, by Vicke Lindstrand, engraved signature "Kosta LH." 1950s 7¼in (18.5cm) high $6,000-7,000 FLD

A suffragette postcard, by Millar & Lang, reading "SUFFRAGETTES ATTACKING THE HOUSE OF COMMONS." $80-90 LOCK

Nostalgia underpins many developments in the collectibles market. For example, on the BBC's *Antiques Roadshow*, we see a large number of postcards, many in elaborate albums. The majority are worth, at most, a few dollars. However, as you can see in this guide, early photographic representations of village stores and rare images of railroad stations are as much in demand as liners and soccer teams and, as always, Louis Wain. In this edition we also have included some suffragette postcards. Of course, one generation's nostalgia isn't necessarily another's: Clockwork and Tinplate can be replaced with Dinky and Corgi. In these areas, condition is vital; collectors aim to buy mint examples.

A near-mint Dinky Toys "VOLKSWAGEN KARMANN GHIA COUPE," no.187, in original panel box. $100-120 LSK

There is also the influence of changing aesthetics. What once appeared fresh and pleasing to the eye gradually diminishes, and is replaced by a different look. Ultimately, this is a matter of fashion and explains why, for example, the naturalistic form and decoration of Victorian ceramics and glass is generally fetching lower prices, while more geometric or abstract Art Deco and Mid-Century Modern equivalents, especially Scandinavian and Murano glass, are forging ahead. Meanwhile, 18thC blue-and-white porcelain is growing increasingly affordable, with many pieces now sold at auction in "job lots."

Of course, at some point these trends may reverse. Predicting that tipping point is far from an exact science. I am often asked what people should buy as an investment. My answer is absolutely nothing! Do some research, look in books, go to fairs, auctions, and museums. Find an area you like and start collecting. Buy something that you love. My advice is: If you see something you can nearly afford—buy it. You will only regret it if you don't. Happy collecting!

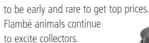

A Clarice Cliff Fantasque Bizarre 365 vase, "House and Bridge" pattern, printed factory mark. 7in (20cm) high $2,300-2,900 WW

Judith Miller

ANTIQUES ARE GREEN

QUICK REFERENCE—ADVERTISING

- **Most of the advertising memorabilia available to collectors today dates from the 20thC.**
- **In general, collectors tend to focus either on a particular kind of advertising item, such as enamel signs or posters, or a particular brand or range of products. Food and drink advertising remains popular, as does tobacco advertising. Signs in mint condition tend to fetch the highest prices.**
- **The advertising collectibles market is driven by a combination of nostalgia and availability. The brands that collectors know well, such as Cadbury's Chocolate and Colman's Mustard, are often popular, as are large brands, such as Coca Cola, Shell, and Michelin, which have produced a huge range of advertising items over a long period of time.**
- **Items that clearly represent a subject area, artistic movement, or time period are also highly collectible, whether from a well-known brand or not. Art Deco advertising items are very popular. "Vintage" 1950s-60s pieces have increased in popularity over the past decade. A design by a major artist will also increase an item's value.**
- **While good condition does increase value, advertising items have often been used over many years, sometimes in outdoor settings, so condition should be consistent with age and use. Reproductions are common in this market, so examine items especially carefully.**

A vintage Allied Breweries Ltd. framed advertising mirror, "DOUBLE DIAMOND BEER."

34in (86.5cm) wide

$90-100 PSA

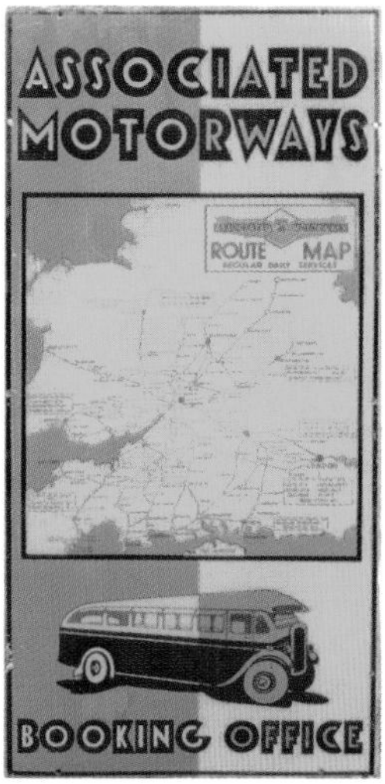

A single-sided enamel sign, "ASSOCIATED MOTORWAYS BOOKING OFFICE," with map showing England and Wales.

34¾in (88.5cm) high

$1,150-1,450 FLD

A Bates cardboard advertising store display sign, "Bates SUPER RUBBER CORD TYRES," slight damage.

1930s *31¼in (79.5cm) high*

$700-850 FLD

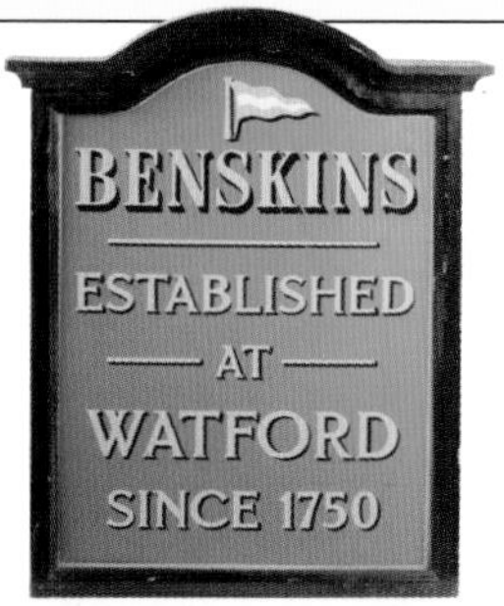

An enamel advertising sign, "BENSKINS ESTABLISHED AT WATFORD SINCE 1750," in a cast iron frame.

17in (43cm) high

$300-400 LOCK

A 19thC C.H.Flooks two-sheet watchmaker's advertising poster, "C.H.FLOOKS 49, PONTMORLAIS CIRCUS, MERTHYR."

59¾in (152cm) high

$260-320 SWO

A Carter pictorial tile advertising panel, "SPORTS BOOKS."

22in (56cm) high

$2,600-3,200 CHOR

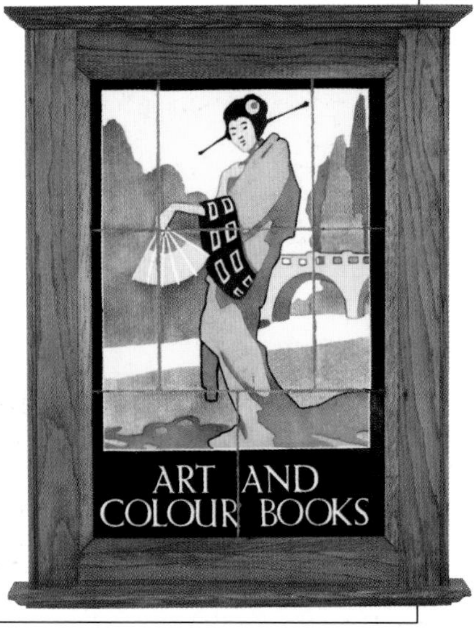

A Carter pictorial tile advertising panel, "ART AND COLOUR BOOKS," slight stain on one of the tiles, grouting missing in places, and the letter "R" in the word "COLOUR" may have been regrouted.

22in (56cm) high

$2,600-3,200 CHOR

ADVERTISING

QUICK REFERENCE—CARTER

- **In 1873, Jesse Carter, a builder and hardware dealer, bought James Walker's struggling pottery near Poole harbor, forming Carter's Industrial Tile Manufactory. The company was then renamed Carter & Co.**
- **Carter & Co. became known for its advertising panels and mosaic flooring, supplying breweries, hospitals, retailers, and schools with glazed decorative and painted tiles. In 1895, Carter purchased the Architectural Pottery in Hamworthy. When Carter retired in 1901, his sons, Charles and Owen, took over the business. In 1921, a subsidiary company, Carter Stabler and Adams, was set up by Charles Carter's son Cyril, silversmith Harold Stabler, and potter John Adams, focusing on decorative pottery and tableware. In the 1920s, Carter & Co. created a series of tile advertising panels for WHSmith stores.**
- **Pilkington Tiles Ltd. bought Carter & Co., along with its subsidiary, in 1964, creating Poole Pottery Ltd.**

A Carter pictorial tile advertising panel, "TRAVEL BOOKS," damaged.

22in (56cm) high

$2,600-3,200 **CHOR**

A French early- to mid-20thC "CHOCOLAT RÉVILLON" tolework advertising clock, in an oeil-de-boeuf or bull's-eye shape, with original brass windup pendulum movement.

23¼in (59cm) high

$850-950 **SWO**

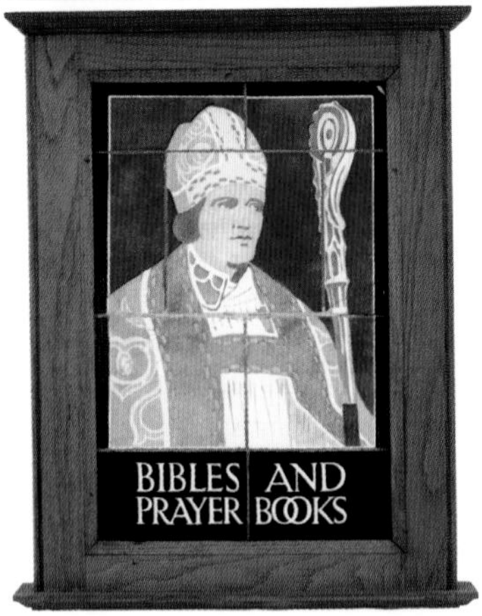

A Carter pictorial tile advertising panel "BIBLES AND PRAYER BOOKS."

22in (56cm) high

$1,250-1,450 **CHOR**

A "CHURCHMAN'S No2" cigarette card advertising sign, "The Cigarette with a pedigree."

26¾in (68cm) high

$160-230 **LOCK**

A Carter textual tile advertising panel for newspaper and periodical deliveries.

25in (63.5cm) high

$1,800-2,300 **CHOR**

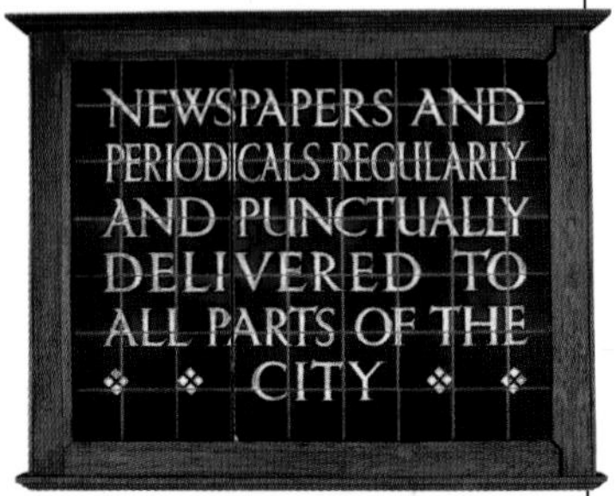

A large "COLEMAN'S D.S.F MUSTARD" enamel sign.

38¼in (97cm) wide

$260-320 **FLD**

A large ceramic model of the Dulux dog.

13in (33cm) high

$130-190 **LOC**

A vintage framed "Dewar's SPECIAL WHISKIES" advertising mirror.

36¼in (92cm) high

$50-80 **PSA**

A "DUNLOP" cardboard advertising store display sign, slight damage.
1930s *30in (76cm) high*
$800-900 **FLD**

A Fry's store display figure of a boy holding a large block of Fry's Chocolate, on a plinth with "JOLLY GOOD! -and a lot for the money," some retouching, wear/flaws.
38½in (98cm) high
$5,200-6,500 **BBR**

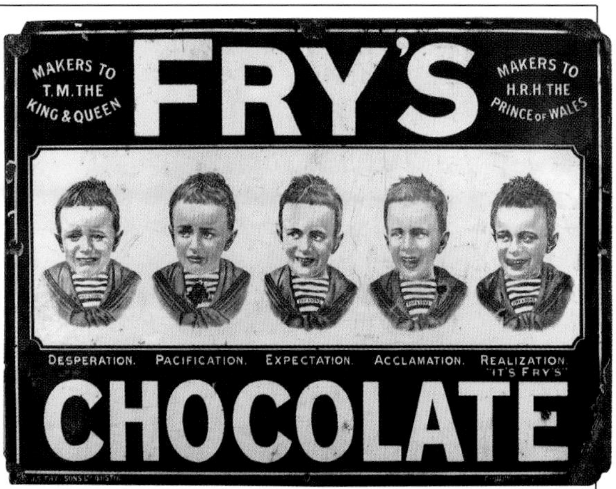

A "FRY'S CHOCOLATE" pictorial enamel sign, by Chromo, with five different expressions on a boy's face, areas of damage and rust.
30in (76cm) wide
$1,800-2,600 **CHEF**

A vintage Holt, Plant & Deakin framed advertising mirror, "HOLT PLANT & DEAKIN LTD HOLTS TRADITIONAL ALES."
38¼in (97cm) wide
$300-350 **PSA**

An early-20thC Edwardian oak fishing tackle display cabinet, with later gilt lettering.
37¾in (96cm) wide
$3,900-4,500 **L&T**

A Hudson's pictorial enamel sign, "A Pail of Water WITH A VERY LITTLE HUDSON'S GOES A VERY LONG WAY," restored.
13in (33cm) high
$190-260 **FLD**

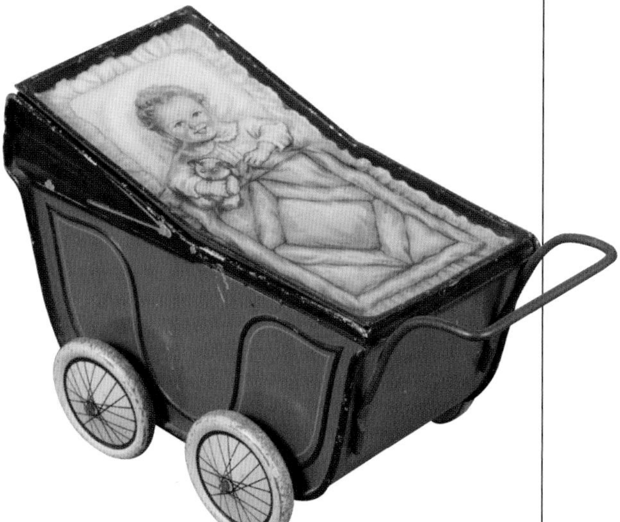

A Huntley & Palmers cookie jar, probably produced by Huntley, Boorne, and Stevens, in lithographed tinplate.
ca. 1930 *8¼in (21cm) long*
$2,600-3,200 **CHEF**

A Hudson's Soap enamel advertising sign, "FOR THE PEOPLE HUDSON'S SOAP," worn.
7in (17.5cm) high
$210-260 **LOCK**

An enamel advertising sign, "JOHN BULL—THE LONG SERVICE TYRE."

48in (122cm) wide

$450-500 **FLD**

An enamel advertising sign, "JOULES STONE ALES," wear on edges.

1920s *22in (56cm) high*

$260-320 **PSA**

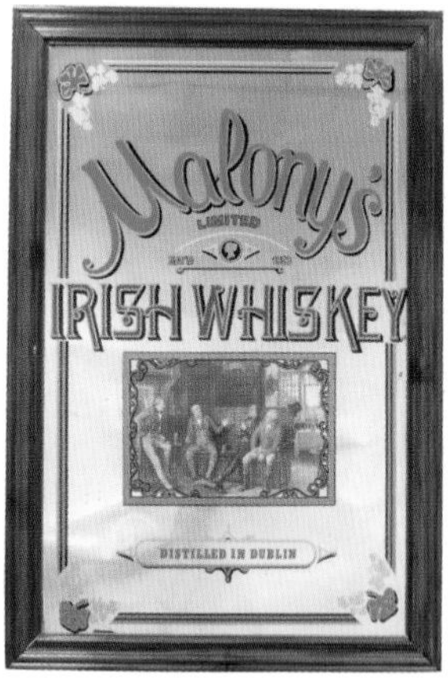

A vintage framed Malony's advertising mirror, "MALONY'S IRISH WHISKEY."

37¾in (96cm) high

$70-80 **PSA**

A French "MATHIS" automobile enamel sign, some damage.

27½in (70cm) diam

$260-320 **BELL**

An enameled "NECTAR TEA" advertising sign, further stamped "Patent Enamel Co. Ltd. B'ham & London."

21in (53.5cm) wide

$300-350 **APAR**

An American mid-20thC carved and painted Northern Pike fish trade sign.

55in (139.5cm) long

$1,900-2,600 **POOK**

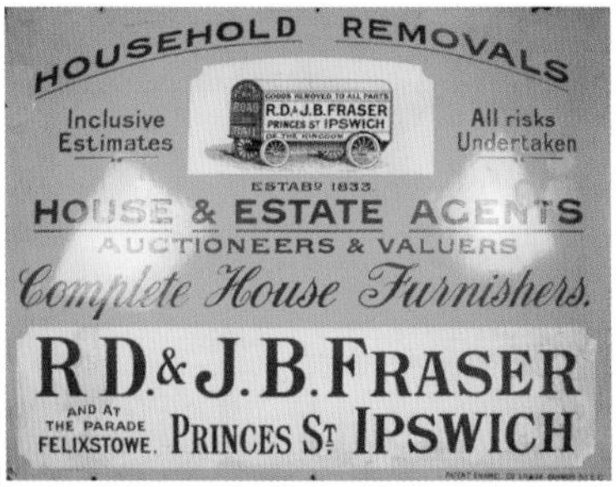

An early- to mid-20thC enamel advertising sign, "HOUSE & ESTATE AGENTS AUCTIONEERS & VALUERS RD. & J.B. FRASER," made by Patent Enamel Co., Ltd., some restoration.

30in (76cm) high

$500-650 **LOCK**

A "Rowntree's ELECT Cocoa" cardboard show card.

19in (48.5cm) high

$160-230 **FLD**

A vintage advertising mirror, "THE SHAMROCK WHISKY DUBLIN."

39in (99cm) high

$190-260 **PSA**

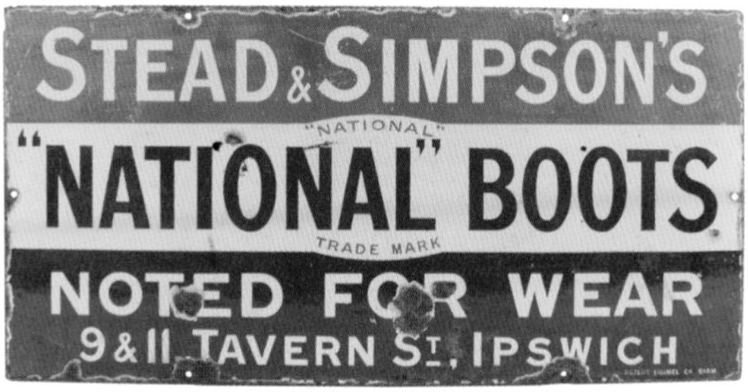

A "STEAD & SIMPSON'S" enamel advertising sign, "'NATIONAL' BOOTS NOTED FOR WEAR."

12in (30.5cm) high

$260-320 **LOCK**

A double-sided enamel WHSmith advertising sign, "The Newsboy," framed and with hanging chain.

44½in (113cm) high

$1,300-1,900 **CHOR**

A WHSmith enamel advertising sign, "MAKERS W. H. SMITH & Co. LTD. WHITCHURCH."

14¼in (36cm) high

$60-80 **LOCK**

An Art Deco shipping line advertising wall calendar, "CIE DE NAVIGATION PAQUET," by J. Tonelli, perpetual day, date, and month window with levers on side, mounted on a wooden board.

19in (48.5cm) high

$600-700 **DUK**

A George V "THE TELEPHONE" cardboard advertising sign, with further motto "A SPEAKING INVESTMENT."

14¾in (37.5cm) high

$260-320 **APAR**

A painted metal "MICHELIN" Man advertising figure.

6in (15cm) high

$60-80 **LOCK**

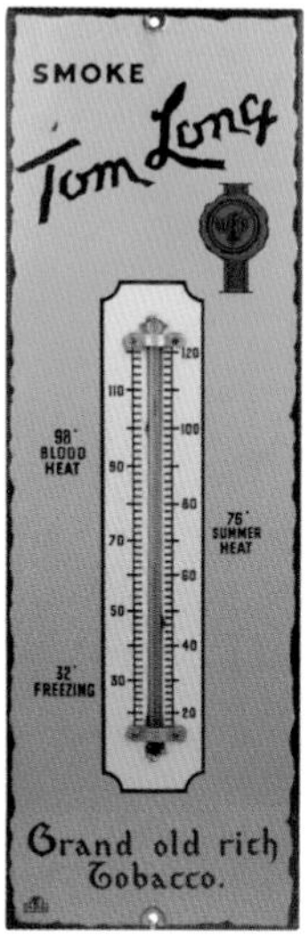

An advertising thermometer, "SMOKE Tom Long Grand old rich Tobacco."

22¾in (58cm) high

$260-320 **LOCK**

QUICK REFERENCE—ANTIQUITIES

- **Antiquities are items belonging to ancient civilizations predating the Middle Ages, such as the ancient Greeks, the Romans, and the ancient Egyptians.**
- **The earliest glass objects discovered date from ca. 2500 BC. In the 1stC BC, glassblowing was invented, with the glassblowing furnace invented in AD 1. Prior to this, glass vessels were usually opaque, due to air bubbles and impurities in the material being common.**
- **Many Roman glass vessels were buried underground in the intervening centuries since their production, with the exposure to sand, soil, heat, and minerals causing iridescence—the rainbow effect often seen on the vessels' surfaces.**

An ancient Roman medical glass flask.
AD 100 *3¾in (9.5cm) high*
$80-100 **LOCK**

A Roman marble-effect glass cup, with finger rim on body.
AD 2ndC-4thC *2¾in (7cm) diam*
$500-560 **FLD**

A Roman glass bowl, with traces of iridescence and internal center-line band.
AD 2ndC-4thC *5in (12.5cm) wide*
$450-500 **FLD**

A Roman amber glass beaker, some damage.
AD 2ndC-4thC *3in (7.5cm) high*
$130-180 **FLD**

A Roman iridescent glass beaker, with slashed ribs on the base.
AD 2ndC-3rdC *2¾in (7cm) high*
$400-500 **FLD**

A Roman glass bowl, with ribbed body and applied lattice decoration, slight damage.
AD 2ndC-4thC *3in (7.5cm) high*
$500-650 **FLD**

A Roman miniature cobalt blue glass flask, decorated with white beehive-style bands.
AD 2ndC-4thC *1½in (4cm) high*
$400-450 **FLD**

A Roman miniature glass flask.
AD 2ndC-4thC *2½in (6.5cm) high*
$450-500 **FLD**

A Roman iridescent deep amber glass pitcher, with applied clear ribbed handle.
AD 2ndC-4thC *5¼in (13.5cm) high*
$700-850 **FLD**

A Roman miniature glass pitcher, with yellow zigzag bands of decoration on the shoulder.
AD 2ndC-4thC *3in (7.5cm) high*
$1,250-1,450 **FLD**

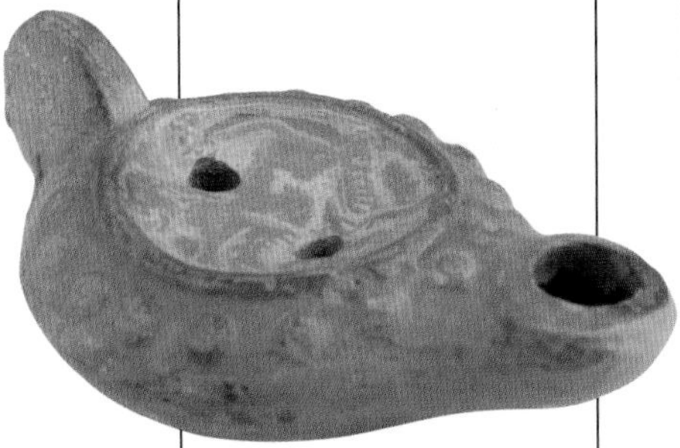

An Ancient Roman terracotta oil lamp, depicitng a lion.
C AD 200
$260-320 **LOCK**

A Roman gold ring, the band consisting of four braided wires, set with a jasper intaglio engraved with a reclining figure, possibly a Genius or personification of a river.
AD 1stC-4thC *0.12 oz*
$1,300-1,800 **HAN**

A Roman olive glass pendant, impressed with a standing lion and glass bangle.
AD 2ndC-4thC *2½in (6.5cm) diam*
$100-120 **FLD**

A Roman string of glass beads.
AD 2ndC-4thC *16¼in (41.5cm) long*
$170-260 **FLD**

A Roman string of speckle millefiori colored glass beads.
AD 2ndC-4thC *9¼in (23.5cm) long*
$160-210 **FLD**

A Roman string of lapis lazuli blue beads, with a spiral lentoid section.
AD 2ndC-4thC *9½in (24cm) long*
$120-140 **FLD**

A Roman string of iridescent and lunar drop beads, with interspaced blue stones and centered fantail pendant.
AD 2ndC-4thC *17¼in (44cm) long*
$500-650 **FLD**

An Allwins oak-cased "24 WINNINGS CUPS" amusement machine, one penny operation.

35in (89cm) high

$650-800 **FLD**

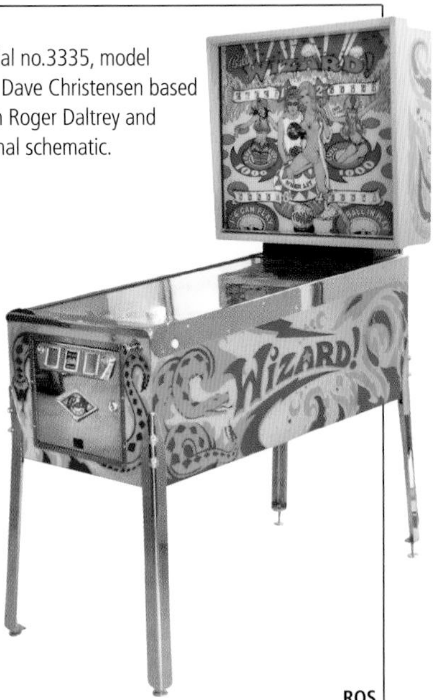

An electromechanical "WIZARD!" pinball machine, serial no.3335, model no.1027, by Bally, designed by Greg Kmiec, artwork by Dave Christensen based on the Ken Russell film *Tommy*, original back glass with Roger Daltrey and Ann-Margret pictured, cabinet and playfield, with original schematic.

The WIZARD! was Bally's first megahit pinball machine, breaking the 10,000 production mark; 10,005 units were built; 5 units were distributed to the 5 top executives of Bally with the 10,005th going to Tom Neymens, Head of Sales. The artwork was franchised from the film *Tommy*, a rock musical fantasy based on The Who's 1969 rock opera about a "seemingly disabled" boy who becomes a pinball champion. It had an important impact on pinball games because it was the first machine to successfully use a popular theme. Nearly every arcade had a WIZARD! and most were placed near the door to attract players. This pinball machine was sold with a six-month warranty for parts and labor for mainland UK buyers, with one free call-out visit.

1975

$5,200-6,500 **ROS**

A Bryans "ELEVENSES FOUR-SQUARE" penny arcade game, the top section with four coin-operated games, mounted on a later square base with cigarette holders on the corners and sides painted with "FUN FAIR" and "2p A Go!."

1930s *30in (76cm) wide*

$3,200-4,500 **L&T**

A "Championnat" soccer table, each team with 11 wooden soccer players, controlled by four rods per team, the oak table with coin-operated mechanism, four corner chrome mounted ashtrays, with abacus-style scoring system.

$3,200-3,900 **DUK**

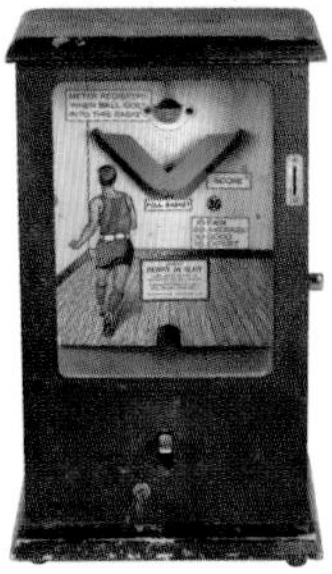

A painted iron penny tabletop basketball trade stimulator, PEO Mfg. Corp., with original paper, from the William Seibt Confectionary Store in St. Louis, Missouri, has the door key, no basketballs, some wear.

ca. 1930 *14½in (37cm) high*

$600-700 **POOK**

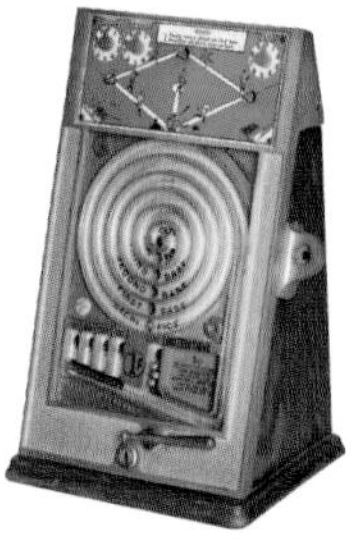

A miniature "BASEBALL WORLD CHAMPION" penny tabletop trade stimulator, PEO Mfg. Corp., with nickel front panel, upper painted panel with pop-up runners, from the William Seibt Confectionary Store in St. Louis, Missouri, has door key.

ca. 1930 *17in (43cm) high*

$900-1,150 **POOK**

A Santa Claus fairground ball game, with bust of Santa Claus with open mouth above the playing area, with painted numbers and instructions, on a painted wooden base.

30in (76cm) high

$500-650 **DUK**

A Jennings Nevada Club 25-cent light-up slot machine.

60½in (153.5cm) high

$1,700-2,100 **POOK**

A Chinese Wanli-period, blue-and-white shipwreck porcelain "Peacock" dish.

Produced from the Wanli period (1573-1619), "Kraak" is the Dutch term for Chinese blue-and-white wares named after the Portuguese ships called "carracks," which were used to export the ware from China.

10¾in (27.5cm) diam

$130-180 JN

A Chinese early-19thC export blue-and-white meat plate, slight damage.

10in (25.5cm) long

$80-90 FLD

QUICK REFERENCE—CHINESE BLUE-AND-WHITE CERAMICS

- **Dating from the Tang dynasty, the use of blue underglaze decoration in China became increasingly important in the late 13thC and 14thC.**
- **During the late 14thC, Ming Emperor Hongwu imposed a trade embargo, reducing the availability of foreign cobalt. Copper oxide, which fires red, was used more widely.**
- **Imported cobalt became widely available again during the early 15thC. Cobalt imported from Persia produced a darker blue than locally sourced ores.**
- **Blue-and-white wares in the 19th and 20thC often imitated that of the Ming dynasty, with precisely spaced decoration.**

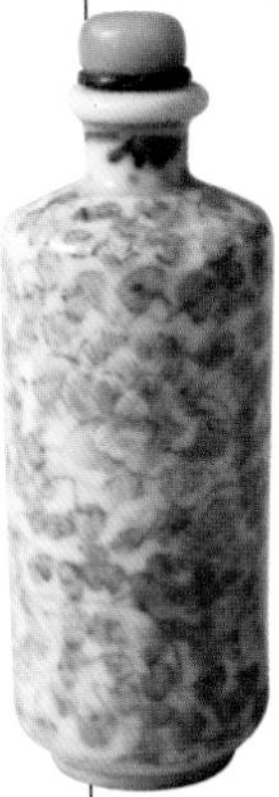

A Chinese 19thC blue-and-white porcelain snuff bottle, with a hard stone/jadeite stopper and ivory spoon, the base with a four character Yongzheng mark.

3¼in (8.5cm) high

$230-290 JN

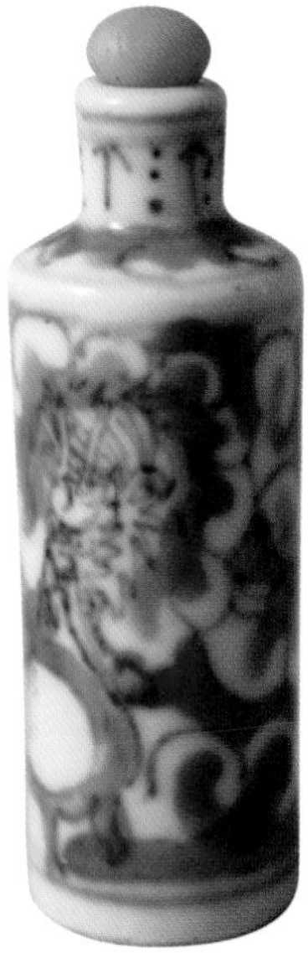

A Chinese 19thC blue-and-white porcelain snuff bottle.

3¼in (8.5cm) high

$100-130 JN

A Chinese early-19thC porcelain platter, small chip on top left edge.

14¾in (37.5cm) wide

$120-160 PSA

A Chinese 19thC blue-and-white underglaze-red porcelain snuff bottle, depicting the scene of a five claw dragon, the base with a six-character Qianlong mark.

3¼in (8.5cm) high

$300-400 JN

A Chinese 19thC landscape-decorated plate, four-character mark on base, nip on outer rim.

16in (40.5cm) diam

$300-350 PSA

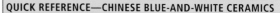

A Chinese Tongzhi-period (1862-74) bowl, painted with scrolling lotus above false gadroon borders, six-character Tongzhi mark.

1862-74 *6¼in (16cm) diam*

$2,600-3,200 SWO

A Chinese 19thC vase, painted with vignettes depicting figures, double ring mark on base, and bearing old paper label "No.149/10," riveted repair and cracks, small chip on foot rim.

13in (33cm) high

$850-950 **APAR**

A Chinese 19thC blue-and-white "Rouleau" porcelain vase, the base with a four-character Kangxi mark.

4¾in (12cm) high

$260-320 **JN**

A Chinese 19thC blue-and-white tea caddy, decorated with landscape scenes.

4½in (11.5cm) high

$60-80 **JN**

A Chinese perhaps 19thC or Republican "Bats and Peaches" saucer dish, Yongzheng six-character mark within double circle, the exterior with pairs of bats each incorporating a shou medallion.

The Republican period covers ca. 1911–1949, when the Republic of China was a sovereign country. The Republic of China formed following the Xinhai Revolution, which overthrew the Qing dynasty.

8½in (21.5cm) diam

$3,200-3,900 **DN**

A Chinese 19thC blue-and-white prunus porcelain spill vase.

4¾in (12cm) high

$25-40 **JN**

A Chinese early-20thC blue-and-white porcelain bottle vase, with decoration of a dragon, with a Ruyi-style border, the base with a double blue ring.

8¼in (21cm) high

$180-230 **JN**

A set of four Chinese early-20thC blue-and-white porcelain-framed panels, depicting landscape scenes, the frames with handles and carved-and-pierced panels of bats.

30¾in (78cm) high

$450-500 **JN**

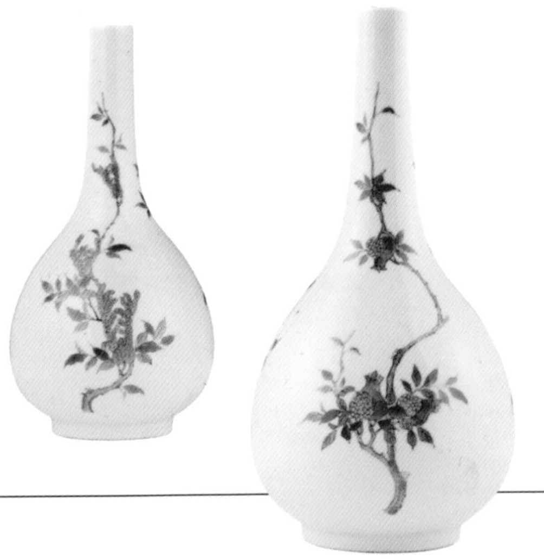

A pair of Chinese Republican-period (1911-49) vases, with fruiting and flowering sprays of the "Three Abundances"—pomegranate, fingered citron, and peach—the base with a six-character Qianlong seal mark.

9¼in (23.5cm) high

$2,900-3,600 **L&T**

A Chinese late-20thC decorative Yen Yen vase, unmarked.

15½in(39.5cm) high

$60-80 **APAR**

QUICK REFERENCE—FAMILLE ROSE

- **Created in the 18thC, famille rose ware typically features flowers, foliage, figures, and symbols in shades of pink and carmine. Painters blended and shaped colors using opaque yellow and white. Gold was often use for embellishments. The colors were seen as foreign in China, where they were introduced from Europe in the 17thC.**
- **Famille rose was popular among wealthy Europeans, with large numbers of dinner services exported to Europe. This palette was copied by European factories, including Meissen and Chelsea.**
- **Famille verte ware, characterized by green, iron red, blue, purple, and yellow, was produced during the Kangxi period (1661-1722). The use of a yellow ground with this palette is called famille jaune, while the use of a green-black ground is called famille noire.**

A famille rose snuff bottle, painted with military figures by the gate of a fortified city, four-character Xianfeng iron red seal mark.

1851-61 *3in (7.5cm) high*

$800-900 **L&T**

A Chinese famille rose box and cover, six-character Tongzhi mark, the interior divided into six compartments.

ca. 1862-74

$950-1,100 **WW**

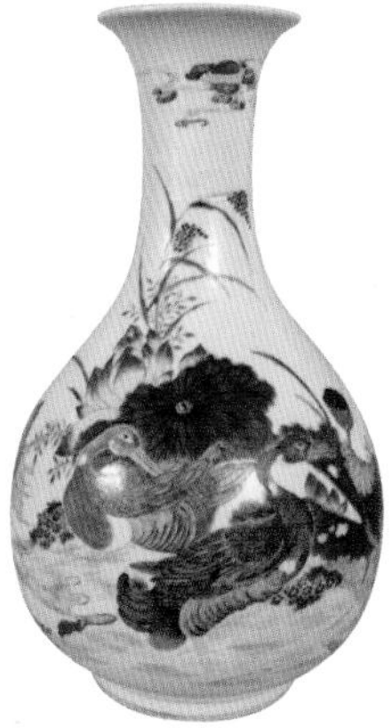

A Chinese 19thC famille rose porcelain bottle vase, painted with ducks in a lotus pond, the neck interior and base turquoise.

13in (33cm) high

$500-650 **JN**

A Chinese 19thC famille rose jardinière and stand, with Canton enameling.

7in (18cm) high

$600-650 **TRI**

A Chinese 19thC famille rose ginger jar and lid, decorated with cartouches of birds.

9in (23cm) high

$500-600 **TRI**

A pair of Chinese 19thC porcelain famille rose baluster vases.

7½in (19cm) high

$800-900 **WW**

A Chinese 19thC Canton famille rose porcelain vase/lamp, lamp fittings in the interior.

21in (53.5cm) high

$450-500 **JN**

A Chinese 19thC celadon famille rose porcelain bowl, the base with an iron-red four-character mark.

8¼in (21cm) diam

$230-290 **JN**

A Chinese 19thC famille rose porcelain bowl, with decoration of Chinese symbols, the base with a blue stylized seal mark.

8in (20.5cm) diam

$80-90 **JN**

A Chinese late-19thC famille rose pedestal dish, exterior sides painted with six immortal gods.

2¾in (7cm) high

$230-290 **FLD**

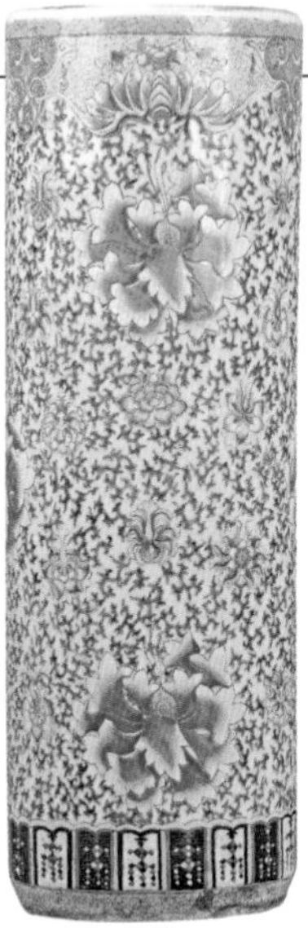

A Chinese famille rose stick stand.

ca. 1900 *26in (66cm) high*

$650-800 **BELL**

A Chinese 20thC famille rose porcelain figurine, modeled as a standing official, seal marks.

15½in (39.5cm) high

$650-800 **DUK**

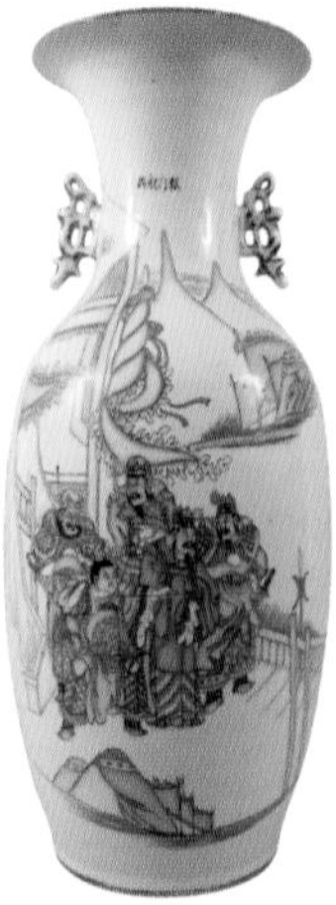

A Chinese 20thC famille rose large porcelain vase, the verso with Chinese calligraphy.

22½in (57cm) high

$180-230 **JN**

A Chinese early-20thC famille rose footed diamond-shaped dish, decorated with panels with alternate figures and sprays of flowers.

14¼in (36cm) long

$400-450 **FLD**

A Chinese Republic-period famille rose vase, iron-red four-character Shen De Tang zhi (made for the Hall of Prudent virtue) mark on base, there is a shallow indentation to one side, done at time of manufacture, which has been painted over with a pomegranate.

16in (40.5cm) high

$1,700-2,100 **BELL**

A Chinese Republican-style famille rose porcelain panel/tile, the upper right section with Chinese calligraphy/poem and seal.

12½in (32cm) high

$500-650 **JN**

A Chinese 19thC famille noire vase, the base with a scroll mark.

19¾in (50cm) high

$650-800 **WW**

A Chinese early 19thC celadon vase, with lying dog decoration on handles, some damage, hairline crack on the body.

First used during the Song dynasty, celadon is a semi-opaque, green-tinted glaze. Between ca. 960-1126, celadon produced in northern China had a thin olive-green glaze, while the later southern celadon had a thicker, cooler green glaze.

24¾in (63cm) high

$450-600 PSA

A Chinese 19thC vase, with blue-and-yellow glazed ground with applied relief details depicting vases, other ceramic wares, insects, and flowers, handles missing, major crack on neck.

22¾in (58cm) high

$230-290 FELL

A Chinese 19thC double-bodied vase, with floral and dragon decoration, Chien Lung square mark on the base, on stand.

13in (33cm) high

$300-350 PSA

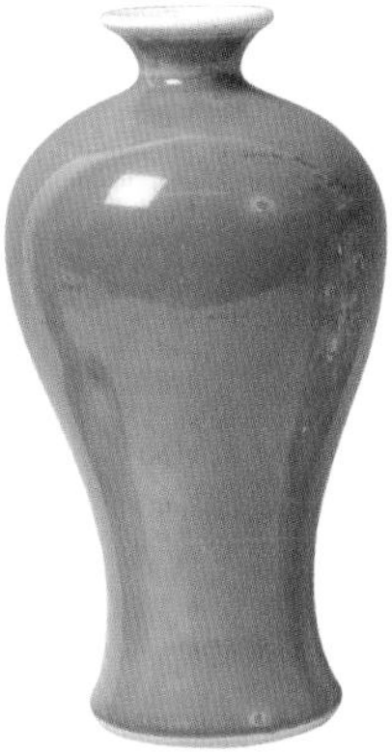

A Chinese 19thC sang-de-boeuf stoneware vase.

Chinese porcelain of the 19thC included Ming-style blue-and-white wares and monochromes. Most export, imperial, and domestic porcelain of the 19thC and 20thC was given reign marks.

11in (28cm) high

$850-950 LSK

A Chinese claire-de-lune porcelain dragon vase, with high-relief molded dragons, the base with a six-character mark.

21½in (54.5cm) high

$950-1,100 JN

A Chinese 20thC sang-de-boeuf Fanghu porcelain vase, with streaked glaze.

10in (25.5cm) high

$400-450 JN

A Chinese 20thC vase, with branches of peaches and bats, gilt rim, seal mark.

17in (43cm) high

$1,900-2,600 GWA

A Chinese Republic-period stem cup, the white glazed body with three burnt-red carp, blue six-character mark to the pedestal inner.

4½in (11.5cm) high

$130-190 FLD

A Chinese Tang dynasty water pot, with a spotted Sancai glaze stopping short of the foot.

The Tang dynasty period is from AD 618 to ca. 906.

$450-500 **WW**

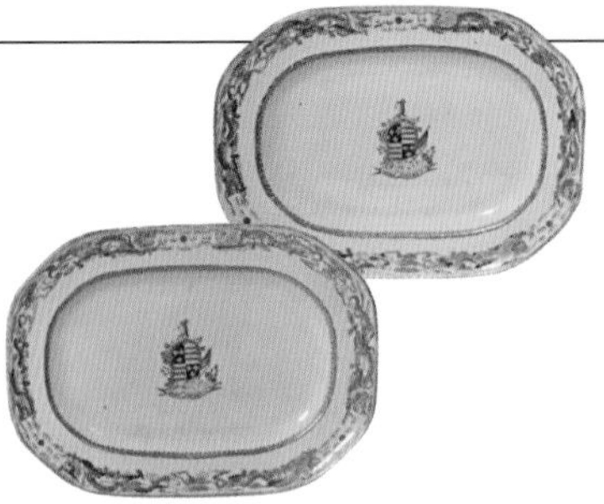

A pair of Chinese early 19thC armorial oval dishes, decorated with the arms of Hay with the motto "Spare Nought," the rims with confronting dragons chasing sacred jewels.

11in (28cm) wide

$600-700 **WW**

A Chinese pottery figure of Guanyin.

12in (30.5cm) high

$500-650 **JN**

A pair of Chinese 19thC pottery "Scholar" figures.

15in (38cm) high

$650-800 **JN**

A pair of Chinese 19th/20thC huge glazed porcelain Buddhistic temple/lion dogs on stands.

42½in (108cm) high

$1,100-1,250 **JN**

A Chinese 19thC Kangxi-style Sancai porcelain official sitting in a dragon chair, with a carved and fitted hardwood stand with carved lion dog head feet.

11¼in (28.5cm) high

$1,050-1,150 **JN**

A Chinese 19thC Yixing teapot and cover, the base with three lines of calligraphy, signed "Yigong Zhi."

$1,150-1,300 **WW**

A Chinese 19thC Yixing Zisha teapot and cover, with a turquoise glaze, one seal on base reads "Shilin He shi" and another on underside of cover reads "Xinzhou."

Produced in the Jiangsu Province, Yixing ware is red stoneware. It was exported to Europe from the mid-17thC to the late 18thC, with the most popular ware being teapots and cups. From the late 17thC, potteries in Staffordshire produced Yixing imitation ware.

6½in (16.5cm) long

$1,100-1,250 **SWO**

A Chinese 19thC Yixing teapot and cover, the base inscribed with a short poem and with a Meng Chen mark.

$900-1,050 **WW**

A Chinese pale jade abstinence plaque/ pendant, carved in low relief with a "grass script" text, the other side with a scholar.

2in (5cm) high

$3,200-3,900 **HAN**

A Chinese late-Qing dynasty (1644-1911) jade plaque, in the shape of a dragon with engraved archaic scrolls.

2¾in (7cm) long

$300-400 **SWO**

A Chinese 19thC red-overlay glass "carps" snuff bottle.

2½in (6.5cm) high

$850-950 **WW**

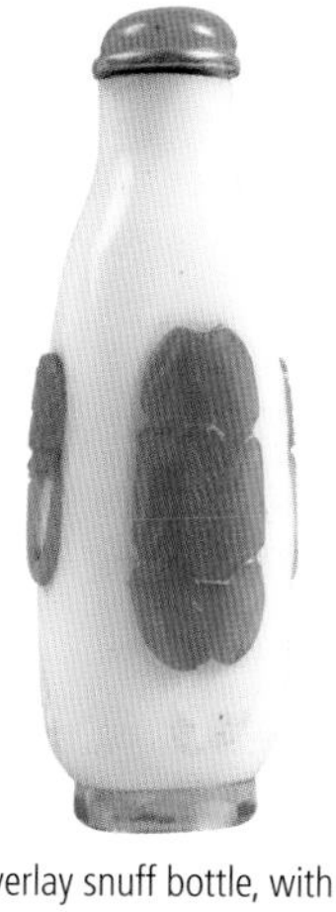

A Chinese overlay snuff bottle, with emblems.

$400-500 **JN**

A Chinese late 19thC to early 20thC enameled silver wine cup, maker's marks on base.

1¼oz

$190-260 **JN**

A Chinese early 20thC hexagonal silver bowl, by Kwan Ho, decorated with a plum tree, a dragon, floral display, interior of a house, bamboo, and Chinese warriors.

3in (7.5cm) high

$700-800 **MART**

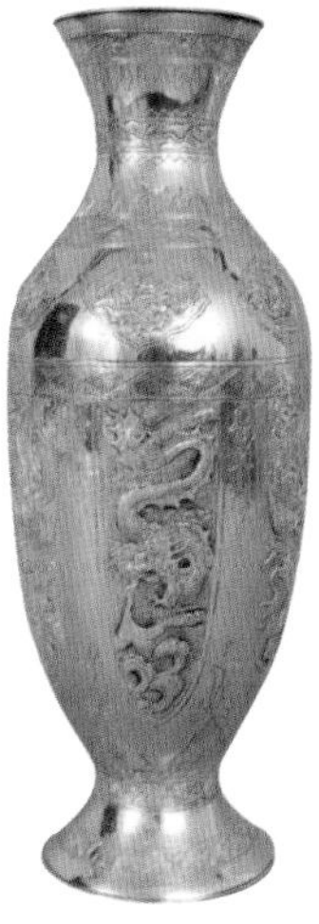

A Chinese silver-metal vase, possibly made for the Straits Chinese market, embossed with dragon and phoenix panels, unmarked.

12in (30.5cm) high

$900-1,050 **JN**

A Chinese 20thC silver bowl, with a dragon wrapped around the body, incised with the initials "B D A" and with a commemorative note in Chinese on the reverse, a punch mark on the base.

8oz

$900-1,050 **WW**

A Chinese Republic-period lobed Paktong teapot and cover, two impressed marks of "yunbai" (Paktong from Yunnan Province) and "qiutianbao" (hallmark) to the base.

Qiutianbao was one of the oldest Chinese jewelry brands in existence, the first store opened in the 1820s in Shanghai.

6in (15cm) long

$450-500 **DN**

A Chinese 20thC bronze censer and cover, the cover surmounted with a guardian lion, the body with phoenix birds.

9in (23cm) high

$650-800 **LC**

A Chinese bronze ding censer, with tauti mask decoration, archaistic-style four-character mark.

8in (20.5cm) high

$700-800 **LC**

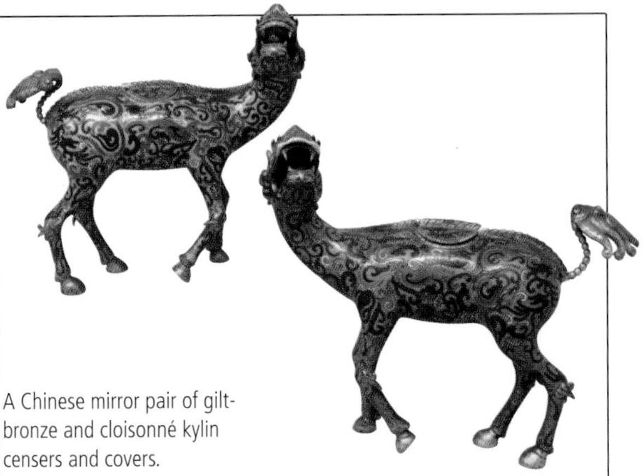

A Chinese mirror pair of gilt-bronze and cloisonné kylin censers and covers.

First made in China in the 14thC, cloisonné is a technique and the resulting ware, in which enamel is fired into compartments (or "cloisons") made from metal wires attached to a metal surface. The early palette was limited to dark green, cobalt blue, red, yellow, and white, on a turquoise background.

10in (25.5cm) long

$850-950 **JN**

A Chinese late-Qing cloisonné ewer and stand, with red-and-green enameled dragon handle, some damage.

12in (30.5cm) high

$1,150-1,450 **DN**

A Chinese 20thC cloisonné plaque, depicting a landscape.

23in (58.5cm) high

$1,700-2,100 **DN**

A Chinese late-19thC cloisonné enameled vase, decorated with dragons and floral scenes.

5½in (14cm) high

$70-80 **PSA**

A Chinese carved soapstone "Dog of Fo," on wooden base.

7¾in (19.5cm) high

$130-190 **PSA**

A Chinese Shoushan stone mythical lion seal, in hardwood box, with collector's label on box.

box 3¾in (9.5cm) high

$650-800 **DN**

A Chinese Qing dynasty or later boxwood carving of a carp.

8in (20.5cm) high

$600-650 **WW**

QUICK REFERENCE—SATSUMA

- **Produced from the mid-19thC in the Japanese towns of Satsuma and Kyoto, Satsuma designs incorporate a cream ground, a finely crackled glaze, and enameled or gilded decoration. The town of Satsuma was important to porcelain production from 16thC but is best known for these designs. The decoration often includes depictions of landscapes or scenes, with elaborate borders. Most Satsuma ware is signed on the base.**

A Japanese Satsuma koro and cover, by Kinkozan, the stylized lion finial above floral and pierced cover, twin elephant mask handles, the main body decorated with panels of figures, signed on base, tiny chip on lion, minor rubbing to the gilding.

5¼in (13.5cm) high

$1,300-1,800 APAR

A pair of Japanese Meiji (1868-1912) Satsuma "cockerel" vases, hen and chicks among flowers and rockwork, gilt and impressed Kinkozan mark.

11½in (29cm) high

$1,600-2,100 L&T

A Japanese Meiji-period Satsuma "chicken" vase, Kinkozan mark, signed on the base in gilt "Kinkozan zo."

7in (18cm) high

$2,600-3,200 L&T

A Japanese Satsuma vase, by Kinkozan, decorated with figures among clouds, signed, minor rubbing to the gilding.

7½in (19cm) high

$1,300-1,600 APAR

QUICK REFERENCE—KINKOZAN

- **The Kinkozan family have been producing ceramics since ca. 1645 in Kyoto. From the late 19thC to the early 20thC, the Kinkozan studio became a significant producer of Satsuma ware.**
- **The studio was run by the Kinkozan family, with Kinkozan Sobei IV (1824-84) and his son exporting their work overseas. Kinkozan produced paneled wares, with scenes of everyday activities.**
- **The studio closed in 1927 after the death of Kinkozan V (1868-1927).**

A Japanese Meiji Satsuma vase, by Kinkozan, painted with mandarin ducks on a stream, signed "Kinkozan zo" in gilt on the base.

11¾in (30cm) high

$3,200-3,900 WW

A Japanese Satsuma vase, by Kinkozan, painted with figures in a landscape, signed within the decoration, neck has been broken off and restored, minor rubbing to the gilding.

9in (23cm) high

$1,050-1,150 APAR

A Japanese Meiji Satsuma earthenware dish, depicting a Daimyo's procession, Kinkozan seal mark.

A Daimyo was a feudal lord in shogunal Japan, subordinate only to the Shogun.

11in (28cm) diam

$1,400-1,900 JN

A Japanese Meiji-period Satsuma vase, signed by Yozan, panels depict characters in a wooded setting, a village scene before a mountainous backdrop.

The artist is referred to in the Louis Lawrence Satsuma book *The Romance of Japan.*

10in (25.5cm) high

$2,900-3,600 K&O

A Japanese Satsuma vase, by Gyokurui and Koshida, decorated with fish beside a rock with a further fish leaping toward branches, signed on base, minor rubbing to the gilding.

4¼in (11cm) high

$800-900 APAR

A pair of Japanese Meiji-period Satsuma millefleur vases, enameled with butterflies hovering above blossoming chrysanthemum sprays, signed "taizan," also signed "Dai Nippon Taizan" on the base.

12in (30.5cm) high

$1,600-2,100 L&T

A Japanese Meiji Satsuma vase, decorated with chrysanthemums below a ryui head and ogee border, eight-character mark.

5¼in (13.5cm) high

$350-440 K&O

A Japanese Meiji-period Satsuma millefleur bowl, decorated with thousand flowers decoration highlighted with gilt, the base with a seal mark.

3½in (9cm) diam

$50-60 JN

A Japanese Meiji-period Satsuma porcelain plate, decorated with figures by a riverside with temple buildings, the base with a black seal signature mark.

7½in (19cm) diam

$100-120 JN

A Japanese 19thC Meiji Imperial Satsuma teapot and cover.

2½in (6.5cm) high

$1,300-1,800 HANN

QUICK REFERENCE—IMARI

- **Imari porcelain, named after a town on the island of Kyushu, has two different interpretations; in Japan, Shoki and Ko Imari refer to blue-and-white wares produced in Arita.**
- **In the West, Imari refers to export porcelain, usually decorated with an underglaze blue, iron red, and gilding, but it can also include green, brown, yellow ,and turquoise. There are also subcategories, such as green family and Kenjo Imari, within Imari wares. Some Imari wares of the late 17thC and 18thC are inscribed with imitation Chinese reign marks.**

A Japanese blue-and-white Arita-style porcelain bowl, the outer glaze apple green.

7in (18cm) diam

$50-80 **JN**

A Japanese Arita Imari jar and cover, the cover with a Buddhist lion knop.

ca. 1720 *24in (61cm) high*

$400-500 **SWO**

A Japanese Edo-period large Imari vase, decorated with chrysanthemums and birch.

17in (43cm) high

$450-500 **JN**

A pair of Japanese 18thC Imari porcelain fluted-rim vases, highlighted with gilt.

10½in (26.5cm) high

$300-400 **JN**

A Japanese 18thC Imari porcelain sake bottle.

7½in (19cm) high

$260-320 **JN**

A Japanese Edo-period Arita blue-and-white porcelain dish, the base with a single blue ring enclosing a factory seal.

The Edo Period began in 1603 and ended in 1868 with the Meiji Restoration. This was a political revolution that overthrew the military government and returned Japan to imperial control. The Meiji period ran from 1868 to 1912.

8in (20.5cm) diam

$230-290 **JN**

A Japanese 19thC Imari porcelain dish, with blue-and-white bamboo decoration and panels of landscape scenes, with panels of iron-red decoration, the base with a four-character mark.

8¼in (21cm) wide

$400-450 **JN**

A Japanese Meiji-period Fukagawa-style Arita porcelain bottle vase, the top section decorated with Imari palette, the base with an iron-red seal mark.

8in (20.5cm) high

$100-160 **JN**

A Japanese Meiji-period Tokyo School Imari porcelain charger, with ladies underneath hanging foliage having tea.

15¾in (40cm) diam

$190-260 **JN**

A Japanese Meiji-period Imari porcelain dish, the base with a blue seal mark.

11½in (29cm) wide

$60-90 **JN**

A Japanese 19thC Imari Arita blue-and-white dish, with arrays of ikebana and prunus blossom borders.

11¾in (30cm) wide

$100-160 **JN**

A Japanese 20thC Imari porcelain baluster vase, with a three-claw dragon in relief around neck, unmarked, with associated hardwood cover.

36¼in (92cm) high

$260-320 **APAR**

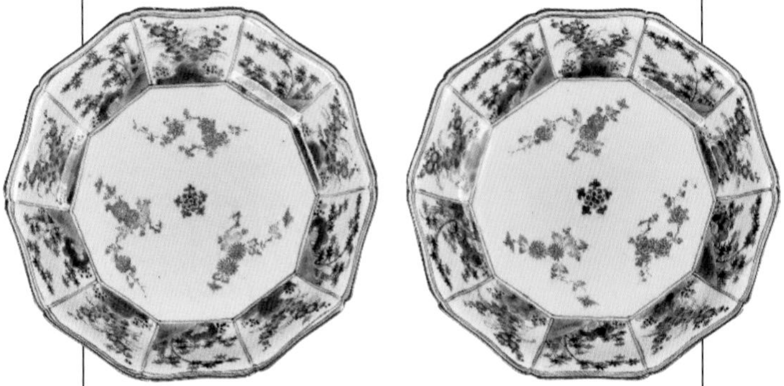

A pair of Japanese Edo-period Kakiemon-style dishes, blue fuku mark, one dish has a riveted repair on the rim, the other with a minor chip and some nicks on the rim.

Made predominantly between 1603 and 1867, Kakiemon porcelain is a type of Arita ware made by the Sakaida family. Kakiemon ware includes small dishes, bottles, bowl and vases, often in octagonal or square shapes.

9½in (24cm) wide

$900-1,050 **BELL**

A pair of Japanese Meiji-period Nabeshima fan-shaped porcelain dishes.

Between the late 17thC and ca. 1870, Nabeshima porcelain, named after the Nabeshima clan, was produced in the Okawachi region, north of Arita. It was made for the ruling Shogun (military ruler) and feudal lords.

9in (23cm) wide

$450-500 **JN**

A Japanese cloisonné enamel charger with centered scene of bird perched on cherry blossom tree, hairlines and surface scratches.

First made in China in the 14thC, cloisonné is a technique and the resulting ware, in which enamel is fired into compartments (or "cloisons") made from metal wires attached to a metal surface.

14½in (37cm) diam

$100-110 **APAR**

A Japanese 19thC cloisonné enamel dish, with flowers and birds.

12in (30.5cm) diam

$70-80 **JN**

A Japanese Meiji/Taisho-period cloisonné dragon fish vase, by Ando, with a dragon fish crashing through waves of water, the rims silvered, the base with the Ando factory mark.

9in (23cm) high

$400-500 **JN**

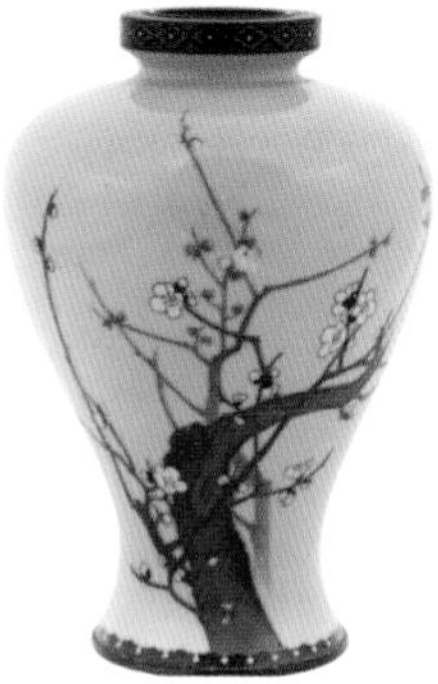

A Japanese early-20thC cloisonné vase, of musen-shippo style with a blossoming prunus tree.

7¼in (18.5cm) high

$300-350 **SWO**

A pair of Japanese white-ground cloisonné enamel vases, with colored bamboo.

7½in (19cm) high

$230-290 **JN**

A Japanese Meiji-period cloisonné vase, with scrolling vine and flora, possibly gold wire.

9in (23cm) high

$140-190 **JN**

A Japanese Meiji-period cloisonné vase, with wired decoration of birds among native flora, mounted with silver/silvered mounts.

4¾in (12cm) high

$100-160 **JN**

A Japanese Meiji/Taisho-period cloisonné temple vase, by Ando, with temples among clouds in moonlight, the moon silver, the rims silver mounted, the base with the Ando factory mark.

9¾in (24.5cm) high

$650-800 **JN**

QUICK REFERENCE - NETSUKE

- **Netsuke are decorative toggles used to secure possessions, including pipes and tobacco pouches, to traditional Japanese clothing, which didn't feature pockets. By the early 20thC, with the spread of Western dress, these items became obsolete.**
- **Netsuke were predominantly made from wood and ivory, with some inlaid or lacquered. Designs vary, with the natural world, mythology and religion acting as inspiration.**

A Japanese 19thC mask netsuke, of a long-nosed man, pale boxwood, unsigned with kaô.

Peter E. Müller Japanese Mask Collection no.12.

2in (5cm) high

$1,900-2,600 MAB

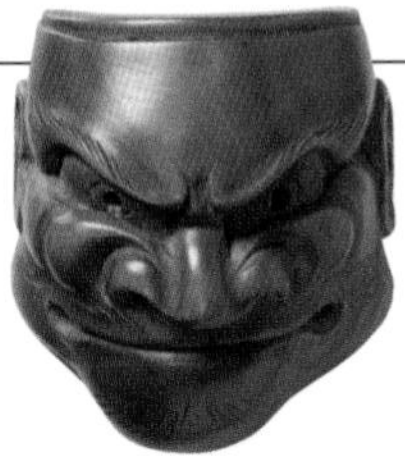

A Japanese 19thC mask netsuke of Beshimi, pale boxwood, unsigned.

Peter E. Müller Japanese Mask Collection no.71.

1½in (4cm) high

$700-800 MAB

A Japanese early 20thC mask netsuke of Okina, by Ryumin, dark stained boxwood, signed 'Ryumin saku'.

Ryumin and Hozan have characteristics in common.

2in (5cm) high

$1,900-2,600 MAB

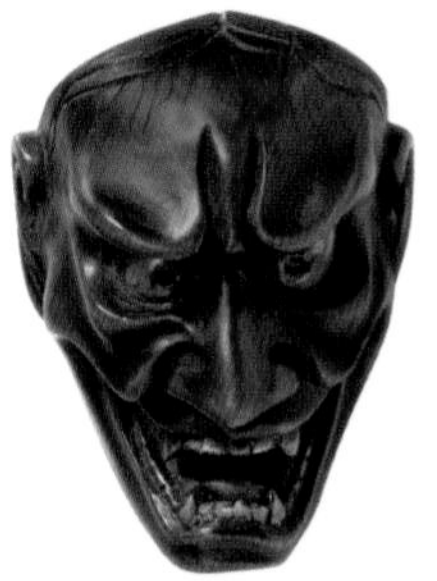

A Japanese 19thC mask netsuke of Shikami, stained boxwood with gold lacquer teeth and eyes, unsigned.

Peter E. Müller Japanese Mask Collection no.62.

1¾in (4.5cm) high

$1,050-1,150 MAB

A Japanese mid-19thC mask netsuke of karasu-tengu, by Jogetsu, dark wood, signed 'Jogetsu to'.

Peter E. Müller Japanese Mask Collection no.219.

1½in (4cm) high

$1,050-1,150 MAB

A Japanese Edo/Meiji-period wood netsuke, carved as a puppy, with the eyes inlaid in horn, signed 'Ransen'.

1½in (4cm) high

$1,100-1,250 WW

A Japanese Meiji-period (1868-1912) four-case lacquer inrō, decorated in takaramaki-e on a nashiji ground, some details in aogai, unsigned.

2½in (6.5cm) high

$700-850 WW

A pair of Japanese early 20thC bronze rats.

3in (7.5cm) wide

$450-500 CHEF

A Japanese early 20thC straw work model of a pagoda-type house, associated display case and stand.

16½in (42cm) high

$650-800 FLD

A Japanese Meiji/Taisho era silver vase, in the form of a koro, decorated in relief and kebori with sparrows and a boat on a river, incised signature.

5in (12.5cm) high

$1,900-2,600 DN

QUICK REFERENCE—AUSTRIAN BRONZES

- **From the late 19thC onward, miniature and tabletop bronze figures were created in Vienna, Austria. Around 50 manufacturers were present in Vienna at the time. Vienna bronzes were considered luxury pieces and quickly attracted the attention of collectors. They depicted lifelike subjects, including pets, farm, forest, and exotic animals, and travel-inspired subjects that reflected aspects of the East.**
- **Vienna bronzes required a high level of craftsmanship. The casting molds that were used to produce the bronzes were designed by artists who simply sold their work to bronze manufacturers and had no further influence on the production of the figures. Sometimes, a bronze figure was cast in separate parts and then welded together.**
- **Cold-painting, one of the main elements of Austrian bronzes, is a technique that involved applying several layers of lead-base paint to the bronze. The cold-painting determined to a significant extent the quality and desirability of the final piece.**
- **Franz Bergman was the most well-known maker of the day. He took over from his father and was the main instigator of the Vienna bronze boom. Carl Kauba is another collectible bronze maker who is perhaps not as well-known as Bergman. His most impressive pieces depict Native Americans and cowboys.**

A cold-painted bronze model, by Franz Bergman, of an Arab riding a camel, foundry stamp, with part of a Nam-Greb signature, some paint loss to the rear leg.

Bergman signed his bronzes with either a letter "B" in an urn-shaped cartouche or "Nam Greb"—Bergman in reverse.

5in (12.5cm) high

$1,050-1,150 GORL

An Austrian cold-painted cast group, by Franz Bergman, circular mark.

4½in (11.5cm) high

$900-1,050 JN

An Austrian cold-painted bronze coffee seller, in the style of Franz Bergman.

9in (23cm) high

$1,050-1,150 BRI

An Austrian cold-painted bronze dancer, by Franz Bergman, with hinged skirt, barefoot on a draped carpet base, foundry mark.

7¼in (18.5cm) high

$1,900-2,600 HT

An Austrian cold-painted bronze model of a Levantine carpet seller, by Franz Bergman, the underside inscribed with "B" and "GESCH" within an urn in the maquette.

ca. 1900 *6in (15cm) long*

$850-950 DN

An Austrian cold-painted cast group, of two Arab men on a rug.

7in (17.5cm) high

$800-900 JN

An erotic bronze study of an owl and nude, by Franz Bergman, the owl with sprung door, opening to reveal a gilt-bronze nude, signed "Namgreb" in the bronze, stamped "B" within urn symbol.

7¾in (19.5cm) high

$5,200-6,500 **PC**

A Franz Bergman cold-painted bronze figure group, cast as four Arabic boys, on a palm tree, cast maker's mark "4888."

ca. 1910 *9.75in (25cm) wide*

$3,900-5,200 **PC**

An Austrian cold-painted cast man reading a book.

4¼in (11cm) wide

$1,100-1,250 **JN**

An Austrian cold-painted cast man, smoking a hookah pipe.

2¼in (5.5cm) wide

$300-400 **JN**

An Austrian cold-painted bronze Arab man sitting on a prayer mat.

4¼in (11cm) wide

$180-260 **LOCK**

An Austrian Bergman-style cold-painted bronze figurine of a water carrier.

8in (20.5cm) high

$500-650 **BRI**

A late-19thC to early-20thC Austrian cold-painted bronze lamp, with a palm tree above a partly stone building with an arch and small glazed door and two Moors with prayer rugs, the interior accommodating a lightbulb, wired for electricity.

15in (38cm) high

$900-1,050 **L&T**

QUICK REFERENCE—FRANZ BERGMAN

- **Franz Bergman (1861-1939) was one of the most important makers of bronze figures in Vienna from the end of the 19thC. The Bergman factory was founded in 1860 by his father, also called Franz Bergman, (1838-94), and was taken over by Franz Bergman Jr. after his father's death.**
- **Bergman was one of the key instigators of the Vienna bronze boom in the late 19thC and early 20thC. His factory produced a range of bronze sculptures, including Asian figures, birds, and animals, and a line of erotic models. The bronzes were highly detailed and cold-painted with vibrant colors.**
- **Bergman bronzes were stamped with a capital "B" within a twin-handled urn or vase. Like many other Austrian bronzes of the time, Bergman models were often inscribed "Geschutzt," German for "protected" or "copyrighted." Some erotic and other figures were marked "Namgreb," which is Bergman backward.**

A cold-painted bronze cockerel, by Franz Bergman, impressed amphora mark, "4263," and "GESCHUTZT."

6¾in (17cm) high

$2,600-3,200 L&T

A late-19thC cold-painted bronze inkwell, by Franz Bergman, stamped "GESCHUTZT" and initialed "F B."

2½in (6.5cm) high

$950-1,100 HUTC

A cold-painted bronze kingfisher, by Franz Bergman, on veined marble dish, impressed marks to cast, broken at ankles.

4¾in (12cm) long

$450-600 WW

A cold-painted bronze bird's nest, by Franz Bergman, stamped "Geschutzt."

6¼in (16cm) wide

$300-400 WHP

An early-20thC Austrian cold-painted bronze model of an owl, in the manner of Bergman, on a marble plinth.

6in (15cm) high

$650-800 WW

A late-19thC Austrian cold-painted bronze sculpture, attributed to Franz Bergman, on marble base, back of tail stamped "GAZSHUTZT 4268."

7½in (19cm) high

$1,100-1,250 HUTC

A 19thC cold-painted bronze inkwell and pen holder, by Franz Bergman, a starling on a branch, stamped "Geschutzt," numbered "459."

4¼in (11cm) high

$400-500 HUTC

An early-20thC Austrian cold-painted bronze bird and nest, in the manner of Bergman, stamped "Geschutzt, Depose."

4¼in (11cm) wide

$400-450 MOR

An early-20thC Austrian cold-painted bronze robin, stamped to the tail "GESCHUTZT."

2¼in (6cm) long

$230-290 **FLD**

A late-19thC cold-painted bronze sculpture, by Franz Bergman, formed as a partridge with three young, stamped "GESCHUTZT" and "DEPOSE" on tail feathers and base.

2½in (6.5cm) high

$950-1,100 **HUTC**

An early-20thC large Austrian cold-painted bronze setter, by Franz Bergman, impressed maker's marks, numbers, and marked "GESCHUTZT."

11¾in (30cm) long

$1,900-2,600 **L&T**

A late-19thC Austrian cold-painted bronze bulldog, by Franz Bergman, with teeth exposed.

6in (15cm) long

$450-500 **HANN**

An Austrian cold-painted bronze setter.

9½in (24cm) long

$450-500 **BRI**

A CLOSER LOOK AT A BERGMAN BRONZE BIRD

The bronze is superbly and naturalistically modeled.

The paint appears to be original. These figues have often been repainted.

The base also appears to be original. There are fastening screws extending below the birds feet, showing it was designed to have a base.

The bronze is stamped on the underside of the tail feathers with the "B" inside an urn, for the Bergman manufactory.

An Austrian cold-painted bronze model of a game bird, by Franz Bergman, on a wooden base, stamped "B" within urn.

ca. 1900 *10½in (26.5cm) high*

$3,200-3,900 **DN**

A late-19thC cold-painted bronze inkwell, attributed to Franz Bergman, of a recumbent dog, with hinged head, stamped "503 Geschutzt" and with "Déposé" stamp and registration mark on base.

3½in (9cm) high

$850-950 **HUTC**

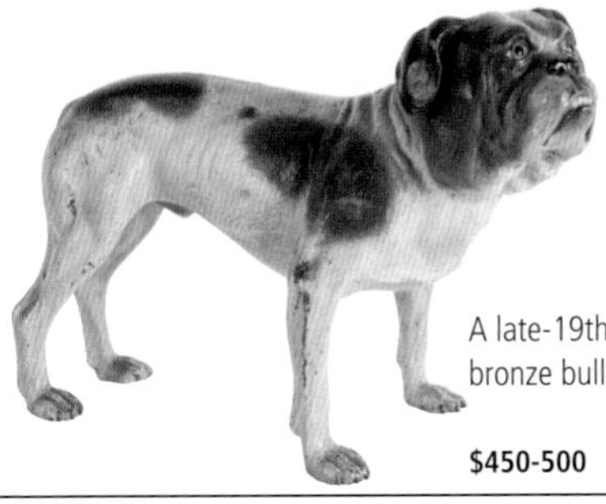

A late-19thC Austrian cold-painted bronze bulldog.

7in (18cm) long

$450-500 **HANN**

A late-19thC cold-painted bronze bulldog, paint finish dirty.

7¼in (18.5cm) long

$850-950 **GORL**

A 19thC Austrian cold-painted bronze bulldog, stamped "VIENNA ST. B."

4in (10cm) high

$500-650 **HUTC**

An Austrian cold-painted cast-bronze dog inkwell, with hinged head, Victorian registration stamp.

7in (18cm) long

$500-650 **JN**

An early-20thC Austrian cold-painted bronze cat, by Franz Bergman, foundry mark, light wear.

3in (7.5cm) wide

$400-450 **APAR**

A 19thC cold-painted bronze stoat, attributed to Franz Bergman, stamped "Geschutzt" and numbered "2865."

2½in (6.5cm) high

$850-950 **HUTC**

An early-20thC Austrian cold-painted bronze model of a hare, on onyx dished base.

4¾in (12cm) diam

$400-450 **WW**

An early-20thC Austrian cold-painted bronze lizard.

7¼in (18.5cm) long

$950-1,100 **WW**

A late-19thC to early-20thC Austrian cold-painted bronze snake.

11¾in (30cm) long

$700-850 **L&T**

QUICK REFERENCE—AUTOMOBILIA

- **Automobilia can refer to any motoring memorabilia. There is a market for car badges, fuel cans, scale models, car accessories, instruction manuals, car mascots, and much more.**
- **Popular from the 1920s to 1950s, car mascots are small sculptural models fitted to the front of a car, often to the radiator grille. They were chiefly made of glass or metal, usually zinc, pewter, or aluminum. They declined in popularity in the 1960s due to safety restrictions.**
- **While some car mascots were added by owners to personalize their cars, many were produced by car manufacturers and fitted as standard to new models. Manufacturers commissioned sculptors and designers to create mascots to become part of the company's brand.**

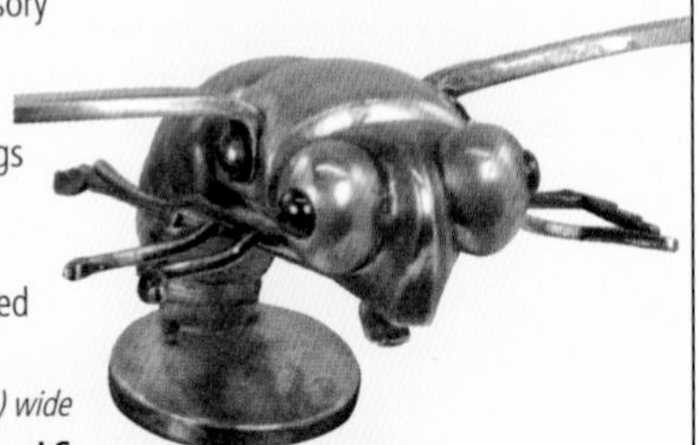

A "Flying Hornet" accessory mascot, red glass eyes, tooling to the wings, separately mounted wings and legs in the correct method, nickel-plated, display mounted, inscribed "Asprey."

7¾in (19.5cm) wide

$950-1,100 **LC**

A bronze model of a hare, made for an Alvis car, with the remains of painted decoration.

4½in (11.5cm) high

$190-260 **LC**

A Bentley "Flying B" nickel-silver mascot, of the type used with 4½-, 6½-, and 8-liter models, with "B" insignia, detailed wings, a rusting threaded mounting stud, mounted.

8½in (21.5cm) wide

$1,100-1250 **LC**

A 1920s to early 1930s Casimir Brau "Leaping Gazelle" mascot, nickel-plated on bronze, signed "C. Brau," stamped "Depose," finish a little rubbed.

6in (15cm) long

$1,600-2,100 **LC**

A rare Bentley "Icarus" nickel-plated mascot, designed and inscribed by F. Gordon Crosby, believed to have been commissioned by W.O. Bentley as an alternative to the "Flying B" design.

Frederick Gordon Crosby (1885-1943) was a self-taught British automotive artist and illustrator. He worked for *Autocar* magazine.

1920s *5½in (14cm) high*

$2,300-2,900 **LC**

A 1920s to early 1930s Casimir Brau "Leaping Lion" mascot, nickel-plated on bronze, signed "C. Brau," stamped "Depose," finish a little worn.

This is one of the popular set of Casimir Brau-designed leaping animal mascots.

8in (20.5cm) long

$1,700-2,100 **LC**

A "Leaping Jaguar" mascot, often fitted to Jaguar SS100 cars, chromium-plated, mounted on a period Jaguar threaded radiator cap, usually retailed by Desmo.

This mascot was not favored by William Lyons and, by December 1937, F. Gordon Crosby had designed a new mascot for the marque, making these mascots largely redundant.

1930s *7½in (19cm) long*

$160-210 **LC**

A John Hassall (1868-1948) "Policeman" brass car mascot, with ceramic movable head, signed "Hassall."

5¼in (13.5cm) high

$160-230 **DUK**

A "Running Hare" mascot, by Augustine & Emile Lejeune, nickel-plated, in German silver, with fur detail and facial expression, with "AEL" and "Copyright" engraved at the rear, display mounted.

3½in (9cm) high

$500-650 LC

A Telcote Pup "Bonzo" mascot, by Augustine & Emile Lejeune, depicting the cartoon character, a hollow-cast bronze body, with diamond-cut red glass eyes, "Bonzo" stamped on the side, "Telcote Pup" impressed in his collar, and "AEL Copyright" at the rear, the larger of two sizes available in the 1920s, not mounted.

Augustine and Emile Lejeune established AE Lejeune in 1910. The company produced ornamental bronze items, including car mascots. The couple's son took over in 1933, renaming the company Louis Lejeune Ltd. It was then bought by Sir David Hughes in 1978 and passed to his son in 1998.

mid-1920s *5½in (14cm) long*

$1,250-1,450 LC

A Rolls-Royce "Spirit of Ecstasy" mascot, as mounted to 1914 40/50hp automobiles, in German silver, embossed "Rolls-Royce Ltd. Feb 6 1911," original mounting stud.

$2,600-3,200 LC

A Rolls-Royce trade gift, engine-turned and decorated desk inkwell, with a miniature Rolls-Royce mascot on the lid, mounted onto an onyx base with a pen holder and chamfered corners, bun feet, and brass base.

6in (15cm) long

$400-450 LC

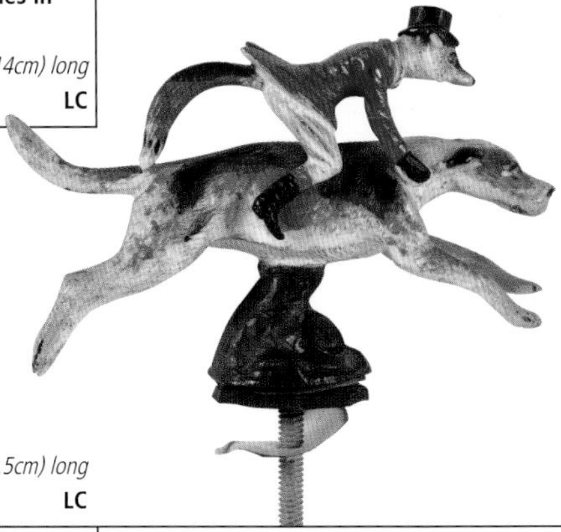

A car mascot, of a fox in a top hat riding a hound, with a metal fastening, marked "Made in England" and "LL" for Louis Lejeune.

5in (12.5cm) long

$400-500 LC

A Sabino vaseline glass "Leaping Gazelle" mascot, mounted on a nickel-silver base, intaglio "Sabino Paris" on the side, small chip on the foot.

4in (10cm) high

$300-450 LC

A "Cock-A-Snook" car mascot, sometimes called a "Devil" mascot, of a satyrlike figurine with original red enamel finish and black tail, designed to be fitted to the rear of a vehicle, display mounted.

1920s

$450-600 LC

A chrome-plated car mascot, of a horse jumping a fence, with a screw attachment on the base.

6¼in (16cm) long

$130-190 LC

A seven-color chrome-plated Brooklands Automobile Racing Club full member's badge, designed by F. Gordon Crosby, with the member's access bridge, numbered "979."

1930 *5in (12.5cm) high*

$850-950 LC

A first issue type-1 Circle of 19thC Motorists badge, with enamels within an escutcheon, with "1900" intaglio at the apex, with a winged wheel supporter, with "MEMBER" raised and a dashboard mount, plated in nickel-silver, the reverse inscribed "Claude Gouldesbrough," in distressed condition.

The Circle of 19thC Motorists, founded in 1927, was the most exclusive of English Motoring Clubs, where to be a member you were required to prove that you had driven a car extensively before the turn of the 20thC. The number of members never exceeded 220, and, with the passing of time, the membership reduced to a point where the last meeting was a Memorial Lunch in 1952. While most of the members names are recorded, Claude Gouldesbrough does not appear to be on any known lists of members.

1927 *4¼in (11cm) high*

$260-320 LC

A St. Christopher car badge, by J.R. Gaunt London, enamel on chrome, "Made in England."

$45-60 PSA

A J.R. Gaunt of London chrome and enamel car badge, on original card with details on the reverse of the card, boxed.

$50-60 APAR

A pair of B.R.C. "Alpha" self-contained brass Boa-Rodrigues & Company acetylene gas head lamps, factory-made for Maison Labourdette, with parabolic nickel-silver reflectors with mirror lenses, both numbered "135," the generators retain their gas taps, carbide of calcium cylinders, and bayonet locking.

1903-10 *14in (35.5cm) high*

$3,200-3,900 LC

A self-contained German-manufactured motorcycle acetylene gas lamp, nickel-plated, with front lens cover, shatter-proof front glass, burner, and component parts, with a rear storage cover, in working order.

ca. 1908

$300-400 LC

A pair of Lucas "Kings Own" side lamps, in black enamel and with nickel-plated fittings, marked "F141."

8¼in (21cm) high

$130-190 LC

An early 20thC Dietz of New York brass lamp, with manufacturer's and patent stamps, general wear.

13½in (34.5cm) high

$120-160 APAR

A pair of early-20thC brass car lamps, each with two sides with beveled glass panels.

11in (28cm) long

$120-160 **FLD**

A Cicca of France four-trumpet car horn, no.9511, nickel-plated.

ca. 1920s *26¾in (68cm) long*

$300-400 **DUK**

A Bentley chromed radiator hip flask, by Ruddspeed Ltd., no.909777.

8in (20.5cm) high

$500-650 **FLD**

A Rolls-Royce floor mat, purported to have come from Rolls-Royce Head Office, inscribed "Sunlight," rubber backed with small "studs" for grip.

45in (114.5cm) long

$90-100 **APAR**

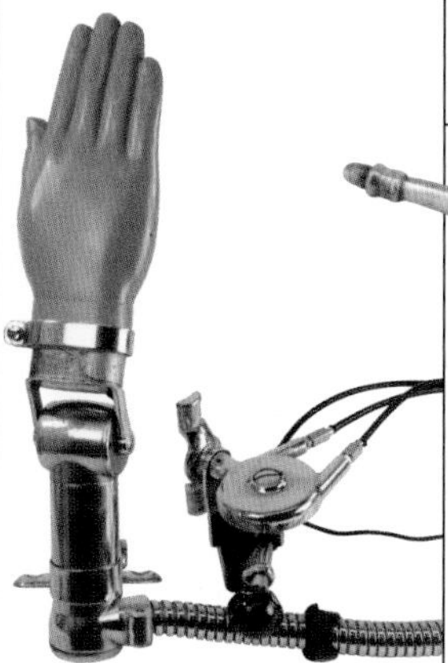

A Birglow "Auto Single Hand" indicator, fitted to the right-hand side of a car, with a multidirectional control for signaling.

$300-400 **LC**

A Lucas Ltd. polished brass "Motor Oiler," no.38, in a discus shape, to be used in fitted toolboxes.

$140-190 **LC**

A Ford "Moto-Lita" steering wheel.

13½in (34.5cm) diam

$70-80 **APAR**

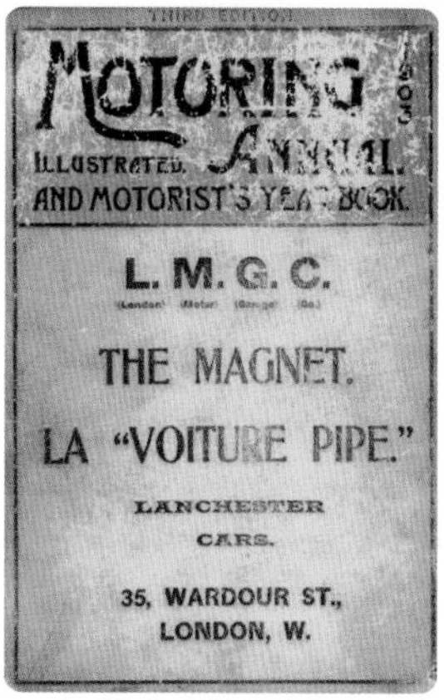

Motoring Annual, third edition, with advertisements, the cover rubbed and a loose spine.

1903

$80-100 **LC**

An MG Car Company promotional nickle-plated vesta case, inscribed "Distinctive Coachwork Designs," with a profile of a ca. 1926 14/28 MG bullnose Salonette on the front, and "The Morris Garages, Oxford" and armorial on the reverse, signs of wear.

$230-290 **LC**

An unusual flip sign, cast in alloy, with a hinging semicircular shape for altering the wording to, "WAITING LIMITED TO 20MINS IN ANY HOUR."

20in (51cm) diam

$300-400 **LC**

A cast alloy sign, single-sided, with catseye glasses, one missing, some original paint.

27½in (70cm) wide

$230-290 **LC**

A vintage "Ferrari" painted wood wall sign.

71in (180.5cm) long

$300-450 **DUK**

An oil on canvas automobile racing scene, by Dion Pears, showing the 1930 Le Mans with Sir Henry "Tim" Birkin driving the Bentley 4.5-liter Blower being overtaken by Woolf Barnato in the Bentley Speed 6, signed, framed, damaged.

British artist, Dion Pears (1929-85) was born in Richmond, UK. His paintings were commissioned by car manufacturers, including Renault, Bentley, and Ferrari, and autmobile racing drivers.

35½in (90cm) wide

$1,050-1,300 **APAR**

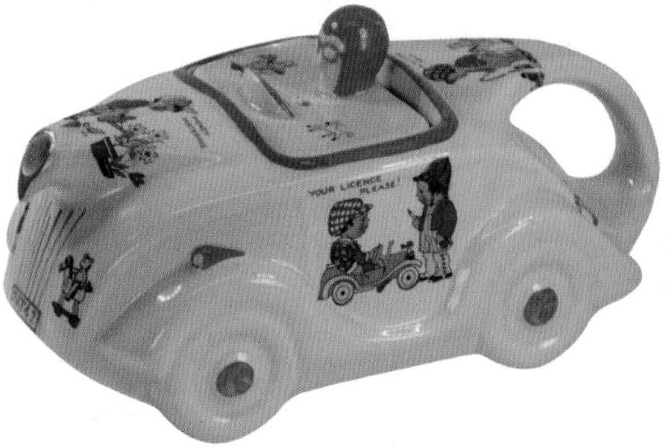

A Sadler OKT42 novelty teapot, so-called "Mabel Lucie Attwell" example, with a transfer underglaze design, impressed "Made in England - Registered No 820236," and a six-hole strainer and a seven bar radiator grille variant, with orange hubs and cockpit outline.

1930s

$300-400 **LC**

An Austin pedal car, restored with correct parts, triple chrome plating in Sheffield, some rust.

1950s *60¾in (154.5cm) long*

$2,300-2,900 **APAR**

QUICK REFERENCE—BOOKS

- **The first print run of a first edition will always be the most valuable. A copy from the first print run of a first edition of a hardback book is called a "true" first edition. Paperback first editions tend to fetch lower prices than hardback first editions. The quantity of the first print run of a book affects the value of its first editions. Iconic titles may well be desirable, but more obscure works or those from an author's early career, which were printed in smaller quantities, are often more expensive. An author's signature often adds value to a first edition. To identify a first edition, check that the publishing date and copyright date match and confirm the original publishing date and publisher with a reliable source. Also, look for the number "1" in the series of numbers on the imprint/copyright page. The first editions that fetch the highest prices are undamaged and come with the original dust jacket.**

Buchan, John, *The Dancing Floor*, first edition, published by Hodder and Stoughton, London, 8vo., blue cloth, dust jacket repaired and soiled, some foxing, 311 pages, four leaves of advertisements.
1926 *7½in (19cm) high*
$450-600 **L&T**

Burnett, W.R., *Little Caesar*, first edition, published by Lincoln MacVeagh, The Dial Press, original blue cloth, in original issue pictorial dust jacket, small scattered chips, with the "$2.00" price at head of front flap.
1929
$7,000-8,000 **FRE**

Blixen, Karen, *Out of Africa*, first edition, published by Putnam, London, 8vo, original red cloth gilt, a little foxing, facsimile dust jacket.
1937
$450-600 **L&T**

Chandler, Raymond, *The Long Good-Bye*, first edition, first printing, preceding the first American edition by a few months, dust jacket designed by Fritz Wegner, slight foxing, 8vo.
1953
$160-210 **DN**

Churchill, Sir Winston Spencer, *My African Journey*, published by Hodder and Stoughton, London, first edition, 8vo., frontispiece, 3 maps, 46 leaves of plates with 60 photographs, original red pictorial cloth gilt, a little foxing, slight fading to covers and spine, endpapers.
1908
$450-600 **L&T**

Dickens, Charles, *A Christmas Carol*, first edition, later issue with "Stave One," title printed in red and blue, original cloth, lower joint splitting, with crack across, slightly worn at extremities, Chapman and Hall, London.
1843
$2,300-2,900 **DN**

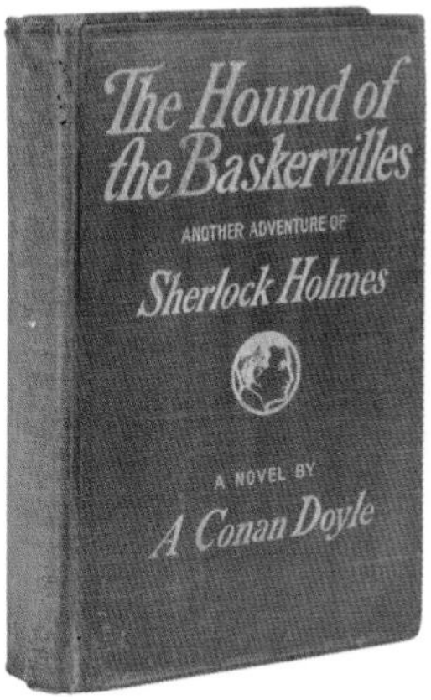

Doyle, A. Conan, *The Hound of the Baskervilles*, first American edition, third state, published by McClure, Phillips & Co., New York, 12mo., Green & Gibson A26 c.ii.
1902
$180-230 **FRE**

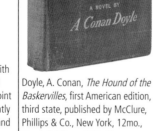

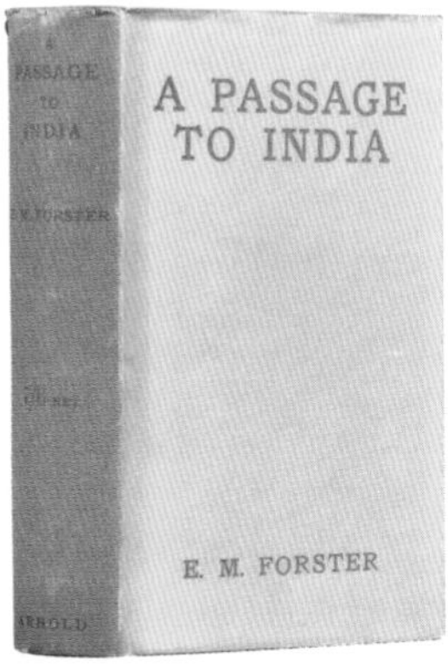

Forster, E.M., *A Passage To India*, first edition, 8vo., published by Edward Arnold, page tops foxed, spine dulled, slight chipping on corners, original cloth, three-page advertisement at end.
1924
$5,200-5,800 **BELL**

Fleming, Ian, *Casino Royale*, first edition, published by Jonathan Cape, London, first issue without Sunday Times Review, 8vo., dust jacket, not price clipped, inscribed by Ian Fleming, reading "Alastair, from the Author - Read & Burn," slight wear to jacket spine and corners.

The Alastair in the inscription has been identified in pencil as Alastair McKinley. This matches other works signed by Fleming.

1953

$70,000-80,000 L&T

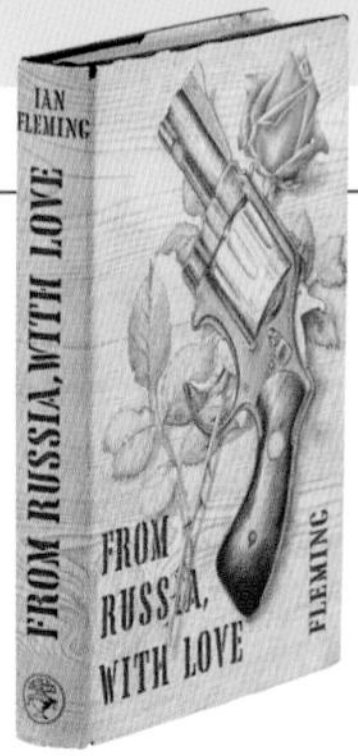

Fleming, Ian, *From Russia, with Love*, published by Jonathan Cape, first edition, first impression, 8vo., original black cloth with gun and rose motif, dust jacket with chipping, some foxing stains, small closed tear, light internal marks.

1957

$800-900 L&T

Fleming, Ian, *The Spy Who Loved Me*, first edition, published by Jonathan Cape, London, 8vo., original black cloth with silver dagger motif, dust jacket not price clipped.

1962

$450-600 L&T

Fleming, Ian, *Diamonds are Forever*, first edition, published by Jonathan Cape, London, first impression with "Boofy" for "Dolly' on p. 134, 8vo.

1956

$3,200-3,900 L&T

Fleming, Ian, *Goldfinger*, first edition, published by Jonathan Cape, London, 8vo., signed "Best wishes, Honor Blackman, Pussy Galore."

1959

$1,900-2,600 L&T

Fleming, Ian, *Live and Let Die*, first edition, published by Jonathan Cape, London, first issue, inscribed "To Robert Bartlett from the Author 1954," some slight edge wear.

Robert Bartlett was the artist who provided the pencil sketch of Fleming for the rear cover of the dust jacket of *Casino Royale*. Bartlett was a fellow officer of Fleming's during World War II, both men serving in the Naval Intelligence Division.

1954

$39,000-45,000 L&T

Fleming, Ian, *For Your Eyes Only*, first edition, published by Jonathan Cape, London, 8vo.

1960

$950-1,100 L&T

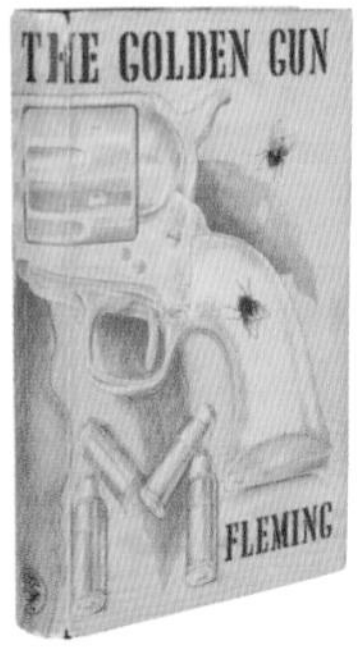

Fleming, Ian, *The Man with the Golden Gun*, first edition, published by Jonathan Cape, London, with 18s. net price on inner flap, minor discoloration to golden gun motif.

Only around 940 copies of the first issue of *The Man with the Golden Gun* were produced before the cost of adding the golden gun motif to each upper board became too great. It is consequently rare to find a copy of this work, particularly one including its intact dust wrapper.

1965

$6,500-8,000 L&T

Golding, William, *Lord of the Flies*, first edition, published by Jonathan Cape, London, 8vo., original cloth, some browning, spotting, and small tears, price intact "12s 6d," bookplate of Desmond Young.
1954
$3,200-3,900 **LC**

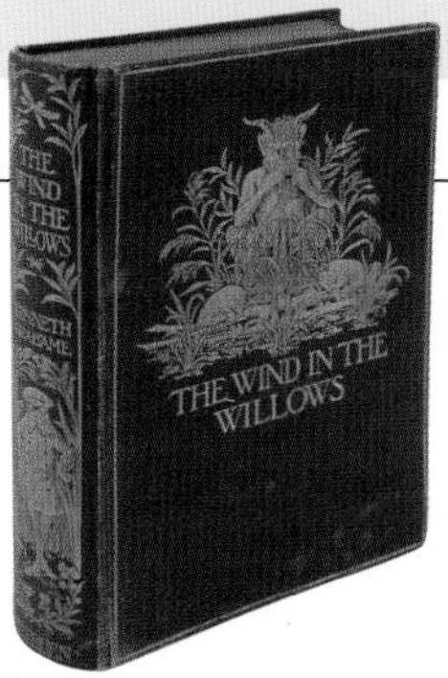

Grahame, Kenneth, *The Wind in the Willows*, first edition, published by Methuen & Co., half title, frontispiece by W. Graham Robertson, 8vo.
1908
$1,600-2,100 **LC**

QUICK REFERENCE—THE NEGRO TRAVELERS' GREEN BOOK

- **This book was once a travel guide for African-American families, from a time when long-distance travel and finding lodging and gasoline would be a cause for apprehension. Friendly service stations, hotels, nightclubs, and restaurants are arranged by state across the country.**
- **The cover of this edition states "Carry your Green Book with you . . . You may need it!" This copy was clearly used by its original owners. The entries for the YMCA in Manhattan and a hotel at Niagara Falls are underlined, and a three-page article on parks has several sections underlined as well, particularly regarding national parks' nondiscriminatory policies—Yellowstone and Mesa Verde are marked as potential destinations. The last "Green Book" was printed in 1966. The recent award-winning film *Green Book* features a copy of the book as a plot point.**
- **It was first published in 1936 and publication stopped in 1966. This copy is a relatively late spring 1958 issue, and sold for much more than expected.**
- **Victor Hugo Green, a New York mailman, launched the book, which grew to cover most of North America, including parts of Canada, Mexico, the Caribbean, and Bermuda.**

Hemingway, Ernest, *A Farewell to Arms*, first trade edition, first issue without legal disclaimer, published by Charles Scribner's Sons, New York, 8vo., some tears and small nicks to spine panel tips.
1929
$1,300-1,700 **SWA**

Ransome, Arthur, *We Didn't Mean to go to Sea*, first edition, published by Jonathan Cape, London, 8vo., original cloth, dust jacket, not price clipped.
1937
$260-320 **L&T**

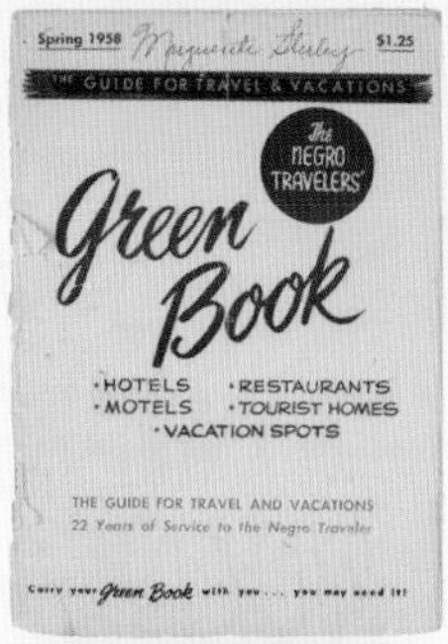

Green, Victor H. (Editor), *The Negro Travelers' Green Book*, original colored wrappers, original owner's signature on front wrapper, worn and detached, moderate damp staining, vertical fold, staple holes in upper corner, other minor wear.
1958
$22,000-26,000 **SWA**

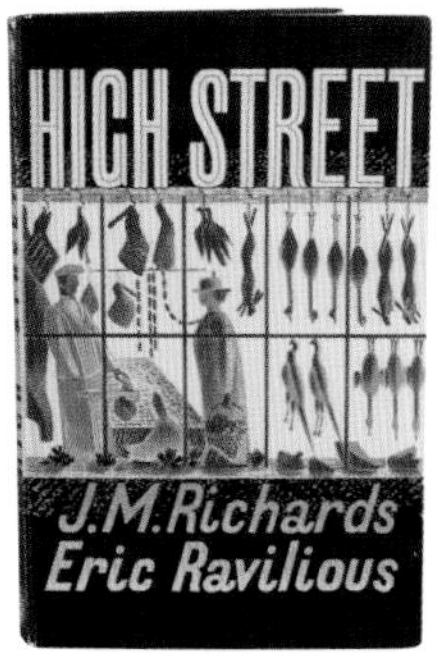

Richards, J.M., *High Street*, first edition, illustrated by Eric Ravilious, published by Country Life, London, printed at the Curwen Press, with 24 color lithographic plates, woodcut vignette title page, publisher's pictorial boards.
1938
$3,200-3,900 **HAN**

Sassoon, Siegfried, *Memoirs of a Fox-Hunting Man*, published by Faber and Faber, London, with illustrations by William Nicholson, no.139 of 300 copies, signed by the author and artist, seven full-page plates and other illustrations, original full vellum, top edge gilt, others uncut, 8vo.
1929
$650-800 **LC**

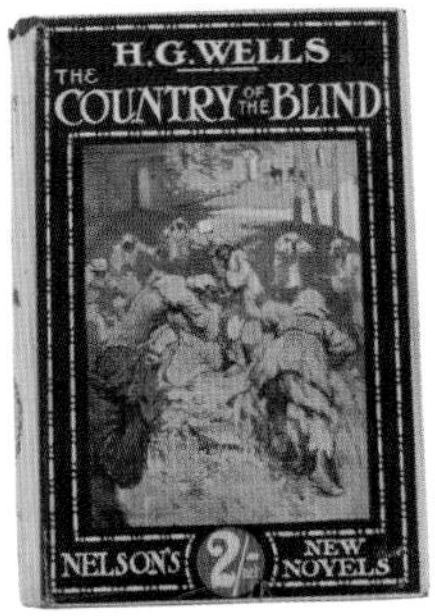

Wells, H.G., *The Country Of The Blind And Other Stories*, published by Thomas Nelson & Sons, seemingly first edition, in rare original dust jacket, mark at base of front cover.
ca. 1911
$5,200-5,800 **CUTW**

Yeats, William Butler, *Poems*, first edition, published by T. Fisher Unwin, London, one of 750 copies, half title, decorated title page, tissue guard, original cloth decorated gilt, untrimmed, spine dulled, 8vo.
1895
$400-500 **LC**

Artzybasheff, Boris, *As I See*, first edition, published by Dodd, Mead & Company, New York, 4to., in original dust jacket.

1954

$80-100 **FRE**

Brown, Margaret Wise, *Goodnight, Moon*, first edition, published by Harper & Brothers, New York, oblong 8vo., illustrated by Clement Hurd, lacking dust jacket, minor wear to spine.

1947

$1,250-1,450 **FRE**

Brown, Palmer, *The Silver Nutmeg*, first edition, published by Harper & Brothers, New York, 8vo., 138 pages, original dust jacket, price clipped, light toning to text.

1956

$160-210 **FRE**

Brunhoff, Jean de, *Histoire de Babar le petit elephant*, first edition, published by Editions du Jardin de Modes, Paris, first issue, with no elephant on copyright page, illustrated in color, moderate wear, boards lightly rubbed.

The adventures of Babar, known as the most famous Frenchman in the world, continue to this day.

1931

$650-800 **FRE**

Burton, Virginia Lee, *Katy and the Big Snow*, first edition, published by Houghton Mifflin Company, Boston, oblong 8vo.

1943

$80-90 **FRE**

Burton, Virginia Lee, *Mike Mulligan and His Steam Shovel*, first edition, published by Houghton Mifflin Company, Boston, oblong 8vo., inscribed by Burton on front free endpaper "Greetings from Virginia Lee Burton."

1939

$600-700 **FRE**

Dahl, Roald, *Charlie and the Chocolate Factory*, first edition, first issue, published by Knopf, New York, illustrated by Joseph Scindelman, 8vo.

1964

$1,150-1,450 **FRE**

Dulac, Edmund (Illustrator), *Sinbad the Sailor & Other Stories from the Arabian Nights*, published by Hodder & Stoughton, some wear and dirt to exterior, some foxing.

$160-230 **APAR**

Grahame, Kenneth, *Dream Days*, published by John Lane, The Bodley Head, London and New York, illustrated by Maxfield Parrish, 8vo., 228 pages, without advertisements at rear, spine stamped in gilt with "John Lane Company," pictorial endpapers, markings in ink at heads of endpapers.

ca. 1902

$140-210 **FRE**

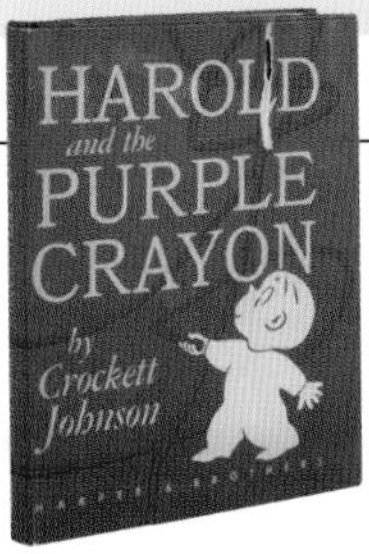

Johnson, Crockett, *Harold and the Purple Crayon*, first edition, published by Harper & Brothers, New York, with Library of Congress catalog card no.55-7683 on title page, in early issue dust jacket with no price at top of front flap, with code "30-60/No.5671A," some light foxing.

One of several variants of the first edition of this book.

1955

$600-700 FRE

Lang, Andrew, *The Red Fairy Book*, first edition, published by David McKay Company, Philadelphia, large 8vo., illustrated by Gustaf Tenggren, with eight colorplates.

1924

$120-160 FRE

MacDonald, George, *At the Back of the North Wind*, first edition, published by David McKay, Philadelphia, 4to., illustrated by Jessie Willcox Smith, signed by Smith, very lightly worn.

1919

$140-210 FRE

Milne, A.A., *The House At Pooh Corner*, first trade edition, published by Methuen & Co. Ltd., London, small 8vo., illustrated with frontispiece and text illustrations, ownership signature on half title, very lightly rubbed.

1928

$260-390 FRE

Milne, A.A., *The House at Pooh Corner*, first edition, published by Methuen & Co. Ltd., London, illustrated by Ernest W. Shepard. first printing, 8vo., spine faded and slightly cocked.

1928

$500-650 FRE

Potter, Beatrix, *The Tale of Peter Rabbit*, published by Frederick Warne and Co., London, first trade edition, fourth impression, with owner's inscription to half title, pale gray leaf-patterned endpapers, color pastedown illustration on upper board, color frontispiece, and another 30 color illustrations throughout.

1902

$480-500 HAN

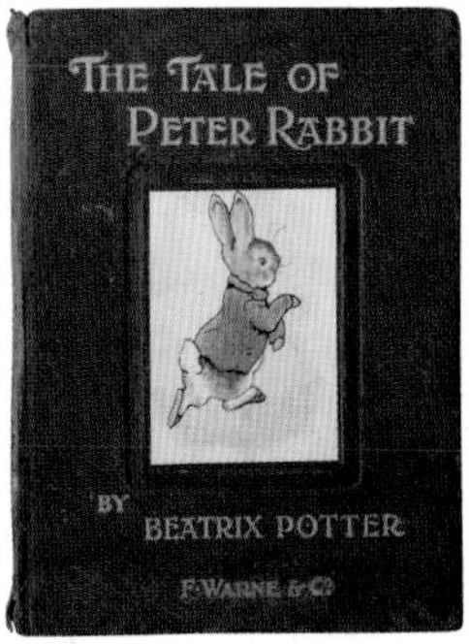

Rowling, J.K., *Harry Potter and the Goblet of Fire*, published by Bloomsbury, signed by Rowling on the dedication page, with golden ticket for the "Hogwart's Express Book Tour" signing event in York laid in.

2000

$1,100-1,300 HT

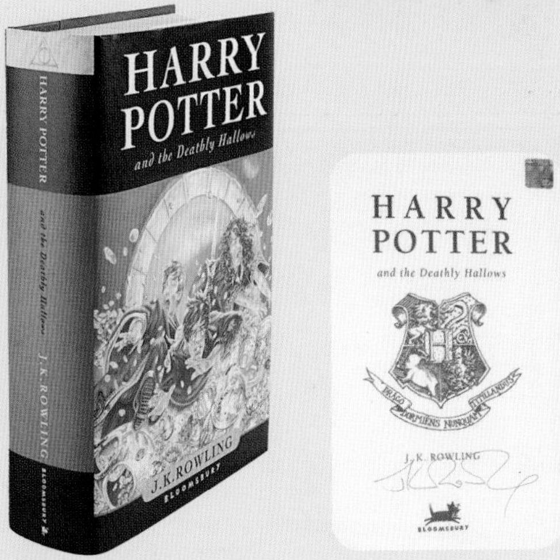

Rowling, J.K., *Harry Potter and The Deathly Hallows*, first edition, published by Bloomsbury, London, 8vo., signed on title page by Rowling and with small holograph sticker dated "21/07/07" at top of title page, original cloth, dust wrapper.

2007

$2,300-2,900 L&T

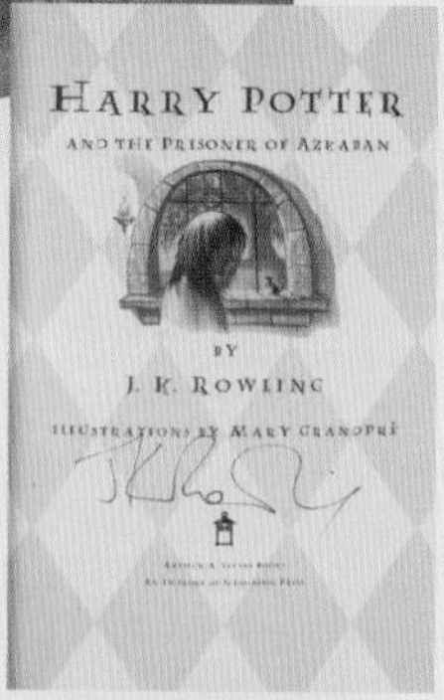

Rowling, J.K., *Harry Potter and the Prisoner of Azkaban*, first American edition, published by Scholastic Press, New York, first printing, 8vo., signed on the title page by Rowling.

1999

$650-800 **FRE**

Rowling, J.K., *The Tales of Beedle the Bard*, first edition, for Children's High Level Group, 8vo., with hologram sticker on front marbled free endpaper, presentation copy inscribed "Christmas 2008. To Di, with lots of love, J.K. Rowling (Jo) x" on half title, original brown calf binding embellished with metal skull, corner pieces, and clasp incorporating replica blue gemstones, maroon morocco bag, with envelope of Collector's Edition Prints containing ten prints, housed in a velvet-lined brown calf box, lettered and decorated on upper cover, with the publisher's lightly rubbed and creased white card sleeve printed in black on the upper panel "This Side Up."

J.K. Rowling produced a deluxe copy of *The Tales of Beedle the Bard* in aid of the charity Children's High Level Group (now Lumos). Rowling signed 100 copies of this book and they were randomly distributed to buyers on Amazon.com, who were surprised to receive a special copy of the book in the mail. This book is an out-of-series copy, signed by Rowling.

2008

$7,000-8,000 **L&T**

Schulz, Charles M., *A Charlie Brown Christmas*, first edition, published by The World Publishing Company, Cleveland and New York, square 8vo.

1965

$450-600 **FRE**

Sendak, Maurice, *In the Night Kitchen*, first edition, published by Harper & Row, New York, small 4to., lightly worn.

1970

$80-100 **FRE**

Seuss, Dr. (Theodor Seuss Geisel), *Green Eggs and Ham*, first edition, Younger and Hirsch 27, published by Beginner Books, INC., New York, second state with the "50 Word Vocabulary" box printed on front panel of dust jacket, 8vo., 62 pages.

1960

$230-290 **FRE**

Travers, P.L., *Mary Poppins Opens the Door*, first edition, published by Reynal & Hitchcock, New York, 8vo. 239 pages, signed by Travers.

1943

$500-650 **FRE**

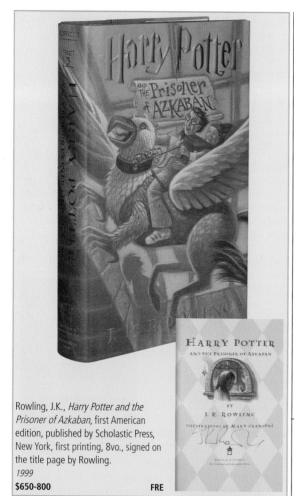

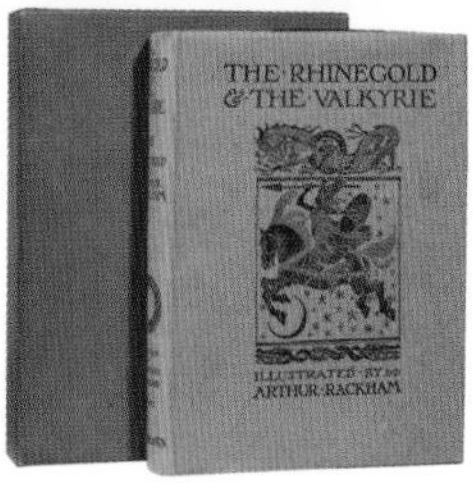

Wagner, Richard, *The Rhinegold & the Valkyrie*, first trade edition, published by William Heinemann and Doubleday, Page & Co., London and New York, illustrated by Arthur Rackham, translated by Margaret Armour, 8vo., 161 pages.

$800-900 **FRE**

QUICK REFERENCE—TEA CADDIES

- **Tea first came to Europe in the early 17thC but was imported in large chests and sold loose, so buyers required a smaller method of storage. Early tea caddies were made of European or Chinese porcelain, with the lid used as a measure.**
- **Most tea caddies on the market are from the 18thC and 19thC, when it was common to lock up tea to prevent spillage or theft by servants. Tea was still a relative luxury, meaning that many tea caddies were produced to high standards and made of expensive materials, such as ivory, tortoiseshell, and exotic woods.**
- **It is worth checking the condition of boxes carefully. Replaced locks, panels, or hinges can reduce the value. Prestigious makers or high-quality locks often add value.**

A two division tea caddy, with silk embroidered panels, one glass panel on lid is broken, the silk panels are heavily stained.

ca. 1780s *7½in (19cm) long*

$900-1,050 **APAR**

A Chinese 19thC export scarlet, gilt and black lacquer tea caddy, with pewter twin-lidded interior, lacquer rubbed, one foot replaced.

10in (25.5cm) wide

$650-800 **BELL**

A 19thC large inlaid mahogany tea caddy, with marquetry detail on the cover "Tea," with two canisters centered by a later mixing bowl.

13½in (34.5cm) wide

$190-260 **FLD**

An early Victorian coromandel and mother-of-pearl inlaid tea caddy, the lid enclosing two dome coromandel lidded tea boxes with centered reservoir set with associated bowl.

13¾in (35cm) wide

$160-210 **APAR**

An early Victorian rosewood tea caddy, with two rosewood veneered lidded tea boxes, associated glass bowl.

13¾in (35cm) wide

$100-130 **APAR**

A 19thC tortoiseshell two-division tea caddy, with pewter stringing, small cracks on lid, small chips on the tortoiseshell lids in the interior, handles replaced.

6¼in (16cm) wide

$260-320 **APAR**

A 19thC tortoiseshell tea caddy, with ivory stringing, with two lidded compartments, on four silvered ball feet, slight damage.

5½in (14cm) high

$600-700 **FLD**

An Edward VII hallmarked silver tea caddy, by Henry Bourne, with stoneware body, some of the silver applied decoration lifts in parts, crazing, and surface wear.

1908 *5¼in (13.5cm) high*

$100-140 **APAR**

A late George III oak and mahogany crossbanded and inlaid candle box, with front centered with an inlaid bird, the back section hinge has been replaced, some damage.

20in (51cm) high

$100-110 **APAR**

A George III oak spoon rack and salt box, general wear.

10in (25.5cm) wide

$190-260 **APAR**

A late Georgian mahogany candle box, with pierced backplate.

9¼in (23.5cm) wide

$60-80 **APAR**

A late Victorian carved oak wall-mounted letter box, the shaped back rail inscribed "LETTERS," old crude repair to backplate, general surface wear.

17in (43cm) wide

$130-180 **APAR**

A 19thC burr maple string box, on brass ball feet.

4in (10cm) high

$260-320 **LC**

A 19thC turned lignum vitae string box, the screw-on lid centered with a blade, small losses to the base section of the lid.

5¼in (13.5cm) diam

$160-210 **APAR**

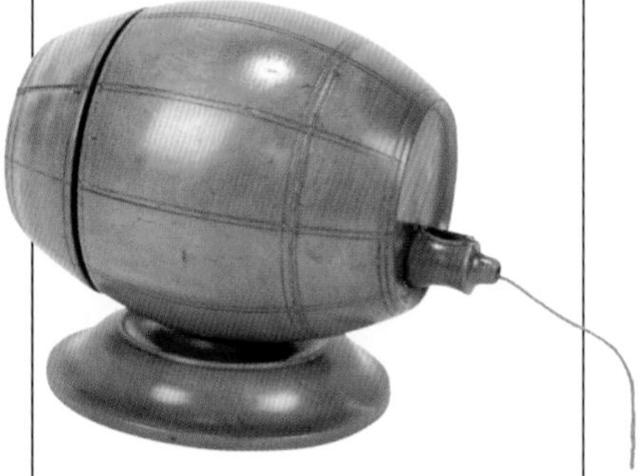

A 19thC fruitwood string box, with screw-on rear section and metal blade attached to the "tap," general wear.

4¼in (11cm) long

$180-230 **APAR**

A 19thC turned lignum vitae box and cover, signs of woodworm to the body.

5¼in (13.5cm) diam

$130-190 **APAR**

A Scandinavian 19thC pine lidded box, with traces of incised floral decoration and original paintwork, surface wear.

8¾in (22cm) diam

$230-290 **APAR**

A Victorian mahogany sewing box, with a fabric lined interior, with two base drawers, with twin brass lion mask ring handles, overall wear and tear.

18¼in (46.5cm) wide

$260-320 **APAR**

An early Victorian rosewood and mother-of-pearl inlaid sewing box, with fitted interior with thread reels, small jars, and accoutrements with further sewing related items in the base, some losses to the mother-of-pearl, a split on base.

14¾in (37.5cm) wide

$800-900 **APAR**

A 19thC Killarney ware inlaid arbutus twin-lidded box, with swing-over handle.

Killarney ware, produced in Killarney and the Gap of Dunloe, Ireland, in the mid- to late-19thC, is often made out of local wood, such as arbutus. The ware can feature local buildings/sites or traditional Irish symbols.

9½in (24cm) wide

$500-600 **BELL**

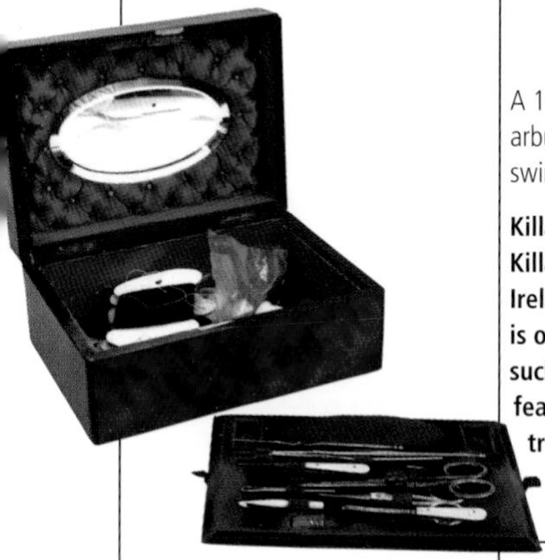

A Victorian amboyna and rosewood crossbanded sewing box, with related sewing tools.

10in (25.5cm) wide

$120-160 **APAR**

A mid-Victorian figured walnut traveling cabinet, with pen tray and inkwell at the front.

12¼in (31.5cm) high

$130-190 **APAR**

An early Victorian rosewood and mother-of-pearl inlaid traveling case or vanity box, with lift-out tray revealing a jewelry compartment, three splits on the top, dents, and surface scratches.

10¾in (27.5cm) wide

$100-130 **APAR**

A 19thC teak and brass-bound gentleman's traveling box, the lid set with a folding mirror, the interior with lift-out tray with a hip flask, razor, scissors, a pewter measure, and a pewter bowl, wear as expected from a campaign piece.

7in (18cm) wide

$160-210 **APAR**

A late-19thC mahogany miniature bureau, on clear glass feet.

12¼in (31cm) high

$160-210 **APAR**

An early-20thC mahogany store display cabinet, for "J. & P. COATS SEWING COTTON."

21¼in (54cm) wide

$300-400 **LOCK**

A 19thC mahogany apothecary box, with seven bottles, a measuring pitcher, and a further drawer of bottles.

10in (25.5cm) wide

$500-650 **FLD**

An H. Bahlsen sheet-metal cookie jar, designed by Emanuel Josef Margold, inscribed with exhibition history.

ca. 1911-12 *7½in (19cm) long*

$450-500 **QU**

An early-20thC enameled glass glove casket, attributed to Moser, decorated with songbirds, on gilt-brass wirework legs, unmarked.

13in (33cm) wide

$1,250-1,450 **L&T**

A 19thC lighthouse keeper's brass tinder box, one cover stamped "US LIGHT HOUSE ESTABLISHMENT," the other "US L H DEPOT 3 DIST. LAMP SHOP, STATEN ISLAND," the interior fitted with a tray, a box and holders for wicks, matches, oil, and funnels.

12¼in (31cm) long

$1,400-1,900 **NA**

A 19thC traveling tradesman's gilt-metal-mounted tortoiseshell veneered vitrine.

14¼in (36cm) high

$400-500 **BELL**

A mid-19thC Jennens & Bettridge writing box, with patent inlaid gems, with a fitted interior and a gilt-decorated papier-mâché frame.

Gem laying was introduced by Theodore Jennens in 1847.

13¾in (35cm) wide

$210-260 **BELL**

A Victorian brass-bound mahogany artist's box, inscribed "COLOURS FOR HERALDIC & MISSAL PAINTING C. ROWNEY & CO." on inside of lid.

10in (25.5cm) wide

$300-400 **BELL**

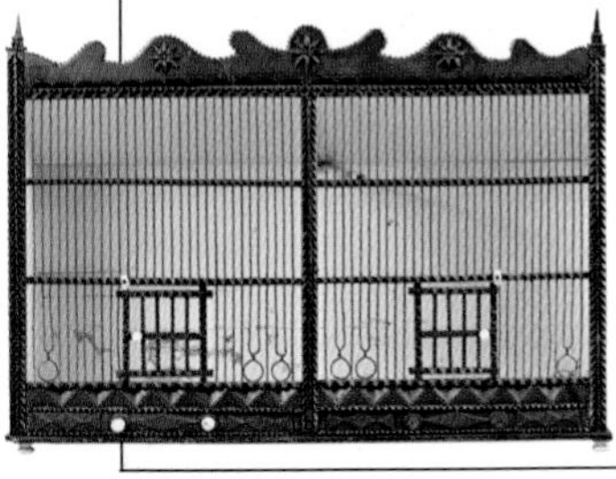

A 19thC birdcage, in the American "Tramp Art" manner.

32¼in (82cm) wide

$500-650 **BELL**

A German St. Bernard candy container, in white and brown artificial silk plush, glass eyes, oil-cloth collar, and head removed to reveal candy container.

1930s *12in (30.5cm) long*

$300-400 **SAS**

An Agfa Super Isolette 120 CRF camera, with Solinar 75mm f3.5 lens and "Ever Ready" case.

$450-500 **AST**

A Canon Pellix camera with FL 50mm f1.4 lens.

$100-130 **AST**

A Canon VI L Rangefinder camera, working, with Canon 28mm f2.8 lens and clip-on finder.

$600-700 **AST**

A Corfield Periflex 1 camera, with Lumar-X 50mm f3.5 lens, no.3434, with torpedo finder and case.

$260-320 **AST**

A 3B Quick Focus Kodak camera, for postcard-size prints.

In use, the focus distance is preset on the side-mounted scale and when a button is pressed the front lens board springs forward.

$130-180 **AST**

A Kodak Regent II Medium Format Rangefinder camera, fitted with Xenar 10.5cm f3.5, shutter linkage needs adjustment.

$700-850 **AST**

A Leica M2 N0 10108277 camera, Elmar 5 cm f2.8 no.1590916, with original leather case and instructions.

$950-1,100 **DUK**

A Leica IIIC no. 465037 camera, collapsible Elmar 50 mm f2.8 no.1669820 lens cap and original leather case.

$400-500 **DUK**

A rare Leica M4 Rangefinder chrome camera, serial no.331A, with Leitz Summicron-M f/2 50mm lens, serial no.3357940.

The top plate of the camera with serial no.331A indicates that this was originally part of a dummy camera and therefore the body and top plate may not be original to each other.

$1,900-2,600 **GORL**

A Leica model 1a camera, serial no.32019, with Letz Elmar1:3,5 F=50mm lens, in fitted leather case, with a cased Excelsior light meter.

$650-800 **FLD**

A Mamiya RZ67 120 professional camera, serial no.101027, with Mamiya Sekor Z f=90mm 1:35 lens, with instructions.

$500-650 **FLD**

A Meyer Planovista Primarette folding 6x4.5cm camera.

It is designed like two cameras, one on top of the other, the top for viewing and the bottom for taking.

$500-650 **AST**

A Mycro leather-cased IIIA miniature camera, with Mycro Una 1:4.5 F=20mm lens.

$25-40 **APAR**

A Penta Asahiflex camera, named for the South African Market, no.230406, slight wear to chrome.

In 1959, Pentax were in dispute with Zeiss, so their cameras for the South African market could not use the Pentax name. Their problems did not last long, so only a few had the Penta name before the Pentax name could legally be used. They are now extremely difficult to find.

$300-400 **AST**

A Nikon F5 film camera body, in maker's box.

$260-390 **AST**

A Ross & Co., London, plate camera, with a leather bellows and a leather and brass-mounted case, 8 x 5 rapid symmetrical brass lens, within fitted case with two Thornton-Pickard roller shutters, leather cased Zeiss Convertible Anastigmat 14in lens and other accessories.

$650-800 **WHP**

An uncommon Shew Twin Lens Xit.

It looks like a stereo camera, but one lens enables viewing on ground glass screen, the other is the taking lens.

$1,900-2,600 **AST**

A Seaside Photographer's camera and Taylor Hobson Lens, based on a Thornton Pickard Reflex plate cameras, no.30, with a Taylor Hobson Wide Angle 6 1/4inch f6.5 lens.

It was probably converted in the late 1940s by Sunbeam Photos, in Margate, UK, to accept rolls of photographic paper.

$180-230 **AST**

QUICK REFERENCE—CANES

- **Decorated canes first became popular during the 16thC, but they reached their golden age in terms of variety and quality in the late 18thC and 19thC. Favored by the upper classes and the bourgeoisie, they largely went out of fashion after World War I. As well as being of practical use, they acted as a status symbol.**
- **The shaft is usually made from wood. The handle or pommel can be made from ivory, bone, silver, gold, or wood. The tip of the stick or cane is typically tipped in metal to prevent it from being worn.**
- **Most canes found today date from the Victorian (19thC) or Edwardian (1901-10) period and can be divided into two types: decorative canes and gadget canes. The latter have a second function, such as containing something useful, for example, a small bottle or a telescope. Some canes cross into folk art and can attract large sums, particularly for rare and desirable American examples.**
- **In all instances, the quality of the decoration or objects inside, and of the material used, counts greatly toward value. Also consider the age and place of manufacture. Many sticks do not bear maker's marks, but may have hallmarks if in a precious metal, or a retailer's mark, such as Swaine & Adeney. Condition is also important—always examine carving all over to be sure parts are not missing.**

A George III gold and enamel-mounted walking cane, the handle with initials "SB" within chased laurel leaf borders, interspersed with oval paterae and with five oval panels decorated "en grisaille" with the muses, with an indistinct maker's mark, with an ebony tapering shaft.

37¾in (96cm) long

$2,300-2,900 WW

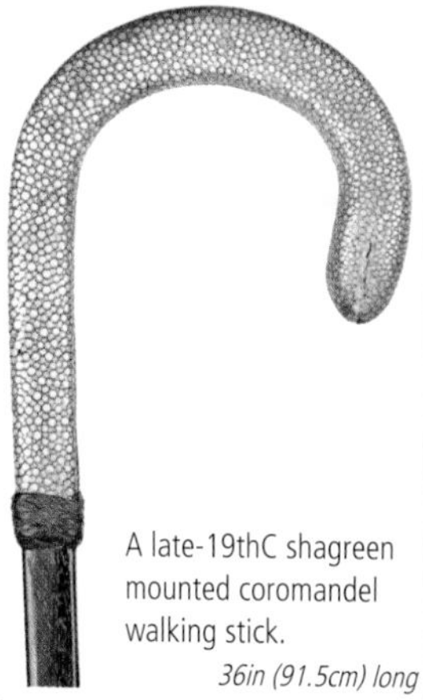

A late-19thC shagreen mounted coromandel walking stick.

36in (91.5cm) long

$260-320 BELL

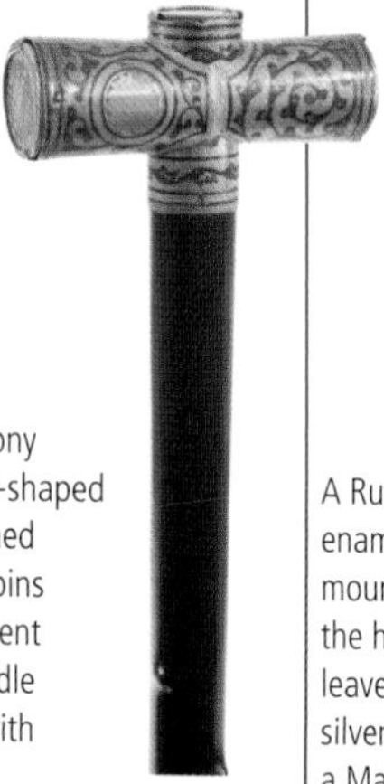

A Russian ebony cane, with a T-shaped handle designed to dispense coins of three different sizes, the handle is engraved with niello work.

35in (89cm) long

$1,900-2,600 SWO

A Russian cloisonné enamel and silver-mounted walking cane, the handle decorated with leaves and flowers, the silver marked "84," with a Malacca shaft.

35in (89cm) long

$650-800 WW

A late-19thC Continental gold-mounted snakewood walking cane.

36¼in (92cm) long

$1,250-1,450 BELL

A late-19thC Continental ivory walking cane, the handle in the form of a military gentleman, wearing the Order of the Golden Fleece and the Order of St. Esprit, with malacca shaft and bone ferrule.

32¾in (83cm) long

$650-800 ROS

An Edwardian walking stick, with bone carved handle, after DALI.

$190-260 JN

A Victorian folk art treen blackthorn walking cane, the handle carved with a grotesque bust of Punch, with glass eyes.

42in (106.5cm) long

$650-800 WW

A rare 19thC sharkskin boxed tortoiseshell walking cane, Toledo work handle with a Ducal crown on the end and initials for the Duke of Bivona, the ferrule is also in Toledo work, the sharkskin case with three metal fasteners and lined in satin, a small piece of wooden core is visible at the bottom of the stick.

box 38½in (98cm) long

$4,500-5,200 CHOR

A CLOSER LOOK AT A WALKING CANE

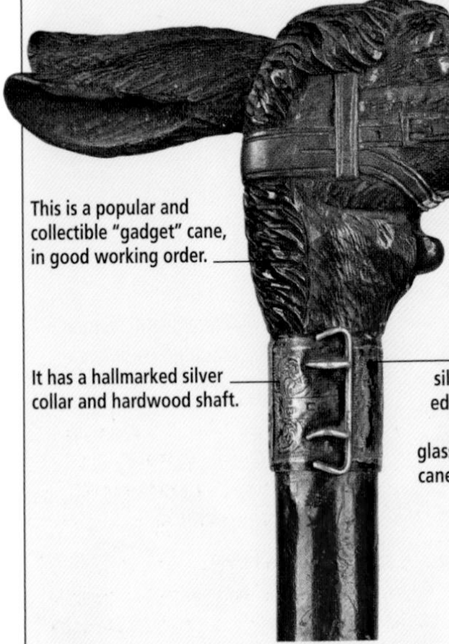

This is a popular and collectible "gadget" cane, in good working order.

The handle is carved as a donkey's head with automated ears and jaw.

It has a hallmarked silver collar and hardwood shaft.

Even with damage—the silver collar possibly a later edition, stick a little shorter than normal, lacking left glass eye, general wear—this cane is desirable because it is rare and interesting.

A late-19thC Black Forest walking cane.

32½in (82.5cm) long

$1,300-1,900 **BELL**

A thorn wood walking cane, the handle modeled as the head of a dog, with white metal collar at neck with engraved initials, handle and cane associated.

34½in (87.5cm) long

$260-390 **FELL**

A late-19thC silver-mounted blackthorn walking stick, the handle carved as a dog's head, in a silver muzzle, indistinctly hallmarked "London 18??."

34½in (87.5cm) long

$300-350 **BELL**

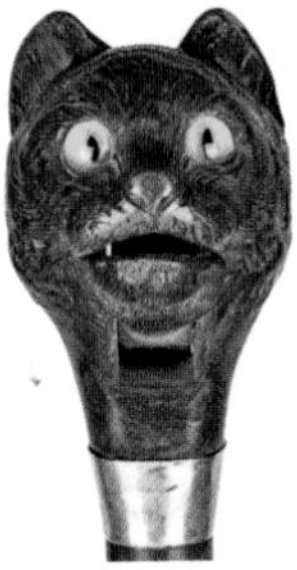

A late-19thC Black Forest novelty walking cane, the carved cat's head pommel with automated jaw, glass eyes, white metal collar, and hardwood shaft.

37in (94cm) long

$400-450 **BELL**

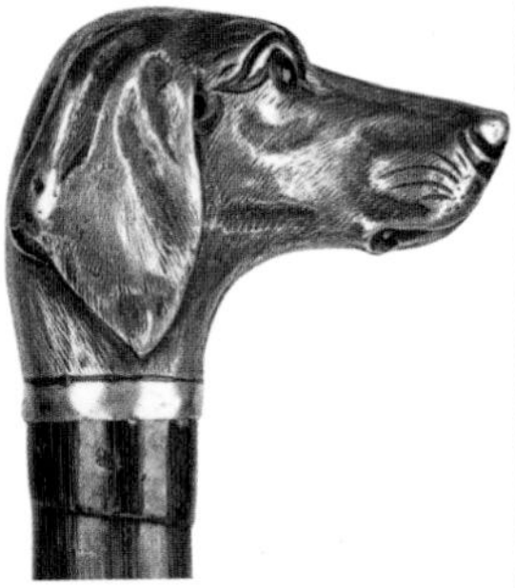

A silver-mounted bamboo walking cane, the handle cast as a dog's head with inset glass eyes, hallmarked "London 1889."

34in (86.5cm) long

$230-290 **BELL**

A malacca walking stick, with silver collar, the ivory handle carved as a pug head with glass eyes.

This stick contains an element of pre-1947 ivory or other organic material that may be subject to export restrictions.

$190-260 **CHOR**

A knotted wood walking stick, with brass collar and greyhound handle with beaded eyes.

This stick contains an element of pre-1947 ivory or other organic material that may be subject to export restrictions.

$230-290 **CHOR**

A rosewood walking stick, with gilt-copper collar and carved ivory bullmastiff handle.

This stick contains an element of pre-1947 ivory or other organic material that may be subject to export restrictions.

$190-260 **CHOR**

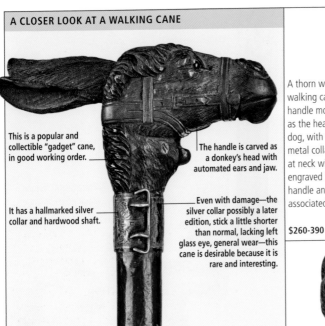

An Edwardian carved ivory walking cane, modeled as a bulldog's head, with engraved silver band.

This stick contains an element of pre-1947 ivory or other organic material that may be subject to export restrictions.

34in (86.5cm) long

$400-450 **JN**

A walking stick, with plated collar and ivory handle carved as a hound.

This stick contains an element of pre-1947 ivory or other organic material that may be subject to export restrictions.

$230-290 **CHOR**

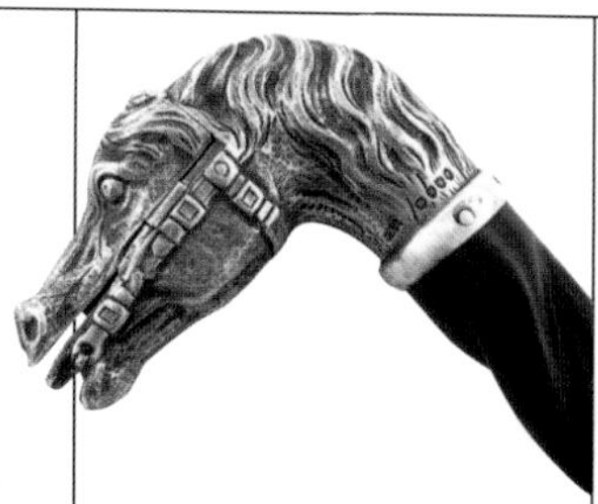

A late-Victorian novelty silver-mounted walking cane, maker's mark WH?, the handle modeled as a horse's head, the hinged cover opens to reveal a vesta compartment and hinged striker, and a hole, possibly for a lighting cord, carved wooden shaft.

1887 *36¼in (92cm) long*

$1,600-2,300 **WW**

A rosewood walking stick, with silver collar, the ivory handle carved as the hare and tortoise, the hare has a slight crack from eyes to the base of head, slight staining, stick slightly scatched, with no stop end.

This stick contains an element of pre-1947 ivory or other organic material that may be subject to export restrictions.

35in (89cm) long

$500-650 **CHOR**

A rosewood walking stick, the ivory handle with python and elephant finial, elephant is split and neck and trunk reglued, minor splits to elephant back, some minor straining throughout.

This stick contains an element of pre-1947 ivory or other organic material that may be subject to export restrictions.

35½in (90cm) long

$230-290 **CHOR**

A rosewood walking stick, with silver collar, the ivory handle carved as a horse with foal, stick is scratched and pitted, no stop end.

This stick contains an element of pre-1947 ivory or other organic material that may be subject to export restrictions.

35¾in (91cm) long

$1,900-2,600 **CHOR**

A Malacca shafted cane, concealing a horse measurer up to 17 hands, with a silver knop, the measuring arm concealing a level.

1895 *37in (94cm) long*

$600-650 **SWO**

An early-20thC Black Forest carved wooden bulldog umbrella handle, with automated mouth and ears, with a gilt metal collar, bamboo handle, and silk shade.

36¾in (93.5cm) long

$300-400 **BELL**

An Edwardian novelty silver-mounted carved wooden umbrella/pencil, by Charles Dumenil, retailed by Brigg, London, the handle carved as a snake head, set with green eyes, also with a pull-out fully marked silver pencil.

1908 *36¾in (93.5cm) long*

$500-600 **WW**

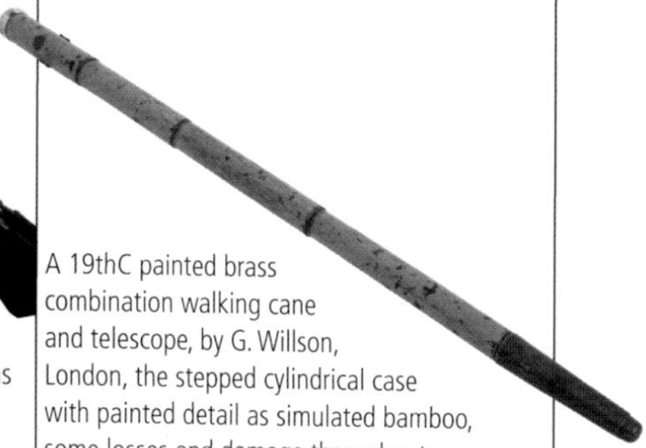

A 19thC painted brass combination walking cane and telescope, by G. Willson, London, the stepped cylindrical case with painted detail as simulated bamboo, some losses and damage throughout.

34in (86.5cm) long

$450-500 **KEY**

A 19thC Malacca mandarin cane, with a large silver cap, when unscrewed it releases a matching knife, fork, and a pair of chopsticks, the cap is engraved "To master Seaman Houghton from Colonel Raveunull."

34½in (87.5cm) long

$1,700-2,100 **SWO**

A triple function dog owner's cane, with a tapered ebony cane and cast handle including a whistle and a spring-loaded collar catch, with Ackwell's patent.

ca. 1895 *34¾in (88.5cm) long*

$950-1,100 **SWO**

A cane with a Brigg silver handle and a taxicab-hailing whistle, the forward part of the handle containing a press fit cap with a small tube holding a pencil, the handle hallmarked London and marked with initials on the cap, marked "69 St George's Square SW" on the stem.

1893 *36¼in (92cm) long*

$950-1,100 **SWO**

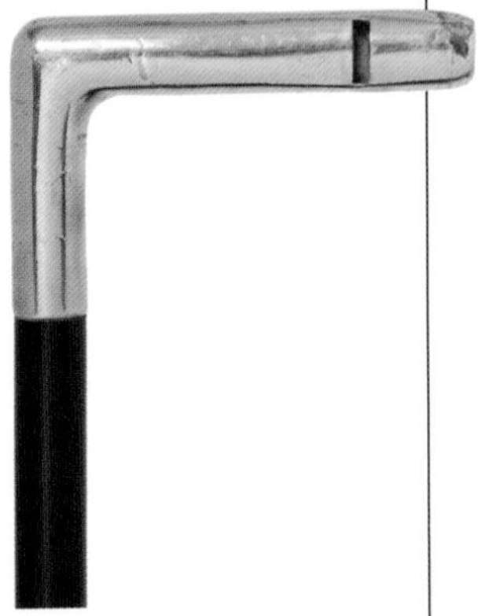

An Edwardian gold-mounted whistle walking cane, with a 9ct gold L-shaped handle, inscribed "Rd No 31680 J C Vicery 181-183 Regent St," with an ebonized shaft and horn ferrule.

1906 *34½in (88cm) long*

$650-800 **ROS**

A Victorian umbrella, modeled as an German shepherd's head, Black Forest carved wood handle, with glass eyes and bone teeth.

30¼in (77cm) long

$500-650 **JN**

A walking stick, with a silver knop, concealing a sword marked on one side of the blade "Defence not Defiance," and the other "Peace with Honour," the sword with a twist-release action.

1891 *35¾in (91cm) long*

$950-1,100 **SWO**

A stout square-section stiletto cane, with four silver straps at intervals along the length, with a silver cap, engraved "Lieut. Col. Thomas Brooke who carried the cane during the Peninsular War," with a concealed "flick" dagger in the handle.

35in (89cm) long

$1,050-1,150 **SWO**

A black knurled sword cane, with a short 12½in (32cm) blade, mounted atop a silver-plated watch that unscrews from the shaft, and is rewound by rotating the bezel in a counterclockwise direction, time adjustment is achieved by raising the hinged glass cover and rotating the centered knob.

ca. 1900 *35¼in (89.5cm) long*

$2,600-3,200 **SWO**

An unusual watch cane, possibly manufactured in Russia, with a French clock decorated with an enamel surround below the cap, the shaft of ebonized mahogany, the time is altered by rotating the rim of the watch after depressing a small catch, and it is rewound by rotating the outer rim in a counterclockwise direction.

ca. 1890 *34in (86.5cm) long*

$3,200-3,900 **SWO**

QUICK REFERENCE—BESWICK POTTERY

- **The Beswick Pottery was founded in Loughton, Staffordshire, in 1894, by James Wright Beswick and his sons John and Gilbert. It initially focused on tableware and vases, then began to produce figurines from 1900.**
- **Beswick was sold to Royal Doulton in 1969, but production continued under the name "Beswick" until 1989, when Beswick and Doulton animal figurines were combined as "Royal Doulton." The name "Beswick" returned to use in 1999 until the factory closed in 2002.**
- **Produced from 1900, Beswick's animal figurines remain its most desirable wares. By 1930, these figurines were successful and a major part of the factory's production—aided by the company's introduction of high-fired bone china in 1934. Beatrix Potter figurines, produced from 1946, and Disney figurines produced from 1952, are also popular.**
- **Prices for Beswick wares rose after the closure of the factory in 2002, and prices for rare figurines remain high. Early pieces, limited edition, or prototype figurines fetch the highest prices. However, it is difficult to identify early pieces, because figurines were not backstamped or numbered until 1934. Limited editions, even from the 1990s, can be valuable if the edition was small and you have documentation.**

A rare Beswick "Foal," designed by Arthur Gredington, model no.763, first version, blue gloss glazed.

First version has long ears. Second version has short ears.

1940-Unknown *3½in (9cm) high*

$700-850 PSA

A rare Beswick "Shire Mare," designed by Arthur Gredington, model no.818, first version, piebald gloss glazed.

8½in (21.5cm) high

$3,200-3,900 PSA

A rare Beswick "Shire Mare," designed by Arthur Gredington, model no.818, first version, chestnut gloss glazed.

1958-67 *8½in (21.5cm) high*

$1,900-2,600 PSA

A rare Beswick "Shire Mare," designed by Arthur Gredington, model no.818, first version, skewbald gloss glazed.

8½in (21.5cm) high

$5,200-6,500 PSA

A Beswick "Shire Mare," designed by Arthur Gredington, model no.818, first version, black gloss glazed.

In recognition of 50 years of production of model no.818, a black gloss shire mare was commissioned by the Beswick Collectors Circle in 1990. Approximately 135 of these were issued with a gold backstamp for Circle Members.

1990 *8½in (21.5cm) high*

$900-1,050 PSA

A Beswick "Foal," designed by Arthur Gredington, model no.836, in rocking horse gray, with early hint of blue colors.

5in (12.5cm) high

$850-950 PSA

A Beswick "Stocky Jogging Mare," designed by Arthur Gredington, model no.855, third version, black gloss glazed, Royal Doulton backstamp "DA44," produced for the Beswick Collectors Club.

Model no.855 third version was transferred to the Royal Doulton backstamp (DA44) in 1989.

2005 *6in (15cm) high*

$160-230 PSA

A Beswick "Stocky Jogging Mare," designed by Arthur Gredington, model no.855, third version, rocking horse gray gloss glazed.

ca. 947-62 *6in (15cm) high*

$700-850 PSA

A rare Beswick "Huntsman on Rearing Horse," designed by Arthur Gredington, model no.868, style one, rocking horse gray gloss glazed, restoration to back legs, tail, and one front leg.

1940-52 *10in (25.5cm) high*

$1,900-2,600 PSA

A Beswick "Huntsman on Rearing Horse," designed by Arthur Gredington, model no.868, second version, painted white gloss, slight crazing.

1965-71 *10in (25.5cm) high*

$500-650 **PSA**

A Beswick large "Shire Foal," designed by Arthur Gredington, model no.951, chestnut gloss glazed.

1958-67 *6¼in (16cm) high*

$700-850 **PSA**

A Beswick "Cantering Shire," designed by Arthur Gredington, model no.975, black gloss glazed, Collectors Club Special, boxed.

Model no.975 was transferred to the Royal Doulton Backstamp (DA45) in 1989.

1996 *8¾in (22cm) high*

$260-320 **PSA**

A Beswick "Cantering Shire," designed by Arthur Gredington, model no.975, palomino gloss glazed.

1961-70 *8¾in (22cm) high*

$700-850 **PSA**

A rare Beswick "Woolly Shetland Mare," designed by Arthur Gredington, model no.1033, chestnut gloss glazed, restoration to one ear.

5¾in (14.6cm) high

$6,000-6,500 **PSA**

A Beswick "Racehorse and Jockey," designed by Arthur Gredington, model no.1037, brown gloss glazed, with stripes on saddlecloth, one broken leg.

Colorway no.1 has stripes on the saddlecloth. Colorway no.2 has a number on the saddlecloth.

1945-Unknown *8½in (21.5cm) high*

$300-350 **PSA**

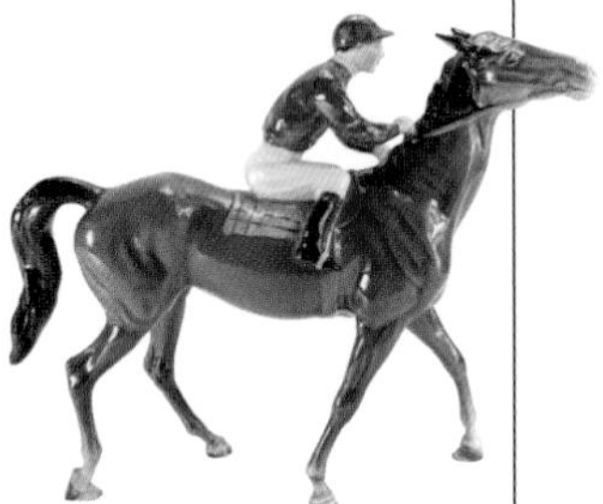

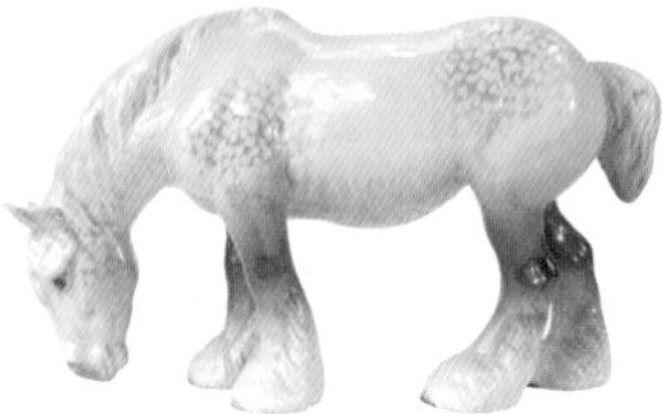

A Beswick "Grazing Shire," designed by Arthur Gredington, model no.1050, in gray gloss.

5½in (14cm) high

$500-650 **PSA**

A Beswick "Knight in Armour - The Earl of Warwick," designed by Arthur Gredington, model no.1145, gray gloss glazed.

1949-73 *10¾in (27.5cm) high*

$800-900 **PSA**

A Beswick "Swish Tail Horse," designed by Arthur Gredington, model no.1182, first version, chestnut gloss glazed.

1958-67 *8¾in (22cm) high*

$500-650 **PSA**

A Beswick "Pony," designed by Arthur Gredington, model no.1197, with head up, rocking horse gray gloss glazed.

ca. 1951-62 *5½in (14cm) high*

$600-700 **PSA**

A Beswick "Suffolk Punch Champion – Hasse Dainty," designed by Mr. Orwell, model no.1359, dark chestnut gloss glazed.

Unknown-1971 *8in (20.5cm) high*

$260-320 **PSA**

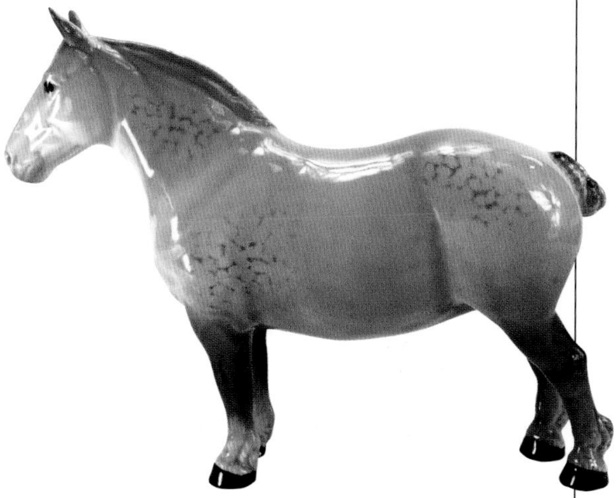

A rare Beswick "Suffolk Punch Champion – Hasse Dainty," designed by Mr. Orwell, model no.1359, gray gloss glazed, three chips on rear hoof.

1965 *8in (20.5cm) high*

$3,200-3,900 **PSA**

A Beswick "Pinto Pony," designed by Arthur Gredington, model no.1373, first version, palomino gloss glazed.

The tail of the first version is attached to the hind leg from the hock down.

1961-70 *6½in (16.5cm) high*

$1,150-1,450 **PSA**

A Beswick "Canadian Mounted Cowboy," designed by Mr. Orwell, model no.1377, palomino gloss glazed, tail restored.

1955-73 *8¾in (22cm) high*

$500-600 **CHT**

A Beswick "Mounted Indian," designed by Mr. Orwell, model no.1391, skewbald gloss glazed.

1955-90 *8½in (21.5cm) high*

$350-480 **PSA**

A rare Beswick "Girl's Pony," designed by Arthur Gredington, model no.1483, rocking horse gray gloss glazed.

1957-62 *5in (12.5cm) high*

$950-1,100 **PSA**

A Beswick "Girl on Pony," designed by Arthur Gredington, model no.1499, skewbald gloss glazed.

The pony used for model no.1499 was also available separately as model no.1483 "Girl's Pony."

1957-65 *5½in (14cm) high*

$400-450 **PSA**

A rare Beswick "Girl on Pony," designed by Arthur Gredington, model no.1499, with light green jacket.

5½in (14cm) high

$1,900-2,600 **PSA**

A rare Beswick model of a boy on chestnut pony, designed by Arthur Gredington, model no.1499, with green jacket.

5½in (14cm) high

$1,900-2,600 **PSA**

A rare Beswick "Huntsman," designed by Arthur Gredington, model no.1501, on rocking horse gray horse, restoration to all legs.

8¼in (21cm) high

$1,300-1,900 **PSA**

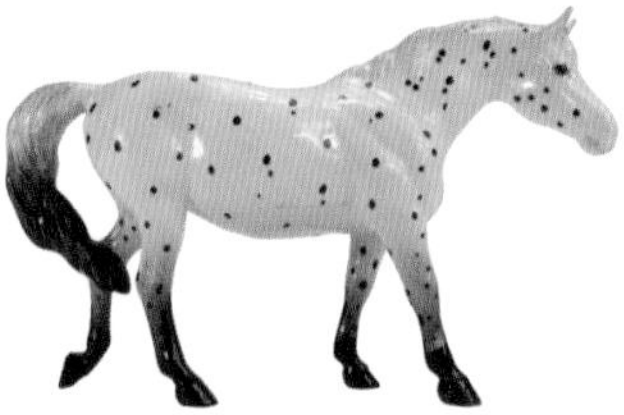

A Beswick "Appaloosa Spotted Walking Pony," designed by Arthur Gredington, model no.1516, gloss glazed.

1957-66 *5¼in (13.5cm) high*

$500-600 **PSA**

A Beswick "Horse," designed by Pal Zalmen, model no.1549, first version, chestnut gloss glazed.

The tail of the first version is angled toward the off-hind hock.

1958-67 *7½in (19cm) high*

$800-900 **PSA**

A Beswick "Fell Pony - Dene Dauntless," designed by Arthur Gredington, model no.1647, black gloss glazed.

This model is part of the "Mountain and Moorland Ponies" series.

1961-82 *6¾in (17cm) high*

$160-230 **PSA**

A Beswick "Huntswoman," designed by Arthur Gredington, model no.1730, style two, gray gloss glazed.

1960-95 *8¼in (21cm) high*

$260-320 **PSA**

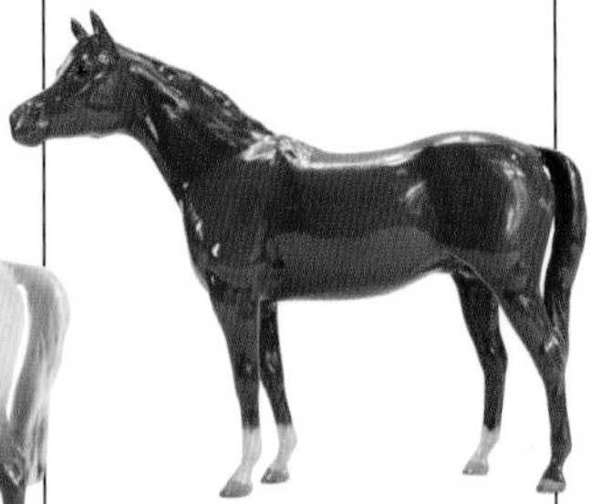

A Beswick horse, "Arab Bahram," designed by Arthur Gredington, model no.1771, chestnut gloss glazed.

From the "Connoiseur Horses" series.

1961-67 *7½in (19cm) high*

$800-900 **PSA**

A rare Beswick "Thoroughbred Foal," designed by Arthur Gredington, model no.1817, piebald gloss glazed.

3¼in (8.5cm) high

$400-500 **PSA**

A Beswick "Horse and Jockey," designed by Arthur Gredington, model no.1862, style two, light dapple gray gloss glazed, ear reglued.

1963-83 *8in (20.5cm) high*

$190-260 **PSA**

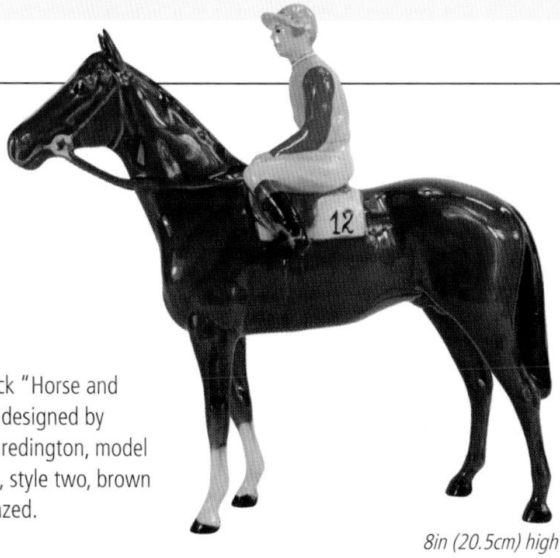

A Beswick "Horse and Jockey," designed by Arthur Gredington, model no.1862, style two, brown gloss glazed.

1963-84 *8in (20.5cm) high*

$230-290 **PSA**

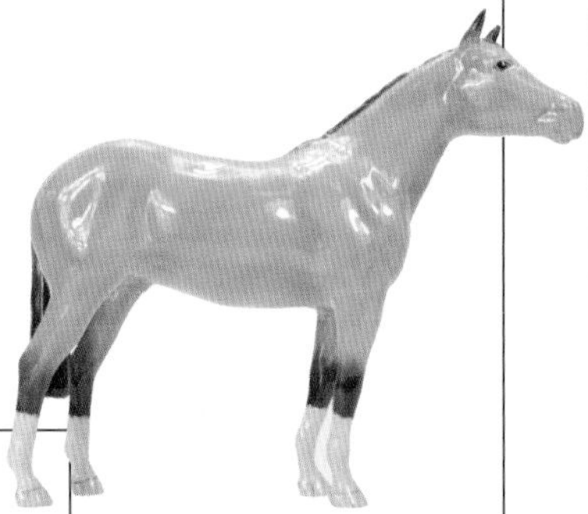

A Beswick "Dun Stallion," model no.2007, limited-edition Collectors Club piece, boxed.

$190-260 **PSA**

A small Beswick "T'ang Horse," designed by Graham Tongue, model no.2137, green/bronze gloss glazed.

1967-72 *8in (20.5cm) high*

$350-440 **PSA**

A large Beswick "T'ang Horse," designed by Graham Tongue, model no.2205, green/bronze gloss glazed.

1968-72 *13in (33cm) high*

$450-500 **PSA**

A Beswick "Highwayman on Rearing Horse," designed by Albert Hallam, model no.2210, bay mat glazed, on a wooden plinth.

From the "Connoisseur Horses" series.

1970-75 *13¾in (35cm) high*

$500-650 **PSA**

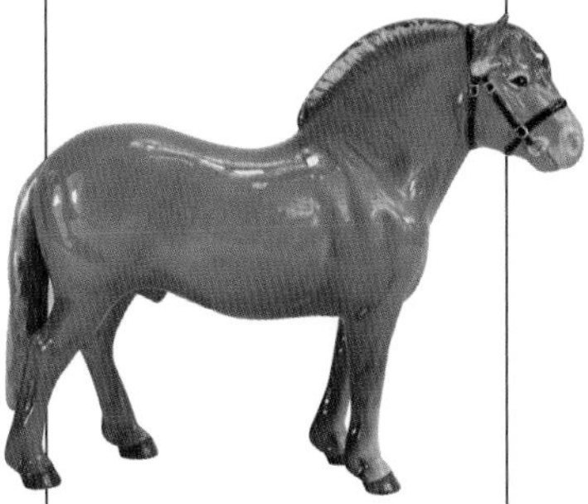

A Beswick "Norwegian Fjord Horse," designed by Albert Hallam, model no.2282, dun gloss glazed.

1970-75 *6½in (16.5cm) high*

$260-390 **PSA**

A rare Beswick "White Horse Whisky," designed by Alan Maslankowski, model no.2514, white gloss glazed.

This model is part of the "Advertising" series.

1974 *6¾in (17cm) high*

$700-800 **PSA**

A Beswick "Red Rum with Brian Fletcher Up," designed by Graham Tongue, model no.2511, bay mat glazed, on a wooden base.

From the "Connoisseur Horses" series.

1975-82 *12¼in (31cm) high*

$400-450 **PSA**

A Beswick "Lifeguard," designed by Graham Tongue, model no.2562, style two, black gloss glazed, on a wooden base.

This is from the "Connoisseur Horses" series. Model no.2562 was transferred to the Royal Doulton backstamp (DA22) in 1989.

1977-89 *14½in (37cm) high*

$140-190 **PSA**

A Royal Doulton "Chestnut Punch Peon" galloping shire horse, designed by W.M. Chance, model no.HN2623.

1950-60 *7½in (19cm) high*

$210-260 **PSA**

A Beswick "Rearing Cancara," designed by Graham Tongue, model no.3426, mat black, made for the Beswick centenary, on a wooden base, boxed.

Model no.3426 was transferred to the Royal Doulton backstamp (DA234) in 1989. It reverted to the Beswick backstamp in September 1999. Modeled from the "Downland Cancara" graded Trakehner stallion famous for advertising Lloyds Bank.

1994 *16½in (42cm) high*

$210-260 **PSA**

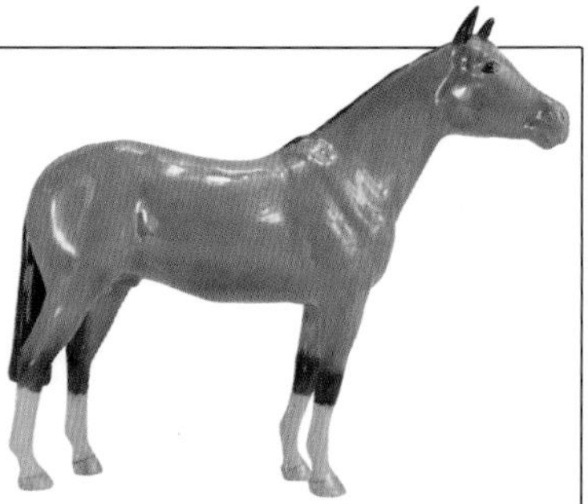

A Beswick "Stallion," model no.BCC2007, dun gloss glazed, produced for the Beswick Collectors Club.

2007 *7½in (19cm) high*

$130-190 **PSA**

A Beswick Connoisseur "Champion Welsh Mountain Pony," designed by Graham Tongue, black gloss glazed, produced for the Beswick Collectors Club, boxed.

The "Champion Welsh Mountain Pony" was issued in a limited edition of 580. Model DA247 was transferred from the Royal Doulton backstamp in September 1999.

1999 *8¼in (21cm) high*

$260-320 **PSA**

A Beswick "Shetland Pony - Hollydell Dixie," designed by Amanda Hughes-Lubeck, model no.H185, skewbald gloss glazed, produced for the Beswick Collectors Club, boxed.

1995 *5¼in (13.5cm) high*

$190-260 **PSA**

A Beswick "Shetland Pony," designed by Amanda Hughes-Lubeck, dapple gray gloss glazed.

The "Shetland Pony" model was transferred from the Royal Doulton backstamp (DA185) in September 1999.

1992-99

$130-190 **PSA**

A Beswick "Warlord's Mare - Another Bunch," designed by Graham Tongue, bay/brown gloss glazed.

This was the second in a series of specially commissioned models for PR Middleweek & Co. from the John Beswick Studios, limited to 1,500 models.

1997 *6in (15cm) high*

$60-90 **PSA**

Judith Picks

Kruger was the last pit pony to work at the Chatterley Whitfield Colliery and was retired in 1931.

The first model from this set of four was presented to H.R.H. Princess Royal on her visit to Chatterley Whitfield Mining Museum to open the New Pit on October 13, 1987.

A rare Beswick "Spirit of Whitfield," by Graham Tongue, modeled after "Kruger," some tarnishing to the metal plaque.

9½in (24cm) high

$8,000-9,000 **PW**

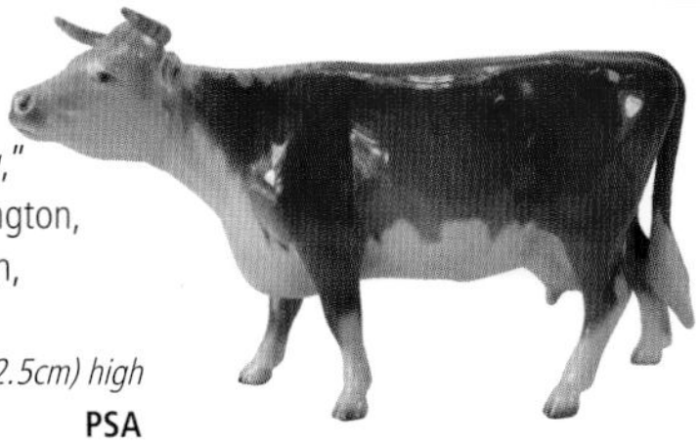

A Beswick "Hereford Cow," designed by Arthur Gredington, model no.948, first version, restored horn.
1941-ca. 1957 *5in (12.5cm) high*
$60-100 **PSA**

An early Beswick "Hereford Bull," designed by Arthur Gredington, model no.949, brown and white gloss glazed.
ca. 1941-57 *5¾in (14.5cm) high*
$130-190 **PSA**

A rare Beswick Lincoln Red Bull, model no.1363A, red gloss glazed, stamped "Beswick England," minor crazing to glaze.
4½in (11.5cm) high
$5,200-5,800 **CHT**

A Beswick "Dairy Shorthorn Calf," desiged by Arthur Gredington, model no.1406C, brown and white with shading gloss glazed, restored ears.
1956-73 *3in (7.5cm) high*
$190-260 **PSA**

A Beswick "Dairy Shorthorn Bull - CH Gwersylt Lord Oxford 74th," designed by Arthur Gredington, model no.1504, brown and white with shading gloss glazed.
1957-73 *5in (12.5cm) high*
$450-500 **PSA**

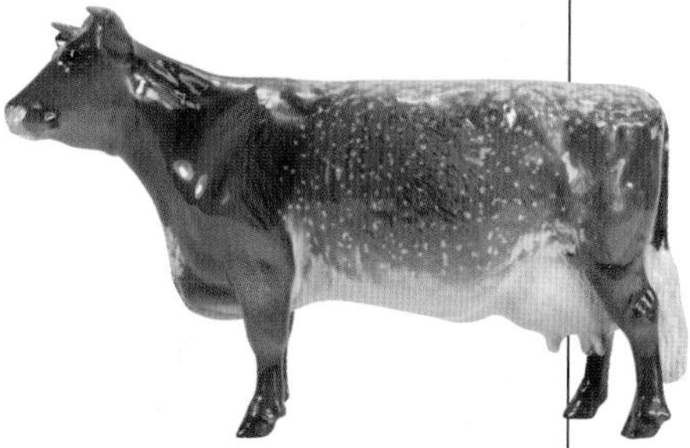

A Beswick "Dairy Shorthorn Cow - CH Eaton Wild Eyes 91st," designed by Arthur Gredington, model no.1510, brown and white with shading gloss glazed, restored front legs.
1957-73 *4¾in (12cm) high*
$450-500 **PSA**

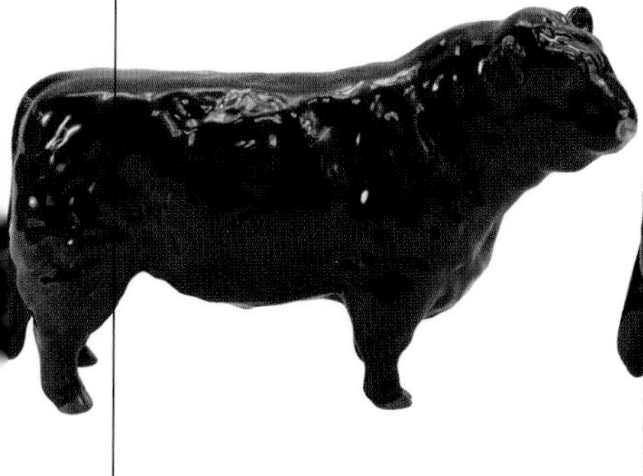

A Beswick "Galloway Bull," designed by Arthur Gredington, model no.1746A, black gloss glazed.
1962-69 *4½in (11.5cm) high*
$950-1,100 **PSA**

A Beswick "Belted Galloway Bull," designed by Arthur Gredington, model no.1746B, black and white gloss glazed.
1963-69 *4½in (11.5cm) high*
$950-1,100 **PSA**

A Beswick "Silver Dunn Galloway Bull," designed by Arthur Gredington, model no.1746C, fawn and brown gloss glazed.
1962-69 *4½in (11.5cm) high*
$900-1,050 **PSA**

A Beswick "Aberdeen Angus Calf," designed by Arthur Gredington, model no.1827A, black gloss glazed.

1985-89 *3in (7.5cm) high*

$100-130 **PSA**

A Beswick "Shetland Cow," designed by Robert Donaldson, model no.4112, black and white gloss glazed.

This model is part of the "Rare Breeds" series.

2001-02 *5¼in (13.5cm) high*

$100-130 **PSA**

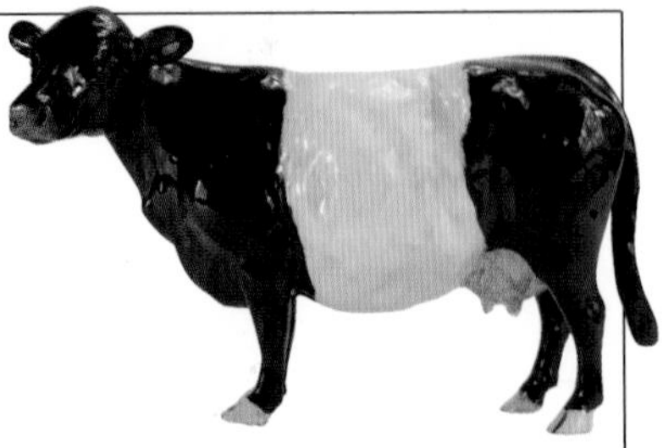

A Beswick "Belted Galloway Cow," designed by Robert Donaldson, model no.4113A, gloss glazed.

2001-02 *5¼in (13.5cm) high*

$140-190 **PSA**

A Beswick "Black Galloway Cow," designed by Robert Donaldson, model no.4113B, gloss glazed, produced for the Beswick Collectors Club.

2002 *5¼in (13.5cm) high*

$160-230 **PSA**

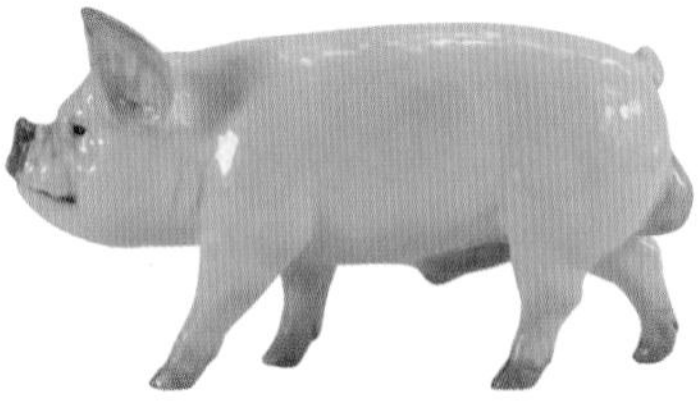

A Beswick "Middlewhite Boar," designed by Robert Donaldson, model no.4117, white gloss glazed.

This model is part of the "Rare Breeds" series.

2001-02 *8in (20.5cm) high*

$130-190 **PSA**

A Beswick "Merino Ram," by Arthur Gredington, model no.1917, gray with white face gloss glazed, oval mark.

1964-67 *4¼in (11cm) high*

$650-800 **FLD**

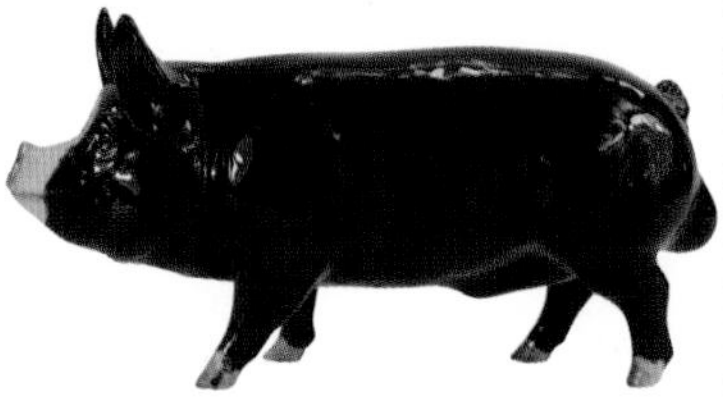

A Beswick "Berkshire Boar," designed by Robert Donaldson, model no.4118, black and gray gloss glazed.

This model is part of the "Rare Breeds" series.

2001-02 *3¼in (8.5cm) high*

$160-210 **PSA**

A Beswick "Tamworth Pig," designed by Amanda Hughes-Lubeck, model no.G215, brown gloss glazed.

Transferred from the Royal Doulton backstamp (DA215) in September 1999.

1999-present *6in (15cm) high*

$80-100 **PSA**

A Beswick "Gloucester Old Spot Pig," designed by Amanda Hughes-Lubeck, model no.G230, pink with black markings gloss glazed.

Transferred from the Royal Doulton backstamp (DA230) in September 1999.

1999-present *3in (7.5cm) high*

$130-190 **PSA**

A Beswick "Seagull on Rock," designed by Arthur Gredington, model no.768, gloss glazed, beak and wing tip restored.

1939-54 *8½in (21.5cm) high*

$600-650 **PSA**

A rare Beswick "Grebie," designed by Arthur Gredington, model no.1006.

This model is part of the "Stylistic Model" series.

1945–54 *5¼in (13.5cm) high*

$1,600-1,900 **WM**

A Beswick "Barnacle Goose," designed by Arthur Gredington, model no.1052, dark gray-blue and white gloss glazed.

1943-68 *6½in (16.5cm) high*

$300-400 **PSA**

A Beswick "Kookaboro," model no.1159.

$80-100 **PSA**

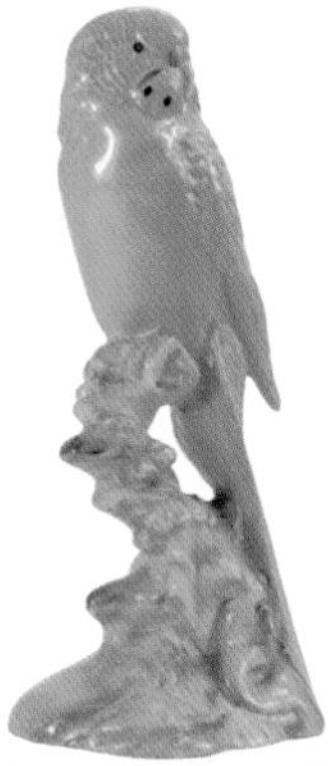

A Beswick "Budgerigar," designed by Arthur Gredington, model no.1216B, second version, yellow gloss glazed.

This version has no flowers on the base.

1970-72 *7in (18cm) high*

$600-700 **PSA**

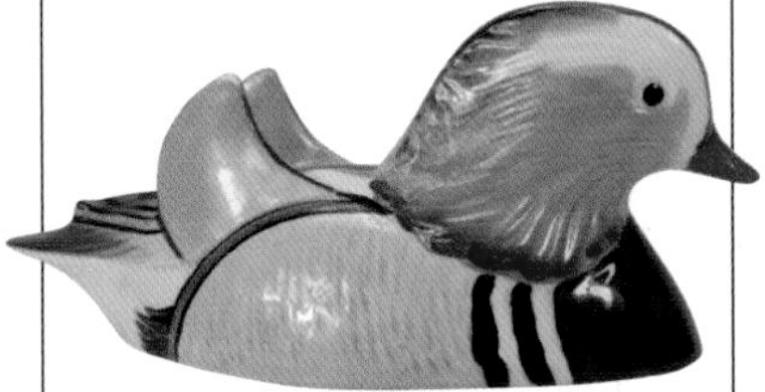

A Beswick "Mandarin Duck," designed by Arthur Gredington, model no.1519-1, approved by Peter Scott.

1958-71

$130-190 **PSA**

A Beswick "Fantail Pigeon," designed by Arthur Gredington, model no.1614, white gloss.

1959-69 *5in (12.5cm) high*

$230-290 **PSA**

A Beswick "Sussex Cockerel," designed by Arthur Gredington, model no.1899, black, white, and pink gloss glazed, minor crazing to glaze.

1963-71 *7in (18cm) high*

$450-500 **WM**

A Beswick "Turkey," designed by Albert Hallam, model no.1957, white gloss glazed.

1964-69 *7¼in (18.5cm) high*

$600-650 **PSA**

A Beswick "Gamecock," designed by Arthur Gredington, model no.2059, gloss glazed.

1966-75 *9½in (24cm) high*

$300-400 **FLD**

A Beswick "Pair of Partridges," designed by Albert Hallam, model no.2064.

1966-75 *5½in (14cm) high*

$300-350 **PSA**

A Beswick "Cedar Waxwing," designed by Graham Tongue, model no.2184, gloss glazed.

1968-73 *4½in (11.5cm) high*

$190-260 **PSA**

A Beswick large "Penguin," designed by Albert Hallam, model no.2357, black and white gloss glazed.

This model is part of the "Fireside Model" series.

1971-76 *12in (30.5cm) high*

$500-650 **PSA**

A Beswick "Penguin Chick," designed by Graham Tongue, model no.2398, gloss glazed.

1971-76 *7in (18cm) high*

$260-390 **PSA**

A Beswick "Penguin Chick," designed by Graham Tongue, model no.2434, sliding, gloss glazed.

1972-76 *8in (20.5cm) wide*

$500-600 **PSA**

A Beswick "Staffordshire Bull Terrier - Bandits Brintiga," designed by Arthur Gredington, model no.1982A, dark brindle gloss glazed.

1964-69 *4¾in (12cm) high*

$260-320 **PSA**

A Beswick large "Fireside Labrador Dog," designed by Graham Tongue, model no.2314, gloss.

1970-89 *13½in (34.5cm) high*

$130-190 **PSA**

A Beswick "Labrador," designed by Alan Maslankowski, model no.3062B, chocolate brown gloss glazed, produced for the Beswick Collectors Club (BCC), boxed.

Produced for the BCC with a special BCC backstamp.

1993 *5in (12.5cm) high*

$400-500 **PSA**

A Beswick "Cat Scratching Ear," designed by Albert Hallam, model no.1877, gray Swiss roll colorway gloss glazed.
1964-66 *6½in (16.5cm) high*
$190-260 **PSA**

A Beswick "Moose," designed by Arthur Gredington, model no.2090, dark brown gloss glazed.
1967-73 *6¼in (16cm) high*
$650-800 **PSA**

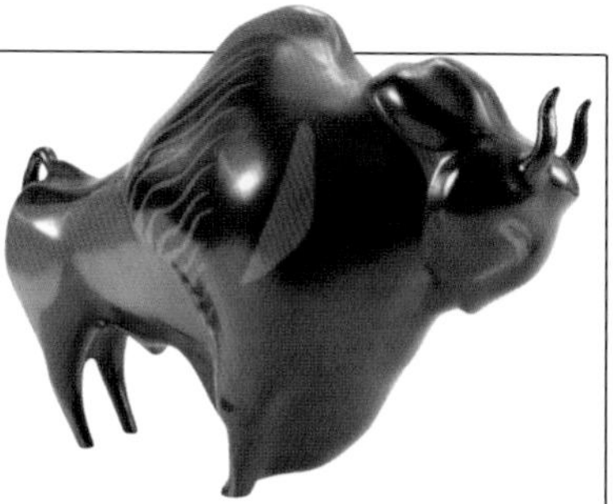

A Beswick "Stylised Bull," designed by Colin Melbourne, brown and black colorway, one horn reglued.
7in (18cm) high
$190-260 **PSA**

A rare Beswick Beatrix Potter "Tailor of Gloucester," modeled by Arthur Gredington, model no.1108, stamped "BP1a."
1949-2002 *3½in (9cm) high*
$5,200-6,500 **CHT**

A rare Beswick Beatrix Potter "Duchess with flowers," designed by Graham Orwell, model no.1355, style one, stamped "BP2a."
1955-67 *3¾in (9.5cm) high*
$1,100-1,250 **PSA**

A Beswick Beatrix Potter "Pickles," modeled by Albert Hallam, model no.2334, stamped "BP3b."
1971-82 *4½in (11.5cm) high*
$80-100 **PSA**

A Beswick Beatrix Potter "Sir Isaac Newton," modeled by Graham Tongue, model no.2425, stamped "BP3b."
1973-84 *3¾in (9.5cm) high*
$130-190 **PSA**

A Beswick Beatrix Potter "Simpkin," modeled by Alan Maslankowski, model no.2508, stamped "BP3b."
1975-83 *4in (10cm) high*
$100-$130 **PSA**

A Beswick Beatrix Potter "Ginger," modeled by David Lyttleton, model no.2559, stamped "BP3b."
1976-82 *3¾in (9.5cm) high*
$100-$130 **PSA**

An Arts and Crafts painted ceramic mug, with text "Some people are always grumbling because roses have thorns; I am so glad that thorns have roses." A. Kapp, the base reads "To be kept for some of A.M.'s best printing for B. or/or R. or M.," signed, dated.
1916 *3¼in (8.5cm) high*
$230-290 **DUK**

QUICK REFERENCE—TRANSFER-PRINTED WARES

- **A cheaper and quicker alternative to painting ceramics by hand, transfer printing was developed between 1757 and 1758 at the Worcester factory.**
- **A design was engraved on a copper sheet and covered in ink. The design could then be transferred to the ceramics surface using paper and sealed under a clear glaze.**
- **Transfer-printed wares were traditionally blue and white, because a cobalt blue underglaze was, at the time, the only one that could withstand the heat of the kiln.**
- **By the 1770s, printed blue-and-white ceramics were being mass produced by factories across England, including at Worcester and Spode. Makers in Staffordshire used this printing method on inexpensive pottery, eventually undermining the porcelain industry.**

An early-19thC dish, perhaps by John Rose, Coalport, transfer printed in underglaze blue, "Dragon" pattern, with twin shell-form handles, unmarked, restored handle.
12in (30.5cm) wide
$130-190 **HALL**

A Baker, Bevans and Irwin meat plate, "Ladies of Llangollen" design, three small restored rim chips.
19in (48.5cm) wide
$190-260 **CHOR**

An early-19thC Davenport blue-and-white pap boat, printed mark.
4¼in (11cm) long
$230-290 **HAN**

A 19thC blue Staffordshire English scenery pitcher and basin, small worn spot to tip of handle.
pitcher 8¾in (22cm) high
$450-600 **POOK**

A Staffordshire nine-piece supper set, "Lace Border" design, with a mahogany two-handled tray of a later date, one lid has a small chip and another a hair crack.
21¼in (54cm) diam
$450-600 **CHOR**

A 19thC Staffordshire footbath, printed in the interior with a large vase of flowers, against a seeded ground scattered with flowers, printed mark "Semi-China."
7¾in (19.5cm) high
$1,900-2,600 **BELL**

An early-19thC creamware "Frederick Duke of York" commemorative mug, entitled "His Royal Highness FREDERICK DUKE of YORK," painted "X" to base, some damage.
4¾in (12cm) high
$120-160 **FLD**

A 19thC Staffordshire pearlware mug, with a transfer Chinoiserie scene, unmarked, slight damage.
5½in (14cm) high
$45-60 **FLD**

A 19thC Staffordshire platter, "Christiansburg Danish Settlement on the Gold Coast of Africa" design.

20¾in (52.5cm) wide

$1,300-1,900 **POOK**

A 19thC Staffordshire platter, "America & Independence" design, impressed Clews.

16¾in (42.5cm) wide

$1,900-2,600 **POOK**

A 19thC Staffordshire platter, "Winter View of Pittsfield, Massachusetts" design, marked Clews, light staining on underside.

14½in (37cm) wide

$700-850 **POOK**

A 19thC Staffordshire platter, "Landing of Lafayette" design, impressed Clews.

17in (43cm) wide

$800-900 **POOK**

A 19thC Staffordshire cup plate, eagle and shield design.

3¾in (9.5cm) diam

$1,900-2,600 **POOK**

A 19thC Staffordshire undertray, "Woodlands Near Philadelphia" design, shallow chip on base.

10½in (26.5cm) wide

$950-1,100 **POOK**

A 19thC Staffordshire platter, depicting "Military School, West Point, New York," rim repair.

17½in (44.5cm) wide

$1,300-1,900 **POOK**

A 19thC Staffordshire fruit bowl, "State House, Boston" design.

11¼in (28.5cm) wide

$3,200-3,900 **POOK**

A 19thC Staffordshire soup tureen, with camel and attendant, the lid with a rabbit, both handles with a few spots of glaze loss, small flake to finial.

10¼in (26cm) high

$850-950 **POOK**

A 19thC Staffordshire soup tureen, depicting NW view of La Grange, the residence of the Marquis Lafayette, with a grapevine pattern ladle, repaired breaks to ladle, repair to rim of tureen.

15in (38cm) wide

$650-800 **POOK**

A Staffordshire fruit bowl, "Esplanade and Castle Garden, New York" design, one small hairline crack.

10in (25.5cm) wide

$3,600-4,500 **POOK**

A 19thC Staffordshire Quadrupeds reticulated tray, with fox and rooster design, inscribed "J Hall."

12¼in (31cm) wide

$3,200-3,900 **POOK**

A Lawrence Mansion Staffordshire transfer-printed wash basin, "Boston (Boston Athenæum)" design, Ralph Stevenson (& Son), Cobridge, impressed "STEVENSON," with the spire of the Octagon Church in the background.

Apparently this view appears only on wash basins, one version with a regular rim, the other the rarer example with white molded gadrooned rim, as on this piece.

1810-35 *12¾in (32.5cm) diam*

$1,300-1,900 **NA**

A 19thC Staffordshire pitcher, "America & Independence" design.

6¾in (17cm) high

$1,900-2,600 **POOK**

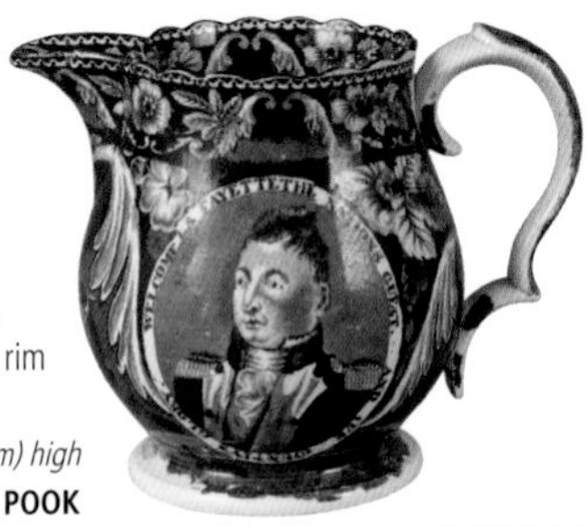

A 19thC Staffordshire pitcher, "Welcome Lafayette" design, rim flake, firing indent on spout.

5¾in (14.5cm) high

$950-1,100 **POOK**

A Staffordshire gravy boat, "Catholic Cathedral" design.

7¾in (19.5cm) wide

$1,300-1,900 **POOK**

A Staffordshire transfer-printed caster, Enoch Wood & Sons, with four figures in a rowboat.

1818-46 *4¼in (11cm) high*

$1,900-2,600 **NA**

QUICK REFERENCE—BURMANTOFTS

- **In the late 19thC, Burmantofts Faience Pottery began as a side project to James Holroyd's brickworks company, and an art pottery studio was opened in Leeds, England, using local deposits of clay. The company specialized in hand-thrown and hand-painted ceramics.**
- **Burmantofts was influenced by the Aesthetic Movement and produced a range of detailed ceramics between 1881 and 1904, when its production of art pottery ceased.**
- **Many wares were hand modeled, often using the French Barbotine technique, where thick slip is used to paint and model ceramics. Some lines, such as the fantastical grotesques and "Partie-Colour", were made from molds, then embellished and painted by hand. Burmantofts monochrome wares of blue, red, and orange-yellow are especially distinctive.**
- **The breadth and variation of Burmantofts' designs demonstrate the freedom the designers had to explore their own ideas. Designer Joseph Walmsley's (1865-1956) repertoire includes "Partie-Colour" and luster-glazed wares.**

A Burmantofts Faience "Anglo-Persian" pitcher, by Leonard King, model no.90, impressed marks, painted "LK" monogram, D.527.

8in (20.5cm) high

$450-600 **WW**

A Burmantofts Faience "Anglo-Persian" vase, by Leonard King, model no.D221, impressed marks, painted marks and "LK" monogram, professionally restored.

10in (25.5cm) high

$500-650 **WW**

A Burmantofts Faience "Partie-Colour" vase, by Joseph Walmsley, impressed marks.

12¼in (31cm) high

$600-700 **WW**

A Burmantofts Faience "Partie-Colour" vase, designed by Joseph Walmsley, model no.2121, decorated with a peacock perched on a bough, the reverse with a crane, impressed and painted marks.

20½in (52cm) high

$1,300-1,900 **WW**

A Burmantofts Faience "Anglo-Persian" vase, by Leonard King, impressed marks, painted "LK" monogram, small glaze nick.

5in (12.5cm) high

$500-650 **WW**

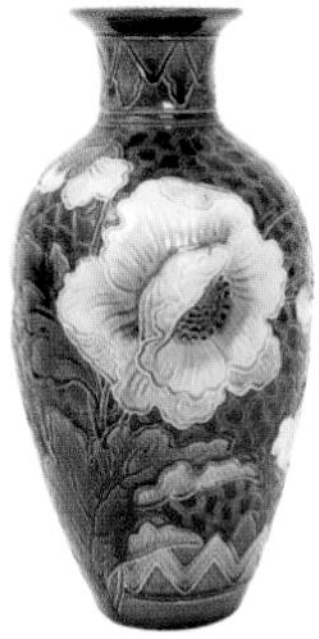

A Burmantofts Faience vase, designed by Joseph Walmsley, model no.2048, impressed and painted marks.

12in (30.5cm) high

$400-450 **WW**

A Burmantofts Faience luster wall plaque, by Joseph Walmsley, painted with an Egyptian queen and hieroglyphs, impressed marks, painted "JW" monogram.

14½in (37cm) diam

$500-650 **WW**

A Burmantofts Faience luster vase, by Joseph Walmsley, model no.1327, impressed marks, painted "JW" and "No1," fine crazing in the ground.

12¼in (31cm) high

$600-700 **WW**

A Burmantofts Faience luster vase, by Joseph Walmsley, painted "JW" monogram.

8½in (21.5cm) high

$600-700 **WW**

A Burmantofts Faience large jardinière, model no.1306, impressed marks, minor glaze chip on top rim.

17¼in (44cm) high

$650-700 **WW**

A Burmantofts Faience jardinière and stand, the jardinière modeled in relief with classical winged cherub, the base with three sitting griffins, impressed marks, chips, glaze loss from water damage to the interior.

34in (86.5cm) high

$450-600 **WW**

A Burmantofts Faience jardinière and stand, model no.2155, modeled in relief with Art Nouveau water lily flowers, impressed and painted marks, two stress crack lines in the bowl's side.

41¼in (105cm) high

$600-700 **WW**

A Burmantofts Faience "Veritas" oil stove and cover, cast with Moorish fan-shaped flower panels, cast "Burmantofts Faience" and "Veritas," light chips and losses.

32¼in (82cm) high

$650-800 **WW**

An unusual Burmantofts Faience "Partie-Colour" wall plaque, slip decorated with flag iris, impressed marks, incised "2309."

12in (30.5cm) diam

$500-650 **WW**

A Burmantofts Faience large floor vase, model no.649, impressed factory marks.

21¼in (54cm) high

$650-800 **WW**

A Burmantofts Faience stick stand, model no.808, impressed mark, a small glaze chip on the rim.

24in (61cm) high

$400-500 **WW**

A Burmantofts Faience pierced Koro cover and stand, the cover with a grotesque anthropomorphic creature, in a sang-de-boeuf glaze, impressed "Burmantofts Faience."

10in (25.5cm) high

$800-900 **WW**

A Burmantofts Faience "Barbotine Pilgrim" flask, model no.298, impressed marks, original paper label, restored chip on foot.

The design on this flask is just to one side.

11¾in (30cm) high

$300-350 **WW**

A Burmantofts Faience "Partie-Colour" vase, impressed marks.

18¼in (46.5cm) high

$500-600 **WW**

A Burmantofts Faience "Partie-Colour" vase, model no.2063, impressed and painted marks.

18¼in (46.5cm) high

$700-850 **WW**

A CLOSER LOOK AT A BURMANTOFTS VASE

This is a good example of a Faience tyg vase with three handles.

It is model no.2203, of waisted cylindrical form.

It is incised with dogs running between foliage on sinuous Art Nouveau stems.

See Jason Wigglesworth, *The History of Burmantofts Pottery*, p. 54, for this vase illustrated.

A Burmantofts vase, impressed marks.

10in (25.5cm) high

$650-800 **WW**

A Burmantofts Faience "Egyptianesque" vase, with hieroglyphs, impressed marks.

12¼in (31cm) high

$650-800 **WW**

A Burmantofts Faience grotesque lizard vase, model no.741, impressed and incised marks, some light wear.

7½in (19cm) high

$650-800 **WW**

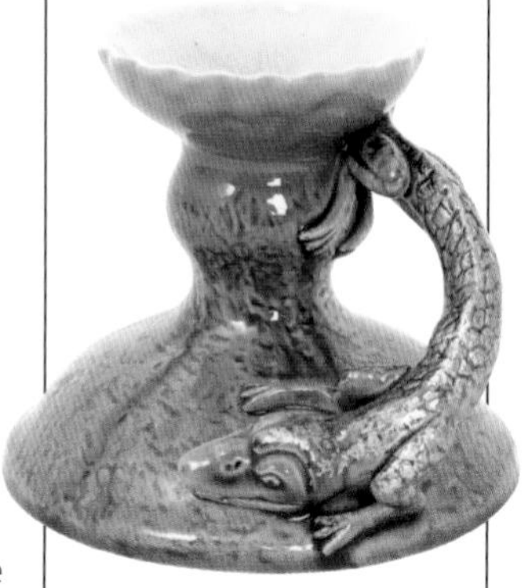

A Burmantofts Faience grotesque alligator chamberstick, model no.884, impressed marks.

4¼in (11cm) high

$400-500 **WW**

A Burmantofts Faience model of a lizard, model no.1993, modeled coiled around a shell eyeing up a spider, with applied glass eyes, impressed marks.

4½in (11.5cm) wide

$850-950 **WW**

A Burmantofts Faience model of a scaly fish, model no.2166, with sang-de-boeuf glaze, with applied glass eyes, impressed marks, restored tail fins.

7in (18cm) wide

$850-950 **WW**

A Burmantofts Faience model of a monkey, model no.797, impressed marks, small hairline on vase.

6in (15cm) high

$650-800 **WW**

A Burmantofts Faience model of a monkey, model no.2000, with applied glass eyes, impressed marks.

3¼in (8.5cm) high

$500-650 **WW**

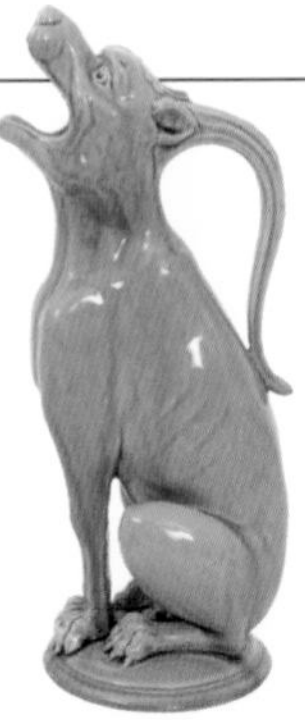

A Burmantofts Faience grotesque ibex creature ewer, model no.555, the horns forming a handle, impressed marks, restoration on handle.

13in (33cm) high

$450-500 **WW**

A Burmantofts Faience grotesque crocodile ewer, model no.554, impressed marks, some minor glaze frits.

11¾in (30cm) high

$600-700 **WW**

A Burmantofts Faience grotesque dragon, impressed marks, restoration on feet.

5¼in (13.5cm) wide

$500-600 **WW**

A Burmantofts Faience grotesque creature, model no.583, impressed marks, small glaze chip on one foot.

7½in (19cm) wide

$600-700 **WW**

A Burmantofts Faience grotesque creature, model no.1906, impressed marks, chips on all four feet, painted to conceal.

6½in (16.5cm) wide

$450-500 **WW**

A Burmantofts Faience model of a Kirin, model no.522, impressed marks, restoration to crest on head, tail, and an ear.

7¾in (19.5cm) high

$500-650 **WW**

A Burmantofts Faience model of a Kirin, model no.1174, impressed marks and incised marks, reglued tail, small frit in the glaze on tail and ear.

4¾in (12cm) wide

$500-650 **WW**

QUICK REFERENCE—CARLTON WARE

- **The Wiltshaw & Robinson Company was founded in 1890 in Stoke, England. It was soon operating under the trade name Carlton Ware.**
- **The founder's son, Frederick Cuthbert Wiltshaw, took over in 1918. With the help of design director Horace Wain and later Enoch Boulton, Wiltshaw launched a range of luster projects featuring flower and animal designs.**

A 1920s Wiltshaw and Robinson Carlton Ware ginger jar and cover, "Barge" pattern, printed mark, some damages to cover.

10¼in (26cm) high

$90-100 FLD

An Art Deco Carlton Ware Tomb jar and cover, "Chinaland" pattern no.2948, highlighted in gilt, printed and painted factory marks, hairline on top rim.

14½in (37cm) high

$300-450 WW

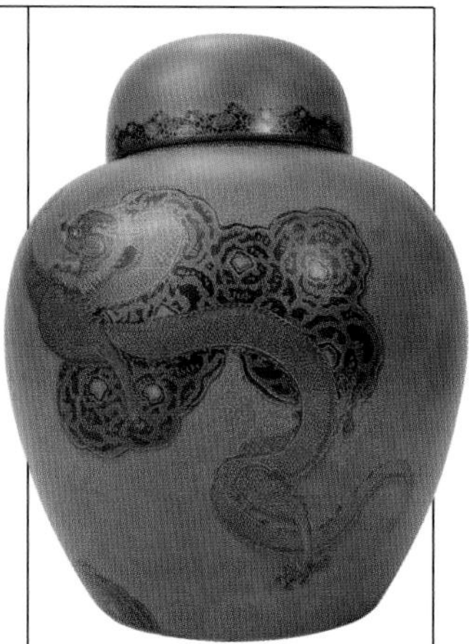

A Carlton Ware ginger jar and cover, "Dragon and Cloud" pattern.

10½in (26.5cm) high

$130-190 PSA

A Carlton Ware ginger jar and cover, "Sunflower Geometric" pattern no.3334, printed and painted, printed factory mark, applied Carlton Ware paper label, cover restored.

The Michael Burningham Collection.

8in (20.5cm) high

$850-950 WW

A Carlton Ware ginger jar and cover, "Devil's Copse" pattern, printed and painted in enamels, highlighted in gilt, printed factory mark, remains of painted mark, original paper retailer's label.

6¾in (17cm) high

$400-500 WW

A Carlton Ware ginger jar and cover, "Chinese Bird and Cloud" pattern no.3327, designed by Violet Elmer, printed and painted in colors highlighted in gilt, printed and painted marks.

10¼in (26cm) high

$500-650 WW

A Carlton Ware ginger jar and cover, "Mandarins Chatting" pattern no.3675, printed and enameled in colors and gilt, printed and painted marks, original paper label.

10½in (26.5cm) high

$600-700 WW

A Carlton Ware ginger jar, "Tutankhamun" pattern no.2711, designed by Enoch Boulton, printed and enameled in colors with hieroglyphs, printed factory marks and special Tut mark.

The "Tutankhamun," or more correctly "Tut," pattern was introduced by Carlton Ware in 1923, the year after Howard Carter discovered the king's tomb in November 1922. Egyptomania spread rapidly across Europe through architecture and the decorative arts.

10¼in (26cm) high

$500-650 WW

A CLOSER LOOK AT A CARLTON WARE VASE

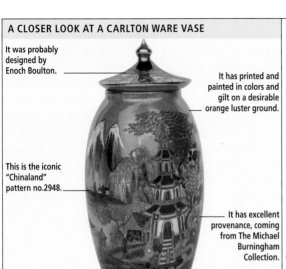

It was probably designed by Enoch Boulton.
It has printed and painted in colors and gilt on a desirable orange luster ground.
This is the iconic "Chinaland" pattern no.2948.
It has excellent provenance, coming from The Michael Burningham Collection.

A Carlton Ware vase and cover, printed and painted factory marks.

7½in (19cm) high

$850-950 **WW**

An Art Deco Carlton Ware vase, "Bluebells" pattern, enameled in colors on a Rouge Royale ground, highlighted in gilt, printed and painted marks.

14in (35.5cm) high

$300-450 **WW**

A Carlton Ware vase, "Hollyhocks" pattern.

4¾in (12cm) high

$90-120 **PSA**

A Carlton Ware vase, "Mandarin's Chatting" pattern no.3653, printed and painted marks.

7¼in (18.5cm) high

$500-650 **WW**

A Carlton Ware vase, "Wagonwheels" pattern no.3814, printed and painted marks, professional restoration to base.

7½in (19cm) high

$500-650 **WW**

A Carlton Ware vase, "Forest Tree" pattern no.3244, printed and painted marks.

12¼in (31cm) high

$400-500 **WW**

An Art Deco Carlton Ware vase, "Devil's Copse" pattern, with an indented collar neck, gilt and enamel decoration, printed script mark.

1930s *8in (20.5cm) high*

$190-260 **FLD**

An Art Deco Carlton Ware vase, "Palm Blossom" pattern, printed script mark.

1930s *8in (20.5cm) high*

$600-700 **FLD**

An Art Deco Carlton Ware vase, "Chinaland" pattern, by Wiltshaw and Robinson, printed mark.

1920s *8¼in (21cm) high*

$160-230 **FLD**

An Art Deco Carlton Ware preserve pot, cover, and stand, "Feathertailed Bird and Flower" pattern, printed script mark.

1930s *stand 4in (10cm) diam*

$130-190 **FLD**

An Art Deco Wiltshaw and Robinson Carlton Ware footed bowl, "Barge" pattern, printed mark.

1930s *12¼in (31cm) long*

$130-190 **FLD**

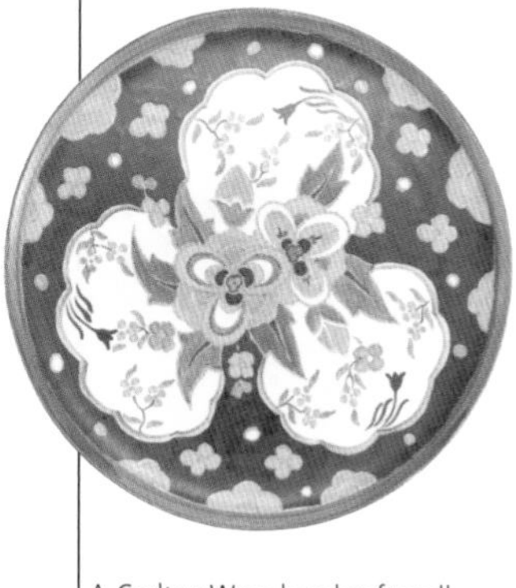

A Carlton Ware handcraft wall plaque, decorated with flowers.

12½in (32cm) diam

$60-80 **PSA**

An Art Deco Carlton Ware tray, "Fan" pattern no.3557, highlighted in gilt, printed and painted marks.

14¼in (36cm) wide

$300-400 **WW**

A rare Carlton Ware charger, "Fighting Cocks" pattern no.4161.

See Dr. Czes and Yvonne Kosniowski *Carlton Ware The Complete Guide*, page 228, for the original design illustrated.

12½in (32cm) high

$400-500 **WW**

A Carlton Ware bowl, "Jazz" pattern no.3361, designed by Enoch Boulton, printed and painted marks, hairline on rim.

8in (20.5cm) diam

$500-650 **WW**

A rare Carlton Ware advertising wall plaque of a toucan next to a glass of Guinness.

Carlton Ware produced ceramics used by Guinness, such as toucans and small animal figurines, for advertising purposes. The toucan was based on John Gilroy's creation of the hapless zoo keeper and his unruly animals for Guinness advertisements in the 1920s-1960s. Many fakes of the pieces have since been created.

7in (18cm) high

$1,900-2,600 **PSA**

A Carlton Ware "Martell Brandy" ceramic advertising figure.

Cognac house Martell was founded in 1715 by Jean Martell. This Carlton Ware advertising piece states, "Make friends with Martell."

8¼in (21cm) high

$300-400 **PSA**

MARKET REPORT

The market in Clarice Cliff is now one of the most established in the field of 20thC ceramics, from its early beginnings in the 1970s to its meteoric rise toward the millennium! Post 2000, there has been a significant readjustment in the market that previously had been driven by the search for knowledge; regardless of what the object was, if it bore Clarice Cliff's name, it was assured to fetch large sums.

Today, the market is much more educated and aware of her story and the products she created, and there has been a definite divide and separate between basic, better, and best! The lower entry-level market has settled down to the point where a basic banded or plain piece of Clarice can be snapped up for as little as a few dollars. However, at the other end of the spectrum, prices continue to rise!

Collectors now know exactly what they want, be it pattern, shape or—better still—the perfect combination of both. Rare patterns, especially in unusual color variants, are still the must-have among collectors, and nowadays the market can be divided into four main categories of Landscapes, Abstracts, Fruits and Florals, and Novelty wares. For many years, the Abstracts and Landscapes have always been the most significantly desirable, with pieces regularly fetching four- and even five-figure sums. However, for me, the Florals perfectly display Clarice Cliff's unique talent for taking simple floral motifs and turning them into bold, bright, and iconic pieces of 1930s ceramics.

It was thought some time ago that we had seen all there was to discover and found all that we were going to find. However, new patterns still emerge even if not as regularly as 30 years ago, and collectors are still left speechless at a new abstract or landscape pattern.

Will Farmer, *Fieldings Auctioneers, Stourbridge*

A Clarice Cliff Bizarre Stamford "Alton" teapot and cover, printed factory marks.

4¾in (12cm) high

$650-800 **WW**

A Clarice Cliff Bizarre fern pot, "Appliqué Avignon" pattern, printed and painted factory marks.

3in (7.5cm) high

$850-950 **WW**

A Clarice Cliff plate, "Appliqué Blossom" pattern, hand painted with stylized flowers and foliage over a patterned ground, printed "APPLIQUÉ" and "Bizarre" mark.

ca. 1931 *8in (22.5cm) wide*

$1,300-1,600 **FLD**

A Clarice Cliff plate, "Appliqué Caravan" pattern, hand painted with a scene of a caravan below a fruiting tree, hand painted "APPLIQUÉ" and "Bizarre" mark.

ca. 1931 *9in (25cm) wide*

$2,600-3,900 **FLD**

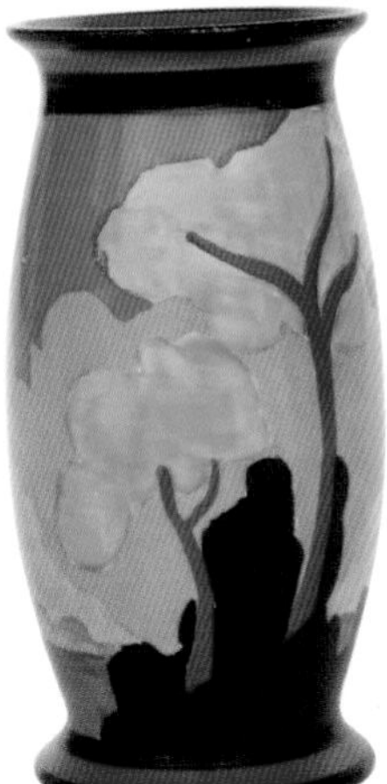

A rare Clarice Cliff Bizarre 265 vase, "Appliqué Etna" pattern, painted with two mountain scenes, printed and painted marks.

6¼in (16cm) high

$6,000-7,000 **WW**

A Clarice Cliff Bizarre plate, "Appliqué Etna" pattern, printed and painted marks, impressed date mark.

1931 *10in (25.5cm) diam*

$3,900-4,500 **WW**

A Clarice Cliff wall plaque, 'Appliqué Idyll" pattern, with a crinoline lady below a flowering tree, signed "Clarice Cliff" to the front and to the reverse "The Property of Threlfalls Brewery," printed "APPLIQUÉ" and "Bizarre" mark.

13in (33cm) diam

$1,900-2,600 **FLD**

A Clarice Cliff dish-form plate, "Appliqué Monsoon" pattern, with a Japanese Torii gate on a hillside, printed "APPLIQUÉ" and "Bizarre" mark.

A Torii gate, literally "bird abode," is a traditional Japanese gate most commonly found at the entrance to or within a Shinto shrine to symbolically mark the transition from the mundane to the sacred.

ca. 1931 *9in (23cm) wide*

$6,500-8,000 **FLD**

A Clarice Cliff Hiawatha bowl, "Appliqué Palermo" pattern, "APPLIQUÉ" and "Bizarre" mark.

ca. 1930 *11in (28cm) wide*

$1,300-1,900 **FLD**

Judith Picks

The "Lotus" or "Isis" pitcher is one of the most characteristic shapes associated with Clarice Cliff. Despite this, it was actually designed in 1919 by her predecessor at Wilkinson's, John Butler, as part of a pitcher and bowl washstand set.

The simple form was intended to suggest antiquity, and it was produced with one or two handles, or no handles. Some examples are stamped "LOTUS" or "ISIS," the original name of the shape.

At the time, examples with handles were classed as functional rather than decorative wares, so they attracted a lower tax. Their popularity means fakes abound—the simplest way to identify one is to look at the inside edge of the handle. If a hole is found, it is a reproduction or fake. Values vary depending on the pattern and condition.

A Clarice Cliff single-handled "Isis" vase, "Blue Autumn" pattern, hand painted with a stylized tree and cottage landscape, double image, "FANTASQUE" and "Bizarre" marks.

ca. 1930 *9¾in (24.5cm) high*

$1,900-2,600 **FLD**

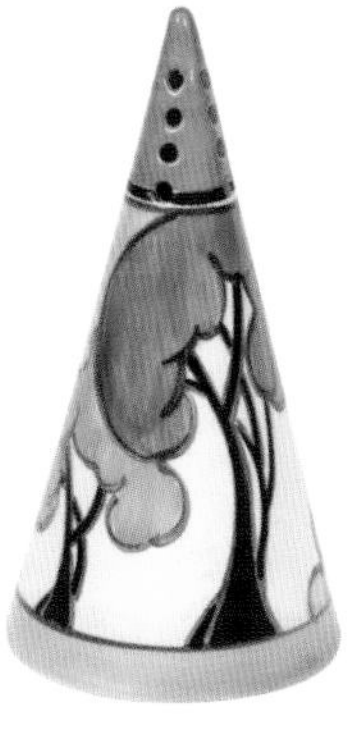

A Clarice Cliff Fantasque Bizarre conical sugar sifter, "Autumn" pattern, printed factory marks, restored base rim and tip.

5½in (14cm) high

$450-500 **WW**

A Clarice Cliff Bizarre conical sugar sifter, "Blue Firs" pattern, printed factory marks, professionally restored.

5½in (14cm) high

$1,150-1,450 **WW**

A Clarice Cliff "Bon Jour" shape preserve pot and cover, "Bridgewater" and "Bizarre" mark, cover restored.

ca. 1933 *4¼in (11cm) high*

$300-350 **FLD**

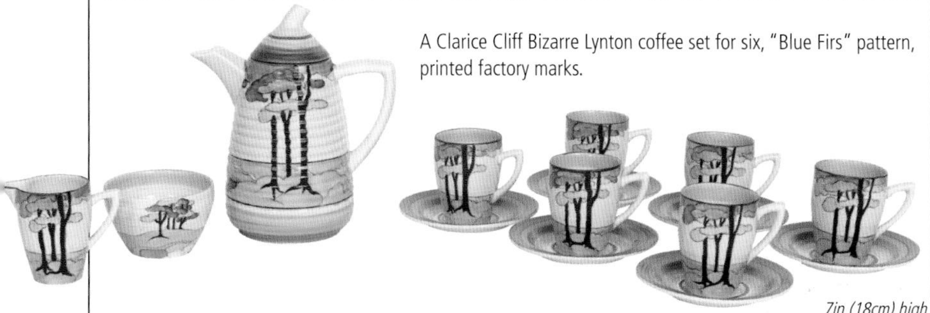

A Clarice Cliff Bizarre Lynton coffee set for six, "Blue Firs" pattern, printed factory marks.

7in (18cm) high

$3,900-5,200 **WW**

A Clarice Cliff "Conical" shape pitcher, "Broth" pattern, "Fantasque" mark.

ca. 1929 *6in (15cm) high*

$700-850 **FLD**

QUICK REFERENCE—CLARICE CLIFF

- **Clarice Cliff (1899-1972) was born in Stoke-on-Trent, England, and began her career as an apprentice enameler at Linguard Webster & Co. in 1912.**
- **In 1916, she moved to A.J. Wilkinson. In the mid-1920s, Wilkinson gave Cliff her own studio, Newport Pottery. Here, she began to work on her earthenware designs, first experimenting by hand painting decoration on blank defective wares.**
- **Her Bizarre and Fantasque ranges were launched in 1928, covering a range of patterns and shapes. The majority of her wares were tableware, although she also designed vases, candlesticks, figurines, and other items.**
- **She trained a group of female decorators to paint her designs by hand. They became known as the "Bizarre Girls."**
- **Clarice Cliff wares were hand painted in thickly applied bright colors, often with thin black outlines around colored elements. Her bold designs include stylized floral patterns, landscapes, and geometric and abstract shapes. Many patterns come in a variety of colors. Orange is commonly found, with pastels and blue and purple being scarcer. There is often variation within one pattern, because the "Bizarre Girls" had the freedom to slightly vary the designs.**
- **In general, the market for Clarice Cliff has remained strong, especially for rarer shapes and patterns. Rare landscapes, such as the "Appliqué" range, "May Avenue," "Luxor," and unusual color variants of classic patterns, such as "Red Autumn" or "Green House," continue to perform well. Geometric patterns, such as "Café," "Sunspots," "Football," and "Tennis" remain strong.**

A Clarice Cliff globe-shaped teapot, "Circle Tree (RAF Tree)" pattern, "Fantasque" mark, small restoration to the spout.

ca. 1929 *4in (10.5cm) high*

$650-800 **FLD**

A Clarice Cliff large shape 14 "Mei Ping" vase, "Butterfly" pattern, Fantasque mark.

16in (41cm) high

$3,200-3,900 **FLD**

A Clarice Cliff shape 368 stepped fern pot, "Orange Chintz" pattern, "Bizarre" mark.

ca. 1932 *9in (23cm) high*

$300-400 **FLD**

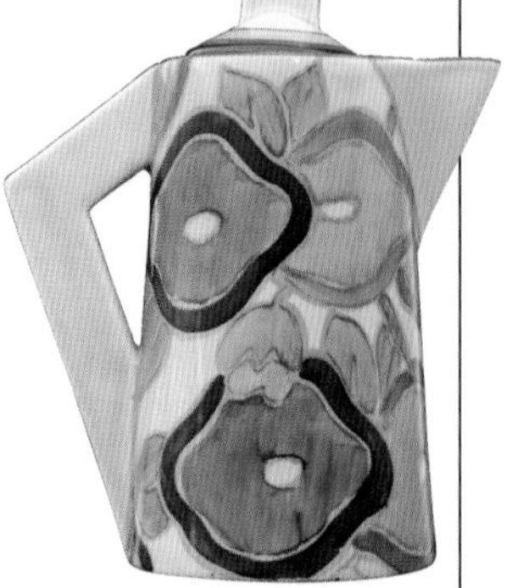

A Clarice Cliff "Conical" shape coffeepot, "Blue Chintz" pattern, "Bizarre" mark with gold "Lawleys" backstamp.

ca. 1932 *7in (18cm) high*

$480-500 **FLD**

A large Clarice Cliff "Perth" shape pitcher, "Circle Tree (RAF Tree)" pattern, "Fantasque" mark.

ca. 1929 *5½in (14cm) high*

$450-600 **FLD**

A Clarice Cliff "Humpty" shape sugar bowl, "Coral Firs" pattern, "Bizarre" mark.

ca. 1933 *3in (8cm) high*

$260-320 **FLD**

A Clarice Cliff Bizarre part-conical tea set, "Delecia Nasturtium" pattern, comprising milk-pitcher and sugar basin, one conical cup, saucer, and side plate, printed factory marks.

$1,150-1,550 **WW**

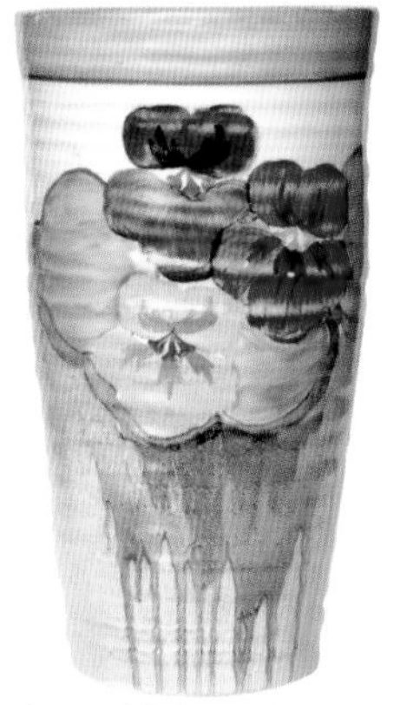

A Clarice Cliff shape 630 vase, "Delecia Pansies," hand painted "PANSIES" and "Bizarre" mark.

ca. 1933 *6in (16.5cm) high*

$300-400 **FLD**

QUICK REFERENCE—CONICAL SUGAR SIFTER

- **The "Conical" sugar sifter is one of Clarice Cliff's most iconic and recognizable designs. It was designed by Cliff herself and issued in 1931 in one height.**
- **It was produced in large quantities and was decorated with a huge number of hand-painted and transfer-printed patterns until around 1938. As a result, some collectors choose to focus on collecting this shape exclusively.**
- **Always examine the edges and particularly the top for damage or restoration, because any damage will affect the value.**

A Clarice Cliff Fantasque Bizarre conical sugar sifter, "Farmhouse" pattern, printed factory marks, minor frits to paintwork on the tip.

5¾in (14.5cm) high

$950-1,100 WW

A pair of Clarice Cliff "Football" "Meiping" vases, printed marks, both restored.

The vendor's grandmother recalls that these were purchased, direct from the factory, on the family's return journey from their summer vacation to Cornwall in around 1930. Subsequently, they were passed down through the family.

14¼in (36cm) high

$5,200-6,500 SWO

A rare Clarice Cliff miniature vase, "Double V" pattern, printed Newport Pottery mark,

These miniature vases were made as tradesman's sample vases taken to show prospective stockists of Clarice's new and vibrant ware.

2¾in (7cm) high

$850-950 WW

A Clarice Cliff shape 360 vase, "Geometric Flowers" pattern, gold "Fantasque" mark.

ca. 1929/30 *8in (20.5cm) high*

$2,900-3,600 FLD

A Clarice Cliff shape 187 vase, "Honolulu" pattern, "Bizarre" mark.

ca. 1933 *7in (18cm) high*

$1,300-1,900 FLD

A Clarice Cliff Bizarre 362 vase, "Honolulu" pattern, printed factory marks.

8in (20.5cm) high

$2,300-2,900 WW

A Clarice Cliff Fantasque Bizarre 365 vase, "House and Bridge" pattern, printed factory mark.

7in (20cm) high

$2,300-2,900 WW

A Clarice Cliff dish-form plate, "Green House" pattern, hand painted with a stylized tree and cottage landscape, "FANTASQUE" and "Bizarre" mark.

ca. 1931 *9in (23cm) wide*

$1,300-1,900 FLD

A Clarice Cliff "Coronet" shape pitcher, "Orange House" pattern, "FANTASQUE" and "Bizarre" mark.

ca. 1930 *7in (18cm) high*

$1,050-1,150 **FLD**

A Clarice Cliff shape 14 "Meiping" vase, "Inspiration Bouquet" pattern, hand painted "INSPIRATION" and "Bizarre" mark, small restoration to the foot.

ca. 1930 *14in (36cm) high*

$1,400-1,900 **FLD**

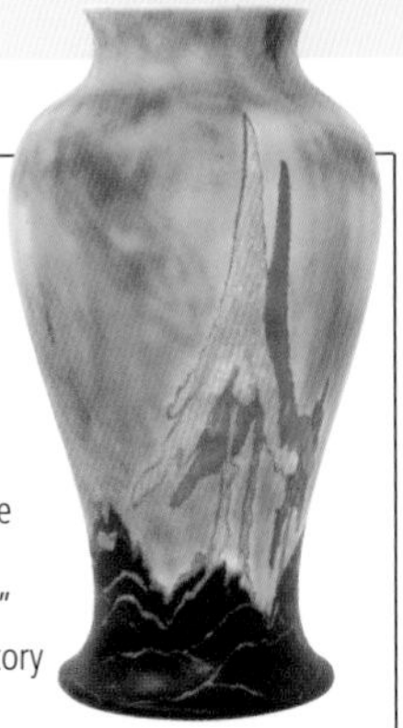

A Clarice Cliff Bizarre "Meiping" vase, "Inspiration Caprice" pattern, painted factory mark, chips on rims.

See Peter Wentworth-Sheilds and Kay Johnson, *Clarice Cliff*, L'Odeon London (1976), page 49, plate 13, for illustration.

14in (37cm) high

$1,050-1,150 **WW**

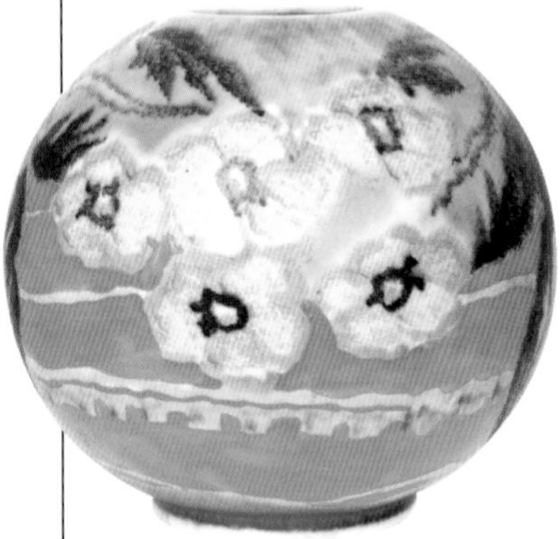

A Clarice Cliff shape 370 "Globe" vase, "Inspiration Clouvre Flowers" pattern, hand painted "CLOUVRE," printed "Bizarre" mark.

ca. 1930 *6in (15cm) high*

$3,600-4,200 **FLD**

A Clarice Cliff shape 386 "Mallet" vase, "Inspiration Clouvre Waterlily" pattern, hand painted "INSPIRATION" and "Bizarre" mark, restored.

ca. 1929 *12in (31cm) high*

$800-900 **FLD**

A Clarice Cliff shape 370 "Globe" vase, "Inspiration Rose" pattern, hand painted ocher "INSPIRATION" mark only, restored.

ca. 1930 *6in (15cm) high*

$1,050-1,150 **FLD**

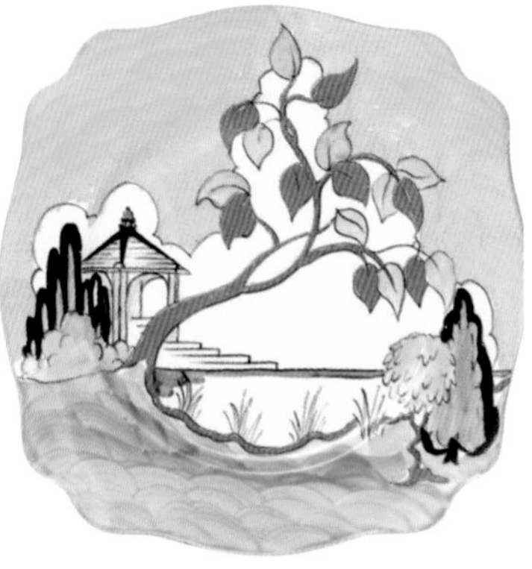

A Clarice Cliff "Leda" shape plate, "Yellow Japan" pattern, with "A.J. Wilkinson" mark only.

ca. 1934 *9in (25cm) wide*

$300-350 **FLD**

A large Clarice Cliff wall plaque, "Latona Red Roses" pattern, hand painted "LATONA" and "Bizarre" mark.

ca. 1930 *13¼in (33.5cm) wide*

$1,600-1,900 **FLD**

A Clarice Cliff Bizarre "Meiping" vase, "Latona Tree" pattern, printed and painted marks.

12in (30.5cm) high

$1,400-1,900 **WW**

A Clarice Cliff advertising bowl, "Limberlost" pattern, hand painted with the words "Bizarre by Clarice Cliff," "Bizarre" mark.

6in (16cm) high

$500-650 FLD

A Clarice Cliff wall plaque, "Luxor" pattern, "Bizarre" mark.

ca. 1930 *13in (33cm) high*

$1,900-2,600 FLD

A Clarice Cliff dish-form wave-edge plaque, "Marigold" pattern, hand painted "MARIGOLD" and "Bizarre" mark.

ca. 1930 *12¼in (31cm) wide*

$1,150-1,550 FLD

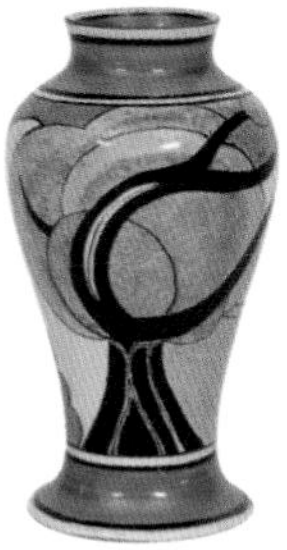

A rare Clarice Cliff Bizarre "Meiping" vase, "May Avenue" pattern, printed factory marks.

6¼in (16cm) high

$3,900-5,200 WW

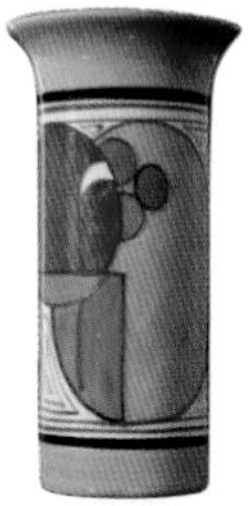

A Clarice Cliff shape 196 vase, "Melon" pattern, "FANTASQUE" and "Bizarre" mark.

ca. 1930 *2½in (6.5cm) high*

$650-800 FLD

A large Clarice Cliff jardinière, "Melon" pattern, "FANTASQUE" and "Bizarre" mark, slightly damaged.

ca. 1929 *8in (20cm) high*

$800-900 FLD

A Clarice Cliff shape 356 "Kidney" vase, "Pastel Melon" pattern, "FANTASQUE" and "Bizarre" mark, small restoration on rim.

ca. 1930 *6¾in (17cm) high*

$500-650 FLD

A CLOSER LOOK AT A "MAY AVENUE" PITCHER

This is a rare and desirable pattern.

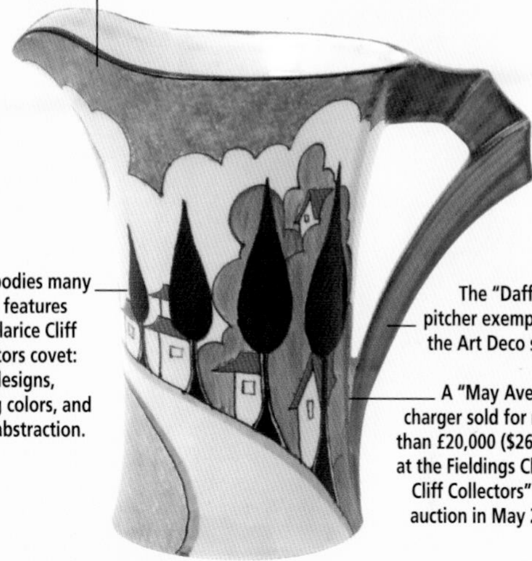

It embodies many of the features that Clarice Cliff collectors covet: bold designs, strong colors, and semi-abstraction.

The "Daffodil" pitcher exemplifies the Art Deco style.

A "May Avenue" charger sold for more than £20,000 ($26,000) at the Fieldings Clarice Cliff Collectors" Club auction in May 2009.

A rare Clarice Cliff Bizarre "Daffodil" pitcher, "May Avenue" pattern, painted in colors, printed factory mark.

6in (17cm) high

$3,200-3,900 WW

A "Conical" shape coffee service, "Melon" pattern, "Fantasque" mark.

ca. 1929-30

$3,900-5,200 FLD

CERAMICS

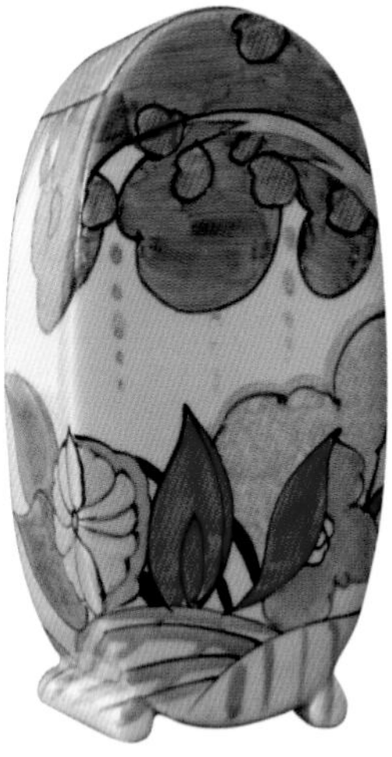

A Clarice Cliff "Bon Jour" sugar sifter, "Moonlight" pattern, partial "Bizarre" mark.

ca. 1933 *5in (12.5cm) high*

$600-700 **FLD**

A Clarice Cliff "Bon Jour" preserve pot, "Newlyn" pattern, with a tonal blue "Delecia" effect sky, script signature.

ca. 1935 *4in (10cm) high*

$400-500 **FLD**

A Clarice Cliff "Humpty" sugar pot, "Oasis" pattern, "FANTASQUE" and "Bizarre" mark.

ca. 1933 *8in (20.5cm) high*

$120-160 **FLD**

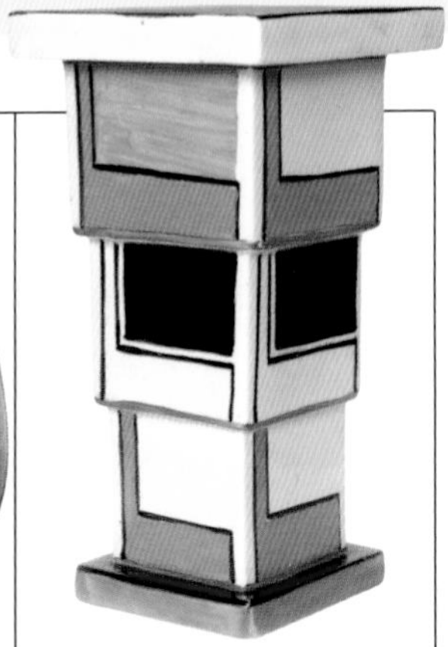

A Clarice Cliff shape 369A vase, "Orange L," hand painted with a repeat abstract linear and block design, "Bizarre" mark, some damages.

ca. 1930 *7in (19.5cm) high*

$1,300-1,900 **FLD**

A Clarice Cliff shape 269 vase, "Original Bizarre" pattern, partial gold "Fantasque" mark.

ca. 1929 *5in (14.5cm) high*

$300-400 **FLD**

A Clarice Cliff shape 120 vase, "Original Bizarre" pattern, gold "Bizarre" mark.

ca. 1928 *10½in (26.5cm) high*

$650-800 **FLD**

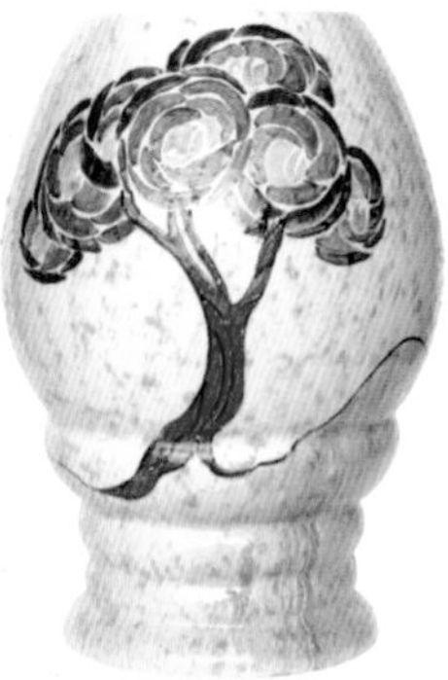

A Clarice Cliff shape 362 vase, "Blue Patina Tree" pattern, decorated with a blue splatter effect, printed "PATINA" and "Bizarre" mark.

ca. 1932-33 *7in (20cm) high*

$500-650 **FLD**

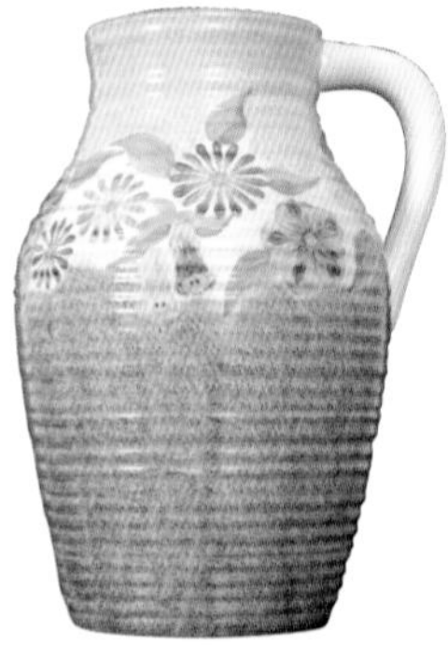

A Clarice Cliff single-handled "Lotus" pitcher, "Petunia" pattern, hand painted with a yellow and brown stippled "Café au Lait"-style ground, "Bizarre" mark.

ca. 1933 *11in (29cm) high*

$450-600 **FLD**

A Clarice Cliff "Conical" bowl, "Red Gardenia Café Au Lait" pattern, "Bizarre" mark.

ca. 1931 *8in (20cm) wide*

$800-900 **FLD**

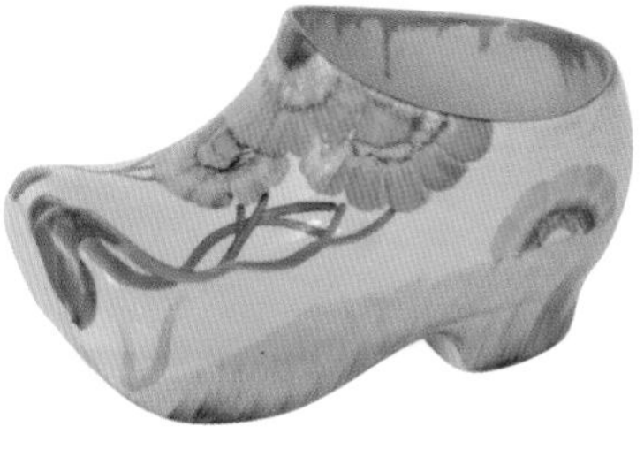

A Clarice Cliff large sabot or clog, "Rhodanthe" pattern, large script signature.
ca. 1935 *5in (14cm) high*
$260-320 **FLD**

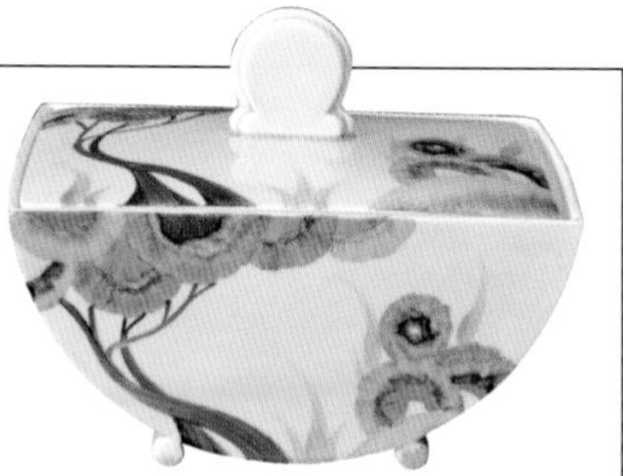

A Clarice Cliff "Bon Jour" vegetable tureen, "Rhodanthe" pattern, script signature and Biarritz mark.
ca 1936 *7¾in (20cm) wide*
$260-320 **FLD**

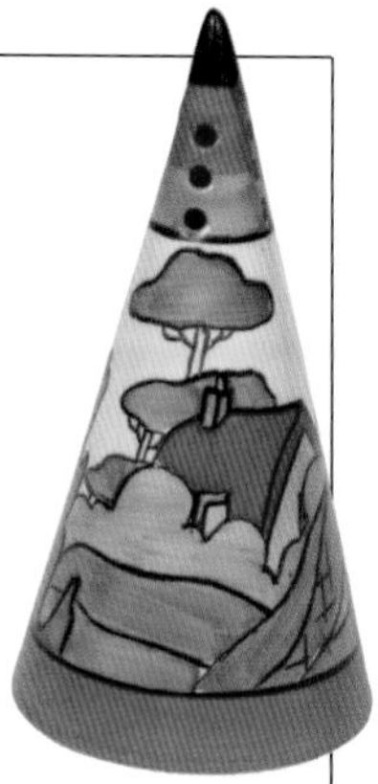

A Clarice Cliff Fantasque Bizarre conical sugar sifter, "Orange Roof Cottage" pattern, printed factory marks, tip restored.
5½in (14cm) high
$500-650 **WW**

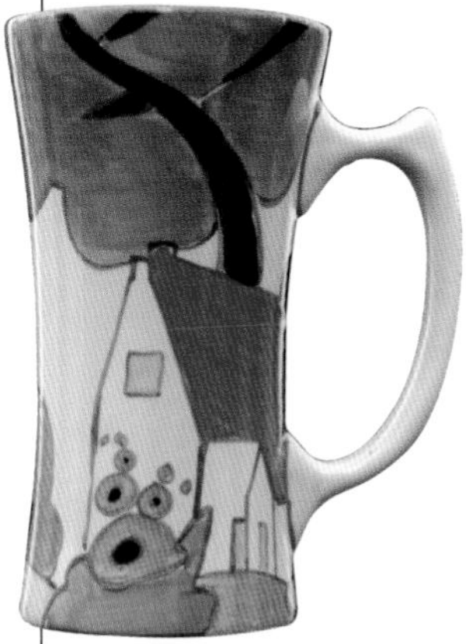

A Clarice Cliff waisted cylindrical mug, "Red Roofs" pattern, "FANTASQUE" and "Bizarre" mark, restored.
ca. 1931 *4¾in (12cm) high*
$300-400 **FLD**

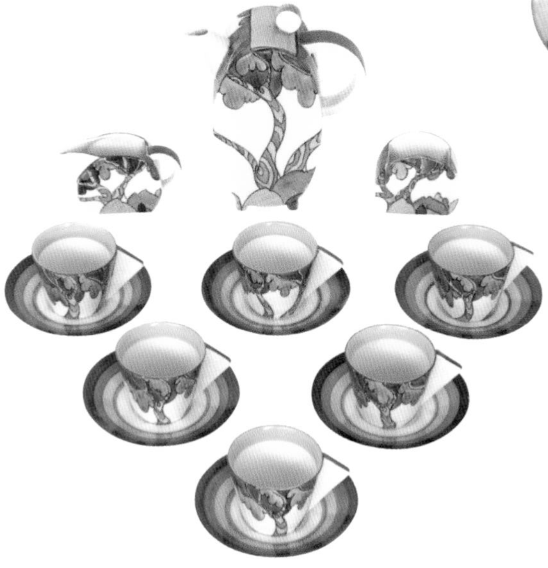

A Clarice Cliff "Bon Jour' coffee service, "Rudyard" pattern.
ca. 1933
$3,200-3,900 **FLD**

A Clarice Cliff shape 54 fruit bowl, "Secrets" pattern, "FANTASQUE" and "Bizarre" mark.
ca. 1933 *19in (48.5cm) wide*
$260-320 **FLD**

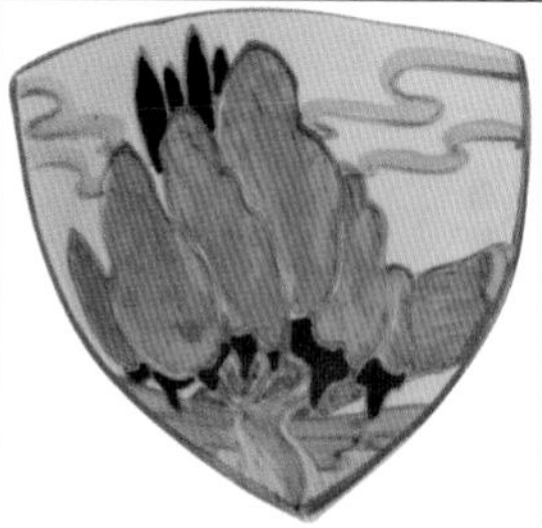

A Clarice Cliff shape 472 bonbon dish, "Solitude" pattern, "FANTASQUE" and "Bizarre" mark.
ca. 1933 *9½in (24cm) wide*
$260-390 **FLD**

A unique Clarice Cliff Bizarre large floor vase, "Sliced Fruit" pattern, printed factory marks.
"Clarice Cliff Giants" by Len Griffin, October 1989, discusses a comparable example of this large vase decorated in the "Branch & Squares" pattern, which was exhibited at L'Odeon's Clarice Cliff exhibition, loaned by Midwinter and now in the Wedgwood collection, after Midwinter closed in 1986.
27½in (70cm) high
$4,200-5,100 **WW**

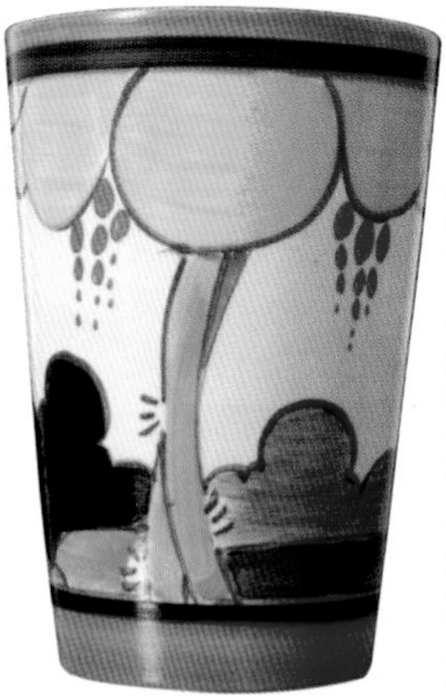

A large Clarice Cliff cup, "Summerhouse" pattern, "Fantasque" and "Bizarre" marks.
ca. 1932 *4½in (11.5cm) high*
$400-500 **FLD**

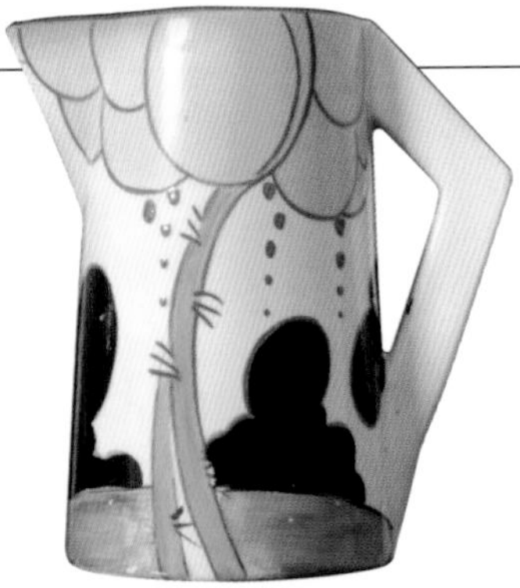

A Clarice Cliff "Conical" pitcher, "Summerhouse" pattern, "Bizarre" mark.

ca. 1932 *4½in (11.5cm) high*

$450-600 **FLD**

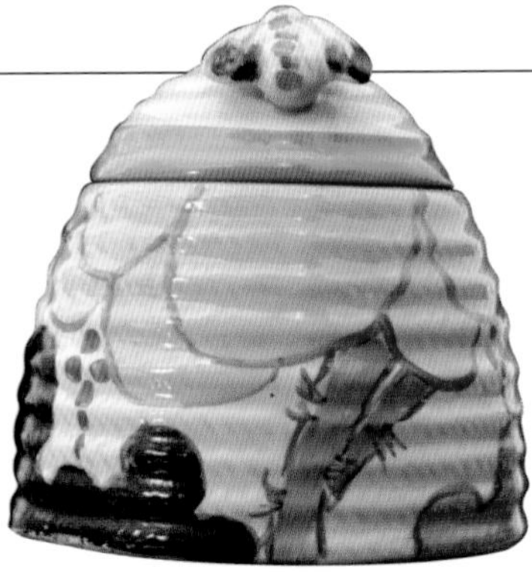

A large Clarice Cliff "Bee Hive" honeypot, "Summerhouse" pattern, "Bizarre" mark.

ca. 1932 *4¼in (10.5cm) high*

$600-700 **FLD**

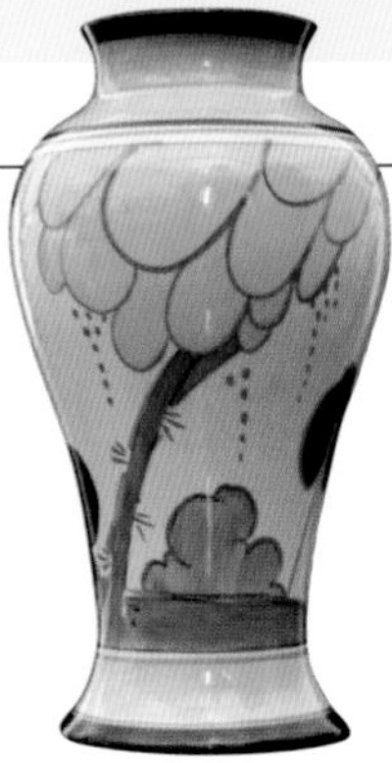

A Clarice Cliff shape 14 "Meiping" vase, "Summerhouse," "FANTASQUE" and "Bizarre" marks, some damages.

ca. 1931 *9in (23cm) high*

$1,100-1,250 **FLD**

A Clarice Cliff Fantasque Bizarre 365 vase, "Summerhouse" pattern, printed factory marks.

8in (20.5cm) high

$2,300-2,900 **WW**

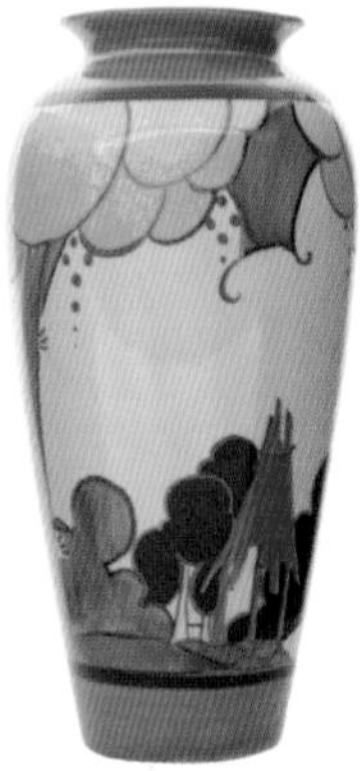

A Clarice Cliff shape 120 vase, "Summerhouse" pattern, "FANTASQUE" and "Bizarre" mark.

ca. 1932 *10¼in (26cm) high*

$1,300-1,900 **FLD**

A Clarice Cliff Bizarre "Conical" teapot and cover, "Sunray" pattern, printed factory marks, paint flakes.

4in (12cm) high

$1,400-1,900 **WW**

A Clarice Cliff globe-shaped teapot, "Sunray (Night and Day)" pattern, matched cover, "Bizarre" mark.

ca. 1929 *6in (15cm) high*

$600-700 **FLD**

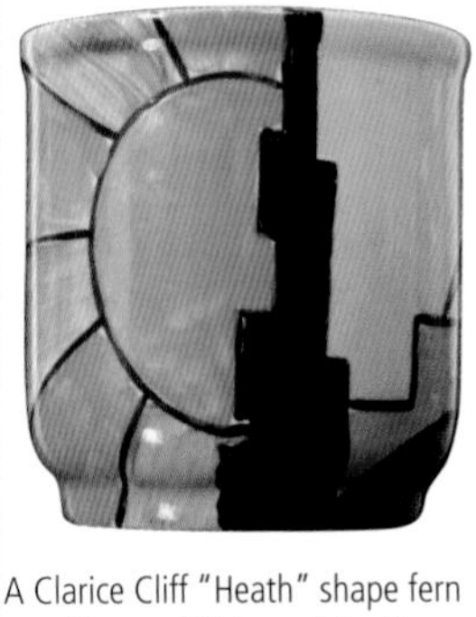

A Clarice Cliff "Heath" shape fern pot, "Sunray (Night and Day)" pattern, "Bizarre" mark.

ca. 1929 *3in (9.5cm) high*

$850-950 **FLD**

A Clarice Cliff side plate, "Tennis" pattern, hand painted with an abstract design with stylized tennis net, "FANTASQUE" and "Bizarre" mark.

ca. 1931 *7in (17.5cm) wide*

$650-800 **FLD**

A Clarice Cliff Fantasque Bizarre "Meiping" vase, "Orange Trees and House" pattern, with printed factory mark.

8in (22.5cm) high

$1,400-1,900 **WW**

A Clarice Cliff shape 278 vase, "Red Trees and House" pattern, "Fantasque" mark.

ca. 1929 *6in (15cm) high*

$700-850 **FLD**

A Clarice Cliff tankard-shaped coffee service, "Red Trees & House" pattern, full and partial "Fantasque" marks.

ca. 1930

$2,600-3,200 **FLD**

A Clarice Cliff Fantasque Bizarre wall charger, "Red Trees and House" pattern, printed factory marks.

17¾in (45cm) diam

$5,200-6,500 **WW**

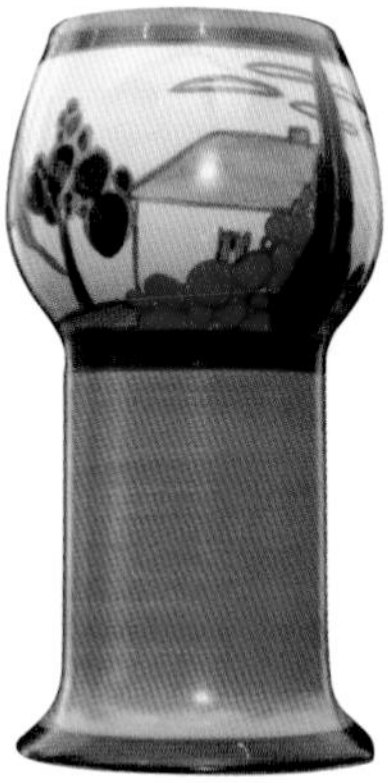

A Clarice Cliff shape 269 vase, "Red Trees and House" pattern, "Fantasque" mark, restored.

ca. 1929 *6in (15.5cm) high*

$450-600 **FLD**

A Clarice Cliff shape 565 vase, "Tulips" pattern, "Bizarre" mark.

ca. 1934 *11½in (29cm) high*

$500-600 **FLD**

A large Clarice Cliff plate, "Windbells" pattern, "Bizarre" mark.

ca. 1933 *9in (23cm) wide*

$400-450 **FLD**

A Clarice Cliff "Isis" vase, "Windbells" pattern, "FANTASQUE" and "Bizarre" mark.

ca. 1933 *9¾in (25cm) high*

$1,600-2,300 **FLD**

QUICK REFERENCE—BRANGWYN PANELS

- **In 1926, Frank Brangwyn was commissioned by Lord Iveagh to paint a pair of large canvases to be displayed in the Royal Gallery at the House of Lords, Westminster. The paintings were to commemorate peers and their family members who had been killed in World War I. Accordingly, Brangwyn painted two battle scenes, which included a scene of life-size troops advancing into battle beside a British tank. When the paintings were unveiled in 1928, the Lords rejected the panels, considering them too grim and disturbing. They recommissioned Brangwyn to produce a series of panels that would celebrate the beauty of the British Empire and the Dominions. Over the next five years, Brangwyn completed 16 panels (that covered 3,000sq ft), which would be known as the British Empire Panels. Five of the panels were displayed in the Royal Gallery for approval by the Lords, but they were again refused on the ground of being "too colorful and lively." In 1934, the 16 panels were purchased by Swansea Counciland are now housed in the Brangwyn Hall, Swansea, Wales.**

A Clarice Cliff framed charger, hand painted after the original from the British Empire Panel with African figures, the reverse with the hand painted mark "The Brangwyn panels designed for the Royal Gallery of the House of Lords 1925, First Exhibited at Olympia 1933. Painted by Clarice Cliff from one of the panels. A.J. Wilkinson, Royal Staffordshire Pottery Burslem, Staffordshire," numbered "17" and signed Frank Brangwyn.

12¾in (32.5cm) diam

$1,900-2,600 FLD

A Clarice Cliff Wilkinson's vase, in the form of a closed book.

7¼in (18.5cm) high

$80-100 WHP

An early Clarice Cliff figurine, "Mrs Puddleduck," on an enameled base, "A.J.Wilkinson" mark.

6¼in (16cm) high

$260-320 FLD

An early Clarice Cliff figurine, "Mr Puddleduck," on an enameled base, "A.J. Wilkinson" mark.

6¼in (16cm) high

$230-290 FLD

A Clarice Cliff novelty candlestick, modeled as an Arab in pantaloons with sash and turban holding a basket.

6in (15cm) high

$190-260 FLD

A Clarice Cliff "United Service" salt pot, printed mark.

4in (10cm) high

$230-290 WW

A rare Clarice Cliff Bizarre "Age of Jazz" table centerpiece, model no.436, modeled as a Jazz piano player and a banjo player, printed factory mark, professional restoration to piano.

5in (13.5cm) high

$16,000-19,000 WW

A Clarice Cliff face mask, "Chahar," "Bizarre" mark.

11in (28cm) high

$1,600-2,100 FLD

A Coalport figurine, "Time," limited edition from "The Millennium Ball" collection, boxed with certificate.

$100-130 **PSA**

A Coalport figurine, "Rain," limited edition from "The Millennium Ball" collection, boxed with certificate.

$100-130 **PSA**

QUICK REFERENCE—COALPORT

- **John Rose established the porcelain factory and began production at Coalport in c1796. It was the first factory established in the Ironbridge Gorge, Shropshire, England.**
- **The Coalport factory began by manufacturing low-cost enameled copies of Chinese patterns, as well as supplying plain white porcelain to independent china painters for decoration. This resulted in a huge variety of designs on Coalport porcelain. By the mid-19thC, Coalport employed in-house decorators.**
- **Porcelain from the factory was also referred to as Coalbrookdale porcelain. In the 1860s, Coalport moved into domestic ware.**
- **In 1967, the Coalport brand was bought by the Wedgwood Group. The original factory buildings at Ironbridge now house the Coalport China Museum.**

A Coalport figurine, "Sun," limited edition from "The Millennium Ball" collection, some small nips on base edge.

$100-130 **PSA**

A Coalport Guinness advertising figurine, "Elephant and Keeper," boxed with certificate.

$130-190 **PSA**

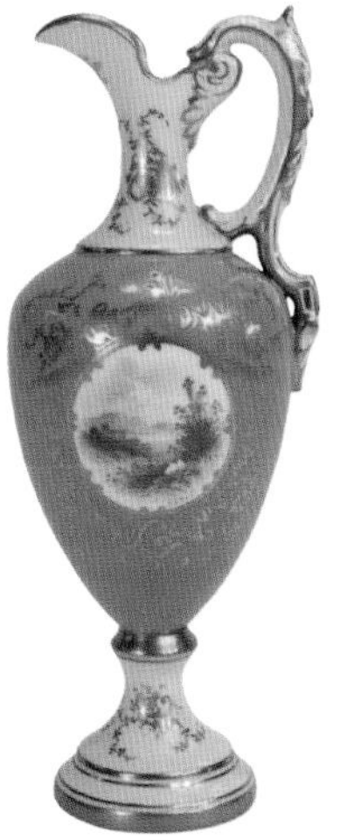

A Coalport ewer, gilded and hand painted, with scenes of Loch Awe by E. Ball.

7½in (19cm) high

$100-110 **PSA**

A Coalport vase, hand painted with castle scene.

6¾in (17cm) high

$140-180 **PSA**

A late 19thC Coalport pâte-sur-pâte vase, painted in white slip with winged putti dancing above a river, with gilt and "jeweled" arabesques and stylized motif, signed "A. Handley," green printed mark.

17¾in (45cm) high

$2,600-3,200 **DUK**

A mid-19thC Coalport porcelain bowl, painted with stag hunting scenes.

10¼in (26cm) wide

$260-320 **DUK**

A Coalport trinket box, with a painted scene of sheep, the lid interior stamped "Coalport AD 1750."

2¾in (7cm) wide

$120-140 **DUK**

QUICK REFERENCE—COBRIDGE

- **Based in Stoke-on-Trent, Cobridge stoneware operated between 1998 and 2005. It was part of Moorcroft Pottery.**
- **After the company's closure, its molds were acquired by Burslem Pottery—owned by Tracey Bentley, a former employee at Cobridge.**
- **Cobridge designer and decorator Anita Harris also worked for Poole Pottery.**

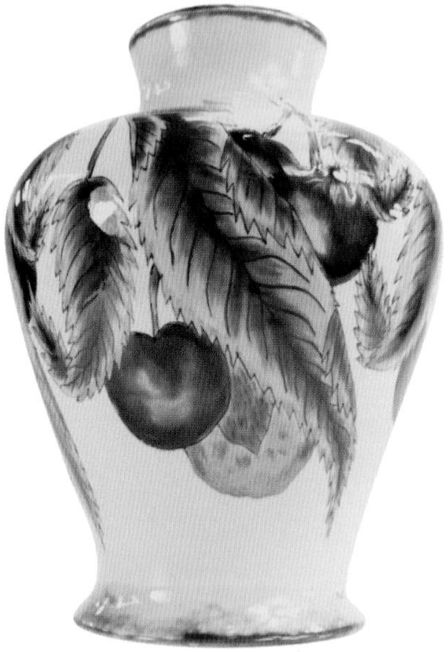

A Cobridge stoneware vase, signed Nicola Slaney.

10½in (26.5cm) high

$130-190 **PSA**

A Cobridge stoneware vase, "Land of the Pharaohs" pattern, impressed and painted marks, painted "Trial 16.11.04," signed Shirley Hayes, boxed.

10¼in (26cm) high

$190-260 **FLD**

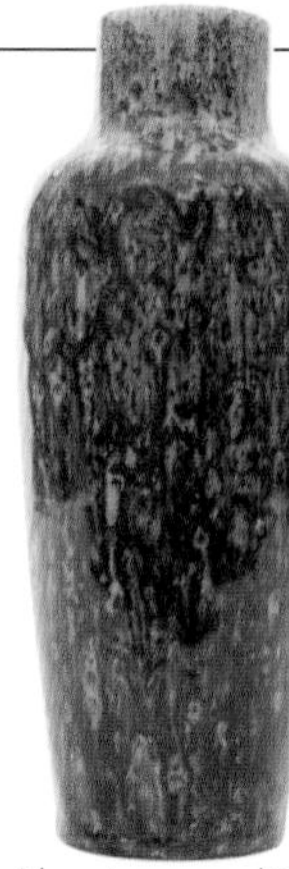

A Cobridge stoneware high-fired vase, impressed marks.

10¾in (27.5cm) high

$260-320 **FLD**

A Cobridge stoneware high-fired barrel vase, impressed marks.

10in (25.5cm) high

$230-300 **FLD**

A Cobridge stoneware high-fired vase, impressed marks.

7¼in (18.5cm) high

$160-210 **FLD**

A pair of Cobridge stoneware vases, designed by Paul Adiamec, "Caledonian Sunset" pattern, impressed marks, limited edition, one numbered 6/25 and the other 8/25, dated.

2003 *10in (25.5cm) high*

$300-450 **LSK**

A pair of Cobridge stoneware vases, designed by Emma Bossons, "Witching Hour" pattern, impressed, monogrammed and dated verso.

2002 *11¾in (30cm) high*

$190-260 **LSK**

A Cobridge stoneware charger, designed by Jackie Strode, "Cobbled Court" pattern, impressed marks, dated, numbered 11/25 verso.

2003 *14¼in (36cm) diam*

$80-100 **LSK**

QUICK REFERENCE—DE MORGAN

- **William De Morgan (1839-1917) studied at the Royal Academy Schools, before meeting and working with William Morris, designing and producing decorative tiles.**
- **De Morgan was inspired by Iznik pottery of the 15thC and 16thC and specialized in Persian ware.**
- **From 1882-1900, P&O Cruises commissioned De Morgan to supply decorative tiles for 12 of their new liners. In 1888, De Morgan set up a pottery at Sands End, London. Here, he developed his "Moonlight" and "Sunlight" series.**
- **De Morgan began writing at the age of 65, producing best sellers, but his work in ceramics had dwindled by 1904.**
- **At the beginning of the 20thC, De Morgan's pottery had become less popular and he is thought to have said, "All my life I have been trying to make beautiful things … and now that I can make them nobody wants them."**

A pair of William De Morgan plastic clay tiles, Fulham, decorated with Persian flowers and foliage, impressed mark.

each 9in (23cm) square

$2,300-2,900 **FLD**

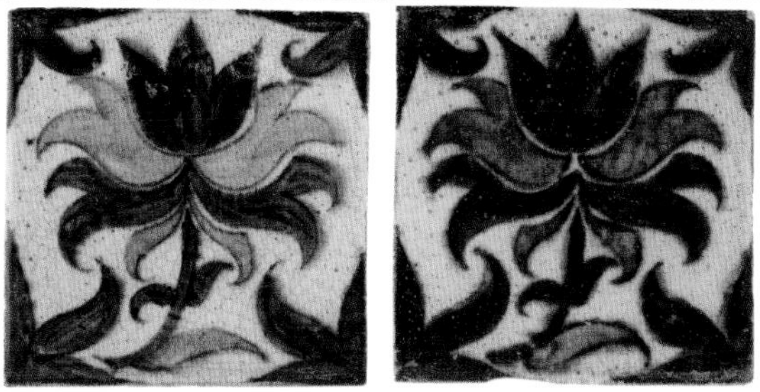

A pair of William De Morgan tiles, impressed marks for Merton Abbey.

ca. 1885 *6¼in (16cm) square*

$300-450 **L&T**

A pair of William De Morgan "Arabia" tiles, Sands End Pottery, with stylized Persian pattern, impressed marks, minor chips.

These tiles were commissioned for the P&O Liner "Arabia."

9in (23cm) square

$4,500-5,200 **WW**

A William De Morgan tile, Sands End Pottery, depicting a galleon in full sail, framed.

ca. 1890 *6in (15cm) square*

$900-1,050 **L&T**

A William De Morgan plastic clay tile, Sands End Pottery, decorated with a hand-painted galleon at sea, impressed mark.

6in (15cm) square

$850-950 **FLD**

A William De Morgan ruby luster "Wild Boar" tile, Merton Abbey, impressed mark.

6in (15cm) square

$3,200-3,900 **WW**

A William De Morgan triple luster "Hoopoe" tile, impressed late-Fulham period mark.

6in (15cm) square

$4,500-5,200 **WW**

A William De Morgan two-tile snake and flower panel, Merton Abbey, impressed mark, chips, mirror glaze nibbles.

1882-88 *8¼in (21cm) square*

$11,000-12,000 **SWO**

QUICK REFERENCE—DENNIS CHINAWORKS

- **Dennis Chinaworks was founded in 1993 in Somerset, UK, by Sally Tuffin and Richard Dennis.**
- **Tuffin graduated from the Royal college of Art and co-ran design house Foale & Tuffin. Between 1986 and 1993, Tuffin was Partner and Design Director of the Moorcroft Pottery.**
- **Richard Dennis trained with Sotheby's before establishing an antique glass and ceramic business and publishing house.**
- **At Dennis Chinaworks, a single decorator works on each pot, with their signature marked on the item's base along with the number, company name, date, and thrower's mark.**

A Dennis Chinaworks "Illyria" vase, designed by Sally Tuffin, B&W Thornton retailer exclusive, limited edition, numbered "4/12," impressed and painted marks.

14¼in (36cm) high

$950-1,100 **FLD**

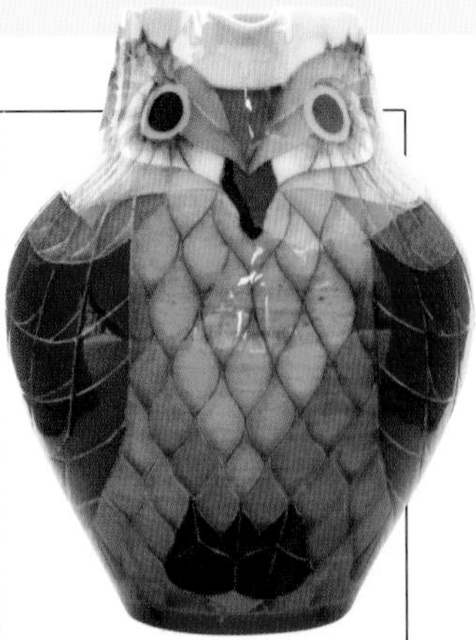

A Dennis Chinaworks pitcher, designed by Sally Tuffin, impressed marks and painted "S.T.des No. 83."

8¾in (22cm) high

$130-190 **FLD**

A Dennis Chinaworks "Moonlight Hare" vase, designed by Sally Tuffin, potted by Rory Mcleod, no.10, impressed and painted marks, dated.

2005 *13½in (34.5cm) high*

$450-500 **WW**

A Dennis Chinaworks "Carp" vase, designed by Sally Tuffin, impressed and painted marks, dated.

2003 *12½in (32cm) high*

$230-290 **WW**

A Dennis Chinaworks "Penguin" jar and cover, designed by Sally Tuffin, impressed and painted marks, dated.

2000 *6¼in (16cm) high*

$180-260 **WW**

A Dennis Chinaworks "Beetle Scarab" Etruscan vase, designed by Sally Tuffin, impressed and painted marks, limited edition, dated.

2004 *11¾in (30cm) high*

$260-320 **WW**

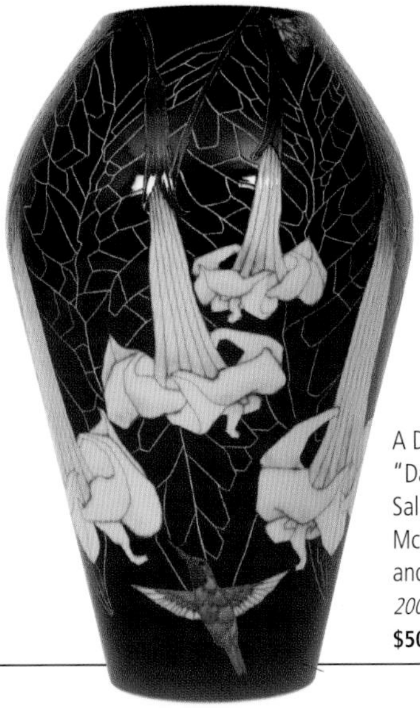

A Dennis Chinaworks large "Datura" vase, designed by Sally Tuffin, potted by Rory Mcleod, no.16, impressed and painted marks, dated.

2004 *18¼in (46.5cm) high*

$500-650 **WW**

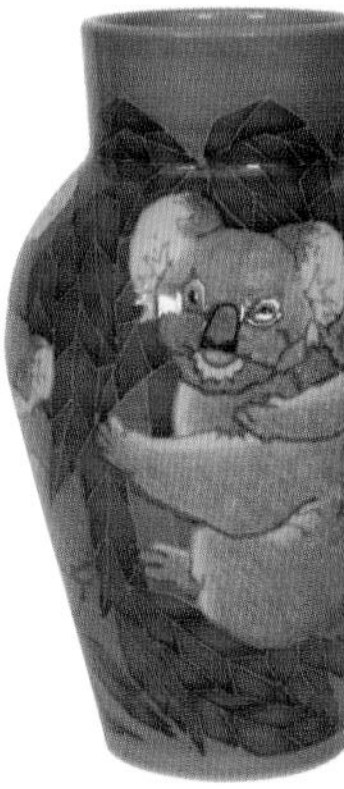

A Dennis Chinaworks "Koala" vase, designed by Sally Tuffin, impressed and painted marks, dated.

2001 *10½in (26.5cm) high*

$300-450 **WW**

A Dennis Chinaworks "Slipper Orchid" vase, designed by Sally Tuffin, painted and impressed marks, dated.

2004 *10¾in (27.5cm) high*

$180-260 **WW**

A Royal Doulton figurine, "Iona," model no.HN1346, designed by L. Harradine.

1929-38 *7½in (19cm) high*

$700-800 **PW**

A Royal Doulton figurine, "The Parson's Daughter," model no.HN1356, designed by H. Tittensor.

1929-38 *9¼in (23.5cm) high*

$300-400 **PSA**

A Royal Doulton figurine, "Love Locked In," model no.HN1474, designed by L. Harradine, restoration to lady's neck and hairline crack to cupid's arm.

Also called "Love in the Stocks."

1931-38 *5in (12.5cm) high*

$600-700 **PSA**

A Royal Doulton figurine, "Gloria," model no.HN1488, designed by L. Harradine.

1932-38 *7¼in (18.5cm) high*

$500-600 **PSA**

A Royal Doulton figurine, "Bonnie Lassie," model no.HN1626, designed by L. Harradine.

1934-53 *5¼in (13.5cm) high*

$190-260 **FLD**

A Royal Doulton figurine, "Miranda," model no.HN1819, designed by L. Harradine.

1937-49 *8½in (21.5cm) high*

$450-500 **FLD**

A Royal Doulton figurine, "Antoinette," model no.HN1851, designed by L. Harradine, small hairline crack in base of pillar.

1938-49 *8in (20.5cm) high*

$260-320 **LOCK**

A Royal Doulton figurine, "Annabella," model no.HN1875, designed by L. Harradine.

1938-49 *4¾in (12cm) high*

$160-210 **PSA**

A Royal Doulton figurine, "Sir Walter Raleigh," model no.HN2015, designed by L. Harradine.

1948-55 *11½in (29cm) high*

$160-210 **PSA**

A Royal Doulton Prestige figurine, "St George," model no.HN2067, designed by S. Thorogood.

1950-79 *15¾in (40cm) high*

$1,050-1,300 **PSA**

A Royal Doulton large Prestige figurine, "Jack Point," model no.HN2080, designed by C.J. Noke.

16in (40.5cm) high

$600-700 **PSA**

A large Royal Doulton figurine, "Jack Point," model no.HN2080, with painted "P.S" and dated "1.12.80" in black.

Produced after the 1918 original by Charles Noke in the "Prestige" series.

1980 *17in (43cm) high*

$800-900 **GWA**

A pair of Royal Doulton figurines, "Oliver Hardy," model no.HN2775 and "Stan Laurel," model no.HN2774, designed by W.K. Harper, limited edition of 9,500.

1990 *10in (25.5cm) and 9¼in (23.5cm) high*

$210-260 **PSA**

A Royal Doulton figurine, "Lord Olivier as Richard III," model no.HN2881, designed by E.J. Griffiths, limited edition of 750, marked "Exhibition only" to base.

1985 *11½in (29cm) high*

$230-290 **PSA**

A Royal Doulton figurine, "Flower Arranging," model no.HN3040, designed by D. Brindley, limited edition of 750, in velvet box with wood base and certificate.

From the "Gentle Arts" series.

1988 *7¼in (18.5cm) high*

$180-230 **PSA**

A Royal Doulton figurine, "Queen Elizabeth I," model no.HN3099, designed by P. Parsons, from a limited edition of 5,000, boxed.

From the "Queens Of The Realm" series.

1987 *9in (23cm) high*

$100-160 **PSA**

A Royal Doulton figurine, "Queen Victoria," model no.HN3125, designed by P. Parsons, from a limited edition of 5,000, with certificate.

From the "Queens Of The Realm" series.

1988 *8in (20.5cm) high*

$100-160 **PSA**

A Royal Doulton figurine, "Queen Anne," model no.HN3141, designed by P. Parsons, limited edition of 5,000, boxed with certificate.

From the "Queens Of The Realm" series.

1988 *9in (23cm) high*

$80-100 **PSA**

A Royal Doulton figurine, "Mary Queen of Scots," model no.HN3142, designed by P. Parsons, boxed with certificate.

A limited edition of 5,000 from the "Queens Of The Realm" series.

1989 *9in (23cm) high*

$100-160 **PSA**

A Royal Doulton figurine, "Henry VIII," model no.HN3458, designed by P. Parsons, limited edition of 9,500, boxed.

1994 *9¼in (23.5cm) high*

$180-230 **PSA**

A set of Royal Doulton figurines, Henry VIII and his six wives, Henry model no.3458, Catherine of Aragon model no.3233, Jane Seymour model no.3349, Anne of Cleves model no.3356, Anne Boleyn model no.3232, Catherine Parr model no.3450, Catherine Howard model no.3449, designed by P. Parsons, limited editions of 9,500.

1990-94

$850-950 **PSA**

A Royal Doulton figurine, "Lady Jane Gray," model no.HN3680, designed by P. Parsons, limited edition of 5,000, boxed.

1995 *8¼in (21cm) high*

$190-260 **PSA**

A Royal Doulton figurine, "Margaret Tudor," model no.HN3838, designed by P. Parsons, limited edition of 5,000, boxed with certificate.

1997 *6½in (16.5cm) high*

$210-260 **PSA**

A Royal Doulton figurine, "Edward VI," model no.HN4263, designed by P. Parsons, numbered 273 from a limited edition of 5,000, printed mark.

8¼in (21cm) high

$350-400 **FLD**

A Royal Doulton figurine, "King Arthur," model no.HN4541, designed by S Ridge, from a limited edition of 950, boxed.

2003 *9in (23cm) high*

$300-400 **PSA**

A Royal Doulton prototype figurine, "Peggy Davies."

ca. 1960s *7¼in (18.5cm) high*

$900-1,050 **PSA**

A Royal Doulton prototype figurine of period sitting lady in garden, marked not for resale.

8¼in (21cm) high

$160-230 **PSA**

QUICK REFERENCE—CHARACTER JUGS

- **Having experimented with stoneware jugs in their early days, Doulton saw the idea revived in the early 1900s when Charles Noke produced "The Kingsware Huntsman," among other Toby jugs portraying various figures from literature, politics, and folklore, and began producing character jugs.**
- **Unlike Toby jugs, which depict the entire figure, character jugs just portray the head and shoulders. These jugs come in three sizes: large, small, and miniature.**
- **Harry Fenton was a prominent designer of Doulton's character jugs, modeling 26 character jugs and 15 Toby jugs. Following Fenton's death in 1953, Max Henk began modeling jugs with a focus on incorporating the handle into the design to a greater degree.**

A Royal Doulton small character jug, "The Jester," model no.D5556, designed by Charles Noke, with special Darley & Son Souvenir backstamp.

1936-60 *3¼in (8.5cm) high*

$260-320 **PSA**

A large Royal Doulton "Red-Haired Clown" character jug, model no.D5610, designed by Harry Fenton.

1936-42 *7½in (19cm) high*

$1,400-1,700 **PSA**

A Royal Doulton large character jug, "Cavalier with Goatee Beard," model no.D6114, designed by Harry Fenton.

1940-50 *7in (18cm) high*

$600-700 **PSA**

A Royal Doulton large character jug, "Field Marshal Smuts," model no.D6198, designed by Harry Fenton.

1946-48 *6½in (16.5cm) high*

$500-650 **PSA**

A Royal Doulton large character jug, "White Haired Clown," model no.D6322, designed by Harry Fenton.

1951-55 *7½in (19cm) high*

$230-290 **PSA**

A Royal Doulton large character jug, "The Poacher," model no.D6429, designed by Mark Henk, different color painted scarf and hat.

1955-95 *7in (18cm) high*

$180-230 **PSA**

A Royal Doulton large double-sided character jug, "Punch and Judy," model no.D6946, designed by Stanley J. Taylor, with certificate.

Created exclusively for the Royal Doulton International Collectors Club in a limited edition of 2,500.

1994 *7in (18cm) high*

$100-130 **PSA**

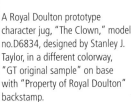

A Royal Doulton prototype character jug, "The Clown," model no.D6834, designed by Stanley J. Taylor, in a different colorway, "GT original sample" on base with "Property of Royal Doulton" backstamp.

$600-650 **K&O**

A Royal Doulton large two-handled character jug, "King Henry VIII," model no.D6888, designed by William K. Harper, boxed.

Issued in a limited edition of 1,991 to commemorate the 500th anniversary of the birth of Henry VIII.

1991 *7in (18cm) high*

$180-230 **PSA**

A Royal Doulton large three-handled character jug, "King Charles I," model no.D6917, designed by William K. Harper, limited edition of 2,500, with certificate.

1992 *7in (18cm) high*

$120-160 **PSA**

A Royal Doulton large character jug, "Phantom of the Opera," model no.D7017, designed by David B. Biggs, from a limited edition of 2,500.

1995 *7in (18cm) high*

$350-440 **PSA**

A Royal Doulton large character jug, "Marley's Ghost," model no.D7142, designed by David B. Biggs, from a limited edition of 2,500, boxed.

1999 *7½in (19cm) high*

$480-500 **PSA**

A Royal Doulton large character jug, "Lord Kitchener," model no.D7148, designed by David B. Biggs, to commemorate the 150th anniversary of his birth, limited edition of 1,500.

2000 *7¼in (18.5cm) high*

$210-260 **PSA**

A Royal Doulton large character jug, "Noah," model no.D7165, designed by David B Biggs, limited edition of 1,000.

2001 *7¼in (18.5cm) high*

$210-260 **PSA**

A Royal Doulton large character jug, "Boudicca," model no.D7221, designed by Caroline Dadd, from "The Great Military Leaders" series, limited edition of 250, with certificate.

2005 *5¾in (14.5cm) high*

$300-400 **PSA**

A Royal Doulton large character jug, "Genghis Khan," model no.D7222, designed by Caroline Dadd, from "The Great Military Leaders" series, limited edition of 250.

2005 *6¾in (17cm) high*

$400-450 **PSA**

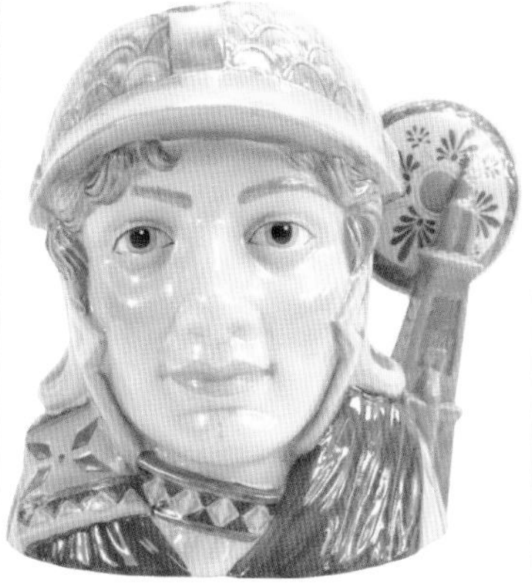

A Royal Doulton large character jug, "Alexander the Great," model no.D7224, designed by Caroline Dadd, from "The Great Military Leaders" series, limited edition of 250.

2005 *6½in (16.5cm) high*

$260-320 **PSA**

A Royal Doulton large character jug, "Attila The Hun," model no.D7225, designed by Caroline Dadd, from "The Great Military Leaders" series, limited edition of 250, with certificate.

$400-450 **PSA**

A Royal Doulton large character jug, "Emperor Kaiser," model no.D7233, from the "World War One Military Leaders" series, limited edition.

$500-650 **PSA**

A Royal Doulton large character jug, "John F. Kennedy," model no.D7246, special commission for Pascoe and Company, boxed.

$190-260 **PSA**

A Royal Doulton character jug, "Joseph Stalin," model no.D7284, from the "World War II Politicians" series, limited edition of 100, with certificate.

2009

$500-650 **PSA**

A Royal Doulton large character jug, "Yuri Andreyevich Zhivago," model no.D7286, from "The Literary Characters" series, limited edition with certificate.

$350-440 **PSA**

A Royal Doulton large character jug, "Erwin Rommel," model no.D7290, from "The Great Generals" series, limited edition.

$650-800 **PSA**

A Royal Doulton large character jug, "Lord Chamberlain," model no.D7296, limited edition with certificate, Pascoe and Company backstamp.

$300-350 **PSA**

A small Royal Doulton prototype "James Dean" character jug, "Property of Royal Doulton" backstamp.

This was designed for the "Celebrity Film Star" collection but never put into production.

2005

$2,600-3,200 **K&O**

A Royal Doulton large prototype character jug, "Maori," "Property of Royal Doulton" backstamp.

$6,000-6,500 **K&O**

QUICK REFERENCE—BUNNYKINS

- **Bunnykins earthenware figurines were introduced in the 1930s. Only six were originally made and the range was discontinued just before World War II. The original six include "Billy," "Mary," "Freddie," and "Reggie" Bunnykin as well as a "Farmer" and "Mother" Bunnykin. They remain rare.**
- **Charles Noke, the art director responsible for the HN range of Royal Doulton figurines, is believed to have modeled them, because they resemble some of his character animals.**
- **After Royal Doulton took over the Beswick factory in 1969, a new Bunnykins range was introduced in 1972 with the DB pattern numbers. A new look was developed by Harry Sales, the design manager of the Beswick factory in the 1980s. From then on, the figurines reflected children's interests. The first such figurine depicted a guitar-playing bunny called "Mr. Bunnybeat Strumming" (DB16) and a space traveler "Astro Bunnykins Rocket Man" (DB20).**

A set of rare Royal Doulton Bunnykins figurines, from the "Oompah Band," in a green colorway, with Sousaphone model no.DB105, Trumpet model no.DB106, Cymbals model no.DB107, Drummer model no.DB108, and Drum Major model no.DB109.

$900-1,050 PSA

A rare Royal Doulton Bunnykins figurine, "Boston College Touchdown," model no.DB29, designed by Harry Sales, in purple colorway.

1985 *3¼in (8.5cm) high*

$450-500 PSA

A Royal Doulton Bunnykins figurine, "Harry the Herald," model no.DB115, designed by Harry Sales, special limited colorway, signed Michael Doulton.

1991 *3¼in (8.5cm) high*

$230-290 PSA

A Royal Doulton Bunnykins figurine, "Clown," model no.DB129, designed by Denise Andrews.

From a limited edition of 250, signed Michael Doulton.

1992 *4¼in (11cm) high*

$260-320 PSA

A Royal Doulton Bunnykins figurine, "Sergeant Mountie," model no.DB136, designed by Graham Tongue, limited edition of 250.

1993 *4in (10cm) high*

$500-650 PSA

A Royal Doulton prototype Bunnykins figurine, "The Jester," model no.DB161, designed by Denise Andrews, in a trial yellow and black colorway.

1995 *4½in (11.5cm) high*

$300-350 PSA

A Royal Doulton prototype Bunnykins figurine, "The Piper," designed by Martyn Alcock, decorated in a different colorway, not for resale backstamp.

1995 *4¼in (11cm) high*

$300-400 PSA

A Royal Doulton prototype Bunnykins figurine, "Shopper," designed by Warren Platt, decorated in a different colorway, not for resale backstamp.

2001 *4½in (11.5cm) high*

$260-320 PSA

A Royal Doulton Bunnykins teapot, designed by Charles Noke.

4¾in (12cm) high

$600-650 LOCK

A rare Royal Doulton model, "Rabbit in morning dress," model no.HN101, designed by Charles Noke, impressed and printed marks.

1913-38 *6½in (16.5cm) high*
$2,300-2,900 **K&O**

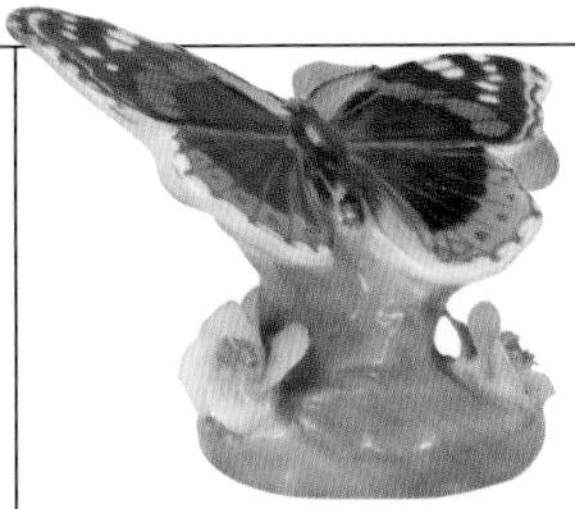

A Royal Doulton model, "Red Admiral Butterfly," model no.HN2607, on embossed floral base, small loss on edge of one petal.

1941-46 *2in (5cm) high*
$260-320 **PSA**

A rare Royal Doulton prototype puppy, playing with ball of string attached to its tail.

1930/40s *4in (10cm) high*
$700-850 **PSA**

A Royal Doulton figurine, "Terrier Puppies in a Basket," model no.HN2588.

1941-58 *3in (7.5cm) high*
$50-60 **JN**

A Royal Doulton porcelain spaniel, model no.HN1987.

$40-50 **JN**

A Royal Doulton figurine, "Cocker Spaniel Chewing Handle of Basket," model no.HN2586.

1941-85 *2¾in (7cm) high*
$50-60 **JN**

A medium Royal Doulton figurine, "English Setter," model no.HN1050.

1931-85 *5¼in (13.5cm) high*
$50-60 **JN**

A Royal Doulton large flambé stalking fox, model no.HN147A.

1912-62 *12½in (32cm) long*
$190-260 **PSA**

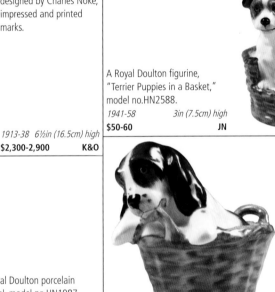

A rare Royal Doulton flambé model of cat lying down, model no.HN233.

1920-36 *3in (7.5cm) high*
$950-1,100 **PSA**

QUICK REFERENCE—FLAMBÉ

- **Taking inspiration from Asian ceramics, Royal Doulton experimented with flambé glaze, applying it to animal figurines in the early 1900s.**
- **Using copper and iron oxide in a glaze, fired in a kiln without oxygen, the vibrant red finish with streaks of purple or blue is achieved.**
- **The resulting pattern of this technique is uncontrollable, meaning pieces with the glaze are not identical.**
- **Noke experimented with variations of the red flambé glaze, creating the mottled Sung, Chang, and Chinese Jade finishes.**
- **While the Chang glaze, produced 1925-39, was the brainchild of Noke, Harry Nixon did most of the decorating, with his monogram often appearing on the base. Several layers of thick glazes were applied to heavy bodies and dripped freely, forming a painterly effect.**
- **Joseph Ledger, art director at Royal Doulton from the 1950s, also experimented with flambé glazes, creating a Mandarin glaze of mottled blue and green, which he used on pieces in his Chatcull series.**

A Royal Doulton flambé pair of snoozing pigs, model no.HN802, signed Noke.

1912-36 *7in (18cm) long*

$400-450 **PSA**

A very rare Royal Doulton flambé group of hugging apes, printed marks.

ca. 1910 *5¾in (14.5cm) high*

$3,900-5,200 **K&O**

A Royal Doulton flambé German sheperd dog, model no.HN899.

1926-46 *3¾in (9.5cm) high*

$350-400 **PSA**

A Royal Doulton large veined flambé owl, model no.2249, designed by A. Maslankowski.

1973-96 *12in (30cm) high*

$190-260 **PSA**

A Royal Doulton flambé Sung pumpkin vase.

6¾in (17cm) high

$500-600 **PSA**

A Royal Doulton large veined flambé dragon, model no.2085, initialled to base "AM."

11in (28cm) long

$180-230 **PSA**

A Royal Doulton prototype flambé model of a group of otters, "Tumbling waters," never put into production with a flambé glaze, printed marks.

14¼in (36cm) high

$3,900-5,200 **K&O**

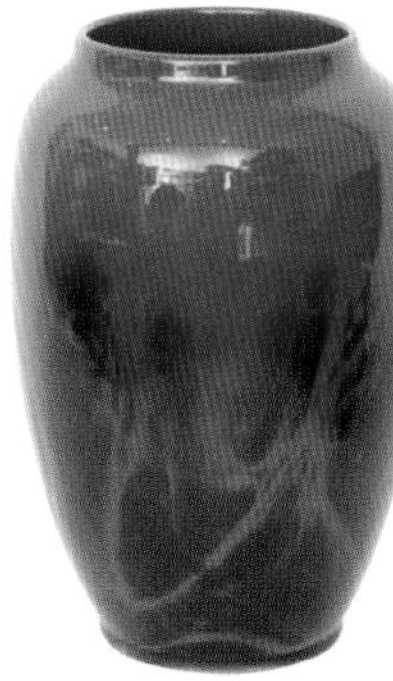

An early-20thC Royal Doulton flambé Sung vase, signed Noke and initialled Fred Moore, decorated mottled and veined tonal glazes over the red ground, printed mark and painted Sung.

6¾in (17cm) high

$300-400 **FLD**

A Fulper large urn, blue and ivory flambé glaze, raised racetrack mark, some darkened crazing lines.
1920s *14½in (37cm) high*
$800-900 DRA

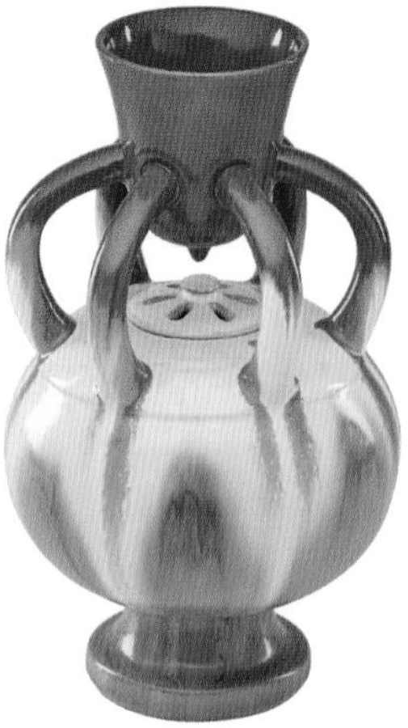

A rare Fulper six-handled incense burner, mahogany-ivory-Flemington green flambé glaze, rectangular ink stamp, with original lid.
1910s *11½in (29cm) high*
$3,200-3,900 DRA

A Fulper salamander vase, cat's eye flambé glaze, rectangular ink stamp, some efflorescence.
ca. 1910 *8in (20.5cm) high*
$800-900 DRA

A Fulper vase, Flemington green flambé glaze, rectangular ink stamp, spider firing line to base, grinding flakes around foot.
1910s *14in (35.5cm) high*
$550-640 DRA

A rare Fulper jardinière, leopard skin crystalline glaze, vertical racetrack ink stamp, long crack on waist with related glaze losses in interior, possibly in the making.

The Fulper Pottery Co., based in Flemington, New Jersey, was incorporated in 1899, having been established ca. 1814. At the turn of the 20thC, under the direction of William H. Fulper II, the company became known for its Arts and Crafts pottery. Ceramics engineer Martin Stangl was employed by Fulper in 1910 and designed the "Vasekraft" lamps. By 1924, Stangl was vice president of the company. In 1935, he closed the original Fulper factory, shifting production focus to hand-painted dinnerware.
1910s-20s *15in (38cm) diam*
$1,050-1,300 DRA

A Fulper vase, cucumber green crystalline glaze, vertical rectangular ink stamp, a few minor grinding chips.
1910s *12½in (32cm) high*
$1,100-1,250 DRA

A Fulper vase, in green, blue, and brown flambé glaze, oval incised mark.
1917-27 *10in (25.5cm) high*
$260-320 DRA

A Fulper vase, brown and black flambé over mustard mat glaze, glazed-over mark.
1910s-20s *7in (18cm) high*
$1,250-1,450 DRA

A Fulper vase, in blue flambé glaze, rectangular ink mark.
1909-17 *9in (23cm) diam*
$230-290 DRA

QUICK REFERENCE—GOLDSCHEIDER

- **Friedrich Goldscheider (1845-97) founded the Goldscheider Manufactory & Majolica Factory in Vienna in 1885. Goldscheider opened retail outlets in Paris, Leipzig, and Florence.**
- **The Goldscheider factory, with sculptors such as Josef Lorenzl (1892-1950) and Stefan Dakon (1904-92), produced Art Deco figurines, tobacco jars, jardinières, and wall masks.**
- **The Art Deco figurines, which portrayed fashionable, carefree women or avant-garde dancers using vivid colors and fine details, are highly collectible.**
- **The factory closed in 1953, with the brand name sold on to Carstens, which continued production until 1963. In the late 1980s, Friedrich's great-grandson, Peter Goldscheider, produced a small number of figurines and objects.**

A Goldscheider figurine of a pair of Spanish dancers, designed by Josef Lorenzl, model no.5775, impressed and printed marks.

17in (43cm) high

$3,900-4,500 K&O

A Goldscheider figurine of a nude woman, by Josef Lorenzl, black printed marks, stamped "5802/489/4," some restoration, crazed all over.

ca. 1926 *11¼in (28.5cm) high*

$600-700 BELL

A Goldscheider "The Egyptian Dancer" figurine, designed by Josef Lorenzl, model no.5281, with eight photographic postcards depicting the dancer Miss Maud Adams in exotic Egyptianesque costume, impressed marks and printed Goldscheider mark, impressed Lorenzl facsimile signature.

See Pinhas, Ora, *Goldscheider*, Richard Dennis Publications, pp. 108-109 for six examples of this figurine illustrated in different colors.

11¼in (28.5cm) high

$1,800-2,600 WW

A Goldscheider figurine of a butterfly girl, by Sailor, model no.5840, stamped and printed marks, extensively restored.

Provenance: The Barbra Streisand Collection of Decorative and Fine Arts and Memorabilia, Part II, March 4, 1994, Christie's.

19¼in (49cm) high

$3,900-5,200 SWO

A Goldscheider large model of a woman in exotic costume, designed by Josef Lorenzl, model no.5927, headdress and purple cape, on domed octagonal base, impressed factory marks, printed marks and impressed facsimile signature, small glaze chip on cloak rim.

17½in (44.5cm) high

$8,500-9,500 WW

A Goldscheider figurine of a dancer, model no.6399, stamped and printed marks, restored left wrist.

11½in (29cm) high

$900-1,050 SWO

An Art Deco Goldscheider figurine of a female dancer, by Josef Lorenzl, model no.6693/49/7, printed and impressed marks, small chip on top, some crazing.

ca. 1930 *7in (18cm) high*

$400-450 BELL

An Art Deco Goldscheider figurine, after Josef Lorenzl, model no.7058, impressed with model number and "2" and "4" on base, some restoration to arms, some crazing.

13in (33cm) high

$1,100-1,250 **PW**

A Goldscheider figurine of a couple ballroom dancing, by Stephan Dakon, model no.7059, stamped and printed marks, restored lady's right arm, left-hand finger retouched, base of plinth chipped.

12in (30.5cm) high

$1,600-2,100 **SWO**

A Goldscheider figurine, by Stephan Dakon, model no.7256, stamped and printed marks, restored and damages.

14½in (37cm) wide

$2,900-3,400 **SWO**

A Goldscheider figurine, by Stephan Dakon, model no.7257, stamped and printed marks, small chip on edge of dress.

12¼in (31cm) high

$850-950 **SWO**

A Goldscheider figurine of an ice skater, by Stephan Dakon, model no.7849, incised on plinth "Dakon," with original silver label, stamped and printed marks.

10¾in (27.5cm) high

$1,700-2,300 **SWO**

A Goldscheider figurine of a dancer, by Stephan Dakon, model no.7857, with remnants of original label, stamped and printed marks, remnants of the label, small flake on left hand.

15¾in (40cm) high

$1,600-2,100 **SWO**

A Goldscheider figurine of a dancer, by Stephan Dakon, model no.8126, stamped "L," printed marks.

15½in (39.5cm) high

$1,250-1,450 **SWO**

A Goldscheider figurine of a dancer, probably by Stephan Dakon, model no.8129, stamped and printed marks, crack on underside of dress, foot restored.

13in (33cm) high

$600-700 **SWO**

A rare Goldscheider figurine of a dancer, model no.8746, stamped, with "Wiener Manufaktur J. Schuster" printed mark.

15½in (39.5cm) high

$1,300-1,800 **SWO**

A Goldscheider figurine, by Josef Lorenzl, model no.7064, incised facsimile signature, stamped and printed marks, minor glaze cracks on cuff.

10¾in (27.5cm) high

$5,200-6,500 **SWO**

An Art Nouveau Goldscheider large bust, by Gambeauche, model no.2437, impressed marks, artist signature to shoulder.

23¼in (59cm) high

$1,900-2,600 **WW**

A Goldscheider figurine, by Claire Weiss, model no. 6769, incised on the plinth "Claire Weiss," stamped and printed marks, chips on the base rim, chip on one arm, glaze cracks.

Hungarian-born Claire Weiss (1906-97), who was also known as Claire Weiss-Herczeg or Klára Herczeg, studied at the Budapest Academy before moving to Paris and Berlin in the late 1920s. Her speciality at Goldscheider was figurines of elegant women, but she modeled lamps and figurines of children, too. She also designed large sculptures for public displays and worked for Rosenthal and Bing & Grøndahl.

8in (20.5cm) high

$950-1,100 **SWO**

A Goldscheider figurine of a girl and a rabbit, model no.7201, stamped and printed marks.

8½in (21.5cm) high

$650-800 **SWO**

A Goldscheider craft pottery figurine, possibly modeled by Kurt Goebel, model no.7845, stamped and printed marks.

10¼in (26cm) high

$500-650 **SWO**

A Goldscheider mask, printed mark "Goldscheider, West Germany," numbered "12," mold "544."

8¾in (22cm) high

$300-400 **SWO**

A Goldscheider wall mask, by Stephan Dakon, model no.7412, incised and printed marks.

10in (25.5cm) high

$260-390 **SWO**

A Goldscheider wall mask, by Stephan Dakon, model no.7412, stamped and printed marks, restored.

10in (25.5cm) high

$160-210 **SWO**

A Goldscheider wall mask of a lady holding a cup, faint printed mark.

8¾in (22cm) high

$160-210 **SWO**

A Peggy Davies Rita Hayworth "Covergirl" figurine, limited edition.
$130-190 **PSA**

A Peggy Davies "Putting on the Ritz" figurine, limited edition.
$190-260 **PSA**

A Peggy Davies "Isadora" figurine, artist's proof by M. Jackson.
$230-290 **PSA**

A Peggy Davies large "The Whisperer" grotesque bird figurine, modeled by Robert Tabbenor, limited edition.
$130-190 **PSA**

A Kevin Francis/Peggy Davies "Lolita Erotic" figurine, in unusual colorway, original artist's proof by M. Jackson.
$450-600 **PSA**

A Kevin Francis/Peggy Davies Ceramics "Isadora" erotic figurine.
$210-260 **PSA**

A Kevin Francis/Peggy Davies "Clarice Cliff, The Artisan" figurine, in red and blue special colorway.
$100-130 **PSA**

QUICK REFERENCE—KEVIN FRANCIS AND PEGGY DAVIES

- **Kevin Francis was founded by Kevin Pearson and Francis Salmon in 1985. It specialized in hand-painted, limited edition figurines and Toby jugs.**
- **Before partnering with Peggy Davies Ceramics (established in 1981), Kevin Francis relied on commissions from Royal Doulton.**

A Kevin Francis/Peggy Davies "Clarice Cliff" figurine, decorating a cup, numbered "1 of 1," signed "Victoria Bourne."
$210-260 **PSA**

A Kevin Francis/Peggy Davies Ceramics "Bubbles" erotic figurine, by Victoria Bourne, limited edition, artist's proof.
$260-320 **PSA**

QUICK REFERENCE—LENCI

- **Lenci was established in Turin, Italy, in 1919, by Helen (Elena) König Scavini and her husband Enrico di Scavini.**
- **The company originally produced felt dolls, but from 1928 they also made earthenware and porcelain figurines, mostly of women.**
- **Distinguishing features of these figurines include elongated limbs, bright yellow hair, and a combination of mat and glossy glazes.**

A Lenci "Il Grattacielo" pottery figurine, by Abele Jacopi, modeled as a young lady with a compact and powder puff, painted mark "Lenci Made in Italy, Torino, 28," some minor chips.

The figurine, titled "Il Grattacielo"—Italian for "skyscraper"—was first shown at the Turin International Exhibition in 1928, around the time that skyscrapers were cropping up across Europe's cities. Designer Abele Jacopi (1882-1957) took inspiration for the figure's outfit from *Vogue* magazine. The figurine sold for a record price for Lenci.

ca. 1930 *17¼in (44cm) high*

$52,00-58,000 BOL

A Lenci "Maternita" figurine, designed by Helen König Scavini, painted factory marks, paper retailers label, professional restoration.

12½in (32cm) high

$2,100-2,600 WW

An Art Deco Lenci porcelain wall mask plaque, probably after a design by Helen König Scavini, minor surface wear and dirt, signature and marks are blurred.

13¾in (35cm) high

$1,250-1,450 APAR

A Lenci "A Teatro" figurine, designed by Helen König Scavini, inscribed "Lenci torino made in Italy," with a flower possibly for Giovanni Ronzan.

11¾in (30cm) high

$950-1,100 SWO

A Lenci "Giovinezza" figurine, possibly by Sandro Vacchetti, model no.442, inscribed "Lenci Torino 4 (XII) made in Italy TK."

7¾in (19.5cm) wide

$6,000-8,500 SWO

A Lenci "Madonna" bust, signed "Lenci Made in Italy."

ca. 1930s *8¾in (22cm) high*

$500-650 FLD

A Lenci "Madonna and Child" earthenware figurine, designed by Sandro Vacchetti, signed "Lenci, IVA, Made in Italy, 31-10-1936."

8¾in (22cm) high

$700-850 ROS

QUICK REFERENCE—LLADRÓ

- **Lladró was founded in 1953 near Valencia, Spain, by bothers Juan, José, and Vicente Lladró. The company started out modeling plates, vases, and ceramic figurines.**
- **In the 1960s, Lladró founded its professional training school, and in 1969 it opened its current headquarters in Tavernes Blanques, Valencia.**
- **Figurines from 1954 to the mid-1960s were stamped with decimal point serial numbers.**
- **Lladró was bought by Spanish investment fund PHI Industrial Group in 2017.**

A Lladró "Romeo and Juliet" figurine group, model no.4750.

18½in (47cm) high

$400-450 **APAR**

A Lladró "Alice in Wonderland" figurine, privilege gold, dated.

2009 *8¼in (21cm) high*

$500-650 **PSA**

A Lladró figurine group, marked "J. Puche & Angeles Cabo no.83," with wooden plinth stand, loss of one flower.

23¾in (60.5cm) high

$850-950 **WM**

A Lladró "Antique Car" figurine group, model no.1146, on a wooden base.

24in (61cm) wide

$1,150-1,450 **APAR**

A pair of Lladró figurines, "Pocket Full Of Wishes" model no.7650, and "A Wish Come True" model no.7676, printed marks.

10¾in (27.5cm) high

$130-180 **FLD**

A pair of Lladró figurines, "Basket Of Love" model no.7622, and "Innocence In Bloom" model no.7644, printed marks.

10in (25.5cm) high

$60-80 **FLD**

A pair of Lladró figurines, "Afternoon Promenade" model no.7636, and "Now & Forever" model no.7642, printed marks.

10¾in (27.5cm) high

$90-100 **FLD**

A pair of Lladró clown figurines, "Circus Sam" model no.5472, and "Sad Sax" model no.5471, printed marks, slight damage.

9in (23cm) high

$80-90 **FLD**

A pair of Lladró figurines, "Jazz Horn" model no.5832, and "Jazz Sax" model no.5833, both with damage.

$140-190 **PSA**

A Lladró "Big Sister" figurine, model no.5735.

7in (18cm) high

$230-290 **PSA**

A Lladró "Sancho Panza" figurine, model no.6633, printed mark.

10in (25.5cm) high

$60-70 **FLD**

A Lladró "Birth of Venus" figurine group, designed by Antonio Ramos, no.32 of an addition of 1,000, with wood base.

2001 *33½in (85cm) wide*

$2,100-2,600 **PW**

A Lladró "Two Horses" figurine group, model no.4597.

17¼in (44cm) high

$300-400 **APAR**

A Lladró large "Horse with Lady Rider" figurine group, factory marks on base.

17¾in (45cm) high

$230-290 **WM**

A Lladró "Pensive Clown" bust, model no.5130, printed mark.

10¾in (27.5cm) high

$120-140 **FLD**

A Lladró "Penguin Love" figurine, model no.2519, mat glazed.

9in (23cm) high

$210-260 **PSA**

CERAMICS

QUICK REFERENCE—LORNA BAILEY

- **Lorna Bailey (b.1978) worked as a painter at her father's firm LJB Ceramics, in Stoke-on-Trent, England.**
- **At the young age of 17, her "House and Path" and "Sunburst" patterns were put into production.**
- **In 2003, LJB Ceramics was renamed Lorna Bailey Artware. Taking inspiration from the Art Deco period, Lorna Bailey Artware produced a range of handcrafted and hand-painted domestic and decorative wares.**
- **Lorna Bailey retired in 2008.**

A Lorna Bailey "Iggy The Cat" prototype.

$60-80 PSA

A Lorna Bailey "Christmas Mayhem The Cat" prototype.

$140-190 PSA

A Lorna Bailey "House and Path" bulbous vase.

7in (18cm) high

$50-60 LOCK

A Lorna Bailey "Poolfields" conical shape sugar sifter.

5¼in (13.5cm) high

$35-45 LOCK

A Lorna Bailey "Ashcroft" pitcher, signed on base.

7in (18cm) high

$60-70 LOCK

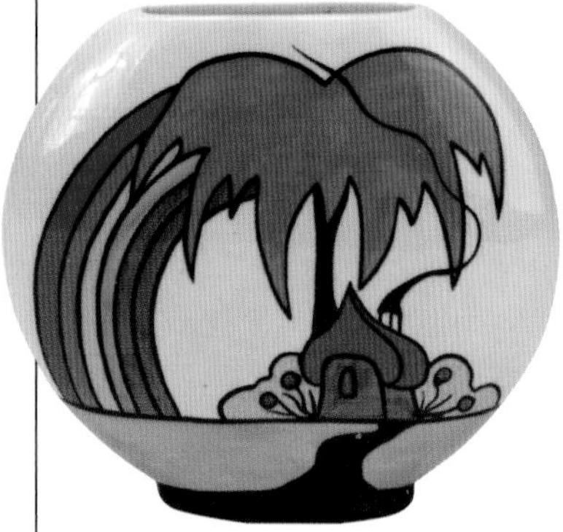

A Lorna Bailey "Brampton Cottage" vase, signed on base.

6¾in (17cm) high

$60-70 LOCK

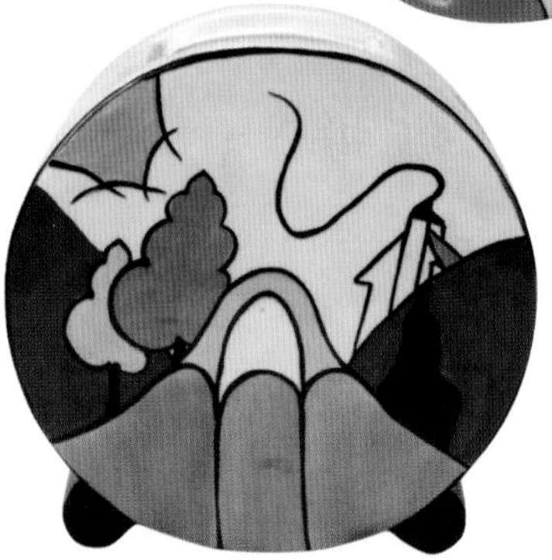

A Lorna Bailey "Bridge and Stream" vase, signed on base.

6¾in (17cm) high

$50-60 LOCK

A Lorna Bailey "Pagoda Garden" pitcher, signed on base.

6¼in (16cm) high

$50-60 LOCK

QUICK REFERENCE—MARTIN BROTHERS

- **Martin Brothers, comprising Robert (1843-1923), Charles (1846-1910), Walter (1857-1912), and Edwin (1860-1915), was established in 1873, in Fulham, London. It moved to Southall in 1877 and production continued until 1923.**
- **Robert Martin's range of birds and grotesques are popular with collectors, as are sgraffito-decorated vases.**
- **Each brother had a role at the business; Robert modeled the figures, Walter threw the pots, Edwin painted and decorated, and Charles ran the store and gallery.**

A Martin Brothers grotesque "Fish" vase, signed "Martin Bros, London and Southall."

ca. 1890 *3¼in (8.5cm) high*

$2,300-2,900 **K&O**

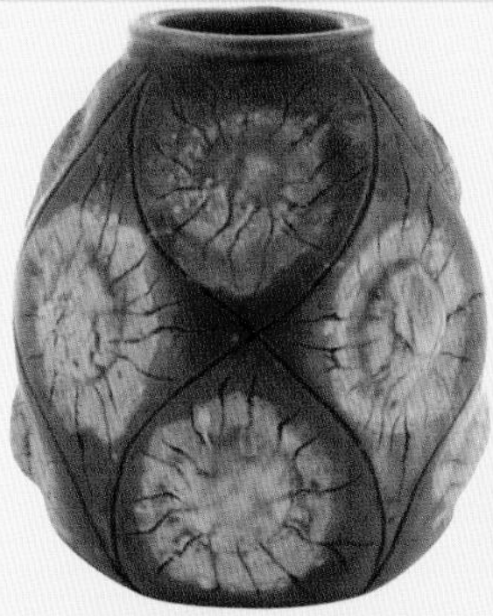

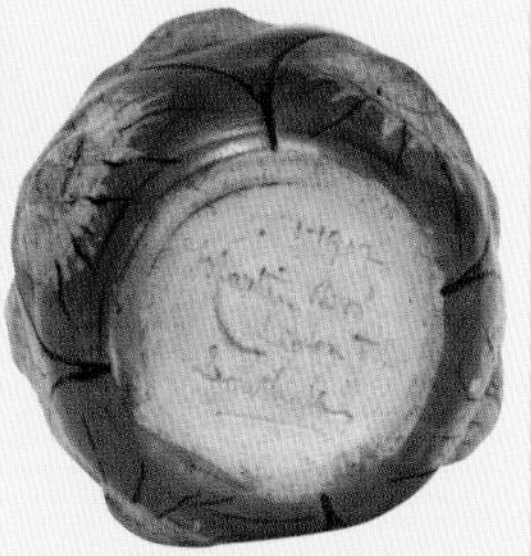

A Martin Brothers stoneware vase, incised mark "Martin ... London & Southall 1-1902."

2¾in (7cm) high

$1,600-2,100 **SWO**

A Martin Brothers stoneware vase, inscribed "21.5.85, Martin Bros., London & Southall."

8¼in (21cm) high

$950-1,100 **CHEF**

A Martin Brothers salt-glazed stoneware vase, incised with a frieze of grotesque birds and a serpent, incised maker's marks "R. W. MARTIN & BROS. LONDON & SOUTHALL 6.1894," chip on rim.

1894 *9in (23cm) high*

$1,900-2,600 **L&T**

An early-20thC Martin Brothers stoneware vase, molded and decorated with a man in medieval dress, incised to the base "Martin Bros, London & Southall," some damages, dated.

1903 *9½in (24cm) high*

$900-1,050 **FLD**

A Martin Brothers stoneware a "Aquatic" miniature vase, by Edwin and Walter Martin, incised "11 Martin Bros London."

1911 *2¼in (5.5cm) high*

$2,600-3,200 **WW**

A Martin Brothers stoneware vase, decorated with anthropomorphic fish, eels, a jellyfish, and seaweed, incised "Martin Bros. London and Southall, 8-1894," restored.

1894 *8¼in (21cm) high*

$1,400-1,800 **SWO**

A Martin Brothers stoneware miniature vase, by Edwin and Walter Martin, incised "12-1903 Martin Bros London," dated.

1903 *2¼in (5.5cm) high*

$700-850 **WW**

QUICK REFERENCE—MEISSEN

- **Meissen was founded in 1710 by Augustus the Strong, Elector of Saxony, in its namesake town in Germany. Its signature of the crossed swords was introduced in 1722. Meissen porcelain was heavily influenced by Asian styles and designs.**
- **In the early 1720s, under the direction of porcelain painter Johann Gregorius Höroldt, Meissen developed the enameling process, increasing the range of colors. From the early 1730s, Meissen produced figurines and table services.**
- **Key modelers include Johann Gottlieb Kirchner (1706-68), Johann Joachim Kändler (1706-75), Peter Reinicke (1715-68), and Michel Victor Acier (1736-99).**
- **New production facilities, still used today, were built in Triebischtal, Germany, from 1861. During World War II, production was hindered and stopped in 1945, with the company returned to the German Democratic Republic in 1950 by occupying Soviet forces.**
- **Since 1991, the company has been owned by the State of Saxony.**

A 20thC Meissen "The Pastry Seller" porcelain figurine, after the original by Peter Reinicke and the "Cris de Paris" series, underglaze blue crossed sword mark, incised "No.60220," further numbered "179."

5¼in (13.5cm) high

$400-500 LSK

A 20thC Meissen "Woman with Triangle" porcelain figurine, after the original by Peter Reinicke from the "Cris de Paris" series, underglaze blue crossed sword mark, incised "No.60223," further numbered "102."

5¼in (13.5cm) high

$400-500 LSK

A 20thC Meissen "Boy with Flute and Drum" porcelain figurine, after the original by Peter Reinicke from the "Cris de Paris" series, underglaze blue crossed sword mark, incised "No.5," further numbered "127."

6in (15cm) high

$400-500 LSK

A 20thC Meissen "The Fruit Seller" porcelain figurine, after the original by Peter Reinicke from the "Cris de Paris" series, underglaze blue crossed sword mark, incised "No.60225," further numbered "126."

6in (15cm) high

$400-500 LSK

A 20thC Meissen "The Carp Seller" porcelain figurine, after the original by Peter Reinicke from the "Cris de Paris" series, underglaze blue crossed sword mark, incised "No.60229," further numbered "733."

5¼in (13.5cm) high

$450-600 LSK

A 19thC/20thC Meissen allegorical "Broken Bridge" figurine group, after the model by Acier, blue crossed swords mark, incised "F63," small amount of restoration.

9¾in (24.5cm) high

$800-900 WW

An early 20thC Meissen "Four Seasons" figural group, painted mark to base.

11½in (29cm) high

$450-600 FLD

A pair of late 19thC Meissen porcelain magpies, blue crossed swords marks.

21in (53.5cm) high

$800-900 DUK

A pair of 20thC Meissen peacock figurines, blue crossed swords marks, one lacking its crest, the other with a small chip to its beak.

5½in (14cm) wide

$400-450 WW

QUICK REFERENCE—MINTON

- **Minton was established in 1793 by Thomas Minton (1765-1836) and Joseph Poulson in Stoke-on-Trent, England. After Thomas's death, he was succeeded by his son, Herbert Minton (1793-1858).**
- **The factory traded under various names, becoming Mintons in 1873. Various parts of the company traded under different names, with its subsidiary tile business separating into Minton & Co. and Minton, Hollins & Co.**
- **Léon Arnoux, Art Director from 1849, developed the tin-glaze used for Minton's tin-glazed majolica range.**
- **Under the direction of Léon Solon, Art Director from 1900–9, the company developed a range of Art Nouveau earthenware, decorated with tube lining and influenced by the Vienna Secession.**
- **The company became part of the Royal Doulton Tableware Group in 1968.**

A Minton plaque, painted freehand with a cherub, signed L. Boullemier (Lucien Emile), in an oak frame.

$230-290 **PSA**

A 19thC/20thC Minton cabinet plate, hand painted with a young woman, by A. Boullemier, gilded to the ribbon edge.

9½in (24cm) diam

$400-450 **PSA**

A Minton's Art Pottery Studio charger, painted by Rebecca Coleman, signed, printed Kensington Gore mark with date code, painted "739" and monogram "WSC," dated.

Rebecca Coleman was the sister of William Stephen Coleman, who was the Art Director at Minton's Art Pottery Studio from 1871-73.

1872 *16½in (42cm) diam*

$3,200-3,900 **SWO**

A Minton bicentenary pâte-sur-pâte dish, with cupids lighting candles, gilded rim.

4¾in (12cm) diam

$140-210 **PSA**

A Minton fruit bowl, heavily gilded.

11½in (29cm) diam

$130-190 **PSA**

An early 20thC Minton pâte-sur-pâte cup and saucer, decorated with portrait panels and raised gilded.

$700-850 **PSA**

An Art Nouveau Minton Secessionist tube-lined vase.

ca. 1900

$140-210 **PSA**

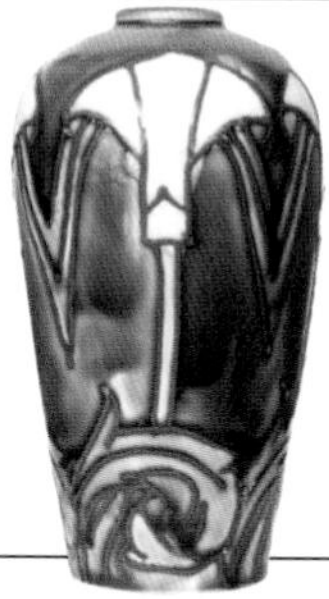

An early-20thC Minton Secessionist vase, decorated with tube-lined stylized flowers, printed mark with "No.7."

5½in (14cm) high

$300-450 **FLD**

A Minton Secessionist jardinière, hairline crack from top rim.

8¾in (22cm) high

$100-160 **PSA**

QUICK REFERENCE—MAJOLICA

- **Majolica (the anglicized term derived from the Italian *maiolica*, meaning "tin-glazed pottery") was inspired by Italian Renaissance pottery and the work of Bernard Palissy (ca. 1510-90), as well as Staffordshire-based Thomas Whieldon (1719-95) and Ralph Wood (1715-72).**
- **Minton & Co., Wedgwood and George Jones & Sons dominated majolica production. Leon Arnoux, at Minton & Co., developed the glaze formulas for the pottery's majolica. Minton & Co. presented their majolica range to the public at London's Great Exhibition of 1851.**

A 19thC Minton majolica monkey teapot, in ocher, cobalt, and green glazes, the interior glazed turquoise, impressed shape no.1844 and date code.

This is the original that the others were inspired by.

1860s *6in (15cm) high*

$500-650 **FLD**

A boxed Minton Archive Collection "Monkey Teapot," modeled on the 1860s majolica original, limited edition no.1694 of 1,793.

8in (20.5cm) long

$160-210 **FLD**

A boxed Minton Archive Collection "Cat and Mouse Teapot," modeled on the late 19thC majolica original, limited edition no.612 of 2,500.

7½in (19cm) long

$300-400 **FLD**

A boxed Minton Archive Collection "Chinaman Teapot," modeled on the 1870s majolica original, limited edition no.571 of 2,500.

8¼in (21cm) long

$180-260 **FLD**

A boxed Minton Archive Collection "Cockerel Teapot," modeled on the late-19thC majolica original, limited edition no.197 of 2,500.

8¾in (22cm) long

$130-180 **FLD**

A boxed Minton Archive Collection "Fish Teapot," modeled on the late-19thC majolica original, limited edition no.646 of 2,500.

9in (23cm) long

$260-320 **FLD**

A boxed Minton Archive Collection "Cockerel and Monkey Teapot," modeled on the 19thC majolica original, limited edition no.577 of 1,000.

8¾in (22cm) long

$190-260 **FLD**

A boxed Minton Archive Collection "Tortoise Teapot," modeled on the 1870s majolica original, limited edition no.111 of 2,500.

8in (20.5cm) long

$140-180 **FLD**

QUICK REFERENCE—MOORCROFT

- **William Moorcroft (1872-1945) studied at the Royal College of Art, London. He began his career at the Staffordshire pottery manufacturers James Macintyre & Co. in 1897 and was soon running the company's art pottery studio.**
- **Moorcroft patterns were often inspired by the natural world. His early designs included the distinctive "Aurelian" and "Florian" wares, decorated with stylized floral and foliate Art Nouveau designs. The later "Hesperian" design portrays fish, and landscapes appeared in patterns, such as "Claremont," "Prunus," "Hazeldene," "Dawn," and "Eventide."**
- **He founded W Moorcroft Ltd. in 1913. With the backing of Liberty of London and other major retailers, the company was quickly successful. In 1928, William Moorcroft was appointed "Potter to HM The Queen."**
- **The designs were produced through "tube lining." Outlines of a pattern were piped onto the surface, leaving a low-relief outline design. The spaces within the pattern were then filled in with colored glazes.**
- **On William's death, his son Walter (1917-2002) took over the company. Moorcroft is still open today and operates from the same factory in Stoke-on-Trent where it was originally founded.**
- **Early ranges from the 1900s-20s, such as "Florian" or "Claremont," tend to be the most valuable, while common patterns, such as "Anemone" and "Pomegranate," are, in general, more affordable. In 2013, a "Claremont" pattern loving cup (ca. 1905) sold for $23,000 at Clars Auction Gallery in Oakland, California. The piece included mounts by the Californian jeweller Shreve & Co.**
- **Many collectors are increasingly interested in contemporary pieces from the 1990s onward by designers such as Rachel Bishop, Emma Bossons, Philip Gibson, Sian Leeper, and Sally Tuffin. Large pieces from limited editions tend to fetch the highest prices.**

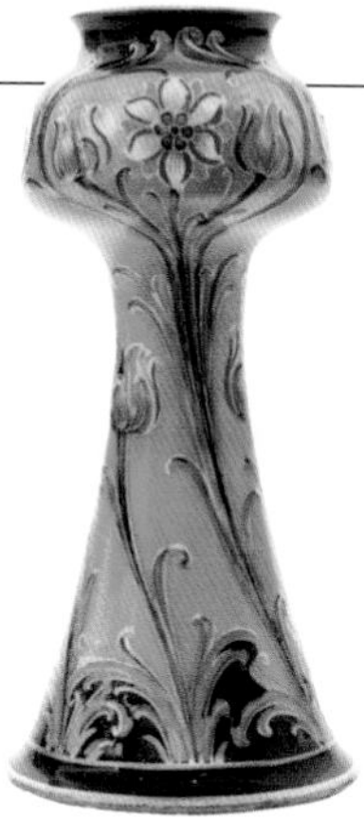

An early-20thC James Macintyre & Co. vase, by William Moorcroft, "Alhambra" pattern, printed mark.

8in (22.5cm) high

$800-900 FLD

An early William Moorcroft Macintyre "Aurelian" ware gilded vase.

5¼in (13.5cm) high

$160-230 PSA

An early-20thC James Macintyre & Co. "Florian" ware vase, by William Moorcroft, "Cornflower" pattern, printed mark and signed in green.

13in (33cm) high

$600-700 FLD

A William Moorcroft Macintyre "Florian" vase, "Cornflower" pattern.

6¼in (16cm) high

$1,600-2,100 PSA

A William Moorcroft Macintyre funnel vase, "Forget-me-nots" pattern.

10in (25cm) high

$650-800 PSA

A William Moorcroft small vase, "Hazeldene" pattern, turquoise green ground, underglaze green signature and date, printed Liberty mark.

ca. 1908 4in (10cm) high

$1,400-1,900 K&O

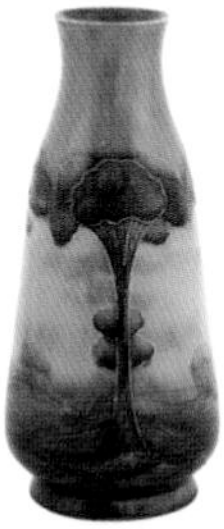

A James Macintyre vase, designed by William Moorcroft, "Hazeldene" pattern, printed marks "Made for Liberty & Co.," "Rd no 397964" and "W. Moorcroft des" in green, crazing on the body.

6¼in (16cm) high

$1,260-2,300 SWO

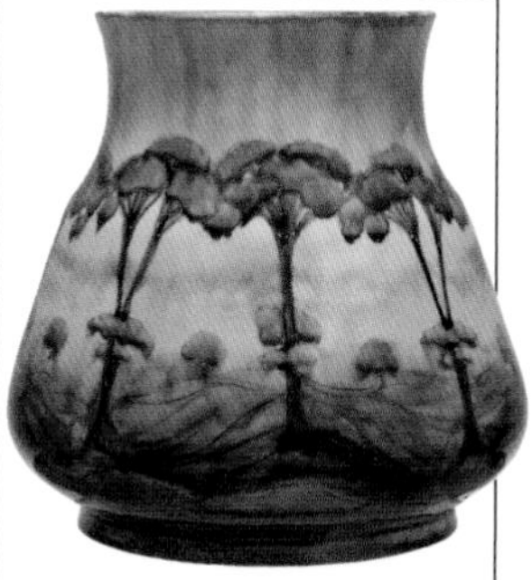

An early-20thC Moorcroft vase, "Hazeldene" pattern, tube-lined green, blue, and yellow streaked colors, signed in green "W. Moorcroft Des," restoration on foot rim.

10in (25.5cm) high

$3,400-3,900 ROS

A William Moorcroft Macintyre vase, "Pansy" pattern.

9in (24.5cm) high

$1,300-1,800 PSA

An early-20thC James Macintyre & Co. "Florian" ware vase, by William Moorcroft, "Peacock" pattern, printed mark, initialed in green.

11in (28cm) high

$650-800 FLD

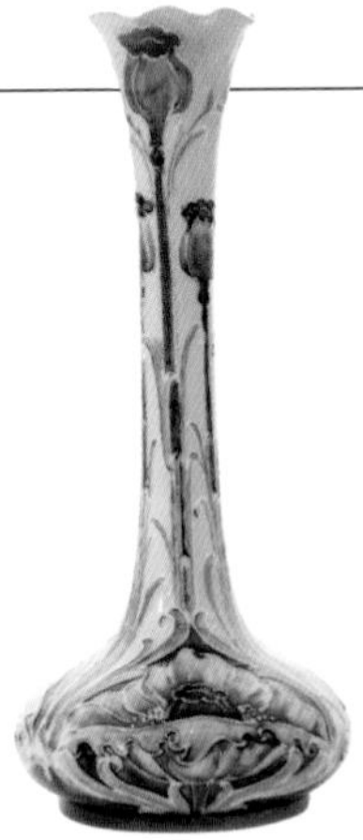

An early-20thC James Macintyre & Co. "Florian" ware vase, by William Moorcroft, "Poppy" pattern, printed mark and signed in green, restored.

9in (25cm) high

$300-400 FLD

A Moorcroft vase, "Rose Garland" pattern, model no.M2837/3, with gilt highlights, signed, printed marks.

11½in (29cm) high

$300-400 DUK

A William Moorcroft Macintrye vase, "Wisteria" pattern, restoration on top rim, dated.

1913 9in (24.5cm) high

$1,700-2,100 PSA

An early-20thC Moorcroft "Florian" vase, "Lilac" pattern, printed marks, signed.

5½in (14cm) high

$900-1,050 FLD

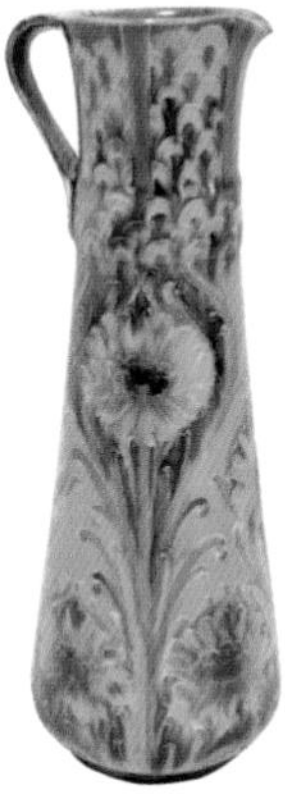

A Moorcroft "Florian" ware ewer, with William Moorcroft signature on the base and inscribed "Made for Liberty & Co.," extensive crazing, some rim restoration.

8in (20.5cm) high

$300-400 APAR

An early-20thC Moorcroft "Florian" vase, decorated with tube-lined poppies and forget-me-nots, printed mark on base, signed.

8in (20.5cm) high

$400-500 FLD

A Macintyre Moorcroft ewer, model no.M2837/3, "Peacock" pattern, printed and painted marks, some glaze running.

8in (22.5cm) high

$900-1,050 CHEF

QUICK REFERENCE—MOORCROFT MINIATURES

- **Small is often considered beautiful by Moorcroft collectors.**
- **Miniature versions of Moorcroft's pieces, measuring only around 2½-3½in (6.5-9cm), can fetch significant prices.**
- **In the 1970s, miniatures sold for around £30 ($40); in the Kingham & Orme sale in June 2019, a series of rare Moorcroft-Macintyre miniatures, some of which are featured on this page, sold for four-figure prices.**
- **Condition of the miniatures can vastly affect price. At the Kingham & Orme sale, a "Harebells" double gourd vase (ca. 1903) with a small flaw sold for £1,600 ($2,100) less than another version of it in good condition.**
- **To collectors, pattern is important, as well as ground color, but as stated the most important consideration is condition.**

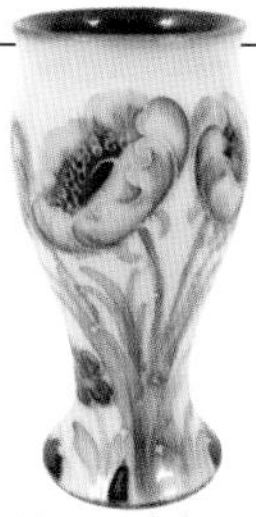

A William Moorcroft for James Macintyre miniature vase, "Yellow Poppy" pattern, printed mark and underglaze green monogram.
ca. 1904 *3in (7.5cm) high*
$5,200-6,500 K&O

A William Moorcroft for James Macintyre miniature vase, "Orange Poppy" pattern, printed mark and underglaze green monogram.
ca. 1903 *3in (7.5cm) high*
$2,100-2,600 K&O

A William Moorcroft for James Macintyre miniature vase, "Blue Poppy" pattern, printed mark and underglaze green monogram.
ca. 1904 *3in (7.5cm) high*
$1,400-2,100 K&O

A William Moorcroft for James Macintyre miniature scent bottle, "Blue Poppy" pattern, with gold screw stopper.

A Macintyre scent bottle is a great rarity although the market has softened recently.
ca. 1904 *1½in (4cm) long*
$4,700-5,200 K&O

A William Moorcroft for James Macintyre miniature vase, "Poppy Garland" pattern, printed mark and underglaze green monogram.
ca. 1904 *2½in (6.5cm) high*
$1,600-2,100 K&O

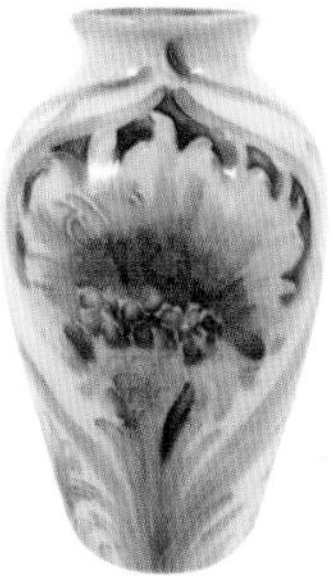

A William Moorcroft for James Macintyre miniature vase, "Cornflower" pattern, printed mark and underglaze green monogram.
ca. 1910 *3¼in (8.5cm) high*
$2,600-3,200 K&O

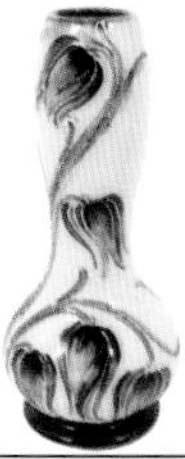

A William Moorcroft for James Macintyre miniature vase, "Blue Harebell" pattern, printed mark and underglaze green monogram.
ca. 1903 *3¼in (8.5cm) high*
$3,900-5,200 K&O

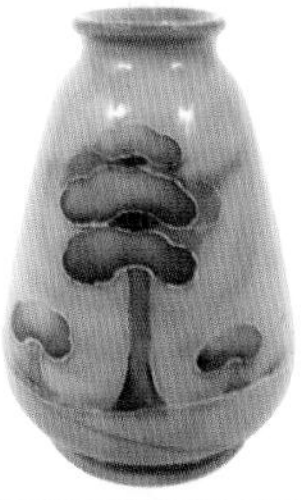

A William Moorcroft for Liberty and Co. miniature vase, "Hazeldene" pattern, printed mark and underglaze green signature.
ca. 1912 *3in (7.5cm) high*
$2,300-2,900 K&O

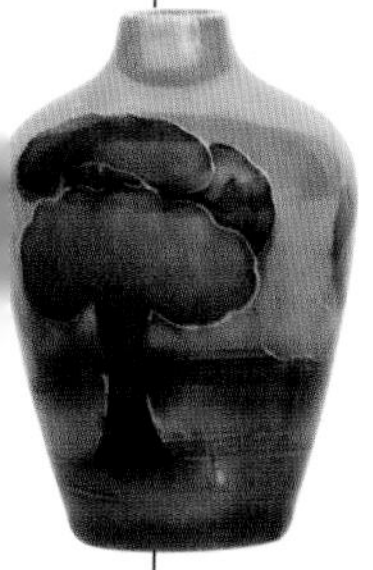

A Moorcroft miniature vase, "Hazeldene" pattern, designed by William Moorcroft, impressed marks, painted green signature.
3¼in (8.5cm) high
$2,600-3,200 WW

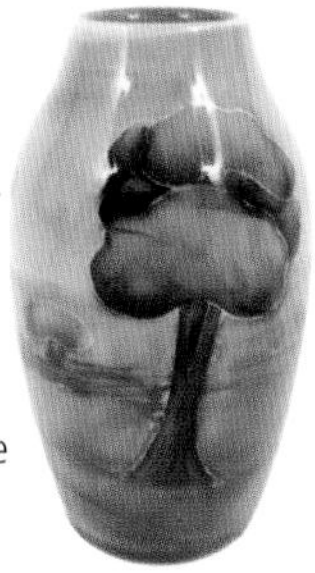

A William Moorcroft miniature vase, "Hazeldene" pattern, impressed Burslem marks and underglaze green signature.
ca. 1914 *3¼in (8.5cm) high*
$1,150-1,450 K&O

A William Moorcroft miniature vase, "Persian" pattern, impressed mark and underglaze green monogram.
ca. 1914 *3in (7.5cm) high*
$2,300-2,900 K&O

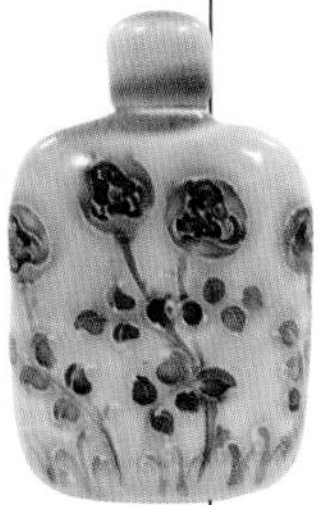

A William Moorcroft for James Macintyre miniature scent bottle, "Tudor Rose" pattern, underlaze green monogram.

This example, although still valuable, has seen a dramatic downturn in price achieved. It sold for close to £5,000 ($6,500) a decade ago.
ca. 1904 *2½in (6.5cm) long*
$2,600-3,200 K&O

QUICK REFERENCE—"CLAREMONT'

- **Instantly recognizable from the toadstool motif, "Claremont" was introduced in October 1903 and named by Liberty. Produced for nearly 40 years, early examples were produced in green and mottled blue backgrounds.**
- **By the 1920s, coloring had become darker and stronger and the drawing had become bolder. During the 1920s and 30s, it was also produced with desirable flambé glazes and in light colors on pale mat grounds.**
- **Despite being so successful, it is considered scarce, particularly when compared to other ranges, such as "Pomegranate." Always desirable, early pieces in unusual and strong forms, from the mid-late 1910s, are in high demand.**

A William Moorcroft vase, "Claremont" pattern.

2¾in (7cm) high

$1,300-1,800 **PSA**

A Moorcroft vase, designed by William Moorcroft, "Claremont" pattern, impressed factory marks.

3in (7.5cm) high

$1,600-2,100 **WW**

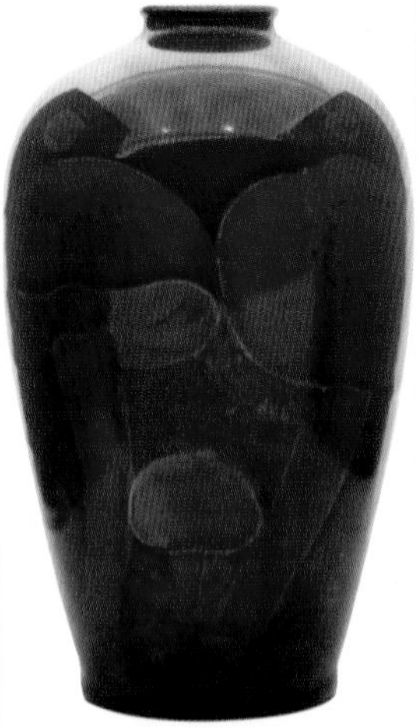

A Moorcroft vase, "Claremont" pattern, with a ruby luster glaze, signed on base.

5½in (14cm) high

$500-650 **FLD**

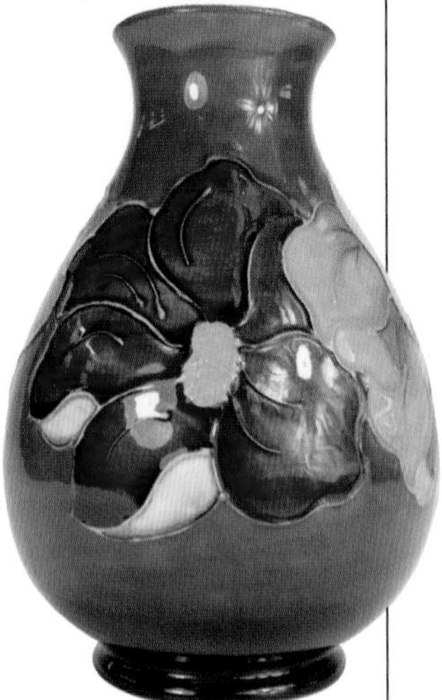

A Walter Moorcroft large vase, "Clematis" pattern.

8½in (21.5cm) high

$180-230 **PSA**

A Moorcroft vase, "Revived Cornflower" pattern, signed "W. Moorcroft XII - 1913" on the base.

9½in (24cm) high

$1,400-1,900 **FLD**

A Moorcroft vase, designed by William Moorcroft, "Dawn" pattern, painted blue signature.

9in (23cm) high

$1,900-2,600 **WW**

A Moorcroft vase, designed by William Moorcroft, "Dawn" pattern, with a light flambé glaze, impressed factory marks.

2¾in (7cm) high

$650-800 **WW**

A Moorcroft plate, "Dawn Landscape" pattern, impressed on base, restored.

6¾in (17cm) diam

$260-320 **FLD**

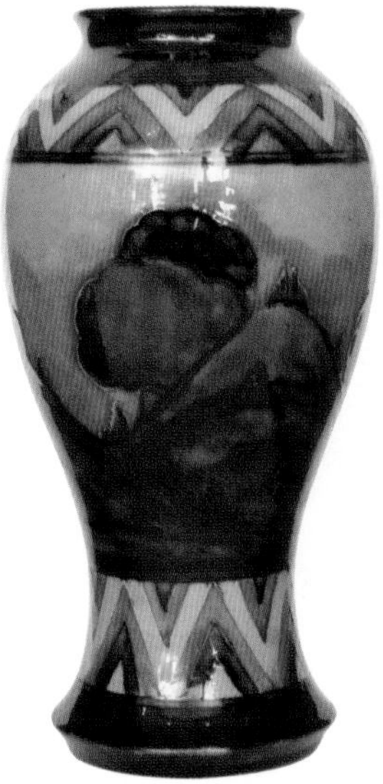

A Moorcroft flambé vase, "Dawn" pattern, impressed mark, initialed, restored.

9in (23cm) high

$1,800-2,300 **FLD**

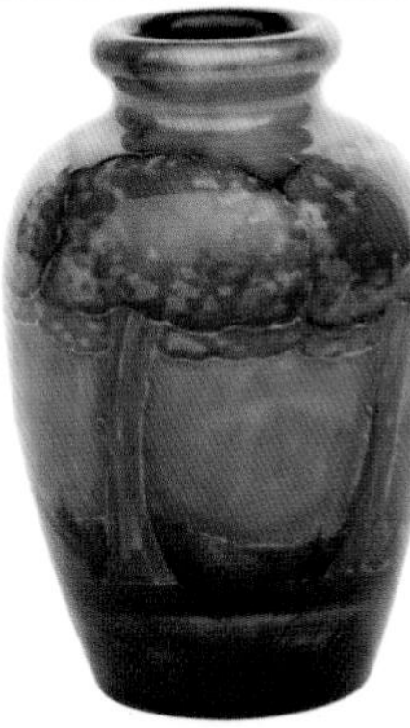

A Moorcroft vase, designed by William Moorcroft, "Eventide" pattern, impressed marks, painted blue signature.

6¼in (16cm) high

$1,600-2,100 **WW**

A 1930s Moorcroft vase, "Fish" pattern, facsimile signature and Royal Warrant.

12¼in (31cm) high

$1,150-1,550 **WAD**

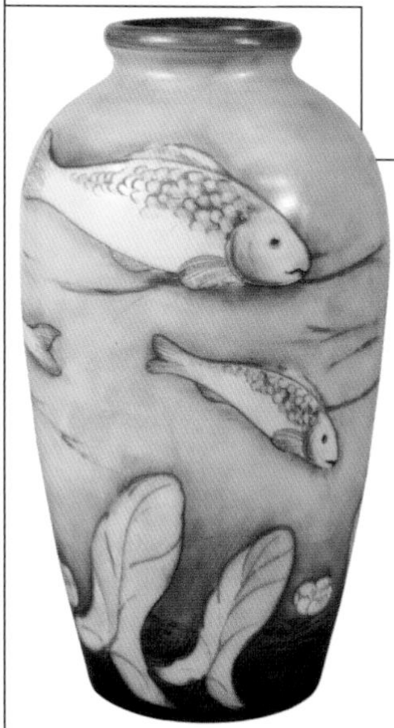

A rare Moorcroft mat glaze vase, "Fish" pattern, painted and impressed marks.

ca. 1930 *12in (30.5cm) high*

$6,500-8,000 **CHEF**

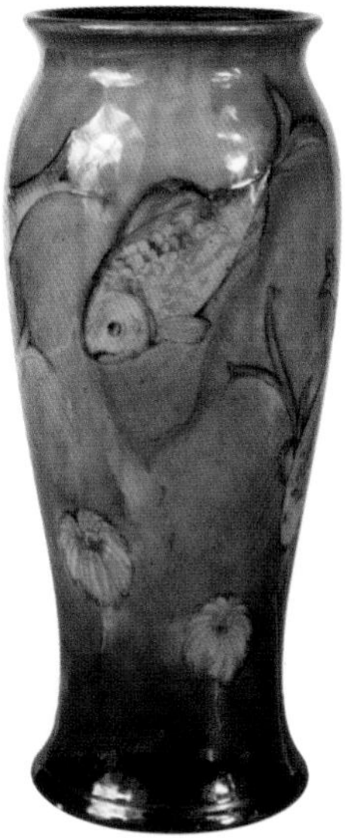

A rare Moorcroft vase, with a flambé glaze, painted and impressed marks, glaze chip on foot rim, some glaze runs.

ca. 1930 *12in (30.5cm) high*

$8,500-9,500 **CHEF**

A William Moorcroft for Liberty & Co. vase, "Hazeldene" pattern, signed "W. Moorcroft," printed marks.

ca. 1907 *4in (10cm) high*

$2,900-3,600 **K&O**

A Moorcroft flambé vase, "Leaf and Berries" pattern, small glaze fault.

3½in (9cm) high

$230-290 **PSA**

A Moorcroft flambé vase, "Leaf and Berries" pattern, with a luster glaze.

4¼in (11cm) high

$300-350 **PSA**

A William Moorcroft flambé vase, "Leaf and Berries" pattern.

14¼in (36cm) high

$700-850 **PSA**

A William Moorcroft tray, "Moonlit Blue" pattern, impressed mark.

13½in (34cm) wide

$1,300-1,800 **FLD**

A William Moorcroft vase, "Moonlit Blue" pattern, signed "WM," impressed marks.

ca. 1925 *7in (18cm) high*

$1,800-2,300 **K&O**

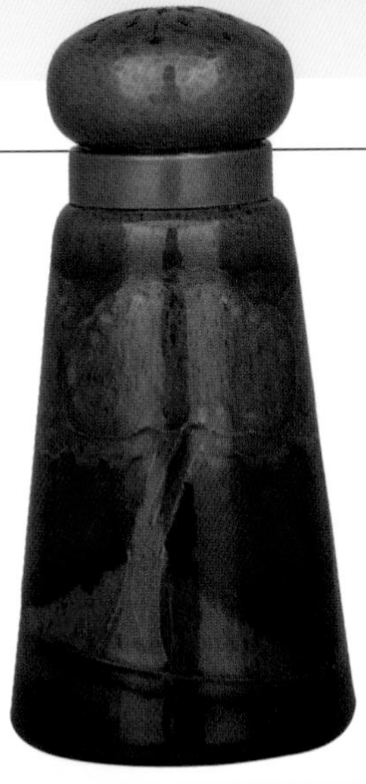

A Moorcroft "Tudric" pewter-mounted sugar caster, "Moonlit Blue" pattern, impressed marks, painted initials, cover stamped "TUDRIC 13."

ca. 1925 *6¾in (17cm) high*

$1,050-1,300 **WAD**

A Walter Moorcroft flambé vase, "Orchid" pattern, small nick on base edge.

6¼in (16cm) high

$400-500 **PSA**

A William Moorcroft small vase, "Pansy" pattern.

2¼in (5.5cm) high

$500-600 **PSA**

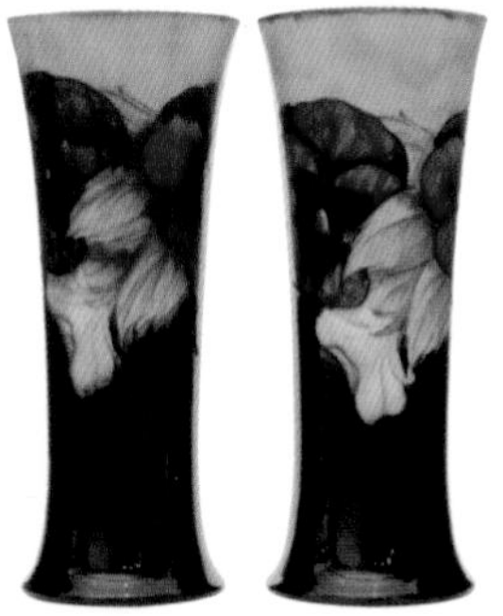

A pair of William Moorcroft vases, "Pansy" pattern, impressed marks, signed in green.

10½in (26.5cm) high

$1,400-1,600 **FLD**

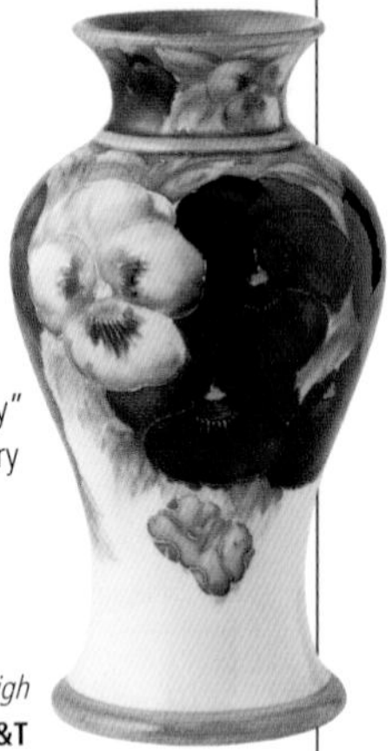

A Moorcroft vase, "Pansy" pattern, impressed factory mark "MOORCROFT BURSLEM 1914," painted signature "W. MOORCROFT," dated.

1914 *8¼in (21cm) high*

$700-850 **L&T**

QUICK REFERENCE—"POMEGRANATE"

- **In the early "Pomegranate" designs, introduced in 1910, the decoration was usually constrained to a particular area, for example, a band circling the piece or just covering the shoulder.**
- **The rest of the piece was usually decorated in a mottled or pale color. In the early pieces, it was in yellows or greens, but it changed to purples and blues by 1916.**
- **"Pomegranate," sold widely by Liberty, was produced until the 1930s and is one of Moorcroft's most popular designs.**

A William Moorcroft Burslem milk pitcher, "Pomegranate" pattern.

5in (12.5cm) high

$500-650 **PSA**

A William Moorcroft Burslem tankard, "Pomegranate" pattern, marked to base "Made for Liberty & Co."

3in (9.5cm) high

$800-900 **PSA**

A William Moorcroft Burslem tankard, "Pomegranate" pattern, marked on base "Made for Liberty & Co."

4½in (11.5cm) high

$400-500 **PSA**

A Moorcroft vase, "Pomegranate" pattern, impressed and painted marks on base, overall crazing.

12½in (32cm) high

$900-1,050 **PW**

A William Moorcroft salt-glazed vase, "Big Poppy" pattern, impressed mark, signed in blue.

7in (19cm) high

$700-850 **FLD**

An early-20thC William Moorcroft for Liberty & Co. vase, "Tudor Rose" pattern, signed in green, scratched out Liberty & Co. mark.

7in (20cm) high

$800-900 **FLD**

A William Moorcroft vase, "Pomegranate" pattern, signed "W. Moorcroft."

ca. 1913 *6¾in (17cm) high*

$1,400-1,800 **K&O**

A William Moorcroft vase, "Poppy" pattern.

8in (21cm) high

$500-650 **PSA**

A Moorcroft pottery vase, "Waving Corn" pattern, impressed marks, painted signature.

12½in (32cm) high

$900-1,050 **WW**

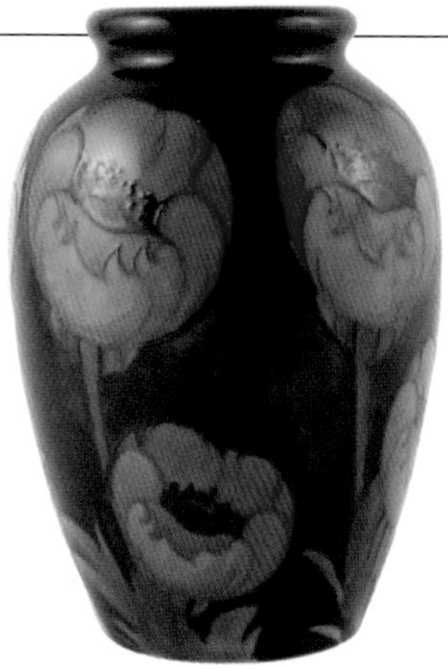

A Moorcroft vase, "Poppy" pattern, impressed mark and painted signature on base.

9in (23cm) high

$1,800-2,300 **PW**

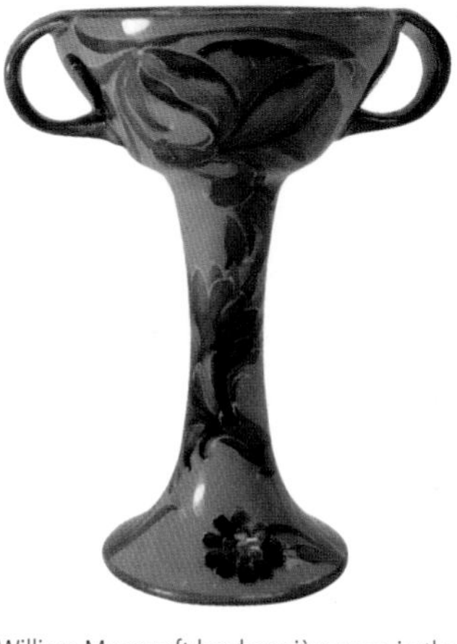

A William Moorcroft bonbonnière vase, in the rare green "Spanish" pattern, ½in (1.5cm) firing crack on top rim.

7in (18cm) high

$500-650 **PSA**

A William Moorcroft vase, "Yacht" pattern, impressed mark and initialled in blue.

1930s *4in (12cm) high*

$260-390 **FLD**

QUICK REFERENCE—SALLY TUFFIN

- **Sally Tuffin (b.1938) studied at Walthamstow Art School and the Royal College of Art.**
- **In the 1960s and 70s, she co-ran a fashion design business, Foale & Tuffin, with her colleague Marion Foale.**
- **In 1986, in an attempt to preserve the security of the Moorcroft pottery, Sally Tuffin, her husband Richard Dennis, and their friends Hugh and Maureen Edwards jointly purchased a 76 percent stake in the company.**
- **From 1986-93, Tuffin worked as art director and designer for Moorcroft. Her numerous pattern designs include "Balloons," "Bramble," "Peacock" and "Sunflower'.**
- **In 1993, she founded Dennis Chinaworks with her husband, Richard Dennis (see pp. 92-93).**

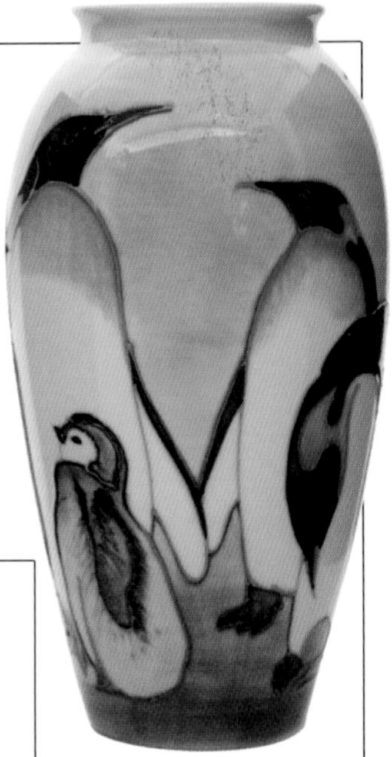

A Moorcroft vase, designed by Sally Tuffin, "Penguin" pattern, painted and impressed marks, numbered "61" of 350.

10in (25.5cm) high

$300-350 FLD

A Moorcroft vase, designed by Sally Tuffin, "Red Tulip" pattern, impressed and painted marks, boxed.

8in (20.5cm) high

$260-320 FLD

A Moorcroft vase, designed by Sally Tuffin, "Polar Bear" pattern, numbered "51" of 250.

This vase is believed to have been made for the Canadian market.

6¾in (17cm) high

$260-320 FLD

A Moorcroft table lamp, designed by Sally Tuffin, "Bramble" pattern, with wooden plinth, marks obscured.

11¾in (30cm) high

$190-260 FLD

A Moorcroft dish, designed by Sally Tuffin, "Finches" pattern, impressed and painted marks.

10¼in (26cm) diam

$130-190 FLD

A Moorcroft year plate, designed by Sally Tuffin, "Carp" pattern, with certificate, numbered "101" from an edition of 250, boxed.

1989 8¾in (22cm) diam

$100-120 FLD

A Moorcroft mantel clock, designed by Sally Tuffin, "Bramble" pattern, impressed mark, the clock movement marked for Wedgwood.

6¼in (16cm) high

$130-190 FLD

A CLOSER LOOK AT A MOORCROFT JARDINIÈRE

Grand statement jardinière and stand, in the "Tree Bark Thief" pattern.
Designed by Rachel Bishop, dated 1998.
An elaborate design painted in colors on a yellow ground.
From a limited edition of 50 pieces, with original paper certificate.

A Moorcroft jardinière and stand, impressed marks, painted signature and number.

1998 *33½in (85cm) high*

$3,200-3,900 **WW**

A Moorcroft vase, designed by Rachel Bishop, "Caravan" pattern, limited edition no.52 of 100, marked "Moorcroft," signed, with a retail label for Watsons of Salisbury, dated.

2003 *16¾in (42.5cm) high*

$1,250-1,450 **LC**

A Moorcroft vase, designed by Rachel Bishop, "Crown of Flowers" pattern, limited edition no.13 of 50, signed, painted, and impressed markings.

ca. 2013 *10¼in (26cm) high*

$230-290 **DUK**

A modern Moorcroft vase, decorated by Rachel Bishop, "England" pattern, impressed and painted marks.

9in (23cm) high

$130-190 **FLD**

A Moorcroft Prestige vase, designed by Rachel Bishop, "Flanders Field" pattern.

Rachel Bishop joined Moorcroft as a designer in 1993 at the age of 24, after receiving a Bachelor of Arts in design (ceramics) at Staffordshire University. Bishop's numbered edition "In Flanders Field" and her "Chocolate Cosmos" and "Phoebe Summer" ranges demonstrate her interest in floral designs.

18½in (47cm) high

$1,100-1,250 **PSA**

A Moorcroft vase, designed by Rachel Bishop, "Kelmscott Dream" pattern, printed marks, numbered "23" of a limited edition of 25.

The "Kelmscott Dream" pattern was designed as a limited edition only available via the Locked Room page on the Moorcroft website.

10in (25.5cm) high

$230-290 **FLD**

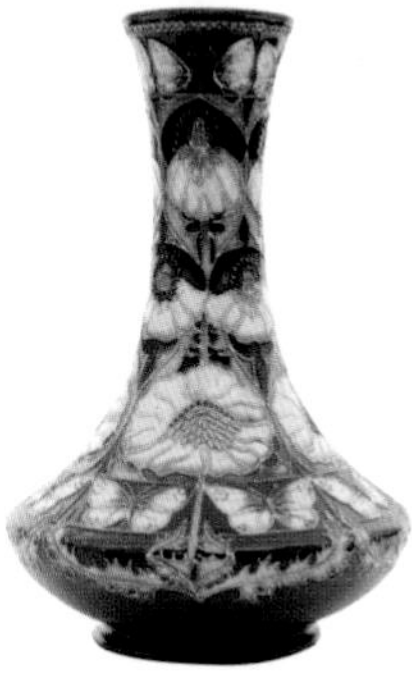

A Moorcroft vase, designed by Rachel Bishop, "Pavion" pattern, impressed and painted marks, numbered "191" from a limited edition of 200, signed.

11¾in (30cm) high

$450-600 **FLD**

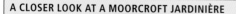

A Moorcroft vase, designed by Rachel Bishop, "Phoenix" pattern, impressed and painted marks.

10½in (26.5cm) high

$230-290 **FLD**

A Moorcroft large vase, known as the "Absentee Pot," designed by Sian Leeper, signed on the base and numbered "4," impressed marks.

The Absentee Pot was awarded to an employee in the production departments, who had not been absent all year, on the day the factory closed for Christmas. If a number of staff had not been absent, all names were put into a hat and one picked out; it was awarded to a different member of staff each year. This has been confirmed by Moorcroft Pottery.

10¾in (27.5cm) high

$800-900 **FLD**

A Moorcroft ginger jar and cover, "Giant Pandas" pattern, in limited edition of 150, signed Sian Leeper, with box, dated.

This is a Collectors Club piece.

2004 *8¼in (21cm) high*

$500-650 **PSA**

A pair of modern Moorcroft vases, designed by Sian Leeper, "Isabella" pattern, signed and dated, limited edition numbered "139" of 250 and "228" of 250.

2004 *10in (25.5cm) high*

$500-650 **LSK**

A Moorcroft vase, designed by Sian Leeper, "Ranthambore" pattern, no.136 of a limited edition of 400, impressed and painted marks on the base, signed, dated.

10.25in (26cm) high

$650-800 **FLD**

A Moorcroft vase, designed by Sian Leeper, "Shamwari" pattern, limited edition no.173 of 300, marked "Moorcroft, "173/300," signed "Sian Leeper," with box, dated.

Having graduated with a Bachelor of Arts in 3D-design from the University of Brighton in 1988, Sian Leeper worked for Moorcroft briefly before going freelance. She returned to Moorcroft as a designer, with her first catalog design, "Pride of Lions," appearing in 2000.

2006 *10½in (26.5cm) high*

$900-1,050 **LC**

A Moorcroft ewer, designed by Sian Leeper, "Shimba Hills" pattern, impressed mark, painted "Trial 8.8.05," signed.

12¼in (31cm) high

$600-700 **FLD**

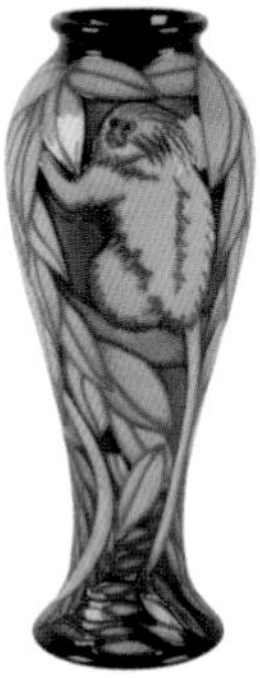

A Moorcroft vase, designed by Sian Leeper, "Tamarin Monkey" pattern, limited edition no.265 of 300, signed, painted, and impressed markings.

10¾in (27.5cm) high

$300-400 **DUK**

A Moorcroft vase, designed by Vicky Lovatt, "Farm Cove" pattern, model no.49, with sailing yachts in a harbor, signed, printed, and impressed markings.

ca. 2015 *4½in (11.5cm) high*

$230-290 **DUK**

A Moorcroft vase, by Nicola Slaney, "Talwin" pattern, Glasgow School-style motifs, printed and impressed marks, with box.

7in (18cm) high

$260-320 **FLD**

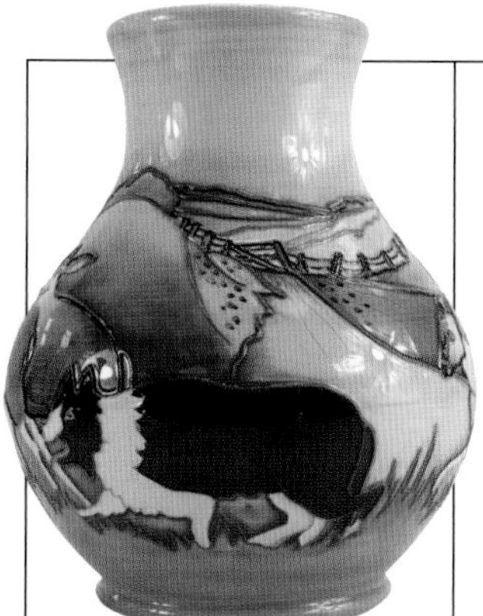

A Moorcroft vase, designed by Kerry Goodwin, "Cheviot Sheep" pattern, limited edition.

This vase is part of the Countryside Collection.

6in (15cm) high

$300-400 **PSA**

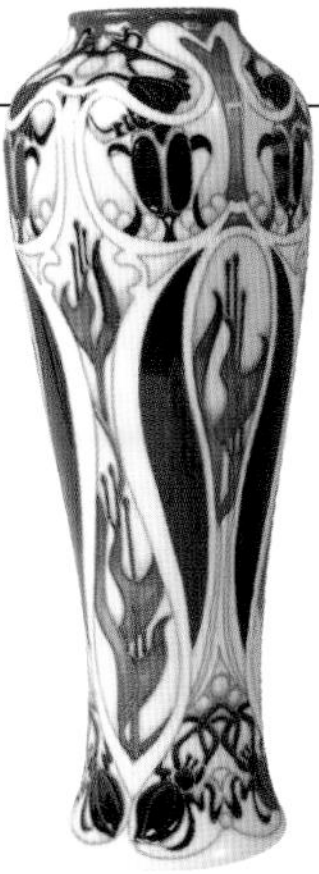

A Moorcroft vase, designed by Kerry Goodwin, "Gardeners" pattern, impressed mark verso, signed, limited edition numbered "23" of 200, dated.

2003 *14½in (37cm) high*

$300-400 **LSK**

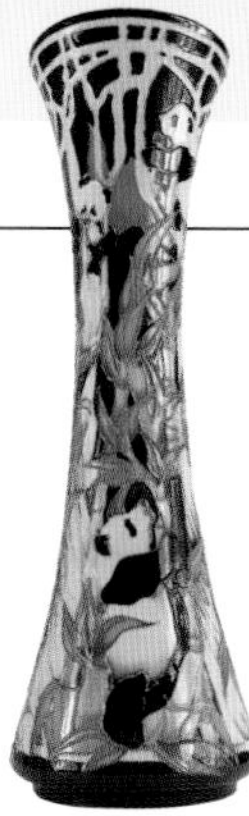

A Moorcroft vase, designed by Kerry Goodwin, "Sichaun Giant Pandas" pattern, trial 16/11/16.

Having joined Moorcroft as a painter in 2000, Kerry Goodwin soon became a designer. Goodwin has become known for her humorous or quirky designs, for example "Potteries in Recession," which depicts a Lowry-like scene of the 2008 recession.

2016 *15¾in (40cm) high*

$500-650 **PSA**

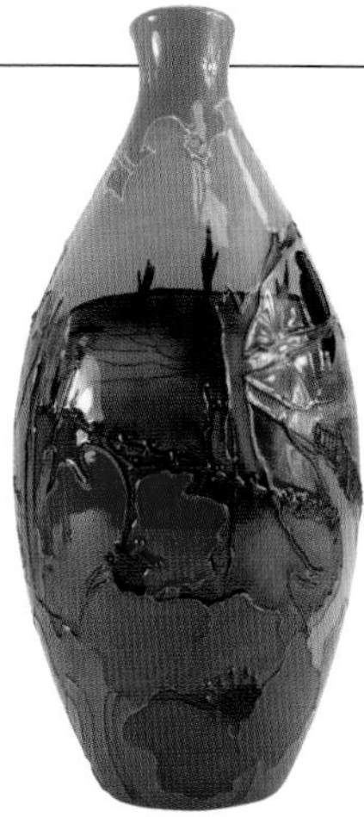

A Moorcroft vase, designed by Kerry Goodwin, "Lest We Forget" pattern, signed.

9½in (24cm) high

$300-400 **PSA**

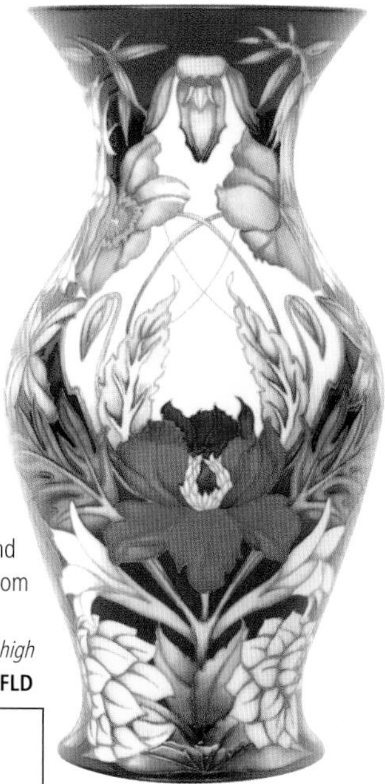

A Moorcroft vase, designed by Philip Gibson, "Hidcote" pattern, impressed and painted marks, numbered "7" from a limited edition of 75, signed.

18½in (47cm) high

$1,050-1,150 **FLD**

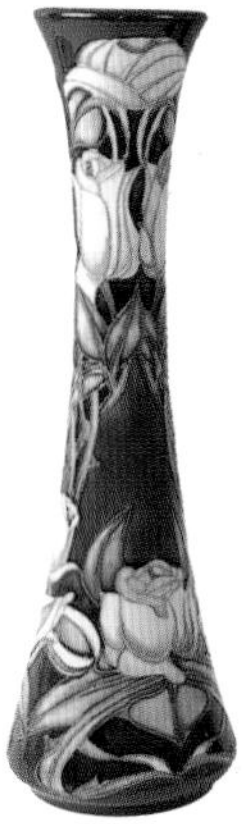

A Moorcroft vase, designed by Philip Gibson, "Moonlight" pattern, impressed mark verso, signed, limited edition numbered "116" of 250, dated, boxed with outer sleeve.

Philip Gibson studied at the Newcastle School of Art and The North Staffordshire Polytechnic, earning a Masters degree in ceramic design. Before going freelance, he worked for Moorcroft and Wedgwood.

2003 *12¼in (31cm) high*

$230-290 **LSK**

A Moorcroft cookie barrel and cover, designed by Philip Gibson, "Puriri Tree" pattern, impressed mark verso and dated.

From the New Zealand Collection.

2004 *6in (15cm) high*

$300-400 **LSK**

A Moorcroft table lamp base, designed by Philip Gibson, "Trout" pattern, with a wooden plinth, marks obscured, retains original Moorcroft shade.

8¾in (22cm) high

$400-500 **FLD**

A Moorcroft vase, designed by Emma Bossons, "Bellahouston" pattern.

8¼in (21cm) high

$130-190 **PSA**

A Moorcroft vase, designed by Emma Bossons, "Sweet Betsy" pattern, limited edition no.29 of 50, signed E Bossons, impressed and painted marks.

16¾in (42.5cm) high

$700-850 **FLD**

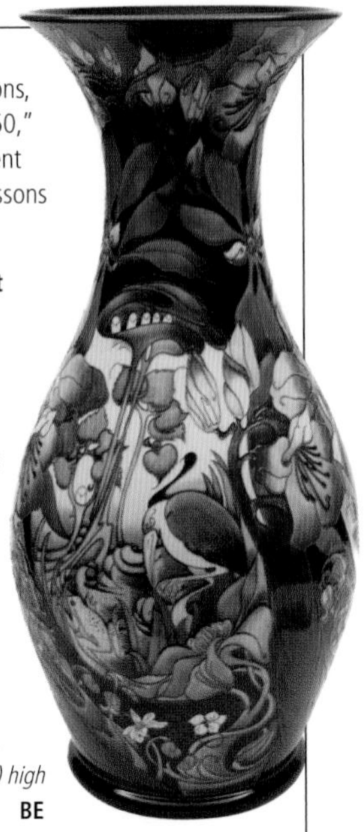

A Moorcroft vase, designed by Emma Bossons, "Hidden Dreams" pattern, numbered "29/50," impressed "Moorcroft Made in Stoke on Trent England," painted signatures for Emma Bossons and Rachel Bishop, dated.

Emma Bossons (b.1976) joined Moorcroft at the age of 20 as a painter before becoming a designer. Her "Hepatica" range of 2000 and her 2001 "Queen's Choice" proved to be successful. At the age of 24, Bossons became the youngest female member of the Fellowship of the Royal Society of Arts. She has looked widely for inspiration for her designs, traveling to Australia, North America, Fiji, New Zealand, and Kiribati. The Queen allowed the use of the Royal Cypher on the base of each piece in Bossons' 2002 Golden Jubilee collection.

2005 *26¾in (68cm) high*

$2,200-2,600 **BE**

A Moorcroft vase, designed by Paul Hilditch, "Charles Dickens" pattern, limited edition no.43 of 75, marked "Moorcroft," signed "Paul Hilditch," with box. 2012.

Paul Hilditch joined Moorcroft as a painter in 1999. His intricate designs convey pictorial scenes, requiring him to research historical periods or figures. Many of Hilditch's designs are recognizable by a fine raised tube lining on the surface.

11¼in (28.5cm) high

$950-1,100 **LC**

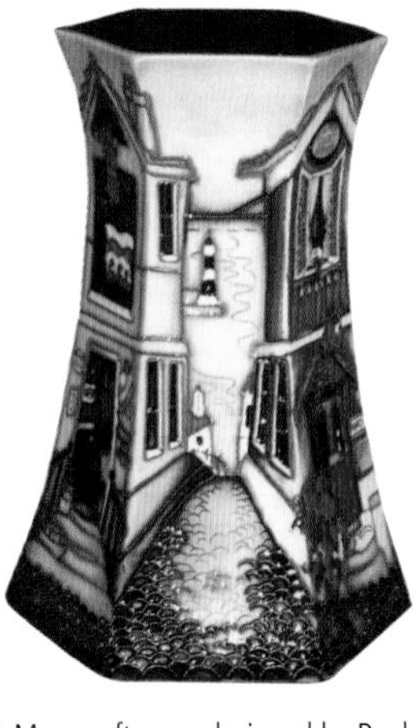

A Moorcroft vase, designed by Paul Hilditch, "Cornish Cove" pattern, limited edition no.81 of 200, marked "Moorcroft," signed "Paul Hilditch," with box.

2008 *7½in (19cm) high*

$800-900 **LC**

A Moorcroft vase, designed by Paul Hilditch, "High Society" pattern, signed, painted, and impressed marks, limited edition no.69 of 100.

ca. 2012 *12¼in (31cm) high*

$300-400 **DUK**

A Moorcroft vase, designed by Paul Hilditch, "Merchants of Venice" pattern, trial 26/7/16.

2016 *12¼in (31cm) high*

$600-700 **PSA**

A Moorcroft pitcher, designed by Paul Hilditch, "Snowdrift" pattern, printed and painted marks, numbered "37" from a limited edition of 50, signed.

10¾in (27.5cm) high

$350-400 **FLD**

A Moorcroft plate, designed by Anji Davenport, "Woodside Farm" pattern, painted marks.

10in (25.5cm) diam

$300-400 **FLD**

A Moorcroft vase, "Blue Nautical" pattern, signed "J. Moorcroft," dated.

1997 *9½in (24cm) high*

$180-230 **PSA**

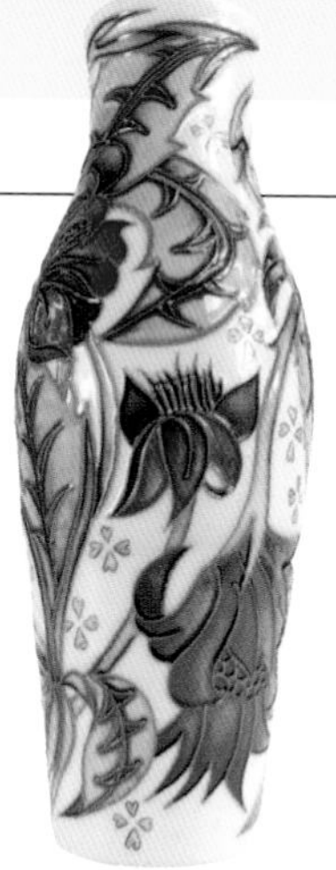

A Moorcroft vase, "Bronwyns Bouquet" pattern, dated.

This is a Collectors Club piece.

2000 *10in (25.5cm) high*

$230-290 **PSA**

QUICK REFERENCE—LISE B. MOORCROFT

- **Lise B. Moorcroft is the fourth generation of the Moorcroft dynasty; great-granddaughter of Thomas Moorcroft, granddaughter of factory founder William Moorcroft, and daughter of Walter Moorcroft OBE. The family situated their famous factory in Burslem, Stoke-on-Trent, England, in August 1913 and were involved in its operations until 1987.**
- **Lise studied at London's Central School of Art and Design, graduating with honors before setting up an independent studio in Stoke, continuing the traditions favored by her illustrious forebears yet adding her individual flair.**
- **Lise's designs, predominantly derived from nature and local environs, are sketched freestyle in pencil onto the clay, making every piece a unique, custom-made piece of art. It is then tube lined onto the surface with colored slip followed by several firings, possibly up to ten. These can include, first, bisque, then numerous applications of underglaze, hand-painted glazes, and lusters. Using this method enables a buildup of colors over many firings, so Lise can achieve the deep color and texture intensity on the surface. Some pieces are then enhanced further by precious metal foils gilding the surface, which is then sealed to protect it.**

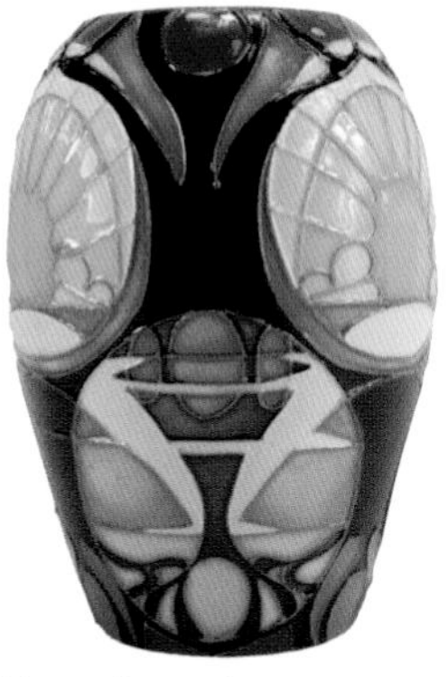

A Moorcroft vase, "Rising Sun" pattern, trial 11/10/16.

2016 *5¼in (13.5cm) high*

$180-230 **PSA**

A Moorcroft vase, "Winter's Feed" pattern.

8¾in (22cm) high

$600-700 **PSA**

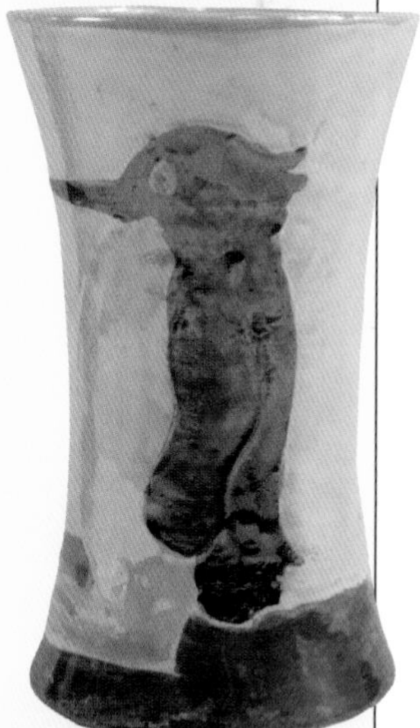

A Lise B. Moorcroft Studio Pottery vase, decorated with penguins.

4¼in (11cm) high

$80-100 **PSA**

A Lise B. Moorcroft Studio Pottery vase, decorated with toadstools.

4¾in (12cm) high

$100-130 **PSA**

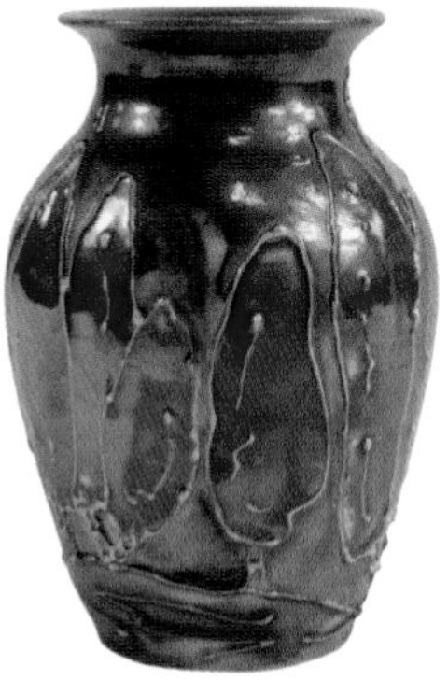

A Lise B. Moorcroft Studio Pottery vase, "Tall Trees" pattern.

4¼in (11cm) high

$120-160 **PSA**

A Lise B. Moorcroft Studio Pottery vase, decorated with pansies.

4¼in (11cm) high

$100-130 **PSA**

QUICK REFERENCE—BERNARD MOORE

- **Known for his use of colored glazes, Bernard Moore was a potter born in 1850 in Longton, UK.**
- **Moore worked at his father's pottery company, Samuel Moore & Son, taking it over upon his father's death in 1867. The firm changed its name to Moore Brothers, exhibiting in the USA in the early 1880s and 1890s.**
- **Moore experimented with flambé and sang-de-boeuf glazes on stoneware in the 1890s.**
- **In 1905, Moore Brothers closed, and Moore opened his own studio in Stoke-on-Trent. He died in 1935.**

A Bernard Moore sang-de-boeuf bottle vase, of chimney form, part glazed in red with mat turquoise rim and shoulder, signed.

5¼in (13.5cm) high

$260-320 **HAN**

A miniature Bernard Moore aventurine glazed bottle vase, signed.

2½in (6.5cm) high

$450-500 **HAN**

A pair of Bernard Moore high-fired vases, speckled sang-de-boeuf and purple flambé glaze, signed.

3½in (9cm) high

$260-390 **HAN**

A Bernard Moore mottled flambé vase.

8in (20.5cm) high

$80-100 **PSA**

A Bernard Moore high-fired flambé vase, decorated with panels of birds, bats, flowers, and trees, glaze fault on foot rim.

4¼in (11cm) high

$230-290 **PSA**

An early-20thC Bernard Moore flambé vase, with an upper band of painted flowers and foliage with patterned banding below, the neck interior with a blood red glaze, signed.

10¾in (27.5cm) high

$800-900 **FLD**

A Bernard Moore flambé vase, decorated with Art Nouveau-style trees, chip on base.

3¾in (9.5cm) high

$90-120 **PSA**

A Bernard Moore small red flambé bust, with original glass eyes.

2¼in (5.5cm) high

$210-260 **PSA**

QUICK REFERENCE—GEORGE OHR

- **From 1880 to ca. 1907, the Biloxi Pottery in Mississippi was worked solely by owner George Ohr (1857-1918). The eccentric Ohr became known as "the mad potter of Biloxi." Ohr's work is characterized by thin walls, a manipulated and pinched asymmetrical form with ridges, and glazing usually in brown, green, and red. During his lifetime, Ohr sold very little, despite producing a vast number of pieces. On his death, his work was left to his family and later bought by antiques dealer James Carpenter, who introduced Ohr's work into the ceramics market.**

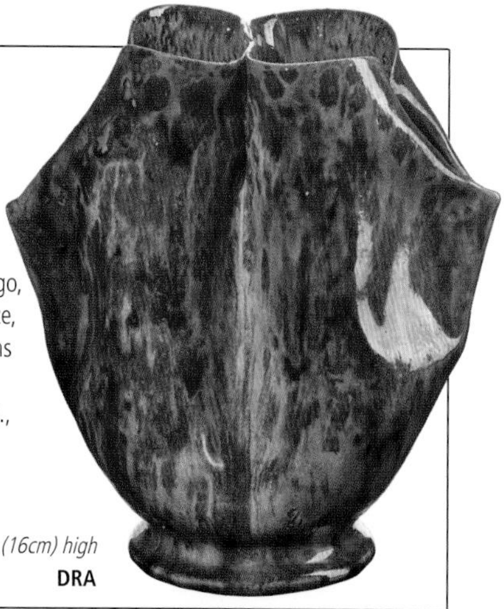

A George Ohr large double-sided vessel, indigo, raspberry, and green glaze, body incised "Marie Evans and Walters" (illegible), base stamped "G.E. OHR., Biloxi, Miss.," partly overglazed mark incised "Sept 189" (illegible).
1897-99 *6¼in (16cm) high*
$52,000-58,000 DRA

A George Ohr vase, multicolor sponged-on glaze, stamped "G.E. OHR. Biloxi, Miss."
1897-1900 *5in (12.5cm) high*
$13,000-16,000 DRA

A George Ohr vase, raspberry and turquoise mottled glaze, stamped "G.E. OHR Biloxi, Miss."
1897-1900 *4½in (11.5cm) wide*
$6,000-7,000 DRA

A George Ohr vase, brown and black speckled and sponged-on glaze, stamped "G.E. OHR Biloxi, Miss."
1897-1900 *5¼in (13.5cm) high*
$6,500-8,000 DRA

A George Ohr vase, with blister glaze, stamped "G.E. OHR, Biloxi, Miss.," some scratches, kiln flaw on shoulder.
1897-1900 *6in (15cm) high*
$3,200-3,900 DRA

A George Ohr vase, with sponged-on glaze, incised "OHR BILOXI," some chips.
1896-1910 *6in (15cm) high*
$1,300-1,900 DRA

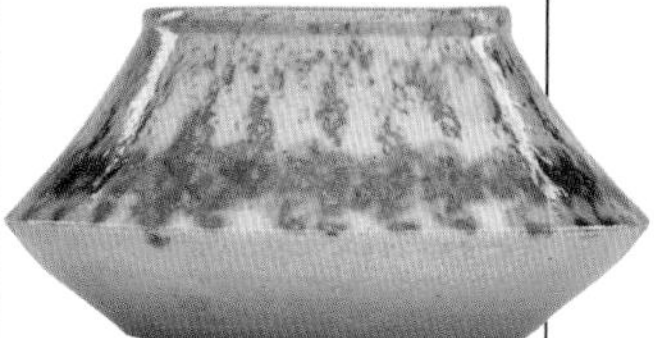

A George Ohr vessel, with sponged-on glaze, stamped "GEO. E. OHR BILOXI MISS.," restoration on rim.
ca. 1895-96 *5in (12.5cm) wide*
$900-1,050 DRA

A George Ohr tall vase, mahogany, gunmetal, and aventurine glaze, stamped "G.E. OHR., Biloxi, Miss."
1897-1900 *6in (15cm) high*
$5,200-6,500 DRA

A George Ohr vessel, mahogany and gunmetal glaze, stamped "G.E. OHR. Biloxi, Miss."
1897-1900 *4in (10cm) high*
$8,500-9,500 DRA

A George Ohr vase, green and gunmetal glaze, script signature, museum deaccession number "L.S.OC.HK.," two grinding chips.

1898-1910 *6½in (16.5cm) high*

$10,500-12,000 **DRA**

A George Ohr bicolor vase, stamped "G.E. OHR Biloxi, Miss.," a few minor touch-ups to ruffles.

1897-1900 *8in (20.5cm) high*

$8,500-9,500 **DRA**

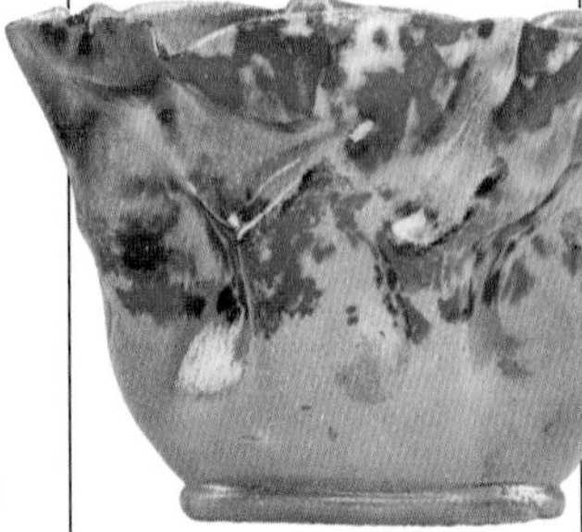

A George Ohr vase, gunmetal and indigo sponged-on glaze, stamped "GEO. E. OHR BILOXI, MISS."

1895-96 *3¾in (9.5cm) high*

$3,900-4,500 **DRA**

A George Ohr vessel, green, gunmetal, and raspberry glaze, stamped "G.E. OHR BILOXI."

1895-96 *4½in (11.5cm) wide*

$12,000-13,000 **DRA**

A George Ohr pinched vase, with two faces, aventurine glaze, stamped "G.E. OHR, Biloxi, Miss.," a few light scratches.

1897-1900 *4in (10cm) wide*

$8,500-9,500 **DRA**

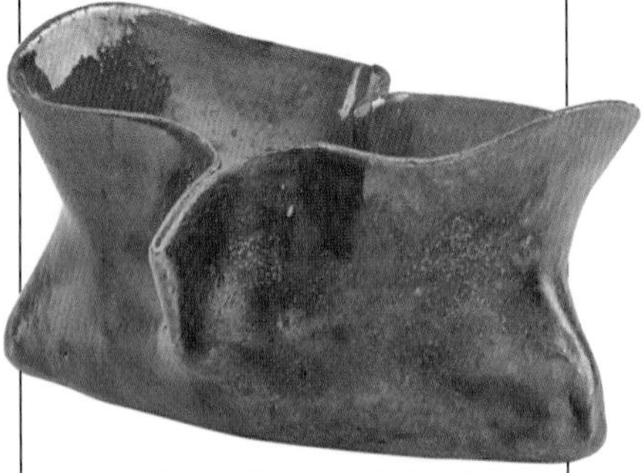

A George Ohr vessel, green and ocher glaze, stamped "G.E. OHR BILOXI."

1895-96 *4in (10cm) wide*

$3,900-4,500 **DRA**

A George Ohr two-sided teapot, deep indigo, speckled green, and gunmetal glaze, stamped "G.E. OHR, Biloxi, Miss."

1897-1900 *6in (15cm) high*

$5,200-5,800 **DRA**

A George Ohr top hat novelty vase, stamped "G.E. OHR Biloxi, Miss."

1897-1900 *3¼in (8.5cm) high*

$1,900-2,600 **DRA**

A George Ohr Cadogan teapot, "Branch" pattern, script signature, dated.

1900 *5in (12.5cm) high*

$4,500-5,200 **DRA**

A pottery bust of King Charles II, by Richard Parkinson (1927-85) and Susan Parkinson (1925-2012), impressed maker's mark.

Richard and Susan Parkinson set up Richard Parkinson Pottery in an oast house near Ashford Kent, in 1951. The work was split, with Richard doing the slip casting, firing, and designing of the functional tableware, while Susan (who trained at the Royal College of Art) designed and decorated the more ornamental pieces, including figurines. The company closed in 1963.

ca. 1950s *13¼in (33.5cm) high*

$1,250-1,450 **L&T**

A pottery figurine of three musicians, by Richard and Susan Parkinson, impressed maker's marks.

1950s *9in (23cm) high*

$500-650 **L&T**

A pottery figurine, "Adam and Eve," by Richard and Susan Parkinson, indistinct molded marks.

ca. 1950s *7½in (19cm) high*

$800-900 **L&T**

A Richard Parkinson Pottery model of a policeman, designed by Susan Parkinson, model no.85, impressed factory marks.

ca. 1958 *12in (32cm) high*

$600-700 **WW**

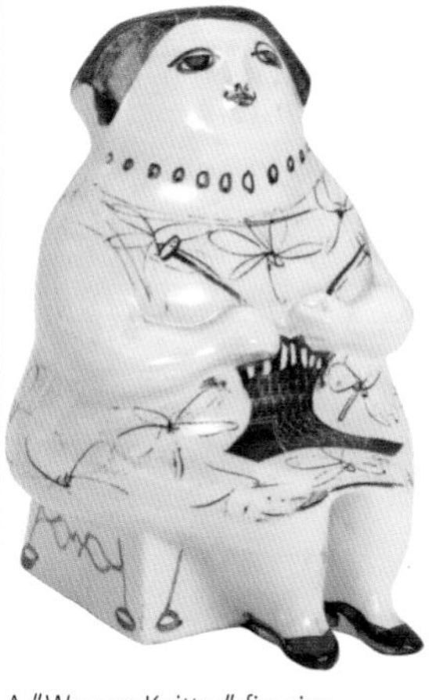

A "Woman Knitter" figurine, model no.110, by Susan Parkinson, impressed marks to feet.

These slightly larger figurines from the early 1960s were "made for a more discerning market" according to Carol Cashmore's 2004 book.

ca. 1960s *7½in (19cm) high*

$500-650 **ROS**

A Richard Parkinson Pottery bust of a lawyer, painted in monochrome, impressed and printed marks.

13in (33cm) high

$650-800 **CHEF**

A Richard Parkinson Pottery figurine, "Golfer," model no.70, designed by Susan Parkinson, impressed marks.

15½in (39cm) high

$500-650 **WW**

QUICK REFERENCE—POOLE POTTERY

- **Poole Pottery was established in 1873 as Carter & Co., trading as Poole Pottery from 1963.**
- **Based in Poole, Dorset, the company combined traditional hand-throwing techniques with hand-painted colorful modern designs.**
- **Key designers include John Adams, Anita Harris, Truda Adams (formerly Truda Carter), Ruth Pavely, and Alan White. Harris also worked at Cobridge Stoneware Pottery, and created designs for Liberty, Harrods and Tiffany.**
- **The company produced many successful ranges, such as "Handcraft" in the 1920s, Truda Carter's "Twintone" in the 1940s, "Contemporary" in the 1950s, and "Delphis" in the 1960s. The "Contemporary" range, designed by Alfred Burgess Read, used geometric or curving linear patterns. The brightly colored "Delphis" range was created by Robert Jefferson, Guy Sydenham, and Tony Morris. The second half of the 20thC also saw the "Atlantis" and "Aegean" ranges.**
- **Factory production was moved away from the Poole quayside in 1999 to the Sopers Lane site in Poole, which closed in 2006. The company was acquired by Denby Holdings in 2011.**

A Poole Pottery "Bush Velt" vase, designed by John Adams, painted by Anne Hatchard, "LZ" pattern, with a lion attacking an antelope, impressed and painted marks.

24½in (62cm) high

$13,000-18,000 DUK

A Poole Pottery "Bush Velt" vase, designed by John Adams, painted by Ruth Pavely, "EZ" pattern, shape no.916, painted and impressed marks.

14½in (37cm) high

$1,300-1,900 DUK

An Art Deco Poole Pottery vase, designed by Truda Carter, "GPA" pattern, impressed and painted marks.

6in (15cm) high

$100-130 WW

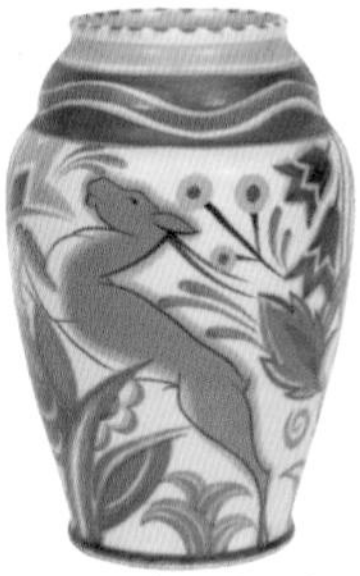

A Poole Pottery "Leaping Gazelle" vase, designed by Truda Carter, painted by Gwendoline Selby, "TZ" pattern, impressed marks, painted artist cipher and mark.

8½in (21.5cm) high

$450-500 WW

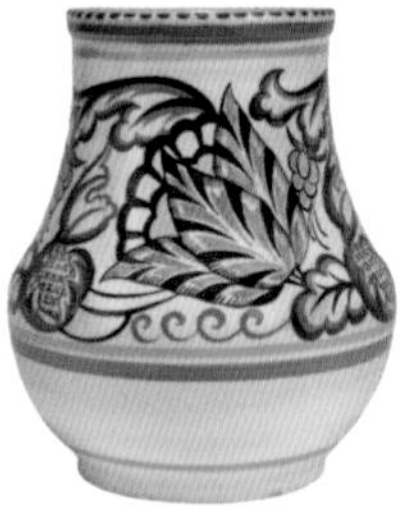

A Poole Pottery glazed red earthenware vase, possibly by Truda Carter, with unusual black and mauve stylized tulips, impressed maker's mark, incised "700 X," painted "/YR."

ca. 1921-34 9¼in (23.5cm) high

$450-500 ROS

A Poole Pottery "Persian Deer" vase, designed by Truda Adams, with printed factory marks, firing flaw on base.

13in (33cm) high

$300-350 WW

A Poole Pottery vase, designed by Truda Adams, painted by Anne Hatchard, "PU" pattern, shape no.337, impressed and painted marks.

9¾in (24.5cm) high

$260-320 DUK

A Poole Pottery "Persian Deer" charger, designed by Truda Adams, painted by Anne Hatchard, "VU" pattern, shape no.528, decorated with a deer, painted and impressed marks.

15in (38cm) diam

$500-650 DUK

A Poole Pottery "Galleon" bookend, designed by Harold Stabler, modeled by Harry Brown, impressed marks.

10½in (26.5cm) high

$450-500 DUK

A Poole Pottery charger, designed by Arthur Bradbury, painted by Ruth Pavely, inscribed with "The Ship of Harry Paye Poole 1400," painted and impressed marks.

ca. 1938 *15in (38cm) diam*

$500-650 **DUK**

A Poole Pottery vase, painted by Anne Hatchard, "ZW" pattern, shape no.684, impressed and painted marks.

14½in (37cm) high

$260-390 **DUK**

A Poole Pottery vase, painted by Margaret Holder, "BR" pattern, shape no.429, impressed and painted marks.

10in (25.5cm) high

$230-290 **DUK**

A Poole Pottery vase, painted by Ruth Pavely, "ER" pattern, impressed and painted marks.

14¼in (36cm) high

$260-320 **DUK**

A Poole Pottery bowl, painted by Pat Summers, "UI" pattern, shape no.686, impressed and painted marks.

9in (23cm) diam

$190-260 **DUK**

A Poole Pottery four-panel tile, designed by E.E. Stickland, "Farmyard" series, made for Dewhurst butchers, impressed marks with painted "FY" mark.

12in (30.5cm) square panel

$300-400 **WW**

A Poole Pottery "Freeform" peanut vase, painted by Gwen Haskins, "WL" pattern, shape no.701, impressed, painted, and printed marks.

12½in (32cm) high

$160-190 **DUK**

A Poole Pottery "Trewellard red" charger, by Sir Terry Frost RA, printed marks, facsimile signature on verso.

"Trewellard Red" was inspired by the colors of the sunset as seen from Trewellard on the north coast of Cornwall near Land's End. Terry decided to paint this special charger to celebrate his 80th birthday. Part of a limited edition of 100, this actual charger was painted by Sir Terry himself at the Poole Pottery Studio.

16in (40.5cm) diam

$450-500 **DUK**

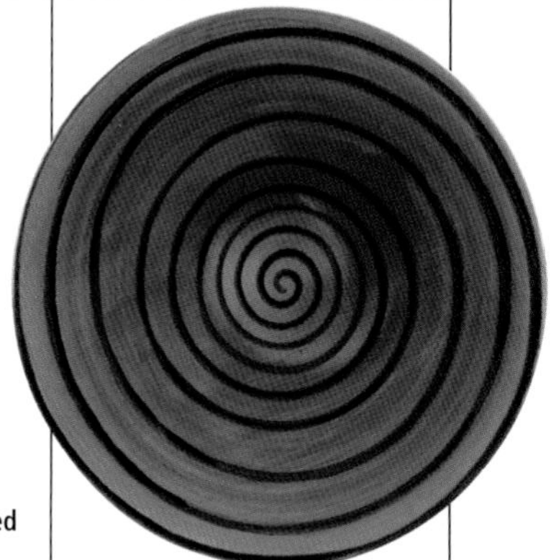

A Poole Pottery "Arizona Blue" charger, by Sir Terry Frost RA, limited edition of 100, painter's marks only.

16in (40.5cm) diam

$300-400 **DUK**

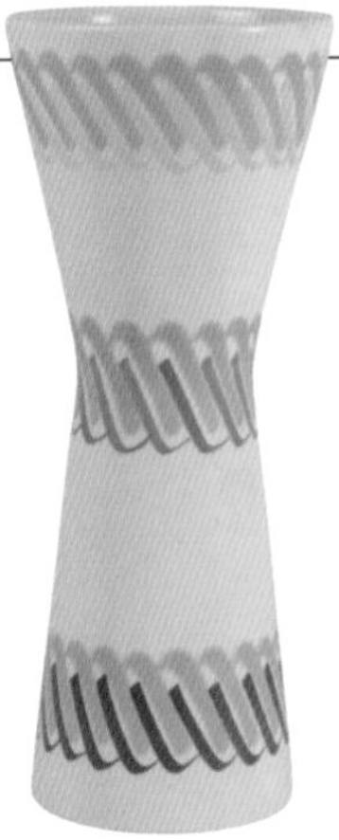

A Poole Pottery "Freeform" Yo Yo vase, designed by Alfred Read, painted by Gwen Haskins, "HYT" pattern, shape no.719, impressed and painted marks.

12½in (32cm) high

$300-400 **DUK**

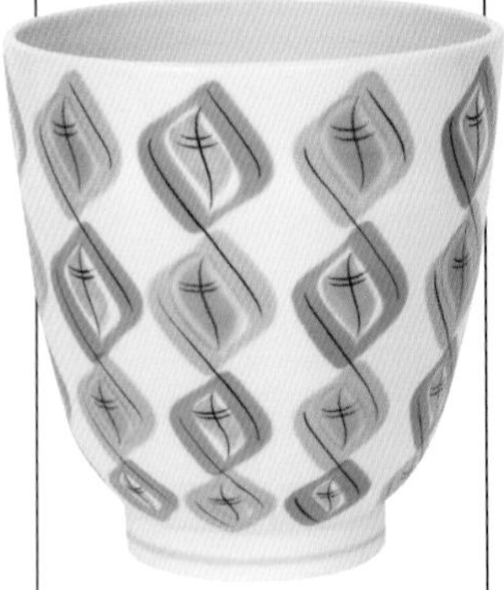

A Poole Pottery "Contemporary" jardinière, designed by Alfred Read and Guy Sydenham, "HOL" pattern, printed and painted marks.

7¼in (18.5cm) high

$260-390 **WW**

A Poole Pottery "Freeform" footed vase, "FST" pattern, shape no.772, impressed and painted marks.

ca. 1950 *9½in (24cm) high*

$120-160 **FLD**

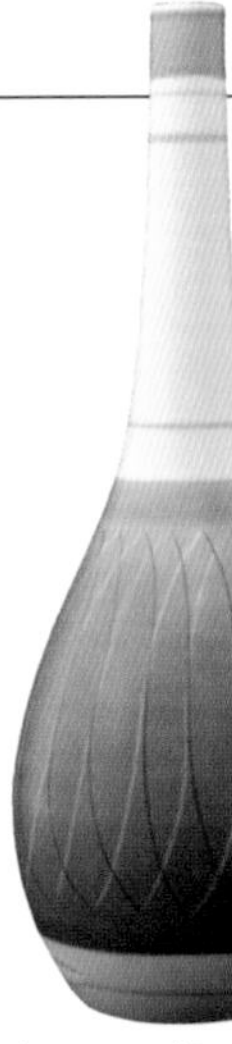

A Poole Pottery "Freeform Skittle" vase, "PRP" pattern, shape no.698, impressed and painted marks.

15¾in (40cm) high

$130-190 **FLD**

A Poole Pottery "Atlantis" vase, designed and thrown by Guy Sydenham, impressed marks.

9½in (24cm) high

$190-260 **DUK**

A Poole Pottery studio charger, with printed "Poole Studio England" mark.

13½in (34.5cm) diam

$170-230 **WW**

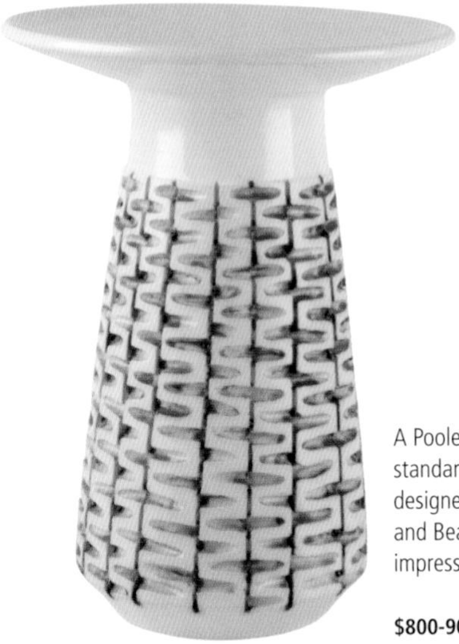

A Poole Pottery exhibition standard "Atlantis" vase, designed by Guy Sydenham and Beatrice Bolton, impressed marks.

12in (30.5cm) high

$800-900 **DUK**

A Poole Pottery studio charger, with printed "Poole Studio England" mark.

13½in (34.5cm) diam

$190-260 **WW**

A later-20thC Poole Pottery studio plaque, by Tony Morris, printed and painted marks on the reverse.

16¼in (41.5cm) diam

$300-450 **FLD**

A Rookwood vase, by Lenore Asbury, iris glaze, with Queen Anne's lace, flame mark "/VIII/1126C/LA," fine crazing, two firing lines do not go through.

1908 *8½in (21.5cm) high*

$1,050-1,150 **DRA**

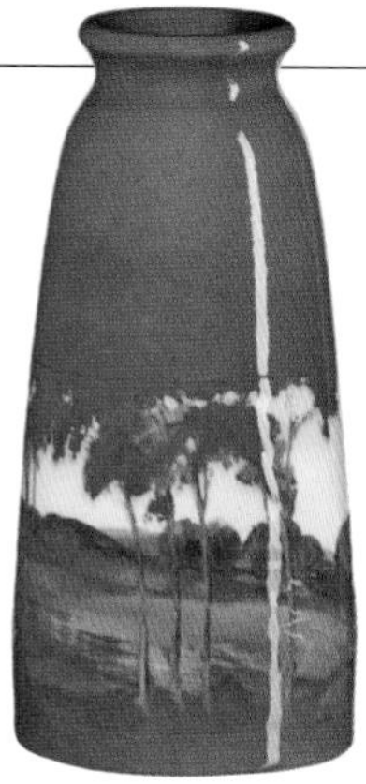

A Rookwood banded scenic vase, by Ed Diers (1871-1947), iris glaze, flame mark "/XI/1658F/ED/W," fine overall crazing.

1911 *6½in (16.5cm) high*

$1,700-2,100 **DRA**

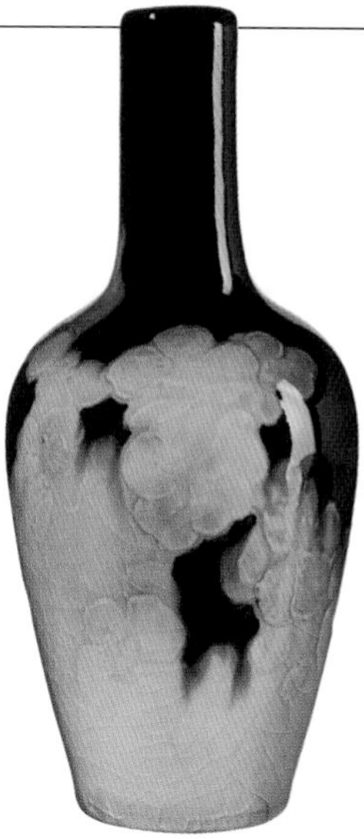

A rare Rookwood "Black Iris" cabinet vase, by Fred Rothenbusch (1876-1937), flame mark "/765L/FR," crazing over flowers.

Rookwood Pottery was established by Maria Longworth Nichols in Cincinnati, Ohio, in 1880. Nichols saw the business as an artistic venture, not a commercial one. Japanese artist Kataro Shirayamadani joined Rookwood in 1887. The factory patented their vellum glaze in 1904. In the late-20thC, Rookwood changed ownership multiple times. In 2009, production moved to the current facility on Race Street, Cincinnati.

1900 *5¼in (13.5) high*

$1,300-1,600 **DRA**

A Rookwood vase with tulips, by Fred Rothenbusch, iris glaze, flame mark "/II/935C/FR."

1902 *8¾in (22cm) high*

$950-1,100 **DRA**

A Rookwood vase, by Sara Sax (1870-1949), iris glaze, with crocuses, flame mark "/VI/904CC/SX."

1906 *9¾in (24.5cm) high*

$1,600-2,100 **DRA**

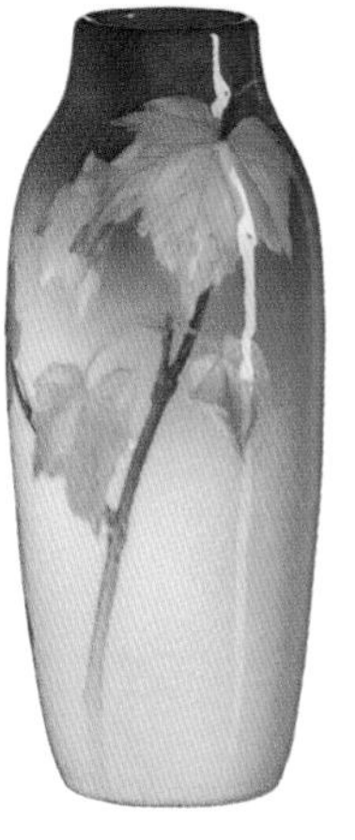

A Rookwood vase, by Josephine Zettel (1874-1954), iris glaze, flame mark "/II/932D/JZ/W," fine overall crazing.

8¾in (22cm) high

$850-950 **DRA**

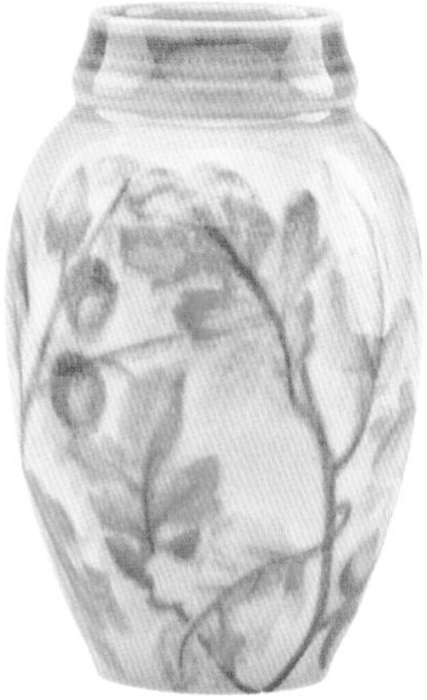

A Rookwood jewel porcelain baluster vase, by Margaret McDonald, shape no.6211, flame mark, artist cipher, "XXXVI."

1936 *10½in (26.5cm) high*

$650-800 **DRA**

A Rookwood mat vase, by Anna Marie Valentien (1862-1947) with daffodils, flame mark "IV/187BZ/V/AMV," fine crazing.

1904 *11½in (29cm) high*

$1,600-1,900 **DRA**

A Rookwood decorated mtt vase, by Margaret McDonald, flame mark, dated, model and artist's cipher.

1928 *7½in (19cm) high*

$450-500 **DRA**

A Rookwood painted mat vase, by Harriet Wilcox (1869-1943), flame mark "/II/192CZ/H.E.W."

The companion piece to this vase is in the permanent collection of the Metropolitan Museum of Art, New York.

1902 *10in (25.5cm) high*

$19,000-21,000 DRA

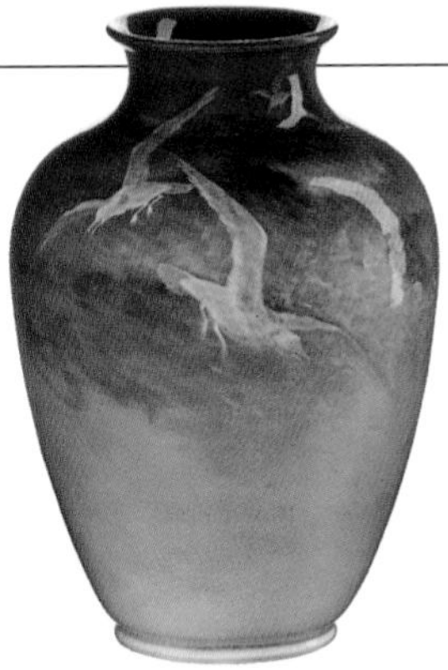

A Rookwood sea-green vase, by Sturgis Laurence (1870-1961), "The Fishers," flame mark "/814/A/G," incised "The Fishers, SL, hb. '97."

1897 *9½in (24cm) high*

$1,700-2,100 DRA

A Rookwood tall vase, by Lenore Asbury, standard glaze, flame mark, dated, model and artist's cipher, professionally restored base.

1903 *14¼in (36cm) high*

$850-950 DRA

A Rookwood scenic vellum vase, by Lenore Asbury, flame mark "/XIX/30F/V/LA," fine overall crazing.

1919 *7in (18cm) high*

$1,050-1,150 DRA

A Rookwood small winter scenic vellum vase, by Sallie Coyne (1876-1939), flame mark "/XXIII/1096V/SEC."

1923 *5in (12.5cm) high*

$1,300-1,900 DRA

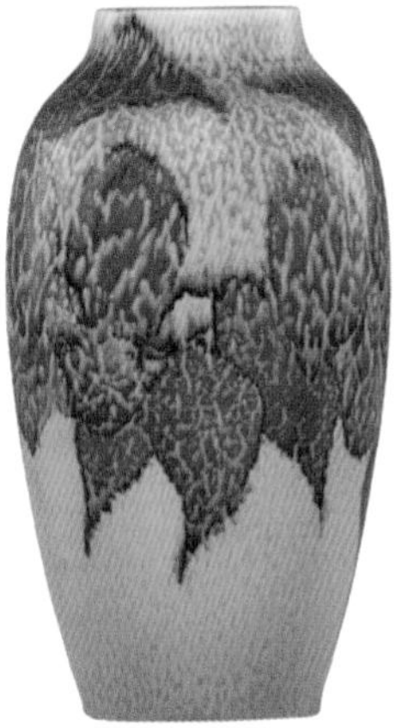

A Rookwood double vellum vase, by William Hentschel (1892-1962), with flowers, flame mark "/XXX/900D/," artist cipher.

1930 *7in (18cm) high*

$800-900 DRA

A Rookwood double vellum vase, by Elizabeth Lincoln (1880-1957), with oak branch and acorns, flame mark "/XXIX/130/LNL," glaze imperfection to widest part of body.

1929 *6½in (16.5cm) high*

$650-800 DRA

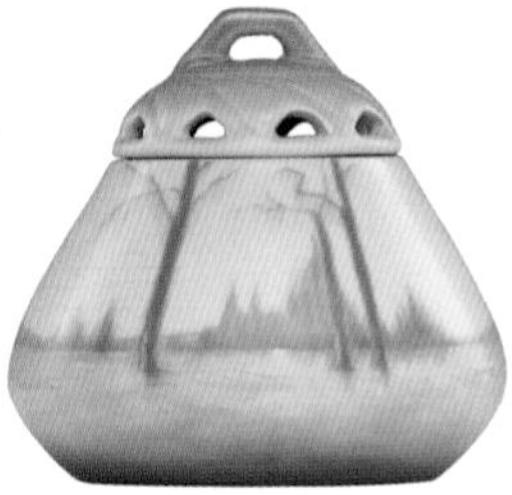

A rare Rookwood winter scenic vellum pot pourri jar, by Elizabeth McDermott (1875-1944), flame mark "/XVII/2337/V/EFM," fine overall crazing, firing line on inner rim in the making.

1917 *4¼in (11cm) high*

$1,150-1,450 DRA

A Rookwood vellum vase, by Sara Sax, with nasturtium border, flame mark, dated, model and artist's cipher.

1908 *9in (23cm) high*

$500-650 DRA

A Roseville "Sunflower" jardinière and pedestal, unmarked, jardinière with a couple of small glazed-over chips in the making, pedestal with one small glaze chip.

Established in 1892 in Roseville, Ohio, Roseville Pottery began producing art wares in 1898. It had produced stoneware since 1890. Roseville launched its first art pottery range, "Rozane," after employing Ross Purdy in 1900. The "Della Robbia" line was designed by Frederick Hurten Rhead (1880-1942) and introduced in 1906. The popular "Futura" line was introduced in 1928. Production ceased in 1954.

1925 *28½in (72.5cm) high*

$1,900-2,600 **DRA**

A Roseville mat green jardinière and pedestal, unmarked, three tight hairlines.

ca. 1910 *12in (30.5cm) high*

$1,050-1,150 **DRA**

A Roseville "Brown Pine Cone" jardinière and pedestal, stamped.

1935 *29in (73.5cm) high*

$850-950 **DRA**

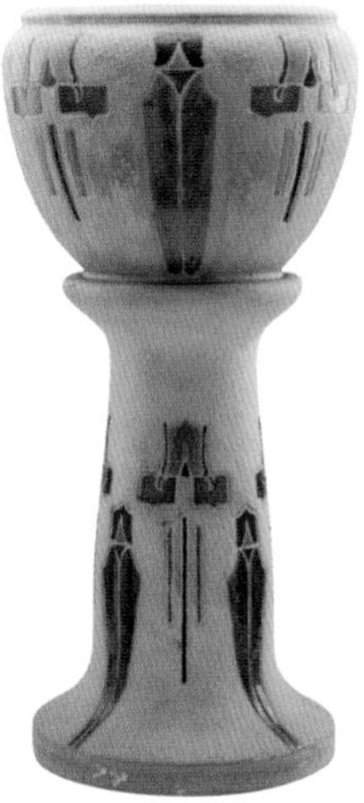

A Roseville "Mostique" jardinière with pedestal, unmarked.

1915 *10in (25.5cm) high*

$1,100-1,250 **DRA**

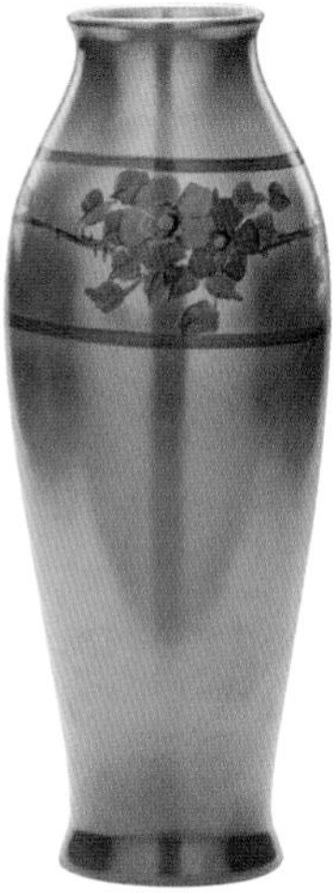

A Roseville "Pauleo" vase, with roses, unmarked, restored base.

ca. 1915 *16in (40.5cm) high*

$260-320 **DRA**

A Roseville "Rozane" ware "Della Robbia" vase, with stylized feathers, raised seal, body incised "E.D.," several chips and touch-ups to high points throughout body.

ca. 1910 *8½in (21.5cm) high*

$7,000-8,000 **DRA**

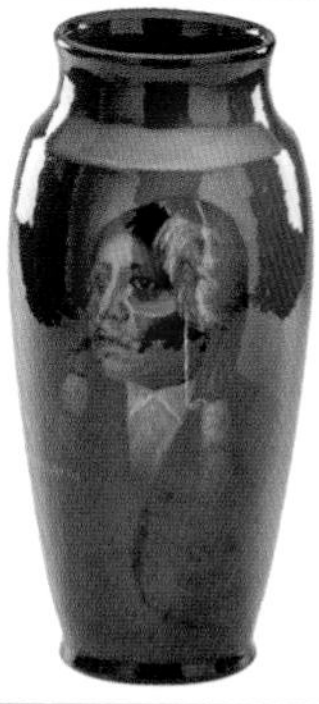

A Roseville "Rozane" ware "Chief Richards" portrait vase, by Arthur Williams, with war paint, marked, professionally restored.

13½in (34.5cm) high

$300-400 **DRA**

A Roseville "Green Rosecraft Nude Panel" fan vase, "RV" blue ink stamp.

1920 *8in (20.5cm) high*

$400-450 **DRA**

A Roseville "Ivory Morning Glory" lamp base, umarked.

1935 *19in (48.5cm) high*

$400-450 **DRA**

QUICK REFERENCE—ROYAL CROWN DERBY

- **The Derby china works was established by Andrew Planché in ca. 1750. The factory was purchased by William Duesbury and John Heath in 1756. After George III granted Duesbury permission to use the royal crown in the company's backstamp in 1775, it became known as Crown Derby.**
- **The company received a royal warrant and became The Royal Crown Derby Porcelain Co. in 1890.**
- **The factory changed hands and sites multiple times over the years. In 2016, businessman and former chief executive of Royal Doulton Kevin Oakes acquired 100 percent of the share capital in Royal Crown Derby.**

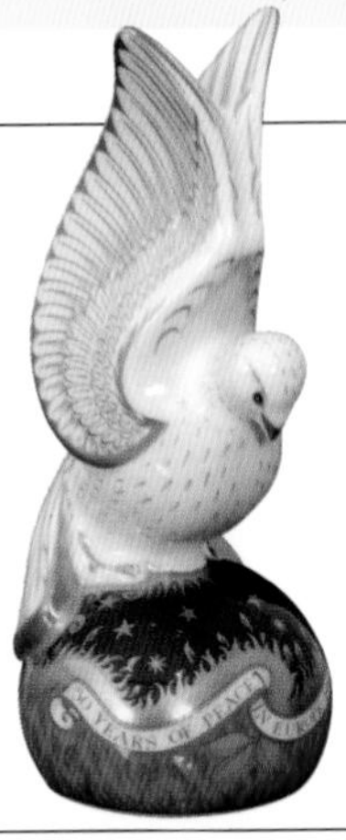

A Royal Crown Derby "Spirit of Peace" paperweight, limted edition no.129 of 150, with gold stopper, boxed.

This paperweight was made as an exclusive edition commissioned by Wheelers of Loughborough to commemorate the 50th anniversary of VE Day.

9in (23cm) high

$700-850 FLD

A Royal Crown Derby "Brown Pelican" paperweight, with gold stopper, boxed.

$50-80 PSA

QUICK REFERENCE—ROYAL CROWN DERBY PAPERWEIGHTS

- **Royal Crown Derby introduced paperweights in 1981 at Chatsworth House, Derbyshire. These paperweights were the "Duck," "Owl," "Penguin," "Quail," "Rabbit," and "Wren," and they continued the Derby tradition of rich decoration. The range became very popular.**

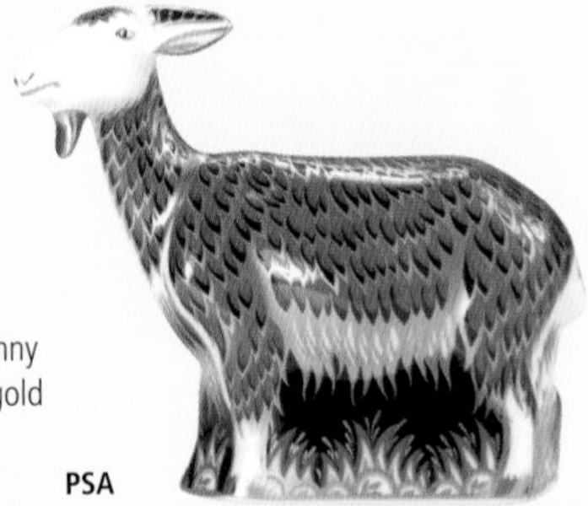

A Royal Crown Derby "Nanny Goat" paperweight, with gold stopper, boxed.

$100-130 PSA

A Royal Crown Derby "Puppy" paperweight, with gold stopper, boxed.

$60-90 PSA

A Royal Crown Derby Jubilee "Black Swan" paperweight, limited edition no.140 of 2,002, with a gold stopper, boxed, with certificate.

$190-260 PSA

A Royal Crown Derby "Cheshire Cat" paperweight, commissioned by John Sinclair, limited edition no.80 of 500, complete with certificate of authenticity and original presentation box.

ca. 1996 *5¼in (13.5cm) high*

$600-700 DUK

A Royal Crown Derby "Thorpe" vase, in the "Old Imari 1128" design, boxed.

11½in (29cm) high

$650-800 PSA

A Royal Crown Derby "Kettle Teapot," in the "Old Imari 1128" design, boxed.

7in (18cm) high

$600-700 PSA

A Royal Crown Derby large candlestick, in the "Old Imari 1128" design, boxed.

10¾in (27.5cm) high

$400-500 PSA

QUICK REFERENCE—ROYAL WORCESTER

- **The Worcester factory was founded in 1751 at Warmstry House, Worcester. After a visit from George III, it was awarded a royal warrant in 1788.**
- **The name and owner of the factory changed multiple times throughout the late 18thC. By 1862, the company was known as Royal Worcester.**
- **The company produced a range of ceramics, including tableware and figurines. Key artists include James Hadley, George Owen, and Charles Toft.**
- **Hadley established a school at Worcester in 1896, using local painters to develop new traditions in porcelain painting. From ca. 1900, painters were allowed to sign their work. Charles Baldwyn painted birds and swans in flight, while Harry Davis (1885-1970) painted fish, sheep, landscapes, and architecture.**
- **Davis (1885-1970) started working for Royal Worcester at the age of 13, becoming foreman of the "Men Painters" department in 1928 and retiring in 1969.**
- **The Stintons were also well-known painters. Harry Stinton painted Highland cattle, James Stinton painted birds, and John Stinton Jr. painted landscapes, castles, and cattle.**
- **Royal Worcester went into administration in 2008. The brand name and intellectual property was bought by Portmerion Pottery Group in 2009.**

A framed Royal Worcester plaque, by Harry Davis, with sheep in a mountainous landscape, signed "H Davis," puce mark on reverse.
plaque 4¼in (11cm) diam
$2,600-3,200 GWA

A Royal Worcester pot pourri, signed "H Ayrton," with printed black marks, includes inner lid.
10¼in (26cm) high
$2,600-3,200 K&O

A Royal Worcester "Stroller and Marion Coakes" figurine, by Doris Lindner, model no.RW3872, limited edition no.537 of 750, with wooden plinth and framed certificate.
11¼in (28.5cm) high
$400-500 FELL

A Royal Worcester "Mill Reef" porcelain figurine, modeled by Doris Lindner, with black printed marks, numbered "150," with wooden plinth.
1974 9¾in (24.5cm) high
$500-650 FELL

A Royal Worcester "The Polo Player" figurine, modeled by Doris Lindner, the bridle missing its wire martingale strap.
7in (20cm) long
$400-500 CHOR

A Royal Worcester "Appaloosa Stallion" figurine, modeled by Doris Lindner, on wooden plinth, with certificate.
1969 10¾in (27.5cm) long
$450-500 WM

A Royal Worcester "Hereford Bull" figurine, modeled by Doris Lindner, on wooden plinth.
1959 10in (25.5cm) long
$300-400 WM

A Royal Worcester "Charolais Bull" figurine, modeled by Doris Lindner, black printed mark and script signature, on a wooden plinth.
11.5in (29cm) long
$450-500 FLD

QUICK REFERENCE—RUSKIN POTTERY

- **Ruskin Pottery was established in 1898 by Edward R. Taylor and William Howson Taylor, in Sandwell, near Birmingham.**
- **Early products included a range of ornamental and useful ware, such as vases, tableware, buttons, and cuff links.**
- **Inspired by Chinese ceramics, William Howson Taylor experimented with glaze techniques, including sang-de-boeuf, flambé, soufflé, and luster glazes.**
- **Shortly before William's death and the factory's closure in 1935, notes and documentation for the unique Ruskin glazes and pottery were deliberately destroyed.**

A Ruskin Pottery high-fired vase and cover, decorated with a deep sang-de-beouf glaze, with lavender patches and copper green spotting, impressed mark, dated.

1909 *10in (25.5cm) high*

$2,100-2,600 **FLD**

A Ruskin Pottery high-fired Meiping vase, decorated with a sang-de-boeuf glaze, impressed mark, dated.

1913 *10¾in (27.5cm) high*

$1,900-2,600 **FLD**

A Ruskin Pottery crystalline vase, decorated in a streaked green over a mottled dark blue with faint crystalline flecks, impressed marks.

15¼in (39cm) high

$450-600 **FLD**

A Ruskin Pottery high-fired vase, decorated in a sang-de-boeuf glaze, impressed mark, dated.

1933 *4in (10cm) high*

$800-900 **FLD**

A Ruskin Pottery high-fired vase, decorated in a sang-de-boeuf glaze, with lavender mottling, impressed marks, dated.

1920 *4in (10cm) high*

$400-450 **FLD**

A Ruskin Pottery high-fired pot pourri and cover, in a sang-de-boeuf glaze with dove gray mottling on the upper half and a flambé red with lavender patches on the lower half, impressed mark, dated.

1927 *3½in (9cm) high*

$600-650 **FLD**

A Ruskin Pottery high-fired flower pitcher, in sang-de-boeuf glaze, with a dove gray body beneath with darker veining, impressed mark, dated.

1933 *9in (23cm) high*

$700-850 **FLD**

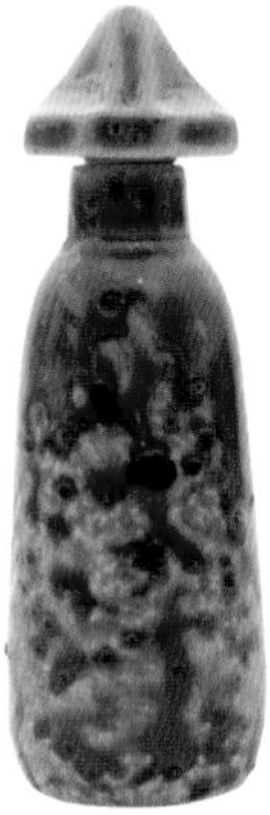

A Ruskin Pottery high-fired pagoda-topped scent bottle, in a sang-de-boeuf glaze with copper green spotting and lavender patches, impressed mark, restored, replacement cover.

5in (12.5cm) high

$650-800 **FLD**

A Ruskin Pottery high-fired "Lily" vase, in a sang-de-boeuf and lavender glaze, impressed mark, painted glaze code "E16" on the base, dated, restored.

1926 *9¾in (24.5cm) high*

$800-1,050 FLD

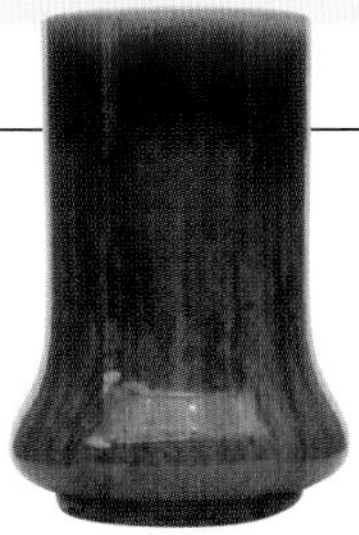

A Ruskin Pottery high-fired "Elephants Foot" vase, in a sang-de-boeuf glaze, with deep lavender streaks and copper green spotting, impressed West Smethwick mark, dated, restored.

See Atterbury, Paul, and Henson, John, *Ruskin Pottery*, Baxendale Press (1993), page 59.

1903 *8in (20.5cm) high*

$1,600-2,100 FLD

Judith Picks

There is something magical about the glazes of the Ruskin Pottery. Some of the Ruskin glazes were gradations of two colors, while some were textured multicolor patterns.

These glazes included misty soufflé glazes, ice crystal-effect glazes—"crystalline," luster glazes resembling metallic finishes, and sang-de-boeuf and flambé glazes, which produced a blood red effect. The sang-de-boeuf glazes were created using a reduction of copper and iron oxides at high temperature.

William Howson Taylor's glazes were leadless, and the decoration was hand painted.

A Ruskin Pottery high-fired vase, with a flambé and tonal lavender glaze, with copper green spotting and dove gray patches, impressed mark.

15½in (39.5cm) high

$3,900-5,200 FLD

A Ruskin Pottery high-fired stoneware vase, by William Howson Taylor, in a sang-de-boeuf and flambé glaze with fine turquoise speckles, impressed marks, dated.

1925 *8in (20.5cm) high*

$500-650 WW

A Ruskin Pottery high-fired stoneware vase, by William Howson Taylor, in a mottled sang-de-boeuf and silver-gray glaze, impressed marks, dated.

1933 *5¼in (13.5cm) high*

$950-1,100 WW

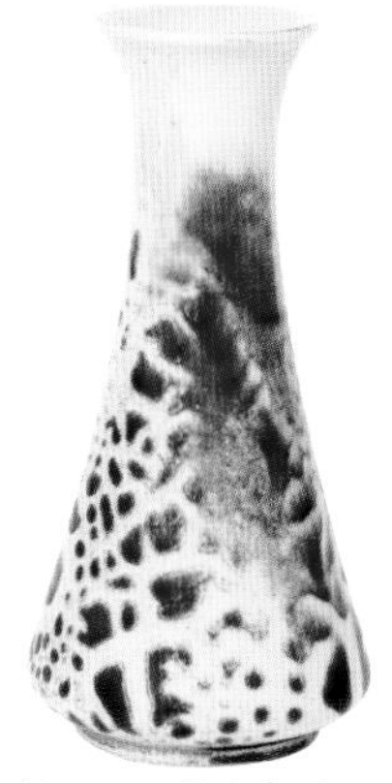

A Ruskin Pottery high-fired stoneware carafe vase, by William Howson Taylor, in a fissured sang-de-boeuf glaze over white impressed marks, dated, professional restoration to neck.

1922 *9¼in (23.5cm) high*

$500-650 WW

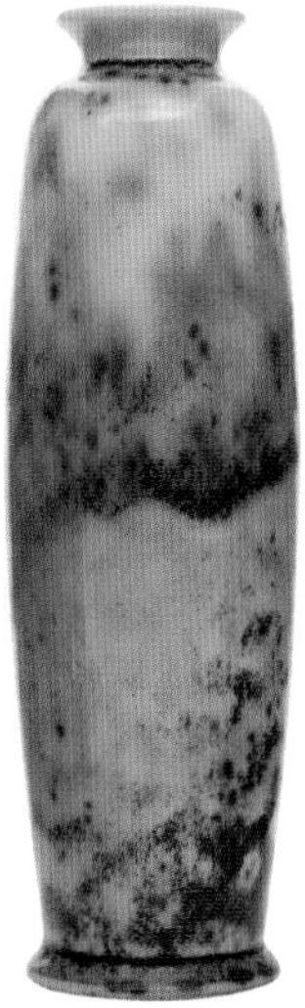

A Ruskin Pottery high-fired vase, in a celadon green with lavender and copper green spotting and sang-de-boeuf patches and pooling, impressed mark, dated, restored.

1910 *8¼in (21cm) high*

$800-900 FLD

A Ruskin high-fired vase, silver-gray and red glaze, impressed marks, dated.

1924 *11½in (29cm) high*

$950-1,100 K&O

A Ruskin Pottery vase, decorated in a Kingfisher blue glaze, impressed marks and dated.

1918 *10in (25.5cm) high*

$1,400-1,900 FLD

A Ruskin high-fired flambé vase and cover, in purple and white with turquoise specks, impressed marks, dated.
1906 *14in (35.5cm) high*
$6,500-8,000 **SWO**

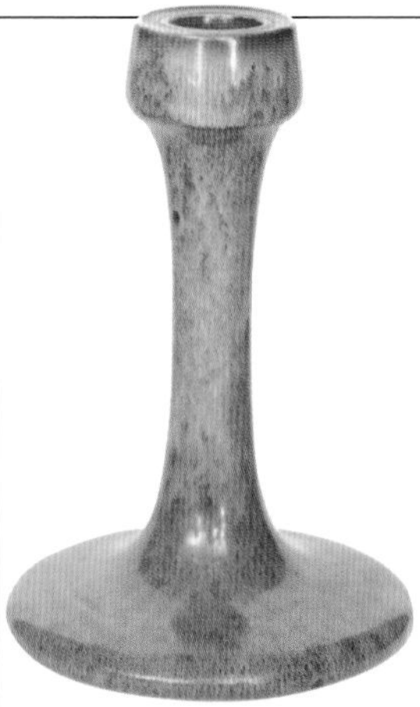

A Ruskin Pottery candlestick, in a Strawberry Crush soufflé glaze, impressed oval "West Smethwick" mark, dated.
1906 *7in (18cm) high*
$120-160 **FLD**

A miniature Ruskin Pottery high-fired vase, in a tonal purple and green glaze with copper green spotting, unmarked, slight damage.
2¾in (7cm) high
$400-500 **FLD**

A Ruskin Pottery high-fired vase, with lavender and red patches over the dove gray ground, impressed mark, dated.
1921 *6in (15cm) high*
$850-950 **FLD**

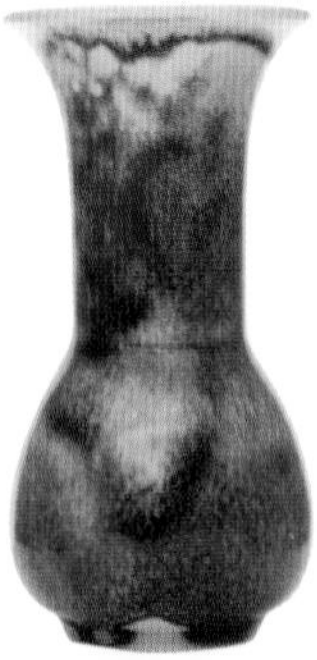

A Ruskin Pottery vase, mat black with hand-painted silver foliate decoration, impressed mark, dated.

See Atterbury, Paul, and Henson, John, *Ruskin Pottery*, Baxendale Press (1993), page 59.
1916 *6¼in (16cm) high*
$2,600-3,900 **FLD**

A Ruskin Pottery high-fired pot pourri and cover, in a green speckled glaze with lavender and dove gray patches beneath, impressed mark, dated.
1911 *3½in (9cm) high*
$1,800-2,300 **FLD**

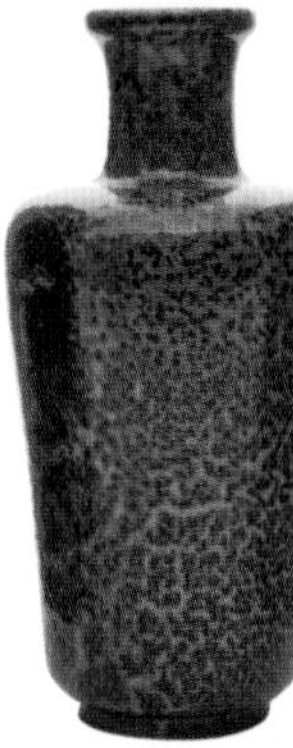

A Ruskin Pottery high-fired vase, in a speckled green with red and purple fissuring, impressed oval "West Smethwick" mark, also impressed "423," dated.
1905 *8in (20.5cm) high*
$5,200-6,500 **FLD**

A Ruskin Pottery high-fired vase, in a flambé glaze against the white ground with copper green spotting, impressed mark, dated.
1932 *12¼in (31cm) high*
$3,200-3,900 **FLD**

A Ruskin Pottery high-fired stoneware vase, by William Howson Taylor, in a fissured purple and blue glaze over white, with flambé patches, impressed marks, dated, professional restoration to neck.
1920 *8in (20.5cm) high*
$850-950 **WW**

A 1950s Michael Andersen & Sons earthernware pitcher, attributed to Marianne Starck, design no.5552, from the "Tribal" range.

This range was originally called the "Negro" range and later become known as the "Tribal" range. Each piece was initially molded, then hand carved, meaning that no two pieces are ever the same.

7in (18cm) high

$210-250 **LYN**

A Swedish Gustavsberg faience studio footed bowl, designed by Stig Lindberg, decorated by Helinä Pitkänen, with impressed mark, painted "SWEDEN 158.T.82," with "G. & hand" cipher and decorator's yellow flower motif.

Established in Sweden in the 1820s, Gustavsberg porcelain factory was run by Wilhelm Kåge (1889-1960) and then Stig Lindberg (1916-82). In 1994, the Dutch company N.V. Koninklijke Sphinx acquired Gustavsberg. The firm is now owned by Villeroy & Boch AG. In its later years, the company moved away from porcelain production to sanitary wares.

1950s *6½in (16.5cm) high*

$190-260 **DAWS**

A Gustavsberg Studio "Farsta" vase, by Wilhelm Kage, turquoise drip glazed with incised decoration in sectioned panels, impressed marks and paper labels.

This vase was reputedly exhibited at the 1955 "Stockholmia 55" Exhibition.

8in (20.5cm) high

$1,600-2,100 **DUK**

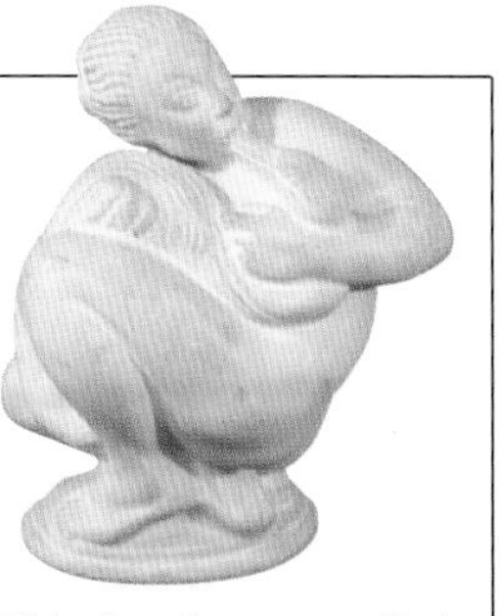

A Kähler Keramik stoneware "Leda & The Swan" figurine, made by Kai Nielson, incised signature "Danmark."

Danish sculptor Kai Nielsen (1882-1924) worked for various factories, including Royal Copenhagen and Bing & Grøndahl.

$160-210 **LC**

A Nymolle ceramic, designed by Bjørn Wiinblad.

$100-130 **LYN**

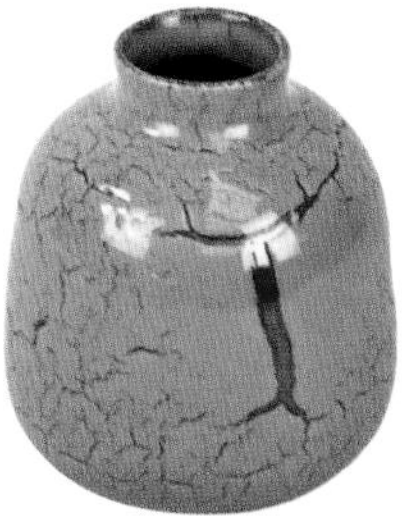

A Rörstrand olive green glazed vase, by Carl-Harry Stålhane, impressed marks on base.

7¼in (18.5cm) high

$160-210 **APAR**

QUICK REFERENCE—ROYAL COPENHAGEN

- **Royal Copenhagen began in Denmark in 1775 as the Royal Porcelain Factory under the patronage of the Royal family.**
- **The Danish Court ran the Royal Porcelain Factory until the late 1860s, when it moved into private hands. The company began producing a Christmas plaque series in 1895, with the design changing annually.**
- **In 1972, Royal Copenhagen acquired the Georg Jensen Silversmithy and in 1985 it merged with Holmegaard Glassworks. It then became part of the Royal Scandinavia group. The company's flagship store is located on Amagertorv, in Copenhagen.**
- **Royal Copenhagen ware is marked with three hand-painted waves, symbolizing Denmark's three important waterways; a crown, showing the royal patronage; and the maker's mark. The crowns changed over time.**

A Royal Copenhagen Mandarin ducks figurine, modeled by Peter Herold, numbered "1863," with printed marks.

8¼in (21cm) wide

$300-450 **SWO**

A pair of Royal Copenhagen herons, designed by Theodor Madsen, with printed backstamps, numbered "532" and "138."

largest 11¼in (28.5cm) high

$650-800 **LSK**

A Royal Copenhagen eagle, signed by Vilhelm Theodor Fischer (1857-1928), marked on base, no.2033, some firing imperfections, dated.

1919 *21in (53.5cm) high*

$1,100-1,250 **APAR**

A Royal Copenhagen porcelain Icelandic falcon, printed backstamp, numbered "109," monogrammed "DR" verso.

16in (40.5cm) high

$400-500 **LSK**

A Royal Copenhagen Hyacinth Macaw parrot, design attributed to Armand Petersen, model no.2235, impressed, printed and painted marks.

16¼in (41.5cm) high

$600-700 **WW**

A Royal Copenhagen barn owl, designed by Thomsen, model no.273, marked "Royal Copenhagen, 273, Denmark."

8½in (21.5cm) high

$300-400 **LC**

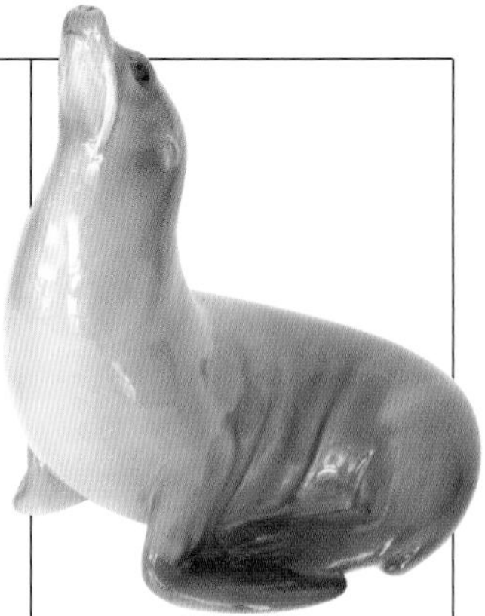

A Royal Copenhagen seal, designed by Theodor Madsen, model no.265, printed mark with date code.

1938 *11½in (29cm) high*

$160-210 **FLD**

A Royal Copenhagen seal with pup, printed backstamp, numbered "090" verso, surface scratches to glaze.

7¾in (19.5cm) high

$90-120 **LSK**

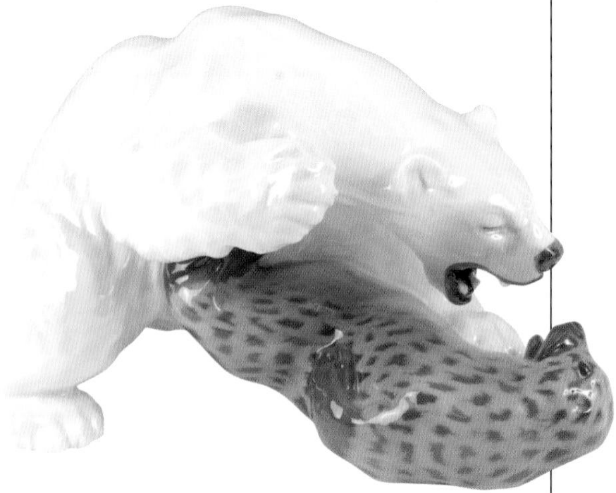

A Royal Copenhagen polar bear attacking a seal, printed backstamp, numbered "1108," monogrammed "OF" verso.

9in (23cm) high

$450-500 **LSK**

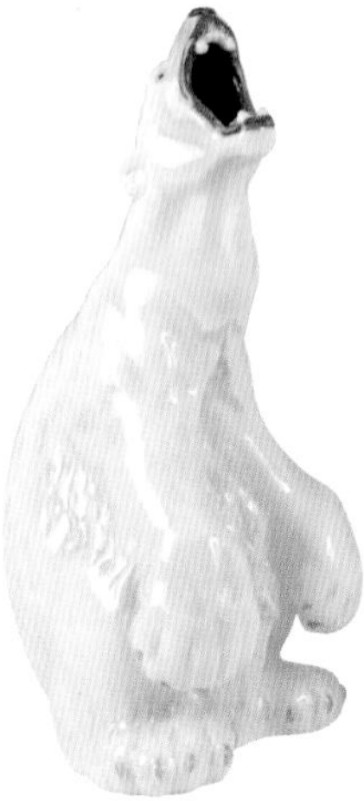

A Royal Copenhagen polar bear, printed backstamp, numbered "060," monogrammed "SM" verso.

12½in (32cm) high

$160-210 **LSK**

A Royal Copenhagen goat, designed by Christian Thomsen, printed backstamp, numbered "466" verso.

11in (28cm) long

$260-320 **LSK**

A Royal Copenhagen Jersey cow, printed backstamp, numbered "4678," with one glazed and three unglazed udder nipples.

10¼in (26cm) long

$400-450 **LSK**

A Royal Copenhagen bull, designed by Knud Kyhn, incised signature, printed backstamp, numbered "1195," small glaze fault.

8in (20.5cm) high

$300-400 **LSK**

A Royal Copenhagen elk, model no.2813, marked to base.

8¼in (21cm) high

$260-320 **CHOR**

A Royal Copenhagen leopardess, printed backstamp, numbered "805" verso.

7in (18cm) high

$160-210 **LSK**

A Royal Copenhagen tiger and two cubs, printed backstamp, numbered "4687" verso.

6in (15cm) high

$650-800 **LSK**

A Royal Copenhagen "The Wave and Rock" figurine, by Theodor Lundberg, marked on base.

17¾in (45cm) high

$600-700 **CHOR**

A Royal Copenhagen "Pan" figurine, printed and painted marks on base, numbered "2113."

7in (18cm) high

$260-320 **APAR**

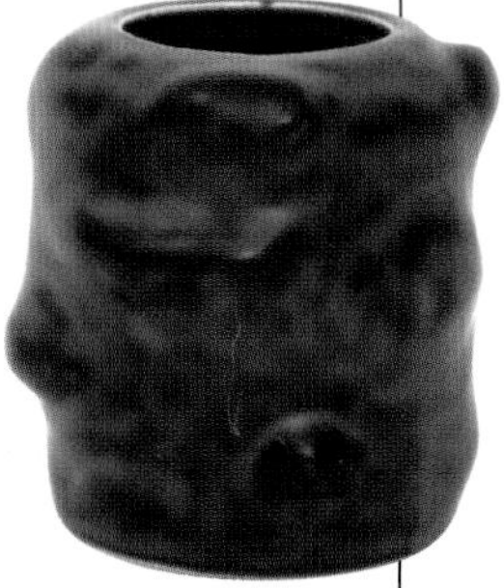

A Royal Copenhagen vase, by Axel Salto, model no.21474, with matt brown "Sung" glaze, printed and painted marks, impressed "Salto" mark, with paper label.

Born in Copenhagen, Axel Salto (1889-1961) studied at the Royal Danish Academy of Fine Arts and worked for Bing & Grøndahl, Saxbo and Royal Copenhagen.

3½in (9cm) high

$300-400 **WW**

A Royal Copenhagen lobster molded shallow bowl, painted and printed marks on the base, numbered "3498," surface dirt.

7¾in (19.5cm) long

$60-80 **APAR**

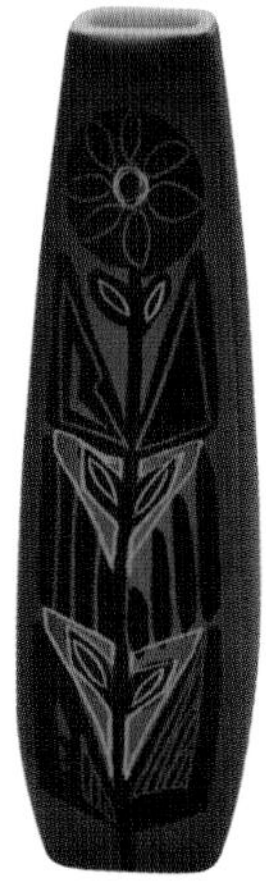

A Soholm vase, by Sven Aage Jensen, with sunflower decoration, shape 2057-2.

1950s *8½in (21.5cm) high*

$100-120 **LYN**

A Soholm vase, designed by Einar Johansen, shape no.3325, with unglazed neck, with factory, designer, and shape marks.

7in (18cm) high

$100-120 **LYN**

A Soholm vase, with geometric raised design, shape 2057-2.

1950s *8½in (21.5cm) high*

$80-90 **LYN**

QUICK REFERENCE—TROIKA

- **Troika was founded in 1962 in St Ives, Cornwall, by potter Benny Sirota, painter Lesley Illsley, and architect Jan Thompson. Thompson left in 1965.**
- **In 1968, Troika ware was sold for the first time by Heal's and Liberty in London. A year later, the company moved to a larger site in Newlyn.**
- **Troika wares were slip molded and decorated by hand. Early pieces had gloss glazes, but textured mat finishes were predominant from 1974. Designs were influenced by Scandinavian ceramics and the Cornish landscape.**
- **The company closed in 1983 following economic troubles and tension between the founders.**

A Troika pottery wheel vase, by Penny Black, one side decorated with a stylized Mosque, the opposing side with raised geometric motifs, painted "Troika England" mark and artist monogram "PB" verso.

1970s *8in (20.5cm) high*

$260-390 **LSK**

A Troika totem vase, by Alison Brigden, signed on base.

8¾in (22cm) high

$210-260 **HAN**

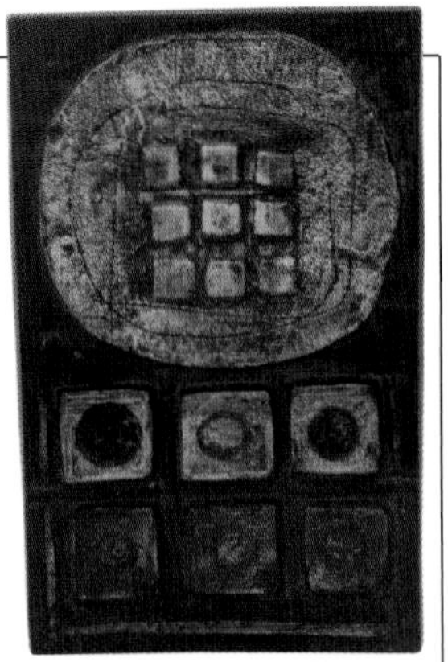

A Troika Pottery wall plaque, by Simone Killburn, painted marks and artist monogram.

12in (30.5cm) high

$700-850 **WW**

A rare Troika Pottery "Love" plaque, designed by Benny Sirota, with stylized couples, painted "Troika" marks, trident mark, artist cipher on back.

14½in (37cm) wide

$1,050-1,300 **WW**

A Troika pottery wheel vase, by Sue Lowe, signed "Troika Cornwall SL."

1976 *6½in (16.5cm) high*

$300-400 **BELL**

A rare Troika Pottery "Thames" wall plaque, designed by Benny Sirota, with the meandering river and buildings, painted "Troika" marks and artist cipher.

10in (25.5cm) high

$950-1,100 **WW**

A Troika Pottery cube-form table lamp base, decorated by Annette Walters, painted marks "Troika Cornwall" and "AW."

8in (20.5cm) high

$260-390 **FLD**

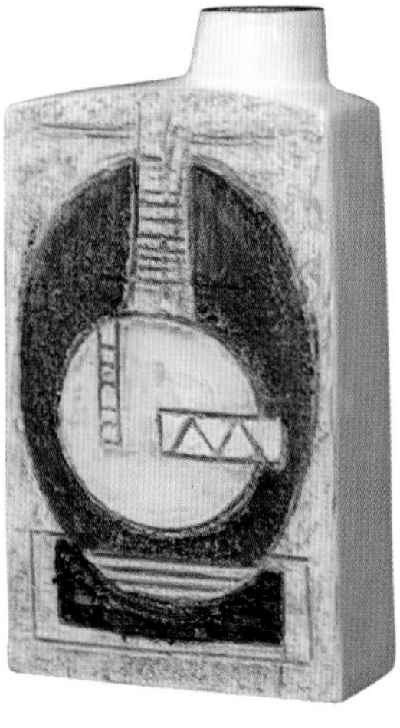

A Troika Pottery chimney vase, signed on base.

8in (20.5cm) high

$300-400 **FLD**

A Troika marmalade pot, signed on base "Troika Cornwall SK."

3½in (9cm) high

$130-190 **LOCK**

QUICK REFERENCE—CHARLES VYSE

- **Charles Vyse (1882-1971) began his career as an apprentice modeler and designer at Doulton in Burslem at the age of 14, and was trained by Charles Noke. He studied at the Royal College of Art and Camberwell School of Art. He was an early pioneer of British studio pottery, experimenting with high-fired stoneware vessels based on medieval Chinese prototypes and producing technically highly accomplished wares throughout the 1930s. After a spell at the Royal College of Art, he produced designs for Doulton in the interwar period, for example, the figurine "Darling." Vyse is, however, best known for the molded and hand-decorated pieces produced by a studio pottery at Cheyne Walk in Chelsea, which he started in 1919 with his wife Nell. Here, they produced figurines based on ordinary people seen around London.**
- **After the Ward War II "Blitz" bombing damaged his studio, Vyse taught at Farnham School of Art and continued producing figurines, before retiring in 1963.**

A Charles Vyse "Barnet Fair" Chelsea figurine, incised maker's marks "C. VYSE/ CHELSEA."

1920s *10¼in (26cm) high*

$3,900-5,200 **L&T**

A Charles Vyse "The Shawl" Chelsea figurine, painted maker's marks under base "CV / CHELSEA / 1926," dated.

1926 *10¾in (27.5cm) high*

$800-1,050 **L&T**

A Charles Vyse "The Piccadilly Rose Woman" Chelsea figurine, painted mark and date on base, minor losses on petals.

1923 *8¼in (21cm) high*

$600-700 **WW**

A Charles Vyse "The Lavender Girl" Chelsea figurine, painted maker's marks under base "CV / CHELSEA / 1922," dated.

1922 *9in (23cm) high*

$650-800 **L&T**

A Charles Vyse "Saturday Night" Chelsea figurine, painted maker's marks under base "CV / CHELSEA / 1927," dated.

1927 *10in (25.5cm) high*

$800-1,050 **L&T**

A Charles Vyse "Seated Tabby Cat" stoneware figurine, painted in shades of tenmoku and ocher, incised "C Vyse Chelsea."

8¾in (22cm) high

$3,900-4,500 **WW**

A Charles Vyse stoneware vase, glazed on the foot with a green celadon, with running iron splashes, incised "C Vyse."

4½in (11.5cm) high

$500-600 **WW**

A Wade "Sunshine" underglaze figurine.

Wade was established in 1810 in Stoke-on-Trent, England, where the company began producing ceramics for the textile and wool spinning industries and bottles for breweries. In 1910, as Sir George Wade joined, the company moved into the Manchester Pottery in Burslem, Staffordshire. In 1930, designer Jessie Van Hallen, known for producing ceramic figurines of celebrities, joined the company. The Wade Whimsies were introduced in 1954. The company opened a new factory in 2010 and production continues today.

6½in (16.5cm) high

$130-190 **PSA**

A Wade "Old Nannie" underglaze figurine.

1930s *9½in (24cm) high*

$160-230 **PSA**

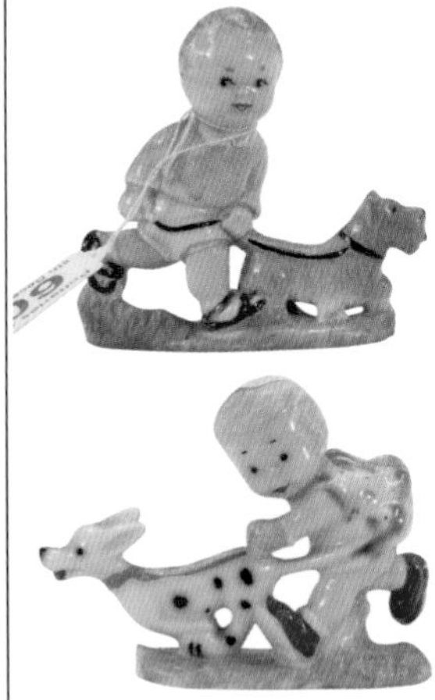

A pair of Wade "Sarah and Sam" porcelain figurines, from the Mabel Lucie Attwell series.

$60-80 **PSA**

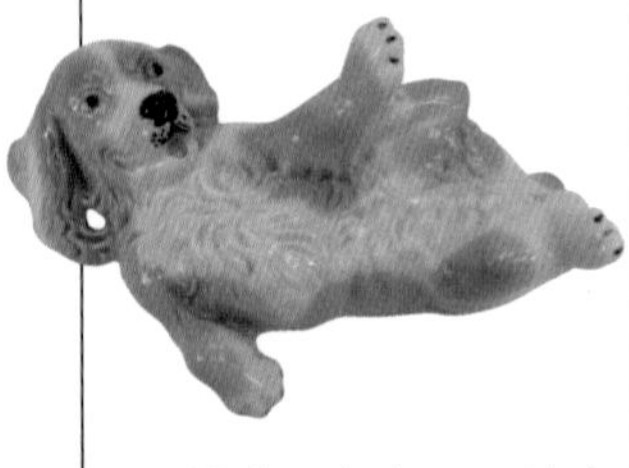

A rare Wade underglaze model of a spaniel dog, Wade porcelain label on base.

6¼in (16cm) long

$500-600 **PSA**

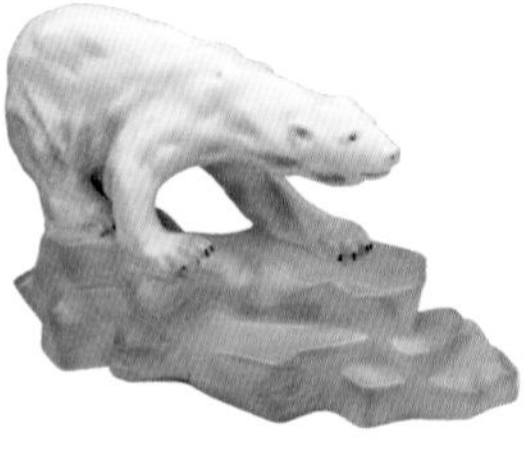

A Wade model of a polar bear, by Faust Lang, signed on base "Wade 1939 Polar Bear," hairline crack.

ca. 1939 *7in (18cm) high*

$450-500 **LOCK**

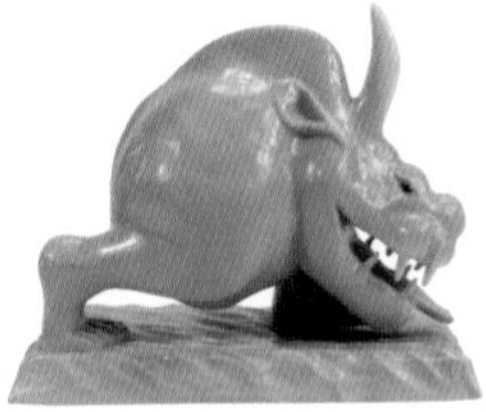

A Wade "Running Spoof" underglaze model, by A.G. Fiddes Watt.

5¼in (13.5cm) high

$350-450 **PSA**

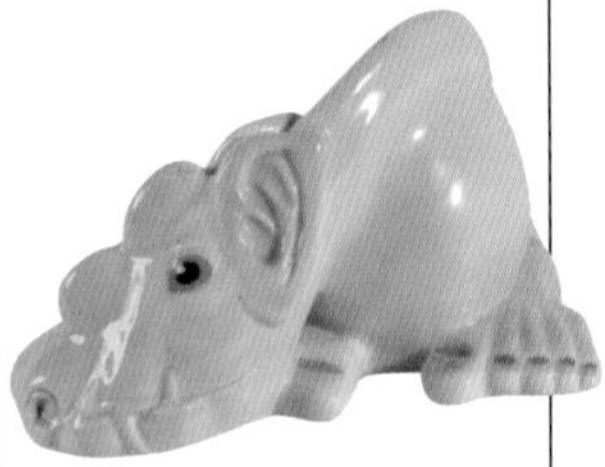

A Wade "Baby Scruple" ceramic glazed model, designed by A.G. Fiddes Watt, printed marks.

5¼in (13.5cm) long

$800-900 **DUK**

A set of Wade "Snow White and the Seven Dwarfs" figurines, some light wear to applied detail.

$70-80 **APAR**

A set of five Wade pig money banks, with Wade plaque.

$30-45 **APAR**

QUICK REFERENCE—WEDGWOOD

- **The Wedgwood Pottery was founded in 1759 in Staffordshire, England, by Josiah Wedgwood. Thomas Bentley soon joined Wedgwood as business partner.**
- **Jasperware, an unglazed vitreous fine stoneware, was developed in ca. 1774.**
- **Key 20thC designers include Daisy Makeig-Jones (1881-1945), Keith Murray (1892-1981), John Skeaping (1901-80), and Eric Ravilious (1903-42).**
- **Ravilious, a painter, illustrator, designer, and wood engraver, worked for Wedgwood between 1936 and 1940. His work included commemorative wares, dinner and tea wares, and nursery ware. In 1942, Ravilious was lost in active service during World War II.**
- **The company went into administration in 2009 and is now part of WWRD Ltd. and the Fiskars Group. Today, Wedgwood pieces are designed in the Wedgwood Design Studio, England, with production facilities across Europe and Asia.**

A Wedgwood coronation mug, designed by Eric Ravilious, with a printed design and highlighted in yellow and pink, printed mark.

1953 *4in (10cm) high*

$400-500 SWO

A Wedgwood commemorative King George VI and Queen Elizabeth coronation bowl, designed by Keith Murray, in gray glaze.

1937 *10¼in (26cm) diam*

$260-320 PSA

A rare Wedgwood Queensware "The Boat Race" bowl, by Eric Ravilious, with scenes from three stages of the boat race and a mermaid, the inside with an oval view of Piccadilly Circus.

$1,300-1,900 HAN

A 20thC Wedgwood Jasperware crimson vase.

3½in (9cm) high

$80-90 PSA

A Wedgwood Queensware "Country Lovers" figural group, by Arnold Machin.

12¼in (31cm) high

$260-320 PSA

A prestige Wedgwood Jasperware "Four Seasons" engine-turned coffee set, limited edition no.5 of 50, boxed with certificate.

$1,300-1,900 PSA

A Wedgwood Pottery ribbed spherical vase, designed by Keith Murray, printed factory mark and facsimile signature.

6¼in (16cm) high

$260-320 WW

A Wedgwood conical bowl, by Keith Murray, printed and impressed marks, a hairline crack on the rim and two small glaze bubbles.

6¼in (16cm) high

$260-390 CHEF

QUICK REFERENCE—WEMYSS WARE

- **Established by Robert Methven Heron (1833-1906) in the 1880s in a pottery in Kirkcaldy, Fife, Scotland, Wemyss Ware was designed and painted by Karel Nekola. Edwin Sandland succeeded Nekola. The company was patronized by Dora Wemyss of Wemyss Castle.**
- **The company closed in 1930 following financial struggles, but production of Wemyss Ware was transferred to Bovey Tracey Pottery Co. in Devon, England, and supervised by Joseph Nekola, Karel's son. Production continued until 1957.**
- **Joseph's apprentice Esther Weeks (née Clark) became head decorator after Joseph's death in 1952.**
- **In 1994, Griselda Hill Pottery in Fife acquired the Wemyss Ware trademark.**

An early-20thC Wemyss Ware model of a pig, painted maker's mark "Wemyss" in black script, crazed all over.

18¼in (46.5cm) long

$2,200-2,600 **BELL**

A Wemyss Ware pink glazed model of a pig, impressed "Wemyss Ware R.H. & S." mark, restored.

6¼in (16cm) long

$260-390 **FLD**

An early-20thC Wemyss Ware model of a pig, "Shamrocks" pattern, painted and impressed mark "WEMYSS."

17in (43cm) long

$5,200-6,500 **L&T**

A Wemyss Ware decanter, modeled as a pig, with black sponged patches, small cork nose, unmarked.

6¼in (16cm) long

$650-800 **FLD**

A Wemyss Ware money box, modeled as a pig, with hand-painted clover leaves and flowers, impressed, restored.

6in (15cm) long

$800-850 **FLD**

A Wemyss Ware model of a cat, decorated with hand-painted clover leaves and painted features, with inset green glass eyes, painted "Wemyss" on base.

13½in (34.5cm) high

$1,600-2,300 **FLD**

A Wemyss Ware heart-shaped tray, "Brown Cockerel and Hens" pattern, impressed mark "WEMYSS," printed retailer's mark "T. GOODE & CO."

ca.1900 11½in (29cm) long

$1,600-2,300 **L&T**

A Wemyss Ware pitcher and bowl, decorated with mallard ducks.

bowl 11½in (29cm) diam

$3,900-5,200 **PSA**

A Wemyss Ware button, decorated by Karel Nekola, depicting a bee, impressed "WEMYSS."

ca. 1900 *1½in (4cm) diam*

$700-850 **L&T**

An early-20thC Wemyss Ware letter rack, "Purple Plums" pattern, painted maker's and retailer's mark "WEMYSS/ T. GOODE & CO.," hairline.

9in (23cm) wide

$500-650 **L&T**

A Wemyss Ware oatmeal bowl, decorated by Karel Nekola, with inscription "WILLIE GARDNER HIS PORRIDGE PLATE," impressed mark "WEMYSS WARE R.H. & S.," painted mark "WEMYSS/ KN/ 1915."

1915 *6½in (16.5cm) diam*

$1,800-2,600 **L&T**

A pair of Wemyss Ware large geese flower holders, impressed marks "WEMYSS WARE/ R.H. & S.," one with printed retailer's mark "T. GOODE AND CO."

ca. 1900 *8in (20.5cm) high*

$1,050-1,300 **L&T**

A Wemyss Ware gordon dessert plate, "Damsons" pattern, impressed mark 'WEMYSS WARE/ R.H. & S."

ca. 1900 *8in (20.5cm) diam*

$950-1,100 **L&T**

An early-20thC Wemyss Ware loving cup, "Carnations" pattern, impressed mark "WEMYSS."

8¼in (21cm) diam

$950-1,100 **L&T**

A near pair of Wemyss Ware candlesticks, "Carnations" pattern, impressed marks "WEMYSS WARE/ R.H. & S."

ca. 1900 *12in (30.5cm) high*

$1,600-2,100 **L&T**

A 20thC Wemyss Ware basin, "Campanula" pattern, impressed mark "WEMYSS," hairlines.

15½in (39.5cm) diam

$1,800-2,300 **L&T**

A Wemyss Ware loving cup, "Tulips" pattern, impressed mark "WEMYSS WARE/ R.H. & S."

ca. 1900 *10in (25.5cm) diam*

$1,600-2,100 **L&T**

An early-20thC Wemyss Ware Kenmore vase, decorated by Karel Nekola, "Cabbage Roses" pattern, impressed mark "WEMYSS," painted retailer's mark "T. GOODE & CO./ LONDON."

14¼in (36cm) high

$1,900-2,600 **L&T**

A Wemyss Ware gypsy jardinière, decorated by Karel Nekola, with cabbage roses and butterflies, painted mark "WEMYSS/ KN/ 1915."

1915 *8¾in (22cm) diam*

$3,200-3,900 **L&T**

An early-20thC Wemyss Ware quaich, decorated by Edwin Sandland, "Strawberries" pattern, painted and impressed mark "WEMYSS."

10¼in (26cm) diam

$1,600-2,100 **L&T**

An early-20thC Wemyss Ware "Fifies" mug, painted with fishing boats on the Fife coast of the Firth of Forth, impressed mark "WEMYSS," printed retailer's mark "T. GOODE AND CO."

3½in (9cm) high

$1,300-1,900 **L&T**

QUICK REFERENCE—WESTERWALD STONEWARE

- **Westerwald stoneware is a type of salt-glazed pottery from the Ransbach-Baumbach and Höhr-Grenzhausen areas of Westerwaldkreis in Rheinland-Pfalz, in West Germany.**
- **The Westerwaldkreis area has large clay quarries of unusually rich and pure quality. These quarries have long encouraged locals to turn to pottery, and there is evidence of ceramic production in the area since 1000 BC.**
- **Traditional salt-glazing was first developed in the mid-15thC, when changing technology allowed kilns to be heated to higher temperatures. The 1960s-70s saw a revival of traditional techniques. These new designs were influenced by Japanese and other Asian ceramics.**
- **Key artists of the mid- to late-20thC movement include Elfriede Balzar-Kopp, Klotilde Giefer-Bahn, Görge Hohlt, Walburga Külz, Wim Mühlendyck, Gisela Schmidt-Reuther and Wendelin Stahl.**

Thanks to Michael G. Lines, *John Newton Antiques.*

A Westerwald pottery pitcher/floor vase, decorated in the studios of Elfriede Balzar-Kopp, design in sgraffito, signed on base.

ca. 1960/70 *16¼in (41.5cm) high*

$600-650 **JNEW**

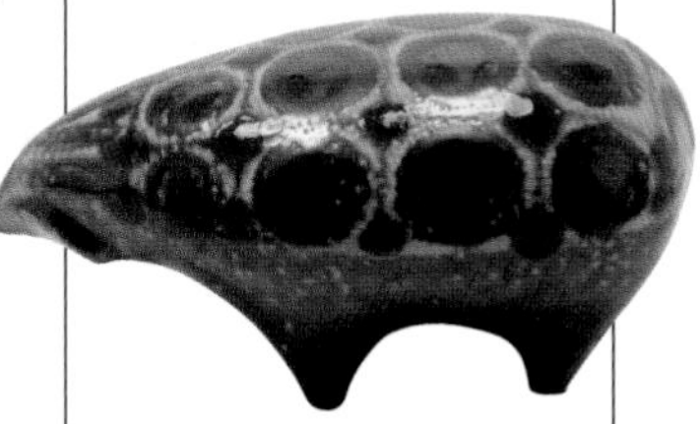

A Westerwald pottery figurine of a badger, decorated in the studios of Elfriede Balzar-Kopp, signed "BK" on base.

ca. 1960/70 *3¾in (9.5cm) high*

$350-450 **JNEW**

A Westerwald lidded pitcher, decorated by Elfriede Balzar-Kopp, with a sgraffito design on a cobalt ground, signed with initials.

Born in Berdorf, Luxembourg in 1904, Elfriede Balzar-Kopp studied and worked at the State Majolica Factory in Karlsruhe, before opening his own studio in 1927. In 1974, he won the Federal Cross of Merit. Balzar-Kopp died in 1983.

ca. 1940s *16½in (42cm) high*

$450-500 **JNEW**

A scarce Westerwald pottery figural group, decorated in the studios of Elfriede Balzar-Kopp, signed on base.

ca. 1960/70s *10¼in (26cm) high*

$950-1,100 **JNEW**

A Westerwald pottery figurine of a rooster, decorated in the studios of Elfriede Balzar-Kopp, signed "BK" oon base.

ca. 1970 *10¼in (26cm) high*

$350-425 **JNEW**

A vase, decorated in the studios of Elfriede Balzar-Kopp, with a design in traditional enamels and salt-glaze.

ca. 1970 *9in (23cm) high*

$180-210 **JNEW**

A figurine of a fish, decorated in the studios of Elfriede Balzar-Kopp.

ca. 1970 *6¼in (16cm) high*

$230-260 **JNEW**

A studio pottery plaque, by Elfriede Balzar-Kopp, decorated with a Modernist design of an owl in sgraffito.

ca. 1970s *11¾in (30cm) diam*

$300-350 **JNEW**

A Modernist studio pottery pitcher, by Heinz Theo Dietz, with sgraffito decoration.

Heinz Theo Dietz (born 1938), studied ceramic engineering in Höhr-Grenzhausen before opening his pottery in 1965. In 1969, he moved to Königswinter and set up a new pottery with his wife, Katherina Dietz. He retired In 2003, and the pottery was transferred to Dietz's daughter.

ca. 1960-70 *9in (23cm) high*
$430-500 **JNEW**

A Modernist studio pottery pitcher, by Heinz Theo Dietz, decorated in sgraffito.

ca. 1960-70 *9in (23cm) high*
$450-500 **JNEW**

A Modernist studio pottery pitcher, by Heinz Theo Dietz, with owls in sgraffito.

ca. 1970s
$160-190 **JNEW**

A studio pottery figurine, made by Heinz Theo Dietz, of a "hybrid creature."

ca. 1980 *10in (25.5cm) high*
$1,300-1,600 **JNEW**

A salt-glaze pitcher, made in the studios of Klotilde Giefer-Bahn, decorated in sgraffito with a retro bird design, signed on base.

Klotilde Giefer-Bahn was born in Koblenz, Germany, in 1924. She trained as a ceramicist and opened her own studio in 1947 in Höhr-Grenzhausen (Rhineland-Palatinate). Following her death in 2008, her son, Roland Giefer, took over her studio.

ca. 1960/70 *12½in (32cm) high*
$430-600 **JNEW**

A scarce Westerwald pottery figurine of a rabbit, decorated in the studios of Klotilde Giefer-Bahn, with cobalt and traditional glaze and enamels, signed "Giefer Bahn" on base.

ca. 1960s *4¾in (12cm) high*
$290-350 **JNEW**

A Westerwald pottery figurine of a fox, decorated in the studios of Klotilde Giefer-Bahn, with a traditional salt glaze and enamels, signed "Giefer Bahn" on base.

Klotilde Giefer-Bahn's son Roland Giefer produced another version of this figurine in the 1980s, but the later version has paler enamels and is signed Roland Giefer.

ca. 1970 *5¾in (14.5cm) high*
$290-350 **JNEW**

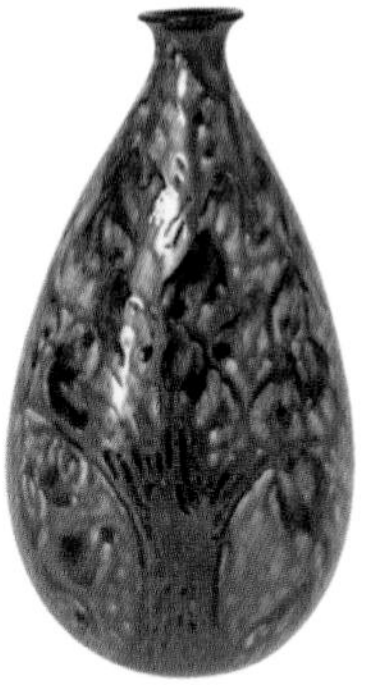

A Modernist salt-glaze vase, by Klotilde Giefer-Bahn, decorated with an abstract design of a tree, in cobalt blue and earthy enamels, signed on base.

ca. 1970s *9¾in (24.5cm) high*
$350-450 **JNEW**

A Westerwald pottery figurine of a toucan, decorated in the studios of Klotilde Giefer-Bahn by her son Roland Giefer, with cobalt and traditional salt glaze and enamels, signed "Giefer Bahn" to base.

ca. 1980 *7¾in (19.5cm) high*
$290-350 **JNEW**

A studio vase, made by Gerhard Liebenthron, with layered erupted/pitted earthy glaze, with Liebenthron's monogram and year code on base.

Born in 1925 in Neustrelitz, Germany, Gerhard Liebenthron studied at the North German Art College before opening his own workshop in 1952 in Bremen. He was a member of the Arts and Crafts Working Group in Bremen. Liebenthron died in 2005.

1962 *7in (18cm) high*

$160-190 **JNEW**

A studio vase, made by Gerhard Liebenthron, with a flowing layered glaze, with Liebenthron's monogram and year code on base.

1963 *6¼in (16cm) high*

$230-290 **JNEW**

A studio vase, made by Gerhard Liebenthron, with a flowing layered glaze, with Liebenthron's monogram and year code on base.

1973 *10in (25.5cm) high*

$260-320 **JNEW**

A studio vase, made by Gerhard Liebenthron, with a layered glaze, with Liebenthron's monogram and year code on base.

1977 *10¼in (26cm) high*

$230-290 **JNEW**

A studio vase, made by Gerhard Liebenthron, with a flowing layered glaze giving the illusion of looking out onto an exotic landscape, with Liebenthron's monogram and year code on base.

1979 *5in (12.5cm) high*

$260-320 **JNEW**

A Modernist studio pottery pitcher, made by Gerhard Liebenthron, with a multilayered flowing earthy glaze, with Liebenthron's monogram and year code on base.

1980 *10¾in (27.5cm) high*

$360-430 **JNEW**

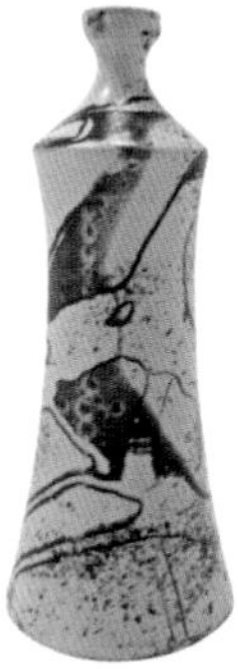

A studio pottery vase, made by Gerhard Liebenthron, with a multilayered flowing glaze, with a calligraphy-type design, with Liebenthron's monogram and year code on base.

1983 *7in (18cm) high*

$230-290 **JNEW**

A Modernist/Space Age-inspired studio vase, made by Gerhard Liebenthron, with a layered glaze, with Liebenthron's monogram and year code on base.

1984 *9¾in (24.5cm) high*

$260-320 **JNEW**

A stoneware vase, made by Gerhard Liebenthron, painted with a graffiti design, in the style of Picasso, with an earthy glaze, with Liebenthron's monogram and year code on base.

1991 *15¾in (40cm) high*

$800-950 **JNEW**

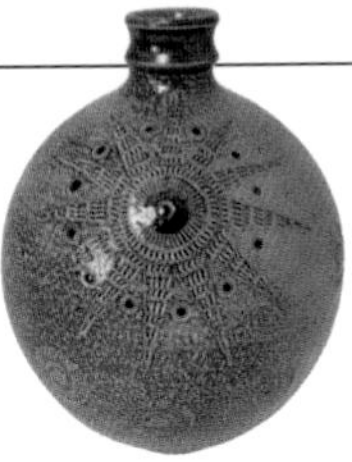

A stoneware pitcher, by Wim Mühlendyck, decorated in sgraffito, salt glaze and earth enamels.

Born in 1905 in Porz, Cologne, Wim Mühlendyck studied at the State Ceramic Technical School in Höhr-Grenzhausen, before training as a teacher in Cologne. He opened his own workshop in 1931 in Höhr-Grenzhausen. Mühlendyck worked closely with his wife, Bita Mühlendyck, and Elfriede Balzar-Kopp. Wim Mühlendyck died in 1986.

ca. 1950 *7½in (19cm) high*

$160-190 **JNEW**

A stoneware salt-glaze lidded decanter, by Wim Mühlendyck, decorated in sgraffito, with a traditional study of forest animals, with Mühlendyck's signature and studio mark.

ca. 1960 *14in (35.5cm) high*

$500-600 **JNEW**

A Westerwald salt-glazed pitcher, decorated in sgraffito by Wim Mühlendyck, with a stylized design of a leaping horse, signed on base.

ca. 1960 *9¼in (23.5cm) high*

$430-500 **JNEW**

A salt-glazed stein, by Wim Mühlendyck, decorated in sgraffito, with a stylized elephant.

ca. 1960/70 *6¼in (16cm) high*

$190-230 **JNEW**

A Westerwald salt-glazed pottery pitcher, decorated in sgraffito by Wim Mühlendyck, with owls, signed on the base.

ca. 1960/70s *11in (28cm) high*

$300-400 **JNEW**

A stoneware lidded tankard, by Wim Mühlendyck, decorated in sgraffito, with a wild boar, finished with a metallic oxide and salt glaze, signed "Wim Mühlendyck."

ca. 1960s *5¾in (14.5cm) high*

$190-230 **JNEW**

A German stoneware pitcher, by Wim Mühlendyck, decorated in sgraffito, with a leaping stag, finished with rich salt glaze, with Mühlendyck's studio mark.

ca. 1960s *13in (33cm) high*

$300-350 **JNEW**

A salt-glazed and cobalt blue-ground jar and cover, by Wim Mühlendyck, decorated in sgraffito, with stylized sea horses.

ca. 1970 *4in (10cm) high*

$190-230 **JNEW**

A globular-shaped tea caddy, by Wim Mühlendyck, decorated with a stylized design in sgraffito, with a cobalt blue and salt-glazed ground.

ca. 1970 *4in (10cm) high*

$190-230 **JNEW**

A salt-glaze liquor flask, made in the studios of Wim Mühlendyck, decorated with a Modernist Space Age design, studio mark on base.

ca. 1970 *6¼in (16cm) high*

$190-230 **JNEW**

A salt-glazed and cobalt blue-ground cigarette-ash jar and cover, by Wim Mühlendyck, decorated in sgraffito, with stylized fish.

ca. 1970 *3in (7.5cm) high*

$190-230 **JNEW**

A stoneware lidded tobacco jar, by Wim Mühlendyck, decorated with stylized owls in sgraffito and rich enamels, with Mühlendyck's signature and studio mark on the base.

ca. 1970 *6in (15cm) high*

$290-300 **JNEW**

A Westerwald salt-glazed "Milk Churn" pitcher, decorated in sgraffito by Wim Mühlendyck, with a stylized leaping horse, signed on base, dated.

1973 *9½in (24cm) high*

$300-350 **JNEW**

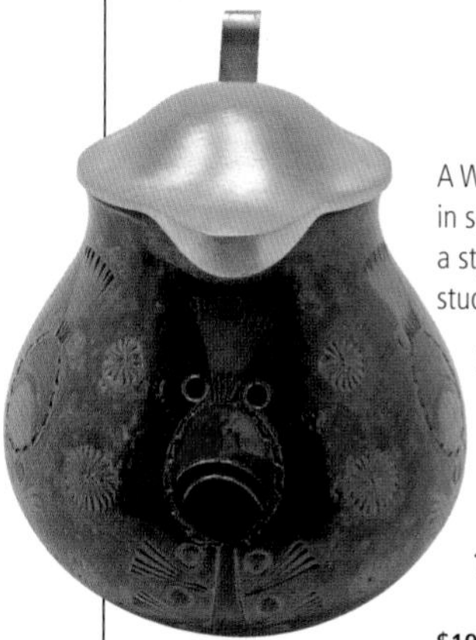

A Westerwald salt-glazed pitcher, decorated in sgraffito by Johannas Mühlendyck, with a stylized design and rich glaze, bears the studio mark "MJ" for Johannes Mühlendyc.

Born in 1933 to Wim and Bita Mühlendyck, Johannes Mühlendyck studied at the College of Ceramics in Landshut, Germany, before working in his parents' pottery studio from 1956-86. He died in 2013.

6¼in (16cm) high

$190-230 **JNEW**

A Westerwald salt-glazed pitcher, decorated in sgraffito by Johannes Mühlendyck, with musical instruments.

ca. 1970 *8½in (21.5cm) high*

$230-290 **JNEW**

A studio pottery vase, made by Rudi Stahl, with a variegated earthy blue glaze, signed on base.

Born in 1918 in Westerwald, Germany, Rudi Stahl studied pottery under Wim Mühlendyck, before attending the State Ceramic Technical School in Höhr-Grenzhausen. In 1938, he founded his own pottery in Höhr-Grenzhausen. Stahl died in 1987.

ca. 1960 *11in (28cm) high*

$300-350 **JNEW**

A studio pottery vase, made by Rudi Stahl, with a variegated earthy glaze, decorated with a Greek key-type design, signed on base.

ca. 1960s *9¾in (24.5cm) high*

$300-400 **JNEW**

A studio pottery vase, made by Rudi Stahl, with a variegated earthy glaze, decorated with a Greek key-type design, signed on base.

ca. 1960s *8in (20.5cm) high*

$300-400 **JNEW**

A Bing & Grøndahl figurine of a cow, modeled by Lauritz Jensen, numbered "2161," with artist's monogram.

9½in (24cm) long

$300-350 SWO

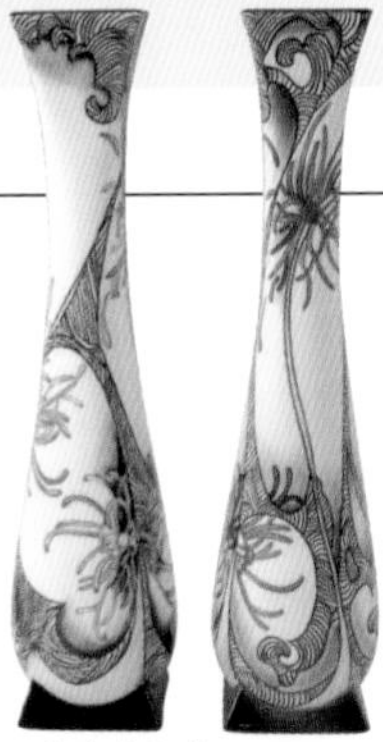

A pair of Black Ryden pottery vases, designed by Kerry Goodwin, "Summers End" pattern, impressed mark verso, signed, limited edition no.12/100 and no.14/100, dated.

2003 14in (35.5cm) high

$260-320 LSK

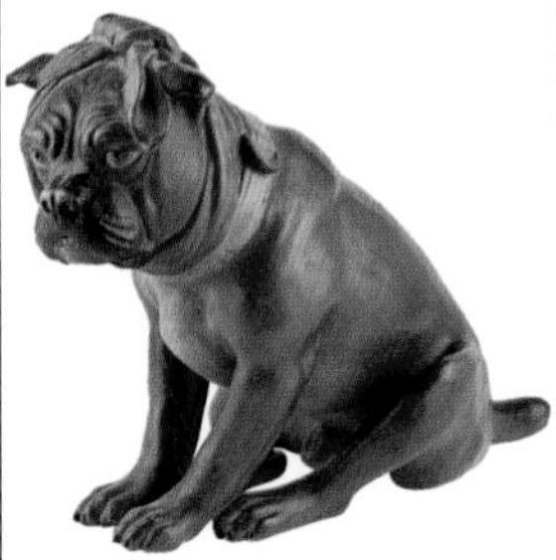

A late-19thC to early-20thC painted terra-cotta boxer, by Bernard Bloch, impressed "4380/ BB."

9¼in (23.5cm) high

$650-800 L&T

A C.H. Brannam Barum Pottery "Mr Punch" money box, possibly retailed by Liberty & Co., incised "C.H. Brannam, Barum, 1901," incised "rd" mark, dated.

1901 3½in (9cm) high

$950-1,100 WW

QUICK REFERENCE—BRETBY ART POTTERY

- **In ca. 1883, Henry Tooth and William Ault set up the Bretby Art Pottery in Derbyshire, producing decorative and novelty wares. Bretby also created ceramic pieces imitating other materials, such as copper and pewter. The company traded as Tooth & Co. Ault left the business to set up his own pottery in 1887.**
- **After ca. 1920, production shifted away from decorative and novelty ware and after changing hands multiple times the factory closed in ca. 1996.**

A pair of Bretby Art Pottery glazed earthenware bookends, model no.3072, impressed Pottery marks.

ca. 1930 8in (20.5cm) high

$90-100 ROS

An early-20thC Cantagalli maiolica charger, decorated with Renaissance-style roundel depicting St. Martin of Tours, painted cockerel mark.

18½in (47cm) diam

$1,600-2,100 FLD

A British W.T. Copeland & Sons stoneware beer pitcher, with "ARCTIC EXPEDITION 1875" transfer crest, with maker's transfer anchor mark on the base, impressed "12," inscribed "DISCOVERY," chip on the rim on the left of the spout.

For this expedition, which was led by Sir George Strong Nares, Copeland produced special services for both HM Ships "Alert" and "Discovery" in stoneware and porcelain using either blue or sepia transfers. Sent by the Admiralty in an attempt to reach the North Pole by way of Smith Sound, it culminated in Commander Albert Hastings Markham's Farthest North of 83° 20'26"N (May 12, 1876), a record latitude at the time.

1875 8in (20cm) high

$1,900-2,600 CM

A Caulden handled vase, by S. Pope.

8in (20.5cm) high

$60-90 PSA

A pair of Compton Potters" Art Guild bookends, depicting St. Joan on horseback.

ca. 1920 7½in (19cm) high

$450-600 L&T

A late-19thC Walter Crane dust-pressed tile, decorated with "Mary Mary Quite Contrary," from "The Baby's Opera," painted onto a Minton Hollins blank.

1877 *6in (15cm) square*

$190-260 **FLD**

A Max Emanuel & Co. ceramic pig spill vase, by Louis Wain, painted in colors, signed on the body "LOUIS WAIN," with printed maker's marks and molded registration mark.

Louis Wain (1860-1939) was an English artist and illustrator, best known for his depictions of anthropomorphized cats. His work appeared in children's books, journals, and on postcards. Wain struggled with his mental health and was diagnosed with schizophrenia. In 1924, he was admitted to Springfield Mental Hospital and later moved to Bethlem Royal Hospital.

ca. 1914 *4¾in (12cm) high*

$650-800 **L&T**

A Karl Ens "Emperor Penguins" ceramic figural group.

1930s

$140-190 **PSA**

A Della Robbia terra-cotta bottle vase, by Charles Collis, base numbered "573," drilled.

13½in (34.5cm) high

$650-800 **WHP**

A Max Emanuel & Co. ceramic cat spill vase, by Louis Wain, signed on the body "LOUIS WAIN," with printed maker's marks and registration mark "RD NO 638317," printed mark "MADE IN ENGLAND."

ca. 1914 *5¼in (13.5cm) high*

$500-650 **L&T**

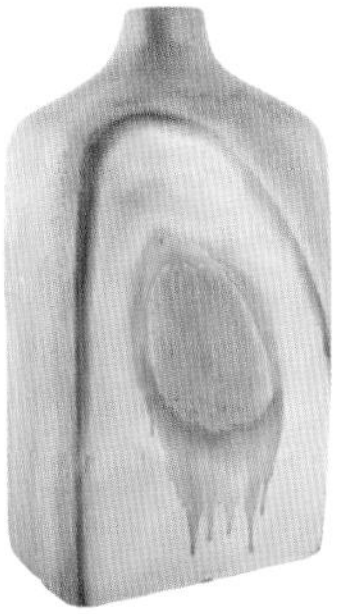

An Italian Marcello Fantoni bottle vase, signed "Fantoni, Italy," slight scratches on the base.

1960s *15in (38cm) high*

$300-450 **DAWS**

A Bourne Denby stoneware hot water bottle.

10in (25.5cm) wide

$50-60 **PSA**

A Dudson luster chalice, by Gordon Forsyth, dated.

1923 *6in (15cm) high*

$600-700 **PSA**

A Della Robbia vase, painted by Annie Smith, incised by Harry Fletcher, incised marks on base.

11in (28cm) high

$700-850 **PW**

A Fielding's "Fairy Castle" Crown Devon vase, designed by Enoch Boulton, pattern no.2414, printed and painted marks, restored.

Simon Fielding established an earthenware manufacturer in ca. 1870 at The Railway Pottery, Stoke. The company became known as S. Fielding & Co. The Crown Devon line of pottery was developed. In the early 20thC, the factory was renamed the Devon Pottery. The pottery was knocked down in 1987.

9in (23cm) high

$300-350 WW

An early-20thC Gallé-style faience "Barrister" pug, with inset glass eyes.

12½in (32cm) high

$950-1,100 BE

An early-20thC Gallé-style nodding pottery cat, with inset glass eyes.

11in (28cm) long

$850-950 BE

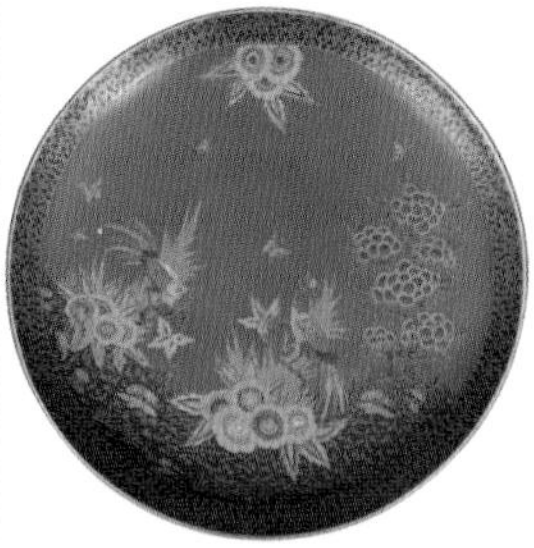

A Fielding's "Crown Devon" charger, pattern no.2130, printed and painted marks.

15½in (39.5cm) diam

$230-290 WW

An early-20thC Gallé-style pottery cat, with inset glass eyes.

13¾in (35cm) high

$800-900 BE

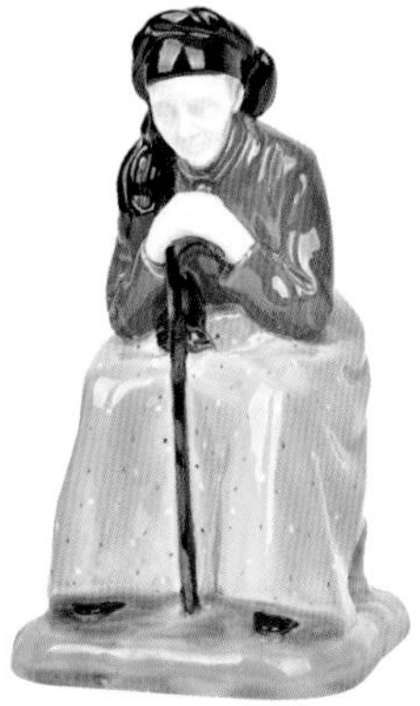

An Austrian Gmundner Keramik pottery figurine, model no.359, impressed marks, remnants of paper label, some crazing.

ca. 1930 *8¼in (21cm) high*

$190-260 BELL

A "Flesh Pots" pitcher, designed by Morris Rushton, printed factory mark.

"Flesh Pots" was a small, humorous pottery launched in Stoke on Trent in 1978 by founder Morris Rushton. Although small and short lived, it influenced, among others, Next, a British chain store, with its avant garde designs, while also producing a more traditional range retailed by the National Trust.

9¼in (23.5cm) high

$400-450 WW

A Fulham Pottery bowl, decorated by Quentin Bell, with an incised portrait of Virginia Woolf, incised "Fulham Pottery, Quentin Bell."

5¾in (14.5cm) wide

$500-650 FLD

Judith Picks

William Henry Goss (1833-1906) studied at the School of Design at Somerset House before working for William Taylor Copeland. In ca. 1858, Goss established his own porcelain business. At the turn of the century, Goss's pieces were hugely popular. Following a decline in popularity after World War I, Goss sold the factory in 1929, but production continued there until the late 1930s. We are often asked on the *Antiques Roadshow* TV show how we decide on our valuations. There are many factors but rarity and desirability are critical. Many Goss pieces can be purchased for under $25 but this tiger is a rare model and hence the price achieved.

A W.H. Goss model of a tiger.

3¾in (9.5cm) high

$1,050-1,150 PSA

QUICK REFERENCE—GRUEBY

- **William Henry Grueby (1867-1925) trained at the Low Art Tile Works, before founding the Grueby Faience Company in Boston, Massachusetts, in 1894.**
- **Most of the pottery was handmade and decorated by a team of young women from Boston's Museum of Fine Arts and other schools.**
- **Grueby experimented with glazes and developed a distinctive mat finish, in contrast to the glossy glazes popular at the time. Grueby received much critical acclaim for his art pottery, but the company struggled financially in the early 1900s, reducing its decorative pottery production and filing for bankruptcy.**
- **Grueby then founded the Grueby Faience and Tile Company, which was bought out by the C. Pardee Works in the late 1910s.**

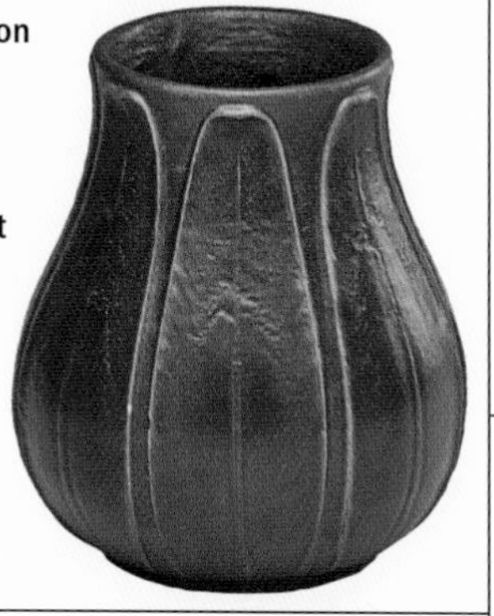

A Grueby vase, circular pottery stamp, incised "FR," some hairlines, some flecks on leaves.
ca. 1905 *8in (20.5cm) high*
$3,900-5,200 DRA

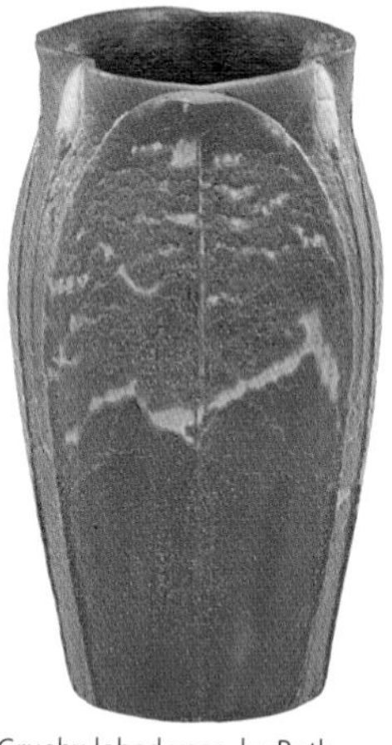

A Grueby lobed vase, by Ruth Erickson, with yellow buds, circular pottery stamp "RE/BL/13-08," one touched-up chip, minor nicks.
ca. 1905 *8½in (21.5cm) high*
$2,600-3,200 DRA

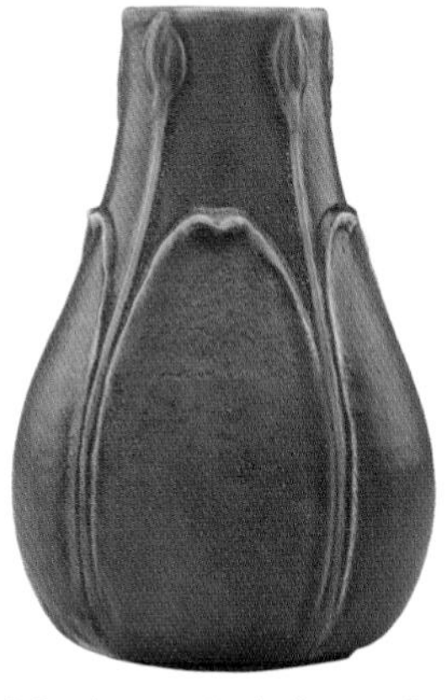

A Grueby vase, circular "Faience" stamp.
ca. 1902 *7in (18cm) high*
$3,200-3,900 DRA

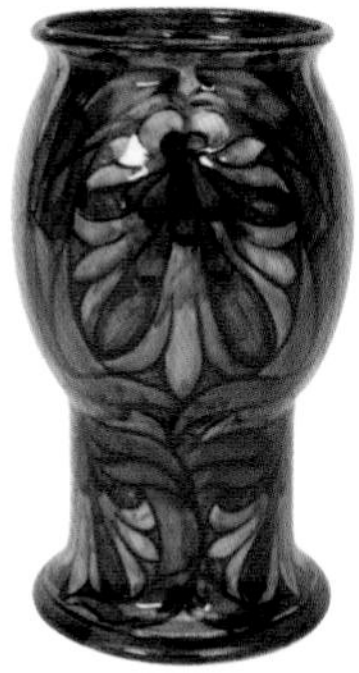

A Hancock & Sons "Morrisware" vase, designed by George Cartlidge, model no.C99-1, printed factory mark, painted mark "C99-1."

Founded in Tunstall, Staffordshire, England, in the mid-to-late 1800s, Sampson Hancock & Sons produced tableware, home ware, and crested china. Following Sampson Hancock's death in ca. 1900, his sons took over the business. Key designers include George Cartlidge, F.X. Abraham, and Edith Gater. The company closed in 1937.

11in (28cm) high
$700-850 WW

A Hancock & Sons "Morrisware" flower bowl, designed by George Cartlidge, model no.C19-28, printed factory mark, facsimile signature.
11in (28cm) diam
$190-260 WW

A Hancock & Sons "Morrisware" vase, designed by George Cartlidge, model no.C17-10, printed factory mark, painted facsimile signature.

See Tony Johnson, *The Morris Ware, Tiles and Art of George Cartlidge*, MakingSpace (2004), page 97, catalog no.264, for comparable vases.
11¾in (30cm) high
$450-600 WW

A Hancock & Sons "Morrisware" table lamp base, by George Cartlidge, model no.C20-6, printed mark, slight damage.
13½in (34.5cm) high
$300-350 FLD

An early-20thC Hancock & Sons "Morrisware" pot pourri, by George Cartlidge, model no.C56-1, decorated with the tube-lined verse "Essences of Past Summers," lacks cover, printed mark, restored.
8in (20.5cm) high
$260-320 FLD

A Howson high-fired flambé vase, dated.
1911 *8in (20.5cm) high*
$90-120 PSA

QUICK REFERENCE—HERTWIG AND CO., KATZHÜTTE

- **Christoph Hertwig, Benjamin Beyermann, and Carl Birkner founded the Hertwig and Co. porcelain factory in 1864 at the Lower Hammer Mill in Katzhütte, Germany. Production started in 1865.**
- **After Birkner quit and Beyermann died, Hertwig ran the business until 1886, when his sons took over.**
- **By 1890, the factory had a workforce of more than 300 people, as well as homeworkers in surrounding villages, producing decorative ceramics, dolls, and stoneware. Production of porcelain figurines began in 1900.**
- **Sculptor Stefan Dakon worked at the factory as a designer. Dakon produced Art Deco-style bronze figurines and ceramics, and also worked for Goldscheider and Keramos.**
- **The Katzhütte factory was passed down the Hertwig family, and, by 1937, was run by Christoph Hertwig's grandsons.**
- **Production was limited to decorative ceramics after nationalization in 1958. The factory closed in 1990.**

A Katzhütte "Ballet Russes" figurine, printed maker's marks, impressed "Germany."
ca. 1920 *8¾in (22cm) high*
$300-400 **ROS**

A Katzhütte Pottery large figurine, by Stephan Dakon, printed factory mark, impressed Dakon.
17in (43cm) high
$600-700 **WW**

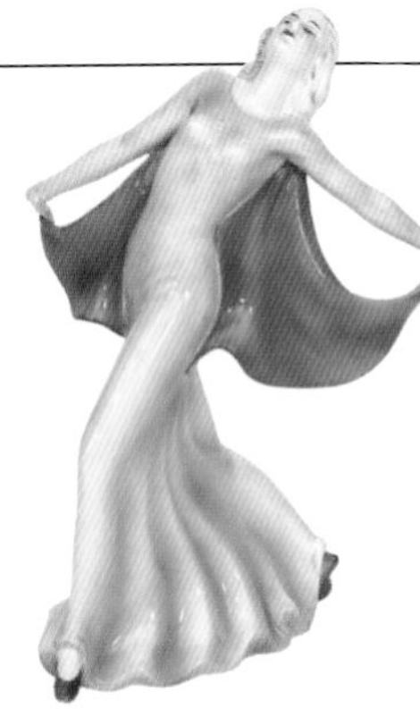

A Katzhütte figurine, printed factory mark.
9¾in (24.5cm) high
$190-260 **WW**

An Art Deco Katzhütte figurine, of a lady walking her Borzoi hound, green stamp below, chain leash is loose.
12½in (32cm) high
$450-500 **CHOR**

An Austrian Keramos "Junge Frau im Kleid" (Young Woman in a Dress) figurine, printed and painted mark "R17," restoration on bonnet.
ca. 1920 *15¾in (40cm) high*
$260-320 **BELL**

A rare Morris and Co. "Cinderella in the Kitchen" tile, designed by Edward Burne-Jones, glaze chips and small hairline on base rim.
6in (15cm) high
$4,500-5,200 **WW**

A Plichta model of a cat, with hand-painted thistle decoration, with inset glass eyes, with printed mark.

Jan Plichta ran a glass and pottery wholesalers in London in the early- to mid-1900s. He commissioned pieces from the Bovey Pottery, the Elton Pottery, and sold some Wemyss Ware. Some of these pieces were marked "Plichta." Records of Plichta after the 1950s are vague.
10¼in (26cm) high
$160-210 **FLD**

A Plichta model of a pig, decorated by Joseph Nekola, printed mark with Nekola Pinxt in script.
6¼in (16cm) high
$300-400 **FLD**

A 19thC Portobello pottery figurine, of a sitting Scotsman in kilt and tam-o'-shanter, on stepped base.
9¼in (23.5cm) high
$1,150-1,300 **GWA**

A pair of Royal Bonn pottery vases, printed and impressed marks, one handle reset.

15¾in (40cm) high

$500-650 **SWO**

A Meissen-style "Nodding Chinaman" sitting figurine, possibly by Samson of Paris.

9½in (24cm) high

$400-500 **JN**

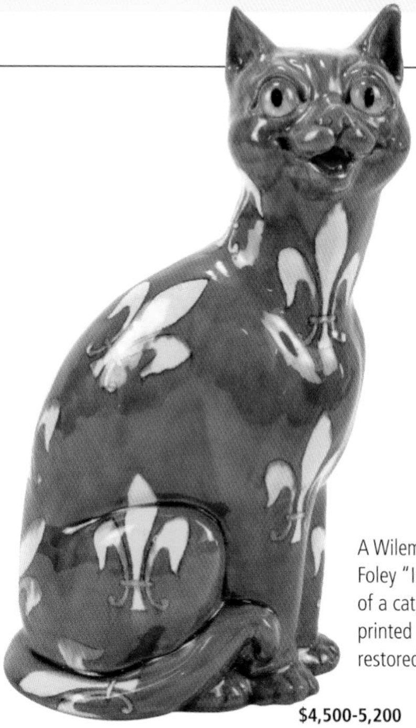

A Wileman & Co. rare Foley "Intarsio" model of a cat, with glass eyes, printed marks "3321," ears restored.

9¾in (24.5cm) high

$4,500-5,200 **APAR**

QUICK REFERENCE—WILEMAN & CO.

- **Based in Staffordshire, England, and known as Wileman & Co. until the early 20thC, as well as Foley Potteries, Shelley Potteries produced ceramics until 1966.**
- **Joseph Ball Shelley joined the firm in 1862, leaving his son Percy Shelley in charge after his death in 1896. The company became known for its Art Deco fine bone china teaware.**
- **Percy Shelley took on ceramic designer Frederick Rhead as art director in 1896.**
- **Rhead produced the "Intarsio" and "Urbato" ranges of decorative earthenware before leaving the company in 1905. Rhead was succeeded by Walter Slater and, by 1914, the company was moving into the production of dinnerware.**
- **In 1925, Percy Shelley trademarked the name Shelley, after failing to trademark Foley years previously.**
- **In the 1920s, illustrator Hilda Cowham designed a range of nursery ware for the company, depicting children playing and seaside scenes. Another illustrator, Mabel Lucie Attwell, joined Shelley Potteries in 1926, producing designs featuring children, the "Boo Boo" elves, and animals.**
- **In the 1930s, Shelley stopped producing earthenware to focus on fine bone china. Shelley Potteries changed its name to Shelley China in 1965 and traded until 1966, when it was bought out by the Allied English Potteries.**

A Shelley Art Deco preserve jar, "Melody" pattern.

4¼in (11cm) high

$50-60 **PSA**

A pair of Foley "Intarsio" vases, designed by Frederick Rhead, pattern no.3159, printed factory marks on base.

12¼in (31cm) high

$850-950 **WW**

A Shelley "Boo Boo" milk pitcher, by Mabel Lucie Attwell, printed mark.

6in (15cm) high

$90-120 **FLD**

A Shelley luster ginger jar, designed by Walter Slater, unmarked, wear and scratches.

13in (33cm) high

$120-160 **WW**

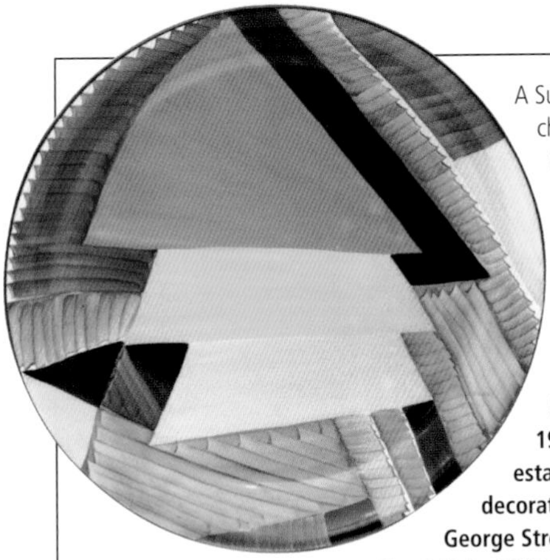

A Susie Cooper wall charger, Grays Pottery Galleon mark.

Susie Cooper (1902-95) studied at the Burslem School of Art before joining AE Gray & Co. in 1922. By 1929, Cooper had established a ceramic decoration company at George Street Pottery in Tunstall. By 1932, she was designing her own shapes, produced by Wood & Sons, in Staffordshire, where she had her own production unit called Crown Works.

1930s *15½in (39.5cm) wide*

$1,250-1,450 FLD

An Art Nouveau Spencer Edge pottery ewer, printed factory mark.

10in (25.5cm) high

$130-190 WW

A Spode cup, commemorative of Great Britain's entry into the Common Market, limited edition no.341 of 500, with certificate signed by Lord Harlech, in a fitted case.

$80-100 CHOR

A plate, printed "by Susie Cooper" mark.

1930s *8in (20.5cm) diam*

$300-400 FLD

A Wiener Werkstätte earthenware figurine, by Michael Powolny, impressed marks.

8in (20.5cm) long

$900-1,050 DUK

An earthenware "Sherwood Forest" wall plaque, hand painted and signed "UKC Wallace," in gilt frame.

14½in (37cm) high

$60-90 PSA

A 19thC Yorkshire-type Toby jug, the handle formed as a ship's figurehead, painted "2G1 Black" on the base.

10¼in (26cm) high

$400-450 FLD

An early-20thC Continental figurine of a dog, with "Votes For Women" molded on the base, unmarked.

3¼in (8.5cm) high

$160-210 FLD

A French 20thC Art Deco earthenware group.

11¾in (30cm) high

$190-260 BELL

A Czechoslovakian wall mask, model no.1172, printed and molded marks.

10in (25.5cm) high

$210-260 **SWO**

A Czechoslovakian double wall mask, model no.15187, printed and molded mark, crack to back, some minor paint flakes.

11¾in (30cm) high

$210-260 **SWO**

A Czechoslovakian wall mask, modeled as a female jester, printed "Czechoslovakia," impressed "15175."

1930s *7¼in (18.5cm) high*

$190-260 **FLD**

A Czechoslovakian wall mask, printed "Made in Czechoslovakia," impressed "15380," slight damage.

1930s *8¾in (22cm) high*

$130-190 **FLD**

A late-20thC Crown Devon hand-painted wall mask, "Dorothy Ann," printed mark.

11in (28cm) long

$45-60 **FLD**

QUICK REFERENCE—ROYAL DUX

- **In 1860, Eduard Eichler founded E. Eichler Thonwaren-Fabrik (which would become Duxer Porzellan-Manufaktur, then Royal Dux) in Dux, Bohemia, now Duchcov, Czech Republic.**
- **Eichler ran the company until his death in 1887.**
- **By the late 19thC/early 20thC, the firm was focusing on porcelain statues, figurines, Art Nouveau busts, masks, and vases.**
- **Production was interrupted by the two world wars, with the company struggling financially. However, it maintained its popularity. Royal Dux is now a member of the Czech Porcelain Group.**

A Goebel wall mask, modeled as a female with side glancing eyes, impressed crown mark "FX 61/2," slight damage.

1930s *6¾in (17cm) high*

$160-230 **FLD**

A Keramos Pottery wall mask, designed by Stephan Dakon, model no.2058, stamped and printed "Keramos Wien."

12¾in (32.5cm) high

$400-500 **SWO**

A Royal Dux wall mask, printed mark, impressed "CZECHOSLOVAKIA" and illegible number.

1930s *6¼in (16cm) high*

$400-450 **FLD**

QUICK REFERENCE—STUDIO POTTERY

- **The term "studio pottery" is used to describe pieces made by the pottery owner or by others under his or her supervision. Studio potteries are typically small in size. Early studio pottery-type establishments were founded in the 19thC.**
- **Each piece can be both handmade and hand decorated. Many designs hark back to traditional pottery or techniques, such as slipware glazes, or Asian designs, particularly from China and Japan. Much is derived from the pioneering work of Bernard Leach (1887-1979) and Shoji Hamada (1894-1978). Leach's and Hamada's influence continues to be felt today.**
- **The most important, often valuable, work was made by a first generation of studio potters, including Leach and his family, Hamada, Lucie Rie (1902-95), and Hans Coper (1920-81).**
- **The work of a second generation, such as Alan Caiger-Smith MBE (b.1930) and Michael Cardew (1901-83), is also highly collected. In some cases, their works are perceived as the "antiques of the future." Many contemporary potters, such as Grayson Perry (b.1966), use pottery to convey a message.**
- **Look on the base of a studio pot for an impressed, printed, painted, or incised mark, which may be in the form of a motif, monogram, or signature. It will help to identify the potter and may help to date the pot. Always look for skill and quality in terms of potting, form, and overall design.**

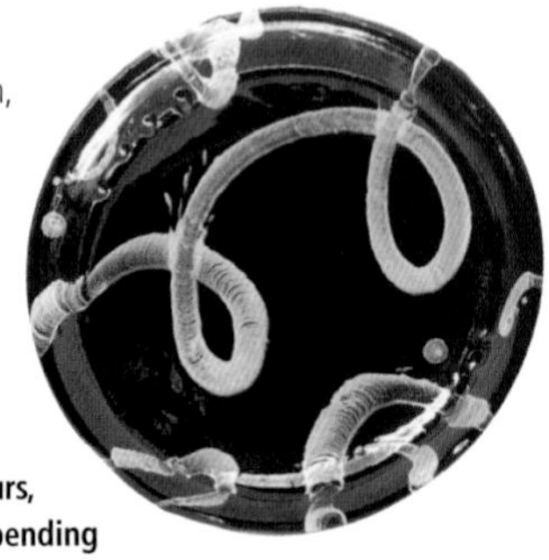

A large platter, by Dylan Bowen, slip decorated earthenware.

Dylan Bowen makes slip-decorated earthenware using both traditional and contemporary materials and techniques. The clay can be thrown, hand built, carved, or assembled. Dylan then pours, trails, or brushes on slips, depending on what is suggested by the form. He aims to capture some of the spontaneity and action of the making process in the finished work. Dylan lives and works in Oxfordshire, England, and is a Fellow of the Craft Potters Association.

17¼in (44cm) diam

$400-450 FLD

A Winchcombe Pottery earthenware wall vase or pocket, by Michael Cardew, impressed seals on base.

ca. 1930-40 *9in (23cm) high*

$160-230 ROS

An Aldermaston Pottery tin-glazed pottery bowl, by Alan Caiger-Smith MBE, printed factory mark, painted monogram, date mark.

1961 *18in (47cm) diam*

$950-1,100 WW

An Aldermaston pottery red luster bowl, by Alan Caiger-Smith MBE, painted mark, date code, a few minor pits in glaze.

The Aldermaston Pottery operated in Berkshire, England, from 1955-2006. It was founded by Alan Caiger-Smith MBE, who studied ceramics at Central School of Arts and Crafts in London, and was joined a year later by Geoffrey Eastop (1921-2014).

1983 *11in (28cm) diam*

$1,600-2,100 DN

A large stoneware crock jar and cover, by Richard Batterham (b.1936), with a celadon-green ash glaze, unsigned, incised "WF" to base, applied paper label numbered 30, small chips.

15½in (39.5cm) high

$950-1,100 WW

A stoneware casserole dish and cover, by Michael Cardew, brush detailing to a cream ground, impressed marks on base, slight blemishes to glaze.

7in (18cm) high

$700-850 CHOR

QUICK REFERENCE—PETER BEARD

- **Peter Beard obtained a degree in Industrial and Furniture Design at Ravensbourne College of Art, London and, on graduating, immediately began his career in ceramics. He has been working professionally since 1973 and, during his career, has taken part in many one-person shows and group exhibitions around the world. Beard's work is represented in many public and private collections and he has held masterclasses in many countries. Beard is a Fellow of the Craft Potters Association and is currently serving on its council as well as serving a three-year period as the Chair of Ceramic Art London. He has been granted various international awards and been invited to partake in residencies in several countries, including the USA, Japan, and Hungary.**

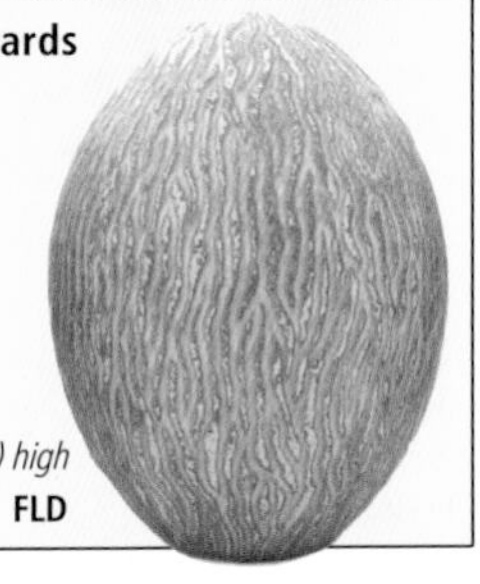

A porcelain vessel, by Peter Beard.

8¾in (22cm) high

$950-1,100 FLD

An owl figurine, produced by Cinque Ports, Rye.

When Richard and Susan Parkinson closed their pottery in 1963; the molds were purchased by George Gray of Cinque Ports Pottery. Most of these molds are believed to have been destroyed.

ca. 1960s

$190-260 **FLD**

A late-20thC to early-21stC wood-fired globular jar, by Nic Collins, signed on base.

19¾in (50cm) high

$400-500 **ROS**

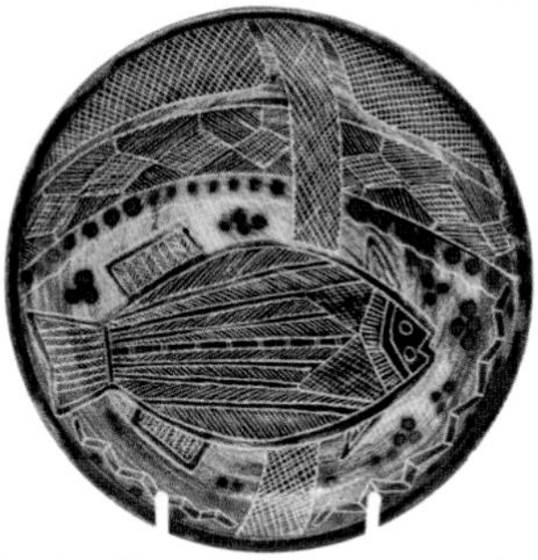

A saucer dish, designed by Carl Cooper (1912-66), with an aboriginal design of a fish, with earth glazes, signed and dated.

1954 *6¾in (17cm) diam*

$260-390 **HAN**

A porcelain vase, by Joanna Constantinidis (1927-2000), in a pale cleadon glaze with cobalt blue swirl, impressed seal mark, hairline crack.

7¼in (18.5cm) high

$1,050-1,150 **WW**

A stoneware vase, by Hans Coper, glazed with iron manganese on rim and white slips on body, impressed seal mark.

5¼in (13.5cm) high

$23,000-29,000 **WW**

A large vase, by Tony Dasent, with slip decoration, makers mark.

14½in (37cm) high

$190-260 **BELL**

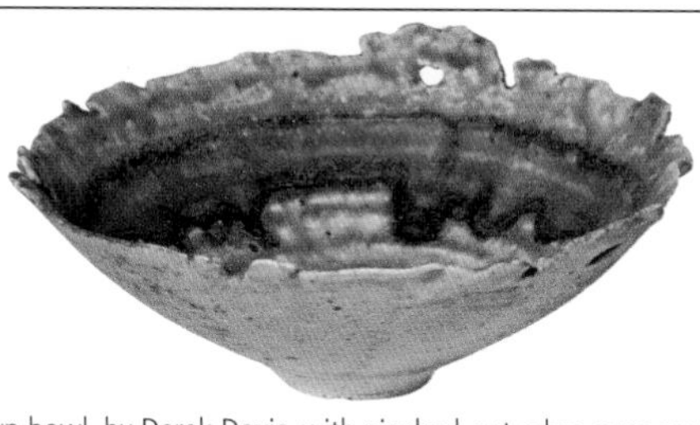

A thrown bowl, by Derek Davis, with pinched-out edge, copper with barium and ash glaze, signed.

1980s *7in (18cm) diam*

$500-600 **BELL**

A lidded celadon glazed porcelain jar, by Edmund de Waal (b.1964), on a wooden base, impressed marks, lid restored.

ca. 1998 *12¼in (31cm) high*

$2,900-3,900 **ROS**

A Winchcombe Pottery stoneware vase, by Ray Finch, with Tenmoku glaze.

13¾in (35cm) high

$190-260 CHOR

A high-fired stoneware flask, by Robert Fournier.

13in (33cm) high

$260-320 BELL

A late-20thC David Frith dish, with a brown wave and linear design, twin seal mark.

14½in (37cm) wide

$230-290 FLD

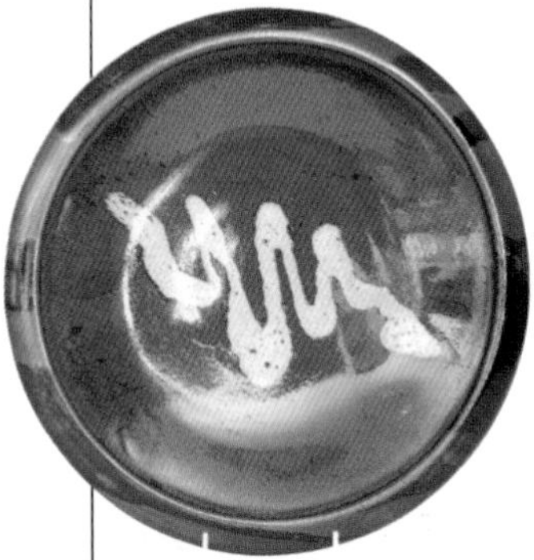

A late-20thC David Frith studio pottery shallow dish, with a brown tenmoku border edge, twin seal mark.

12½in (32cm) diam

$300-400 FLD

A stoneware vase, by Henry Hammond (1914-89), with a celadon glaze, painted in rust with a willow tree design, impressed seal mark, some restoration.

1990 *9in (23cm) high*

$500-650 WW

QUICK REFERENCE—ADAM FREW

- **Adam Frew's work centers on the potters wheel. Traditional Eastern forms inspire him, but spontaneity as a means of personal expression is key to his work. The exuberant action of throwing is enhanced by a continued experimentation through process, form, and color. Frew's mark-making is related to form, the process of making or a personal narrative. While studying at Belfast Art College, Frew spent time at the historic Winchcombe Pottery as well as a year working for Judy Makela on the Finnish island Aland. Upon graduating, he undertook a two-year apprenticeship with Lisa Hammond at her Greenwich-based pottery, where he gained the experience to set out on his own. Frew works in his studio on the north coast of Northern Ireland. He was most recently invited to exhibit and demonstrate at the Mungyeong International Ceramics Festival in South Korea. His work is in several major collections, including the Mungyeong Ceramic Musuem, the Univeristy of Ulster, and the Arts Council of Northern Ireland.**

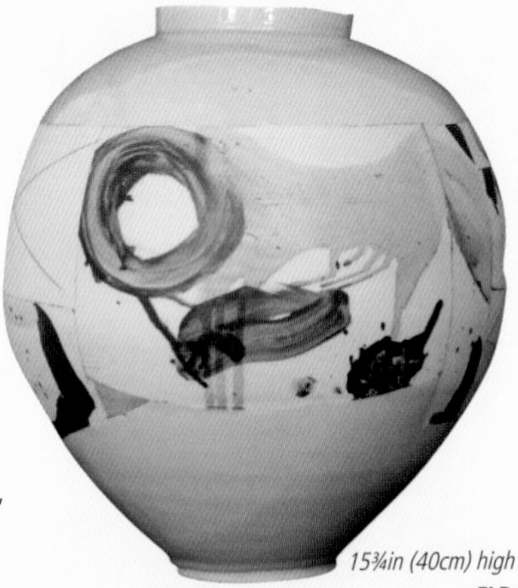

A "Pot with Mint Foot" porcelain vessel, by Adam Frew.

15¾in (40cm) high

$1,050-1,150 FLD

A "Small Round Pot," carved raku, by Ashraf Hanna, handbuilt.

7in (18cm) diam

$850-950 FLD

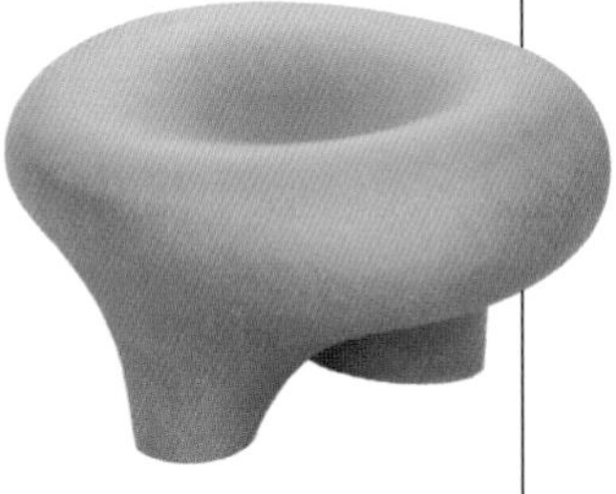

A "Bowl Form" hand-built vessel, by Ashraf Hanna, surface treatment terra sigillata slips.

15¾in (40cm) wide

$1,600-1,900 FLD

A "Disc with Blue Wave" raku, by Peter Hayes.

Peter Hayes creates sculptures using ceramics, bronze, glass, marble, and stone from his studio on Bath's Cleveland Bridge. During his career, he has created commissions for office spaces, hotels, yachts, and private homes. His work has been exhibited globally. Having lived and traveled in Africa and India, he is naturally drawn to the shapes of artifacts and objects from other cultures and other times but that remain timeless.

19in (48.5cm) high

$1,050-1,150 **FLD**

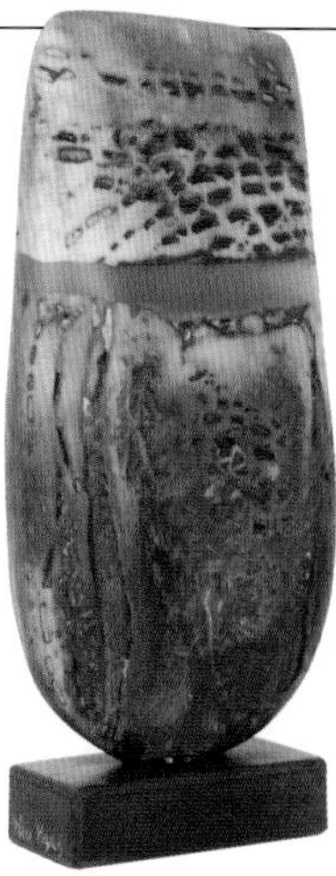

A "Bowl with Disc and Blue Wave" raku, by Peter Hayes.

10¾in (27.5cm) high

$500-650 **FLD**

A Margaret "Margi" Hine (1927-87) earthenwarе platter, slip decorated with a flying angel, signed and dated.

1951 *15½in (39cm) wide*

$900-1,050 **WW**

A Margaret "Margi" Hine "Girl on a Horse" stoneware sculture, painted signature, minor professional restoration.

17in (43cm) high

$6,500-8,000 **WW**

A porcelain bowl, by Don Jones, painted cobalt blue with pink, gold, and white stripes.

18¼in (46cm) diam

$500-650 **CHOR**

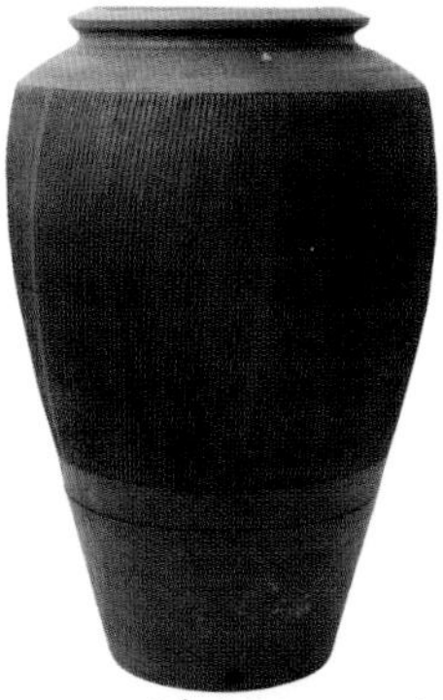

A monumental stoneware garden vase, by Jenifer Jones (b.1940), impressed seal mark, garden patinantion.

25½in (65cm) high

$9,000-10,500 **WW**

A contemporary conical bowl, by Tony Laverick, initialed, dated.

2009 *6in (15cm) diam*

$170-230 **FLD**

A large handbuilt stoneware vase, by Janet Leach, the form having open cracks, multiple incisions, and marks.

By repute, this was the funerary jar that Janet Leach made to commemorate the life of her husband Bernard Leach.

ca. 1980s *11½in (29cm) high*

$400-450 **ROS**

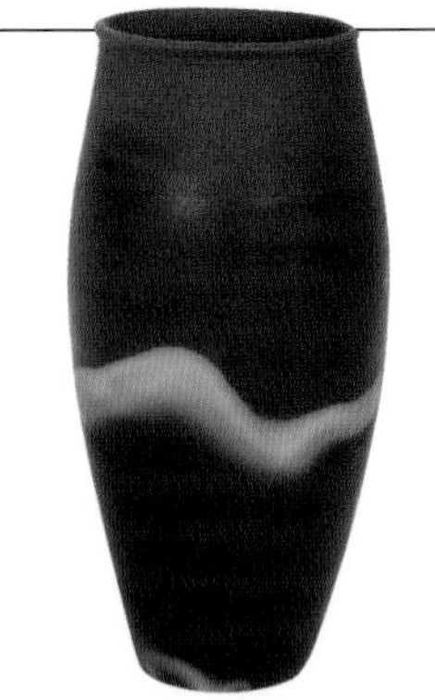

A Muchelney Pottery wood-fired burnished stoneware vase, by John Leach, decorated with a smoked, wave design, stamped marks on base.

9in (23cm) high

$160-230 WW

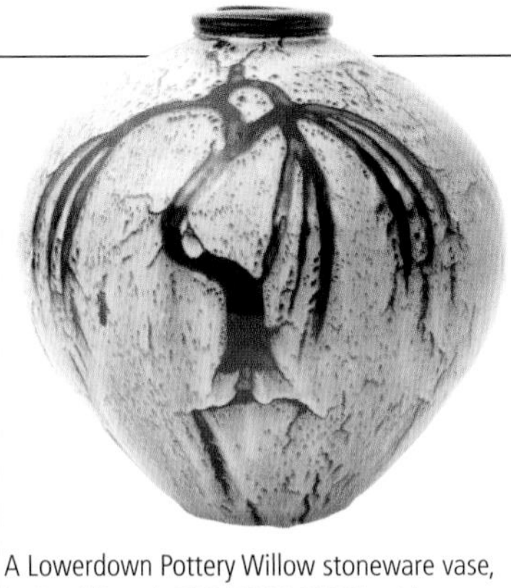

A Lowerdown Pottery Willow stoneware vase, by David Leach OBE (1911-2005), with a tenmoku willow tree, under thick and running Dolomite glaze, impressed seal mark.

11in (28cm) high

$2,600-3,200 WW

An Ainstable Pottery stoneware bottle vase, by Jim Malone, incised with willow tree motif, glazed in hakeme, under a celadon glaze, impressed seal marks.

16in (40.5cm) high

$500-650 WW

An early pottery flowerhead wall plaque, by Kate Malone (b.1959), impressed seal marks and date.

1933 *8¼in (21cm) diam*

$400-500 WW

A stoneware sculpture on a slate base, by John Maltby, "Three Figures and a Wall," signed and titled on base, artist's paper label, a small chip on the slate base, which is in manufacture.

John Maltby (b.1936) studied pottery with David Leach from 1962-63 before founding his own pottery at Stoneshill, near Crediton, Devon, in 1964. He focused on producing unique pieces that are artistic objects. His influences are rooted in modern, abstract art. Maltby was inspired by abstract paintings by St Ives School artists Ben Nicholson, Christopher Wood, Terry Frost, and Alfred Wallis. Pablo Picasso and Paul Klee are also influences, as is the Cornish landscape.

10¼in (26cm) high

$1,150-1,450 WW

A tall spade vase, by John Maltby, "Small Suffolk Seaport," painted on one side with houses, the reverse with a boat, painted "Maltby" on base.

1991 *8in (20.5cm) high*

$2,600-3,200 WW

A John Maltby stoneware sculpture, painted with graveyard crosses, signed.

Produced in a limited edition of two for an exhibition at the New Craftsman Gallery, St Ives. It is believed this example was kept by John Maltby.

22in (56cm) high

$5,200-6,500 WW

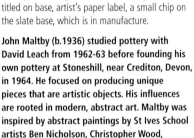

A contemporary sculpture, by John Maltby, entitled on the base "Bird and Five Fish," seal mark on the side, hand-written title, dated.

2011 *16½in (42cm) high*

$800-900 FLD

A cut-sided stoneware bottle vase, by William "Bill" Marshall (1923-2007), in a pitted celadon green ash glaze, impressed seal mark.

19in (48.5cm) high

$1,700-2,100 **WW**

QUICK REFERENCE—PICASSO POTTERY

- **In the latter part of his life, Pablo Picasso (1881-1973) became interested in creating pottery. In 1949, he met and began working with Georges and Suzanne Ramié, owners of the Madoura pottery.**
- **Producing more than 3,500 ceramic designs, Picasso combined techniques of painting, sculpture, and printmaking. Human and animal faces appear frequently on his pieces. His second wife, Jacqueline Roque, also appeared on and inspired his ceramic works.**
- **The pieces were not only decorative, but functional, too. Picasso used his plates and bowls in his home.**
- **Each piece is marked or stamped, however, these changed over time. The edition number also appears on some pieces.**

A Madoura "Pichet Têtes" earthenware pitcher, by Pablo Picasso, from a limited edition of 500, stamped and marked.

designed 1956 *4¾in (12cm) high*

$3,900-5,200 **DN**

A swollen cylindrical stoneware vase, by Katharine Pleydell-Bouverie, with incised vertical petal motif, impressed seal mark, painted glaze mark.

6¾in (17cm) high

$450-500 **WW**

A stoneware vase, by Katharine Pleydell-Bouverie, impressed seal, glaze codes on base.

ca. 1930-40 *7in (18cm) high*

$260-320 **ROS**

QUICK REFERENCE—LAURENCE MCGOWAN

- **Laurence McGowan was born in Salisbury, England, in 1942. After an earlier career in land surveying, he resolved to become a potter. He received workshop training, first with Pru Greene at Alvingham Pottery, Lincolnshire, and then with Alan Caiger-Smith at Aldermaston. In 1979, he returned to his native Wiltshire and established his own workshop at Collingbourne Kingston.**
- **Trained in the traditional majolica or in-glaze technique of pottery decoration, McGowan now applies this knowledge to enhance his thrown stoneware pots with ever-changing brushwork patterns distilled from plant and animal forms.**

A Laurence McGowan earthenware owl, tin glazed and painted, signed marks.

8¼in (21cm) high

$400-500 **DUK**

A Fulham Pottery tile, by John Piper (1903-92), with a stylized face in green, impressed Fulham Pottery mark.

6¼in (16cm) square

$210-260 **HAN**

A porcelain bottle vase, by Dame Lucie Rie, with sgrafitto or "knitted" decoration, impressed personal seal.

Having studied at the Vienna School of Arts and Crafts, Lucie Rie (1902-95) emigrated to the UK in 1938. She set up a studio in Paddington in London and, during World War II, produced ceramic buttons for the fashion industry. She was joined in the studio by Hans Coper in 1946. Initially, the studio produced functional tableware, with Rie moving on to make stoneware and porcelain, including bowls, urns, and vases. She became known for her decorative yet functional domestic ceramics, as well as the delicate appearance of her pieces contrasting to the durable material from which they are made.

9½in (24cm) high

$29,000-36,000 **BE**

CERAMICS

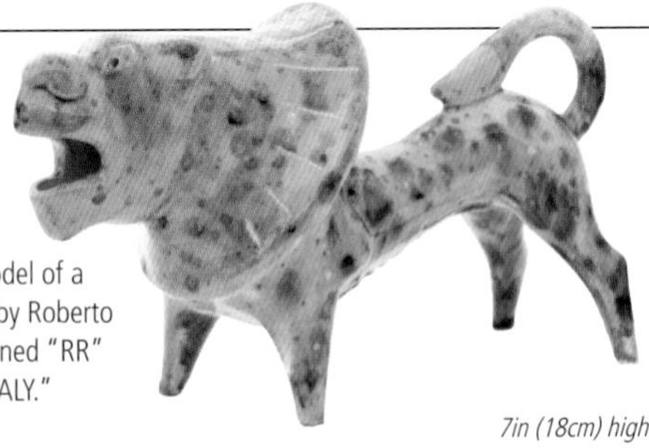

An Italian model of a stylized lion, by Roberto Rigon, tube lined "RR" mark and "ITALY."

7in (18cm) high

$190-260 **FLD**

A porcelain vase, by Julian Stair (b.1955), impressed seal mark.

8¼in (21cm) high

$1,900-2,600 **WW**

A porcelain bowl, by Alan Spencer-Green (1932-2003), incised with leaves, unsigned.

7in (18cm) diam

$190-260 **SWO**

A flared stoneware bowl, by William Staite Murray (1881-1962), with abstract brushed and resist decoration, impressed seal oo foot.

ca. 1930 *3¾in (9.5cm) high*

$400-500 **ROS**

QUICK REFERENCE—CLARE SUTCLIFFE

- **Clare Sutcliffe (1943-2019) spent 27 years making traditional wood-fired stoneware pots. She trained at Wenford Bridge Pottery, Cornwall, as Seth Cardew's first student and worked in the Leach/Cardew tradition. She made her own glazes from different wood ashes and local stream clays, and fired her pots in a wood-burning kiln to 2,375°F with a firing cycle of up to 20 hours. During the course of the glaze firing, additional wood ash was drawn on the flame through the kiln, where it settled on the pots, melting to create soft colors and incidental effects, making each pot unique.**
- **Sutcliffe had an earlier career as an actress appearing in such films as *The Ploughman's Lunch*, *I Start Counting*, and *The Best Pair of Legs in the Business*, but was regularly seen on British television in *Play for Today*, *Coronation Street*, *Z Cars*, *Softly Softly*, and *On the Buses*.**

A stoneware globular vase, by William Staite Murray, impressed seal on side of foot.

ca. 1930-40 *6½in (16.5cm) high*

$350-400 **ROS**

A rimmed bowl, by Clare Sutcliffe, with reed design and copper red glaze, maker's mark.

12½in (32cm) diam

$190-260 **BELL**

A vase, by Clare Sutcliffe, with shino glaze, maker's mark.

7½in (19cm) high

$160-210 **BELL**

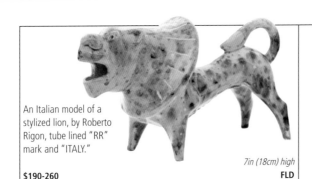

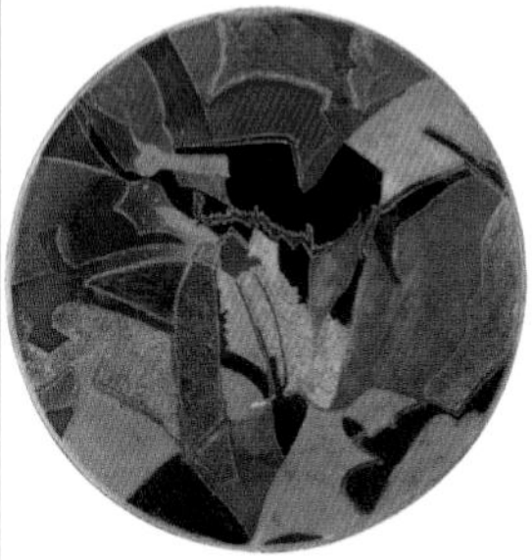

An earthenware bowl, by Sutton Taylor (b.1943), on narrow foot, paper label no.44, with a hairline crack.

18¼in (46.5cm) diam

$1,150-1,450 **WW**

QUICK REFERENCE—MARVEL

- Marvel Comics' precursor, Timely Comics, began in October 1939. Its first publication was called *Marvel Comics no.1* and featured the Human Torch. Several other superheroes were added to the company's repertoire in the 1940s, including Captain America and Miss Marvel—this was the Golden Age of comic books. In 1951, Timely Comics became Atlas Magazines. In the early 1960s, Atlas Magazines became Marvel Comics.
- Many Marvel comics were created by Marvel's head writer and editor, Stan Lee, and illustrated by artist Jack Kirby. In the 1960s, they worked together to create famous superhero comics, such as *The Fantastic Four, The Incredible Hulk, The Amazing Spider-Man*, and *The X-Men*. The Silver Age refers to comics produced between ca. 1956 and ca. 1969. In 2009, the Walt Disney Company bought Marvel's parent company. The success of the Marvel film franchise has pushed up prices for key comic book issues.

The AMAZING SPIDER-MAN, "RETURN of DOCTOR OCTOPUS!," volume 1, no.11, Silver Age, edge wear and creases, yellowed.
1963
$130-190 VEC

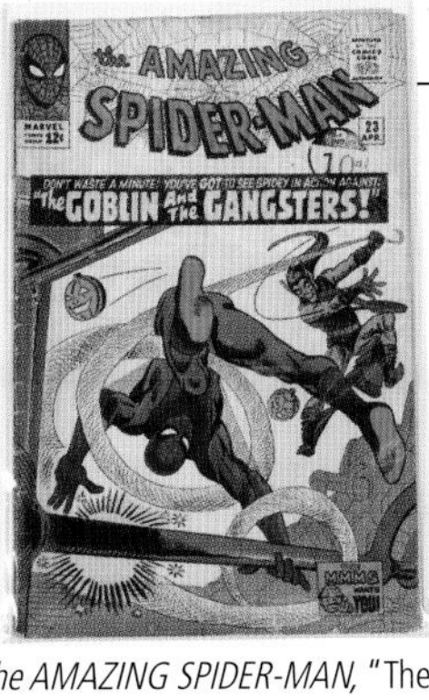

The AMAZING SPIDER-MAN, "The GOBLIN And The GANGSTERS!," volume 1, no.23, Silver Age, early Green Goblin appearance, edge wear tears and creases, yellowed.
1963
$100-130 VEC

The AMAZING SPIDER-MAN, "SPIDER-MAN GOES MAD!," volume 1, no.24, Silver Age, edge wear and creases, yellowed.
1963
$100-130 VEC

The AMAZING SPIDER-MAN, "THE MAN IN THE CRIME-MASTER'S MASK!," volume 1, no.26, Silver Age, edge wear and creases, yellowed.
1963
$80-90 VEC

The AMAZING SPIDER-MAN, "THE THRILL OF THE HUNT!," volume 1, no.34, Silver Age, edge wear and creases, yellowed.
$60-80 VEC

The AMAZING SPIDER-MAN, "THE SINISTER SHOCKER!," volume 1, no.46, Silver Age, edge wear and tears, creases, front page is creased top to bottom, yellowed.
1963
$100-120 VEC

The AMAZING SPIDER-MAN, "RHINO ON THE RAMPAGE!," volume 1, no.43, Silver Age, edge wear and tears, creases, front page is creased top to bottom, yellowed.
1963
$100-130 VEC

The AMAZING SPIDER-MAN, "WOULD'JA BELIEVE ... KRAVEN THE HUNTER!," volume 1, no.47, Silver Age, edge wear and tears, creases, yellowed.
1963
$80-90 VEC

The AMAZING SPIDER-MAN, "SPIDEY and the GREEN GOBLIN...BOTH UNMASKED!," volume 1, no.39, Silver Age, edge wear and creases, yellowed.
1963
$160-190 VEC

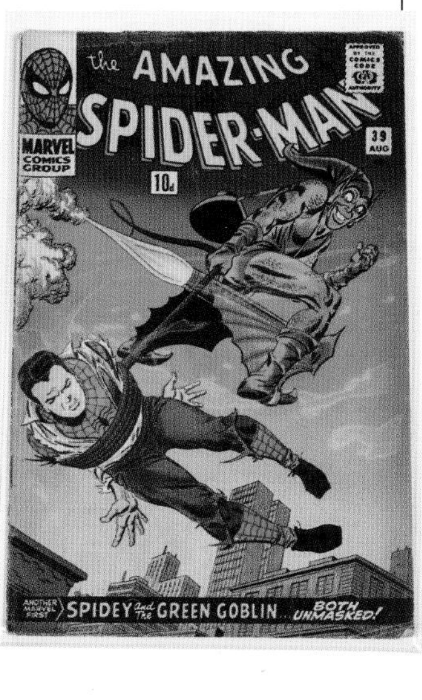

The AMAZING SPIDER-MAN, "SPIDEY SAVES THE DAY!," volume 1, no.40, Silver Age, edge wear and creases, yellowed.
1963
$100-130 **VEC**

The AMAZING SPIDER-MAN, "THE VULTURE'S BACK ... AND SPIDEY'S GOT 'IM," volume 1, no.48, "Silver Age," edge wear and tears, creases, yellowed.
1963
$80-90 **VEC**

TALES OF SUSPENSE, no.48, with story by Stan Lee, featuring the first appearance of "Iron Man's" new armour drawn by Steve Ditko, UK variant.
1963
$60-80 **AST**

FANTASTIC FOUR, "AMONG US HIDE ... THE INHUMANS!," volume 1, no.45, Silver Age, script by Stan Lee, cover pencils by Jack Kirby, inks by Joe Sinnott, first appearance of the Inhumans, edge wear and tears, creases, yellowed.
1964
$120-140 **VEC**

Fantastic Four, "THOSE WHO WOULD DESTROY US!," volume 1, no.46, Silver Age, script by Stan Lee, pencils by Jack Kirby, inks by Joe Sinnott, second appearance of the Inhumans, wear and tears, creases, yellowed.
1964
$80-90 **VEC**

THE MIGHTY THOR, "WHOM THE GODS WOULD DESTROY!," volume 1, no.126, Silver Age, title previously *Journey Into Mystery With Thor*, script by Stan Lee, pencils by Jack Kirby, inks by Vince Colletta, wear and tears, creases, yellowed.
1964
$60-80 **VEC**

THE AVENGERS, no.4, featuring Jack Kirby cover art of Captain America joining the Avengers in his first Silver Age appearance, wear on the spine and a small back cover section missing, UK variant.
1964
$180-210 **AST**

TALES OF SUSPENSE, no.49, featuring Iron Man drawn by Steve Ditko, first X-Men crossover, first Avengers crossover, and second appearance of The Watcher, UK pence variant.
1964
$80-90 **AST**

Fantastic Four, "THE COMING OF GALACTUS!," volume 1, no.46, Silver Age, script by Stan Lee, pencils by Jack Kirby, inks by Joe Sinnott, first appearance of Galactus and the Silver Surfer, wear and tears, creases, yellowed.
1964
$230-290 **VEC**

The AMAZING SPIDER-MAN, "RETURN of DOCTOR OCTOPUS!," no.11, featuring the first appearance of Bennett Brant and the second appearance of Doctor Octopus, art by Steve Ditko, UK variant.
1964
$130-180 AST

The AMAZING SPIDER-MAN, "UNMASKED BY DR. OCTOPUS!", no.12, UK variant.
1964
$120-140 AST

The AMAZING SPIDER-MAN, "SPIDEY BATTLES DAREDEVIL!," no.16, art by Steve Ditko, UK variant.
1964
$100-130 AST

The AMAZING SPIDER-MAN, "KRAVEN, THE HUNTER!," no.15, art by Steve Ditko first appearance of Kraven the Hunter, first mention of Mary Jane Watson, UK variant.
1964
$230-290 AST

HERE COMES ...DAREDEVIL, THE MAN WITHOUT FEAR!, no.1, the first appearance of Daredevil, written by Stan Lee, illustrated by Bill Everett, UK cover version, wear on the edges, slight mark above Daredevil's arm, tear on the back cover, the pages have been chipped.
1964
$650-800 AST

STRANGE TALES OF SUSPENSE, SECRETS OF THE UNKNOWN, no.38, with art by Jack Kirby, featuring Thor and the lead story from *Journey into Mystery* no.84.
1966
$30-40 AST

THE INVINCIBLE IRON MAN, no.1, featuring the origin of Iron Man, with art by Gene Colan, UK cover stamped.
1968
$130-160 AST

EXCITING COMICS, no.46, with cover art by Alex Schomburg, Golden Age, cover is loose.
1946
$60-80 **AST**

THE BEANO, no.452, including the first appearance of Dennis the Menace, duotone illustrations, original color printed wrappers.

***The Beano* is the longest running British children's comic and is published by DC Thomson. The first issue was published in the 1930s and, by the 1950s, its weekly circulation was nearly two million copies. The 1950s also saw the introduction of new characters, such as Roger the Dodger, The Bash Street Kids, and Minnie the Minx. In 2015, the 3,800th issue of *The Beano* was published.**
1951
$350-400 **LOCK**

THE BEANO BOOK, personalized inscriptions on inside cover, some minor marks on the covers.
1951
$190-260 **LOC**

THE FLASH, "THE BIG FREEZE!," no.114, Silver Age, cover edges are worn with some tears, creasing, yellowed.

DC began in the 1930s as National Allied Publications, founded by Malcolm Wheeler-Nicholson. Following the company changing hands and a series of mergers, the name "DC Comics" was officially adopted in 1977. *Superman* appeared in 1938 and *Batman* in 1939. Today, DC's parent company, DC Entertainment, is a subsidiary of Time Warner Inc.
1960
$45-60 **VEC**

THE FLASH, "INVASION of the CLOUD CREATURES!," no.111, Silver Age, cover edges worn, tears, back page has tape repair, creasing, yellowed.
1960
$40-45 **VEC**

BATMAN, no.181, with art by Carmine Infantino, first appearance of Poison Ivy, with centerfold pinup page of Batman and Robin.
1966
$350-400 **AST**

DETECTIVE COMICS, no.359, first appearance of new-look Bat-Girl (Barbara Gordon), UK cover stamped.
1967
$350-400 **AST**

A French early-19thC papier-mâché doll, with painted hair and features, the rigid body with leather arms, stitched fingers and separate thumbs, with original clothing, all embroidered in red with "VI," and with a period dress.

ca. 1835 *14¼in (36cm) high*

$400-450 **LC**

A mid-19thC papier-mâché doll, with molded hair and painted features, fabric body with painted wood lower limbs, in original dress.

10in (25.5cm) high

$500-600 **HT**

An English 19thC poured-wax doll, with implanted hair, glass eyes, smiling mouth, with a fabric body and leather lower arms.

ca. 1865 *17in (43cm) high*

$300-400 **LC**

A poured-wax child doll, inserted hair in ringlets, stuffed body with wax limbs, Princess-line silk dress with bustle and train, underclothes and brown shoes, hair sparse on top of head, some fraying to silk, a later hat.

1870s *24½in (62cm) high*

$1,050-1,150 **SAS**

A French 19thC bisque-head fashion doll, with fixed blue eyes, closed mouth, and pierced ears, with a leather body, a dress and hat, marked "H5," impressed "6."

Bisque (or biscuit) is porcelain or earthenware that has been fired but not glazed. Features of bisque dolls appear realistic. Bisque-head dolls were manufactured in Germany in the 1850s, selling throughout Europe. From the 1860s to the 1890s, French bisque dolls became popular.

15½in (39.5cm) high

$1,050-1,150 **LC**

A French fashion doll, in the style of Barrois, with glass eyes, closed mouth, and later mohair wig, on wooden articulated body, in 1870s-style walking dress, the head incised "4," green stamp on leather collar attaching shoulder to body reading "Poupee Passage de L'Opera Paris."

Madame Barrois was a maker of china and bisque dolls in Paris, France, active between 1844-77. In the late 1870s, the company was bought by Aristide M. Halopeau.

16in (40.5cm) high

$3,200-3,900 **MORP**

A French 19thC fashion doll, possibly by Barrois, with fixed eyes, painted closed mouth, and pierced ears, with a bisque shoulder plate and a leather body and arms, in a period clothing, marked on the side of each shoulder "00."

10in (25.5cm) high

$1,150-1,450 **LC**

A Bru Bébé bisque-head doll in the "Circle/Dot" style, with glass paperweight eyes, open mouth, and sheepskin wig, on original leather body with bisque forearms, the shoulder incised "4."

16in (40.5cm) high

$8,000-9,000 **MORP**

A DEP closed-mouth child doll, with fixed eyes, closed mouth, pierced ears, jointed papier-mâché French body, floral sprig printed dress, black velvet coat and matching hat, Ermin muff, pink corset, underclothes, and leather shoes.

19in (48.5cm) high

$1,900-2,600 **SAS**

A Simon & Halbig for Heinrich Handwerck "Bébé Cosmopolite" doll, with weighted eyes, open mouth, and jointed composition body, with a Bébé Cosmopolite box, probably original, marked "Simon & Halbig, Heinrich Handwerck, 2½."

21in (53.5cm) high

$600-650 **LC**

A Simon & Halbig for Heinrich Handwerck child doll, with sleeping eyes, pierced ears, synthetic wig, jointed composition body.

29½in (75cm) high

$400-450 **SAS**

A German Heinrich Handwerck/S. & H. bisque-head doll, with weighted glass eyes, real lashes, open mouth, upper teeth, pierced ears, on a fully jointed wood and composition body, with original clothing.

ca. 1910 *31½in (80cm) high*

$500-650 **C&T**

A German Imhoff bisque mechanical walking doll, patented 1899.

12in (30.5cm) high

$300-400 **BER**

QUICK REFERENCE—JUMEAU

- **Jumeau (1842-99) was founded near Paris, France, in the 1840s by Pierre François Jumeau (1811-95) and Louis-Desire Belton. It designed and manufactured high-end bisque dolls with detailed clothing.**
- **In 1855, Jumeau produced the first Bébé doll—a doll modeled as a little girl.**
- **The company's dolls were highly acclaimed, receiving medals at the 1851 London Great Exhibition and the 1878 Exposition Universelle. In 1875 Jumeau's son, Emile, took over the firm.**
- **Jumeau dolls remain popular with collectors today and those with original costumes in good condition can fetch high prices. In the 1890s, Jumeau joined Société Française de Fabrication de Bébés et Jouets.**

A French Jumeau doll, with glass paperweight eyes, pierced ears, jointed composition body, marked "Depose Tete Jumeau Bte SGDG 9."

19in (48.5cm) high

$800-900 **LC**

A French Jumeau doll, with open mouth, fixed eyes, pierced ears, jointed composition body, with contemporary clothing, marked "12."

27in (68.5cm) high

$700-850 **LC**

A Bébé Jumeau bisque-head doll, with fixed glass paperweight eyes, open mouth, and teeth, pierced ears, mohair wig, jointed composition limbs and body, marked "11," in original box with label and lid.

23in (58.5cm) high

$600-700 **HT**

A Jumeau kiss-throwing and walking doll, the bisque head with fixed eyes, open mouth with upper teeth, with pierced ears and composition body, with clothing and antique shoes, marked on the neck "8."

21in (53.5cm) high

$850-950 **LC**

A CLOSER LOOK AT A JUMEAU BÉBÉ

The doll has a pale bisque head with fixed blue eyes and closed mouth.

It has the original wig over a replaced cork pate.

The doll has a fully jointed body, with clothing and original leather Jumeau size 9 shoes.

It is marked in red "Tete Jumeau, Depose, SGDG, 9," and also stamped on the body in blue.

A Jumeau Bébé bisque-head doll.

20in (51cm) high

$3,200-3,900 **LC**

A Tete Jumeau bisque-head Bébé doll, with later wig, on a fully jointed wood and composition body, with marked size 11 Jumeau shoes, one firing line.

ca. 1890 *25in (63.5cm) high*

$700-850 **C&T**

A Kämmer & Reinhardt bisque-head doll, with glass sleeping eyes, open mouth and teeth, pierced ears, later blonde mohair wig, jointed composition limbs, and body, marked "K&R SIMON & HALBIG 70."

27in (68.5cm) high

$300-400 **HT**

A Jumeau small bisque-socket-head child doll, with glass eyes, mohair wig, on articulated body, in antique (if not original) silk and lace dress, the head stamped "Depose Tete Jumeau 5," the body stamped "Bébé Jumeau Paris," the shoes impressed "5 Paris Depose."

14½in (37cm) high

$3,200-3,900 **MORP**

A Simon & Halbig for Kämmer & Reinhardt child doll, with lashed sleeping eyes, pierced ears, mohair wig, jointed composition body, printed pink cotton body, dirty face.

Kämmer & Reinhardt (1886-ca. 1940) was founded in 1886 in Waltershausen, Germany, by designer Ernest Kämmer and entrepreneur Franz Reinhardt. Kammer designed the heads until his death in 1901, when Simon & Halbig took over production using Kämmer's designs. In 1909-14, Kämmer & Reinhardt produced popular character dolls, with painted eyes, closed mouths, and mohair wigs. The character child dolls are especially collectible.

20½in (52cm) high

$260-320 **SAS**

A Tete Jumeau Bébé no.11, with jointed papier mâché and wood body with blue ink stamp, restoration to head, chipping on fingers.

25in (63.5cm) high

$950-1,100 **SAS**

A Simon & Halbig for Kämmer & Reinhardt doll, with weighted eyes, open mouth, and pierced ears, marked "Simon & Halbig, K & R."

12½in (32cm) high

$190-260 **LC**

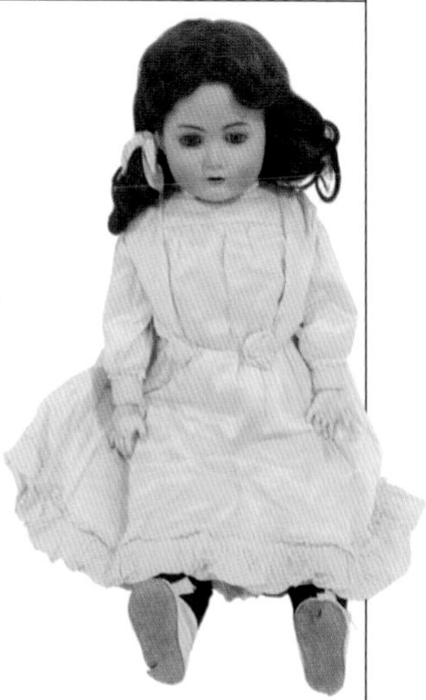

A Simon & Halbig for Kämmer & Reinhardt doll, with weighted eyes, open mouth with tongue, and pierced ears, marked "Simon & Halbig, K & R, 403, Germany."

25in (63.5cm) high

$300-400 **LC**

A Kestner bisque-head doll, with glass sleeping eyes and open mouth, with later mohair wig, marked "16 1/2 171."

Kestner & Co. was founded in 1816 in Thuringia, Germany, by Johannes Daniel Kestner. The company was later taken over by his grandson, Adolphe Kestner. It became known for its child dolls, with high-quality bisque heads, mohair wigs, and blown-glass sleeping eyes. The comparatively rare "200" series, produced ca. 1910, are especially sought after by collectors. Kestner dolls were distributed by George Borgfeldt in the USA. Kestner & Co. merged with Kämmer & Reinhardt in 1930.

ca. 1910 *32in (81.5cm) high*

$650-800 **HT**

A German bisque-head Asian doll, possibly Kestner, with glass sleeping eyes, open mouth and teeth, mohair wig, jointed composition limbs and body, marked "164 Germany 36."

14in (35.5cm) high

$850-950 **HT**

A Kestner bisque-head doll, with glass sleeping eyes, open mouth and teeth, mohair wig, marked "192."

31in (78.5cm) high

$1,150-1,300 **HT**

An Armand Marseille bisque-head doll, marked "AM, Germany."

Armand Marseille was founded in Thuringia, Germany, by Armand Marseille and was active between 1885 and 1930. The company manufactured bisque doll heads until the 1930s, also supplying other manufacturers. Armand Marseille merged with Koppelsdorf in 1919 to form the Koppelsdorf porcelain factory.

36in (91.5cm) high

$130-190 **JN**

An Armand Marseille bisque-head doll, with articulated body.

25in (63.5cm) high

$160-230 **JN**

An Armand Marseille "370" doll, with weighted eyes and open mouth, with original clothing and shoes, impressed marks "AM, 370, Dep."

20in (51cm) high

$160-210 **LC**

An Armand Marseille Oriental "Ellar" doll, with weighted eyes, closed mouth, and bent limb body, marked, "AM, Ellar, Germany, 2K."

10in (25.5cm) high

$190-260 **LC**

An Armand Marseille "390" walking doll, with fixed eyes and open mouth, with a mechanism to move the head as the legs move, impressed marks "390," "Armand Marseille," "Made in Germany."

23in (58.5cm) high

$180-230 **LC**

An Armand Marseille "390" doll, with weighted eyes and open mouth, impressed marks "Armand Marseille," "390," "12."

28in (71cm) high

$190-260 **LC**

A Porzellanfabrik Mengersgereuth bisque-head character doll, with glass sleeping eyes, open mouth and teeth, mohair wig, marked "P.M. 94 14."

$190-260 **HT**

A Bruno Schmidt bisque-head boy doll, with glass sleeping eyes, closed mouth, molded hair, jointed composition limbs and body, marked "2048."

21in (53.5cm) high

$500-600 **HT**

A Schoenau & Hoffmeister "PB Star" bisque-head doll, no.1909, size 7.5.

25in (63.5cm) high

$160-210 **JN**

An SFBJ Paris "301" bisque-head doll.

The Société Française de Fabrication de Bébés et Jouets (SFBJ) was formed in 1899, as an association of leading French doll manufacturers. It formed as a response to increasing competition from German doll manufacturers. SFBJ was based at the Jumeau factory. Despite incorporating highly acclaimed companies, such as Jumeau and Bru Jeune & Cie (1866-83), the need to keep costs down resulted in reduced quality. Character dolls, produced from ca. 1911, were of slightly better quality and proved more successful than the bébé dolls. Production ceased in ca. 1950.

26in (66cm) high

$190-260 **JN**

A large SFBJ, Paris "301" bisque-head doll, with white lace bonnet and dress.

$260-320 **JN**

An SFBJ Paris "60" doll, with weighted eyes, open mouth, and jointed composition body, marked "SFBJ, 60, Paris, 2/0."

15in (38cm) high

$190-260 **LC**

An SFBJ "60" Trouville fisherwoman, with sleeping eyes, mohair wig, pierced ears, jointed composition body, original costume, sabots with "TROUVILLE" written on them.

13½in (34.5cm) high

$300-350 **SAS**

A Simon & Halbig bisque-head doll, model no.121, with open-close eyes and jointed composition body in lace-edged dress.

Based in Thuringia, Simon & Halbig (ca. 1869-ca. 1930) produced bisque dolls and bisque doll parts, which they supplied to other manufacturers, such as Kämmer & Reinhardt and Jumeau. Simon & Halbig's early dolls has fixed glass eyes, closed mouths, and solid, domed heads. Their later dolls had open mouths and socket heads. The company was bought by Kämmer & Reinhardt in ca. 1920 and production continued until the early 1930s. The Simon & Halbig factory was then renamed Keramisches Werk Gräfenhain and production continued until 1943.

22½in (57cm) long

$190-260 **FLD**

A Simon & Halbig doll, with weighted eyes, open mouth, and pierced ears, marked "S & H, 1079, Dep, Germany, 9."

22in (56cm) high

$230-290 **LC**

A Simon & Halbig child doll, with sleeping eyes, mohair wig, jointed composition body, impressed "S & H H X I."

16in (40.5cm) high

$190-260 **SAS**

A Simon & Halbig bisque-head musical automaton doll, with glass eyes, open mouth and teeth, mohair wig, on a base with spinning top action, marked "SH 1300 DEP."

ca. 1900 *18in (45.5cm) high*

$1,300-1,800 **HT**

A British National Dolls "Dollie Walker" hard plastic doll, with original box.

1950s *21in (53.5cm) high*

$60-80 **VEC**

An early 20thC velvet and mohair golly doll, probably by Chad Valley.

11½in (29cm) long

$400-500 **WW**

QUICK REFERENCE—CELLULOID

- **Celluloid is a form of plastic made from camphor and cellulose nitrate. Companies in Japan (where camphor was relatively easily attainable from the native camphor trees), Germany, the USA (where celluloid was patented), France, and Italy used the material to make dolls. The Rhineland Rubber & Celluloid Co. (1873-ca. 1930) produced celluloid dolls from 1873. Kämmer & Reinhardt, Kestner & Co. and Jumeau followed suit. Celluloid was popular because it did not flake, however, it was highly flammable, had a tendency to crack, fade, or dent, and was difficult to restore.**

A Japanese celluloid walking doll, carrying a small baby doll in carriage while holding umbrella, with ringing bell and key-wound walking movemnet, with box.

9¼in (23.5cm) high

$1,100-1,250 **BER**

A Character Novelty Co. "Mickey Mouse" doll, with original corduroy pants, missing one shoelace.

10½in (26.5cm) high

$190-320 **POOK**

A Martha Chase cloth boy doll, small sporadic surface flakes and minor sporadic rubs.

40in (101.5cm) high

$260-320 **POOK**

A Lantiner Cherie child doll, with fixed eyes, open mouth with molded top teeth, pierced ears, jointed papier-mâché body.

20in (51cm) high

$170-210 **SAS**

A Crolly Irish composition doll, musical key-wound mechanism plays "When Irish Eyes are Smiling," weighted eyes, five piece jointed body, original clothing, with card swing label to wrist "CROLLY DOLLIES FACTORY CROLLY CO DONEGAL."

1940s *15in (38cm) high*

$190-260 **VEC**

A mint R. John Wright Genevieve artist-designed felt doll, fully jointed, dress made from custom-printed silk, straw bonnet with felt flowers, hand-cobbled shoes, holding a doll made of resin with cotton stuffed body, with original box, outer sleeve.

This doll was made for the United Federation of Doll Club's Region 14 Conference 2009, limited to 150 pieces, complete with certificate. Second in the Victorian Children series, made as a companion to the Abigail doll.

11½in (29cm) high

$190-260 **VEC**

A Gotz "Jennie" vinyl artist doll, by Sissel-Bjorstad Skille, swing label certificate, with three additional Gotz cardigans.

Designed by Gotz for Trisha Plant's store KR Bears and Dolls, limited edition no.13 of 100.

26in (66cm) high

$400-450 **VEC**

A rare Harwin World War I "Tommy" felt doll, the face with center seam, boot button eyes, painted moustache, eyebrows, and hair, jointed body, khaki green felt uniform, oilcloth Sam Brown, shoes and hat band, small holes, slightly discolored and missing some brass buttons.

13in (33cm) high

$600-700 **SAS**

A mint Heidi Plusczok "Li Wang" vinyl artist designed doll, limited edition 5 of 120, with swing label and certificate, with box, outer trade carton.

12in (30.5cm) high

$230-290 **VEC**

A Lenci pressed felt boy doll, with side glancing eyes, sad expression, mohair wig, swivel head, jointed body, original felt traditional Italian costume, with cloth label on vest and card tag on leg, slight fading.

1930s *19in (48.5cm) high*

$260-320 **SAS**

A Kathy Kruse doll, with original hang tag.

15in (38cm) high

$100-140 **POOK**

A near-mint Annette Himstedt "Kleine Leleti" club mini vinyl artist designed doll.

2003 *13½in (34.5cm) high*

$400-450 **VEC**

A Lenci "300" series boy and girl, with pressed felt face with side-glancing eyes.

17½in (44.5cm) high

$1,150-1,450 **SAS**

A mint Neue Munchner Kinderpuppen H255 artist designed doll, by Elisabeth Pongratz, "83B5111P" to sole of left foot and "NEUE MUNCHNER KINDERPUPPEN ELISABETH PONGRATZ" on sole of right foot, hand-carved wood five-way jointed body, hand-painted eyes, handmade costume, with sewn-in cloth Pongratz embroidered labels.

Elisabeth Pongratz first started to make dolls in 1979.

14in (35.5cm) high

$800-900 **VEC**

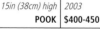

A mint Neue Munchner Kinderpuppen H 199 artist designed doll, by Elisabeth Pongratz, "83B4802P" on sole of left foot and "NEUE MUNCHNER KINDERPUPPEN ELISABETH PONGRATZ" incised on sole of right foot, hand-carved wood five-way jointed body, hand-painted eyes, costume is handmade.

14in (35.5cm) high

$1,250-1,450 **VEC**

DOLLS

A Pedigree "Captain Scarlet" original doll, with gun and cap with metal headset attached, in original box, loss on clear peak on cap.

Between 1945 and the 1950s, hard plastic was used to manufacture dolls by companies such as Pedigree, Rosebud, and British National Dolls Ltd.

1967

$500-650 **LOCK**

A pair of British Pedigree hard plastic vintage dolls.

1950s *tallest 20in (51cm) high*

$60-90 **VEC**

A pair of British Pedigree hard plastic vintage dolls, baby is in original clothing, other doll is in handmade clothing.

1950s *tallest 18in (45.5cm) high*

$100-120 **VEC**

A Pedigree "Sindy Pretty Pose" vintage doll, with original sweater and jeans, missing shoes, within Fair box.

From the 1950s, vinyl was used. "Barbie" was launched in 1959 by Mattel and in 1962 Pedigree made the vinyl doll "Sindy."

$60-70 **VEC**

A Pedigree "Sindy" vintage doll.

$30-35 **VEC**

A near-mint Pedigree "Active Sindy" vintage doll, marked "033055" on back of head, original clothing, within Fair box.

11in (28cm) high

$70-80 **VEC**

A mint Heidi Plusczok "Candy" vinyl artist designed doll, limited edition 28 of 120, with swing label certificate, with box, outer trade carton.

10¼in (26cm) high

$190-260 **VEC**

A Plush "Uncle Wiggly" cloth rabbit doll, in original outfit, some fading.

17in (43cm) high

$120-160 **POOK**

A Trendon "Sasha Gregor" boy doll, in original wool sweater and denim jeans.

$60-80 **SAS**

A Trendon "Sasha" doll, probably original white boots.

Swiss designer Sasha Morgenthaler created the vinyl doll "Sasha" in ca. 1970.

$50-60 **SAS**

A Sebastian of London fashion doll, with closing eyes, in a faux leather coat and a pair of faux leather boots.

ca. 1969 *2in (56cm) high*

$80-90 **LOCK**

A Steiff "Little Red Riding Hood" doll, in original box, small break in plastic box lid.

18in (45.5cm) high

$140-210 **POOK**

A Norah Wellings fairy doll, with a label on the wrist "Made in England by Norah Wellings."

18½in (47cm) high

$400-500 **ROS**

A set of three "Wynken," "Blynken," and "Nod" cloth artist-designed baby dolls, by Jan Shackelford, limited edition 2 of 30, each signed on the torso by the artist, with cloth tag stating "JAN SHACKELFORD ORIGINALS, INC," cotton stockinette, dated.

1996 *17in (43cm) high*

$60-90 **VEC**

A vintage "Action Man" doll, dressed in camouflage.

$30-35 **WHP**

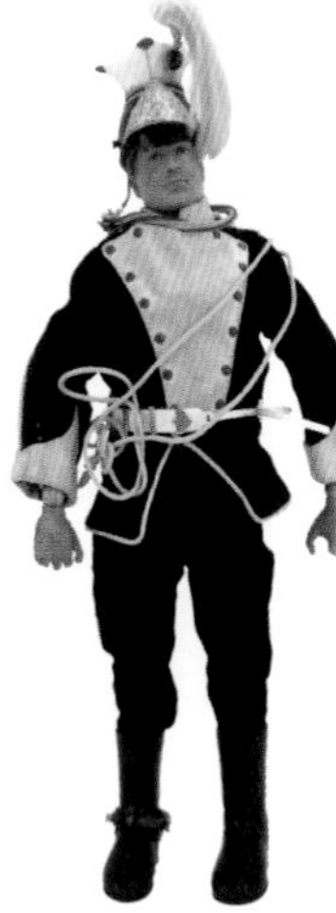

A vintage "Action Man" doll, dressed as a lancer.

$60-70 **WHP**

A rare Moritz Göttschalk large dollhouse, brick and stone external papers, three stories with attic rooms, hanging two-story celestial window on each side, dormer windows, front opening to reveal six rooms, centered staircase with generous hall and landings, mainly original wall papers, and door-bell mechanism on the first floor, some overpainting on balconies, front steps replaced, lacks glazing, other damage and repairs, some slight worm.

This house appears in the reproduced 1895 catalog on page 33 of "Ciesliks Reprints 'Moritz Göttschalk 1892-1931.'"
German dollhouse manufacturer Mortiz Göttschalk specialized in French-style dollhouses. Produced from ca. 1880-1910, Göttschalk's blue roof series used blue lithographic printed paper to imitate slate tiles. Dollhouses with red roofs were more frequently produced by the company from 1910. Göttschalk was one of the few makers to create a Modernist house. After Göttschalk's death in the early 1900s, the company remained in the family until its closure in the late 20thC.

ca. 1895 *58in (147.5cm) high*

$6,500-8,000 **SAS**

A Moritz Göttschalk furnished blue-roof dollhouse, with brick and stone facade, two rooms with original papers, furniture, and chattels, including soft metal upright piano, single bed, dressing table, and tinplate and soft metal fireplace, Erhard fender, wall clock and Rococo chair, two bisque shoulder-head dolls, and other items.

20½in (52cm) high

$2,300-2,900 **SAS**

A German red-roof border control dollhouse, possibly Göttschalk, with center office with desk and shelving, "Contor" and "Spedition" sign, storage attic, slight wear.

18¾in (47.5cm) wide

$260-320 **SAS**

A Göttschalk red-roof front-opening dollhouse, lithographed paper floor, furnished with several pieces of painted cardboard and wood Göttschalk furniture, electrified, side railing incomplete.

15¼in (38.5cm) high

$500-650 **POOK**

A G. & J. Lines "The Clock House" dollhouse, no.34, timbered on left and clock dormer with working clock, front opening in the middle to reveal four rooms with fireplaces and range, original interior papers, some restoration.

G. & J. Lines was founded by Joseph and George Lines in the 1870s. The company produced dollhouses from ca. 1895.
Joseph Lines' son established Lines Brothers in 1919, selling modern-style dollhouses under the name Triang from the mid-1920s. When Joseph Lines died in the early 1930s, Lines Brothers acquired the G. & J. Lines trade name and marks. Lines Brothers went into liquidation in 1971.

ca. 1910 *32in (81.5cm) high*

$190-260 **SAS**

A G. & J. Lines dollhouse, no.32, two-story large bay on left and three windows on right with balustraded garden, mansard roof with dormer window, andwidow's walk, and two chimneys, front opening in the middle to reveal four rooms with fireplaces and dresser, completely restored.

ca. 1909 *33½in (85cm) high*

$260-390 **SAS**

An unusal German Moko dollhouse, windows with printed paper shutters, dormer window with four shuttered windows, and front opening to reveal an attic room, with two rooms with original wall and flower papers, Moko label on base, one chimney replaced, general wear.

24¾in (63cm) wide

$300-450 **SAS**

A late-19thC/early-20thC six-room painted-wood dollhouse, the facade with rusticated corner stones, with arched front door with lead light window and steps to two doors, on turned feet, the two doors opening to rooms around a center flight of stairs over three levels, each room with a fireplace, panel doors, and wall paper to interior, with a collection of furniture and figures.

This dollhouse was owned by the Duke of Bedford. This item includes documentation and letters between a previous owner and the duke, explaining that he had sought to build a collection of dollhouses and games to amuse the younger visitors to Woburn, but with the rise in value of his collection of Japanese porcelain he thought it wise to display that in the cases reserved for the toys, hence his decision to sell the dollhouses.

62½in (159cm) high

$6,000-7,000 **ROS**

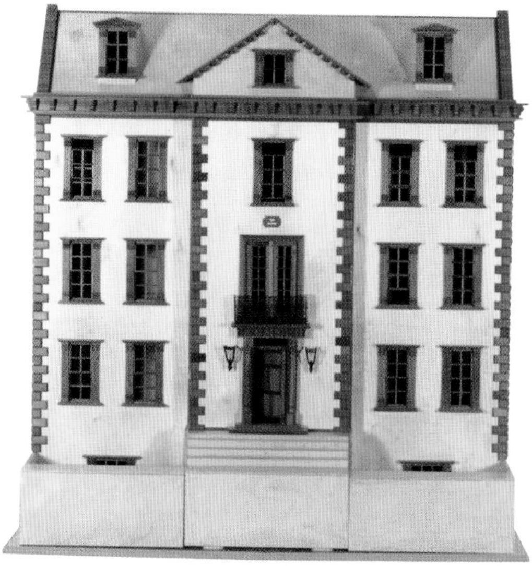

A contemporary double-fronted three-story dollhouse, Regency style, with basement and attic rooms, opening sash windows and doors, with internal staircases, fitted internal lighting but lacking transformer.

48in (122cm) high

$3,200-3,900 **FLD**

An early to mid-20thC dollhouse, damaged.

21¾in (55cm) wide

$30-45 **LOCK**

A rare English mahogany two-room dollhouse, "The Travelling Baby House," of the type mentioned in Jonathan Swift's *Guilliver's Travels*, the windows are painted on the reverse with glazing bars and curtains, and there are two inlaid lozenges of mother-of-pearl, with brass finials, brass lion mask ring handles, and a brass carrying handle on the roof, the front is hinged on one side, there are two rooms, one above the other, each with dark green painted walls, wooden dado, and white painted fireplace mantelpiece.

From the Vivien Greene Collection. Purchased at Bonham's Sale, December, 1998, by the children's charity Tara's Palace Trust and displayed at Powerscourt House, Enniskerry.

ca. 1810 *17¼in (44cm) high*

$60,000-65,000 **FOM**

A handcrafted six-room plantation-style dollhouse, with removable front, widow's walk or observatory, of lithographed paper on wood construction, with wood railing, trim, and miniature tile cornerstones, unmarked, a few minor pieces need regluing.

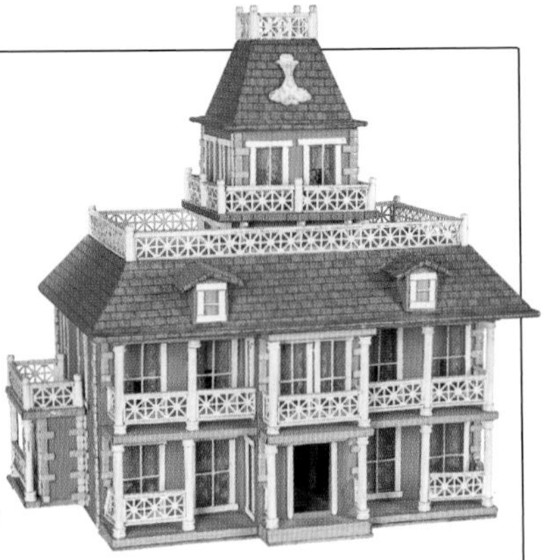

30in (76cm) high

$190-260 **POOK**

A German red-roof wooden dollhouse, with brick-paper facade, front door with steps to veranda, gable, and front opening to reveal two rooms with original papers, repainted roof and other restoration.

23in (58.5cm) high

$190-260 **SAS**

An Asian-themed miniature music room box, attributed to Robert Bernhard, with oriental paper-covered walls and mirrors, furnished with Rosemarie Torre chinoiserie hand-painted, signed, and dated pieces, including collectors chest on stand, a side table, a trinket chest on stand, and two armchairs, with a cello, a violin, a harp, guitars, a shamisen, and a Steinway spinet piano by Ralph Partelow.

From the Carolyn Sunstein Collection.

1981 *25in (63.5cm) wide*

$650-900 **POOK**

A German large-scale room box, with lithographed folding card walls, silk upholstered and wood stained furniture, including a day bed with canopy, mirrored cupboard, four chairs, table, and mantel cabinet, with ormolu accessories, including a mirror, rare figural E.P. mantel clock, and two oval portraits, some light wear on bed drapes and upholstery.

21½in (54.5cm) wide

$1,300-1,900 **POOK**

A Georgian dining room diorama, attributed to Robert Bernhard, with inlaid parquet flooring, corner cupboards, a panoramic lithographed panelled wallpaper scene, and a crystal chandelier, furnished with fine artisan furniture, including a Federal-style sideboard, three-pedestal table, Chippendale side and arm chairs, and a cellarette, with a bisque gentleman, with numerous porcelain, china, silver, and metal accessories, figurines, and a birdcage with a tiny wax bird.

From the Carolyn Sunstein Collection

28in (71cm) wide

$3,900-5,200 **POOK**

A German painted composition butcher's store, with a figural butcher at a butcher block, with a cut of meat and sausage with a cat below, the window with various cuts of meat and bread, the back wall with carcasses and ducks, the pediment inscribed "D. CAIRNS BUTCHER & POULTERER."

8½in (21.5cm) high

$1,700-2,300 **POOK**

A European-style butcher's store diorama, with two carved and painted butchers, two butcher blocks and rows of carcasses of various cuts of meat, with a painted brick facade with container plants, age cracks on facade of store.

21¾in (55cm) high

$9,500-11,000 **POOK**

A 19thC butcher's storefront diorama, the painted butcher figure standing in the center with his display before a four-window building, surmounted by a gilt Royal coat of arms, all in a glazed wood case, scuffs and light damages on case, much of the internal leather fringing now lost.

26¾in (68cm) wide

$26,000-32,000 **CHEF**

A rare Rock & Graner dollhouse tinplate half-tester bed, painted grained finish, with gold-painted classical scroll motif.
1870s *7¾in (19.5cm) high*
$500-650 **SAS**

A mid-19thC stained beech doll's half-tester bed, with a molded canopy, footboard with knob finials, feather pillows, eiderdown-and-hair mattress.
39in (99cm) high
$400-500 **L&T**

A rare Rock & Graner dollhouse tinplate square piano, painted grained finish, three keys that should pluck three metal strings, slight flaking, one leg soldered.
1870s *5¼in (13.5cm) wide*
$950-1,100 **SAS**

A toy/doll's upright piano, of grained wood, brass carrying handles, candle sconces, bone keys, and inside lid printed with musical scales, missing one sconce.
ca. 1900 *15¾in (40cm) wide*
$100-120 **SAS**

A rare Rock & Graner dollhouse tinplate secrétaire, painted grained finish, yellow painted interior and serpent legs.
1870s *5in (12.5cm) high*
$400-500 **SAS**

A rare Rock & Graner dollhouse tinplate desk, painted grained finish.
1870s *6¼in (16cm) high*
$400-450 **SAS**

A miniature tilt-top breakfast table, with burl walnut top, inlaid with boxwood stringing, and carved tripod legs.
5½in (14cm) high
$70-100 **SAS**

A Marklin painted tin doll's carriage, with flower and pinstripe stenciling, fabric replaced, some paint wear.
8in (20.5cm) high
$1,050-1,300 **POOK**

A German all-bisque dollhouse doll, with glass eyes, closed mouth, mohair wig, socket head, peg joints at shoulders and hips, original clothing, impressed "4," arms and head need restringing.
4½in (11.5cm) high
$400-450 **SAS**

A Davenport doll's part dinner service, printed and impressed marks "DAVENPORT" and "7-64," with 2 soup tureens with covers, 1 with broken ladle, 2 platters with covers, 5 ashets, 2 platters, 2 sauceboats, 6 soup plates, 6 side plates, 11 dinner plates, and 6 dessert plates.
ca. 1860
$400-500 **L&T**

An 18thC fan, with pierced ivory sticks with cherubs and swags, the leaf painted figures in a landscape, in a gilt glazed case, minor tears to leaf where there are folds.

Contains an element of pre-1947 ivory so export restrictions may apply.

$4,500-5,200 **CHOR**

An 18thC fan, with carved and pierced ivory guards and sticks, double paper leaf showing a mythological procession.

11¾in (30cm) long

$4,500-5,200 **K&O**

A miniature Italian Grand Tour fan, with carved and pierced ivory guards and sticks, the double leaf painted recto with the bay of Naples with Vesuvius smoking in the background, in the foreground are ships and figures with the city beyond, in contemporary box.

ca. 1800 *6¾in (17cm) long*

$4,500-5,200 **K&O**

A late-18thC bone fan, the guards pierced and carved, the sticks centered by an Aesop's Fable panel, the paper leaf painted with a side-to-side Arcadian scene, in a card box.

10¾in (27.5cm) long

$1,100-1,250 **DN**

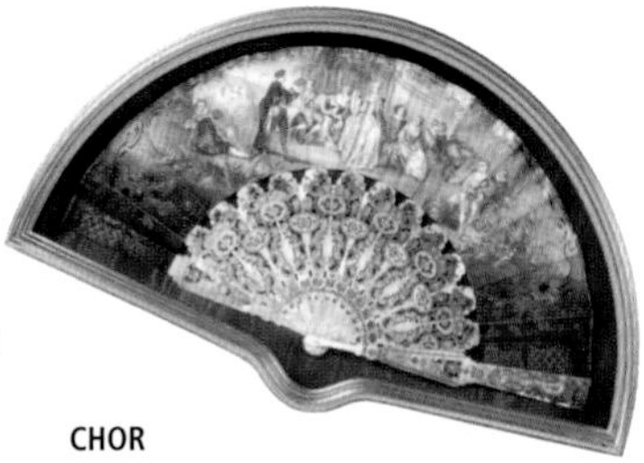

A 19thC fan, the leaf printed with an 18thC "fęte champętre," with pierced and gilt mother-of-pearl sticks, in a gilt-glazed case.

$1,250-1,450 **CHOR**

A Chinese mid-19thC Canton export black lacquer "Applied Faces" or "Mandarin" fan, painted in two-color gilt with figures and building, the paper leaf painted with figures with applied ivory faces and silk robes.

15½in (39.5cm) long

$1,300-1,800 **DN**

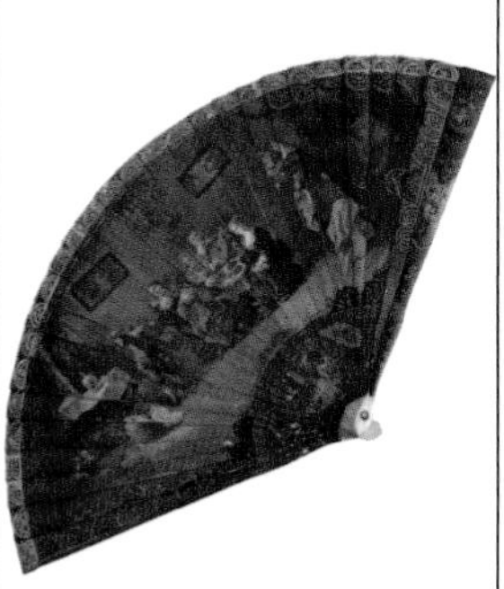

A 19thC ivory brisé fan, painted with "An Allegory of the Five Senses" after David Teniers the Younger.

7in (18cm) long

$190-260 **DN**

A Japanese 19thC Shibayama white metal lacquered fan, inlaid with mother-of-pearl, decorated with cockerels in a landscape, metal tarnished.

15¾in (40cm) wide

$8,500-9,500 **ECGW**

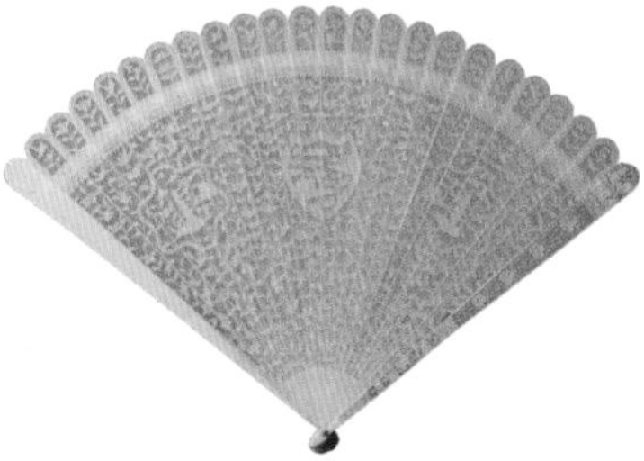

A Cantonese 19thC ivory fan, foliate carved and pierced decoration with a Chinese landscape flanked by two pagodas, stick guard.

10¾in (27.5cm) wide

$950-1,100 BELL

A Japanese late-19thC ivory fan, with three female figures representing "speak no evil, hear no evil, see no evil," stick guard, with a Japanese ivory Shibayama comb.

9½in (24cm) wide

$1,250-1,450 BELL

A Chinese 19thC ivory fan, pierced and carved with Chinese figures and animals, stick guard.

17¾in (19.5cm) wide

$700-850 BELL

A paper fan, with wooden sticks commemorating the Battle of Trafalgar, printed and hand colored with Nelson's coat of arms and his baronial arms, with a portrait of Nelson, the reverse with a plan of the Battle of Trafalgar and a caption "Plan of the Brilliant Action of Trafalgar."

ca. 1805 *8in (20.5cm) long*

$1,600-2,100 FLD

An early-19thC fan, the leaf with adults and children in a cottage tavern, in a glazed gilt frame.

19¾in (50cm) wide

$600-700 BLEA

A Chinese Qing dynasty painted bamboo lacquer and paper fan, with a courtly scene with ivory-faced figures with their clothes made of silk, and reverse painted with vignettes of country scenes, Macao.

ca. 1860 *21¼in (54cm) wide*

$1,100-1,250 DN

A Chinese Qing dynasty lacquered bamboo brisé fan, painted on both sides in colors with figures, pagodas, and foliage, Macao.

ca. 1860 *9in (23cm) wide*

$1,700-2,100 DN

A mother-of-pearl fan, the paper leaf painted in gouache with a hunt in full cry, signed "Van Garden," the reverse with a hunting trophy ferns and foliage, in a card box from Duvelleroy.

Van Garden worked at the famous French fan factory Duvelleroy. He also painted fan leaves for the Henrik Wigstrom workshop for retailing by Fabergé.

ca. 1900 *15½in (39.5cm) long*

$1,100-1,250 DN

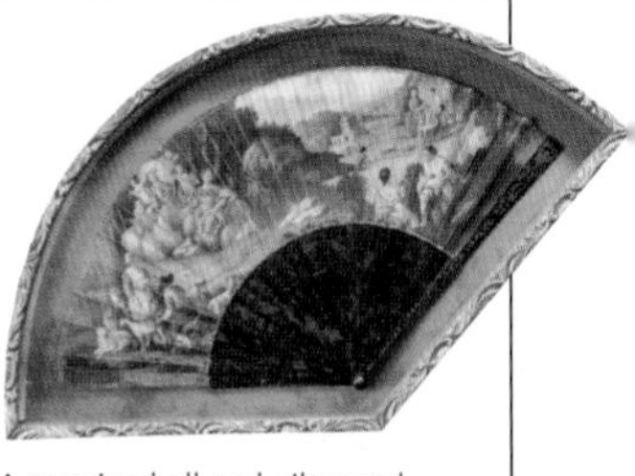

A tortoiseshell and gilt metal inlaid-handle fan, painted with pastoral and allegorical figures in a landscape, within a glazed gilt frame.

According to a pencil note on the reverse, "This fan belonged to Ellen Terry."

25¼in (64cm) wide

$2,600-3,200 CHEF

A Christian Dior sillk scarf, with the maker's monogram print in black on a cream background.

30¾in (78cm) wide

$230-290 **FELL**

A Gucci cotton scarf.

34¾in (88.5cm) square

$100-160 **FELL**

A Hermès "Couvertures Et Tenues De Jour" silk scarf, designed by Jacques Eudel.

ca. 1970 *35½in (90cm) square*

$230-290 **DUK**

A Gucci cotton scarf, with a nautical theme.

35in (89cm) wide

$100-160 **FELL**

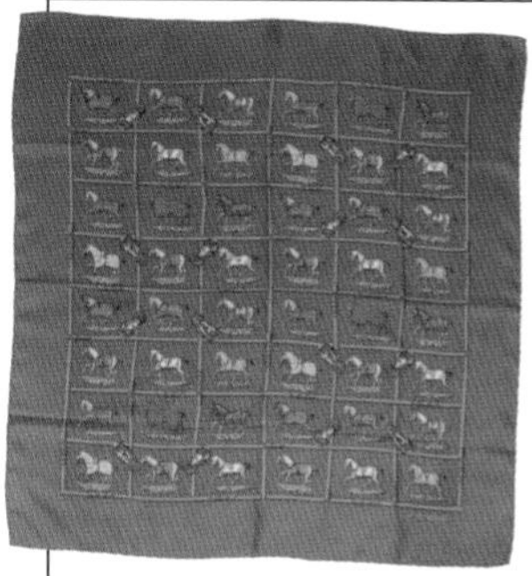

A Hermès "Petits Chevaux" silk scarf, designed by Jacques Eudel.

ca. 1974 *33½in (85cm) square*

$190-260 **DUK**

A Hermès "Chasse À Vol" silk scarf, designed by Henri de Linares, boxed.

ca. 1962 *35½in (90cm) square*

$170-210 **DUK**

A Hermès "Rouages" silk scarf, designed by Francois Heron, with 55¼in (140.5cm) of Hermès brown gift ribbon.

ca. 1966 *35½in (90cm) square*

$230-290 **DUK**

A Hermès "Faune Et Flore Du Texas" silk scarf, designed by Kermit Oliver.

ca. 1992 *35½in (90cm) square*

$120-160 **DUK**

A Hermès "République Française Liberté Égalité Fraternité 1789" silk scarf, designed by Joachim Metz, first issued in 1989.

35½in (90cm) square

$400-450 **FELL**

A Hermès "Cheval Turc" scarf, originally designed in 1969 by Christiane Vauzelles.

35½in (90cm) wide

$130-190 **FELL**

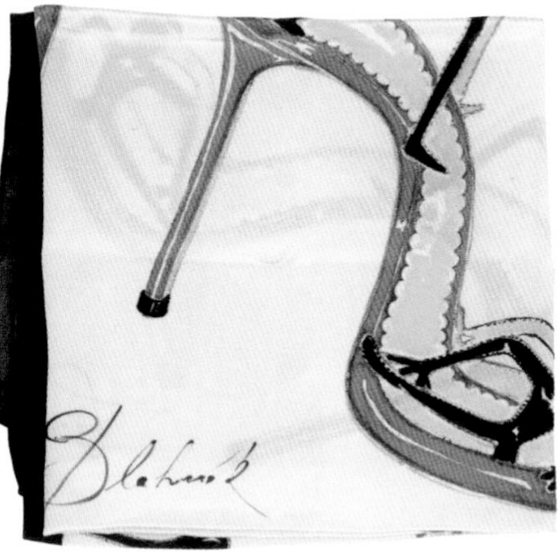

A Manolo Blahnik for Liberty scarf.

32¼in (82cm) long

$400-500 **FELL**

A Louis Vuitton limited edition "Yayoi Kusama Monogram Dots" cotton scarf.

21¾in (55cm) square

$450-500 **FELL**

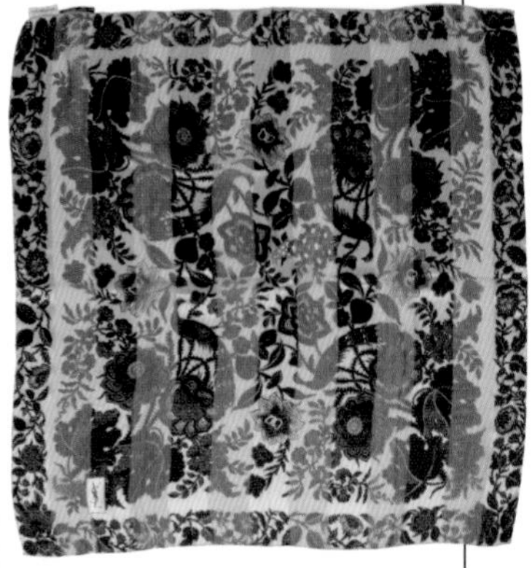

An Yves Saint Laurent silk scarf.

33½in (85cm) square

$60-100 **DUK**

An Austrian sterling silver and guilloche enamel novelty powder compact, modeled in the form of a lady's dressing mirror, impressed marks.

4in (10cm) long

$650-800 **WM**

An Art Deco Richard Hudnut "Deauville Idie Aiuviolioie" powder compact, with enameled silhouette, the hinged cover lifts to enclose spring-loaded mirror, impressed marks, with lipstick holder and chain.

One of the first American cosmetic manufacturers, Richard Hudnut began selling perfumes and cosmetics from his father's pharmacy in New York in the late 19thC. He went on to form his own company, Richard Hudnut's Pharmacy Co., which sold perfumes and cosmetics in pharmacies and department stores.

5in (12.5cm) long

$140-190 **WM**

A rare Art Deco Richard Hudnut "Three Flowers" powder compact, the hinged cover lifts to enclose spring loaded mirror, impressed marks.

ca. 1930 *2¼in (5.5cm) diam*

$230-290 **WM**

A George VI hallmarked silver and enamel powder compact, made by Deakin & Francis Ltd.

1947 *3in (7.5cm) diam*

$230-290 **WM**

An Art Deco Evans Of America sterling silver compact.

4in (10cm) diam

$260-320 **WM**

A German 935 Rodica butterscotch guilloche enamel powder compact, cover with silver border, with perfume bottle.

2½in (6.5cm) long

$950-1,100 **WM**

A pair of Cartier Aviator sunglasses, stamped "Cartier 62 12," with maker's pouch.

$600-700 **FELL**

A pair of Fendi rimless sunglasses, with maker's FF zucca-patterned acetate arms.

$160-230 **FELL**

A pair of Ray-Ban Traditional B&L sunglasses, with imitation tortoiseshell acetate frames, signed "Ray-Ban, Style B 54 18," with maker's case.

$120-160 **FELL**

A pair of Dunhill gentleman's silver cuff links, of Scottish terrier form, inscribed "dunhill," in a fitted case.

$450-500 **DUK**

A pair of Tiffany & Co. sunglasses, with nude brown acetate frames, with maker's case.

$190-260 **FELL**

A pair of Dunhill gentleman's jade and silver cuff links, of tortoise form, inscribed "ALFRED DUNHILL," in a fitted case.

$450-600 **DUK**

A Dunhill gentleman's alligator and silver cuff links, inscribed "dunhill," with clip connections, in a fitted case.

$170-230 **DUK**

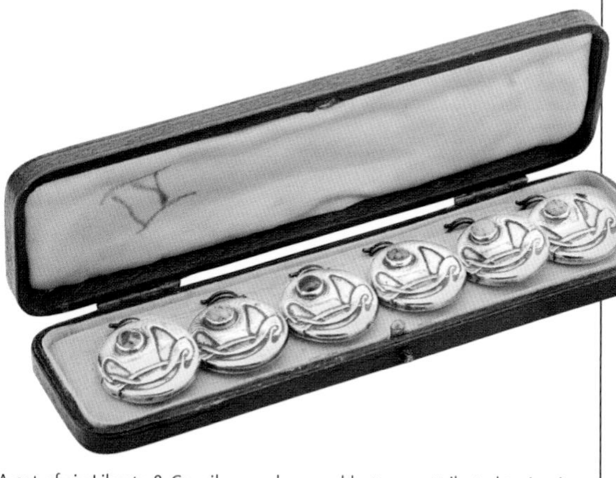

A set of six Liberty & Co. silver and enamel buttons, attributed to Jessie M. King, London, stamped maker's marks, hallmarked for Birmingham, with original box.

1906 *each 1in (2.5cm) diam*

$700-800 **L&T**

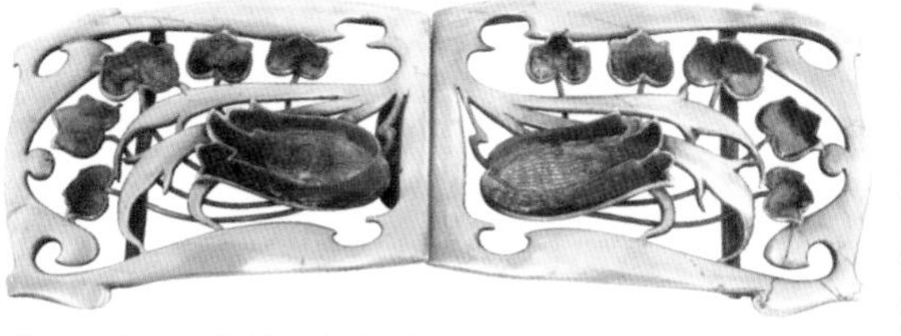

A silver and enameled buckle, by Liberty & Co.

1908 *4¾in (12cm) wide*

$650-800 **SWO**

A Balenciaga logo wallet, with a black leather exterior, with multiple card slots and slip pockets, with maker's care card and box.

4¼in (11cm) wide

$160-230 **FELL**

A Patek Philippe leather card holder, with the maker's logo crest, with maker's box.

4in (10cm) long

$160-230 **FELL**

A Louis Vuitton "Eye-Trunk" iPhone 7 Plus case, designed to replicate the maker's trunks, with maker's cleaning cloth and care guides.

6½in (16.5cm) long

$600-650 **FELL**

A Cartier black leather belt, with silver-tone hardware, with garnet cabochon details, stamped "Cartier Paris," with maker's box and authenticity card.

$230-290 **FELL**

A Chanel black leather and gilt-metal coin belt, buckle stamped "Chanel Paris," size marked "85/34."

2in (5cm) wide

$900-1,050 **ROS**

A pair of Hermès gentleman's brown alligator skin penny loafers.

size 8 (UK)

$600-650 **DUK**

A pair of Gianni Versace patent leather shoes, loafer-style, with gold chain and medallion trim.

size 6½ (UK)

$100-140 **DUK**

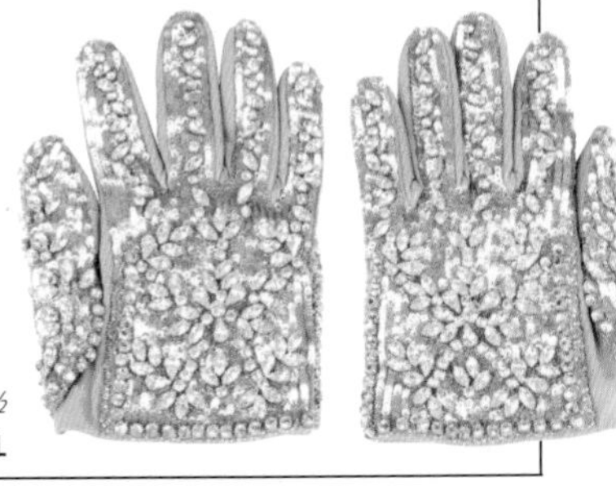

A pair of Dolce & Gabbana embellished leather gloves, with rhinestones and sequins on soft beige leather, labeled "Dolce & Gabbana," with maker's box.

size 7½

$450-500 **FELL**

An Armani Collezioni three quarter-length virgin wool coat with fur trim, labeled "Armani Collezioni."

size 48

$80-100 **FELL**

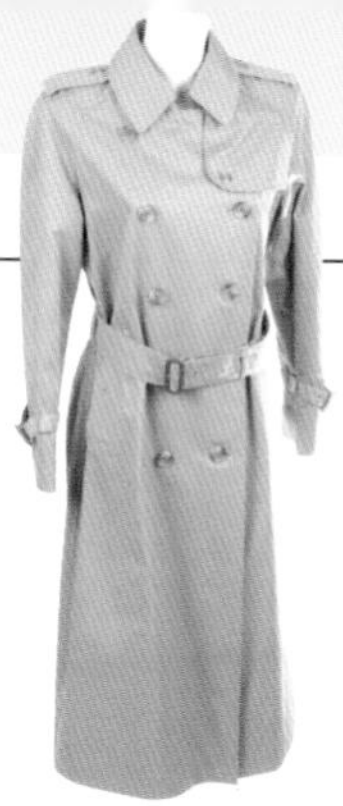

A Burberry women's classic trench coat, with buttoned epaulettes, a storm flap on the left side, labeled "Burberrys."

size 12

$260-320 **FELL**

QUICK REFERENCE—BURBERRY

- **Burberry was founded in 1856 by Thomas Burberry, who went on to develop gabardine, a waterproof and breathable fabric. The company patented the fabric.**
- **In 1912, gabardine was used to make the Tielocken coat, a predecessor to the trench coat. The Tielocken coat was worn during the Boer War and, after further development, Burberry supplied around 500,000 to the British Armed Forces during World War I. A single strap and buckle fastened the Tielocken coat.**
- **The Burberry check (or nova check) was introduced in the 1920s as a coat lining. It is now trademarked.**

A Burberry wool and camel hair knee-length coat, labeled "Burberrys."

chest 42in (106.5cm)

$130-190 **FELL**

A Chanel cream satin and black velvet camellia dress, look no.49 from the Fall 2014 Runway, front CC button accents, slip pockets on sides and concealed zipper closure at the rear, labeled "Chanel," with maker's hanger and dust bag.

size 50

$300-400 **FELL**

A Jean Paul Gaultier blue denim jacket, with black leather trim, labeled "JPG Jeans."

size 10

$140-190 **FELL**

QUICK REFERENCE—JOHN GALLIANO

- **Having studied at St Martin's School of Art, John Galliano (b.1960) started his own fashion label in East London and despite financial trouble, he went on to win the British Fashion Council Designer of the Year in 1987, 1994, 1995, and 1997 (the latter award was shared with Alexander McQueen).**
- **Galliano was appointed Head Designer of Givenchy in 1995 and then Designer in Chief at Dior in 1996.**
- **In 2011, Galliano was accused of making racist remarks and was fired from Dior and his namesake fashion house. Galliano briefly retired from the public eye, before collaborating on an Oscar de la Renta collection in 2013 and then taking up the role of creative director at Maison Margiela.**

A John Galliano silk bias cut spaghetti strap dress.

1990s

$450-600 **SWO**

A Michael Kors white double-breasted virgin wool pea jacket, with two decorative style pockets, labeled "Michael Kors."

size 10

$80-100 **FELL**

An Yves Saint Laurent fur-lined, knee-length coat, with black metallic leather with black fur lining, labeled "Yves Saint Laurent Fourrures."

chest 34in (86.5cm)

$850-950 **FELL**

A Missoni three quarter-length wool-blend coat, lined with a multicolored foliate-patterned fabric, labeled "Missoni."

size 12

$140-210 **FELL**

A Love Moschino longline coat, with gold-tone front button fastenings, labeled "Love Moschino," with maker's original tags attached.

size 14

$140-210 **FELL**

A Loro Piana shearling cape, with a brown leather exterior, hkahi wool lining, labeled "Loro Piana."

one size

$500-650 **FELL**

QUICK REFERENCE—EMILIO PUCCI

- **Emilio Pucci (1914-92) began his fashion career in the late 1940s. He became known for his vividly printed silk jersey clothing, as well as his so-called "Pucci pants." These lightweight vivid prints were popular in the 1960s and were revived in the 1980s and 90s.**
- **In 2000, French conglomerate LVMH acquired 67 percent of the Pucci company.**

An Emilio Pucci cotton jacket, with the maker's psychedelic colorful print, front zipper fastening, and optional foldout hood, labeled "Emilio Pucci."

size 8

$140-210 **FELL**

A Valentino "Red" black three-quarter length coat, with a Peter Pan collar, labeled "Red Valentino."

size 12 (UK)

$190-260 **FELL**

A Vivienne Westwood striped shirt dress, with long sleeves, full-length button fastening and a gathered ruffle detail on the front, labeled "Vivienne Westwood."

size 40

$100-160 **FELL**

A Vivienne Westwood and Malcolm McLaren "Devil" white linen sleeveless top, with a printed design of a stylized dog barking the word "devil" in different languages, Velcro fastening on the reverse, with original Worlds End label, "Born in England."

$450-600 **SWO**

A lady's vintage blonde mink fur long coat.

size 10/12

$130-190 **PSA**

A lady's vintage gray mink fur jacket, label "Firs of Canada."

size 10/12

$300-400 **PSA**

A dark ranch mink shawl, with mink tail tasseled trim and one hook-and-eye front fastening.

May be subject to export restrictions.

one size

$260-390 **FELL**

A full-length mink and silver fox fur coat, labeled "Faulkes Edgbaston Birmingham."

size 10

$500-650 **FELL**

A knee-length green cashmere and mink lined coat, with a lapel collar, labeled "Habsburg."

size 16

$1,050-1,150 **FELL**

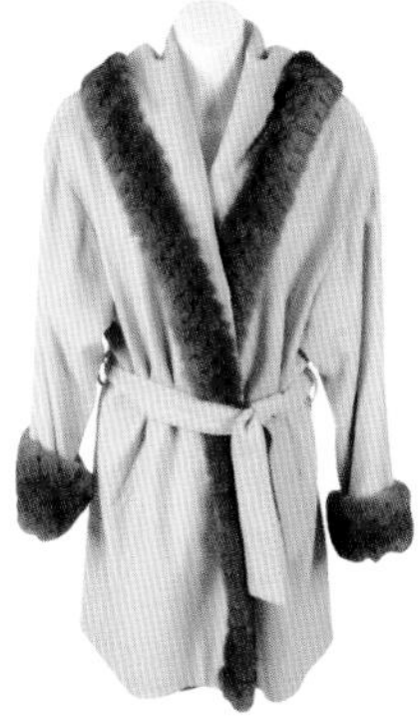

A cream hooded jacket, with mink fur trim, wool, angora, and cashmere blend jacket, labeled "Jan-Rone Paris."

chest 50in (127cm)

$170-230 **FELL**

A knee-length tapestry coat, with a large brown beaver lamp notched lapel collar.

chest 32in (81.5cm)

$230-290 **FELL**

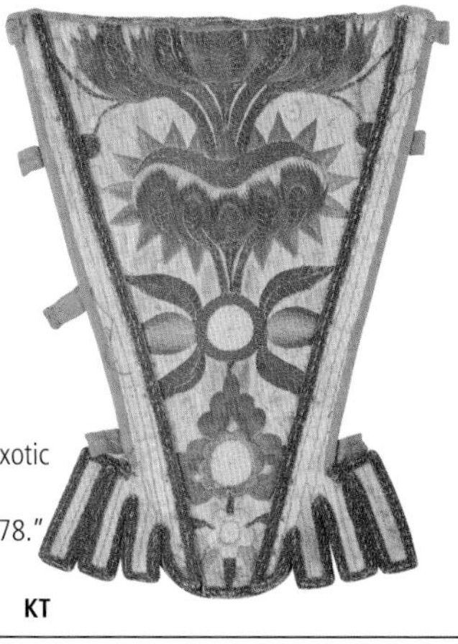

An English embroidered linen stomacher, embroidered with exotic blooms and pods in floss silks, annotated in pencil "R.A.C. 1778."

ca. 1710

$850-950 **KT**

A hand-painted organza ball gown, with black tulle petticoat, additional dark red taffeta skirt, and inner skirt of black linen.

1950s *UK size 6*

$100-160 **CHEF**

QUICK REFERENCE—HANDBAGS

- **Handbags and purses have become a desirable fashion accessory. Collectors will pay hundreds or even thousands of dollars for new or vintage examples by top designers, such as Chanel, Hermès, Judith Leiber, Louis Vuitton, and Gucci. Sometimes second-hand luxury handbags that are still in production will change hands on the vintage market for more money than they would if they were new.**
- **However, many handbags by less well-known makers are equally desirable and do not have such a high price tag.**
- **If you want to collect designer handbags and purses, it's important to buy them from a reputable source, because there are many fakes and copies on the market.**

A Bottega Veneta "Nappa Intrecciato Veneta" hobo handbag, in calfskin leather, with maker's small hand mirror, slight wear on the bottom corners.

19in (48.5cm) wide

$700-850 **FELL**

A Burberry "Nova Check" hobo handbag, top zipper fastening and one interior side pocket, with maker's dust bag.

16½in (42cm) wide

$300-450 **FELL**

A vintage Cartier top handle "Happy Birthday Bordeaux" handbag, with a twist-lock fastening and two interior side pockets, with maker's authenticity card, dust bag, and box.

11in (28cm) wide

$850-950 **FELL**

A Céline khaki leather "Trapeze" handbag, with optional suede side wings, with maker's dust bag and care cards, some scuffs and scratches.

12½in (34cm) wide

$500-650 **FELL**

An Aspinal of London snakeskin letterbox saddle handbag, with gold-tone hardware accents, with maker's dust bag and box.

10in (25.5cm) wide

$300-400 **FELL**

A Berluti leather "Deux Jours" briefcase, optional shoulder strap, with maker's dust bag and box.

15¾in (40cm) wide

$1,300-1,800 **FELL**

A Bottega Veneta "Intrecciato Knot Grosgrain" clutch, cream lizard skin trim, with maker's dust bag and care card.

9¼in (23.5cm) wide

$600-700 **FELL**

MARKET REPORT

The demand for top-quality handbags and accessories (such as scarves) is really high.

Auction is a great way to get your hands on items that are incredibly sought-after yet hard to come by. Designer bags made from good-quality materials will stand the test of time. They might also retain their value over time.

In terms of trends and prices, if the piece is very worn, it will be reflected in the estimate. The more pristine an item, the higher price it commands. The material it is made of will also be a factor. The exotic leathers demand a much higher price than the standard ones.

Limited edition pieces also tend to surpass their estimates. Auction is a good way to get your hands on a piece that was released in limited quantities or other items, such as Hermès Birkin bags, which are hard to come by. According to a 2016 study, Birkin handbags have increased in value year on year. Indeed, the Birkin's value has never fluctuated downward and it offers an average annual increase in value of 14.2 percent. Even at its lowest annual increase in 1986, the value of a Birkin went up from 1985 by 2.1 percent.

As far as record-breaking lots are concerned, Fellows Auctioneers broke a house record for price achieved on a Louis Vuitton Neverfull handbag in February 2019. The limited edition "Pumpkin Dot Neverfull MM" handbag more than doubled its estimate and sold for £2,041.60 (about $2,667).

Furthermore, in October 2016, Fellows sold a "Rouge Porosus Crocodile Birkin 35" handbag by Hermès for a full price of £22,968 (about $30,079). Other brands to look out for are Chanel, Louis Vuitton, and Gucci.

Sophie Higgs, Specialist for
The Designer Collection, Fellows Auctioneers

QUICK REFERENCE—CHANEL

- **Gabrielle Chanel (1883-1971) opened her first store in Paris, Chanel Modes, in 1910, and her first couture house in Biarritz, in 1915. The Chanel brand produced many bags that remain instantly recognizable today.**
- **In 1955, Chanel launched the "2.55" bag (referring to the month and year the bag was introduced) combining quilted leather and a gold chain. An iconic design, the bag was also practical, with various compartments and a shoulder strap, allowing for women to keep their hands free. Celebrities of the time, including Elizabeth Taylor, Brigitte Bardot, and Jane Fonda, were seen wearing Chanel's bag.**
- **The brand continued after Gabrielle Chanel's death in 1971, with Karl Lagerfeld (1933-2019) becoming artistic director in 1983.**
- **Lagerfeld's 2011 "11.12" version of the "2.55" bag was a more rigidly structured design and featured a more heavy-duty chain. Lagerfeld also introduced the interlocking Cs logo, known as the mademoiselle lock.**
- **Under Lagerfeld's direction, Chanel created more instantly recognizable bags, including the "Grand Shopping Tote," the "Chanel Gabrielle," and the "Boy" bag.**

A Chanel 50th anniversary limited edition "2.55" reissue quilted "Classic Flap" handbag, antique gold-tone chain strap and mademoiselle turn-lock fastening, with maker's dust bag and box, metalwork purposefully distressed from gold to silver.

In 2005, this commemorative 50th anniversary edition marked the official relaunch of the "2.55" bag.

10in (25.5cm) wide

$2,600-3,900 FELL

A small Chanel "Classic Double Flap" handbag, serial no.1403263, featuring maker's iconic black quilted lambskin leather exterior with gold-tone hardware, with maker's authenticity card.

1989-91 *9in (23cm) wide*

$2,600-3,900 FELL

A beaded Chanel "Camellia Flap" lambskin leather handbag, serial no.16503618, with beaded and embroidered camellia flower embellishments, "CC" fastening, silver-tone hardware, with maker's authenticity card, care pamphlet, and dust bag, signs of light use.

10¼in (26cm) wide

$3,900-4,500 FELL

A Chanel suede quilted handbag, serial no.3581503.

11¾in (30m) wide

$1,050-1,150 ROS

A Chanel small quilted duffle bag, of soft black lambskin leather, with maker's authenticity card.

11¾in (30cm) wide

$1,300-1,900 FELL

A vintage Chanel "Medium Classic Double Flap" handbag, with quilted lambskin leather exterior, with maker's authenticity card.

10in (25.5cm) wide

$1,900-2,600 FELL

A Chloe "Madeleine" lambskin-leather handbag, with "Chloe Authenticity card BOFMX8" and dust cover.

13½in (34.5cm) wide

$650-800 DUK

A Coyard "Chevron Okinawa PM" handbag, with maker's dust bag.

14¼in (36cm) wide

$1,300-1,900 FELL

A Christian Dior "Cannage Quilted Lady Dior MM" handbag, with maker's dust bag, care guide, and authenticity card.

9in (23cm) wide

$1,600-2,300 FELL

A Dunhill prototype alligator document briefcase, inscribed "Alfred Dunhill."

15¾in (40cm) wide

$1,600-2,300 **DUK**

A Fendi "3Jours" leather bicolor handbag, with maker's dust bag and care guide.

13¾in (35cm) wide

$600-700 **FELL**

A Gucci "Horsebit" hobo handbag, serial no.232961 213317, made from maker's "GG" canvas, minor wear.

14in (35.5cm) wide

$400-500 **FELL**

A Gucci "Unskilled Worker Matelassé Marmont" camera handbag, an online exclusive in collaboration with Unskilled Worker for the 2017 "Capsule" collection, with maker's care guide, dust bag, and box.

9½in (24cm) wide

$1,050-1,150 **FELL**

QUICK REFERENCE—HERMÈS

- **Hermès was founded in 1837 and is best known for its handbags, most famously the "Kelly," designed in the 1930s and used by Grace Kelly from 1956, and the "Birkin," designed for actress Jane Birkin in 1984, adapted from a 1894 design.**
- **Hermès bags are produced in a wide variety of different leathers and skins. Depending on the bag and its material, prices can vary from under $130 to more than $130,000.**
- **Condition can affect value considerably. Fakes are common and can be extremely good, so if in doubt, it is worth taking a bag to Hermès for identification.**

A Hermès tan "Epson Birkin 35" handbag, with tan stamped-grain leather and rolled leather handles, with polished silver-tone turn-lock fastening, minor wear.

ca. 2007 *13in (33cm) wide*

$9,000-10,500 **FELL**

A Hermès "Kaba" red handbag, date stamp "U," minor scratches.

ca. 1991 *15in (38cm) wide*

$1,300-1,900 **FELL**

A Hermès "Birkin 35" handbag, maker's padlock with detachable clochette and keys and four protective base feet, with maker's dust bag and box.

2008 *13¾in (35cm) wide*

$9,000-10,500 **FELL**

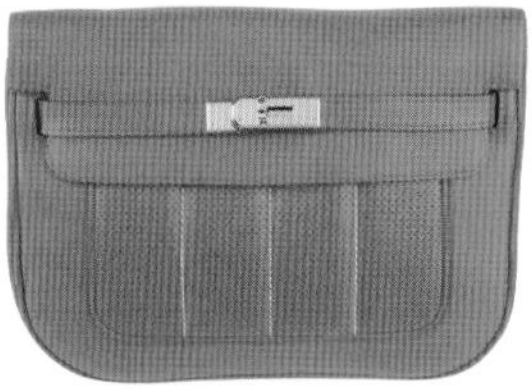

A Hermès "Padded Berline" messenger bag, with the "Kelly" strap closure with center turn-lock fastening, with maker's dust bag, blind stamp "T."

ca. 2015 *11in (28cm) wide*

$3,900-5,200 **FELL**

A Hermès Kelly Sport MM black leather bag, date letter "W" within circle for 1993.

1993 *9½in (24cm) wide*

$1,900-2,600 **ROS**

A Miu Miu matelassé crystal leather handbag, with silver-tone hardware, with maker's care card and dust bag.

13in (33cm) wide

$800-900 **FELL**

QUICK REFERENCE—MULBERRY

- **Founded by Roger Saul in 1971, Mulberry began designing buckled leather belts before moving on to accessories, bags, and womenswear in 1979. Saul's sister designed the iconic tree logo.**
- **Mulberry opened its first factory, The Rookery, in 1989 in Chilcompton in Somerset, England, with just 100 employees. The Rookery now employs nearly 300 skilled workers. The Willows, Mulberry's second UK factory, opened in 2013 in Bridgewater.**
- **Mulberry Green, the company's signature color, was created in 2015. It is used on Mulberry's packaging, shoe insoles, and outerwear linings. Now, the company has more than 120 stores worldwide.**

A Mulberry mini Boston "Roxanne" leather handbag,internal pocket with zipper, wear and scuffing.

7in (18cm) wide

$180-260 **CHEF**

A Mulberry "Mocha" ostrich-leather handbag, serial no.1706018, with a detachable embossed key fob.

14¼in (36cm) wide

$300-450 **DUK**

A Mulberry ostrich-leather handbag, silver tone hardware with the Mulberry tree logo, with a detachable embossed key fob.

14¼in (36cm) wide

$1,050-1,150 **DUK**

A Mulberry embossed "Bayswater" handbag, serial no,656188, with postman's lock fastening, minor wear.

14¼in (36cm) wide

$1,150-1,450 **FELL**

A Prada backpack, with a black leather-trimmed quilted velvet exterior, with maker's dust bag, care card, and authenticity card, dusty exterior.

11in (28cm) high

$800-900 **FELL**

A Prada caramel saffiano leather handbag, with gold-tone hardware, with maker's authenticity card and dust bag.

14¼in (36cm) wide

$850-950 **FELL**

A Valentino Garavani leather flower handbag, some wear.

15in (38cm) wide

$230-290 **FELL**

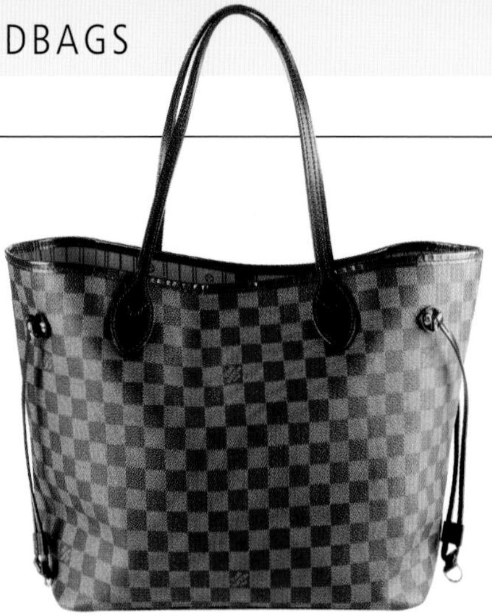

A Louis Vuitton "Damier Neverfull MM" handbag, with maker's archive details, date code "GI4112," faint marks to red canvas lined interior.

18¼in (46.5cm) wide

$1,050-1,300 **FELL**

A Louis Vuitton "Monogram Montsouris" backpack, serial no.SP1907, minor marks, wear, and tarnishing to hardware, lining faded.

ca. 1997 *11in (28cm) high*

$600-700 **FELL**

A Louis Vuitton "Ribera MM" lady's handbag, in Damier Ebene canvas leather, a cell phone pocket and another in the interior.

13in (33cm) long

$300-450 **CHEF**

A Louis Vuitton "Monogram Graffiti Pochette Accessoires" handbag, serial no.AR0051, with maker's dust bag, minor scratches on gold-tone hardware.

8in (20.5cm) wide

$300-350 **FELL**

A Louis Vuitton "Cherry Blossom Sac Retro" handbag, serial no.CA0023, with maker's dust bag, minor scattered water marks.

ca. 2003 *11in (28cm) wide*

$450-600 **FELL**

A Louis Vuitton "Multicolor Monogram Accessories Pochette" handbag, serial no.SL0053, with bolt key holder, signs of light use, with maker's dust bag.

5in (21.5cm) wide

$300-450 **FELL**

A Louis Vuitton "Epi Gobelins" backpack, serial no.VI1909, with maker's dust bag, padlock and keys, some minor scuff marks.

ca. 1999 *13in (33cm) high*

$650-800 **FELL**

A Louis Vuitton "Monogram Vernis Alma GM" handbag.

15in (38cm) wide

$1,150-1,450 **FELL**

A Louis Vuitton "Speedy" Epi leather handbag, with two keys, hardware, and padlock stamped "Louis Vuitton."

$650-800 **DUK**

QUICK REFERENCE—LOUIS VUITTON

- **Louis Vuitton (1821-92) founded his namesake fashion company and retailer in 1854.**
- **The company's success sparked from its "Trianon" trunk, produced in 1858. This trunk was waterproof, canvas covered, and airtight. Previously, trunks had domed or sloping tops to let water run off, but because Vuitton's trunk was already waterproof, it could have a flat top. This allowed for it to stack when being transported.**
- **In 1876, Louis Vuitton introduced beige and brown striped canvas to differentiate its products from its competitors and imitators. Its checked "Damier" was introduced in 1888, followed in 1896 by the "LV" monogram canvas, which is still used by Louis Vuitton today.**
- **Vintage Louis Vuitton pieces are highly popular today. Specially commissioned pieces or those with niche uses, such as musical instrument cases, can get especially large sums.**

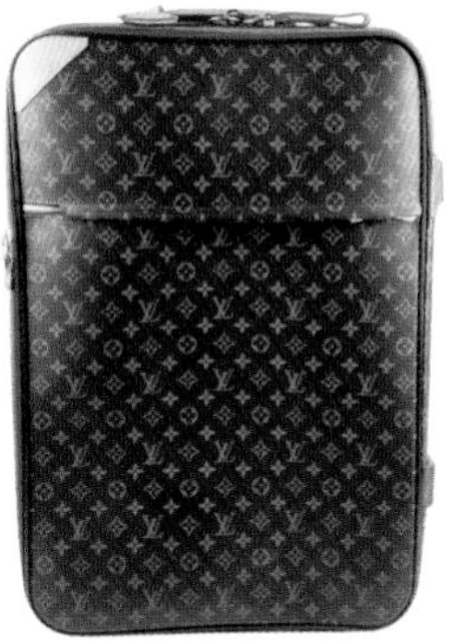

A Louis Vuitton monogram "Pégase 65" rolling suitcase, a canvas-lined interior with removable garment cover, heat stamped initials on leather tag.

25½in (65cm) high

$1,900-2,600 **FELL**

An early-20thC Louis Vuitton wooden and leather-bound traveling trunk, the brass flip catch signed "70. Champs Elysees, Paris, Louis VUITTON, London 149 New Bond Street," with attached iron wheels underneath.

40in (101.5cm) wide

$11,000-12,000 **T&F**

A Louis Vuitton attaché case, serial no.1030479, with two keys.

17¾in (45cm) wide

$1,050-1,150 **BELL**

A 20thC Louis Vuitton vanity case, serial no.915955, the lid with internal mirror, with two keys.

16in (40.5cm) wide

$1,600-2,100 **ROS**

A Louis Vuitton "Boite Chapeaux 50" hat box, with leather card holder and two keys.

19¾in (50cm) diam

$1,900-2,600 **BELL**

A Louis Vuitton cigar humidor, of briefcase form, the lock plate stamped with London and Paris addresses and "082946," the interior with hygrometer.

15¾in (40cm) wide

$3,200-3,900 **CHOR**

An early-20thC Louis Vuitton leather trunk, with leather banding and brass fittings, the lock stamped with serial no.023361, the interior with paper label and stamped no.151369, the side with monogram "K.C.K."

24in (61cm) wide

$8,000-9,000 **L&T**

An early-20thC Louis Vuitton leather touring trunk, the lock plate stamped "70 CHAMPS ELYSEES PARIS LOUIS VUITTON LONDON 149 BOND STREET," the relined interior with paper trade label.

30¼in (77cm) wide

$9,000-10,500 **L&T**

A Louis Vuitton "Epi Keepall 55" luggage bag, a few creases on the exterior.

18in (45.5cm) wide

$800-900 **FELL**

A Cartier "Must De Cartier" travel vanity case, the emblazoned suede and leather box with gold-tone hardware accents, interior mirror missing, with maker's dust cover.

12in (30.5cm) long

$800-900 **FELL**

A Mulberry Scotchgrain and tan leather suit carrier and a holdall ensuite, both with detachable shoulder straps.

$300-400 **CHEF**

An early-20thC Goldsmiths & Silversmiths Co. Ltd. crocodile-skin suitcase, with gilt-embossed maker's name and address "12 REGENT STREET LONDON W."

24in (61cm) wide

$900-1,050 **L&T**

An early-20thC small crocodile-skin Gladstone bag, stamped "J.C. VICKERY 179, 181 & 183 REGENT ST. W." and "TO THEIR MAJESTIES THE KING AND QUEEN."

Contains material that may be subject to import/export restrictions, especially outside the EU, due to CITES regulations.

13¾in (35cm) wide

$650-800 **L&T**

A Goyard steamer trunk, leather-bound chevron fabric with brass fittings, the interior with cream linen-covered drawers with leather tab handles on one side, extending chrome rail, and four original clothes hangers, stamped "Goyard Aine, Monte-Carlo, Biarritz, Paris," one strap handle missing.

ca. 1900 *22in (56cm) wide*

$17,000-23,000 **ROS**

A leather-covered and brass-bound shipping trunk, the lid decorated with a painted vignette of a sailing ship being towed by a steam-powered tugboat, inscribed "The Barque Marion Johnstone," further inscribed "Joshua Brown: Master," dated.

1847 *61½in (156cm) long*

$1,400-1,800 **DUK**

A stitched leather suitcase, stamped "Churchill" below a crown.

26½in (67.5cm) wide

$130-190 **FLD**

A 20thC leather car trunk, with gilt-metal hardware and original lined interior.

33¾in (85.5cm) wide

$650-900 **L&T**

A vintage Kenner *Star Wars* vinyl cape "Jawa" figure, small pinhole in cape.

3¾in (9.5cm) high

$1,300-1,800 **VEC**

A Kenner *Star Wars* vintage "Imperial Gunner" figure.

3¾in (9.5cm) high

$160-210 **VEC**

A Kenner *Star Wars* vintage "Lando Calrissian General" figure.

3¾in (9.5cm) high

$190-260 **VEC**

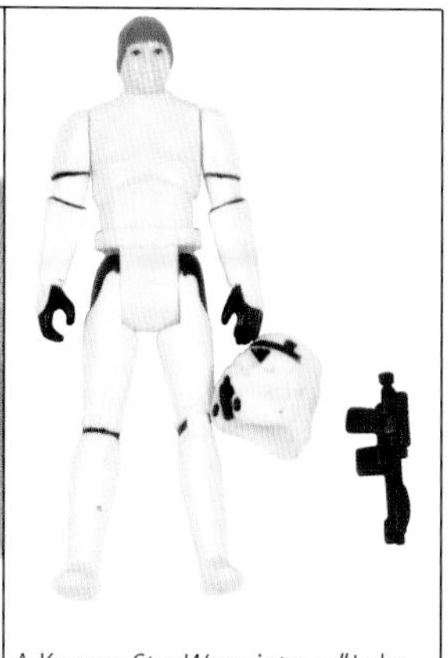

A Kenner *Star Wars* vintage "Luke Skywalker Stormtrooper" figure, yellow paint on inside of helmet.

3¾in (9.5cm) high

$190-260 **VEC**

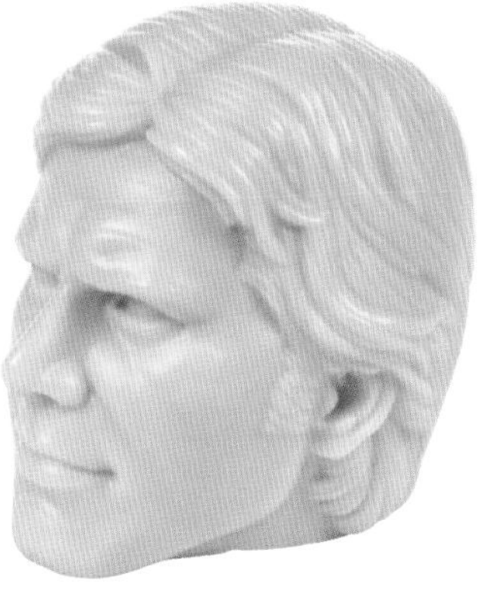

A Hasbro *Star Wars* "Han Solo" modern hard-copy prototype figure head.

12in (30.5cm) high

$300-450 **VEC**

A Hasbro *Star Wars* "RETURN OF THE JEDI, SCOUT WALKER AT-ST," the vintage collection, near-mint packaging.

$100-110 **VEC**

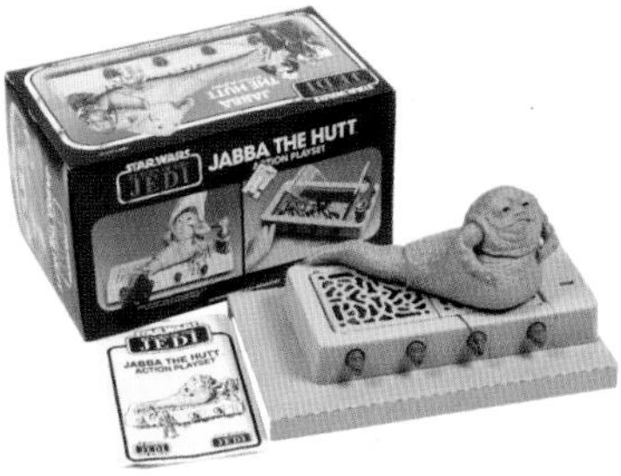

A vintage Kenner *Star Wars* "RETURN OF THE JEDI, JABBA THE HUTT, ACTION PLAYSET," missing pipe, within near-mint packaging, with instructions and inserts.

$230-290 **VEC**

A vintage Kenner *Star Wars* "LAND SPEEDER."

$160-190 **VEC**

A vintage Kenner *Star Wars* "RETURN OF THE JEDI, Han Solo" figure, near mint, creasing of 65C back punched card.

figure 3¾in (9.5cm) high

$300-400 **VEC**

A vintage Kenner *Star Wars* "Han Solo, LARGE SIZE ACTION FIGURE," mint, within scuffed sealed packaging.

figure 12in (30.5cm) high

$500-650 **VEC**

A vintage Palitoy *Star Wars* "THE EMPIRE STRIKES BACK, AT-AT ALL TERRAIN ARMOURED TRANSPORT," missing chin guns, with inserts.
$170-210 **VEC**

A near-mint vintage Palitoy *Star Wars* "BLASTER PISTOL," within scuffed packaging, includes Acrylic display case.
$1,150-1,450 **VEC**

A vintage Palitoy/General Mills *Star Wars* "RETURN OF THE JEDI, HOTH WAMPA ACTION FIGURE," with insert.
$230-290 **VEC**

A vintage Palitoy/General Mills tri-logo *Star Wars* "RETURN OF THE JEDI, RANCOR MONSTER FIGURE," with insert and poster, creased packaging.
$160-210 **VEC**

A vintage Palitoy/General Mills tri-logo *Star Wars* "RETURN OF THE JEDI, Sy Snootles and the Rebo band," broken microphone.
$230-290 **VEC**

A vintage Palitoy/General Mills *Star Wars* "RETURN OF THE JEDI, MILLENNIUM FALCON VEHICLE," with instructions.
$230-290 **VEC**

A vintage Palitoy/General Mills tri-Logo *Star Wars* "RETURN OF THE JEDI, Artoo-Detoo (R2-D2) with pop-up Lightsabre."
figure 3¾in (9.5cm) high
$400-500 **VEC**

A vintage Palitoy/General Mills tri-logo *Star Wars* "RETURN OF THE JEDI, Yak Face" figure, mispackaged with "Sand People" weapon.
figure 3¾in (9.5cm) high
$1,800-2,300 **VEC**

A *Star Wars* floor-standing life-size "Ewok" figure, complete with bow, quiver with feather arrows.

The "Ewok" is a character played by Warwick Davis in Star Wars. The Ewoks became very popular, having their own film *Caravan of Courage: An Ewok Adventure.*

44in (112cm) high
$300-400 **AST**

QUICK REFERENCE—LEGO *STAR WARS*

- **LEGO signed a licensing agreement with LucasFilm Ltd., producer of the *Star Wars* films, in 1998 to produce LEGO versions of the film's characters, locations, starships, and other vehicles.**
- **This line of products was launched in 1999 at the International Toy Fair, New York. In the same year, LEGO's first new male hairpiece in 20 years was designed for "Qui Gon Jinn" and the first specially designed minifigure head was made for "Jar Jar Binks."**
- **In 2011, the "UCS Super Star Destroyer" was launched. At 48¾in (124cm) long, it is the longest LEGO product made.**
- **In 2013, the world's largest LEGO model of the X-Wing Starfighter went on display in Times Square, New York.**
- **In 2017, LEGO launched its "Ultimate Collector Series Millennium Falcon #75192." It has 7,541 pieces.**

A LEGO *Star Wars* "10143, Death Star II," in dusty box with some undulation, box seals have been broken.

$950-1,100 **AST**

A LEGO *Star Wars* "10188, Death Star," box seals have been broken.

$350-400 **AST**

A LEGO *Star Wars* "4483, AT-AT," box with some undulation and creasing.

$180-230 **AST**

A LEGO *Star Wars* "10236, Ewok Village," sealed in box.

$260-320 **AST**

A LEGO *Star Wars* "10030, IMPERIAL STAR DESTROYER," box seals have been broken.

$950-1,100 **AST**

A LEGO *Star Wars* "10240, Red Five X-wing Starfighter," box has been opened.

$190-260 **AST**

A LEGO *Star Wars* "7964, Republic Frigate," box has been opened.

$80-100 **AST**

A LEGO *Star Wars* "10225, R2-D2," box has been opened.

$230-290 **AST**

A Universal Studios Lon Chaney as "The Hunchback Of Notre Dame" diorama, assembled resin 1:6 scale Garage Model Kit.

1923 *12in (30.5cm) high*

$190-260 VEC

A Universal Studios Boris Karloff as "The Mummy" diorama, assembled resin 1:6 scale Garage Model Kit, sculpted by Jeff Yagher for the Janus Company, painted by Darren Kefford.

17in (43cm) high

$300-400 VEC

A Universal Studios Boris Karloff as "The Mummy" diorama, assembled resin 1:6 scale Garage Model Kit, painted by Darren Kefford.

12in (30.5cm) high

$190-260 VEC

A Universal Studios "King Kong" diorama, assembled resin 1:6 scale Garage Model Kit, painted by Darren Kefford.

1933 *11in (28cm) high*

$190-260 VEC

A Universal Studios Lon Chaney Jr. as "The Wolf Man," with Harry Talbot, diorama, assembled resin 1:6 scale Garage Model Kit, sculpted by Mike Hill for the Janus Company, painted by Darren Kefford.

12in (30.5cm) high

$190-260 VEC

A Universal Studios Bela Lugosi as "Dracula" diorama, assembled resin 1:6 scale Garage Model Kits creating one diorama, sculpted by Mike Hill for the Janus Company.

ca. 1999 *22in (56cm) high*

$300-400 VEC

A Hammer Films "Dracula" diorama, starring Christopher Lee and Veronica Carlson, assembled resin 1:6 scale Garage Model Kit, painted by Darren Kefford.

2005 *16in (40.5cm) high*

$190-260 VEC

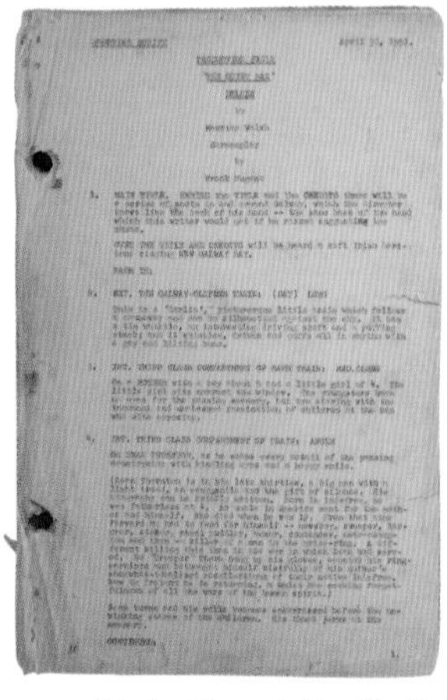

A mimeographed manuscript shooting script for *The Quiet Man*, by Frank Nugent, from a story by Maurice Walsh, 146 pages, legal folio.

Acquired from a cast member.

1951

$5,200-5,800 WHYT

A *The Horror of Frankenstein* script, from the sound department's boom operator Keith Batten, 124 pages detailing the screenplay by Jimmy Sangster and Jeremy Burham for Hammer Film Productions Ltd., signed, with underlinings but without annotations, a loose additional dialogue page for scene 70, p.66.

$230-290 AST

A Lone Star "JAMES BOND 007 MOONRAKER SPACE GUN," some wear, opened packaging, one torn flap.

$130-190 VEC

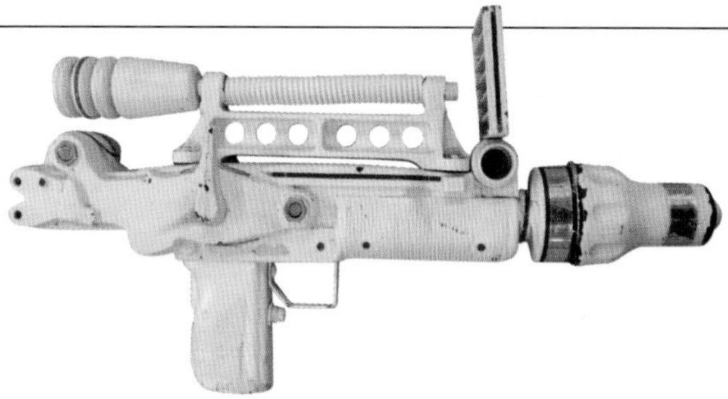

A James Bond *Moonraker* laser rifle, created for the film, features a telescopic sight with rotating grid metal trigger guard.

This is one of only a few surviving examples of these props. This item belonged to the late Brian Bailey, who worked with Cubby Broccoli at Pinewood Studios. Bailey was the production accountant and is named in the end credits of *Moonraker*.

1979 *20in (51cm) long*

$35,000-39,000 AST

A James Bond *The World is Not Enough* Russian cylindrical screen-used barrel, with certificate of authenticity.

$90-100 AST

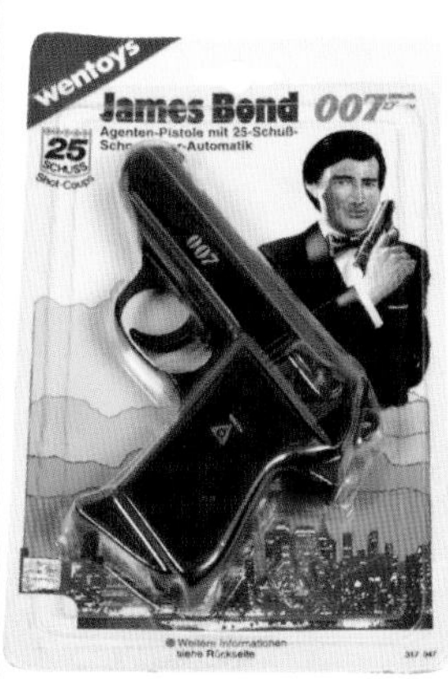

A Wentoy's "James Bond 007" toy pistol, in unopened German packaging.

$50-60 VEC

A Swatch 40th Anniversary "James Bond 007" watch, unused, includes instructions.

$60-90 VEC

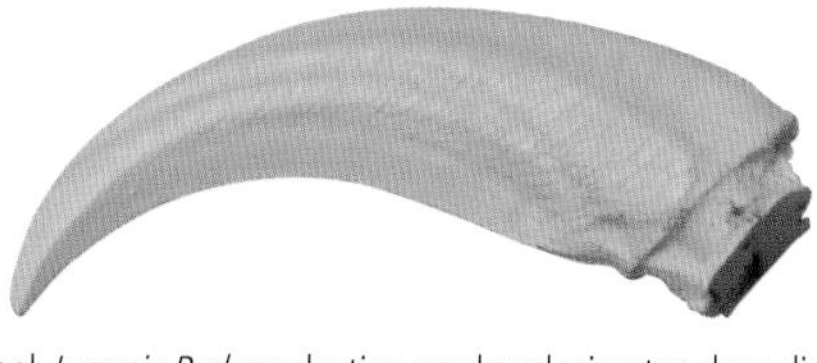

An original *Jurassic Park* production-made velociraptor claw, directed by Steven Spielberg, all the life-size animatronic dinosaurs were created by the Stan Winston Studios.

This item was made during production but unfinished, so it was never used on screen. It is constructed from a type of resin and remains in an excellent production-used condition.

1993 *4½in (11.5cm) long*

$500-600 AST

A "Blade Runner" special edition box set, containing film poster, screen play, film cell, and DVD.

2002

$30-40 LSK

A Marx Toys vintage "The Black Hole" bagatelle.

$80-100 VEC

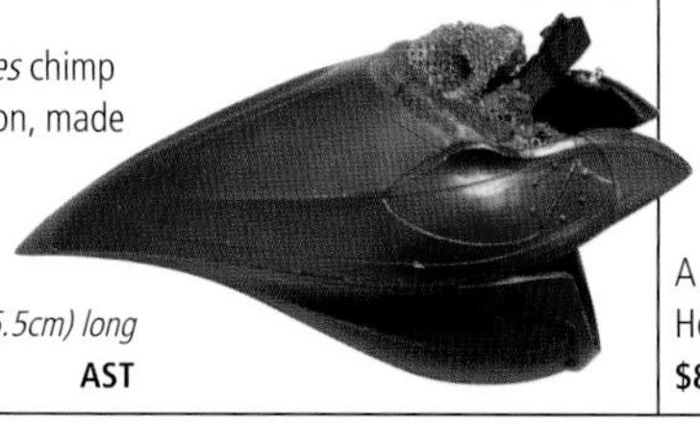

An original *Planet of the Apes* chimp helmet, directed by Tim Burton, made from fiberglass, with a chin strap and chain mail, with a foam interior lining.

2001 *18in (45.5cm) long*

$500-650 AST

An original *Garfield: The Movie!* animation maquette, made by Rhythm and Hues Studio, with production markings on the bottom of the maquette "CB-03."

2004 *9in (23cm) high*

$500-600 **AST**

A "Corpse Bride" character head maquette for *The Maid*, production used, made of resin, with photocopied certificate.

2005 *4in (10cm) wide*

$120-140 **AST**

A "BOHEMIAN PHAPSODY" carpet, from the Queen-inspired light installation switch-on in celebration of the release of the film *Bohemian Rhapsody* on October 21, 2018, at Carnaby Street, London.

192.5in (489cm) wide

$80-100 **AST**

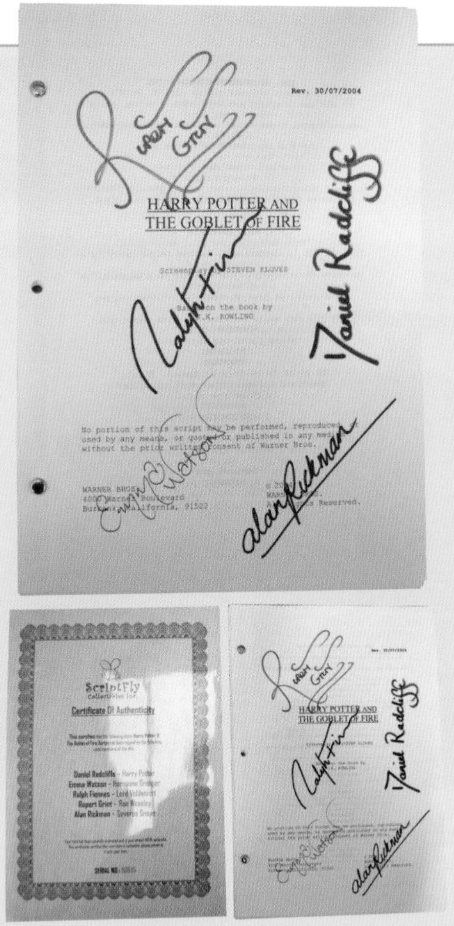

A *Harry Potter and the Goblet of Fire* original script, signed by Daniel Radcliffe as "Harry Potter," Emma Watson as "Hermione Granger," Ralph Fiennes as "Lord Voldemort," Rupert Grint as "Ron Weasley," and Alan Rickman as "Severus Snape," the script is dated "30/07/2004," screenplay by Steven Kloves, with a letter from Warner Bros. Pictures concerning the provenance of the script.

2004

$650-800 **AST**

A Jakks Pacific large-scale DC Comics "Batman" figure, mint, with box.

31in (78.5cm) high

$40-50 **VEC**

A Dapol "Doctor WHO, DAVROS, Creator of the Daleks" black card figure, BBC Enterprises Ltd., CAS graded 75 C80 B70 F80, real grade 76.4, upon punched card, with certificate.

1987

$50-60 **VEC**

A Dapol "Doctor WHO, THE FOURTH DOCTOR" black card figure, BBC Enterprises Ltd. series two, AFA graded 80NM C80 B80 F85, upon punched card.

1988

$80-100 **VEC**

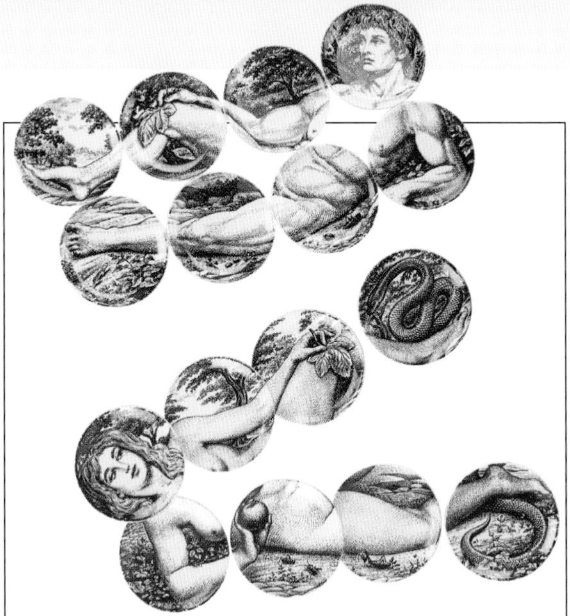

A set of 16 Fornasetti "Adam and Eve" coasters, in two original boxes, marked "Fornasetti Italy."

Piero Fornasetti (1913-88) was an Italian artist and designer of furniture, ceramics, glass, and homeware. He attended and was expelled from Milan's Brera Art Academy. Fornasetti's designs were highly decorative and often featured Surrealist imagery. He died in 1988 in Milan, Italy.

ca. 1965 *4in (10cm) diam*

$1,300-1,900 **DRA**

A pair of Fornasetti "Astrolabio" and "Melodramma" plates, designed by Piero Fornasetti, printed and gilt, printed mark "Weihnachten 1967" and "Melodramma 15," gilt wear on both.

largest 10½in (26.5cm) diam

$500-650 **SWO**

A Fornasetti porcelain inkwell and penholder, decorated with classical verse on a gold luster ground, printed marks.

2¾in (7cm) high

$180-230 **SWO**

A Fornasetti trash can, lithographed with a repeating design of a soldier on horseback, with a brass collar, printed "Fornasetti Milano Made in Italy."

11in (28cm) high

$1,400-1,900 **SWO**

A Fornasetti transfer-printed and brass-bound umbrella stand, "Losanghe" pattern, printed mark "Fornasetti Milano, Made in Italy."

ca. 1950s *22¾in (58cm) high*

$1,100-1,250 **ROS**

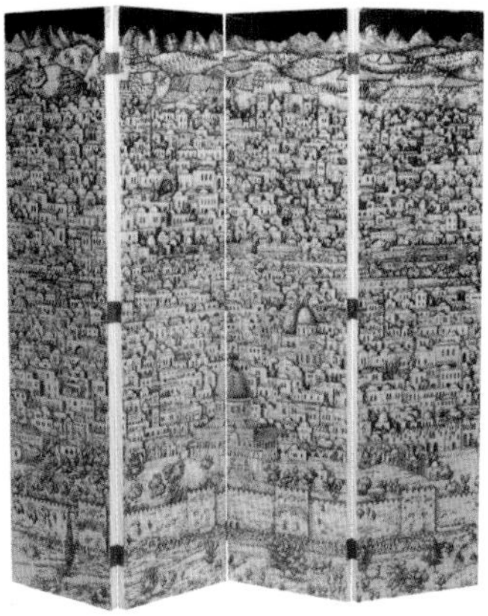

A Fornasetti four-fold "Jerusalem" lacquer screen, transfer-printed and painted, the reverse with playing cards, factory label, some scuffs.

78¾in (200cm) high

$15,000-19,000 **DN**

A Fornasetti four-fold dressing screen, printed on one side with "The Clockmaker's Shop" design, the reverse in plain painted finish, unmarked.

ca. 1950s *51¼in (130cm) high*

$2,600-3,200 **FLD**

An "Onion" bottle, patches of iridescence on the green ground.
ca. 1680-1700 *5½in (14cm) high* **$850-950** **FLD**

An 18thC olive green glass wine bottle, of mallet form, applied lip.
14½in (37cm) high
$900-1,050 **FLD**

A Haywards amber glass hand fire grenade.
6in (15cm) high
$130-180 **FLD**

A Harden Star cobalt blue glass fire grenade, unopened.
7in (18cm) high
$90-100 **FLD**

A French amber "Unic" glass fire grenade.
5½in (14cm) high
$120-140 **FLD**

Judith Picks

The Coca Cola bottle shown here is no ordinary Coca-Cola bottle. For nearly a decade after its introduction in the mid-1880s, Coca-Cola was sold by the glass from store-installed soda fountains, but as its popularity grew, the owners of the company realized bottling it was the best way to expand the business. They were right. By 1915, there were some 1,000 contracted or subcontracted bottling plants in existence.

There was, however, a problem. Diversity in the types of bottles used, together with inconsistent labeling, made it easy for the brand to be confused with a growing number of imitations from competitors. What was needed was a standardized and highly distinctive, indeed, unique bottle, so the company asked several large glass manufacturers to submit potential designs.

Conceived by Earl R. Dean, working at the Root Glass Company, the winning design—with its contoured sides that made it distinguishable even in the dark—was confidentially tested and, after reducing the center diameter to make it more stable on a conveyor belt, went into national production in 1917.

It had been long thought that all the pre-1917 prototypes of these bottles had been broken and discarded at the bottling plants. Until, that is, this bottle (made in 1915 at the Atlanta, Georgia, plant) surfaced among the collection of Coca-Cola artifacts of a retired bottling plant employee. Its huge current value is testament to not only an iconic design, but also one of the world's biggest and most enduring brands.

A Coca-Cola Root Glass Co. modified prototype bottle.
7¾in (19.5cm) high
$120,000-$130,000 **MORP**

An early-20thC Harrach cameo glass vase, cased in blue over pale pink and cut with trailing flowers, cameo signature on body.

10¼in (26cm) high

$400-500 **FLD**

A late-19thC Harrach cameo glass pot pourri, with pierced gilt-metal fitting, the body cased in ruby over a citron rose and acorn air trap ground, numbered on base.

9in (23cm) high

$2,600-3,200 **FLD**

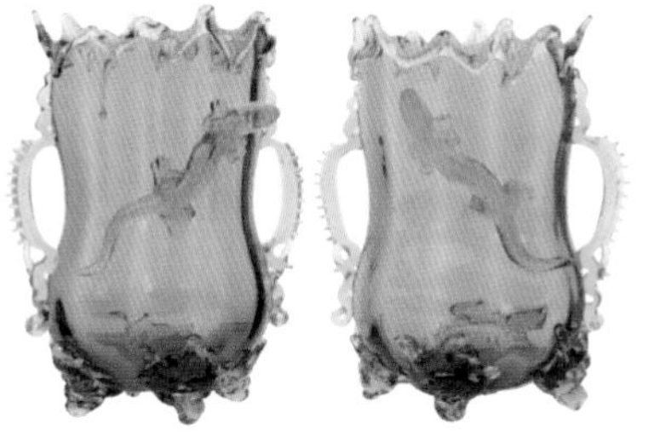

A pair of late-19thC Harrach lizard vases, in pale cinnamon with applied blue crimped handles, rustic form feet and lizards, unmarked.

11½in (29cm) high

$450-600 **FLD**

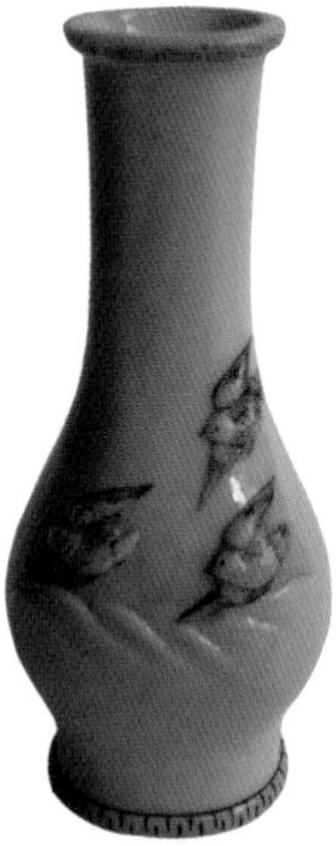

A Harrach "Chinoiserie" vase, with birds flying over mountains.

ca. 1895 *6in (15cm) high*

$300-450 **M&DM**

A late-19thC Harrach glass vase, with collar neck in maroon cased over opal, printed propeller mark on base.

6¾in (17cm) high

$650-800 **FLD**

QUICK REFERENCE—HARRACH

- **In the early 18thC, Elias Müller (1672–1730) took over operation of the glassworks on the Harrach estate in Neuwelt (now Nový Svet in the Czech Republic). There had been a glassworks in the area since the middle of the 17thC, founded by Count Harrach.**
- **Colored glass, high-quality tableware, and milk glass were produced from the 18thC. In 1764, Graf Ernst Guido Harrach ran the company.**
- **In the early 19thC, Johann Pohl managed the glassworks. It produced Lithyalin glass (a polished opaque glass), as well as Hyalith, engraved, enameled, cut, and cameo glass.**
- **The glassworks became a pioneer of Art Nouveau glassware under the management of Jan Mallin in the early 20thC. It produced glass for Czech companies, including J. & L. Lobmeyr and Moser.**
- **The company was nationalized in 1948, becoming part of The Glassworks of Železný Brod, then The Glassworks of Nový Bor and, finally, Crystalex Nový Bor in 1974. In 1993, the glassworks were bought by František Novosad. To support the glassworks' production of luxury and decorative glassware, a microbrewery was built in 2002.**

A pair of Harrach uranium green over red drip vases.

ca. 1890 *5in (12.5cm) high*

$300-450 **M&DM**

A Harrach cameo and intaglio-cut vase, blue over clear and gilded.

ca. 1900 *14in (35.5cm) high*

$650-800 **M&DM**

A Harrach "Lilies and Sun" cameo vase, white on green, gilded.

ca. 1899 *4in (10cm) high*

$1,300-1,600 **M&DM**

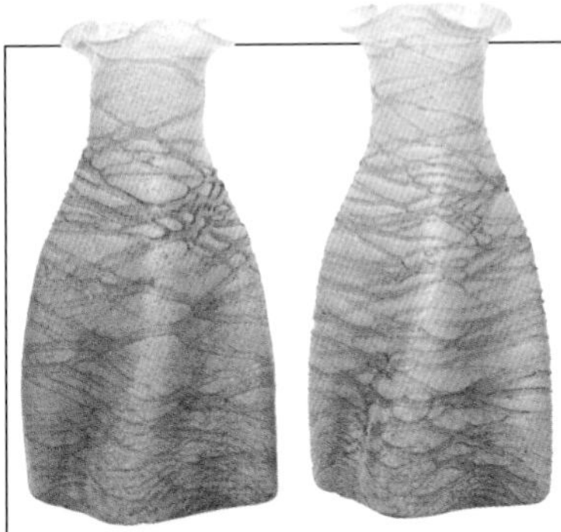

A pair of late-19thC Kralik glass vases, of propeller form, with a crackle finish over the graduated ruby and silvered ground and overlaid with green trails.

The Wilhelm Kralik Söhne glassworks was originally founded by Josef Meyr in Bohemia in 1815 under the factory name Adolfshütte. It passed to his son and then his son's nephews, Josef Taschek and Wilhelm Kralik. After Kralik's death in 1877, the company's factories were divided into what became the Wilhelm Kralik Söhne glassworks and the Meyr's Neffe glassworks. Wilhelm Kralik Söhne, known as Kralik, continued production until World War II.

9in (23cm) high

$190-260 **FLD**

A late-19thC Kralik bronze ware vase, decorated with random whiplash lines over the iridescent ground.

6¼in (16cm) high

$130-190 **FLD**

A Kralik large vase, with applied green flower.

ca. 1900 *14in (35.5cm) high*

$600-700 **M&DM**

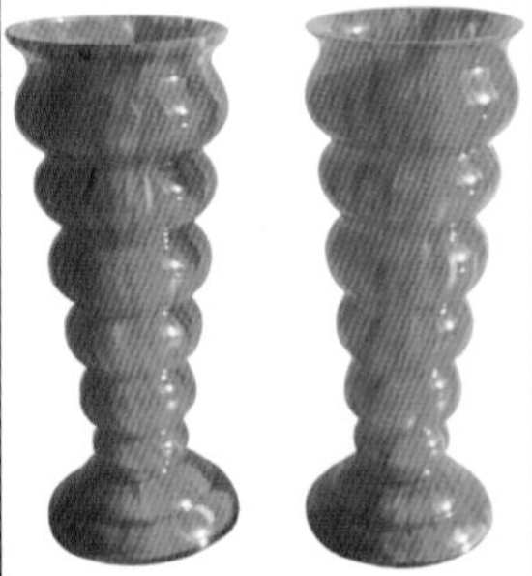

A pair of Kralik vases, by Franz Tomschick.

ca. 1925 *8in (20.5cm) high*

$500-650 **M&DM**

A Kralik giant cut-to-clear/cameo vase.

This is one of the few pieces of Kralik to be documented, pattern no.5089/6.

ca. 1935 *13in (33cm) high*

$650-800 **M&DM**

A Moser "Alexandrit" trio of dishes, signed "Moser Alexandrit."

Color-change glass, depending on light—goes from purple to blue.

Ludwig Moser (1833-1916) founded a glassworks in Karlsbad, Bohemia (now Karlovy Vary, Czech Republic) in 1857. The company specialized in polishing, engraving, and cutting glass, and it began making its own glass from 1893. In the 1930s, the Depression caused Moser difficulties and the family sold their shares in 1938. The company was nationalized in 1948, changed hands multiple times, and became Moser a.s. in 1991.

ca. 1929 *2in (5cm) high*

$400-500 **M&DM**

A late-19thC Moser spirit flask, cased in amber over clear crystal and cut with wild poppies, gilded handle and thumb-lift cover.

9in (23cm) high

$300-400 **FLD**

A Moser "Alexandrit" vase, designed by H. Hussmann.

The glass changes color from pink to blue, depending on light.

ca. 1928 *5in (12.5cm) high*

$400-450 **M&DM**

A Moser cameo bowl, by Otto Tauschek, signed.

ca. 1915 *6in (15cm) diam*

$1,300-1,600 **M&DM**

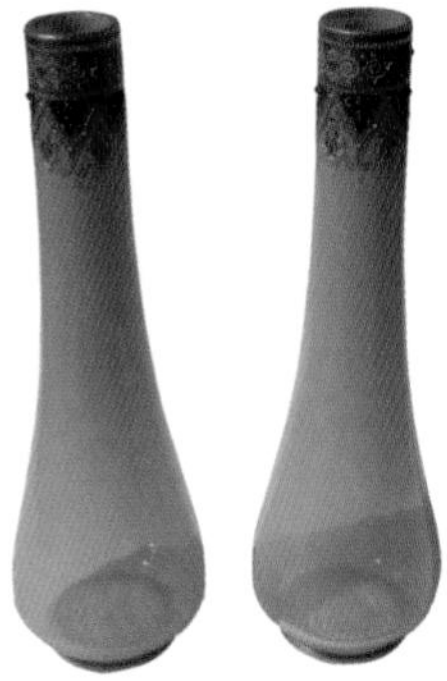

A pair of Moser jeweled vases, on Loetz blanks, pink shading to clear, faintly signed.

ca. 1890 *10in (25.5cm) high*

$1,300-1,600 **M&DM**

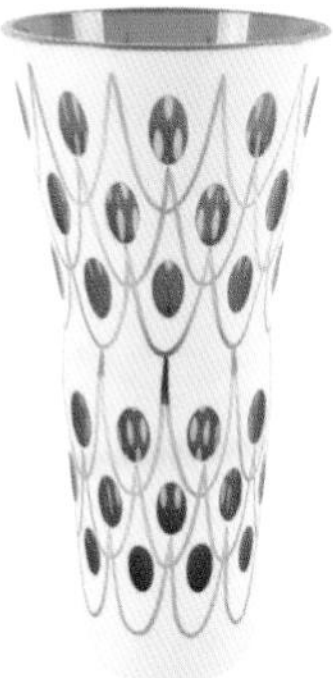

A Czech Borské Sklo "Expo 58" vase, designed by Jaroslav Lebeda for the 1958 World Exposition in Brussels.

A similar, but smaller, shape was included in the commemorative supplement for the Brussels Expo produced by Czechoslovak Glass Review in 1958.

designed 1957 *12in (30.5cm) high*

$700-850 **DAWS**

A rare late-1950s Czechoslovakian Borské Sklo cased, cut, enameled, and gilded "Expo "58" bottle, designed by Jaroslav Lebeda in 1957, the red-pink core overlaid with opaque white glass and cut through with miter cut curving lines in a grid pattern, yellow and gilt embossed foil "Expo "58" paper label, light rubbing.

This is the most iconic form from this series of vases, bottles, and bowls produced for the Czechoslovakian pavilion at the World Expo in Brussels in 1958. Each element of the design updated historic Bohemian glass traditions, from the colors to the style of the casing and cutting, and the Picasso-eques, Modern art-inspired choice of motifs for enameling. Glass was not considered to convey a social, ideological, or political message, so many artists were free to use glass as a medium to express themselves in a modern manner.

Mark Hill, *Dawson's Auctioneers*

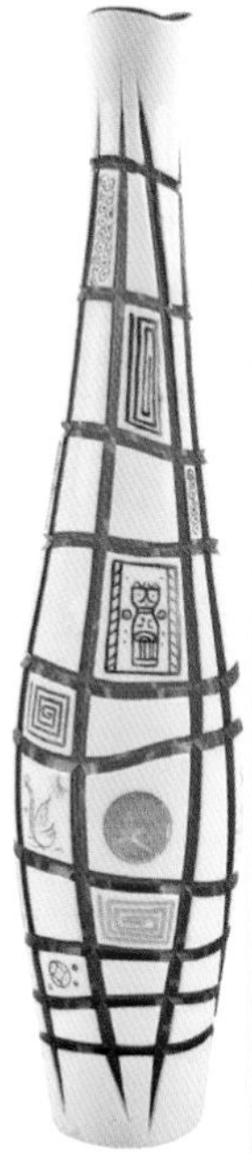

12¾in (32.5cm) high

$1,600-1,900 **DAWS**

A pair of Carl Goldberg vases, silver overlaid with a silver "Gui" (mistletoe) pattern.

ca. 1900 *4in (10cm) high*

$400-500 **M&DM**

A pair of Meyr's Neffe glasses, white over clear, made for Bakalowits using Otto Prutscher designs, on an unknown designer's shape.

ca. 1906 *4in (10cm) high*

$1,150-1,450 **M&DM**

A Meyr's Neffe liqueur set, including decanter and six shot glasses, after a design by Hoffmann.

ca. 1907 *decanter 9in (23cm) high*

$1,050-1,150 **M&DM**

A Czech Novy Bor cased and cut-glass conical vase, possibly designed by Karel Wünsch, with Borocrystal distributor's paper label.

1960s *15in (38cm) high*

$300-400 **DAWS**

A large "Splatter" vase, possibly Ruckl.

ca. 1925 *12in (30.5cm) high*

$260-320 **M&DM**

A Welz vase, "Octopus" pattern.

The pattern was named because of the oval suckers.

ca. 1925 *8in (20.5cm) high*

$300-400 **M&DM**

A pair of Welz "Splatter" vases.

ca. 1925 *6in (15cm) high*

$300-400 **M&DM**

A Ruckl "Splatter" salts jar, with original lid, retailer's label "BATH CRYSTALS Old English Lavender."

ca. 1925 *10in (25.5cm) high*

$160-190 **M&DM**

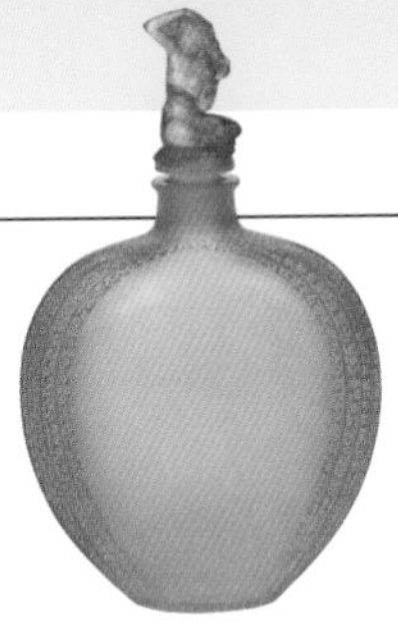

A Lalique "Myosotis" frosted glass scent bottle and stopper, designed by Rene Lalique, with sepia staining, etched "R. Lalique France 611," stopper repaired.

11¾in (30cm) high

$2,300-2,900 **WW**

A Lalique "Lapin" Topaz glass seal, script-etched maker's mark "R. LALIQUE."

ca. 1925 *2¼in (5.5cm) high*

$400-500 **L&T**

A late-20thC Lalique powder box, after designs by René Lalique, relief molded with a serpent, with original box.

$300-450 **FLD**

QUICK REFERENCE—LALIQUE

- **Jewelry designer René Lalique (1860-1945) moved into glassware production in the early 20thC, founding the Verrerie d'Alsace glassworks at Wingen-sur-Moder, Alsace, in 1921.**
- **The Lalique glassworks produced glass screens, lamps, car mascots, fountains, lights, and vases. These were primarily mold blown or pressed, of frosted white, opalescent glass.**
- **Lalique participated in the 1925 International Exposition of Modern Industrial and Decorative Arts in Paris. He was also commissioned for various projects, including decorating the Côte d'Azur Pullman Express carriages in 1929 and producing a temporary fountain for the Galerie des Champs-Elysées in Paris. In 1935, the Lalique shop at 11 rue Royale, Paris, opened.**
- **In 1945, René Lalique died and was succeeded by his son Marc. René Lalique's designs remained in production after his death, but a new crystal glass was also used. Marc's daughter Marie-Claude took over management of the company in 1977 and created the fragrance "Lalique de Lalique" in 1992.**
- **In 2008, Lalique was acquired by Art & Fragrance. The Lalique museum opened in 2011 and the Villa René Lalique, a restaurant and hotel, opened in 2015 in Wingen-sur-Moder.**

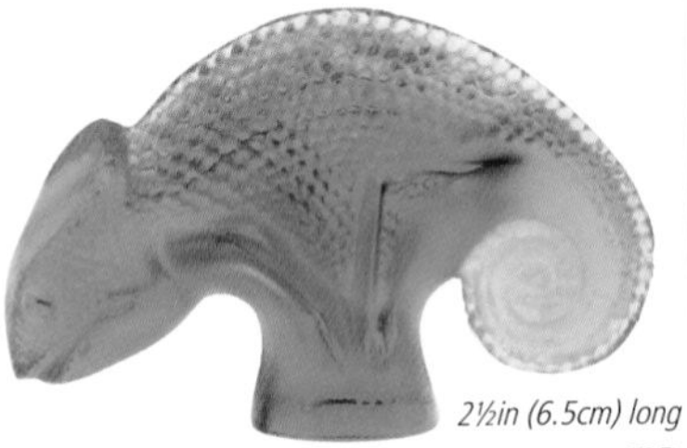

A Lalique chameleon figurine, engraved signature.

2½in (6.5cm) long

$170-230 **FLD**

A 20thC Lalique "Sidonie" turtle figurine, in light green with a frosted finish, engraved signature.

3¼in (8.5cm) long

$50-60 **FLD**

A Lalique "Sainte-Christophe" clear and frosted glass paperweight/car mascot, model no.1142, intaglio molded "R. Lalique France."

1928 *4½in (11.5cm) high*

$1,300-1,900 **ROS**

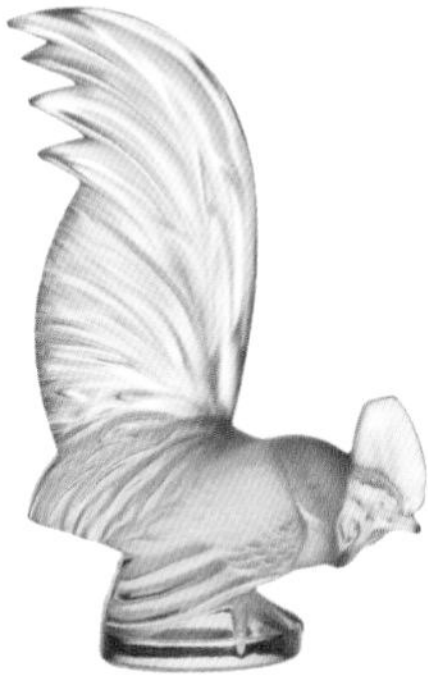

A Lalique "Coq Nain" clear and frosted glass paperweight, designed 1928, model no.11-800, engraved "Lalique ® France," Cristal Lalique Paris label.

post 1951 *8in (20.5cm) high*

$260-320 **ROS**

A René Lalique clear and frosted glass "Pinsons" bowl, no.11-016, designed 1933, molded with sparrows and foliage, engraved "Lalique ® France," "Cristal Lalique Paris" label.

post 1951 *9¼in (23.5cm) diam*

$300-400 **ROS**

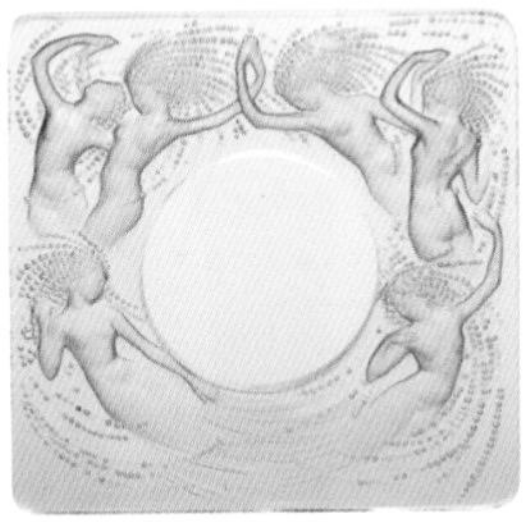

A René Lalique clear and frosted glass "Naiades" clock face, no.764, designed 1926, intaglio molded with water nymphs, without movement, engraved "R. Lalique France."

4½in (11.5cm) square

$1,600-1,900 **ROS**

QUICK REFERENCE—LOETZ

- **In 1836, Johann Eisner founded a glassworks factory in Klostermühle, Bohemia (now Klášterský Mlýn, Czech Republic). The factory was acquired by Susanne Loetz, widow of glassmaker Johann Loetz.**
- **In 1879, the factory, known as Johann Loetz Witwe, passed to Maximilian von Spaun. Along with Eduard Prochaska, von Spaun modernized and expanded production. Notable designers include Franz Hofstätter, Michael Powolny, Koloman Moser, and Josef Hoffmann.**
- **After World War I, two major fires, and the Depression, the factory declared bankruptcy, finally closing in 1947, having produced utilitarian glassware during World War II.**
- **Loetz's best-known ranges are iridescent and trailed in the Art Nouveau style.**

A late-19thC Loetz "Aesthetic" glass vase, relief enameled and gilt oriental dragon on the tangerine to opal ground rising to a gilt band with black enameled characters.

7½in (19cm) high

$650-800 **FLD**

A late-19thC Loetz bowl, with relief gilded fir boughs over a graduated white to pink Burmese-style ground, unmarked.

5¼in (13.5cm) high

$300-400 **FLD**

A Loetz brown-to-cream yellow vase, enameled with birds on blooming branches, enameler's codes on base.

ca. 1888 *4in (10cm) high*

$400-600 **M&DM**

A Loetz vase, "Rubin PG 6893 Phänomen Genres" pattern, with silver to electric blue iridescent wave lines over a ruby-colored ground, unmarked.

ca. 1898-1900 *10in (25.5cm) high*

$2,600-3,200 **FLD**

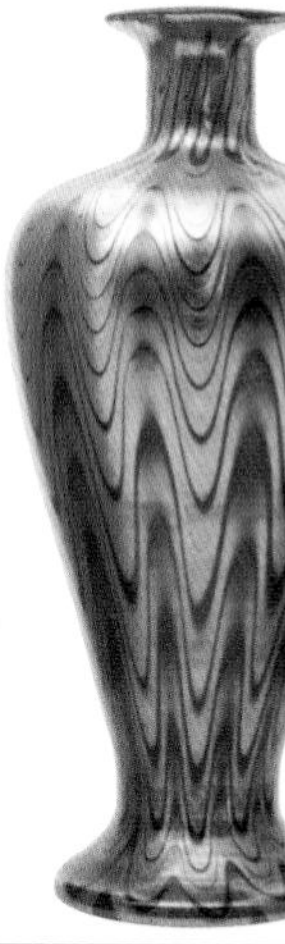

A Loetz two-handled vibrant pink bowl/vase, gilded with one of the classic French Rococo patterns.

ca. 1893 *7in (18cm) wide*

$800-900 **M&DM**

A Loetz handled vase, in opal blue mountain, with enamel flowers.

ca. 1898 *8in (20.5cm) high*

$1,300-1,600 **M&DM**

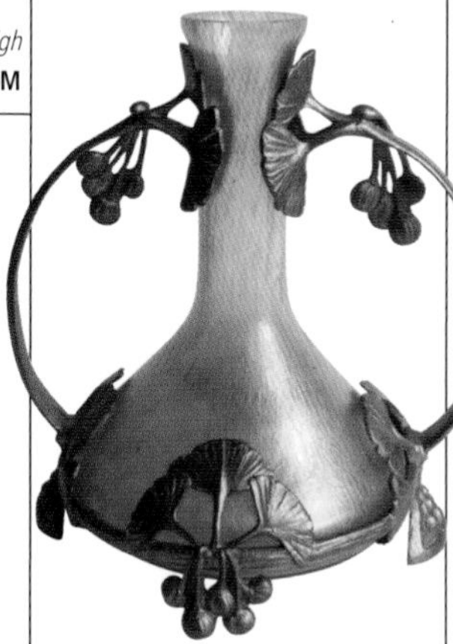

A Loetz "Candia Papillon" vase, in an original gold-plated over pewter mount, decorated with ginkgo.

1898 *6in (15cm) high*

$2,300-2,900 **M&DM**

A Loetz "Dec I/255" vase, on an apparently undocumented Loetz early "Phänomen" genre, marked.

ca. 1898 *5in (12.5cm) high*

$1,150-1,450 **M&DM**

A Loetz "Candia Phan 6893 85/3681" vase, made for Bacalowitz, often called "The Broken Egg," on original bronze stand.
1899 *5in (12.5cm) high*
$2,600-3,200 **M&DM**

A Loetz "Phan 7773" vase, with rare early signature of two crossed arrows and stars in a circle.

Only a handful of pieces have been found with this signature.
1899 *5in (12.5cm) high*
$3,200-3,900 **M&DM**

A Loetz iridescent glass vase, of shell form decorated with blue "Papillon."
ca. 1900 *10¼in (26cm) long*
$400-450 **ROS**

A Loetz "Phänomen PG 85/3780" may green vase, made for Bakalowits.
1900 *6in (15cm) high*
$1,900-2,600 **M&DM**

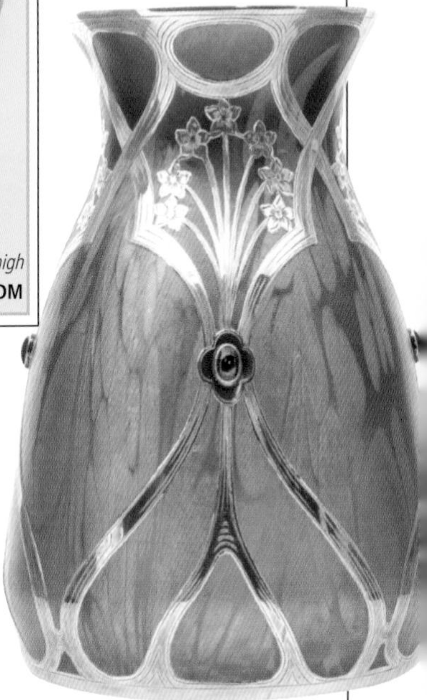

A Loetz silver overlay vase, with a "PG 1/475" type ground, overlaid in silver with interlaced whiplash lines with sprays of flowers and centered cabochon garnets, unmarked.
ca. 1901 *6¾in (17cm) high*
$6,000-6,500 **FLD**

A Loetz "Phänomen PG 2/187" vase, dark blue on opal.
1902 *4in (10cm) high*
$3,900-4,500 **M&DM**

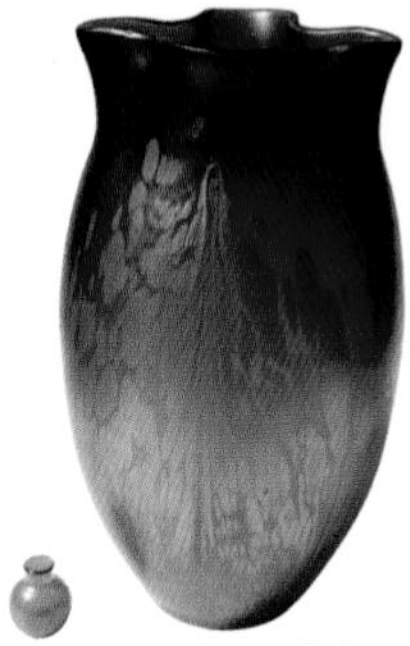

A Loetz giant "Medici" vase, "Phan 2/484," spreading peach color.

Shown with a Loetz miniature to illustrate size difference.
ca. 1902 *14in (35.5cm) high*
$3,200-3,900 **M&DM**

A Loetz "Green Metalin" vase, with silver overlay, with US silver marks.
ca. 1907 *5in (12.5cm) high*
$1,900-2,300 **M&DM**

A pair of Loetz silver-mounted iridescent glass vases, green with pink tints, overlay with flowers, unmarked.

ca. 1910 *11in (28cm) high*

$1,050-1,300 **DN**

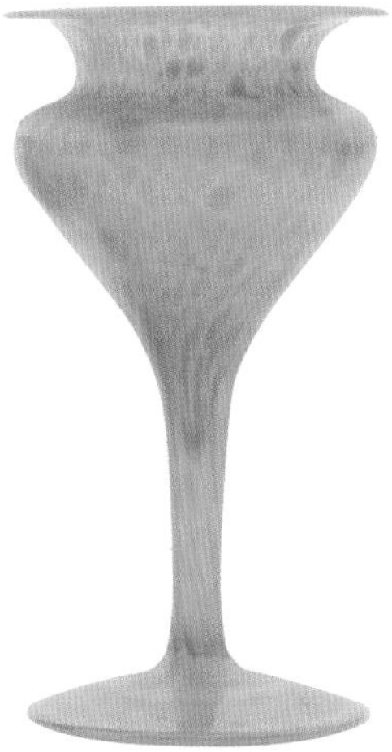

An early-20thC Loetz vase, decorated in green "Papillon" over an opalescent ground.

7¼in (18.5cm) high

$260-320 **FLD**

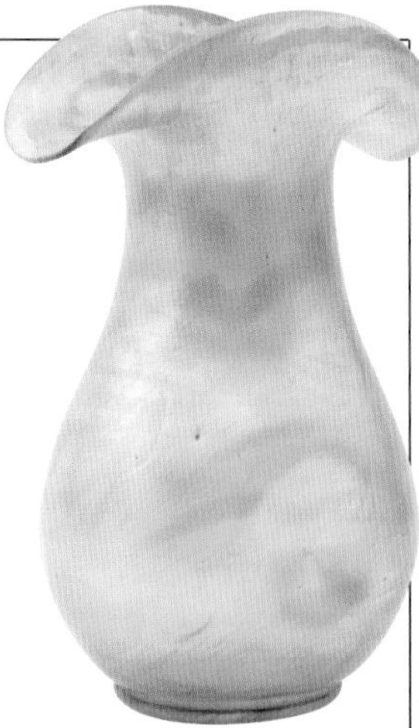

An early-20thC Loetz vase, decorated in a "Phänomen" genre decor with pulled threads over a "Papillon" ground.

9in (23cm) high

$300-400 **FLD**

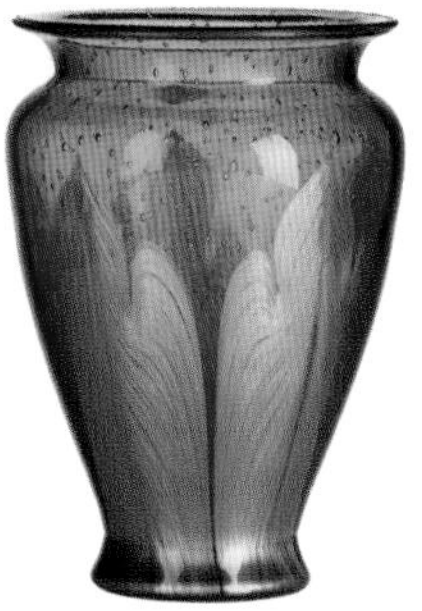

A Loetz "Titania" iridescent glass vase, the ruby body with pulled silver iridescent frieze and bubble inclusions.

ca. 1910 *7¾in (19.5cm) high*

$1,800-2,300 **L&T**

A Loetz "Ausfuehrung 157" vase, black piped onto orange.

1914 *8in (20.5cm) high*

$450-600 **M&DM**

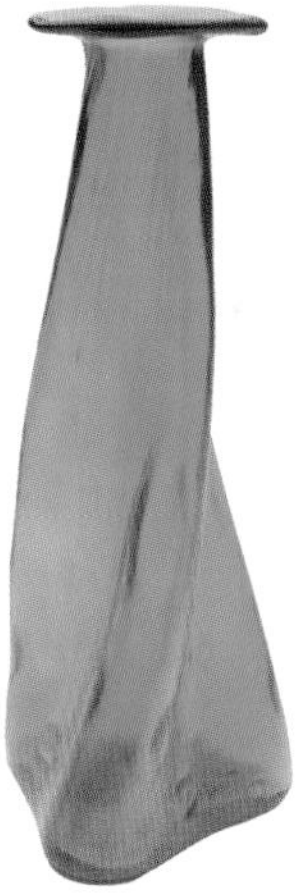

A Loetz "Propeller" iridescent glass vase, triangular section with brim top.

12½in (32cm) high

$650-800 **K&O**

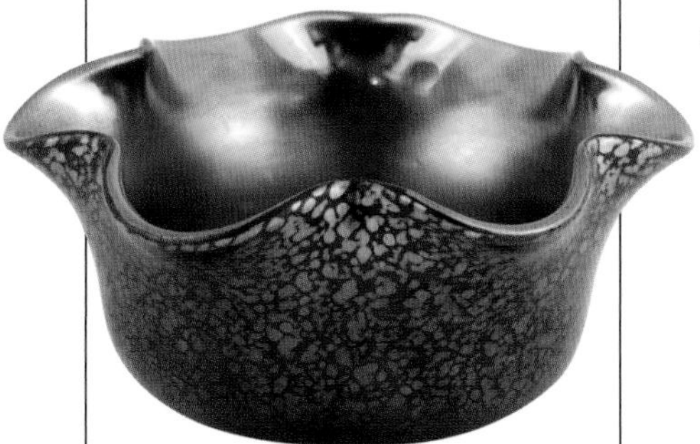

A Loetz glass bowl, the shaped rim with a plain iridescent center.

6½in (16.5cm) diam

$500-600 **SWO**

A Loetz "Ausf 181 Mandarin Mit Schwarz" vase.

ca. 1914 *8in (20.5cm) high*

$400-500 **M&DM**

A Loetz "Ausf 226" atomizer, in metallic yellow and cobalt "Papillon," with all its original fitments, including the puffer with metal valve.

ca. 1925 *6in (15cm) high*

$800-950 **M&DM**

QUICK REFERENCE—MDINA

- **Mdina Glass was established in 1968 by Eric Dobson and Michael Harris in Malta. Shortly afterward, glassmaker Joseph Said joined the company, eventually becoming Production Manager in 1975.**
- **Harris left the company in 1972 and Dobson left in 1985, with Said taking over. Harris went on to establish the Isle of White Studio Glass works near Ventnor, Isle of White, UK, with his wife. When Harris died in 1994, his son Timothy Harris took over.**
- **When the company went into liquidation in 2012, Michael Harris' brother bought most of the company's assets and its name and, with Timothy, set up the company again in a new location near Newport, Isle of White.**

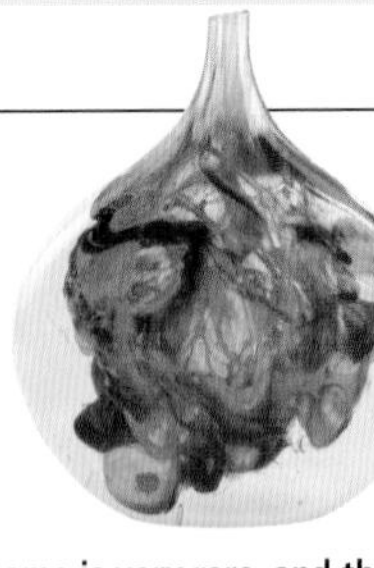

A rare late 1960s Mdina "Cut Ice" glass vase, designed and made by Michael Harris, the colorless flat, ovoid body containing swirls in silver chloride beige, green, blue, and browny-purple, one face cut with large polished facets, the base signed "Michael Harris Mdina Glass Malta."

Glass signed by Michael Harris with his name is very rare, and the presence of his signature usually indicates that he made the piece. The plethora of small "seeds" in the colorless casing and the slight green tinge may indicate that this is an early piece. If it is early, it is almost certain that Harris made this piece due to only him having the skills and experience needed to make it at the time.

8¾in (22cm) high

$1,150-1,450 **DAWS**

A Mdina large "Fish" glass vase, the centered compressed globe and shaft section decorated with ocher and blue streaking over a cinnamon to ruby ground, heavily cased with clear crystal squared shoulders with angular crystal strapping, signed "Michael Harris - Mdina Glass - Malta."

11½in (29cm) high

$2,300-2,900 **FLD**

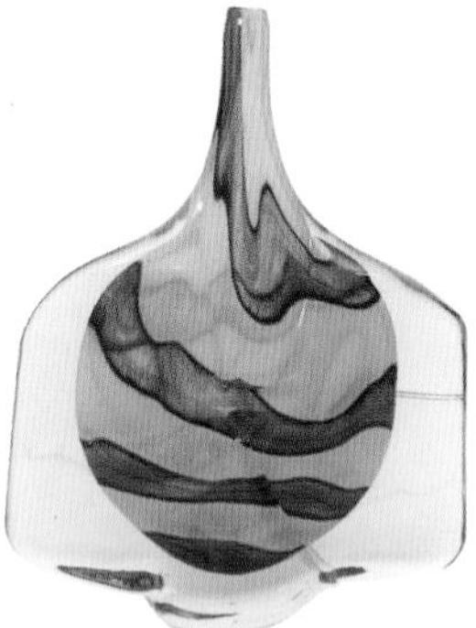

A Mdina "Fish" cased glass vase, designed by Michael Harris, etched "Mdina."

1981 *11in (28cm) high*

$180-230 **WW**

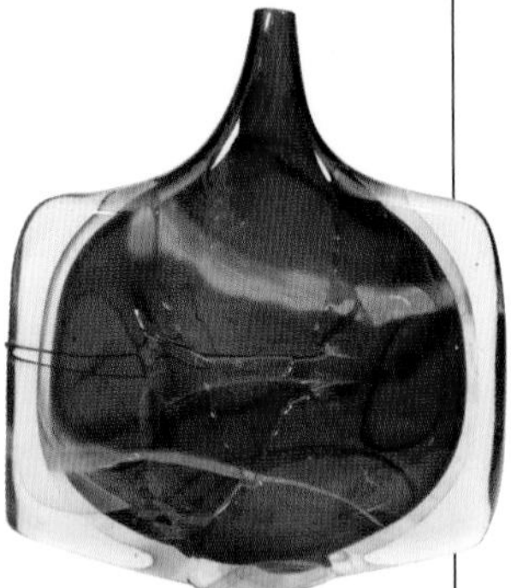

A Mdina "Fish" cased glass vase, designed by Michael Harris, etched marks on base.

9¾in (24.5cm) high

$400-500 **WW**

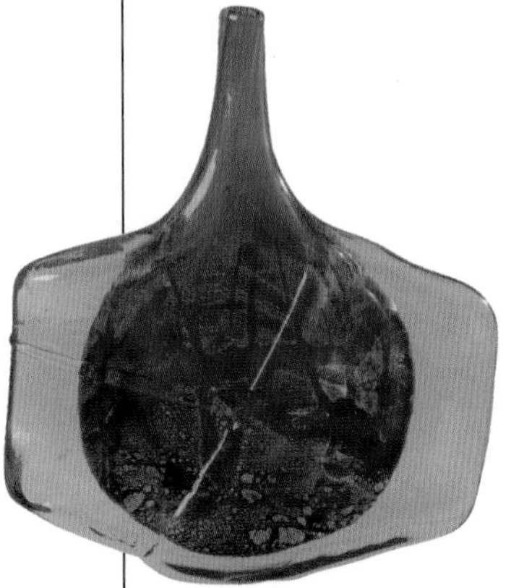

A Mdina "Fish" glass vase, designed by Michael Harris, green mottled center and cased in clear.

8¾in (22cm) high

$260-320 **DUK**

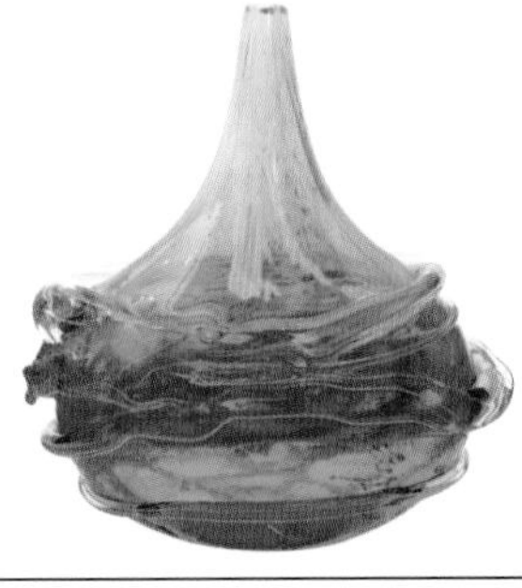

A Mdina large wrapped "Fish" vase, unmarked.

9½in (24cm) high

$300-450 **FLD**

A Mdina glass vase, by Michael Harris, the green to blue swirling ground detailed with black linear designs, signed.

6¾in (17cm) high

$300-450 **FLD**

A late-20thC Mdina "Attenuated Bottle" vase, by Michael Harris, with applied deep blue strapping over an amethyst ground, signed.

16¼in (41.5cm) high

$850-950 **FLD**

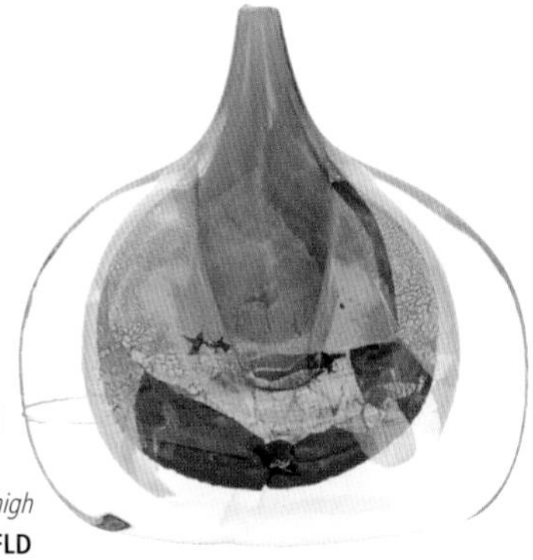

An Isle of Wight "Fish" green azurene glass vase, the green ground with silver leaf, signed "Michael Harris."

7¾in (19.5cm) high

$500-650 FLD

A late-20thC Isle of Wight large "Seascape Bell" vase, by Michael Harris, with veined blue patches over an opal and gold aventurine ground, numbered "46/500," signed.

This piece was formerly in the Ronald Stennett-Willson Collection.

9in (23cm) high

$950-1,100 FLD

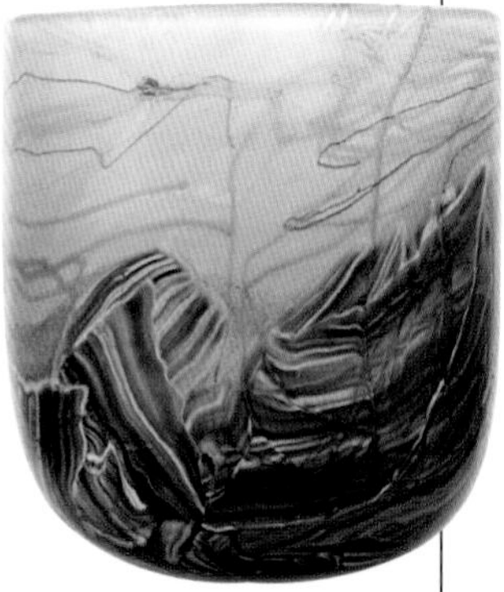

A late-20thC Isle of Wight "Undercliff" vase, by Michael Harris, with a stylized tree landscape over mottled ground, full engraved signature.

8¼in (21cm) high

$800-900 FLD

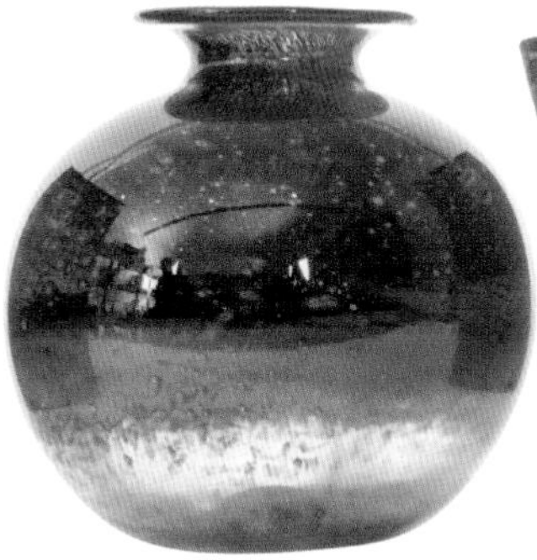

A late-20thC Isle of Wight "Aurene" blue glass globe jar, signed by Michael Harris.

7½in (19cm) high

$130-190 FLD

An Isle of Wight "Undercliff" glass bowl, with blue, yellow, and green concentric designs, signed "Michael Harris."

5in (12.5cm) high

$500-650 FLD

An Isle of Wight "Seascape" glass box vase, by Michael Harris, signed.

12½in (32cm) high

$450-600 FLD

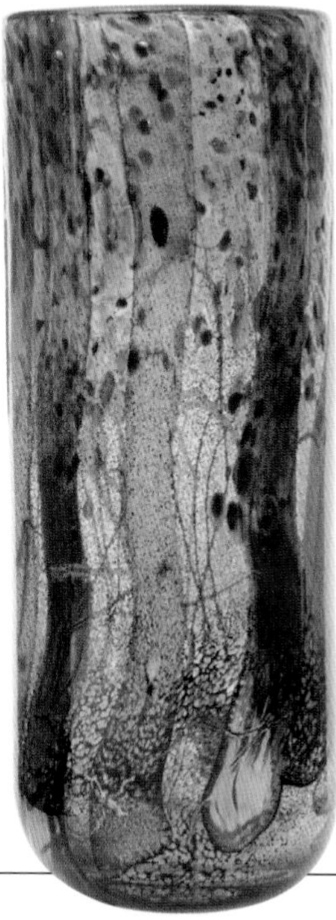

An Isle of Wight "Undercliff" glass vase, by Michael Harris, with trees on the exterior side, picked out in brown, green, and azurene, before a mottled ground, signed.

13¾in (35cm) high

$900-1,050 FLD

A late-20thC Isle of Wight "Kyoto" glass perfume bottle.

6in (15cm) high

$160-210 FLD

Judith Picks

I first came across Monart as a homesick Scot in London. Monart glass was made at the Moncrieff Glassworks in Perth, Scotland, from 1926-61. It was a collaboration between the Spanish glassmaker Salvador Ysart and Isobel Moncrieff, the wife of the factory's owner. "Monart" comes from "Moncrieff" and "Ysart." Salvador Ysart and his son Paul Ysart designed more than 300 shapes, including vases, bowls, dishes, and lamps. Most pieces were free blown and typically have vibrant colors and mottled patterns. Monart glass is not signed but bears a distinctive pontil mark. Before leaving the factory, every piece was given an adhesive paper label. These were very often lost over time, so it is a great treat to a collector to discover one with the original paper label still present.

A Moncrieff's Monart Ware glass vase, mottled green shoulder graduating to purple and blue with eggplant veins, cased in clear.

8in (20.5cm) high

$300-400 **WW**

A Monart stoneware vase, of ovoid form with collar neck, shape A.

1930s *6¾in (17cm) high*

$1,150-1,550 **FLD**

A Monart vase, shape CF.

ca. 1935 *6in (15cm) diam*

$300-450 **M&DM**

A Moncrieff's Monart Ware vase, shape F, orange glass with green and ocher pulled stripes, unsigned.

8½in (21.5cm) high

$700-850 **WW**

A Monart vase, shape GA, with stoneware finish, raised pontil.

1930s *9in (23cm) high*

$1,300-1,800 **FLD**

A Monart vase, shape HF, color 187, mottled purple and red over a cloisonné-type internally crackled turquoise body.

9½in (24cm) high

$500-650 **K&O**

A 20thC Monart cloisonné glass vase, shape MF, with crackled-surface decoration.

10¼in (26cm) high

$400-500 **ROS**

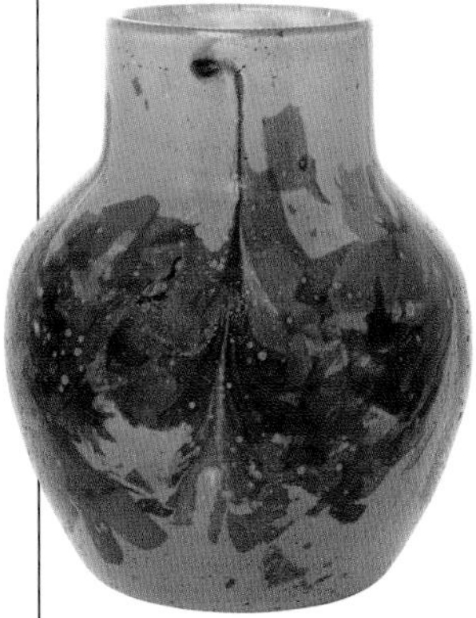

A Monart stoneware glass vase, shape N.

9½in (24cm) high

$650-800 **ROS**

A Monart vase, shape PA, in orange.

ca. 1935

$450-600 **M&DM**

A Monart vase, shape SA.

ca. 1935 *7in (18cm) high*

$400-500 **M&DM**

An unusual Moncrieff's Monart Ware vase, clear glass surface decorated with yellow, blue, and metallic crackled patches, unsigned.

7in (18cm) high

$650-800 **WW**

A Monart glass vase, by John Moncrieff Ltd., "Paisley" pattern, overlaid with swirls in silver, red, and blue on a green body.

ca. 1930 *10in (25.5cm) high*

$2,300-2,900 **L&T**

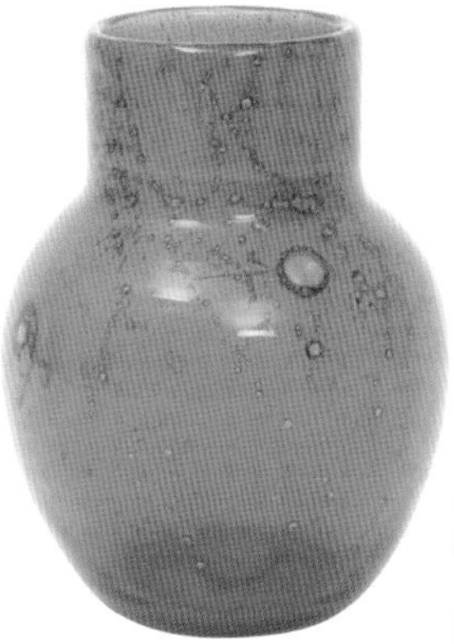

A Monart glass vase, stress cracks on base.

6½in (16.5cm) high

$300-400 **WW**

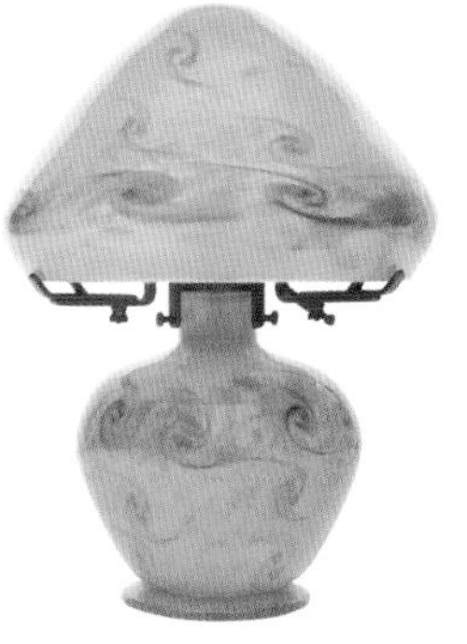

A Moncrieff's Monart Ware glass lamp base and shade, model VII, with brass tripod mount, unmarked.

See Ian Turner, *Ysart Glass*, Volo Editions (1990), pp.86-89 for two comparable mushroom-shaped lamps.

12½in (32cm) high

$2,600-3,200 **WW**

A Moncrieff's Monart Ware vase, decorated with yellow and lustered white stripes, applied collection label for the Ian Turner Collection.

This technique was achieved by blowing the glass into a dip mold with vertical grooves and then rolled in colored glass powder.

5¼in (13.5cm) high

$1,050-1,300 **WW**

A Moncrieff's Monart Ware glass mushroom lamp and shade, with bronze tripod mount, applied retail paper label for Watson's China Hall, Perth.

13¾in (35cm) high

$2,100-2,600 **WW**

QUICK REFERENCE—VENINI & C.

- **A prominent figure in Italian glassmaking, Paolo Venini (1895-1959) founded Venini & C. in Murano, Italy, in 1921, with Giacomo Cappellin.**
- **The company produced Art Deco glassware using Venetian glassmaking techniques.**
- **Designer Fulvio Bianconi (1915-96) worked with Venini, creating the Handkerchief vases in ca. 1949. Other key designers include Napoleone Martinuzzi, Gio Ponti, and Carlo Scarpa.**
- **In 2001, Venini was bought by Italian Luxury Industries.**

A rare Venini "Pezzato" glass vase, by Fulvio Bianconi, "Istanbul" color variation, with original manufacturer's label.

See *Venetian Glass: The Nancy Olnick and Giorgio Spanu Collection*, Edizioni Charta (2000), fig. 87.

ca. 1951

$9,500-11,000 FIS

A mid-20thC Venini "Laguna" vase, by Tomaso Buzzi, the coral-colored body with aventurene highlights.

8¾in (22cm) high

$1,300-1,900 FLD

A set of 12 Venini "A Canne" glasses, designed by Gio Ponti, including a pitcher and a carafe.

highest 10¼in (26cm) high

$5,200-6,500 SWO

A Venini "Tessuto" vase, by Carlo Scarpa, the body with a series of vertical green running lines before a sectioned black-and-white ground, acid etched mark on base.

1950s 11½in (29cm) high

$2,100-2,600 FLD

A Venini & C. "Sommerso a Bollicine" shell, designed by Carlo Scarpa, stamped "venini murano MADE IN ITALY."

ca. 1934 2¾in (7cm) high

$850-950 QU

A Venini & C. "A fili molato" vase, by Carlo Scarpa, clear glass, applied threads, unsigned.

ca. 1942 7¾in (19.5cm) high

$6,000-6,500 QU

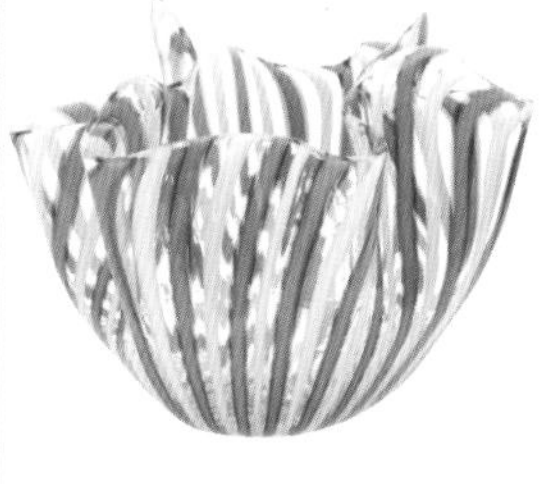

A postwar Venini glass Fazzoletto "A Canne" vase, designed by Paolo Venini, remnant of label on base, acid-marked signature.

3¼in (8.5cm) high

$120-160 FLD

A postwar Italian Murano Venini glass "Fazzoletto" vase, designed by Paolo Venini, acid-marked signature on base.

11in (28cm) high

$130-190 FLD

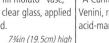

A Versace for Venini vase, with alternating panels of red, mauve, and white glass, separated with vertical black lines, signed and dated on base.

ca. 2010 8in (20.5cm) high

$600-700 ROS

QUICK REFERENCE—BAROVIER & TOSO

- **The merging of Fratelli Barovier and Ferro Toso in 1936 formed the glassmaker that became known as Barovier & Toso in 1942. One of Barovier & Toso's leading designers was Ercole Barovier (1889-1974). Having worked at Fratelli Barovier, experimenting with new methods of bringing color and texture to glass, Barovier produced pieces incorporating fused mosaic and "Intarsio" glass, made up of geometric patterns in colored glass.**

A Barovier & Toso "Oriente" vase, designed by Ercole Barovier, model no.24335, multicolored ribbon rods and wavy threads, with original paper label.
1940 *10¾in (27.5cm) high*
$6,000-6,500 **FIS**

A rare Barovier & Toso iridescent vase, by Ercole Barovier, thick wall, colorless glass with inserted air bubbles, decoration of stylized fish.
ca. 1940 *11½in (29cm) high*
$7,000-8,000 **FIS**

A Barovier Seguso & Ferro "Laguna Oro" glass bowl, designed by Flavio Poli and Alfredo Barbini.
ca. 1936 *5¼in (13.5cm) high*
$1,100-1,250 **FIS**

A Barovier & Toso blown iridescent glass vase, by Ercole Barovier.
1938 *12½in (32cm) high*
$1,700-2,100 **FIS**

A postwar Italian Murano glass vase, by Barovier & Toso, engraved signature on base.
13¾in (35cm) high
$190-260 **FLD**

An Italian 20thC Murano glass vase, in the style of Barovier, in clear crystal cased over deep red with internal trails of gold aventurine.
10in (25.5cm) high
$130-180 **FLD**

A 20thC Italian Murano glass duck, in the style of Barovier, the amber and gold aventurine interior encased with clear glass and applied black detailing on eyes, bill, and neck.
11in (28cm) long
$130-190 **FLD**

A 20thC Italian Murano stylized glass bird, in the style of Barovier.
4½in (11.5cm) high
$90-130 **FLD**

A Fratelli Toso "Murrine Redentore" vase, by Ermanno Toso, colorless glass with scattered multicolored "Murrine Redentore," surface acid-matted, with original label.

Fratelli Toso was established in 1854 by the Toso family. The six Toso brothers (Angelo, Giovanni, Carlo, Ferdinando, Liberato and Gregorio) were joined by Ermanno Toso in 1924. The company was known for producing colorful murrina pieces.

ca. 1955 *13¼in (33.5cm) high*

$6,500-8,000 **FIS**

A Murano glass vase, possibly by Dino Martens for Aureliano Toso, of tapering form, with polychrome inclusions, with a label "MADE IN ITALY," numbered "3509" in red.

See Marc Heiremans, *Vetreria Aureliano Toso, Murano 1938-1968: Designs by Dino Martens, Enrico Potz and Gino Poli*, Arnoldsche Art Publishers (2016), for similar designs by Dino Martens. The number "3509" relates to the model list and, although this is incomplete, the date of similar numbers is 1952.

ca. 1952 *14½in (37cm) high*

$1,600-2,100 **SWO**

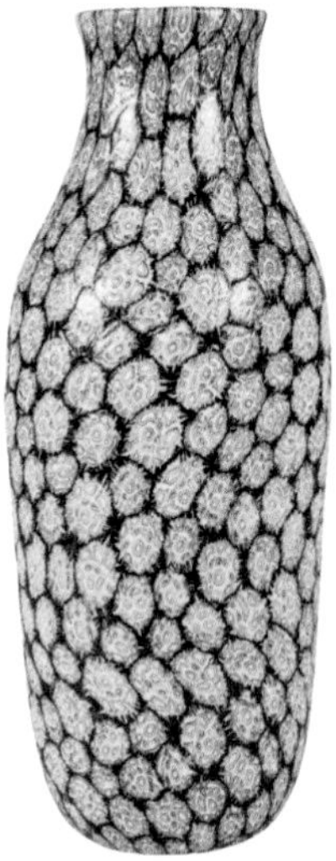

A rare Fratelli Toso vase, designed by Ermanno Toso, colorless glass with remelted murrine terrazzo, framed with "nerox," original manufacturer's label.

1930s *13½in (34.5cm) high*

$3,900-5,200 **FIS**

A Fratelli Toso "Murrine Strisce con Nerox" vase, by Ermanno Toso, framed with "Nerox," manufacturer's label.

ca. 1930 *12in (30.5cm) high*

$8,000-9,000 **FIS**

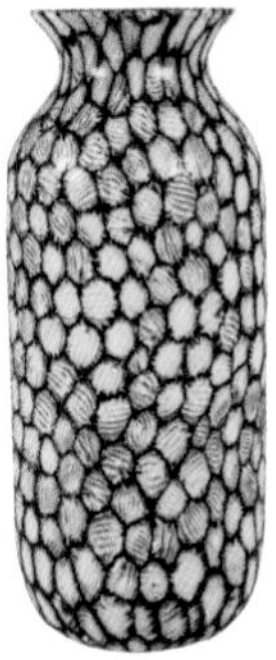

A Fratelli Toso vase.

ca. 1910 *8in (20.5cm) high*

$850-950 **FIS**

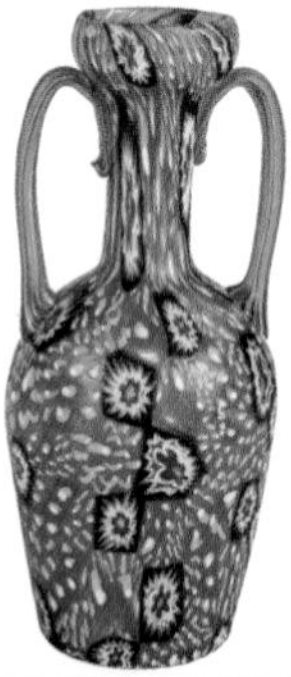

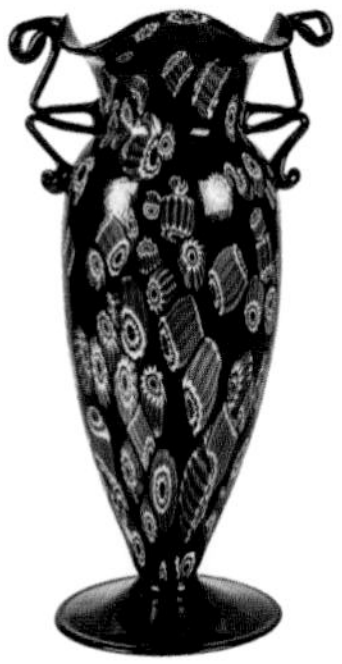

A Fratelli Toso "Black Violet" glass vase, with scattered melted murrine in white and purple.

ca. 1925 *14¾in (37.5cm) high*

$800-900 **FIS**

A Fratelli Toso vase, by Ermanno Toso, colorless glass with melted murrine no.41, manufacturer's label.

This was acquired from the sample collection of the manufactory, which makes it rare and desirable.

ca. 1930 *10½in (26.5cm) high*

$13,000-16,000 **FIS**

A Fratelli Toso "Millefiori" vase, by Ermanno Toso, blue and yellow murrines, before a purple ground, signed "S. Nicola."

1976 *6¾in (17cm) high*

$1,900-2,600 **FLD**

An Arte Vetraria Muranese (A.VE.M.) vase, by Aldo Nason, cased in translucent pink and blue over a foil aventurine ground with deep blue interior, unsigned.
10¾in (27.5cm) high
$3,200-3,900 **FLD**

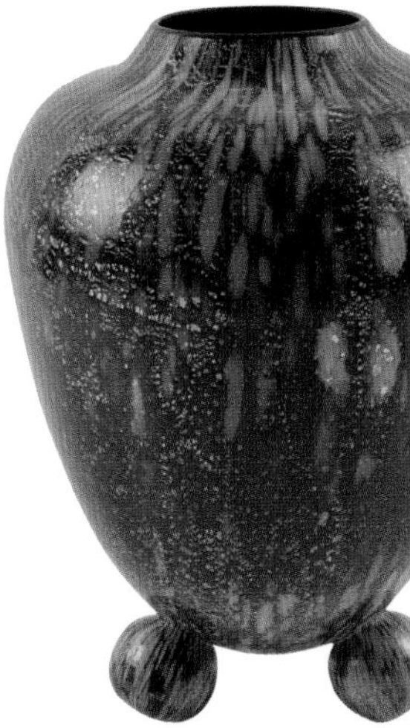

An Italian A.VE.M. glass vase, designed by Giulio Radi.
1960s *11in (28cm) high*
$260-320 **DAWS**

A rare "Fenicio" vase, designed by Carlo Scarpa, Maestri Vetrai Muranesi, Cappellin & Co.
ca. 1928/29 *9in (23cm) high*
$3,200-3,900 **FIS**

A Salviati "Soffici" glass vase, by Christian Ghion, with a miter-cut linear grid design over the black ground, with original box.
ca. 2004 *8in (20.5cm) high*
$260-320 **FLD**

A Seguso Vetri d'Arte sommerso vase.
ca. 1960 *9¾in (24.5cm) high*
$80-100 **FIS**

A Seguso Vetri d'Arte bowl, designed by Flavio Poli.
ca. 1937 *4¼in (11cm) high*
$210-260 **FIS**

A pair of Seguso Vetri d'Arte vases, the clear glass decorated with mottled gold aventurine inclusions, unpolished pontil marks.
1940s *14½in (37cm) high*
$450-500 **FLD**

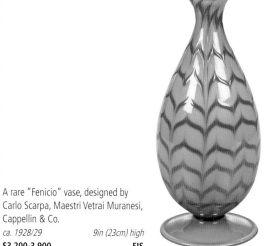

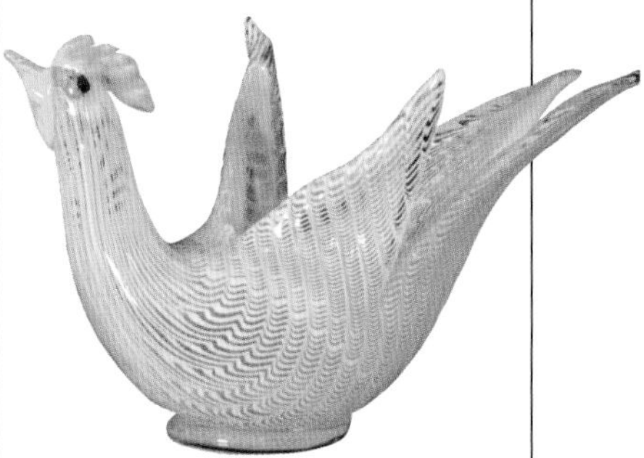

An Aureliano Toso "Trina" vase, designed by Dino Martens, in the form of a stylized chicken, slight damage.
1950 *8¾in (22cm) long*
$190-260 **FLD**

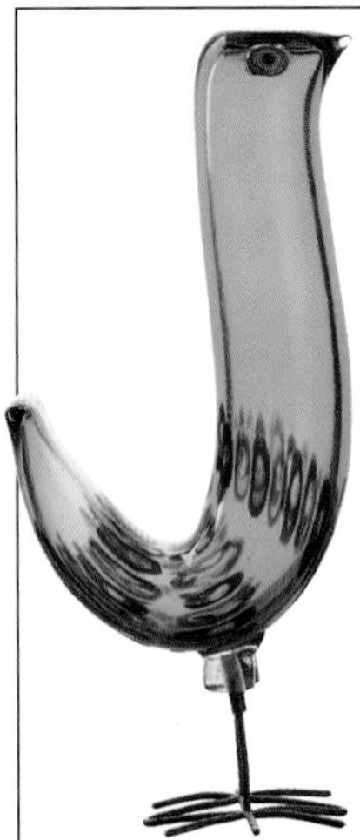

A Murano Vistosi "Pulcini" bird, by Alessandro Pianon, blown glass, murrines, patinated copper, unmarked, some scuffs.

1960s *12in (30.5cm) high*

$6,500-8,000 DRA

A Murano Vistosi "Pulcini" glass bird, by Alessandro Pianon, with a triangular pale blue body, dark blue spiral line, and murrine glass eyes above clear crystal base with copper wire legs.

ca. 1963 *6¼in (16cm) high*

$12,000-14,000 FLD

Judith Picks

And now my particular favorites! Established in Murano in 1945 by the Vistosi family, Vistosi became known for its lighting design but also produced bright glassworks. Alessandro Pianon (1931-84) worked for Vistosi from 1956. His "Pulcini" series of 1962 consisted of five colored glass birds.

Each bird was handblown into a mold. Some had textured surfaces applied or were decorated with murrines, slices of multicolored glass. The beaks and tails were pinched on and the metal sockets for the copper legs were set in clear glass applied after the making of the body. The "Pulcini" birds were made in limited numbers and were expensive.

They are particularly difficult to give price ranges, because prices vary considerably. They also have different personalities, with some being more appealing than others!

A Murano Vistosi "Pulcini" bird, by Alessandro Pianon (1931-84), blown glass, murrine, patinated copper, unmarked, scratches to body, pitting to chest, residue to interior.

1960s *9½in (24cm) high*

$6,500-8,000 DRA

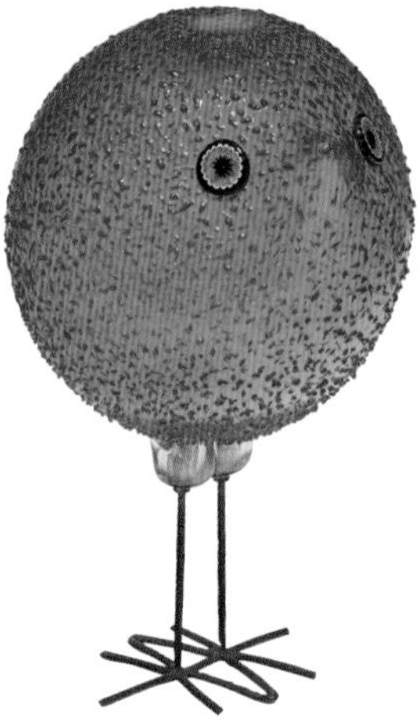

A Murano Vistosi "Pulcino" bird, by Alessandro Pianon, with applied glass eyes standing on copper legs, unsigned.

ca. 1960s *8¾in (22cm) high*

$6,000-6,500 ROS

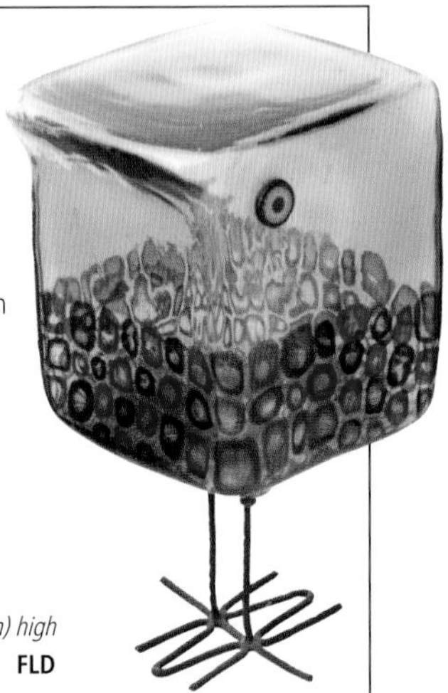

A Murano Vistosi "Pulcini" glass bird, designed by Alessandro Pianon, with an olive green glass body, internal applied murrines in blue and orange, millefiori glass eyes, on copper wire feet.

This example was purchased by the vendor new, directly from Vistosi in Murano on a family vacation, having driven there from the UK in 1964.

ca. 1964 *8¼in (21cm) high*

$14,000-17,000 FLD

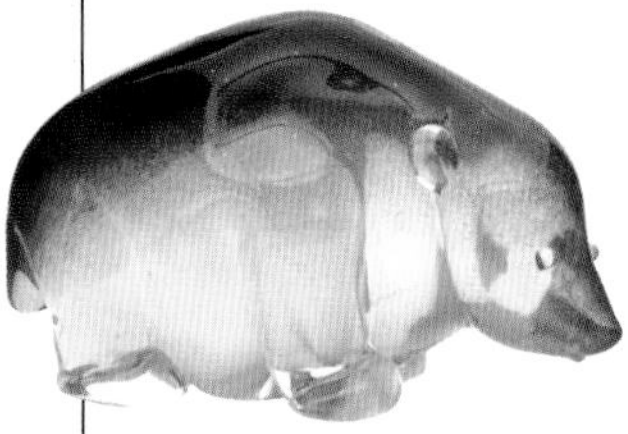

A mid-20thC Italian Murano sommerso glass stylized bear figurine, designed by Archimede Seguso, unmarked.

9½in (24cm) long

$130-190 FLD

A mid-20thC A.VE.M. glass model of a stylized aardvark, in the manner of Archimede Seguso, slight damage.

10in (25.5cm) long

$300-400 FLD

A postwar Italian Murano glass stylized seagull, in the manner of Seguso, on a clear crystal stylized wave, unmarked.

10¼in (26cm) high

$190-260 FLD

A postwar Kosta "Unika" glass vase, by Vicke Lindstrand, internally decorated, marked "UNIKA 1713," engraved signature.

5in (13cm) high

$1,600-2,100 FLD

A Kosta "Winter" glass vase, by Vicke Lindstrand, engraved signature "Kosta LH."

1950s *7¼in (18.5cm) high*

$6,000-7,000 FLD

A Kosta "Trees in Fog" glass vase, designed by Vicke Lindstrand, internally decorated with onyx stylized branches, acid stamped "LIND-STRAND KOSTA LU2005."

ca. 1951 *13¼in (33.5cm) high*

$3,200-3,900 FLD

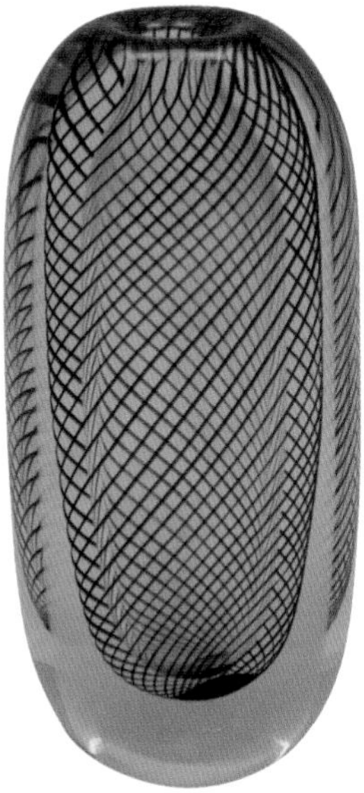

A Kosta Boda sommerso vase, designed by Vicke Lindstrand, marked "LH1361."

ca. 1959

$350-430 LYN

QUICK REFERENCE—KOSTA

- **Kosta glassworks was founded in 1742 by Anders Koskull and Georg Bogislaus Staël von Holstein in Småland, Sweden.**
- **Kosta designers include Vicke Lindstrand (1904-83), Bertil Vallien (b.1938), Elis Bergh (1881-1954), Anna Ehrner (b.1948), and Sven-Erik Skawonius (1908-81).**
- **Between 1950 and 1973, Lindstrand was art director at Kosta. He worked with engraved decoration on clear and colored glass.**
- **A merging of glassworks in the areas of Kosta, Boda, and Åfors bought the company under the control of the Afors Group in the early 1970s. In 1976, the company changed its name to Kosta Boda AB and became part of Orrefors Kosta Boda AB from 1989.**

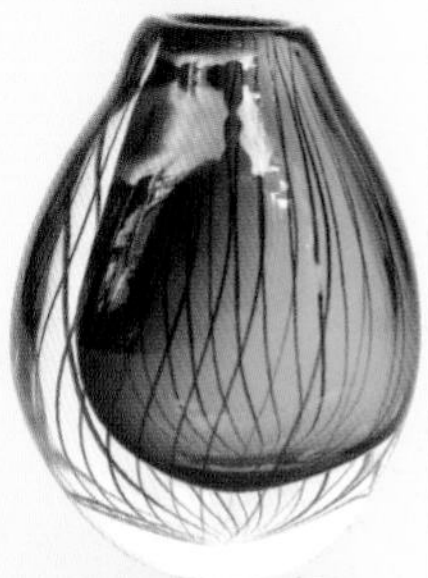

A Kosta crystal glass vase, designed by Vicke Lindstrand, the turquoise core surrounded by purple threads, engraved "Kosta, LH 1720."

ca. 1958-62 *6in (15cm) high*

$500-650 FLD

A Kosta Boda "Moonlanding" glass vase, designed by Monica Backström, original label, engraved signature.

ca. 2000 *8¼in (21cm) diam*

$300-400 SWO

A late-20thC Kosta Boda "Satellite" vase, by Bertil Vallien, original label, engraved signature.

11½in (29cm) high

$130-190 FLD

A late-20thC Kosta Boda bowl, designed by Bertil Vallien, "Galaxy" pattern, no markings.

6¼in (16cm) diam

$100-160 FLD

A contemporary Artist's Collection Kosta Boda glass vase, designed by Bertil Vallien, engraved signature.

7½in (19cm) high

$190-260 FLD

QUICK REFERENCE—ORREFORS

- **Established in 1898 in Småland, Sweden, Orrefors began producing bottles and tableware. From the 1920s, the company's focus moved to art glass. It experimented with cameo glass, graal engraving, and cut and engraved glass produced using a copper wheel.**
- **Key designers include Simon Gate (1883-1945), Edvard Hald (1883-1980), Ingeborg Lundin (1921-92), Sven Palmqvist (1906-84), Edvin Öhrström (1906-94), and Vicke Lindstrand (1904-83). Lindstrand worked for Orrefors between 1928 and 1941.**
- **The graal technique was developed by Knut Bergqvist. It featured internal decoration with a clear glass exterior. Graal came in various colors.**
- **In 1989, Orrefors merged with Kosta Boda.**

An Orrefors graal vase, designed by Eva Englund, marked "v968-75," "Orrefors" and "Eva Englund."

Normally, Graal vases have thick walls; unusually, in this vase the glass is extremley thin, having the appearance of medieval or Roman glass.

6¼in (16cm) high

$300-320 LYN

An Orrefors graal "Fish" vase, by Edvard Hald, signed "ORREFORS GRAAL 17980 Edvard Hald."

ca. 1955 5in (12.5cm) high

$450-500 BELL

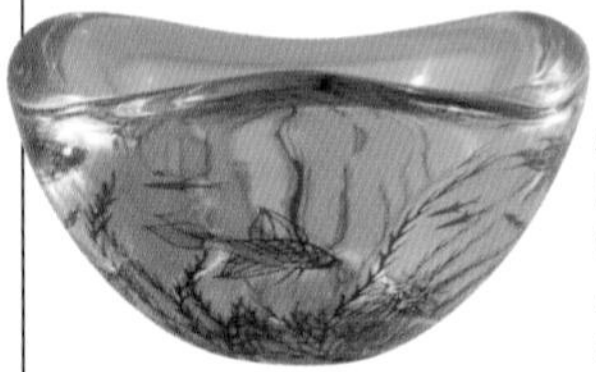

An Orrefors graal fish bowl, by Edvard Hald, signed "ORREFORS GRAAL 4390 Edvard Hald."

ca. 1955 7¾in (19.5cm) high

$500-650 BELL

An Orrefors graal glass paperweight vase, by Edvard Hald, signed marks.

ca. 1930 5in (12.5cm) high

$650-800 DUK

An Orrefors "Ariel" glass vase, by Ingeborg Lundin, signed "ORREFORS No 179 E3 INGEBORG LUNDIN."

ca. 1973 6¼in (16cm) high

$500-650 BELL

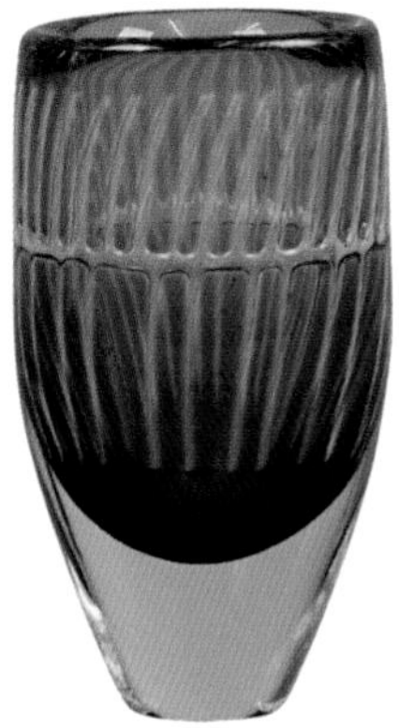

An Orrefors "Ariel" glass vase, by Ingeborg Lundin, signed "ORREFORS ARIEL No 718N INGEBORG LUNDIN."

ca. 1964 8in (20.5cm) high

$500-650 BELL

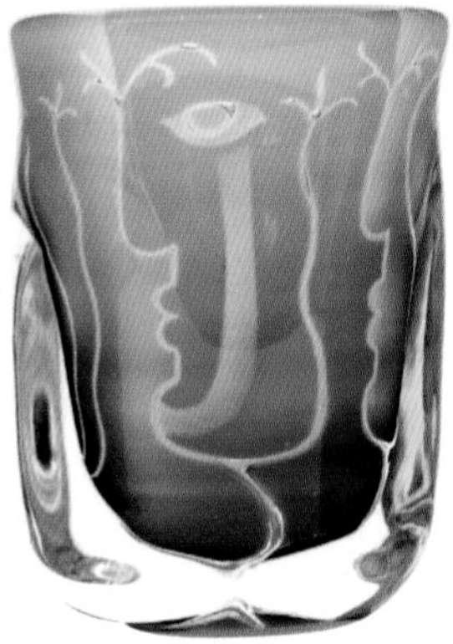

A postwar Orrefors "Ariel Faces" glass vase, by Ingeborg Lundin, internally decorated with stylized Picasso-esque faces with ariel band detailing, engraved signature.

7in (18cm) high

$3,900-4,500 FLD

An Orrefors "Ariel" glass vase, designed by Edvin Öhrström, etched signature and number "957913" with "Orrefors Sweden" sticker.

8in (20.5cm) high

$1,600-2,100 SWO

An Orrefors "Kraka" vase, by Sven Palmqvist, with engraved signature on the base.

ca. 1954 8¼in (21cm) high

$700-850 FLD

A Flygsfors glass vase, etched mark.

17¼in (44cm) high

$130-190 SWO

A Hadeland slab-sided glass vase, by Hermann Bongaard, signed.

4¾in (12cm) high

$190-260 HAN

A Holmegaard Carnaby vase or candlestick, designed by Per Lutken.

The more common version of this vase has three layers of glass, not two, and an inner white core.

10¼in (26cm) high

$220-250 LYN

A pair of green glass "Gulvvase" bottle decanters and ball stoppers, in the style of Holmegaard.

15½in (39.5cm) high

$260-320 SWO

A "Stellaria" large serving bowl, designed by Tapio Wirkkala, manufactured by Iittala, Finland, signed on base.

ca. 1960s 11½in (29cm) diam

$160-230 ROS

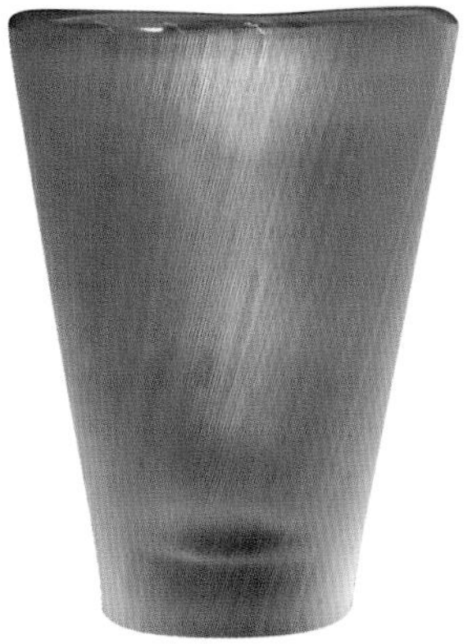

A postwar Iittala bamboo vase, designed by Tapio Wirkkala, engraved signature.

ca. 1950s 6¾in (17cm) high

$400-450 FLD

A Nuutajärvi Notsjo glass "Sieppo" or "Flycatcher" figurine, designed by Oiva Toikka, original label, engraved signature.

ca. 1972 5in (12.5cm) high

$400-450 FLD

A Nuutajärvi "Ariel" glass bowl, by Kaj Frank, acid mark on the base.

4¼in (11cm) wide

$90-120 FLD

A Nuutajärvi Notsjo sommerso glass vase, designed by Kaj Franck, engraved signature, dated.

1961 4in (10cm) high

$190-260 FLD

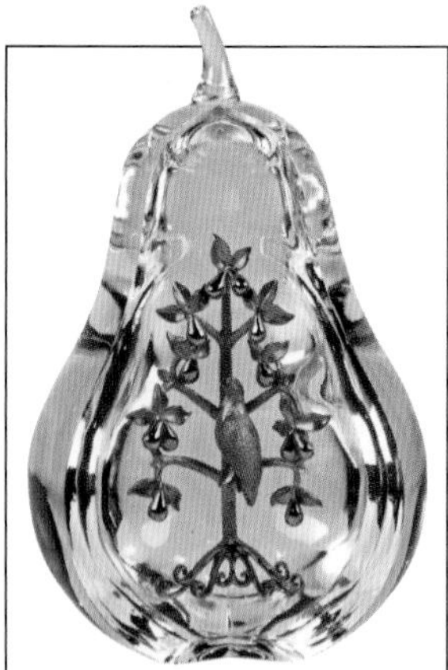

A Steuben "Partridge In A Pear Tree" sculpture, designed by Lloyd Atkins, signed "Steuben" on base, with box.

designed 1968 *6in (15cm) high*

$900-1,050 **CLAR**

A 20thC Steuben blue "Aurene" vase, marked, shallow chip on underside of base.

10½in (26.5cm) high

$950-1,100 **DRA**

An early-20thC Steuben "Gold Aurene" trumpet vase, etched signature, numbered "2909," wear on iridescence, scuffs and scratches.

5¾in (14.5cm) high

$260-320 **DRA**

QUICK REFERENCE—STEUBEN

- **Steuben was founded in 1903 in Corning, New York, by Frederick Carder (1863-1963). In 1918, it was acquired by Corning Glass Works, which is now Corning Incorporated.**
- **Carder patented an iridescent glass called "Aurene" in 1904. It was produced in blue, brown, red, and green.**
- **In 1933, a new formula for colorless crystal glass was introduced and Steuben moved away from producing colored pieces.**

A pair of early-20thC Steuben jade cameo glass vases, attributed to Frederick Carder, "Bristol" pattern, unmarked, with scuffs and scratches throughout, ground down rims and bases, chip on one in the body.

12¼in (31cm) high

$2,200-2,900 **DRA**

A Steuben glass vanity jar with threaded stopper, marked, acid-etched fleur-de-lis mark.

1903-33 *6¼in (16cm) high*

$190-260 **DRA**

A 20thC Steuben glass lion sculpture, on lacquered wood base, with original box.

7in (18cm) high

$800-900 **DRA**

A Steuben blue "Aurene" intarsia glass vase, by Frederick Carder, unmarked, repaired crack on rim.

8½in (21.5cm) high

$160-230 **DRA**

An early 20thC Steuben gold "Aurene" blown-glass vase, on carved wood stand, etched "AURENE 2412," wear on iridescent surface.

without stand 8in (20.5cm) high

$600-700 **DRA**

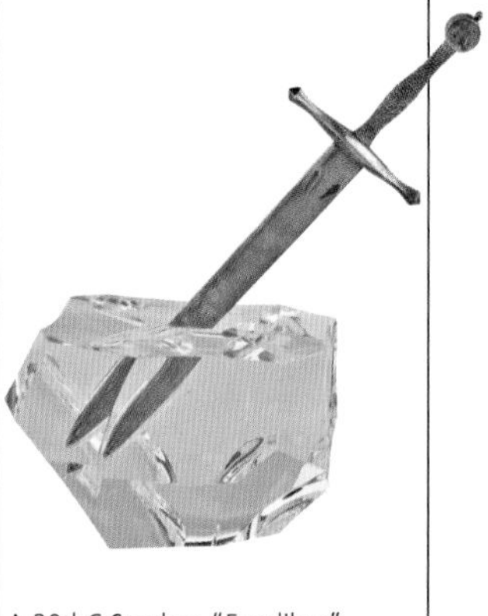

A 20thC Steuben "Excalibur" paperweight, with sword, crystal and sterling silver, 18k gold, original box, marked, some small chips.

11in (28cm) high

$900-1,050 **DRA**

A late-19thC Stevens & Williams Osiris-type vase, on three clear rustic form feet.

Stevens & Williams was established in Stourbridge in 1847 and produced heavily cut crystal glass. The company's "Rockingham" ware is especially sought after. John Northwood was appointed Art Director in the 1880s. In 1919, Stevens & Williams received a Royal Warrant and later changed its name to Royal Brierley Crystal. The company went bankrupt in the 1990s, but in the early 2000s it was reopened under ownership of Dartington Crystal Ltd.

8¾in (22cm) high

$400-450 **FLD**

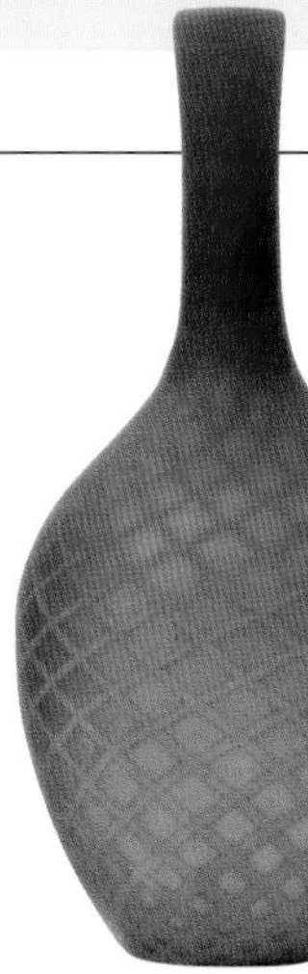

A late-19thC Stevens & Williams satin quilted air trap vase, slight damage.

9½in (24cm) high

$80-100 **FLD**

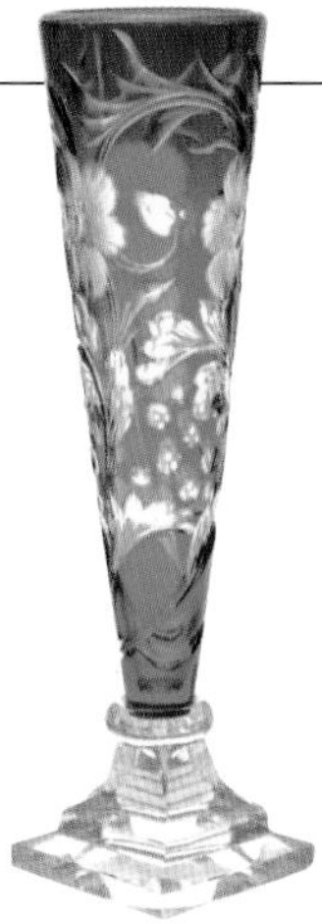

An early-20thC Stevens & Williams posy vase, pattern no.43686, dated.

1912 *8¼in (21cm) high*

$160-210 **FLD**

A Stevens & Williams Royal Brierley footed glass vase, designed by Keith Murray, unsigned.

14¾in (37.5cm) high

$260-320 **WW**

A Stevens & Williams glass tumbler vase.

1940s *8in (20.5cm) high*

$80-100 **FLD**

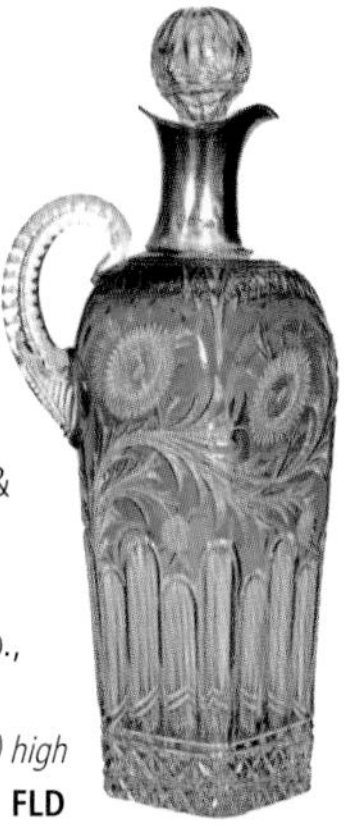

An early-20thC Stevens & Williams decanter, with silver collar, Sheffield, Hammond, Creak and Co., slight damage.

1904 *11in (28cm) high*

$700-850 **FLD**

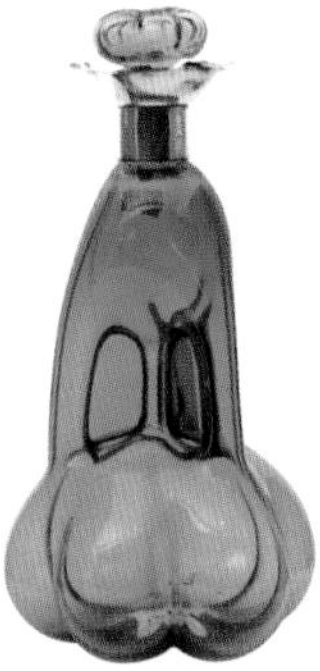

A late-19thC Stevens & Williams "Scrooge" decanter, collar neck with silver mounts, with a matched lobed stopper, hallmarked for Sheffield.

1898 *10¾in (27.5cm) high*

$160-210 **FLD**

A Stevens & Williams intaglio hock drinking glass, probably engraved by T.E. Wood, the bowl cut in the "Willow" pattern.

8in (20.5cm) high

$1,400-1,800 **DUK**

A Stevens & Williams opaline glass bowl, by Will Capewell, with classical figurines in black enamel, unmarked.

1930s *6¼in (16cm) high*

$130-180 **FLD**

QUICK REFERENCE—WEBB

- **Thomas Webb & Sons was founded by Thomas Webb in Stourbridge, England in 1837. When Thomas Webb retired in 1869, his son Thomas Wilkes Webb took over the company. Webb employed freelance decorators, including French decorator and gilder Jules Barbe. The company became known for rock crystal-style glass, "Cameo Fleur" glass, and cameo glass.**
Thomas Webb & Sons became part of Webb's Crystal Glass Co., which was bought by Crown House Ltd. and then the Coloroll Group PLC. The factory closed in 1990.

A late-19thC Thomas Webb & Sons cameo glass vase, by the Thomas & George Woodall workshop, base faintly inscribed "1563."

8in (20.5cm) high

$8,000-9,000 **FLD**

A late-19thC Thomas Webb & Sons cameo glass vase, with white metal collar on the rim.

2½in (6.5cm) high

$500-650 **FLD**

A Thomas Webb & Sons cameo glass vase, wheel-carved convolvulus flowers, insects, and butterflies.

11¾in (30cm) high

$1,700-2,100 **DUK**

A Thomas Webb & Sons miniature cameo glass vase, wheel-carved flowers and insects.

3in (7.5cm) high

$700-850 **DUK**

A Thomas Webb & Sons cameo glass vase, wheel-carved blackberry bush, acanthus leaf border.

6¼in (16cm) high

$900-1,050 **DUK**

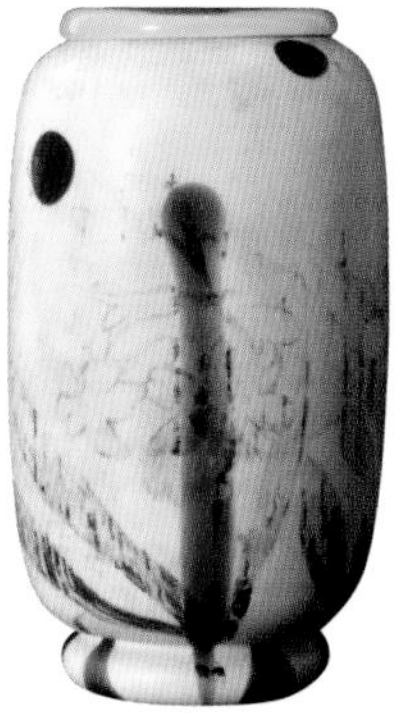

A late-19thC Thomas Webb & Sons unfinished padded cameo glass vase, showing remains of the original pencil outline design.

$800-900 **FLD**

An early-20thC Thomas Webb & Sons glass vase, flash cut with fish in reeds.

10½in (26.5cm) high

$130-180 **FLD**

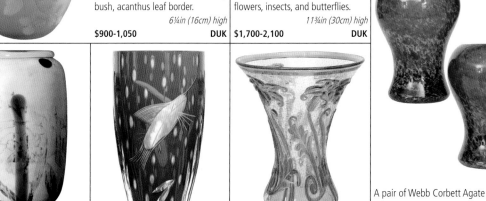

A Webb cameo "Fleur" glass vase, with textured finish, overlaid in pink with flower stems, Webb cameo signature.

8¾in (22cm) high

$260-320 **WW**

A pair of Webb Corbett Agate Flambé glass vases.

Webb Corbett Ltd. was formed in ca. 1897 by Thomas and Herbert Webb, sons of Thomas Wilkes Webb, with George Harry Corbett.

1920s *6¾in (17cm) high*

$130-180 **FLD**

QUICK REFERENCE—WHITEFRIARS

- **In the late 17thC, a glassworks was founded at Whitefriars, near Fleet Street in London. The site was previously a monastery of the Carmelite Fathers, known as the "White Friars" due to their white habits. James Powell took over the glassworks in 1834, renaming it James Powell & Sons.**
- **In 1962, the company changed its name to Whitefriars Glass Ltd. However, glass produced from the 1830s to 1980 is usually referred to as Whitefriars.**
- **The factory struggled financially in the 1970s and closed in the 1980s. Scottish glassmaker Caithness bought the Whitefriars brand name.**

A James Powell & Sons Whitefriars goblet, probably designed by Harry Powell, unsigned.

The melted threads relate to the Minerbi range of glass tableware designed by Harry Powell and produced by James Powell & Sons in 1906 as a 400-piece service for Count Lionel Minerbi.

8¼in (21cm) high

$1,600-2,100 WW

A James Powell & Sons Whitefriars "Alsatian" blue glass goblet vase, designed by Harry Powell, unsigned.

8½in (21.5cm) high

$1,100-1,250 WW

A James Powell & Sons Whitefriars glass inkwell, probably designed by Harry Powell, with blue-and-white swirls and silver inclusions, with silver cover, stamped marks "JP & Ss, London 1906."

3¾in (9.5cm) high

$1,900-2,600 WW

An early-20thC Whitefriars golden amber "Serpent" or "Comet" vase, designed by Harry Powell, pattern no.1218.

9½in (24cm) high

$400-450 FLD

A Whitefriars ribbon-trailed bucket vase, in sea green and sapphire blue.

7¼in (18.5cm) high

$90-130 FLD

A Whitefriars footed bowl, by James Hogan, pattern no.8973.

1930s *8in (20.5cm) diam*

$230-290 FLD

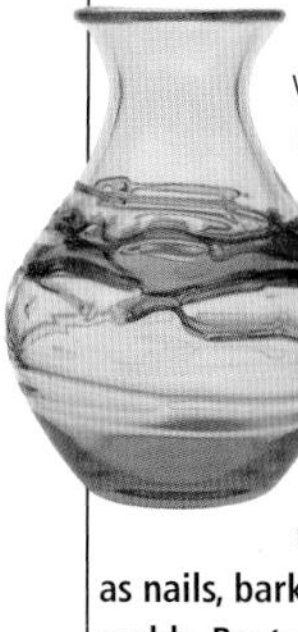

A Whitefriars "New Studio" range vase, by Geoffrey Baxter, pattern no.9886.

Geoffrey Baxter (1922-95) joined James Powell & Sons as a designer in 1954, having studied at the Royal College of Art. Baxter became known for using unusual materials, such as nails, bark, and wire, to make his initial molds. Baxter worked for Whitefriars until the company's closure in 1980.

1970s *7½in (19cm) high*

$260-320 FLD

A Whitefriars vase, designed by Geoffrey Baxter, pattern no.9700.

1960s *7½in (19cm) high*

$130-190 FLD

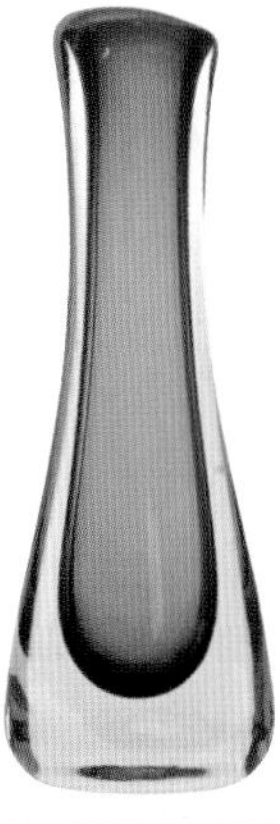

A Whitefriars "Swung Out" vase, designed by Geoffrey Baxter, pattern no.9650, clear crystal cased over willow.

1960s *15¾in (40cm) high*

$260-320 FLD

A Whitefriars "Banjo" vase, designed by Geoffrey Baxter, unsigned, in willow.

12½in (32cm) high

$850-950 **WW**

A Whitefriars "Banjo" vase, designed by Geoffrey Baxter, unsigned, in Kingfisher blue.

12½in (32cm) high

$1,300-1,800 **WW**

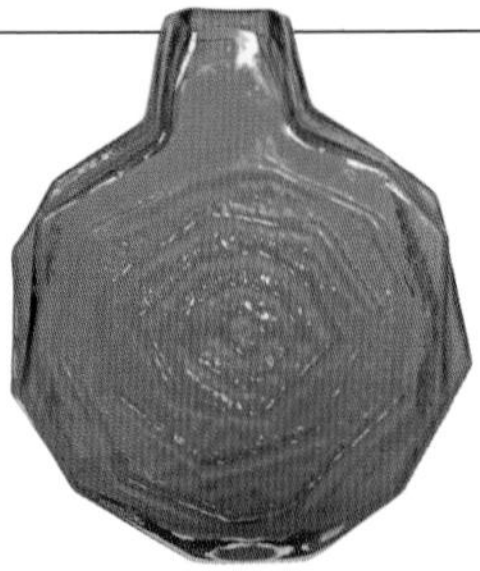

A Whitefriars "Banjo" vase, designed by Geoffrey Baxter, unsigned, paper label on base, in tangerine.

12½in (32cm) high

$1,100-1,250 **WW**

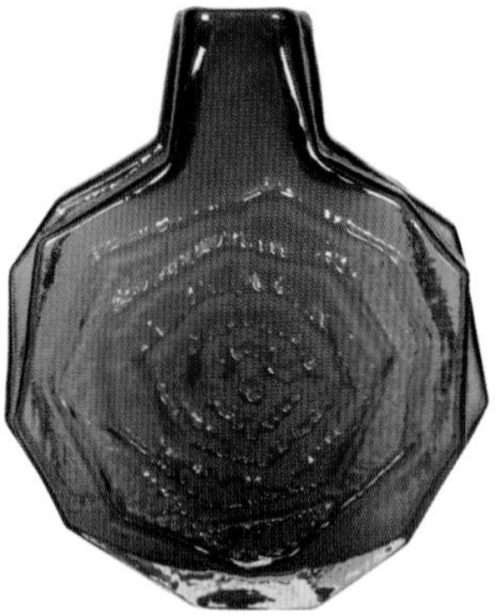

A rare Whitefriars "Banjo" vase, designed by Geoffrey Baxter, unsigned, in eggplant.

12¾in (32.5cm) high

$2,600-3,200 **WW**

A Whitefriars reversed "Drunken Bricklayer" vase, designed by Geoffrey Baxter, in tangerine.

8½in (21.5cm) high

$600-700 **WW**

A Whitefriars "Drunken Bricklayer" vase, designed by Geoffrey Baxter, unsigned, in willow.

13in (33cm) high

$500-650 **WW**

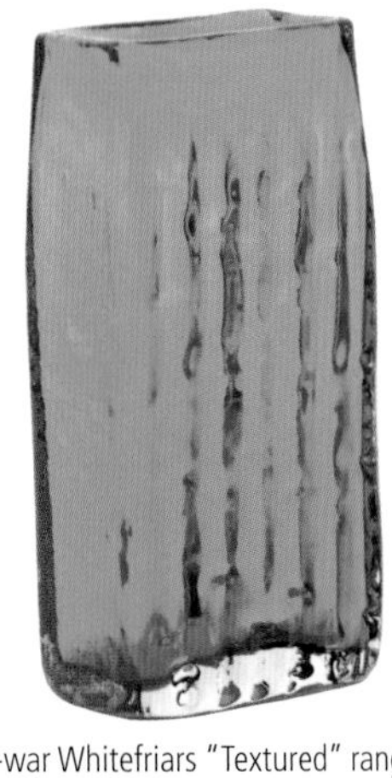

A post-war Whitefriars "Textured" range "Bamboo" vase, designed by Geoffrey Baxter, pattern no.9669, in Kingfisher blue.

8¼in (21cm) high

$130-180 **FLD**

A Whitefriars "Nuts and Bolts" vase, by Geoffrey Baxter, shape no.9668, in cinnamon.

10½in (26.5cm) high

$230-290 **DUK**

A Whitefriars vase, by Geoffrey Baxter, in willow, paper label.

ca. 1967 *12¼in (31cm) high*

$300-400 **DUK**

A pâte-de-verre "Roses/Ranunculus" glass box, by Gabriel Argy-Rousseau, model no.0108, pull-off cover, cast signature.

3¼in (8.5cm) diam

$1,300-1,900 **DUK**

An early-20thC Baccarat cameo glass vase, cased in ruby over citron and acid cut with a flowering bough with faint gilded highlights, unmarked.

6in (15cm) high

$300-400 **FLD**

An Art Deco Boom Glass "Flamingo" vase, by Paul Heller, the black ground cut with a frieze of stylized flamingos on a silvered textured back, foil label.

11¾in (30cm) high

$650-800 **DUK**

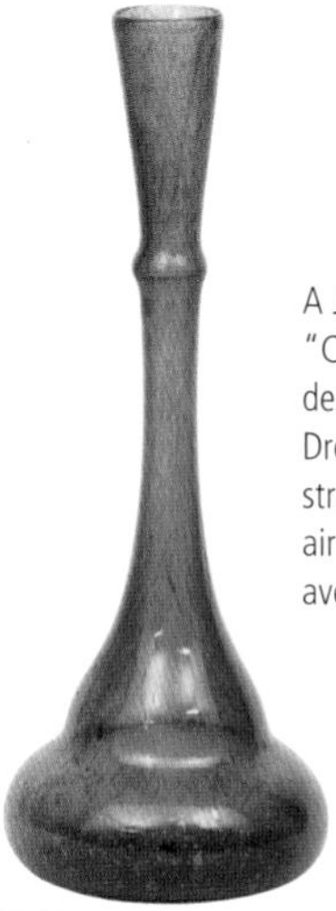

A James Couper & Sons "Clutha" glass vase, designed by Christopher Dresser (1834-1904), streaked green glass with air bubble inclusions and aventurine, unsigned.

15in (38cm) high

$1,900-2,600 **WW**

A James Couper & Sons "Clutha" glass vase, by Christopher Dresser, acid-etched mark with Liberty's Lotus flower trademark, inscribed "CLUTHA DESIGNED BY CD REGISTERED."

ca. 1900 *3¼in (8.5cm) high*

$1,050-1,300 **L&T**

A late-20thC Dartington vase, relief molded with flower designs, all in a pale gray tint.

10in (25.5cm) high

$70-100 **FLD**

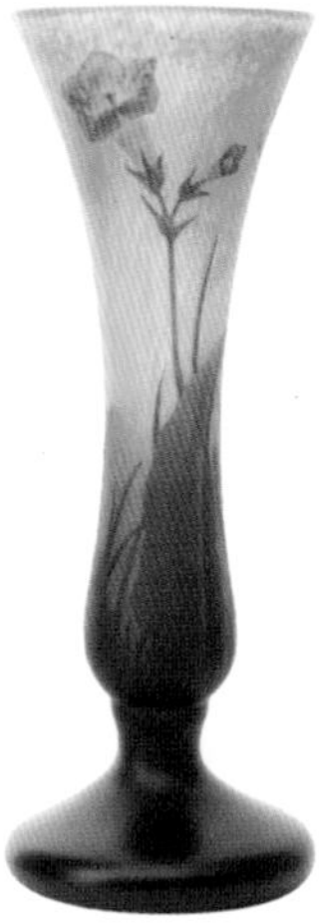

An early-20thC Daum cameo glass vase, cased in magenta over a mottled tonal red to orange ground, cut and engraved with campanula, engraved signature "Daum Nancy," with the cross of Lorraine.

ca. 1900 *13¾in (35cm) high*

$1,250-1,550 **FLD**

A Decorchemont pâte-de-cristal glass coupe, by François-Émile Décorchemont, cast with pairs of budgerigars, impressed seal mark, etched "0808" on base.

8in (20.5cm) wide

$1,600-2,100 **WW**

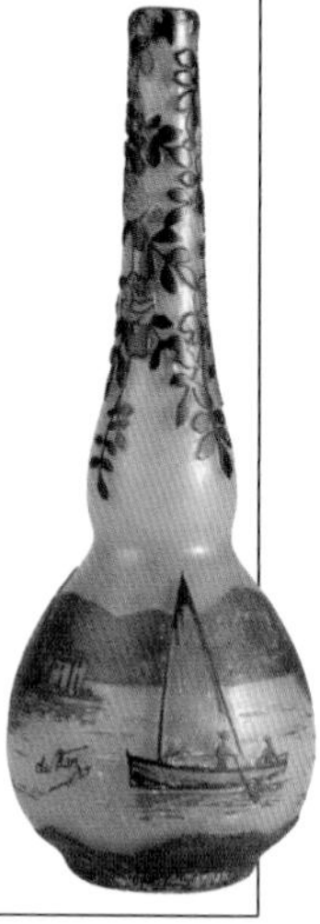

A French Devez cameo glass vase, the body with a sailing boat with mountains in the background, signed marks.

8½in (21.5cm) high

$500-650 **DUK**

A Georges De Feure amethyst glass vase, made for Fauchon, relief molded with classically dressed females, relief molded signature.

5½in (14cm) high

$120-160 **FLD**

A Gallé cameo glass vase, the yellow body overlaid and acid etched with clematis flowers and leaves, signed in cameo "Gallé."

ca. 1910 *5¼in (13.5cm) high*

$850-950 **ROS**

A drinking glass, by Émile Gallé (1846-1904), decorated with enameled flowers with gilt highlights, signed marks.

3¼in (8.5cm) high

$400-500 **DUK**

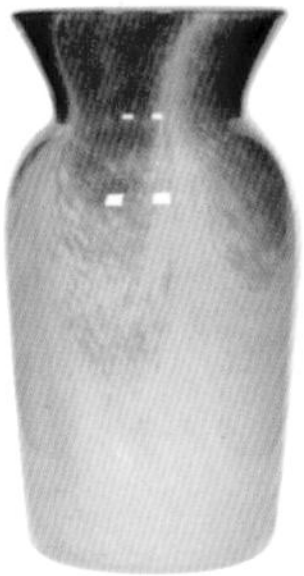

An Elizabeth Graydon-Stannus "Graystan" glass vase, engraved signature.

1930s *7in (18cm) high*

$130-180 **FLD**

An early-20thC Fritz Heckert vase, possibly designed by Max Rade, hand enameled, unmarked.

5¼in (13.5cm) high

$100-120 **FLD**

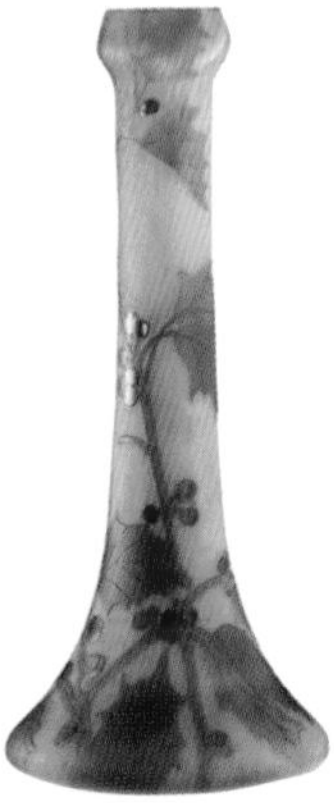

A Legras cameo glass vase, wheel cut with holly leaves, berries, and twigs on a yellow peach ground, signed in cameo.

11¾in (30cm) high

$650-900 **DUK**

An Art Deco Legras "Neptune" glass vase, acid etched and cut with stylized decoration, impressed marks.

17½in (44.5cm) high

$1,150-1,300 **DUK**

A Lobmeyr glass, signed.

Pieces that are produced for the Islamic market usually have Islamic calligraphy on them, but this is the only one with stylized animals.

ca. 1885 *5in (12.5cm) high*

$1,700-2,100 **M&DM**

A late-19thC to early-20thC Mont Joye vase, enamel decorated with stylized flowers.

5¼in (13.5cm) high

$130-210 **FLD**

A Poschinger blue and purple vase, often mistaken for Loetz "Phänomen" but of equal quality.

ca. 1900 *4in (10cm) high*

$1,900-2,300 **M&DM**

A pair of American Quezal iridescent glass bell-shaped shades, signed "Quezal," with a "Gold Aurene" iridescent interior.

ca. 1910 *5in (12.5cm) high*

$300-400 **ROS**

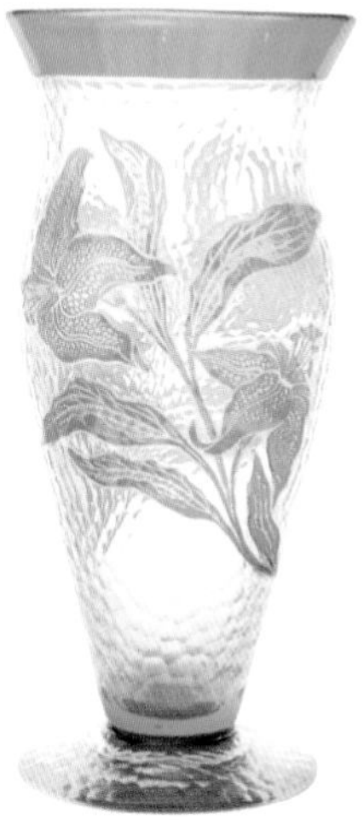

A Richardson's "Rich" cameo vase, with Richardson's "Rich Cameo" mark.

1930s *10in (25.5cm) high*

$130-260 **FLD**

A late-19thC Richardson's glass vase, in opaline with green and gilded decoration around floral panels, Richardson's mark on base.

13½in (34.5cm) high

$300-400 **FLD**

A mid-19thC Richardson's vase, decorated with Richardson's vitrified enamels, depicting Christ and the money lenders, enameled mark.

10in (25.5cm) high

$300-400 **FLD**

A mid-19thC Stourbridge glass vase, probably Richardson's, painted in the Etruscan style, with a classical figure below a Greek key border.

9in (23cm) high

$120-160 **FLD**

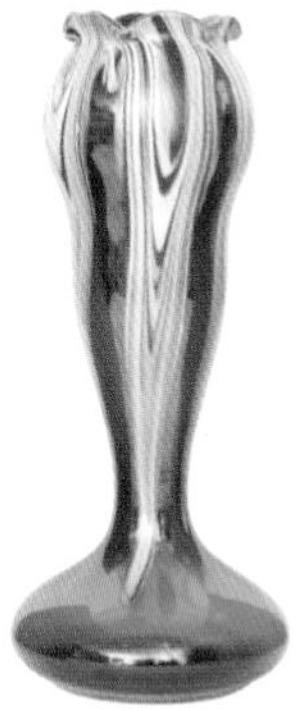

A Rindskopf vase, with a tonal white and purple iridescent pulled and feathered design over the deep green ground.

13in (33cm) high

$300-400 **FLD**

An early-20thC Rindskopf vase, with a wrapped serpent in iridescent green over an iridescent apple green ground.

12¾in (32.5cm) high

$190-260 **FLD**

A large Rosenthal Studio abstract glass flower bowl, designed by Andy Warhol.

20½in (52cm) diam

$100-120 **PSA**

An Art Deco Sabino iridescent powder box and cover, the lid decorated with three relief-molded mermaids, marked on the lid.

1930s *6¼in (16cm) diam*

$300-400 **FLD**

A Schneider "Le Verre Français" cameo glass vase, decorated with dahlias, inscribed "Le Verre Français, France," wear on base.

12½in (31.5cm) high

$650-800 **SWO**

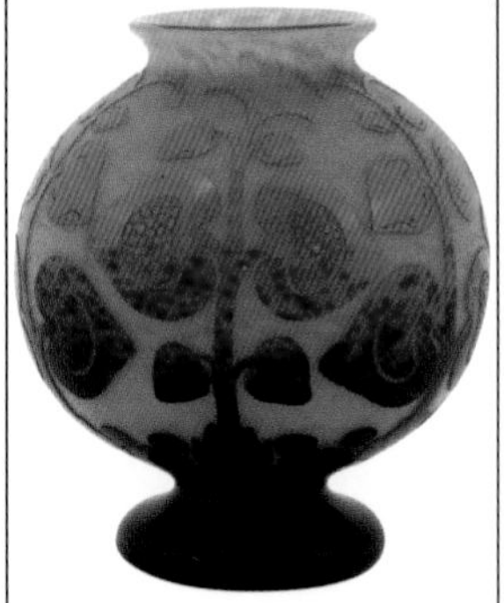

A Schneider cameo glass vase, with mottled amber ground, cut with stylized flowers, in orange and blue.

8in (20.5cm) high

$650-800 **SWO**

A Stourbridge cameo glass vase, with images of parrots in branches, marked "SGC" (Stourbridge Glass Co.), dated.

1983 *17in (43cm) high*

$450-500 **FLD**

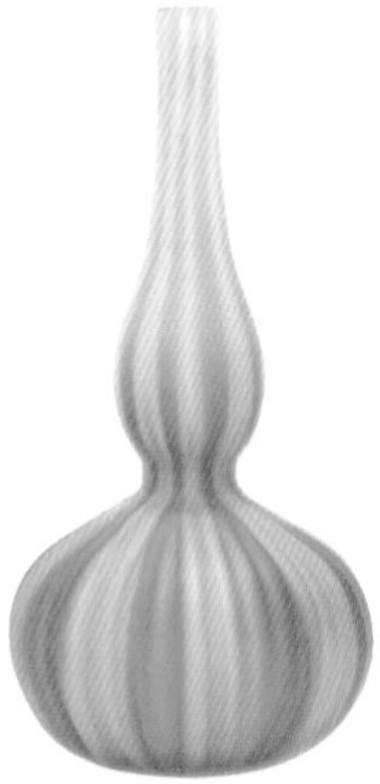

A late-19thC Stourbridge glass vase, ribbed and decorated with a rainbow-striped pattern.

9½in (24cm) high

$120-160 **FLD**

A late-19thC Stourbridge glass strawberry set, in pale ruby with applied white threading.

$60-80 **FLD**

A late-19thC Stuart & Sons vase, with applied clear rigger work garlands and raspberry prunts.

6½in (16.5cm) high

$100-120 **FLD**

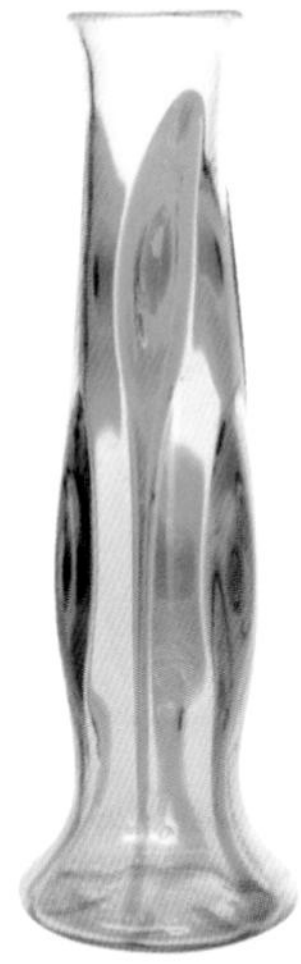

An early-20thC Stuart & Sons glass vase.

11¾in (30cm) high

$190-260 **FLD**

A Stuart & Sons glass cocktail shaker, with chromed fittings, acid marked.

1930s *9in (23cm) high*

$160-210 **FLD**

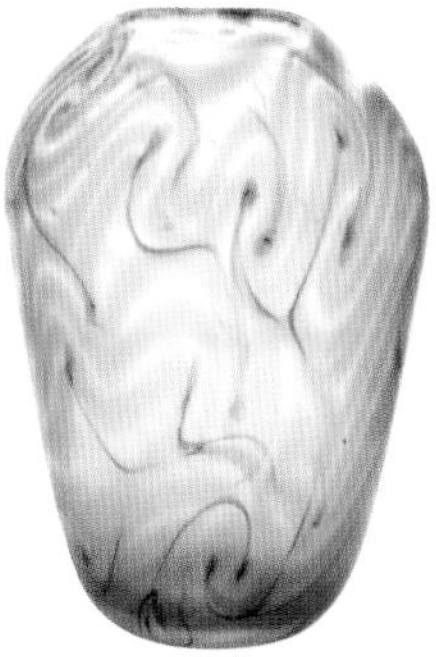

An early-20thC glass vase, by L.C. Tiffany, decorated with a repeat green and pearlized swirl design, full engraved signature.

5½in (14cm) high

$650-800 **FLD**

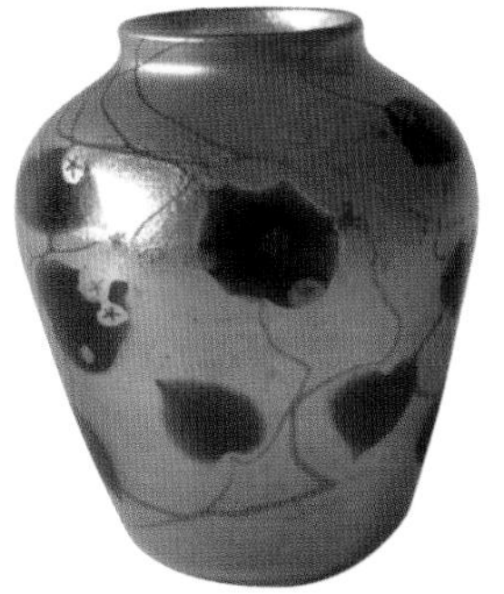

An L.C. Tiffany "Heart and Vine" Favrile vase, decorated with murines (paperweight canes), signed.

ca. 1902 *4in (10cm) high*

$3,200-3,900 **M&DM**

An L.C. Tiffany experimental Favrile vase, coded with an "X," signed.

ca. 1900 *9in (23cm) high*

$2,600-3,200 **M&DM**

A mid-20thC Val St Lambert cut glass vase, "Bolero," by Charles Graffart, signed "Val St Lambert."

8in (20.5cm) high

$100-160 **ROS**

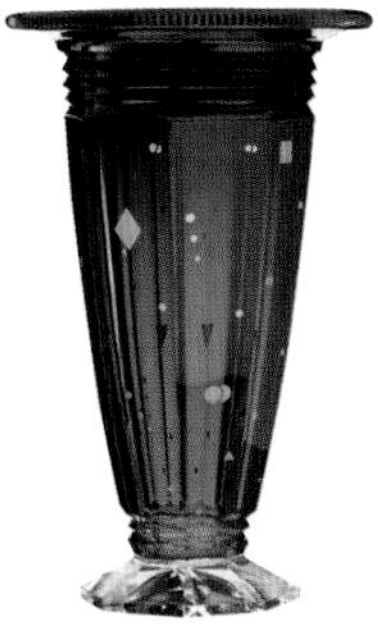

An Art Deco Val St Lambert "Ardennes" glass vase, in an amethyst-brown tint with gilt highlight, stylized decoration.

10¼in (26cm) high

$650-900 **DUK**

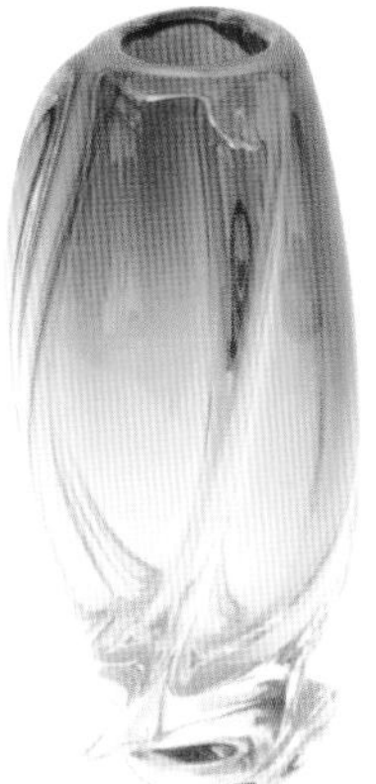

A mid-20thC Val St Lambert "Propeller" vase, engraved signature.

10¾in (27.5cm) high

$80-100 **FLD**

An Art Deco Verart glass vase, acid cut with a repeat abstract panel pattern over the cinnamon ground, signed "VERART Paris."

1930s *12½in (32cm) high*

$190-260 **FLD**

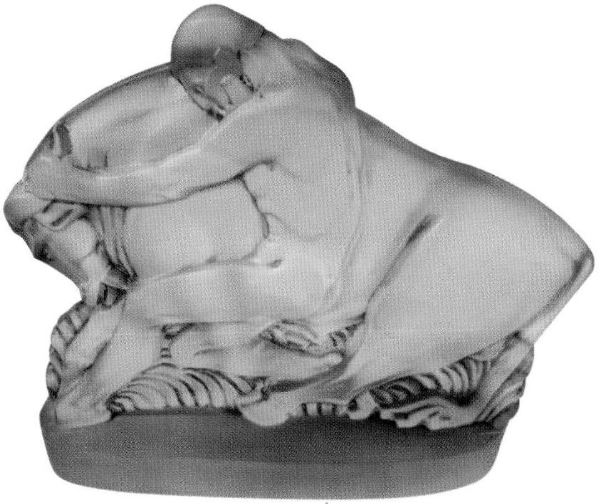

A Walsh Walsh "Vesta" statue, by Walter Gilbert, "Hercules and the Cretan Bull."

ca. 1929 *6½in (16.5cm) high*

$900-1,150 **M&DM**

A late-19thC to early-20thC John Walsh Walsh "Opaline Brocade" vase, unmarked.

11¼in (28.5cm) high

$190-260 **FLD**

A John Walsh Walsh cut-clear glass fan vase, with applied green glass teardrops cut with feather motif, unsigned.

10¼in (26cm) high

$450-500 **WW**

A WMF "Ikora" glass vase, internally decorated with white fissuring over the tonal orange ground, unmarked.

1930s *8¼in (21cm) high*

$100-120 **FLD**

An early-20thC WMF "Myra Crystal" glass vase, with a gold petrol iridescence, unmarked.

3¼in (8.5cm) high

$130-180 **FLD**

A set of five mid-20thC novelty "Mickey Mouse" band cocktail glasses, with lampworked "Mickey Mouse'-style musician figure stems.

4in (10cm) high

$400-500 **FLD**

A late-19thC Continental glass vase, in the style of Mary Gregory with a white enameled female figure.

10¾in (27.5cm) high

$160-210 **FLD**

A late-19thC satin quilted "air trap" pitcher, in a graduated blue to maroon, with a diamond design.

9in (23cm) high

$190-260 **FLD**

A late-19thC to early-20thC twin-handled pedestal vase, engraved with classical profiles.

8in (20.5cm) high

$300-400 **FLD**

A late-19thC Bohemian ruby glass pedestal bowl, with panels of enameled decoration of children, some damage.

7in (18cm) high

$260-320 **FLD**

A late-19thC "Amberina" glass vase, with enameled and gilt trailing flowers.

9in (23cm) high

$60-80 **FLD**

A contemporary studio glass vase, designed by Martin Andrews, from his "Stone" series, with black-and-white mottled and linear design over a deep blue ground, unsigned.

Martin Andrews studied at West Surrey College of Art and Design, graduating in 1991 with a B.A. (Hons) Glass. In 2000, he opened a workshop at the Ruskin Glass Centre, Stourbridge, England. All of Andrews' pieces are handmade and signed.

5½in (14cm) high

$130-190 **FLD**

A handblown "Koi Glass" graal-type vase, by Vic Bamforth, cased in clear crystal with Koi carp, engraved signature, numbered 1 of 1, dated.

Vic Bamforth (b.1952) studied at Buckinghamshire Chilterns University College and Dudley International Glass Centre, graduating with a diploma in Glass Techniques and Technology and an Advanced Diploma in Glass Design. Bamforth is based at the Ruskin Glass Centre, Stourbridge.

2007 *7½in (19cm) high*

$600-700 **FLD**

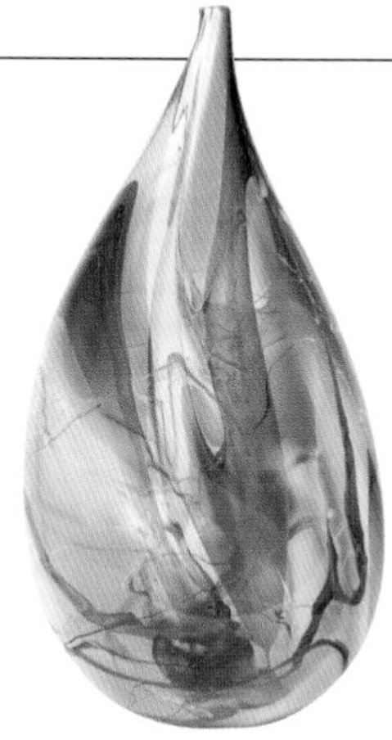

A 21stC glass vase, by Guido van Besouw (b.1951), signed and numbered on base.

Guido van Besouw (b.1951) was apprenticed to glassmaker Anton Voorveld before becoming a full-time glass artist in 1980, producing windows for churches and private residences. Van Besouw set up his own studio and began making glassware in the late 1990s.

20½in (52cm) high

$500-600 **ROS**

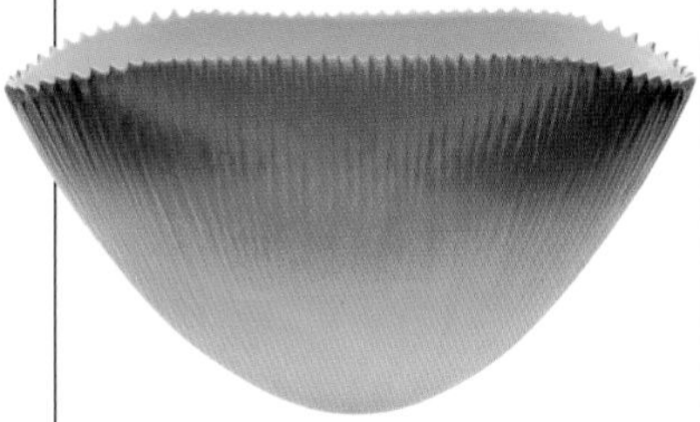

A large "Fin" bowl, by Laura Birdsall, of compressed ovoid form, cased in olive green over white over lime green and cut with a vertical ripple line rising to a fine scalloped rim, engraved signature.

Laura Birdsall is based in North Yorkshire, UK, where she makes blown-glass vessels with strong sculptural qualities. Birdsall's inspiration is often some small detail in nature, such as a seed pod or a fish's fin.

2014 *14½in (37cm) wide*

$650-800 **FLD**

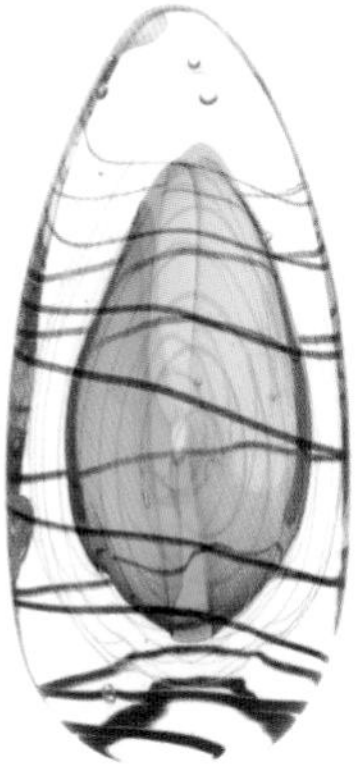

A contemporary glass sculpture, by Tim Boswell, engraved signature on base.

10¾in (27.5cm) high

$260-320 **FLD**

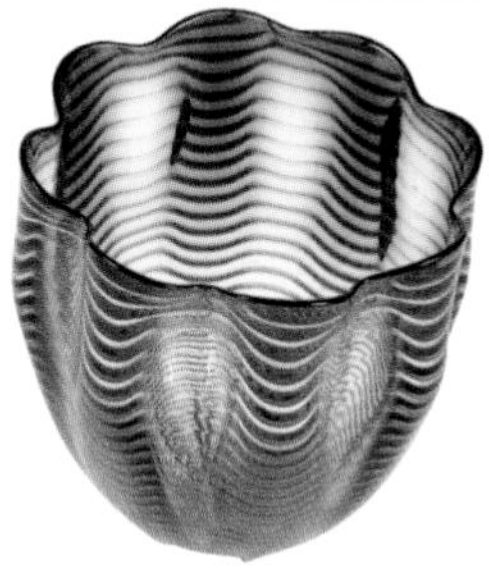

A glass seaform, by Dale Chihuly (b.1941), signed "Chihuly PP97."

8¼in (21cm) high

$3,200-3,900 **POOK**

A late-20thC studio glass vase, by Norman Stuart Clarke, with random whiplash lines over a silver iridescent ground, signed, dated.

1996 *7½in (19cm) high*

$260-390 **FLD**

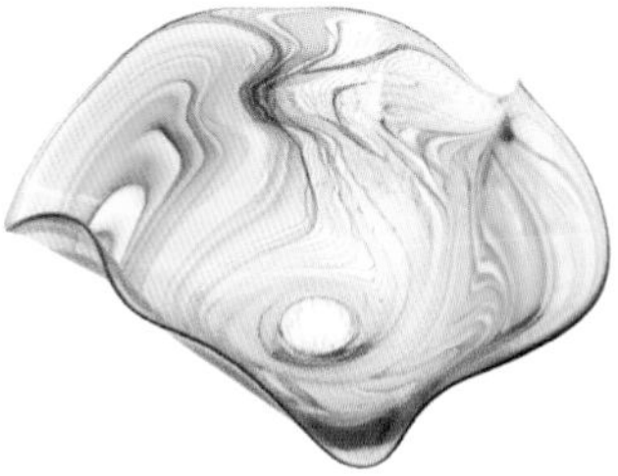

A large "Contour" bowl, by Bob Crooks, in mixed color palette with lattachino thread work, engraved signature.

ca. 2000 *21in (53.5cm) wide*

$1,050-1,150 **FLD**

A Osiris Studio glass vase, by Iestyn Davies, cased in green over deep amethyst and acid cut with a window revealing bamboo shoots, dated.

1986 *11½in (29.5cm) high*

$400-450 **FLD**

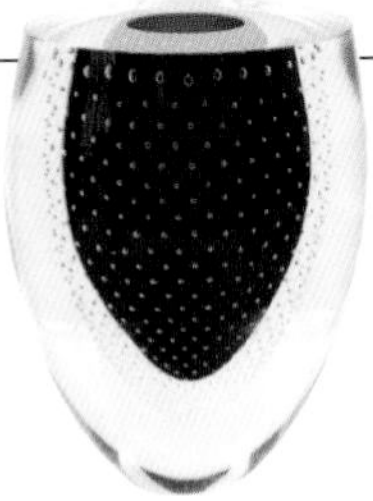

A Salviati "Goccia di Poggia" glass vase, by Christian Ghion, with original box.

ca. 2007 *8¾in (22cm) high*

$300-350 **FLD**

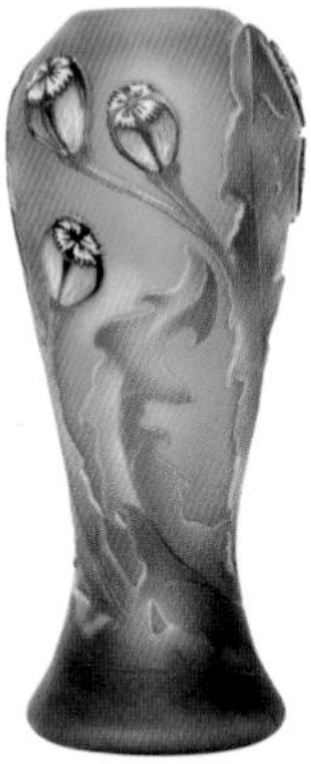

A late-20thC Okra studio cameo glass vase, by Richard P. Golding and Sarah Cowan, cased in green and opal over the red ground cut with poppy heads among leaves and detailed with enameling, numbered 16 of 50, engraved signature.

See Charles R. Hajdamach, *20th Century British Glass*, Antique Collectors' Club Ltd. (2009), for a comparable example.

1 9in (23cm) high

$400-450 **FLD**

A Sam Herman glass vase, cased in clear glass, streaked, etched signature and date.

1970 *7¼in (18.5cm) high*

$300-400 **WW**

A Sam Herman solifleur vase, with metallic oxide pale blue streaked glass body with swollen green knop, unsigned.

11¾in (29.5cm) high

$500-650 **WW**

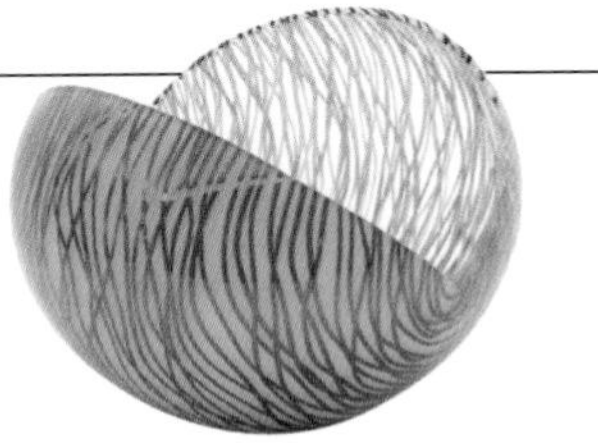

An "Aesculus" bowl, by Stephen Gillies and Kate Jones, cased in purple on the exterior and pale blue in the interior and cut with wave lines over the clear crystal ground, signed, dated.

2004 *11½in (29cm) wide*

$2,900-3,600 **FLD**

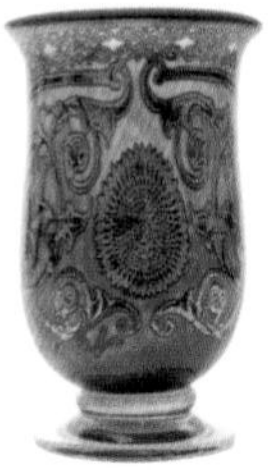

A contemporary Jonathan Harris "Unique Golden Graal" vase, decorated foliate scrolls in gold leaf over a mottled cinnamon ground, engraved signature.

The Jonathan Harris Art Glass Studios was set up in 1999 at the Coalport China Museum at the Ironbridge Gorge, near Telford, England, by Jonathan Harris and his wife Alison. However, Harris had been producing glassware for more than 20 years, focusing on cameo and Graal glass.

2003 *8in (20.5cm) high*

$260-320 **FLD**

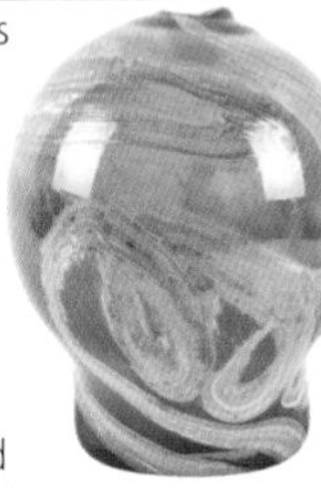

A large British studio glass "Untitled" sculpture, by Sam Herman, made using the wet stick process at the Jam Factory, South Australia, with applied and melted-in, silver chloride trails, and browny-green applied mottles, the base inscribed "Samuel J. Herman 1978 SA1853," with "Sam Herman Glass" Lots Road studio paper label.

Sam Herman introduced the use of the wet stick technique at the Jam Factory in 1974 in order to make the largest pieces he could while working alone. After the body had been partly blown and decorated, a wet stick was forced into the mass. The heat of the glass caused the water in the stick to turn into steam, which caused the body to expand and swell, creating a random bulbous form. This is an example in colors typical of his work in South Australia.

11½in (29cm) high

$1,600-2,300 **DAWS**

A contemporary studio glass sculpture in the form of a pumpkin, by Richard P. Golding, engraved signature.

6¾in (17cm) high

$190-260 **FLD**

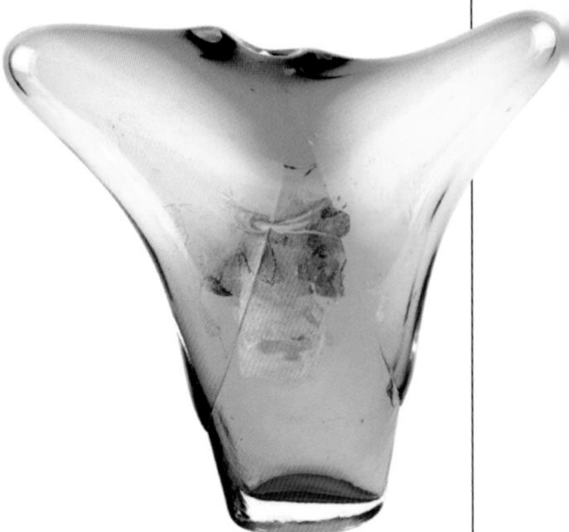

A Loco Glass unique sculptural glass vase, by Sam Herman, with silver leaf inclusions, signed.

From The Private Collection Of Samuel (Sam) J. Herman.

Sam Herman (b.1936) studied at the University of Wisconsin before gaining a Fulbright Scholarship to study at the Edinburgh College of Art in 1965. Herman then became the head of the Royal College of Art's glass and ceramics department, where he remained until 1974. Herman set up the Glasshouse in Covent Garden, London, in 1969. In 1974, Herman opened a glass workshop at the Jam factory in Adelaide, Australia, before returning to the UK in 1979 to set up a studio in London. In 1984, Herman moved to Mallorca and focused on his painting and sculpture work. Since then, he has made glass on only a handful of occasions, at Adam Aaronson's studio in West London in 2007, at Peter Layton's London Glassblowing studio in London in 2012, and at Loco Glass in Gloucestershire in 2015-16. Herman estimates that he made less than 90 pieces of glass between 1984 and 2017, making later vases such as this rare.

15¼in (39cm) high

$2,900-3,600 **DAWS**

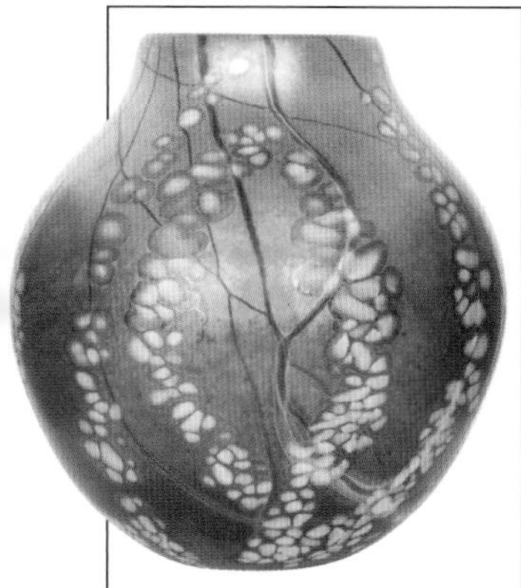

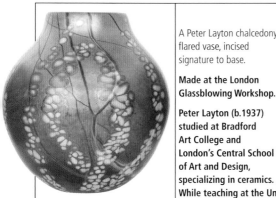

A Brideshead studio glass vase, by Siddy Langley, decorated in a petrol iridescent with white spotting and whiplash lines, engraved signature, dated.

1998 *8¾in (22cm) high*

$350-400 **FLD**

A Peter Layton chalcedony flared vase, incised signature to base.

Made at the London Glassblowing Workshop.

Peter Layton (b.1937) studied at Bradford Art College and London's Central School of Art and Design, specializing in ceramics. While teaching at the University of Iowa in 1965, Layton became interested in glass and enrolled on the university's glass-blowing program. After returning to the UK in 1968, Layton opened a glass studio in the Scottish Highlands. In 1976, he opened the London Glassblowing Workshop at Rotherhithe, before moving the studio to Bermondsey Street.

9½in (24cm) high

$400-450 **WW**

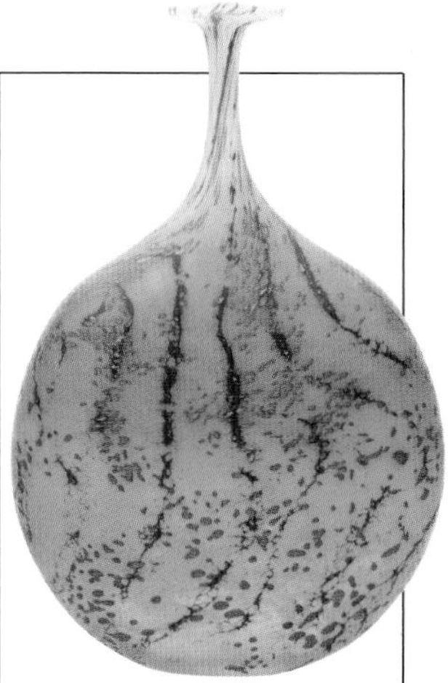

A late-20thC Peter Layton vase, cased in turquoise decorated with blue and ocher flashes over an opal interior, engraved signature.

9in (23cm) high

$300-350 **FLD**

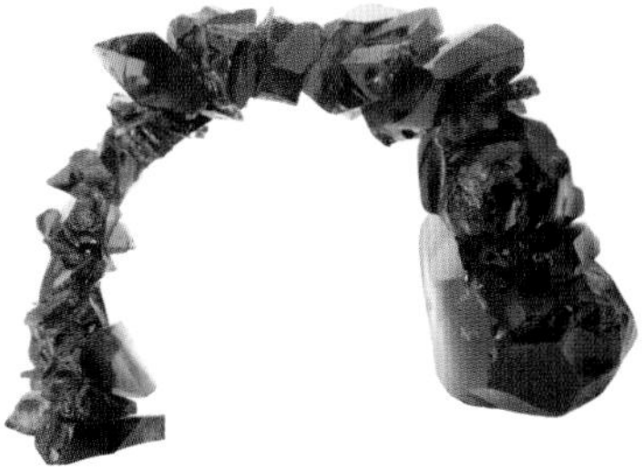

A large contemporary studio glass "Un-refined Arch" sculpture, by Allister Malcolm.

Featured in the 2008 International Festival of Glass British Biennale.

11¾in (30cm) high

$1,900-2,600 **FLD**

A Richard Marquis free-blown teapot, with multicolored murrines, signed "Marquis 1979-4CQ."

1979 *3in (7.5cm) wide*

$3,200-3,900 **FIS**

A late-20thC studio glass vase, by Karlin Rushbrook, engraved signature.

9in (23cm) high

$190-260 **FLD**

A Melting Pot Glassworks studio glass vase, by Robin Smith and Jeff Walker, signed on base.

9¾in (24.5cm) high

$230-290 **CHOR**

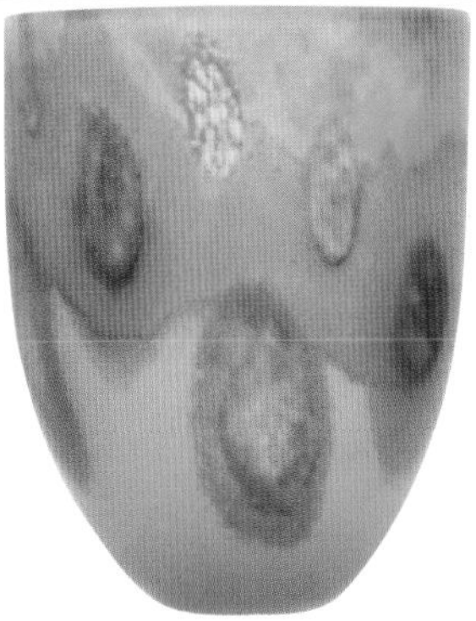

A "Garden" bowl, by Pauline Solven, engraved signature, dated.

1996 *6in (15cm) high*

$190-260 **FLD**

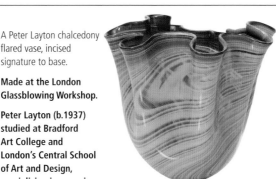

A contemporary "Vertical No.35" glass piece, by Rachael Woodman, mounted on a black slate base, signed, dated.

Rachael Woodman (b.1957) studied at the Orrefors Glass School, in Sweden, and the Royal College of Art, London. Between 1986 and 2005, Woodman worked as a designer for Dartington Crystal.

2004 *6½in (67.5cm) high*

$1,800-2,600 **FLD**

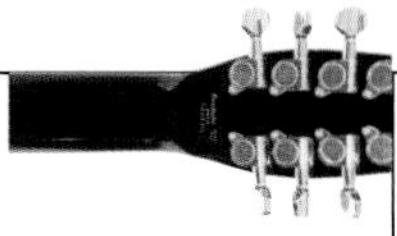

A Danelectro DC59 12-string guitar, the lightweight hollow body with single F-hole, in black finish with white pickguard, fitted with two single-coil "lipstick" pickups, one master volume, one master tone and three-way selector, with padded carry bag.

ca. 2015-16

$300-500 **SWO**

A Danelectro Bellzouki 7020 12-string guitar, in metallic blue finish, with two single coil lipstick pickups, three-way selector switch, volume, tone, and master knobs, and chrome hardware, with soft case, with "Andy's Guitar Workshop, 27 Denmark Street, London" label on the reverse of the headstock.

Developed in the early 1960s by American session guitarist Vinnie Bell, the electric Bellzouki was inspired by the traditional 8-string Greek Bouzouki, an acoustic instrument with a pear-shaped body. The early models of the electric Bellzouki (model no.7010) also had pear-shaped bodies, but the revised models, as shown here (no.7020), feature four notches in the body, making the instrument more stable on the thigh when played sitting down.

ca. 1965

$500-900 **ROS**

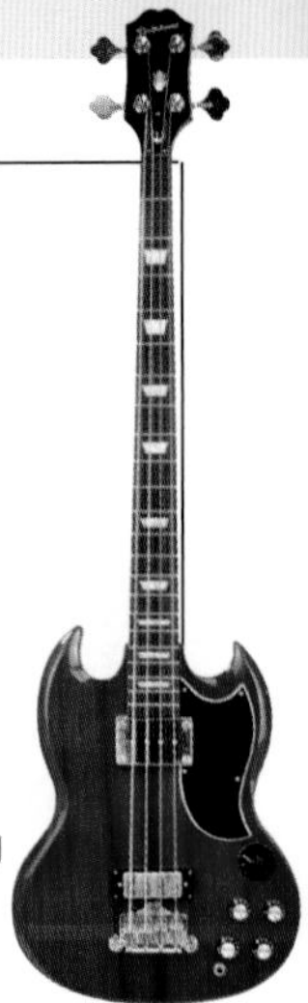

An Epiphone EB-3 bass guitar, with stained mahogany body and mother-of-pearl inlaid rosewood fretboard, serial no.1208201654, light wear and minor surface scratches as expected in the usual places, plus a dent and small area of damage on the edge upper left side of body, and pitting on the metalwork, with hard case.

2012

$190-320 **APAR**

A Fender Stratocaster-style electric guitar, the metallic orange body fitted with Charvel SoCal electrics, including Seymour Duncan "Distortion" pickups, with G&G hard case and strap.

This guitar was constructed from Warmoth parts by the renowned Suffolk-based luthier Andrew Guyton, best-known for his restoration of Queen guitarist Brian May's original and iconic "Red Special," and his internationally acclaimed authorized limited (50) edition replicas of the latter in 2004.

$650-900 **SWO**

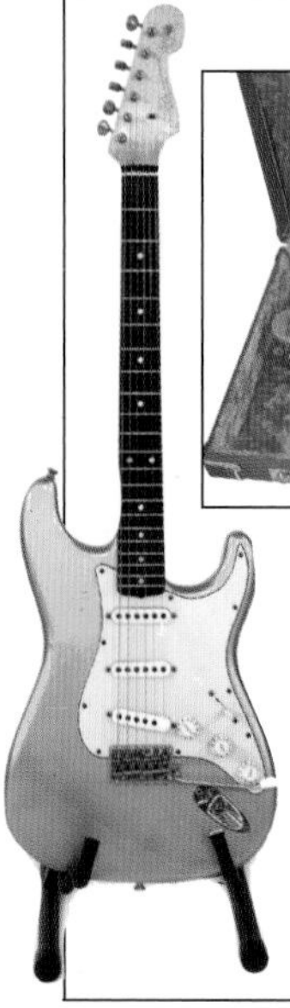

A Fender Custom Shop "61 Relic Stratocaster, the alder body finished in Aztec Gold, complete with original paperwork and tags, with G&G vintage flight case.

2017

$1,900-2,600 **SWO**

Judith Picks

Provenance, and indeed the lack of it, can be an important factor in determining the value of musical instruments (as it is for almost all collectibles). However, there's provenance, and then there's provenance. For example, the mid-1970s-made standard Fender Jazz bass with three-tone sunburst finish shown here, bought in 1981 and subsequently played by bassist Noel Redding (1945-2003), will currently cost you $3,900-5,200. In contrast, exactly the same mid-70s bass, in similar condition but without any affiliation to Noel Redding (or, indeed, any other famous rock musician), would currently set you back about $1,600-2,600. So, this particular provenance roughly doubles the price. However, and this is a big however, if the same Fender Jazz bass had been made in the mid-1960s (as many were), and if it had been the one bought by Noel Redding and played by him from 1966-69 while he was the bass player in one of the most iconic rock bands of all time, namely the Jimi Hendrix Experience, then you would have to dig significantly deeper into your pocket to buy it. Back in 1980, Noel Redding did, in fact, sell his original mid-60s Hendrix-period Jazz bass to a private collector, for the sum of £10,000 ($11,100). Forty years on, I wonder just how many more tens of thousands it would go for!

A Fender Jazz bass guitar, with three-tone sunburst finish, played by Noel Redding, formerly of the Jimi Hendrix Experience, serial no.670644, accompanied by a receipt on signed December 5, 1981, by Noel Redding acknowledging payment of a deposit of £200 ($220) for the guitar.

1975

$3,900-5,200 **WHYT**

A Gibson SG Classic electric guitar, made in the USA, with red-stained solid mahogany body, rosewood fretboard, P90 pickups, with hard case.

2004

$650-900 **SWO**

A Gibson Les Paul 60s Tribute electric guitar, the weight-relieved solid mahogany body with carved maple top and tobacco sunburst finish, rosewood fretboard, P90 pickups, serial no.160055255, with hard case.

2016

$650-900 **SWO**

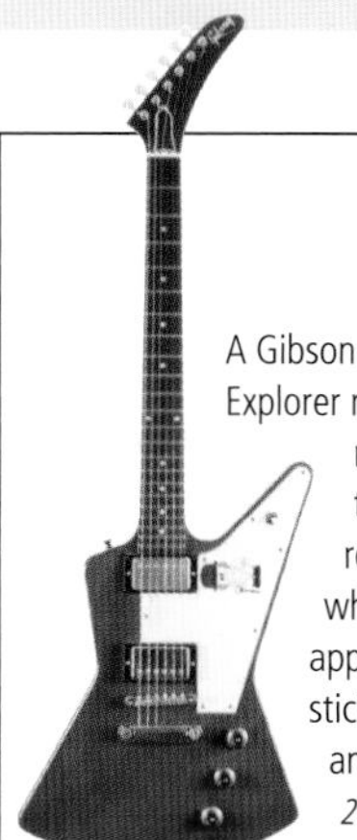

A Gibson Custom Shop 1958 Explorer reissue, the elbow-cut mahogany body with two humbucker pickups, rosewood fretboard, white pickguard with applied Clockwork Orange sticker, with original case and certificates.

2014-18

$2,300-3,200 **GHOU**

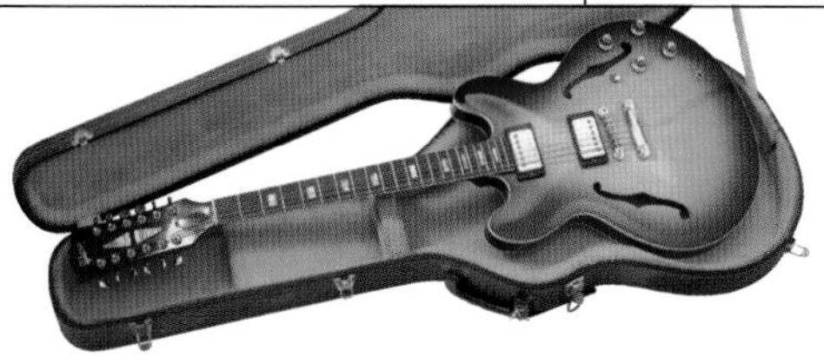

A Gibson ES-335 TD 12-string semihollow electric guitar, made in Kalamazoo, Michigan, in vintage sunburst finish, its Brazilian rosewood fretboard with 22 frets, fitted with two humbucker pickups, three-way toggle pickup selector, two volume and two tone knobs, and chrome stoptail, serial no.403438, in original hard case, with CITIES license no.580443/1.

Introduced by Gibson in 1958, and still in production, the 6-string ES-335 features a double cutaway body with arched top and back constructed of laminated maple, incorporating a sold block of maple running through its center—a semisolid design that produced much of the warmth of hollow body guitars while eliminating much of the feedback associated with the latter. Notable players have included Chuck Berry, Eric Clapton, Keith Richards, and Larry Carlton. The 12-string version, as shown here, was originally produced 1965-70.

1966

$2,600-3,900 **ROS**

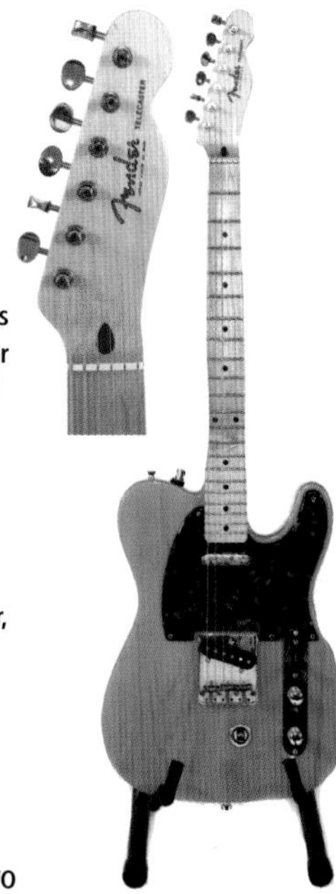

A Luthier-built Fender-style Telecaster, with a Hipshot "String Bender" mechanism, maple neck, and an Asher Guitars tortoiseshell pickguard.

Invented ca. 1968, a "B-Bender" mechanism employs a series of levers or pulleys inside or outside the guitar body that—when activated by a pull or push of either the guitar neck, bridge, or body (as with the Hipshot mechanism)—bends the B string up by as much as a minor third (three frets). The resulting change in tone sounds similar to a pedal steel guitar, and consequently the "B-Bender" is primarily associated with country music. However, rock musicians, notably Jimmy Page, Keith Richards, and Ronnie Wood, have also used it producing a distinctive effect.

$500-650 **SWO**

A Vox V257 Mando 12-string electric guitar, made in Italy, in two-tone dark sunburst finish, with double T-bar neck, two single-coil pickups, a three-way toggle selector, volume and tone knobs, and chrome hardware, serial no.334144, with original hard case, with CITES license No.580443/2.

In 1964, a prototype version of the guitar was given to George Harrison of The Beatles and to Brian Jones of the Rolling Stones.

ca. 1964-66

$1,150-1,550 **ROS**

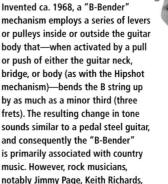

A Vox V251 guitar organ, the maple Phantom body with white polyester finish, the 21-fret maple neck with rosewood fretboard, fitted with two single-coil pickups and six organ tone generator circuits, and chrome hardware, serial no.73059, with original PSU and hard case.

Only approximately 400 of these organ guitars were made. The first, a prototype, was in 1964 given by it's inventor, Vox engineer Dick Denny, to John Lennon of The Beatles. Because of its provenance, this model sold at Sotheby's in 2014 for £179,148 (around $286,000).

ca. 1966

$1,900-3,900 **ROS**

A silver gilt-and-blue enamel butterfly brooch, by Child & Child, the wings engraved with veins and decorated with shaded blue enamel, the body set with demantoid garnets, maker's mark on reverse, fine hairline cracks in enamel, fitted case.

ca. 1905 *2.5in (6cm) wide*

$9,500-11,000 **WW**

An Arts & Crafts silver brooch, attributed to Dorrie Nossiter, set with a cluster of moonstones, native-cut sapphires and zircons with matching polished bead fringe, fitted Dorrie Nossiter case.

ca. 1930 *2¾in (7cm) high*

$5,200-6,500 **WW**

A 19thC 15ct gold and amethyst brooch.

3in (7.5cm) long 0.67oz

$1,300-1,900 **FELL**

An early-19thC gold cameo brooch, the agate cameo carved to depict a lady in profile, with split pearl, single and rose-cut diamond surround, signed "Pestrini," French assay marks.

2½in (6.5cm) long 0.83oz

$3,200-3,900 **FELL**

A 19thC yellow gold opal and diamond tubular scroll drop brooch, in box.

2¾in (7cm) long 0.46oz

$600-700 **PW**

A late-19thC silver and gold opal and diamond brooch, some surface scratches and wear.

1¼in (3cm) diam 0.17oz

$1,150-1,450 **FELL**

A late-19thC gold, diamond, and enamel brooch, with a vari-cut diamond and blue enamel star-set dome, inset in the rose-cut diamond, some surface scratches and wear.

2¼in (5.5cm) long 0.57oz

$1,900-2,600 **FELL**

A 19thC oval cameo pendant/brooch, depicting a Roman gladiator driving a chariot pulled by two prancing horses.

2¾in (7cm) long

$700-850 **BE**

A late-19thC enameled baroque pearl and rose diamond brooch.

1¾in (4.5cm) long 0.56oz

$400-500 **BE**

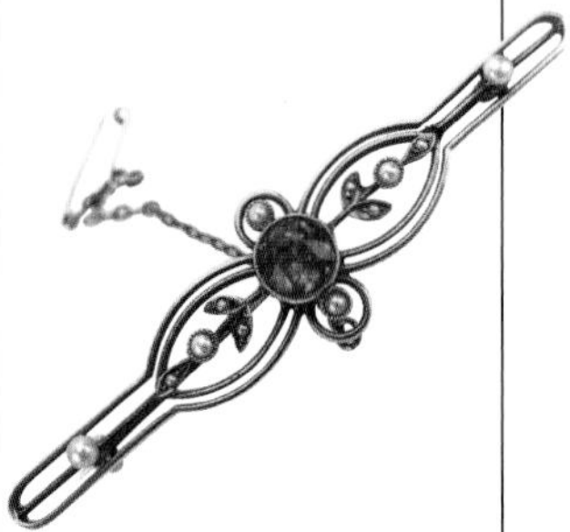

An Edwardian yellow metal bar brooch, set with peridot and small pearls.

0.18oz

$120-140 **WHP**

An Egyptian yellow metal scarab beetle brooch, with hardstones including moss agate, amber, chalcedony, and turquoise, each carved with a different hieroglyph on the reverse, unmarked.

7¾in (19.5cm) long 0.74oz

$450-500 **APAR**

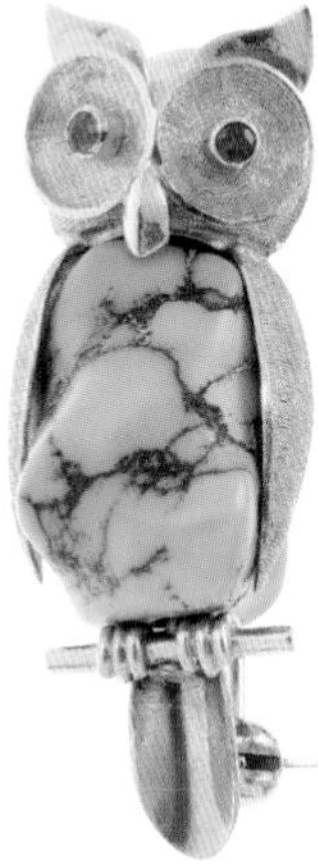

A mid-20thC turquoise and ruby brooch, designed as a textured owl.

1½in (4cm) long 0.43oz

$850-950 **FELL**

A vintage Continental turquoise-set dragonfly brooch, gilt-metal stamped "800," the gilding is thin and worn.

This is an inexpensive example of a popular 19thC theme.

2in (5cm) long

$450-600 **CHEF**

An 18k yellow gold and enameled frog brooch, with red and clear stone eyes.

2in (5cm) long 0.5oz

$650-800 **DUK**

An 18ct gold poodle brooch, diamond collar and ruby eyes.

0.54oz

$700-850 **LOCK**

An enamel ladybug and arrow diamond brooch, mounted in white and yellow metal testing as silver and 9ct, largest rose-cut diamond is 0.33ct, evidence the brooch is made from two pieces.

¾in (7cm) long 0.4oz

$1,900-2,600 **ECGW**

A turquoise and ruby flower head brooch, with petals, stamped "18K."

1960s *1½in (4cm) wide*

$650-800 **DN**

An enamel and diamond cluster brooch, with eight cut-diamond accents, approximately 0.35ct total, stamped "750."

1960s *1¾in (4.5cm) diam*

$800-900 **DN**

A citrine and emerald owl brooch.

1970s *1½in (4cm) long 0.79oz*

$2,600-3,200 **FELL**

A cat brooch, with round-cut emerald eyes, mounted in 18ct yellow gold, hallmarked London.

1980 *1¾in (4.5cm) high 0.41oz*

$650-800 **ECGW**

An early-19thC 18ct gold enamel locket, with inscription "a mon amie" in the interior, Swiss marks.

2½in (6.5cm) long 0.74oz

$1,100-1,250 **FELL**

A 19thC carved coral pendant, mounted in gold.

2½in (6.5cm) high

$300-350 **LC**

A 19thC turquoise gilt-metal set pendant.

1½in (4cm) high

$500-650 **LC**

A Revivalist gold pendant, with enamel portrait, locket compartment on the reverse, on a fine link gold chain, in the style of Falize.

ca. 1885 *pendant 1½in (4cm) high*

$1,600-2,100 **WW**

A 19thC gem-set snake necklace and locket, with three cabochon turquoises and garnet cabochon eyes, with a diagonal stripe of four turquoises separated by a quatrefoil of seed pearls, bordered with black enamel.

15½in (39.5cm) long

$1,100-1,250 **CHEF**

A 19thC hairwork, coral, and seed pearl pendant, unmarked yellow metal tests for gold, with light wear and tear.

2in (5cm) long 0.5oz

$500-650 **CHEF**

A late-19thC gold enamel and diamond pendant, in the manner of Riker Bros., suspending a pearl, on fine-link gold neck chain set with a diamond.

pendant 1¾in (4.5cm) long

$2,300-2,900 **WW**

A 19thC pinchbeck shell cameo necklace, with six oval shell cameo panels, with textured fancy-link connecting chains and push-piece clasp.

16¼in (41.5cm) long

$400-450 **FELL**

A late-19thC gold micromosaic pendant, may be worn as a brooch.

2¼in (5.5cm) long 0.96oz

$3,900-4,500 **FELL**

An Arts and Crafts gold, amethyst, and opal pendant, with a gold-filled chain.

pendant 2in (5cm) long

$1,700-2,100 **NA**

An Arts and Crafts silver-gilt and enamel pendant, by Omar Ramsden, engraved to the reverse "ELLEN MAYNARD LEWIS MAYORESS 1922-23 and OMAR RAMSDEN ME FECIT."

pendant 1¾in (4.5cm) long

$1,600-2,100 WW

An Arts and Crafts silver and enamel pendant, attributed to Ramsden & Carr, decorated with three flower heads, each set with a garnet cabochon, enamel ground cracked.

ca. 1905 pendant 2½in (6.5cm) high

$1,800-2,300 WW

An Art Nouveau Charles Horner silver and enamel pendant necklace, stamped marks, Chester, indistinct date code.

1¼in (3cm) wide

$450-500 WW

An Art Nouveau Murrle Bennett & Co. enameled pendant, set with an oval-cut mother-of-pearl, with an unmarked white metal chain.

17in (43cm) long

$450-500 DUK

An early-20thC gold, sapphire, and diamond pendant, with later trace-link chain, may be worn as a brooch, estimated diamond weight 0.90ct.

pendant 1½in (4cm) long 0.34oz

$1,150-1,300 FELL

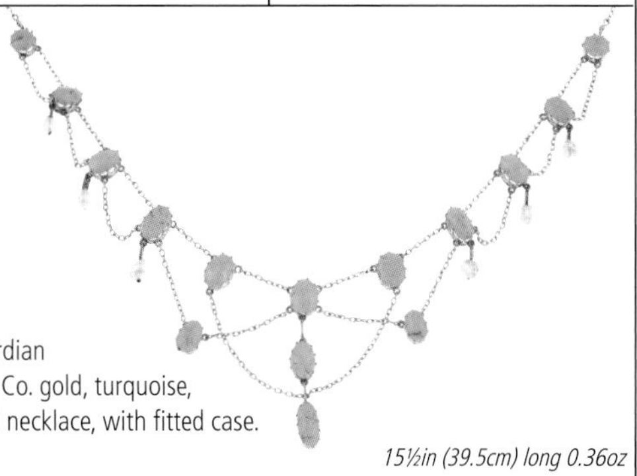

An Edwardian Liberty & Co. gold, turquoise, and pearl necklace, with fitted case.

15½in (39.5cm) long 0.36oz

$3,200-3,900 FELL

A silver and turquoise Navajo "Squash Blossom" necklace, of white metal, with numbers on reverse "499" above "24" above "7387."

10.16oz

$500-650 CHOR

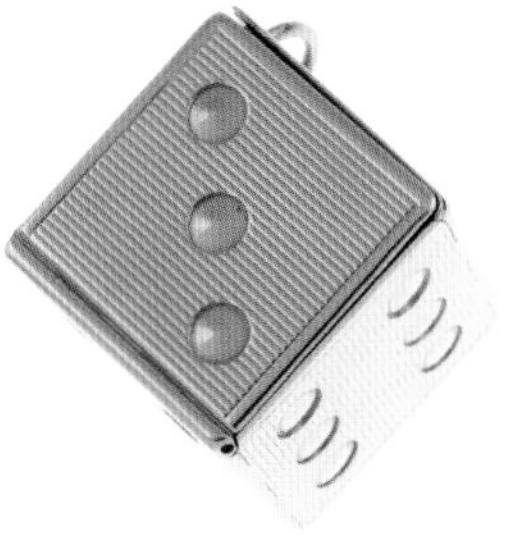

A Cartier 18ct gold dice locket, with four internal compartments, signed "Cartier London, _3352," partly indistinct, hallmarks for London.

1955. 1½in (4cm) long 1.09oz

$2,300-2,900 FELL

A 9ct-gold triangular-link necklace.

14½in (37cm) long 1.5oz

$800-900 BE

An Indian gem-set silver and gold pendant, set with emeralds, rubies, and rose-cut diamonds with a fringe of seed pearls, on a link gold chain set with ruby and emerald beads and seed pearls.

It comes with the original purchase receipt from The Gem Palace, Jaipur, dated March 9, 1998.

pendant 1½in (4cm) high

$800-900 WW

A mid-19thC citrine-set gold bangle, the oval-shaped citrine set within yellow gold rope-twist surround, with seed pearls, French marks.

2½in (6.5cm) diam 2.57oz

$2,300-2,900 **WW**

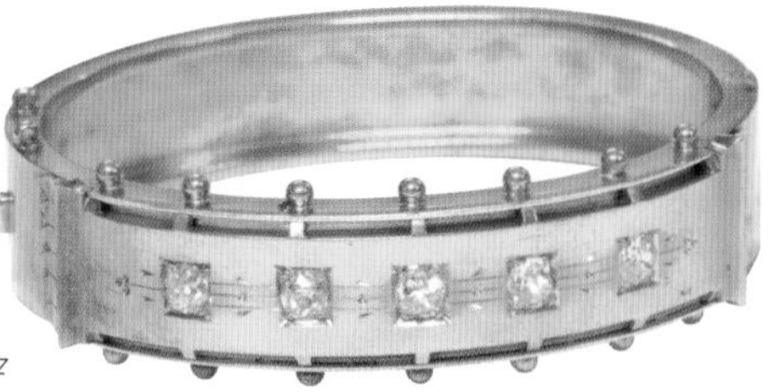

A 19thC yellow metal-hinged snap bangle, set with five old European round and oval-cut diamonds, total 1.10ct, light surface scratches.

2in (5cm) wide 0.85oz

$1,600-2,100 **APAR**

A 19thC Etruscan-style 15ct coral and pearl hinged bangle, unmarked.

$500-650 **FLD**

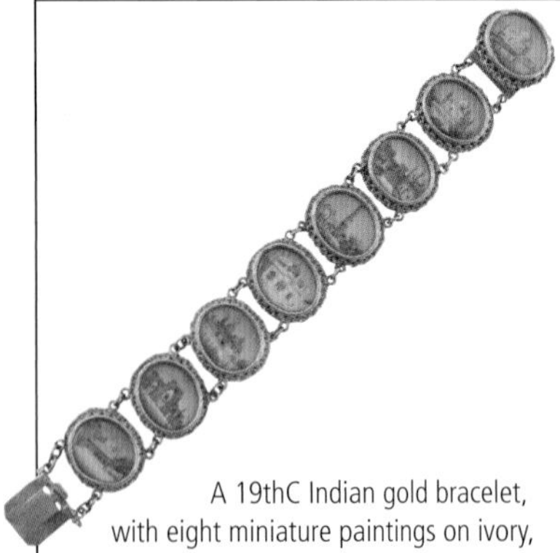

A 19thC Indian gold bracelet, with eight miniature paintings on ivory, depicting famous Indian temples.

7in (18cm) long

$1,100-1,250 **PW**

A 19thC hinged bangle, set with lapis lazuli and pearls, unmarked, tested as 18ct.

$950-1,100 **ECGW**

A lady's yellow metal pearl-encrusted bangle, with centered diamond, test as 14ct gold, three pearls missing.

0.31oz

$400-450 **LOCK**

A silver and green agate foliate bracelet, design no.3, stamped "Sterling Denmark" and with maker's mark.

post-1945 *7¼in (18.5cm) long*

$2,300-2,900 **WW**

A 19thC amethyst five stone ring, set in 15ct gold.

size M½

$220-290 **LC**

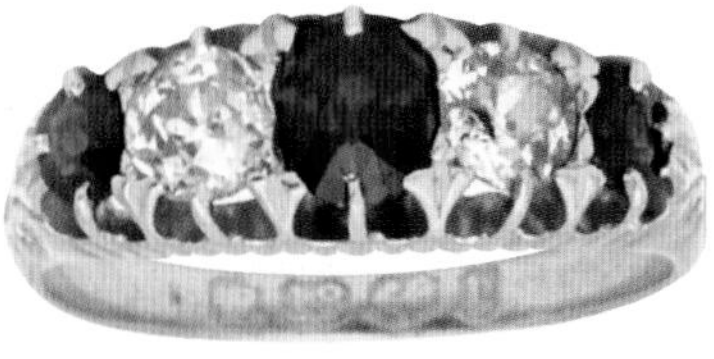

A 19thC 18ct gold, sapphire and diamond-set five stone ring, Birmingham.

1895 *size P½*

$600-650 **BELL**

A late-19thC emerald and diamond panel ring, the old cut diamonds, 0.54ct total, set in 15-18ct gold, emeralds rubbed on the crown, one emerald probably a replacement.

ca. 1900 *size K*

$900-1,050 **DN**

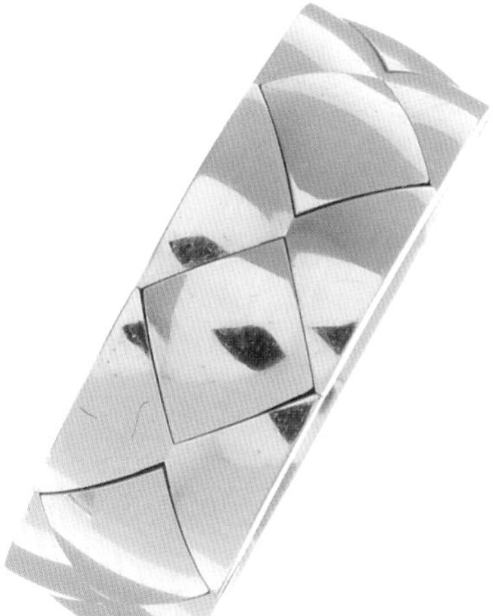

A Chanel "Profil de Camelia" dress ring, signed "Chanel, 20H 2768."

size L

$500-600 **FELL**

A pair of sapphire and diamond earrings, by Child & Child, sapphires approximately 2ct, maker's mark.

ca. 1905 *1¼in (3cm) high*

$2,900-3,600 **WW**

A pair of diamond and sapphire pendant earrings, with Continental hook and clip fittings, white and yellow metal stamped "750."

ca. 1910-25 *1¼in (3cm) long*

$5,200-5,800 **CHEF**

A pair of sapphire and diamond floral earrings, estimated diamond weight 0.25ct.

½in (1.5cm) long ¼oz

$850-900 **FELL**

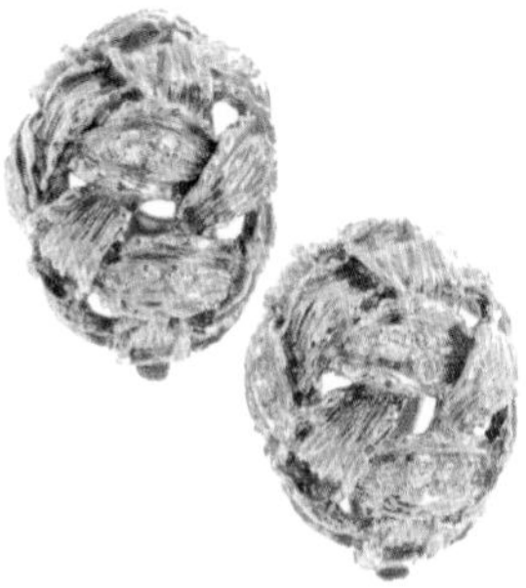

A pair of Kutchinsky 18ct gold diamond earrings, with vari-cut diamond line accents, signed "Kutchinsky," estimated diamond weight 0.80ct, partial hallmarks.

1in (2.5cm) long 1oz

$3,200-3,900 **FELL**

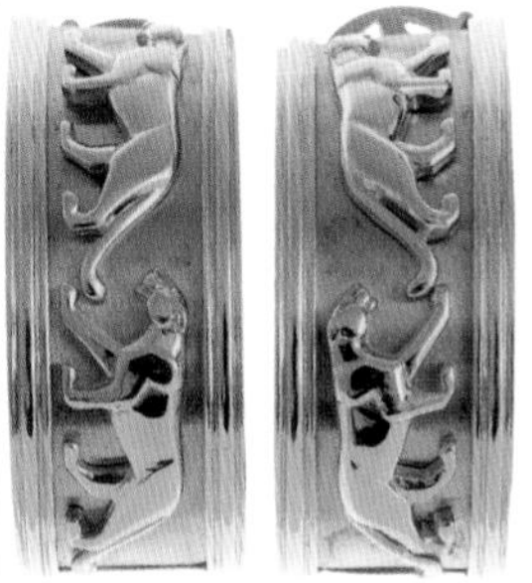

A pair of Cartier 18ct gold "Panthere de Cartier" earrings, with walking panther motif, signed "Cartier, 655935," French assay marks.

1½in (4cm) long 1.64oz

$3,200-3,900 **FELL**

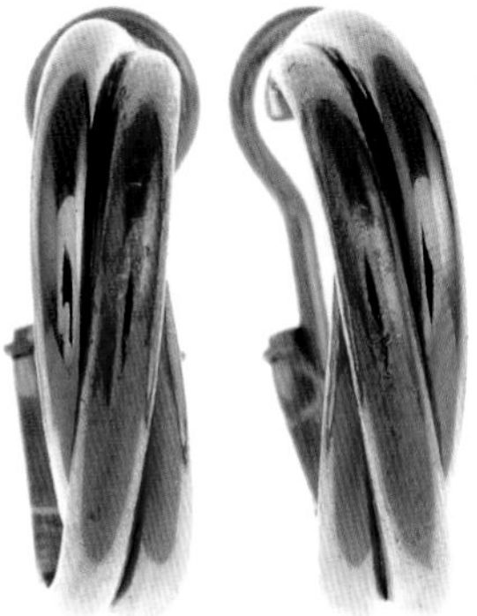

A pair of Cartier "Trinity" earrings, signed "Cartier, 987509," stamped "750."

1in (2.5cm) long

$900-1,050 **FELL**

A pair of Chaumet 18ct gold diamond and ruby earrings, with scattered brilliant-cut diamond and marquise-shape ruby highlights, signed "Chaumet," estimated total diamond weight 0.40ct, import marks for London.

1968 *1¼in (3cm) long 1oz*

$2,600-3,200 **FELL**

A pair of early-20thC emerald and diamond hair clips, emeralds are all abraded or chipped.

1¾in (4.5cm) long

$700-800 **CHEF**

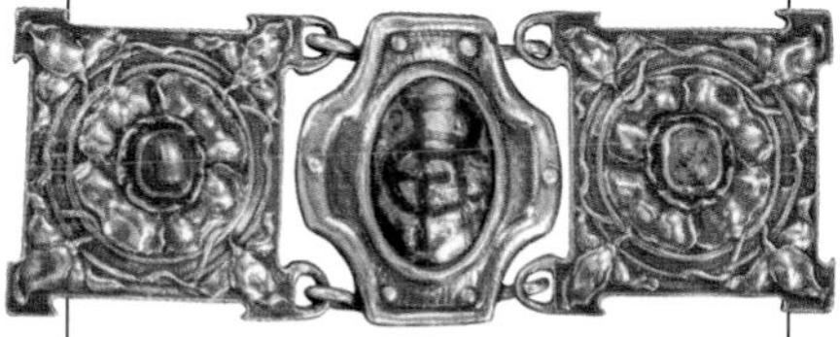

An Arts and Crafts silver belt buckle, by Ramsden & Carr, with an enamel monogram "E*C*R," linked to two embossed side sections, each set with a rough turquoise, London hallmarks, maker's mark, in original fitted box.

1901 *4¾in (12cm) wide*

$1,600-2,100 **WW**

QUICK REFERENCE—GEORG JENSEN

- **Georg Jensen Co. was founded in Copenhagen in 1904 by silversmith and jewelry designer Georg Jensen (1866-1935). Jensen's jewelry designs were inspired by the Arts and Crafts movement as well as Art Nouveau.**
- **Georg Jensen Co. has employed many talented designers, including Johan Rohde (1856-1935), Harald Nielsen (1892-1977), Arno Malinowski (1899-1976), Henning Koppel (1918-81), and Vivianna Torun Bülow-Hübe (1927-2004).**
- **The company is still operational today.**

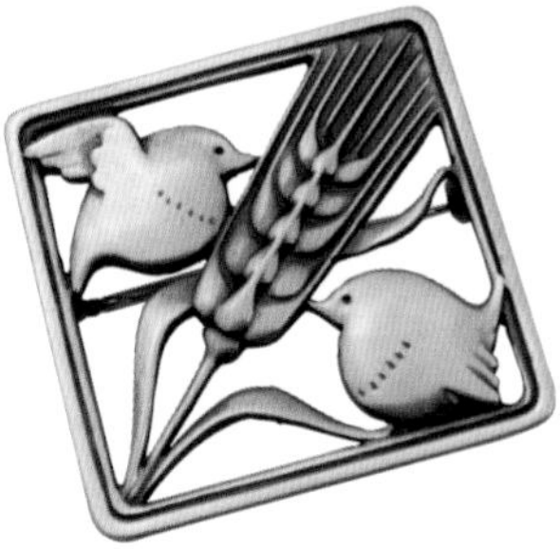

A Georg Jensen sterling silver brooch, designed by Arno Malinowski, no.250.

1½in (4cm) square

$300-350 **LOCK**

A Georg Jensen silver and enamel brooch, designed by Arno Malinowski, no.284, stamped marks.

1¼in (3cm) wide

$700-850 **WW**

A Georg Jenson sterling silver rooster brooch, no.276.

1½in (4cm) square

$300-350 **LOCK**

A Georg Jensen sterling silver dolphin brooch, no.251.

1½in (4cm) wide

$260-320 **LOCK**

A Georg Jensen silver pendant bird necklace, designed by Arno Malinowski, model no.97, stamped marks.

1½in (4cm) high

$400-450 **WW**

A Georg Jensen silver link necklace, model no.826S, cast with flower-head panels, the links set with green chrysoprase, stamped marks.

17½in (44.5cm) long

$2,300-2,900 **WW**

A Georg Jensen silver necklace, model no.270, each link modeled as a stylized seed pod, stamped marks.

17¾in (45cm) long

$1,400-1,900 **WW**

A Georg Jensen silver necklace, designed by Astrid Fog, model no.122, stamped marks.

pendant 2in (5cm) long

$850-950 **WW**

An early-20thC Georg Jensen 18ct gold labradorite ring, maker's mark, "111," stamped "GI, 111, 18k, 765," some surface scratches.

size L½ 0.18oz

$1,900-2,600 **FELL**

A pair of Balenciaga gold-plated metal, blue enamel, plastic, and rhinestone earrings.
1980s *2¼in (5.5cm) long*
$190-260 **GRV**

A pair of Chanel gilt-metal and glass earrings.
1950s *1½in (4cm) long*
$650-800 **GRV**

A pair of Chanel gold-plated metal and Gripoix glass earrings.
1994
$500-600 **GRV**

A pair of Coppola e Toppo gilded-metal and glass earrings.
1960s
$450-600 **GRV**

A pair of Christian Dior silver-tone metal and rhinestone earrings.
1990s
$190-260 **GRV**

A pair of Jomaz green glass, rhinestone, and gold-tone metal earrings.
1960s *2¼in (6cm) long*
$300-400 **GRV**

A pair of Kramer silver-tone metal and rhinestone earrings.
1950s
$100-130 **GRV**

A pair of Christian Lacroix gold-plated metal earrings, with rhinestones, velvet, and faux pearls.
1990s
$300-400 **GRV**

A pair of Napier silver-tone metal and rhinestone earrings.
1950s
$100-130 **GRV**

A pair of Louis Rousselet gold-tone metal and glass earrings.
1940s
$190-260 **GRV**

A pair of Trifari gold-tone metal and enamel earrings.
1960s *2in (5cm) long*
$100-90 **GRV**

A pair of silver, marcasite, carnelian glass, and paste earrings.
1920s
$450-500 **GRV**

A Ciro sterling silver and rhinestone brooch.
1930s *2¼in (6cm) long*
$230-290 **GRV**

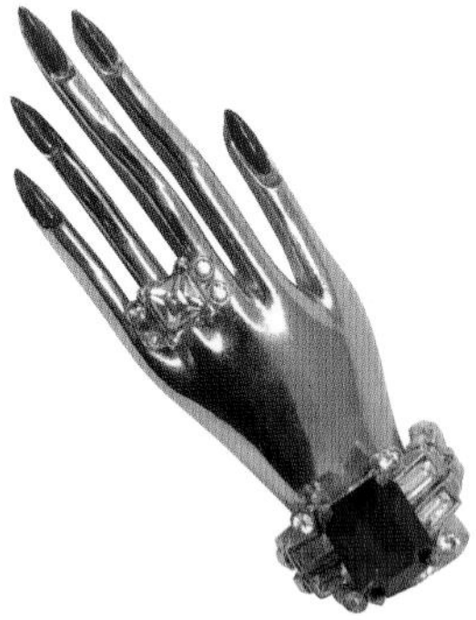

A Coro gold-plated sterling, enamel, and rhinestone brooch.
1944
$190-260 **GRV**

A Christian Dior rhodium-plated metal, rhinestone, and turquoise glass brooch.
1968 *1¾in (4.5cm) long*
$300-400 **GRV**

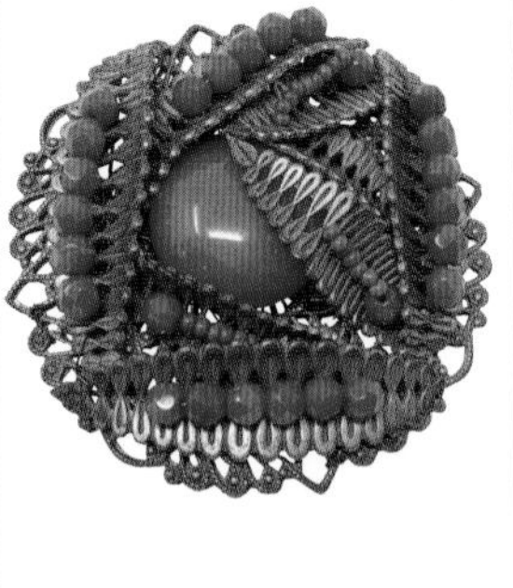

A Miriam Haskell gilded-metal and glass brooch.
1950s
$190-260 **GRV**

A Hobé gold-plated metal, enamel, rhinestone, and glass demi-parure.
1966
$160-230 **GRV**

A Knoll and Pregizer silver and paste brooch.
1930s
$300-400 **GRV**

Judith Picks

I've always loved the glamour of Joseff of Hollywood. Eugène Joseff was born in 1905 in Chicago. In the late 1920s, he moved to Los Angeles to train as a jewelry designer and to exploit one of the few booming industries of the period: Hollywood.

Joseff soon met with incredible success, both as a designer and a supplier of jewelry to the major film studios. He developed a coppery-gold colored mat finish (known as Russian gold), which minimized the problem of over-reflectivity when filming gold jewelry under studio lights. He leased his pieces to the studios and was able to accumulate an archive of nearly three million pieces available to rent.

From 1937, Joseff developed a retail line of jewelry, sold via some 500 "exclusive" stores throughout the USA and abroad. It is these pieces that are now so much in demand. He died in a plane crash in 1948.

A Joseff of Hollywood Russian gold-plate and glass demi-parure.
1940s
$450-500 **GRV**

A Henry Perichon silver and glass brooch.
1960s
$400-450 **GRV**

A Roger Jean Pierre silver, rhinestone, and glass demi-parure.
1950s
$600-700 **GRV**

An Yves Saint Laurent gold-plated metal brooch.
1980s
$100-160 **GRV**

An Archimede Seguso for Chanel glass and gold-tone metal necklace.
1960s
$300-350 **GRV**

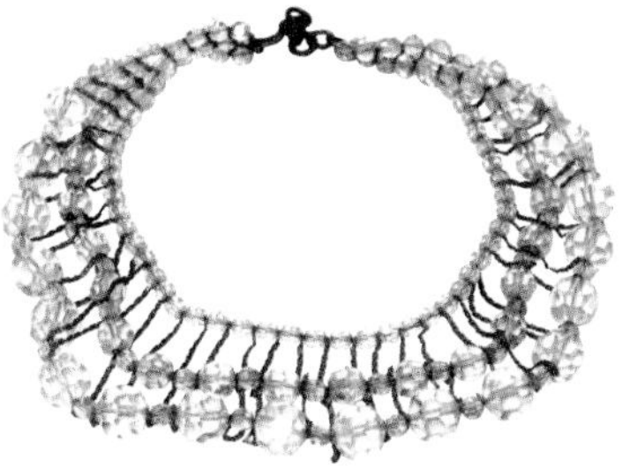

A Christian Dior "Aurora Borealis" crystal necklace, signed.
ca. 1950
$300-400 **SWO**

A Christian Dior gold-plated metal necklace.
1970s
$450-500 **GRV**

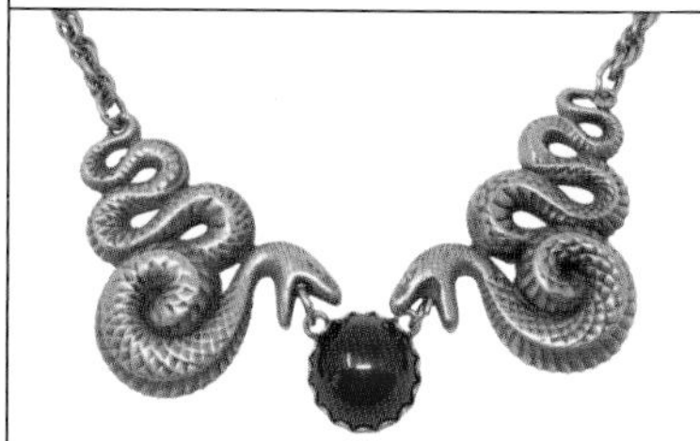

A Joseff of Hollywood Russian gold-plate and glass necklace.
1960s
$600-650 **GRV**

A Ciner gold-plated metal and enamel necklace.
1970s
$190-260 **GRV**

A Christian Dior by Mitchel Maer rhodium-plated metal, glass, and rhinestone full parure.
1952-56
$1,300-1,600 **GRV**

A Jomaz rhodium-plated metal and rhinestone necklace.
1940s
$350-450 **GRV**

A Louis Rousselet Bakelite, glass, faux pearl, and base metal necklace.
1930s *17¼in (44cm) long*
$190-260 **GRV**

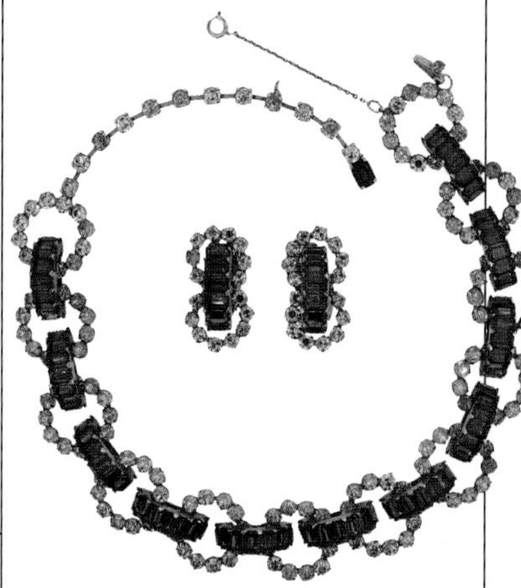

A Christian Dior gold vermeil-plated and green rhinestone necklace and earrings set, designed by Mitchel Maer.
1950s *necklace 14½in (37cm) long*
$950-1,100 **GRV**

QUICK REFERENCE— LAWRENCE VRBA

- **Lawrence (Larry) Vrba worked as a designer for Miriam Haskell in the 1960s and 70s. In the early 1980s, Vrba set up his own jewelry business. He has created pieces for theater productions, including *Wicked* and *Hairspray*, films, and private customers.**

A Lawrence Vrba brass, glass, and plastic demi-parure.
$850-950 **GRV**

A Selro silver-tone metal, thermoset plastic and rhinestone demi-parure.

Selro was founded by Paul Selenger in the 1940s. Selenger was born in Russia in 1911 and emigrated to New York in 1927. Before setting up his own company, Selenger worked for jewelry company H. Pomerantz & Co. in New York. He also made jewelry under the name of Selini. Selro closed in the mid-1970s.

1960s

$300-450 **GRV**

A Czechoslovakian gilt-metal, enamel, glass, and paste necklace.

1910s

$260-320 **GRV**

A chrome-plated metal, glass, and paste necklace.

1920s

$300-450 **GRV**

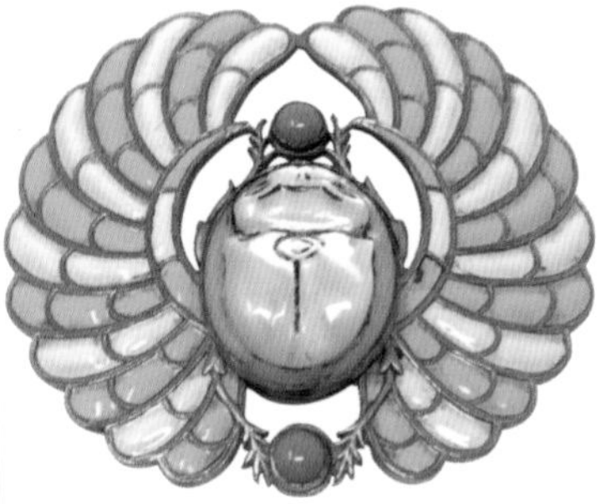

A Piel Frères gilt-metal, enamel, and glass buckle.

ca. 1900

$950-1,100 **GRV**

A Limoges copper and enamel bracelet.

1950s

$190-260 **GRV**

A Jean Painlevé brass and plastic bangle.

1930s

$190-260 **GRV**

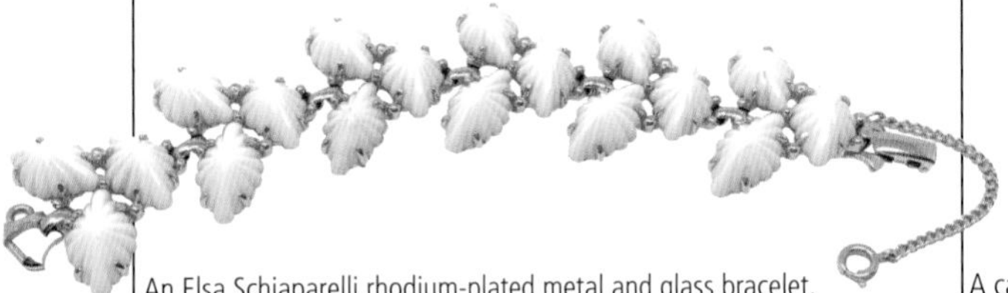

An Elsa Schiaparelli rhodium-plated metal and glass bracelet.

1950s

$300-400 **GRV**

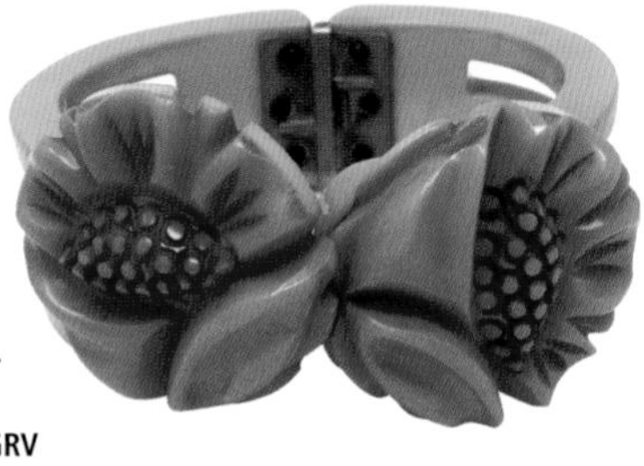

A carved Bakelite bangle.

1930s

$450-500 **GRV**

An Anna Greta Eker silver ring.

1970s

$300-400 **GRV**

A Trifari silver-tone metal and rhinestone ring.

1960s

$100-160 **GRV**

QUICK REFERENCE—OIL LAMPS

- **An oil lamp produces light using an oil-based fuel source. The use of oil lamps began thousands of years ago.**
- **Oil lamps were used as an alternative to candles before the use of electric lights. Starting in 1780, the Argand lamp quickly replaced other oil lamps still in their basic ancient form. These, in turn, were replaced by the kerosene lamp in about 1850.**
- **Sources of fuel for oil lamps include a wide variety of plants, such as nuts (walnuts, almonds) and seeds (sesame, olive, castor, flax). Also widely used were animal fats, including butter, fish oil, shark liver, and whale blubber. Camphine, a blend of turpentine and alcohol, was the first "burning fluid" fuel for lamps after whale oil supplies were depleted. It was replaced by kerosene after the US Congress enacted excise taxes on alcohol to pay for the American Civil War.**

A 19thC oil lamp and shade.

$80-110 **PSA**

A 19thC oil lamp, with brass base and cranberry shade.

$220-260 **PSA**

A 19thC Craighead and Kintz novelty patinated metal owl oil lamp, the oil fitments with marks "OSBERT HENDERSON/ GLASGOW."

19½in (49.5cm) high

$650-900 **L&T**

A 19thC enameled opaque glass and brass oil lamp, with a Palmer & Co. patent fitting and Rococo-style brass base.

35in (89cm) high

$450-600 **L&T**

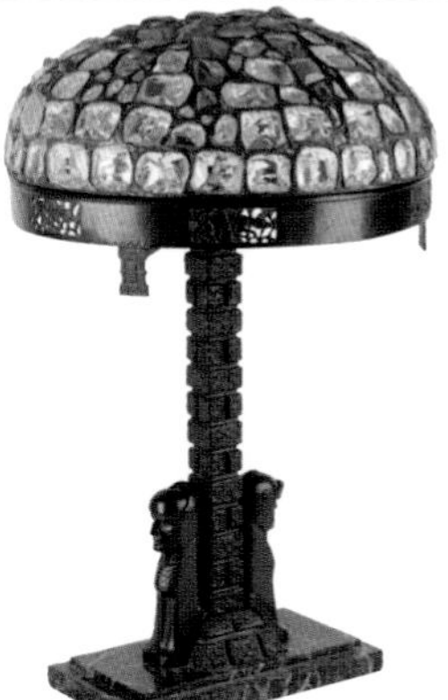

A Continental Arts and Crafts bronze table lamp, the shade inset with glass "jewels," the band pierced with panels depicting a hunting scene, impressed monogram.

23¾in (60.5cm) high

$850-950 **DUK**

An early-20thC silver Corinthian column oil lamp, made by Mappin & Webb, with diamond-cut and engraved frosted glass shade, shade with two chips on bottom rim, burner has been replated.

1902 *30¼in (77cm) high*

$1,100-1,250 **LSK**

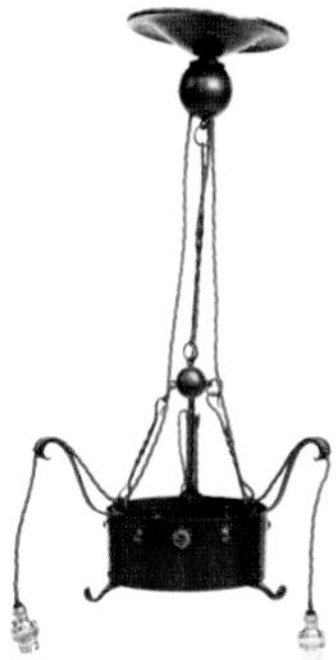

A Jesson Birkett & Co. patinated copper ceiling light, collar set with three Ruskin Pottery turquoise stones, unsigned.

The Birmingham Arts and Crafts metalworking business of R. LL. B. Rathbone, part of which was taken over by the Faulkner Bronze Company in 1902, was reconstituted as Jesson, Birkett & Co. in 1904. This company took over more of Rathbone's business, but was liquidated in 1910.

24¾in (63cm) drop

$2,600-3,200 **WW**

An Art Nouveau "Le Lumiere de Nancy" silvered metal figural table lamp, with Le Verre Français glass shade, signed.

16¼in (41.5cm) high

$400-450 **WW**

A pâte-de-verre "Chrysanthemum" glass lamp, by Gabriel Argy-Rousseau (1885-1953), cast signature, on a tripod bronze base, with incised geometric decoration.

6¼in (16cm) high

$1,150-1,550 **DUK**

A Degué "Cristalleries de Compiègne" cameo glass lamp, with conical glass shade, signed, on a scrolling ironwork base.

8¾in (22cm) diam

$400-450 **CHOR**

An Art Deco Degué "Cristalleries de Compiègne" chandelier, signed, a few shades with minor chips.

31½in (80cm) high

$600-700 **CHOR**

A patinated metal figural table lamp, in the manner of Josef Lorenzl (1892-1950), on alabaster base, with frosted glass shade, unsigned.

8in (20.5cm) wide

$400-450 **WW**

An Art Deco adjustable brass table lamp, the shade inset with four tinted blue glass panels.

13¼in (33.5cm) high

$300-350 **DUK**

An Art Deco-style lamp in the form of a metal figurine of a dancer.

25¼in (64cm) high

$300-350 **CHOR**

An Art Deco table lamp, with a glass globe shade, chrome mounts, and a reeded Bakelite column.

16½in (42cm) high

$300-450 **SWO**

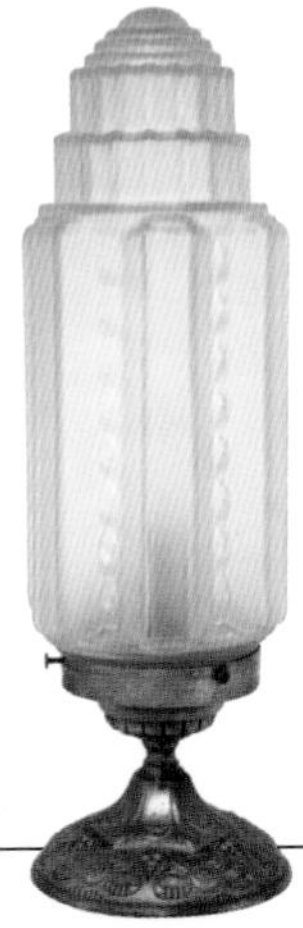

A French Art Deco table lamp, with a frosted glass shade, mounted on a cast plinth.

17¾in (45cm) high

$400-500 **SWO**

An Art Deco cast lamp, with a molded glass shade on a brass and silvered cast stand.

22½in (57cm) high

$400-450 **SWO**

An Italian 14-light chandelier, in the manner of Fontana Arte, with smoky glass shades.

ca. 1950 *20in (51cm) high*

$1,900-2,600 **ROS**

Judith Picks

This is the epitomy of the Art Deco style. Lamps incorporating elegantly posed nude or barely clothed athletic ladies were typical of this period. Their poses were largely based on earlier Modernist ideals about health, exercise, and athletics. Some were, however, based on dance movements or the expensive highly fashionable bronze and ivory figurines designed by top sculptors, such as Ferdinand Preiss. The use of figural forms for lamps (or candlesticks) was not a new idea, from Blackamoors of the 18thC to all kinds of forms from warriors to shepherds during the 19thC. Later examples were often made from spelter alloy, which was less expensive than bronze, lighter in weight, but more brittle. Always look for good proportions and quality in terms of pose, finishing, and details, such as the face and hands.

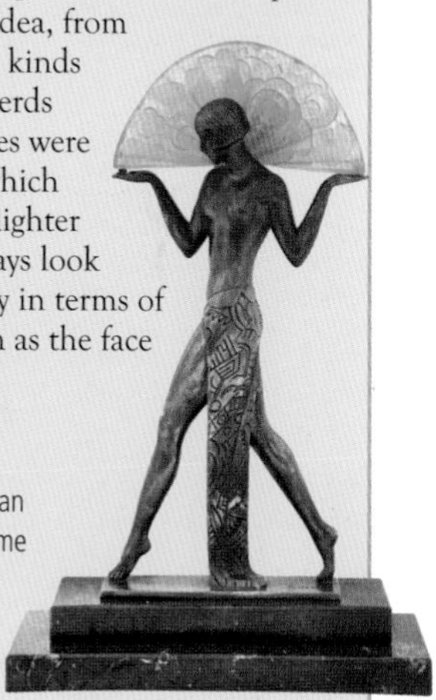

An Art Deco table lamp, modeled as a fan dancer after Guerbe, with signature, some wear on the nude, fan appears plastic (not glass).

19¾in (50cm) high

$2,600-3,200 **SWO**

A Flos "Arco" floor lamp, by Achille and Pier Giacomo Castiglioni, the steel shade, on adjustable arm to Carrera marble base, applied label.

ca. 1990 *86½in (220.5cm) high*

$1,050-1,150 **ROS**

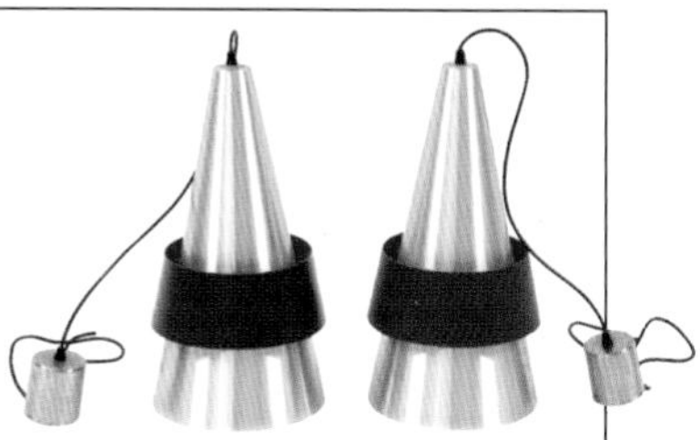

A pair of Fog and Mørup ceiling lights, designed by Jo Hammerborg.

18¼in (46.5cm) high

$160-210 **SWO**

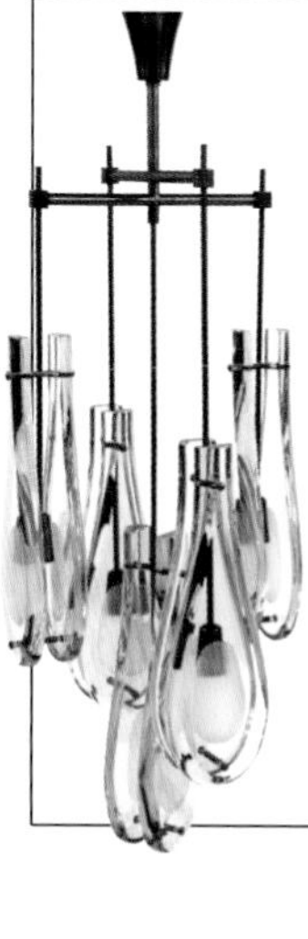

A Fontana Arte Italian glass five-light ceiling light, in the style of Max Ingrand.

67in (170cm) high

$7,000-8,500 **SWO**

A pair of black lacquered and brass desk lamps, by Louis Christian Kalff.

ca. 1950s *15in (38cm) high*

$950-1,100 **ROS**

A J. Lüber AG "SP2" ceiling light, by Verner Panton, in silvered plastic, the mount, with hanging spiral droplets.

ca. 1969 *57½in (146cm) high*

$5,200-6,500 **ROS**

A CLOSER LOOK AT A LUMITRON LAMP

Robert Welch (1929-2000) was a leading British designer best known for his stainless steel tableware.

The range included a spherical-form ceiling light and a taller floor lamp.

In 1986, Robert Welch was commissioned by lighting company Lumitron to design a light. He was inspired by mid-century modern Scandinavian examples. This is shown by the clean lines, acrylic, and silvered metal.

Many examples were retailed through Habitat (founded by Terence Conran in 1964).

A Lumitron table lamp, designed by Robert Welch.

21in (53.5cm) high

$190-260 **WW**

A pair of Martinelli Luce "Pipistrello" table lamps, designed by Gae Aulenti.

34¾in (88.5cm) high

$1,300-1,900 **SWO**

A Memphis "Charleston" standard lamp, by Martine Bedin, with lacquered aluminum frame, with label.

ca. 1984 *77½in (197cm) high*

$1,600-1,900 **ROS**

A gilt-metal ceiling light, by Oliver Messel, of sunburst form, with matching ceiling rose.

ca. 1960 *17¼in (44cm) diam*

$650-800 **L&T**

A 1950s Italian Stilnovo-style chandelier, in gilt metal and enamel.

36¼in (92cm) high

$1,300-1,900 **BELL**

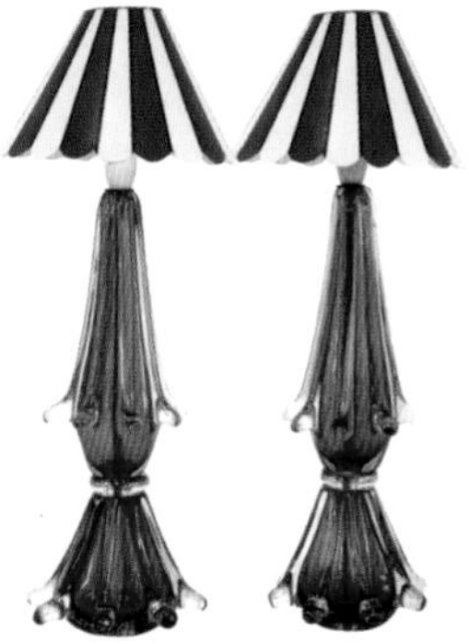

A 1970s pair of large Murano glass lamps, with painted shades.

$400-450 **SWO**

An Italian brushed steel and glass five-light chandelier, by Gaetano Sciolari.

ca. 1970 *27½in (70cm) high*

$500-650 **SWO**

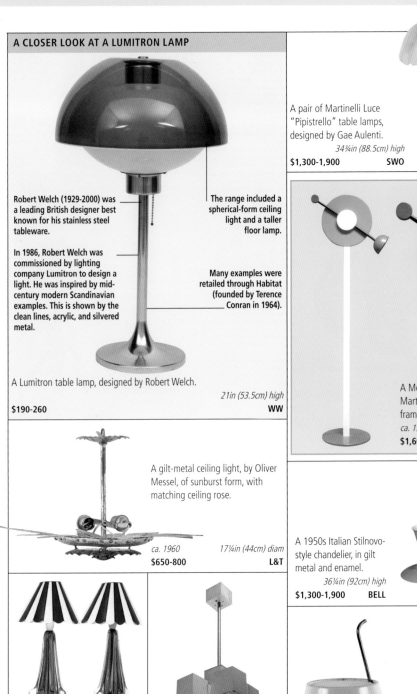

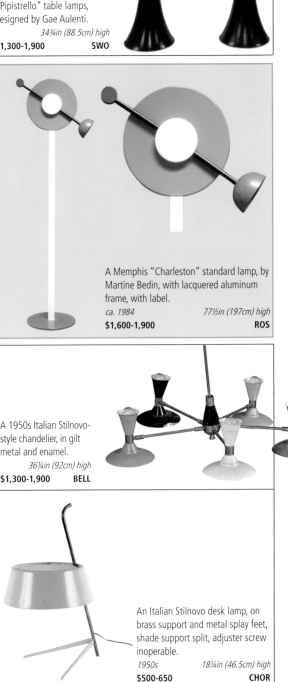

An Italian Stilnovo desk lamp, on brass support and metal splay feet, shade support split, adjuster screw inoperable.

1950s *18¼in (46.5cm) high*

$500-650 **CHOR**

An Ives, Blakeslee & Co. "Bulldog Savings" mechanical bank, clockwork activated, press lever and dog springs forward and bites/swallows coin from man's hands.

ca. 1878

$2,600-3,900 **BER**

A Kyser & Rex "GLOBE SAVINGS FUND" semi-mechanical bank, extensive casting effects with colorful highlights in red and gold, bronze dragons sitting on roof, combination lock on front door.

ca. 1889

$2,600-3,900 **BER**

A Kyser & Rex "Organ Grinder and Performing Bear" mechanical bank, when wound the bear revolves as organ grinder turns organ handle.

ca. 1882

$6,000-7,000 **BER**

A Jerome B. Secor "FREEDMAN'S BANK" mechanical bank, the sitting man thumbs his nose and gives a jeering look to depositors when clockwork is activated, minor repair on head.

This bank gains its inspiration from the Freedman's Bank for newly freed slaves established by the US Congress. Less than ten known examples of this bank still exist in what has come to be considered one of the best-known historically important banks made.

ca. 1880

$130,000-190,000 **BER**

A Kyser & Rex cast iron "Mammy and Child" mechanical bank, with original spoon, trap replaced.

7¾in (19.5cm) high

$2,300-2,900 **POOK**

A J. & E. Stevens Co. classic Americana "Darktown Battery" mechanical bank.

ca. 1888

$12,000-13,000 **BER**

A J. & E. Stevens Co. "Calamity" mechanical bank, place a coin in the slot in front of the full back and press lever, as the players crash together at front, coin drops into the receptacle.

ca. 1904 *7½in (19cm) high*

$4,500-5,800 **BER**

A J. & E. Stevens Co. "Acrobat" mechanical bank.

ca. 1883

$12,000-14,000 **BER**

A rare American "Sewing Machine" mechanical bank, coin slot appears on table.

This bank was reportedly given away by the American Sewing Machine Co.

ca. 1880s

$10,500-12,000 **BER**

A German silver automaton musical box, the hinged lid enclosing a rotating singing bird, stamped "800," in a Tessiers Ltd. New Bond Street retail box, bellows in need of attention.

4¼in (11cm) wide

$2,600-3,200 **BE**

An early-20thC German symphonion, with 32 discs, the double combe with serial number "290472," in a walnut case with brass claw feet.

20in (51cm) wide

$1,150-1,550 **DUK**

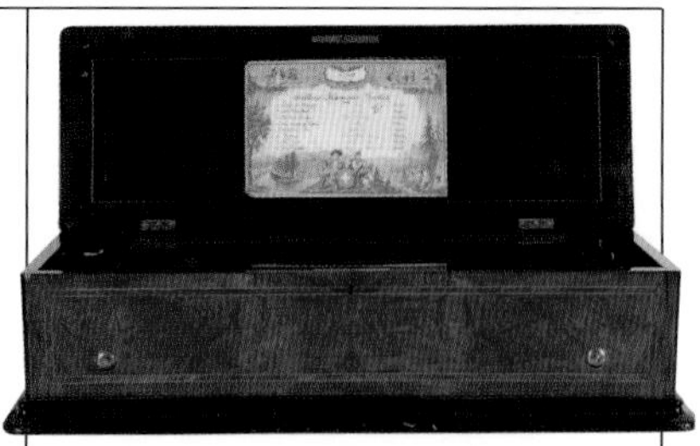

A late-19thC Swiss walnut and rosewood banded music box, the mechanism playing eight airs via pinned brass cylinder and tuned steel combs, the lid with handwritten tune sheet inscribed "no.7219," some wear.

12¼in (31cm) long

$2,600-3,200 **DN**

A Swiss filigree gilt singing bird box.

4in (10cm) long

$3,200-3,900 **JN**

A musical box, playing ten airs, 18-key organ section, tune card, cylinder 9¼in (23.5cm), with crossbanded rosewood lid.

26in (66cm) wide

$2,300-2,900 **FLD**

A 19thC coin-operated walnut wall-mounted polyphon, with twenty-eight 19½in (50cm)-diameter discs.

49¼in (125cm) high

$3,200-3,900 **APAR**

A style 104 upright polyphon, by Nicole Frères, coin operated, carved walnut case playing 19⅝in discs on duplex combs, serial no.8931, on a later bin stand with fall front to reveal 25 discs.

82in (208.5cm) high

$7,000-8,000 **FLD**

A rare American Wurlitzer "Peacock"-type 850 juke box, designed by Paul Fueller, serial no.788323, amusement machine no.3738, expiring June 30, 1948, playing twenty-four 10in 78 rpm records, in veneered wooden case, the front in glass, chrome, Plexiglass and walnut veneer, coin selectors taking 25, 10, and 5-cent pieces.

Launched in 1941, just before the USA entered World War II, the "Peacock" was regarded as the decorative top of the range at the time and is one of the larger and showiest jukeboxes made.

1940s *68in (172.5cm) high*

$23,000-29,000 **HT**

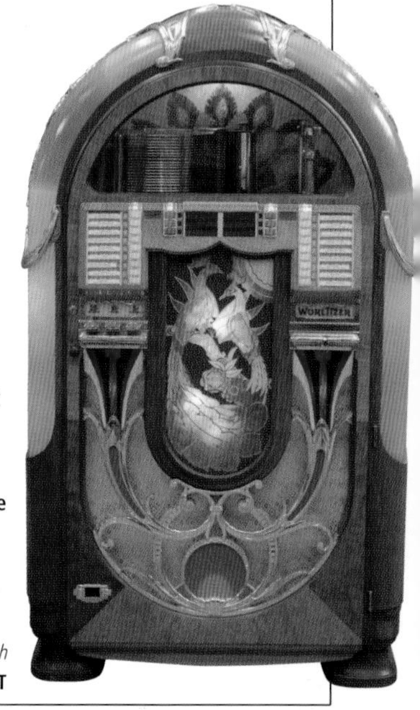

A Continental oak-cased wind-up gramophone, with green tin horn.

1920s *12¼in (31cm) wide*

$450-500 **FLD**

A Graphophone type Q phonograph, with small witches hat-type horn, oak case on plinth base.

10½in (26.5cm) wide

$350-400 **FLD**

A Columbia Graphophone Co. phonograph, with key-wind operation, fixed horn, and original reproducer.

13½in (34.5cm) long

$190-260 **FLD**

An Edison Gem phonograph, serial no.G118804, model C reproducer with horn and six cylinders.

$300-400 **FLD**

An Edison Gem phonograph, serial no.G116835, model B reproducer and key-wind operation, with later aluminum horn.

10in (25.5cm) wide

$350-400 **FLD**

An Edison Standard phonograph, with a brass-finished horn and a group of cased cylinders, in an oak case.

$400-450 **WHP**

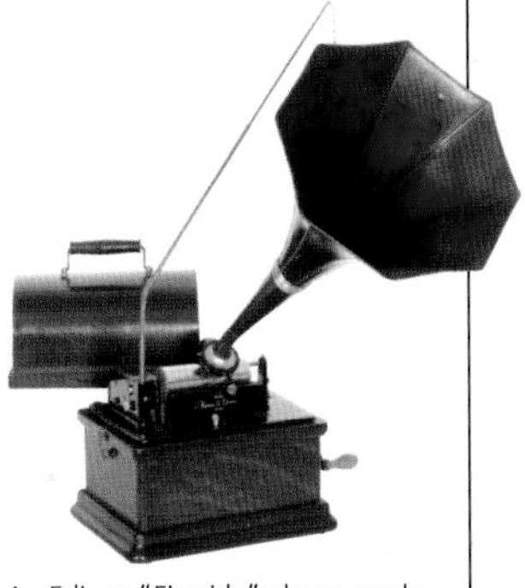

An Edison "Fireside" phonograph, serial no.13685, 4 to 2-minute play, with combination model reproducer, with original fireside horn and crane, in oak case.

11½in (29cm) wide

$700-850 **FLD**

A French Pathé phonograph, later aluminum horn and stenciled walnut case.

11¾in (30cm) wide

$260-320 **FLD**

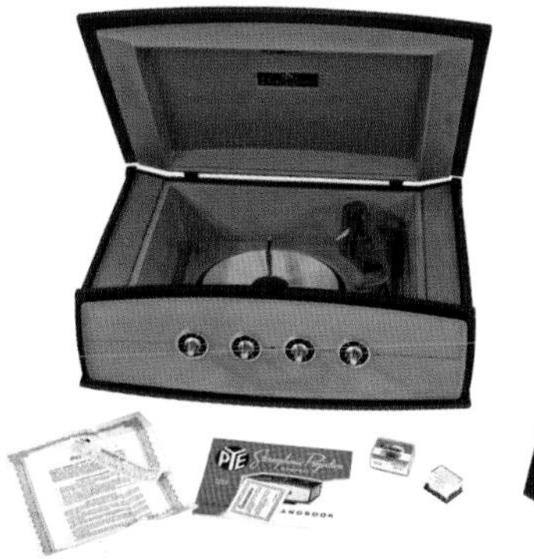

A Pye "Stereophonic Projection System," in a mahogany case, with instructions and guarantee, working order.

1967 *22¼in (56.5cm) wide*

$260-320 **SWO**

An Akai Model X-355 Cross Field Head 4-Track stereo recorder, with original instructions.

$300-400 **SWO**

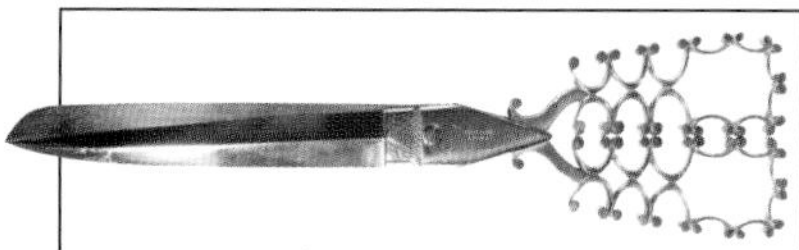

A pair of 19thC steel scissors, by Joseph Cousins, stamped "J. COUSINS & SONS SHEFFIELD."

By repute, these were made for the Great Exhibition at Crystal Palace in 1851.

10½in (26.5cm) long

$450-500 **WW**

A W.A.S. Benson copper and brass hand candlestick, foliate design by George Heywood Sumner, stamped Benson shield mark on brass handle.

9in (23cm) high

$1,050-1,150 **WW**

A 19thC brass dog collar, with padlock.

3in (7.5cm) diam

$160-210 **LOCK**

A late-19thC ornate brass coal bin, with foliate scrolls and shell surmount.

$850-950 **BRI**

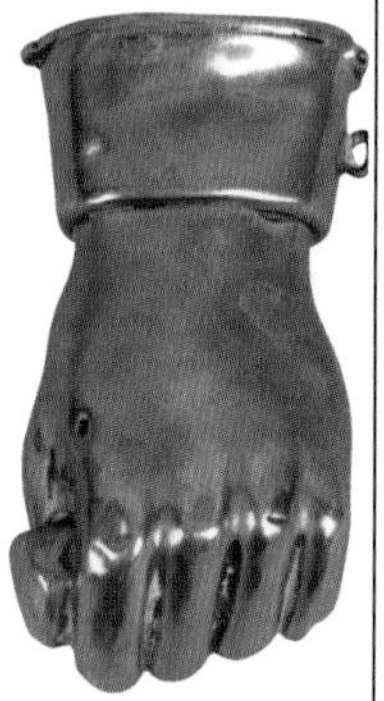

A late-19thC brass vesta case, modeled as a hand clasping a scroll.

For Smoking, see pp. 337-341.

2½in (6.5cm) high

$60-70 **FELL**

A Keswick School of Industrial Art copper letter rack, with repoussé work, titled "Post," stamped.

8in (20.5cm) wide

$300-400 **FLD**

A pair of Stickley Brothers hammered copper candlesticks, with brass bands, marked "131," rims bent out of form.

ca. 1915 *12in (30.5cm) high*

$1,100-1,250 **DRA**

A World War I trench art model of a brass British pillar-shaped mailbox, engraved "GR," inset with an aluminum collection time plaque.

6½in (16.5cm) high

$260-320 **FLD**

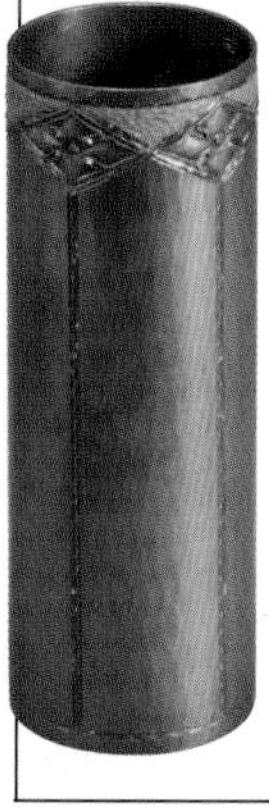

A Roycroft hammered copper and enamel vase, designed by Walter Jennings, with etched dogwood pattern and Italian enamel decoration, incised with orb and cross mark with two dots for Walter Jennings.

The Roycrofters, an Arts and Crafts community, was founded in 1895 in East Aurora, New York, by Elbert Hubbard (1856-1915). While Roycroft began as a publishers, a blacksmiths was added in 1899 and a copper shop in 1902. Copper ware was sold commercially from 1906. Roycroft pieces are patinated. Notable craftsmen include Karl Kipp and Walter Jennings. Production ceased in 1938.

ca. 1915-20 *7in (18cm) high*

$2,900-3,600 **WES**

An Art Deco table mirror, by Émile Jacques Ruhlmann (1879-1933), on a waterfall front walnut stand.

16¼in (41cm) high

$850-900 **DUK**

An American 19thC painted tin folk art weathervane, of a firefighter, traces of original paint, extremely worn, lacking post.

30in (76cm) high

$1,250-1,450 **DRA**

An American 19thC Merino ram molded sheet iron weathervane, horn present but detached, part of head on one side missing, wear throughout.

34in (86.5cm) long

$950-1,150 **DRA**

An American "Polo Players" enameled wrought iron weathervane, by William Hunt Diederich (1884-1953), unmarked, repainted.

46in (117cm) long

$16,000-19,000 **DRA**

A 19thC painted, cast iron fox head doorstop.

5¾in (14.5cm) high

$450-500 **WW**

A 19thC cast iron heraldic doorstop, of a greyhound with its paw resting on a shield, with a faint registration lozenge.

18in (45.5cm) high

$850-950 **WW**

A William IV bronze shell decorated doorstop, on a scroll weighted base.

14½in (37cm) high

$180-230 **WW**

A 19thC brass doorstop, in the form of a basket of fruit and flowers, on a weighted base.

14in (35.5cm) high

$600-700 **WW**

An early-19thC brass doorstop, of a fox emerging from foliage, with a leaf and flower scroll handle.

16½in (42cm) high

$1,700-2,100 **WW**

A 19thC brass sphinx doorstop, on a polished cast iron plinth.

15½in (39.5cm) high

$190-260 **WW**

A 19thC brass lion's paw doorstop, with weighted base.

14½in (37cm) high

$180-230 **WW**

An early-20thC Tiffany Studios blown-out patinated bronze candelabrum, blown glass, stamped "TIFFANY STUDIOS, NEW YORK, S1454 TGDCO," touch ups to original patina.

For Lighting, see pp.269-272.

13in (33cm) high

$2,600-3,200 DRA

An early-20thC Tiffany Studios patinated bronze lamp base, stamped "TIFFANY STUDIOS, NEW YORK, 540," rewired.

13in (33cm) high

$1,900-2,600 DRA

An early-20thC Tiffany Studios fleur-de-lis gilt-bronze candelabrum, stamped "TIFFANY STUDIOS, NEW YORK, 1230," with cipher, some wear.

8¾in (22cm) high

$450-600 DRA

A Tiffany Studios patinated copper and glass outdoor sconce, unmarked, verdigris throughout, original screw/screw caps, all but one glass panel replaced.

ca. 1900 *22½in (57cm) high*

$2,600-3,200 DRA

A 20thC Tiffany style of bamboo patinated and bronzed metal table lamp base, spurious mark, with mottled verdigris patina.

21in (53.5cm) high

$1,900-2,600 DRA

An early-20thC Tiffany Studios "Seven Zodiac" acid-etched gilt-bronze desk set, all marked.

largest 9½in (24cm) long

$1,050-1,150 DRA

A Tiffany Studios "Adam" acid-etched, enameled, and gilt-bronze picture frame, stamped "TIFFANY STUDIOS, NEW YORK, 1610," some light wear, glass possibly replaced.

1920s *12in (30.5cm) high*

$1,100-1,250 DRA

An early-20thC Tiffany Studios "Pine Needle" patinated bronze and slag glass picture frame, stamped "TIFFANY STUDIOS, NEW YORK," etched "147," a Y-line crack on one large piece of glass, few minor dents.

9¼in (23.5cm) high

$1,600-2,100 DRA

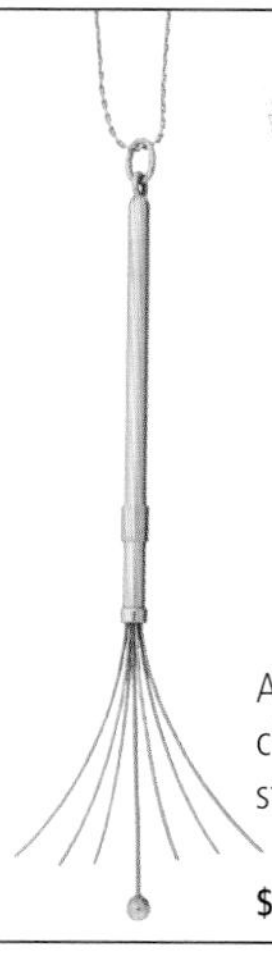

A Tiffany & Co. yellow gold champagne swizzle stick, stamped by the maker.

4¾in (12cm) high

$650-800 DRA

A Victoria Burma medal, awarded to 1418 Corp. S. Helsby 1st Bn. R.W.

$300-350 **PSA**

A Punjab medal, with two clasps for Chilianwala and Goojerat, named to Cornet F.C.J. Brownlow, 1st Bengal Cavy.

1849

$1,100-1,250 **CHEF**

An India General Service medal, with Pegu clasp, named to Lieutenant Colonel G.W. Osborne 19th Madras Native Infantry.

1854-95

$450-600 **CHEF**

An Army of India medal, with Ava clasp, awarded to Captain John Wilson 30th N.I., with ribbon.

1799-1826

$1,100-1,250 **CHEF**

An India General Service Medal, with Perak clasp, named to Lieutenant H.A.Rigg Rl. Arty., with partial ribbon.

1854-95

$300-450 **CHEF**

An Indian Mutiny one-clasp "Delhi" medal, awarded to Captain G.G. McBarnet, 55th Bengal Native Infantry, in frame.

George Gordon McBarnet was the son of Donald McBarnet Kingussie and Insh, Inverness-shire, Scotland. He was born October 8, 1823, and later became captain in the 55th Bengal Native Infantry, attached to the 1st Bengal European Fusiliers. He was killed in action at the assault of Delhi during the Indian Mutiny on September 14, 1857.

1857-58

$1,700-2,100 **BRI**

An India medal, with Punjab Frontier 1897-98 clasp, named to 526 Sergeant J. Smith 3d Bn Rifle Brigade, with copy medal roll.

1896

$300-400 **LOCK**

A Malaya General Service medal, with clasp awarded to "2252647 SIGMN K.T BEAUMONT R.SIGS."

$60-70 **PSA**

A South African medal, awarded to "2621 GNR. J.BIRCH. 19th Bty.R.F.A," with the following clasps, South Africa 1902, South Africa 1901, Transvaal, Orange Free State, Cape Colony.

$190-260 **PSA**

A Naval General Service medal, with renamed inscription for John Brookfield, Copenhagen 1801 bar and ribbon.

$850-950 **HT**

A British South Africa Company medal, with "Rhodesia 1896" reverse, awarded to Trooper R. Dickson, Belingwe Column.

$500-650 **LOCK**

A gilt 19thC 6th Royal Warwickshire Regiment helmet plate.

$1,300-1,800 LOCK

An Austro-Hungarian Empire Austrian pilot's badge, toned.

$160-230 LOCK

A small WM HP, or puggaree, of the Hong Kong Volunteer Corps Garrison Artillery, with slide.

1902-08

$950-1,100 W&W

A possibly World War I London Scottish Regiment unmarked silver officer's Glengarry badge, rusty stout pin on reverse.

1⅜oz

$210-260 LOCK

A Churchill's Secret Army enamel badge, "1-202-3," fitting on the reverse.

$600-650 LOCK

A 19thC officer's gilt- and silver-plated helmet plate, of The Middlesex Regiment.

$230-290 W&W

An officer's gilt- and silver-plated shako plate, of The 65th 2nd Yorkshire N. Riding Regiment, shallow dents to Garter.

1861

$300-400 W&W

A Women's Land Army distinguished service badge, inscribed on the back "E. Brooke 27.11.19."

This is a rare badge, awarded for outstanding devotion to duty or for an act of courage.

$300-350 LOCK

A World War I bronze death plaque, for Thomas William Young.

$120-140 PSA

An early-17thC German "Black and White" comb morion, the base encircled with brass rosette washers, some splits, refreshed with paint.

9¾in (25cm) wide

$1,600-2,100 **TDM**

A Crimean War French shako, with helmet plate and no.3 pommel, with leather sweatband liner.

ca. 1850s

$600-700 **LOCK**

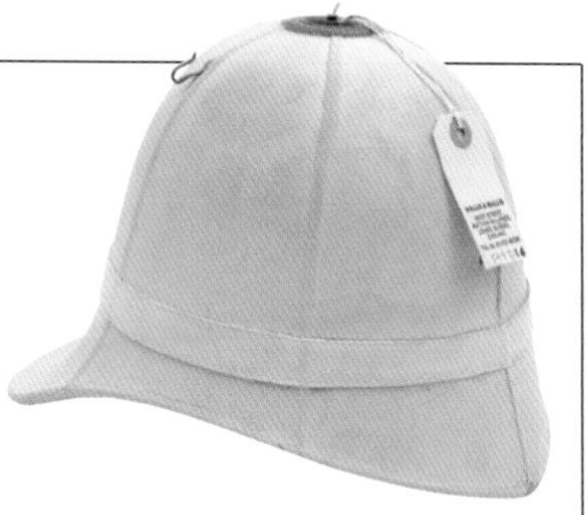

An officer's white cloth tropical helmet, leather and silk headband lining, "By Appointment" label of Military Taylor J.B. Johnston inside, spike and chin chain missing.

$1,900-2,600 **W&W**

A German World War I Sappenpanzer Gesichtsmaske green-painted iron "Elephant Plate" sniper's mask, general surface wear and tear.

11in (28cm) high

$2,900-3,600 **APAR**

A 19thC officer's full-dress embroidered sabretache, of the Second Hants Volunteer Artillery, the Royal Arms with supporters and motto, silver-plated cannon within wreath with title scrolls "Second" above and "Hants Volunteer Artillery" below.

13in (33cm) high

$1,300-1,600 **W&W**

A 19thC officer's full-dress embroidered sabretache, of the Royal Bucks Yeomanry, gilt "VR" cipher, black leather backing and pouch, three buff leather suspension straps with buckles.

$1,800-2,300 **W&W**

A 19thC 16th Queen's Lancers lieutenant's tunic.

ca. 1860

$800-900 **DUK**

An early-19thC officer's mess dress, with silver buttons and silver-gilt cuffs and collar, three buttons precuff, with vest.

$220-260 **DUK**

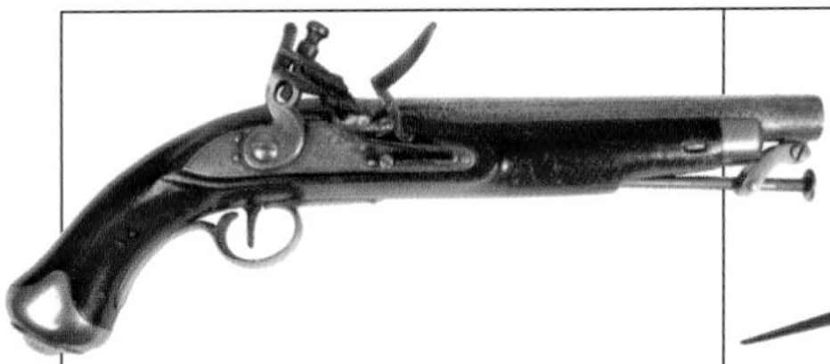

A British Flintlock service pistol, by Tower, with full walnut stock, brass trigger guard, and iron swivel ramrod.

ca. 1808 *15in (38cm) long*

$850-950 **DUK**

A 56-bore flintlock boxlock overcoat pocket pistol, with spring bayonet, signed "Dunderdale, Mabson & Labron," the top safety and walnut slab butt with oval silver escutcheon, some wear.

ca. 1815 *8in (20.5cm) long*

$300-450 **W&W**

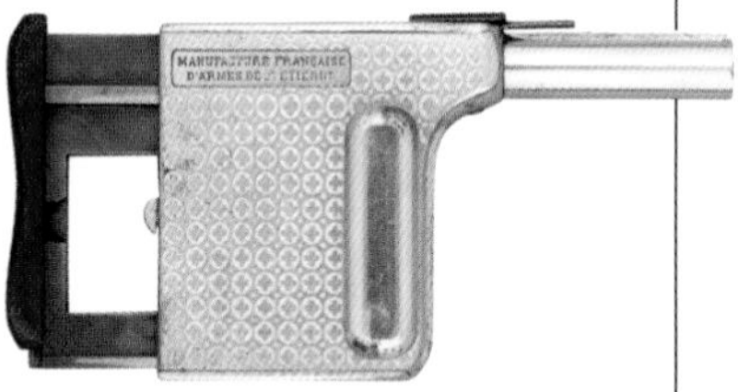

An 8mm french five-shot center-fire gaulois patent palm pistol, by Manufacture d'armes de St Étienne, no.2512, with short barrel stamped "Mitrailleuse."

ca. 1880 *5¼in (13.5cm) long*

$850-950 **TDM**

A six-shot percussion revolver, by E.M. Reilly & Co. Gun Manufacturers of London, with Bakelite grip in oak pistol case, with oil bottle and accessories.

$1,150-1,450 **DUK**

A Colt US 1911A1 transition model second-type pistol, .45 ACP caliber, marked "MODEL OF 1911 U.S. ARMY."

1924 *barrel 5in (12.5cm) long*

$3,900-4,500 **POOK**

An infantry officer's dirk, Lockwood Brothers, Sheffield, the single fuller blade signed, the scabbard set with bi knife and fork, the mounts with applied crown, badge, and initials.

17¾in (45cm) long

$1,600-2,100 **L&T**

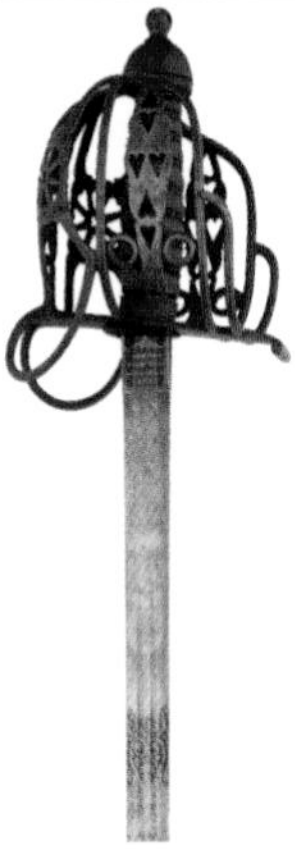

A rare 1st Royal Lanarkshire militia basket-hilted sword, by Henry Wilkinson, London, the blade numbered "16898," with regimental badge and Royal cipher, in original scabbard.

39½in (100.5cm) long

$1,800-2,300 **L&T**

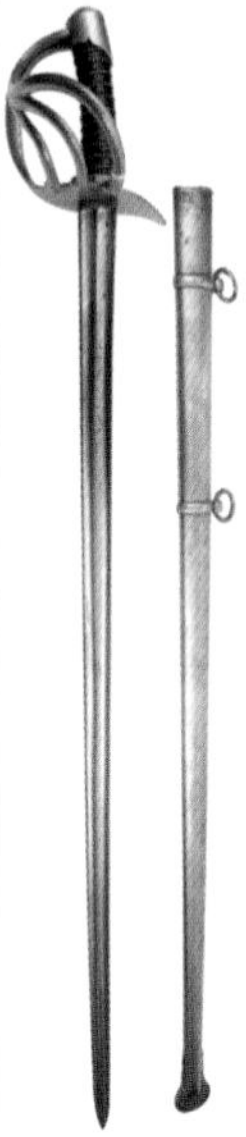

A French M XIII cavalry trooper's sword, straight double fullered blade, marked "Mfture Imple du Klingenthal Octobre."

blade 37½in (95.5cm) long

$1,600-2,100 **W&W**

A 1796 pattern heavy cavalry trooper's sword, in its steel scabbard with two rings, pitting overall, blade heavily cleaned.

blade 34½in (87.5cm) long

$1,800-2,100 **W&W**

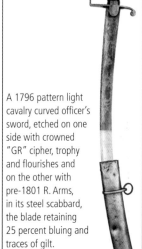

A 1796 pattern light cavalry curved officer's sword, etched on one side with crowned "GR" cipher, trophy and flourishes and on the other with pre-1801 R. Arms, in its steel scabbard, the blade retaining 25 percent bluing and traces of gilt.

blade 32½in (82.5cm) long

$950-1,100 **W&W**

QUICK REFERENCE—BACCARAT PAPERWEIGHTS

- **Although paperweights were first made in Murano, Italy, France became the prominent producer of paperweights in the 19thC, with Clichy, St. Louis, and Baccarat as the leading companies in the 1840s and 50s.**
- **The Compagnie des Cristalleries de Baccarat was founded in Baccarat, France, in 1765. Baccarat produced paperweights from 1845.**
- **Many were made from clear crystal with canes cut to create floral designs. Millefiori paperweights were also common. *Millefiori* is Italian for "thousand flowers" and refers to designs of densely packed stylized decoration often found in paperweights.**
- **Some Baccarat paperweights contain a signature cane, marked with the date the paperweight was made.**

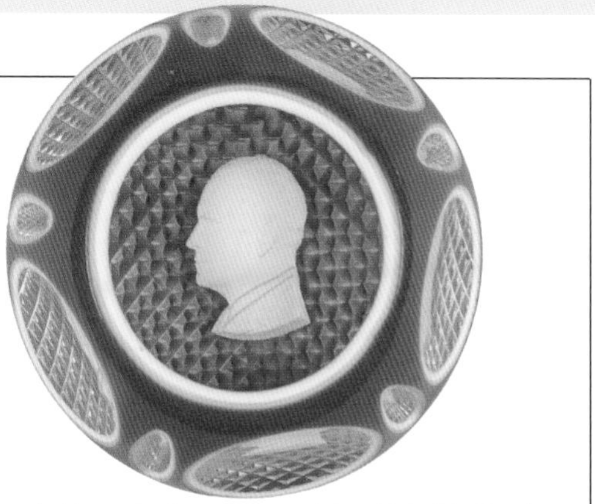

A Baccarat double-overlay faceted paperweight, with Dwight Eisenhower sulfide.

3in (7.5cm) diam

$80-100 **POOK**

A Baccarat flower paperweight, set with a primrose, edged with 11 leaves.

ca. 1850 *3in (7.5cm) diam*

$500-650 **WW**

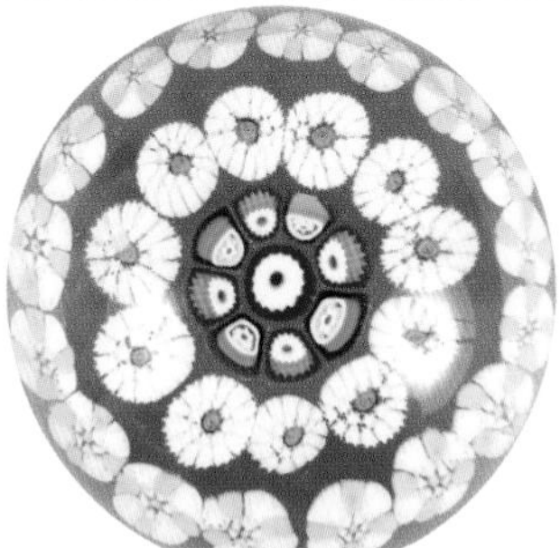

A Baccarat paperweight.

2in (5cm) wide

$130-190 **JN**

A Baccarat paperweight.

2¾in (7cm) wide

$130-190 **JN**

A Baccarat paperweight, with scrabble lacework.

2½in (6.5cm) wide

$80-100 **JN**

A Baccarat paperweight.

2in (5cm) wide

$450-600 **JN**

A Baccarat spaced millefiori glass paperweight, the canes including silhouette canes of a rooster, a stag, a goat, and a dog and the date cane "B1848," two chips on foot rim, some surface scratches.

1848 *2½in (6.5cm) diam*

$700-850 **BELL**

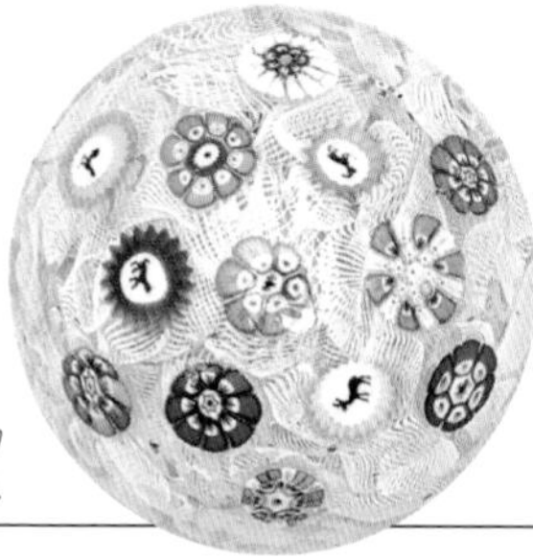

A CLOSER LOOK AT A BACCARAT PAPERWEIGHT

This is a rare antique magnum Baccarat spaced millefiori and griddle canes paperweight.

With assorted complex canes of flower and animal design, including horses, dogs, deer, and elephants.

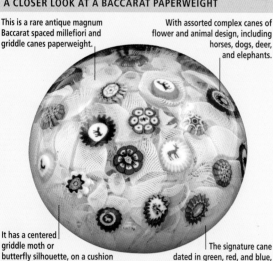

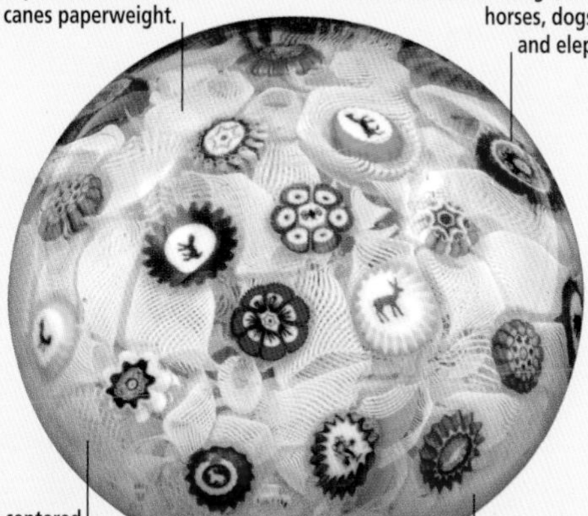

It has a centered griddle moth or butterfly silhouette, on a cushion of white upset latticino cheesecloth.

The signature cane dated in green, red, and blue, marked "b1848."

A Baccarat paperweight, with expected scratching on edge of base.

1848 *3in (7.5cm) diam*

$1,050-1,300 **MART**

A Baccarat paperweight, with flower canes formed into a mushroom, with a spiral ring of white and blue threads.

ca. 1850 *3¼in (8.5cm) diam*

$400-500 **FIS**

A Clichy swirl paperweight.

ca. 1850 *2½in (6.5cm) diam*

$300-450 **WW**

A Clichy spaced paperweight, set with colorful canes including two Clichy roses.

ca. 1850 *3in (7.5cm) diam*

$800-900 **WW**

A Clichy spaced paperweight, set with 37 canes including a Clichy rose, on a twisted latticino ground.

ca. 1850 *3in (7.5cm) diam*

$500-650 **WW**

A Baccarat glass paperweight, internally decorated with floral design, limited edition, numbered "211/250," dated on cane.

1977 *3¼in (8.5cm) diam*

$260-320 **APAR**

A mid-19thC Clichy faceted concentric millefiori paperweight, small chips on edges.

2in (5cm) diam

$400-500 **BELL**

QUICK REFERENCE—CLICHY PAPERWEIGHTS

- **Clichy was founded by Joseph Maës in 1837. It produced paperweights from the 1840s to 1852, after which production was sporadic.**
- **These paperweights are rarely dated, usually marked with only a "C." They were mostly flat with a concave base.**
- **Millefiori patterns were common as were colored swirls and flowers. One common design is a small rose-shaped cane that has become known as the "Clichy rose."**

A contemporary paperweight, by Jim D'Onofrio, depicting a snake approaching a mouse, signed in script "Jim D'Onofrio 01" and "1241."

3½in (9cm) diam

$600-700 **JDJ**

A Millville mushroom footed paperweight.

3¼in (8.5cm) diam

$130-190 **POOK**

A Millville orange crimp rose footed paperweight, by Tony DePalma, stamped on base.

2¾in (7cm) diam

$60-90 **POOK**

QUICK REFERENCE—ST. LOUIS PAPERWEIGHTS

- **The glassworks at Saint-Louis, Lorraine, began making clear crystal wares in the 1780s and paperweights in ca. 1842-45.**
- **Many St. Louis paperweights were made with a latticinio ground, with threads of glass arranged in a lattice design, usually in pink or white. St. Louis paperweights tend to have star-cut bases and high domes.**
- **The St. Louis factory still produces paperweights today.**

A 20thC St. Louis glass paperweight newel post, with millefiori canes, with brass fitting, limited edition, with signature cane, original box, and certificate, dated.

1974 *6¾in (17cm) high*

$1,050-1,150 FLD

A St. Louis glass paperweight vase, the base with radial millefiori cane work below a bell-form bowl with internal latticino decoration, dated, original label, and signature cane, boxed.

1973 *5¼in (13.5cm) high*

$650-800 FLD

A mid-19thC St. Louis glass pansy paperweight, small bruise above foot rim.

3in (7.5cm) diam

$300-400 BELL

A 20thC St Louis glass piedouche paperweight, with a centered ruffle cane and nine varying millefiori rings atop a lattachino foot, limited edition, dated, signature cane, original box, and certificate.

1972 *3in (7.5cm) high*

$800-900 FLD

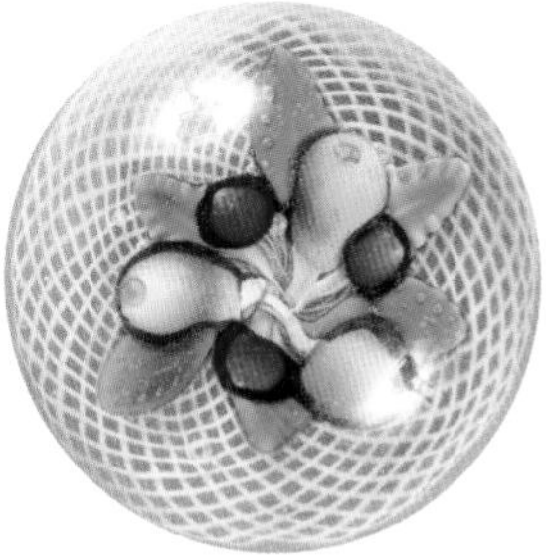

A St. Louis paperweight, with lacework and fruit.

2¼in (5.5cm) wide

$190-260 JN

QUICK REFERENCE—PAUL YSART

- **Paul Ysart (1904-91) is seen by many collectors as one of the most important 20thC paperweight makers. After working at St. Louis and the Leith Flint Glass Co., Paul joined his father at the Moncreiff Glassworks in Perth, Scotland, where he worked until 1963.**
- **He then moved to Caithness Glass, where he worked from 1963-70.**
- **Ysart opened a dedicated paperweight studio in Harland, Wick, which he ran until he retired in 1979. His typically complex and finely made weights are often signed with "PY" or "H" canes.**

A 20thC Paul Ysart glass paperweight inkwell, with a centered five-flower bouquet surrounded by an alternating ring of millefiori canes, cased in clear crystal, rising to the stopper in the conforming pattern with three centered flower heads.

5¼in (13.5cm) high

$800-1,050 FLD

A St. Louis glass paperweight, with a centered lampwork white flower, limited edition, dated, signature cane, original box, and certificate.

1973 *3¼in (8.5cm) diam*

$210-260 FLD

A St. Louis paperweight, set with pears, cherries, and leaves in a basket of spiraling white latticinio threads, minor bruising and chips.

ca. 1850 *2¾in (7cm) diam*

$400-450 BELL

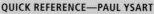

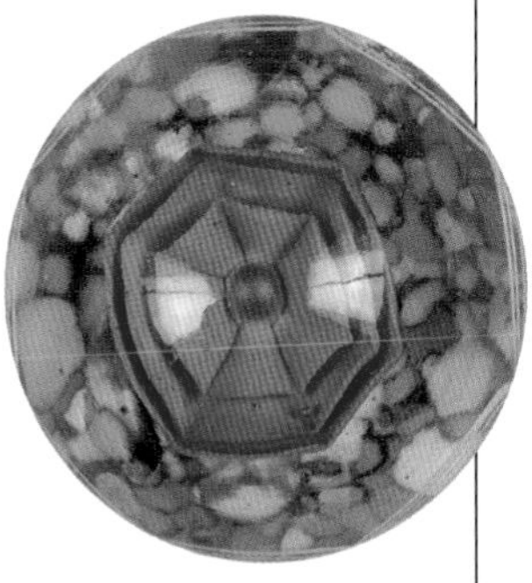

An upright red flower paperweight, probably Czechoslovakian, with a multicolor chip ground and white looping around base.

ca. 1920 *2¾in (7cm) diam*

$80-90 POOK

QUICK REFERENCE—THE KB COLLECTION OF PENCILS

- **The evolution of the mechanical pencil ca. 1822-1930 is documented in the KB Collection of Pencils, which was put together over many decades by Kenneth Bull. Bull, along with Dr. David Shepherd, published a book on the collection.**
- **The collection includes pencils from top makers, such as Sampson Mordan and Co., Cartier, and Tiffany and Co., among others. The majority of the collection's pencils date from 1870 to 1890.**
- **While commercial production of the lead pencil dates from around 1775, a graphite pencil is documented as early as 1686, following the discovery of black lead/plumbago (graphite) near Keswick, UK, in the 16thC. Variety in the hardness of pencils was developed in the 1790s, when Nicholas Conté and Josef Hardtmuth mixed powdered graphite with china clay and fired it.**
- **Many of the pencils in this section come from Kenneth Bull's collection.**

An early-19thC novelty silver pencil and toothpick set, by S. Mordan, modeled as pistols, engraved "July 6, 1840," with a cartridge for leads, in a fitted velvet lined ivory box, with an oval plaque inscribed "S. Mordan Pencil Maker."

1840 *closed 1½in (4cm) long*

$1,050-1,150 **WW**

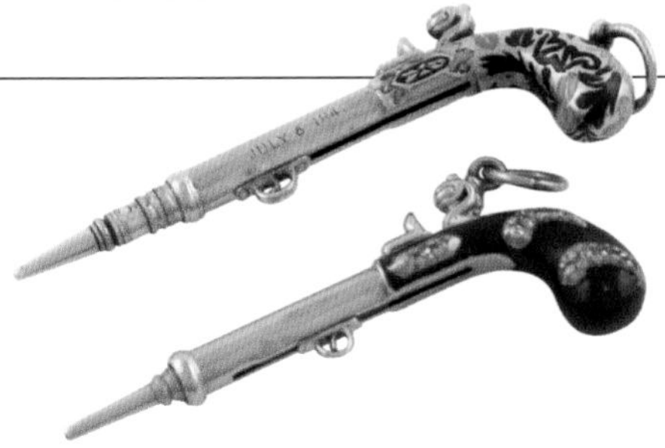

An early-19thC matched pair of novelty gold and enamel pencils, by S. Mordan, modeled as pistols, one of the butts with varicolored enamel decoration, the other with dark blue enamel and set with diamonds, both with ring attachments, one engraved "July 6, 1840."

From the KB Collection of Pencils.

1840 *closed 1½in (4cm) long*

$1,900-2,600 **WW**

An early 19thC novelty gold pencil, by S. Mordan, modeled as a pistol.

From the KB Collection of Pencils.

ca. 1840 *closed 1½in (4cm) long*

$450-600 **WW**

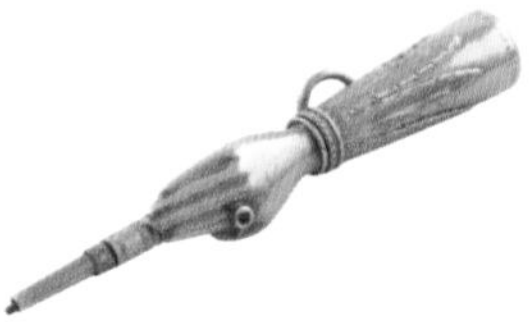

A 19thC novelty gold pencil, by S. Mordan, modeled as a hand and sleeve, the finger with a hardstone ring, with a ring attachment, and with a colored stone matrix terminal, marked "S. Mordan Aug 3, 1842, no.1390," in a later fitted box.

From the KB Collection of Pencils.

ca. 1840 *closed 1½in (4cm) long*

$800-900 **WW**

A 19thC novelty gold pencil, by S. Mordan and Co., modeled as a revolver, with revolving cartridge case, with diamond registration mark for March 8, 1855.

From the KB Collection of Pencils.

closed 2in (5cm) long

$500-650 **WW**

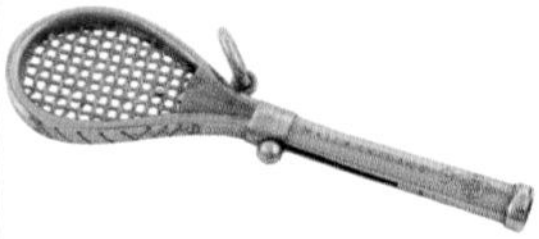

A 19thC novelty ten carat gold pencil, by S. Mordan and Co., modeled as a tennis racket, with a ring attachment, with a design registration for September 1878.

1878 *closed 2½in (6.5cm) long*

$850-950 **WW**

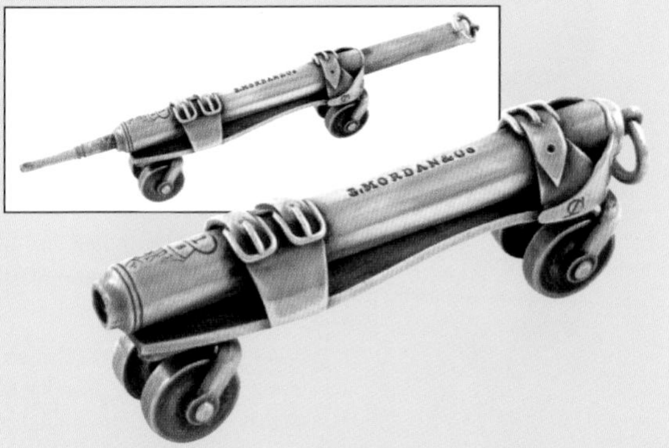

A 19thC novelty silver pencil, by S. Mordan and Co., modeled as a roller skate, with a ring attachment, with a registration lozenge.

From the KB Collection of Pencils.

1879 *closed 2½in (6.5cm) long*

$1,300-1,700 **WW**

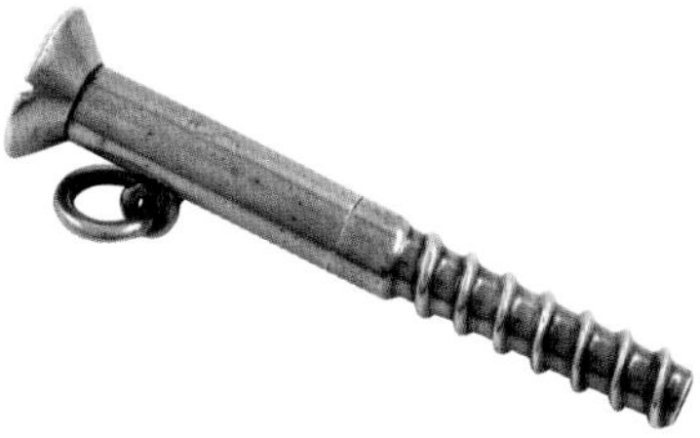

A 19thC novelty silver pencil, by S. Mordan and Co., modeled as a screw, with a ring attachment.

closed 2in (5cm) long

$500-600 **WW**

A 19thC novelty silver pencil, by S. Mordan and Co., modeled as a pistol, with a ring attachment.

closed 1¾in (4.5cm) long

$300-400 **WW**

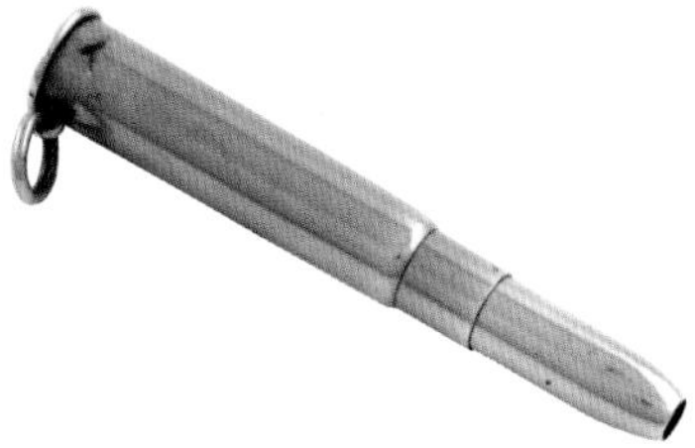

A 19thC novelty silver pencil, by S. Mordan and Co., modeled as a bullet, with a ring attachment.

This pencil is referred to in the 1898 catalogue as "Magazine Rifle Cartridge."

closed 2¼in (5.5cm) long

$400-500 **WW**

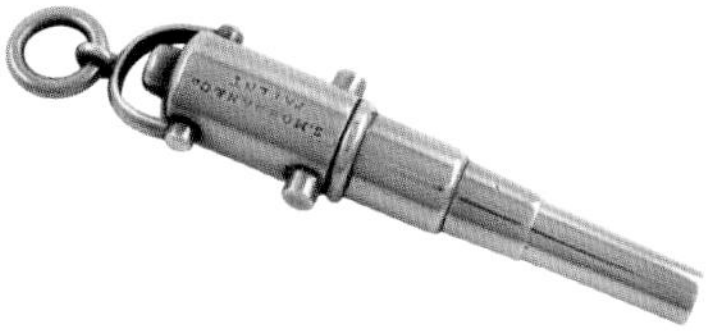

A 19thC novelty silver pencil, by S. Mordan and Co., modeled as a cannon barrel, with a ring attachment, also marked "Patent."

closed 2¾in (7cm) long

$300-400 **WW**

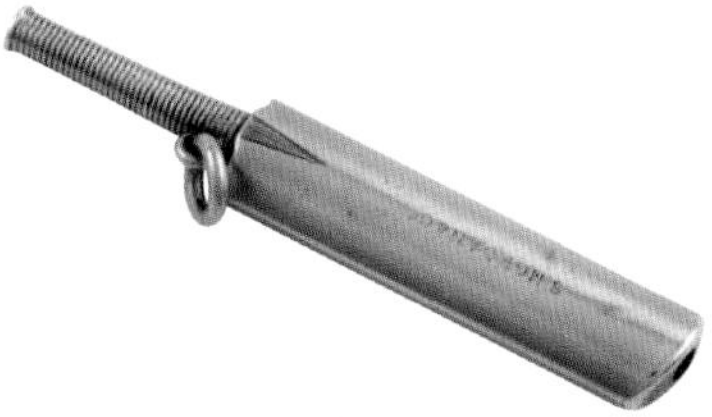

A 19thC novelty silver pencil, by S. Mordan and Co., modeled as a cricket bat, with a ring attachment.

closed 2¼in (5.5cm) long

$600-700 **WW**

A 19thC novelty silver-mounted pencil, by S. Mordan and Co., the ceramic body modeled as a bird's egg, with a ring attachment.

closed 1¼in (3cm) long

$500-650 **WW**

A 19thC novelty silver and enamel pencil, probably by S. Mordan and Co., modeled as an Allsopp's India Pale Ale bottle, with enameled label, unmarked.

ca. 1880 *1¾in (4.5cm) long*

$400-500 **WW**

A 19thC novelty ten-carat gold pencil, by S. Mordan and Co., modeled as a crucifix, with a ring attachment.

closed 1½in (4cm) long

$260-320 **WW**

A 19thC novelty silver and enamel pencil, by S. Mordan and Co., modeled as a Bass beer bottle, the enameled label with the beer details and "S.MORDAN & C/ London," with a ring attachment.

ca. 1880 *2in (5cm) long*

$300-450 **WW**

A 19thC novelty silver and enamel pencil, by S. Mordan and Co., modeled as a Royal Mail pillar-style mailbox, engraved with the "VR" cipher, the enamel panel with "Cleared at 7am and 8pm Sundays Excepted," with a ring attachment.

From the KB Collection of Pencils.

closed 2in (5cm) long

$950-1,100 WW

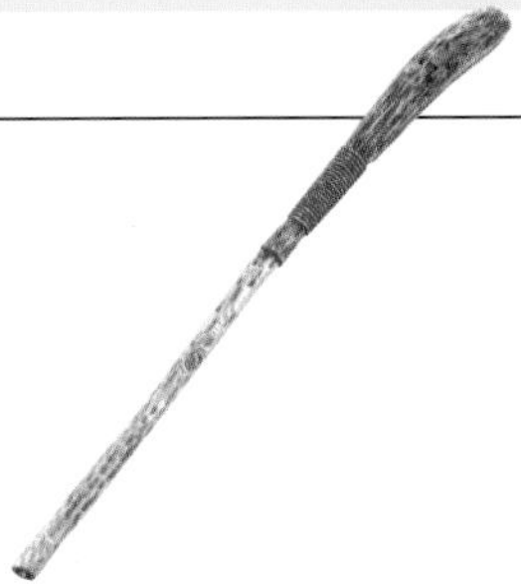

A 19thC novelty silver pencil, by S. Mordan and Co., modeled as a broom.

From the KB Collection of Pencils.

7in (18cm) long

$1,050-1,150 WW

A 19thC novelty silver pencil, by S. Mordan and Co., modeled as a begging dog, with a ring attachment.

From the KB Collection of Pencils.

ca. 1880 *closed 1½in (4cm) long*

$850-950 WW

A 19thC novelty silver pencil, by S. Mordan and Co., modeled as a railroad lamp, with a ring attachment.

From the KB Collection of Pencils.

closed 2¼in (5.5cm) long

$1,050-1,150 WW

QUICK REFERENCE—S. MORDAN AND CO.

- **Sampson Mordan (1790-1843) was a British silversmith. In 1822, he and his associate John Isaac Hawkins patented the first mechanical pencil.**
- **Mordan then went into partnership with Gabriel Riddle, a stationer with whom he manufactured and sold silver propelling pencils. The partnership dissolved in 1837, but Mordan continued to sell his pencils under the trading name of S. Mordan and Co. until his death in 1843, when the company passed to his sons, Sampson Mordan Jr. and Augustus Mordan.**
- **Edmund Johnson, Horace Stewart, Henry Lambert Symonds, and James Pulley joined the company and production was diversified, focusing on smaller pieces. In 1884, Augustus Mordan retired and left the company to his partners.**
- **The company manufactured a wide variety of products, including locks, whistles, boxes, and inkwells, but they were chiefly known for their propelling and telescopic pencils.**
- **S. Mordan and Co. became a limited liability company in 1898.**
- **Following the destruction of their City Road Factory by a bombing raid in 1941, the company stopped trading.**
- **S. Mordan and Co.'s silver and gold-cased "Everpoint" pencils remain popular with collectors today, as do the novelty propelling pencils. These pencils were often shaped as animals, figures, tools, or everyday objects. They were usually made in silver or gold.**

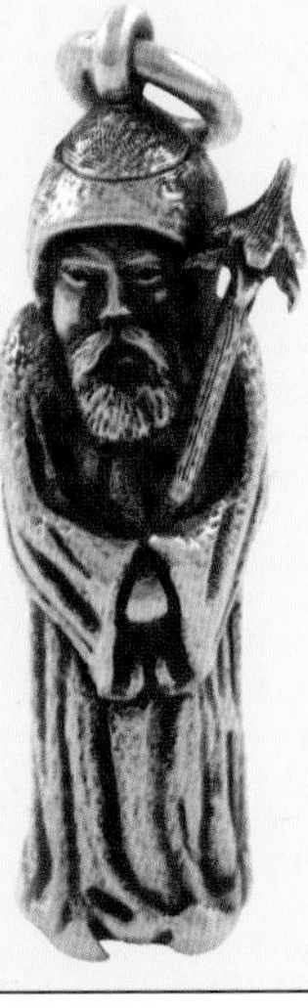

A 19thC novelty silver figural pencil, by S. Mordan and Co., modeled as a man wearing a habit and holding a spear, possibly a disciple, ring attachment, with a registration lozenge.

From the KB Collection of Pencils.

1880 *1½in (4cm) long*

$1,600-2,100 WW

A 19thC novelty silver pencil, by S. Mordan and Co., modeled as a railroad lamp, with a ring attachment.

From the KB Collection of Pencils.

closed 2¼in (5.5cm) long

$1,050-1,150 WW

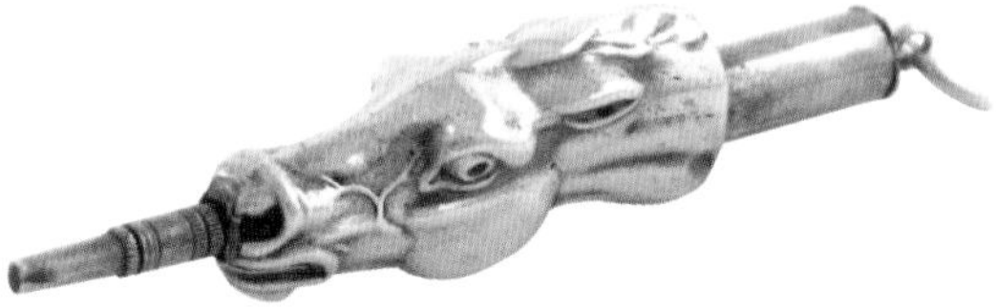

A 19thC novelty silver pencil, by S. Mordan and Co., modeled as a horse's head, with a ring attachment.

From the KB Collection of Pencils.

closed 1½in (4cm) long

$1,100-1,250 WW

A 19thC novelty silver pencil, by S. Mordan and Co., modeled as a cat, with a ring attachment, with a registration lozenge.

From the KB Collection of Pencils.

1881 *closed 1¾in (4.5cm) long*

$1,600-2,100 WW

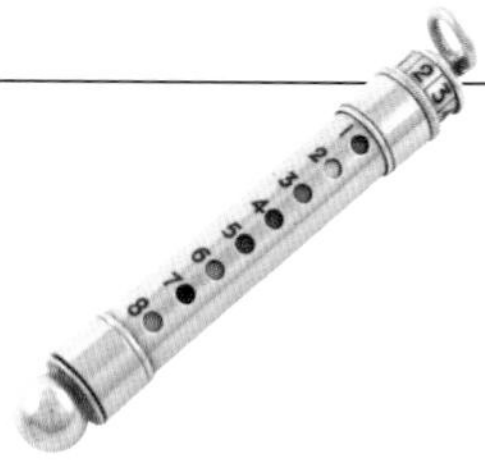

A novelty silver and enamel pencil, by S. Mordan and Co., also marked "Pan Tan patent, sterling silver," the side enameled 1-8 with the varicolored disks, the top enameled 1-8, with a ring attachment.

From the KB Collection of Pencils.

3½in (9cm) long

$600-700 **WW**

A novelty gold pencil, by S. Mordan and Co., modeled as a shoe, also marked "Rd199100."

From the KB Collection of Pencils.

closed 1½in (4cm) long

$800-900 **WW**

A CLOSER LOOK AT A SENTRY BOX PENCIL

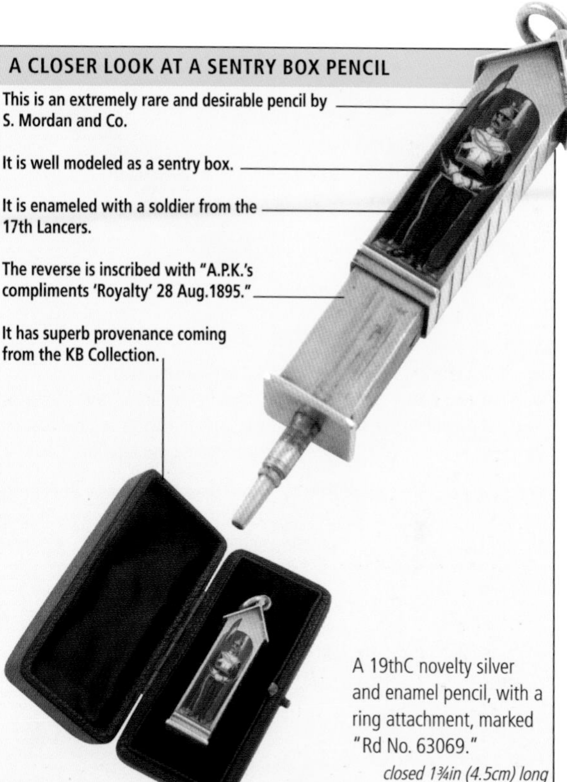

This is an extremely rare and desirable pencil by S. Mordan and Co.

It is well modeled as a sentry box.

It is enameled with a soldier from the 17th Lancers.

The reverse is inscribed with "A.P.K.'s compliments 'Royalty' 28 Aug.1895."

It has superb provenance coming from the KB Collection.

A 19thC novelty silver and enamel pencil, with a ring attachment, marked "Rd No. 63069."

closed 1¾in (4.5cm) long

$3,900-4,500 **WW**

A silver-gilt pencil and aide memoire, by S. Mordan and Co., the fan formed by six ivory sheets.

May be subject to CITES regulations if exported.

From the KB Collection of Pencils.

3¼in (8.5cm) long

$850-950 **WW**

QUICK REFERENCE—CARTIER

- **Louis-François Cartier founded Cartier in Paris in 1847. The company was passed to Cartier's son and remained in the family until it was bought by investors in the mid to late 20thC. The company's headquarters remain in Paris, despite being owned by Switzerland-based Richemont Group.**
- **In the early 20thC, Cartier began producing writing equipment, including fountain and rollerball pens, pen holders, mechanical pencils, and office accessories. Some of the writing equipment included a pen combined with a watch element.**
- **The writing equipment could be made from gold, silver, guilloché enamel, and jade, among other materials, and some items are set with precious stones.**

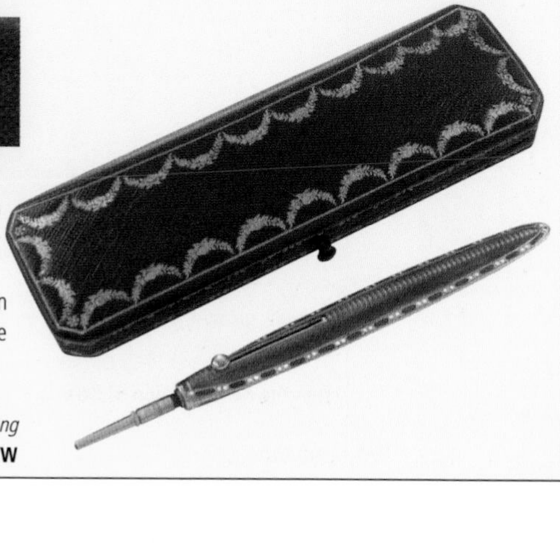

A French gold and enamel pencil, by Cartier, feather quill form, with gray enamel decoration and a gold and white enamel bead border, with a moonstone slider, in a fitted Cartier case, the underside with "Cartier 13, rue de la Paix, and 4, Burlington St."

3¾in (9.5cm) long

$13,000-19,000 **WW**

A rare 19thC novelty silver pencil, by Edward and Son, modeled as a sphinx, with a ring attachment, the base inscribed " Tel-El-Kebir, 13 Sept.1882" and "D. Martin."

From the KB Collection of Pencils.

The battle of Tel-el-Kebir was fought between the Egyptian army, led by Ahmed Urabi, and the British military, near Tel-el-Kebir. After Egyptian officers rebelled in 1882, the British reacted to protect its financial and expansionist interest in the country, and in particular the Suez Canal, which opened to shipping in 1869.

ca. 1882 *closed 1½in (4cm) long*

$1,900-2,600 **WW**

A 19thC novelty silver figural pencil, by Leuchars, modeled as a child wearing a necklace, with a ring attachment, with a registration lozenge.

From the KB Collection of Pencils.

closed 1¾in (4.5cm) long

$1,100-1,250 **WW**

A 19thC novelty gold and enamel pencil, by Thornhill, enameled with the "Jack of Hearts," with a ring attachment, also marked "1761."

From the KB Collection of Pencils.

closed 2in (5cm) long

$800-900 **WW**

A rare American novelty silver pencil, by Tiffany and Co., modeled as The Metropolitan Life Tower, together with an old postcard depicting the tower.

From the KB Collection of Pencils.

The Metropolitan Life Tower is a landmark skyscraper at One Madison Avenue, Manhattan, New York. Designed by the architectural firm Napoleon Brun and Sons, the tower is modeled after the Campanile in Venice. It was constructed in 1909 and was the world's tallest building until 1913, when it was surpassed by the Woolworth Building.

closed 3½in (9cm) long

$3,900-4,500 **WW**

A 19thC novelty silver pencil, by W. Thornhill, modeled as a tortoise, with a ring attachment.

From the KB Collection of Pencils.

closed 1¾in (4.5cm) long

$3,200-3,900 **WW**

A rare novelty silver pencil, modeled as a lobster claw, with a ring handle, unmarked.

From the KB Collection of Pencils.

2in (5cm) long

$800-900 **WW**

A 19thC novelty silver and red enamel pencil, modeled as a heart, unmarked, with a ring attachment.

From the KB Collection of Pencils.

closed 1½in (4cm) long

$700-850 **WW**

A French silver-mounted enamel pencil and scent bottle, decorated with a lady and gentleman, the hinged cover opens to reveal a scent bottle, marked with a French control mark.

From the KB Collection of Pencils.

2¾in (7cm) long

$650-800 **WW**

A novelty papier-mâchè pencil, modeled as a globe, with a ring attachment.

From the KB Collection of Pencils.

1¼in (3cm) long

$500-650 **WW**

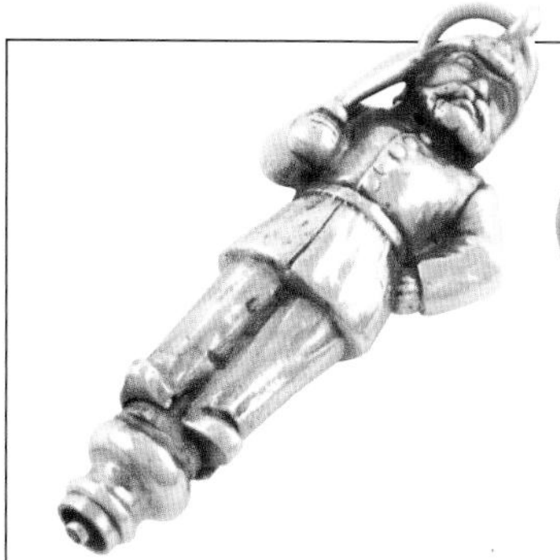

A 19thC novelty figural silver pencil, modeled as a policeman holding his truncheon, with a ring attachment, unmarked.

From the KB Collection of Pencils.

1¾in (4.5cm) long

$450-600 **WW**

A rare 19thC novelty gold pencil, modeled as an elephant, with a ring attachment, unmarked.

From the KB Collection of Pencils.

closed 1½in (4cm) long

$850-950 **WW**

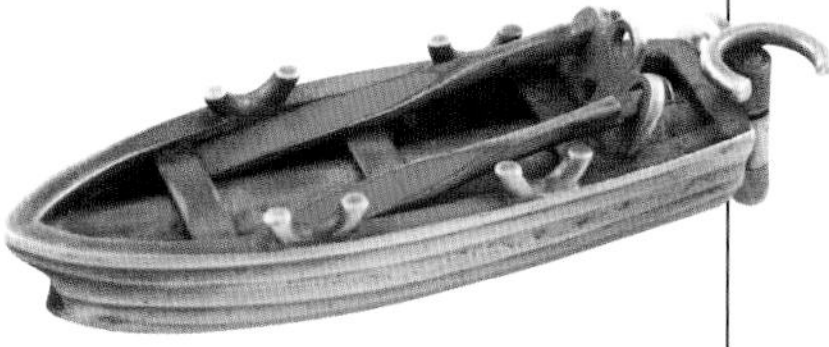

A 19thC novelty parcel-gilt silver pencil, modeled as a rowing boat, with enameled oars, a rudder formed as a ring attachment, unmarked.

From the KB Collection of Pencils.

closed 2in (5cm) long

$600-700 **WW**

A 19thC novelty silver and enamel pencil, modeled as a soda water bottle, with an enameled label, unmarked.

From the KB Collection of Pencils.

1¾in (4.5cm) long

$500-600 **WW**

A 19thC novelty copper and mixed metal figural pencil, modeled as a Japanese man, with a ring attachment, unmarked.

From the KB Collection of Pencils.

1½in (4cm) long

$300-400 **WW**

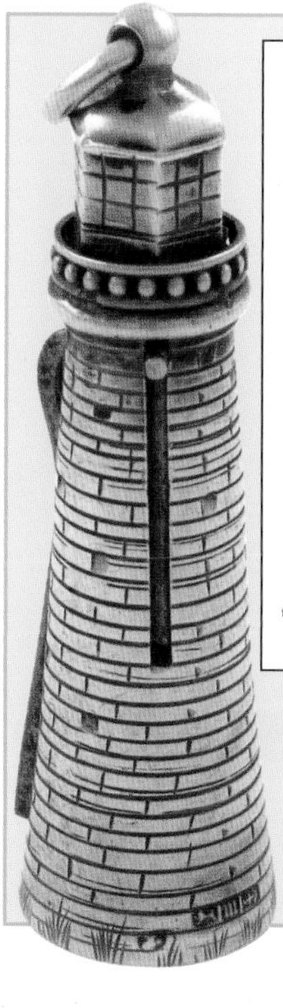

A 19thC novelty silver pencil, modeled as a lighthouse, button hook and pen knife, with a ring attachment.

From the KB Collection of Pencils.

1896 *1¾in (4.5cm) long*

$1,100-1,250 **WW**

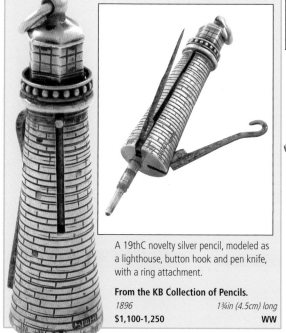

A rare Edwardian novelty gold pencil, modeled as a frog, with gem set eyes, with a ring attachment, unmarked, one eye missing.

From the KB Collection of Pencils.

ca. 1902 *1¼in (3cm) long*

$1,600-2,100 **WW**

QUICK REFERENCE—FOUNTAIN PENS

- **The first commercial fountain pens date from the 1880s, but the "golden age" of the fountain pen was the 1910s to 50s.**
- **Most collectors aim to collect one period or brand of fountain pen. The collectors' market for fountain pens has long been dominated by pens produced in the first half of the 20thC by big names, such as Parker, Waterman, Montblanc, and Dunhill Namiki. However, these pens have become less common in recent years, prompting some collectors to focus on lesser-known brands and contemporary limited edition pens.**
- **The rarity, quality, and material can all affect value. Unusual celluloids or pens with complex metal overlays can be popular, as can classic models, such as the Parker 51 or 75. Limited editions, such as Montblanc's "Lorenzo de Medici" of 1992, are also highly sought after.**
- **Condition is paramount. To ensure value, a pen must come with its original packaging and paperwork. Most collectors do not use the pens or even unpack them. Uninked pens in mint condition and pens still sealed in their cellophane tend to fetch the highest prices.**

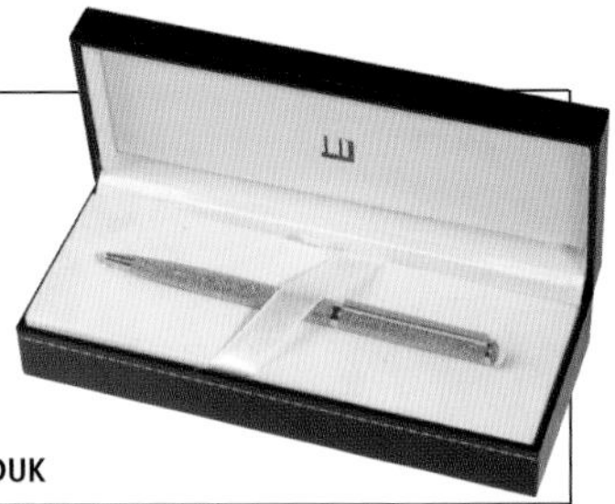

A Dunhill 18ct yellow gold ballpoint pen, with a rope-twist design barrel, stamped 18k, in a fitted presentation case.

$1,600-2,100 **DUK**

An S.T. Dupont "Place Vendome" gold and diamond fountain pen, limited edition no.20/35, the cap and barrel reminiscent of the Vendôme Column, the cap with a clip and set with a band of eight panels of diamonds, the barrel set with conforming diamond set band, the medium nib stamped "750," cartridge filling system, uninked, with an S T Dupont box, guarantee card, instruction booklet, diamond certificate, information booklet, a box of six ink cartridges, cartridge converter, and outer card packaging.

$4,500-5,200 **DN**

A Montblanc "Patron of Art Peter the Great" fountain pen, limited edition no.292 of 888, the cap and barrel with white gold overlay, the cap with a clip and set with a band of emeralds, the medium nib stamped "750 18K," piston filling system, with a Montblanc box, international service certificate book, outer card packaging, and white card sleeve.

1997

$4,500-5,200 **DN**

A Conway Stewart "Dinkie 550" fountain pen and pencil set, green marble effect, in original box with original guarantee certificate.

$210-260 **HAN**

A Montblanc "Patron of Art, Ludovico Sforza [Duke of Milan]" fountain pen, limited edition no.089 of 888, the lacquer cap and barrel with gold trim, stamped "Au750," the nib stamped "18K," uninked, with related Montblanc leaflet.

2013

$2,900-3,900 **DN**

A Montblanc "Patron of Art" fountain pen, by Andrew Carnegie, the black resin body with pistol filling system, silver Art Nouveau foliate overlay marked "Ag 925," the twist-action cap with silver colored clip modeled as a nude female figure, and Montblanc white star emblem on terminal, the bicolor nib decorated with a lily and marked "2002, 18K 750, 4810," limited edition no.0403 of 4810, in maker's fitted lacquer box, some slight tarnishing to silver.

5¾in (14.5cm) long

$1,050-1,150 **FELL**

A Montblanc Meisterstuck Ramses II fountain pen, with certificate, booklet, and cloth, in original case and outer cardboard packaging, unused.

$800-900 **LOCK**

A Montblanc "Johannes Guttenberg 42" fountain pen, limited edition no.30 of 42, the hardwood barrel inlaid with letters, the gold colored cap with enamel checkerboard detail, stamped "750," the medium nib stamped "18K," piston filling system, with a Montblanc box, leaflet, outer card packaging, and white card sleeve.

2007

$16,000-19,000 **DN**

A Montblanc "Meisterstuck" ball point pen, boxed, with paperwork.

$500-600 **PSA**

A Montblanc "Meisterstuck" black fountain pen, no.149.

$300-400 **LOCK**

A rare Montblanc "Pope Julius II" fountain pen, 2005 Patron of the Arts limited edition no.748 of 888, crafted in 18K gold fretwork encasing a guilloche enamel ground, gemstones set in the cap, five diamonds set in the clip, mother-of-pearl Montblanc star insignia to the cap cover, 18ct gold nib engraved with the emblem of the Pope, in lacquer presentation box and Montblanc branded pouch, outer cardboard box and service certificate with matching limited edition number.

Considered to be one of the most influential patrons of art, Pope Julius II consolidated the papal states and transformed Rome into the cultural center of the Renaissance. He supported Michelangelo and Raphael, among others, and commissioned the famous frescoes in the Sistine Chapel and ordered the design and construction of St. Peter's Basilica. Montblanc's tribute pen, their 2005 "Patron of the Arts" version, is limited to just 888 examples.

2005

$6,000-6,500 **HAN**

A rare Montblanc "Sir Winston Churchill" fountain pen, limited edition no.36 of 53, the barrel crafted in 18K pink gold, inlaid with black and brown tortoiseshell lacquer bands, the cap top ringed with 53 diamonds to commemorate the year in which Churchill was knighted and bestowed the Nobel Prize for Literature, the Montblanc star is of lustrous mother-of-pearl, the great statesman's legendary "V for Victory" sign is echoed in the design of the clip, 18K gold nib engraved with Churchill's portrait, with pouch, in a lacquered presentation box with outer cardboard box, plain outer sleeve with two accompanying brochures, signs of light use.

$16,000-21,000 **HAN**

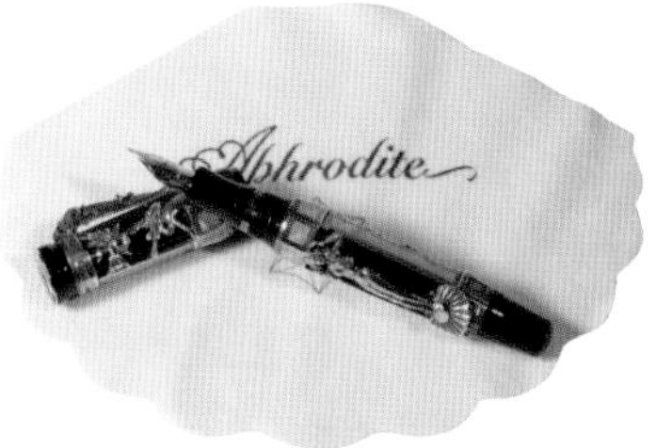

A Montegrappa "Aphrodite" silver fountain pen, limited edition no.1318 of 1912, the resin body and cap decorated with figural silver mounts and mother of pearl panels, 18ct gold nib, with presentation case, outer sleeve and booklets.

$1,300-1,800 **DUK**

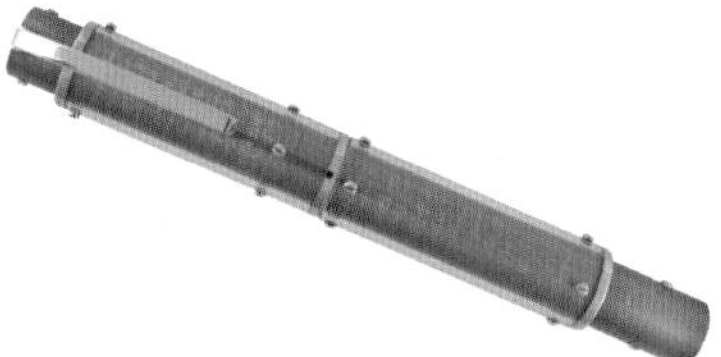

An Omas "Harmonia Mundi" fountain pen, limited edition no. 504 of 950, the titanium cap with gold colored clip and fittings, the cap and barrel etched with the messages of peace in various languages by Clara Halter, the nib stamped "18K 750," piston filling system, in a box, with booklet and outer card packaging.

$1,300-1,800 **DN**

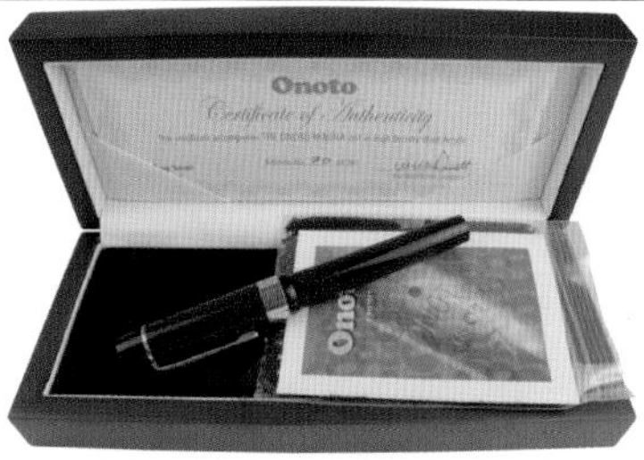

An Onoto Magna "261 High Density" black acrylic fountain pen, with silver gilt hallmarked band, limited edition no.70 of 261, certificate of authenticity, in original case.

$300-400 **LOCK**

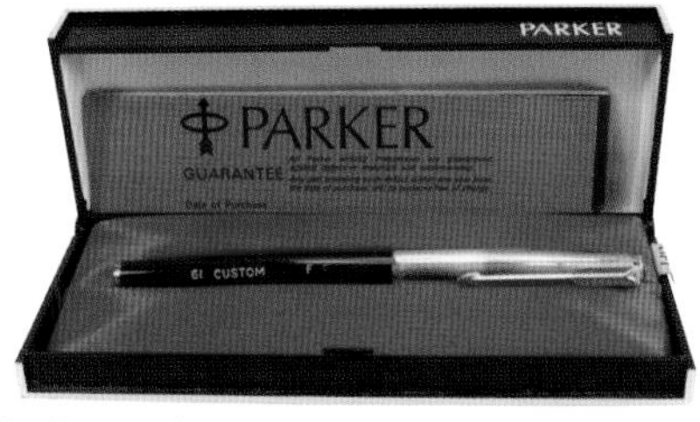

A Parker "61" custom fountain pen, boxed.

$60-90 **PSA**

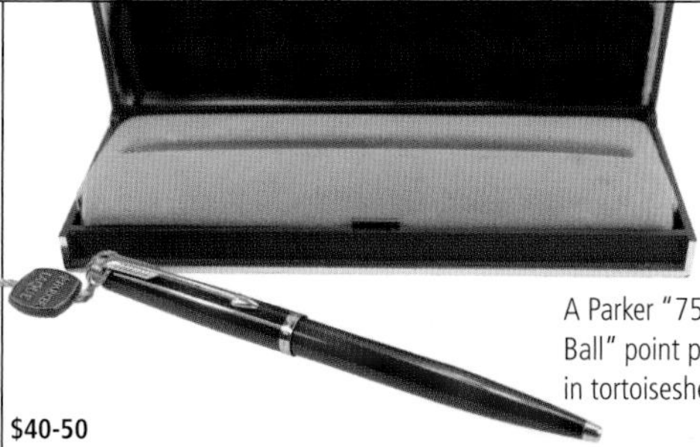

A Parker "75 Laque Ball" point pen, boxed in tortoiseshell.

$40-50 **PSA**

A Parker "Duofold" centennial fountain pen, with 18ct gold nib, blue marbled effect body with gold plated arrow clip and double band cap, cartridge filling system, medium nib.

5½in (14cm) long

$300-350 **DUK**

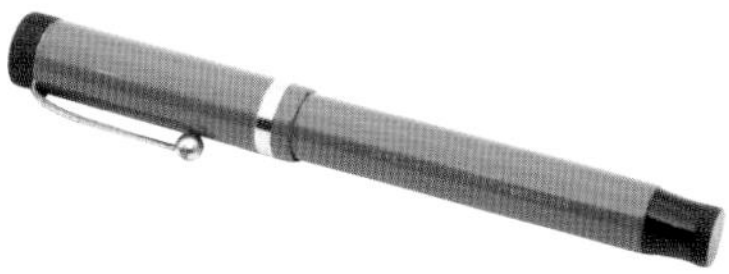

A Parker "Duofold" fountain pen, with orange case.

$300-400 **FLD**

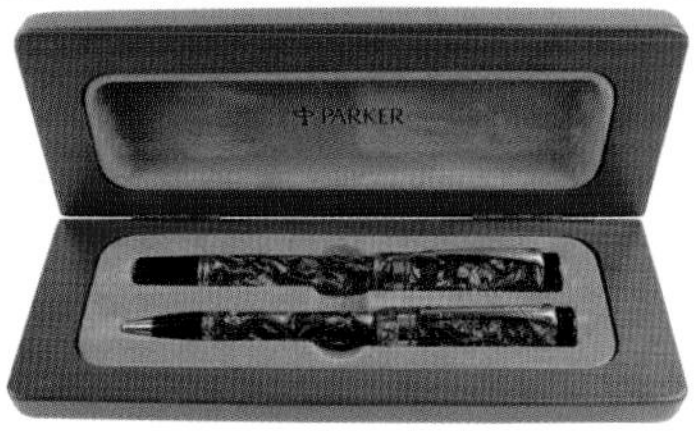

A Parker "Duofold" blue marbled fountain and ballpoint pen set, in original fitted mahogany case.

$300-400 **LOCK**

A leather heart-shaped photograph frame, by Child & Child, gilt center section with guilloche enamel ground, signed to frame.
ca. 1900 *4¾in (12cm) wide*
$3,900-5,200 **WW**

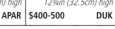

A hallmarked silver-mounted mirror, by Goldsmiths & Silversmiths Company, London, with back stand.
1901 *12¼in (31.5cm) high*
$300-350 **FLD**

An early-20thC silver-mounted photograph frame, on a replacement oak easel reverse, hallmarked E. Jacobs & Co., Birmingham.
1903 *8in (20.5cm) high*
$400-500 **FELL**

An Art Nouveau silver embossed photograph frame, by Henry Charles Freeman, Birmingham, on oak backing, surmounted by a butterfly, stamped "RD No.442132."
1904 *13¼in (33.5cm) high*
$260-320 **LSK**

A matched pair of early-20thC silver-mounted photograph frames, with later cold enamel accents, by E.F. Braham Ltd. and Deakin & Francis Ltd., minor wear.
1904 *5½in (14cm) high*
$950-1,100 **FELL**

A pair of early-20thC Art Nouveau silver-fronted frames, by Synyer & Beddoes, with enamel flower heads, with oak easel backs, minor tarnishing.
1904 *5½in (14cm) high*
$900-1,150 **APAR**

An early-20thC Arts and Crafts hammered pewter photo frame, with Ruskin-type cabochon, with oak easel back.
9½in (24cm) high
$450-600 **APAR**

A pair of early-20thC Art Nouveau silver-fronted photo frames, by William Neale, with enamel flowers, with oak easel backs.
7¾in (20cm) high
$1,900-2,600 **APAR**

A Dunhill walnut photograph frame, by David Linley, easel back, stamped marks, with original box.
12¾in (32.5cm) high
$400-500 **DUK**

A postcard, G.B. Bigwood, Gaiety House storefront, Southend-on-Sea, Essex, UK, with staff, facing the pier.

$32-35 **LOCK**

A real photographic postcard, of a "H.DOWNING STEAM BAKERY" horse-drawn delivery wagon.

$45-50 **LOCK**

A real photographic postcard, of W. Smith's "THE FAVOURITE" dining room on Victoria Dock Road, Canning Town, London.

$130-160 **LOCK**

QUICK REFERENCE—POSTCARDS

- **Postcards have their origins in the mid-19thC, but their golden age was arguably 1890-1910. Postcards continued to be sent throughout the 20thC, but today have largely fallen out of fashion.**
- **As well as being used as greetings cards, postcards in the late 19thC and early 20thC were used as a method of spreading news. People regularly sent commemorative postcards and postcards featuring photographs of fires, mining disasters, shipwrecks, and train crashes.**
- **Postcards were so commonly sent and received in the 20thC that most vintage postcards are worth very little, sometimes only a few pennies. It is only rare postcards that can today achieve high prices. These include postcards depicting rare or now closed railroad stations, postcards of the *Titanic*, and postcards by key designers, such as Louis Wain.**

A China real photographic postcard, "Selling food on street," franked British stamp, with British Army PO 1927 military postmark.

1927

$45-50 **LOCK**

A real photographic postcard, of "THE GASLIGHT & COKE COMPANY BECKTON" horse and cart.

$25-30 **LOCK**

A real photographic postcard, of Loudwater station, interior, C316.

$40-45 **LOCK**

A real photographic postcard, of Newhaven railroad station.

1913

$40-45 **LOCK**

A postcard, of "New Barnet Railway Station."

$60-80 **LOCK**

A real photographic postcard, by Warner Gothard, of "S.E. RAILWAY COLLISION TONBRIDGE JUNCTION MAR. 5TH 1909."

$45-50 **LOCK**

A real photographic postcard, of the disaster at Greenhalgh's Dye Works and Burnley Viaduct.

$62-68 **LOCK**

A real photographic postcard, of the Lincoln typhoid disaster, "TAKING THEIR TURN FOR WATER EASTGATE TYPHOID OUTBREAK LINCOLN 1905."

$94-100 **LOCK**

A postcard, of the RMS *Carpathia*, the ship that rescued the *Titanic*, not as titled the "Cunard Liner, 'Juernia.'"

$130-160 **LOCK**

A postcard, reading "THE ILL-FATED WHITE STAR LINER 'TITANITC' Struck an iceberg off the coast of Newfoundland on her maiden voyage & sunk with over One Thousand and Six Hundred of her Passengers & Crew, Monday morning April 15th 1912."

$90-100 **LOCK**

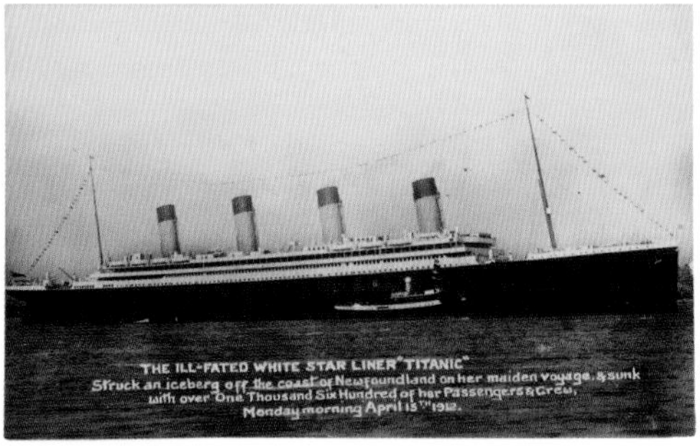

A postcard, signed in ink by "F. Poynton England's Rd Walking Champion 1923," pictured with trophy and in his racing gear.

Poynton's most successful year was 1923; he won the British 20 miles championship and the London to Brighton race.

For Sporting, see pp.342-355.

$24-28 **LOCK**

A postcard, of "R.M.S. TITANIC," wrecked April 1912, F.G.O. Stuart 1697.

$120-130 **LOCK**

A postcard, by Crawford Edmonton, of Tottenham Hotspur FC 1919-20, black-and-white team photo.

For Sporting, see pp.342-355.

$80-90 **LOCK**

A real photographic postcard, of Dover Cycling Club's awards gathering.

$45-50 **LOCK**

A postcard, of Colditz, hand signed by Douglas Bader.

$62-68 **LOCK**

QUICK REFERENCE—SUFFRAGETTES

- **Mary Wollstonecraft's 1792 book *A Vindication of the Rights of Woman* first publicly advocated women's suffrage in Britain. In 1865, the first women's suffrage committee was formed in Manchester, UK, with many following suit across the country. In the late 1800s and early 1900s, Parliament rejected nearly all major suffrage bills brought before it. However, in 1869, Parliament granted the right to vote in municipal elections to women taxpayers. In 1897, the National Union of Women's Suffrage was formed as these committees united.**
- **In 1903, the Women's Social and Political Union (WSPU) was formed. Emmeline Pankhurst (1858-1928) was a founding member of the WPSU. With a call for "Deeds not Words," the WSPU undertook hunger strikes and militant action to bring attention to women's suffrage and initiate social change. In 1918, the parliamentary vote was granted to women, but only those over the age of 30 who owned land or property.**
- **Postcards were used by both sides; pro-suffrage organizations and publishers promoted women's right for the vote, while some commercial publishers used postcards to mock and criticize the movement.**

A suffragette postcard, hand-drawn court size, reading "The New Woman" and "Votes for Women."

$40-45 **LOCK**

A suffragette postcard, reading "WE ONLY WANT WHAT THE MEN HAVE GOT!!!," depicting a woman with a political rosette by a table with a banner reading "VOTES FOR WOMEN MISS ORTOBEE SPANKDFIRST."

$100-120 **LOCK**

A suffragette postcard, by Millar & Lang, reading "SUFFRAGETTES ATTACKING THE HOUSE OF COMMONS."

$80-90 **LOCK**

A suffragette postcard, by Millar & Lang, reading "THE MARTYRS SUFFRAGETTES IN PRISON I WONDER WHAT THEIR OLD MEN ARE DOING JUST NOW."

$80-90 **LOCK**

A suffragette postcard, by Millar & Lang, reading "SUFFRAGETTES IT'S LOVE THAT MAKES THE WORLD GO ROUND."

$80-90 **LOCK**

A real photographic suffragette postcard, of "ST CATHERINE'S CHURCH HATCHAM CLEMENT BROS NUNHEAD DESTROYED BY FIRE MAY 6TH 1913," the arson disaster was said to have been started by militant suffragettes.

$50-60 **LOCK**

A suffragette postcard, "There are things that even a Suffragette cannot do," with a man resting his leg up on wall to tie his shoelaces.

$30-40 **LOCK**

A suffragette postcard, "I want my Vote!," sent to Mrs. A. Pankhurst Dec. 1908 from Alf.

$42-46 **LOCK**

A silk postcard, reading "SOUTH AFRICA INFTY."

$40-45 **LOCK**

A silk postcard, reading "WAAC SOUVENIR DE FRANCE."

$46-50 **LOCK**

A silk postcard, for the Royal Welsh Fusiliers.

$40-45 **LOCK**

A silk postcard, for the Shropshire Light Infantry.

$35-40 **LOCK**

An Art Nouveau postcard, by Alphonse Mucha, of a Byzantine head, "Blonde 427."

$300-400 **LOCK**

A Louis Wain postcard, by Faulkner, "And He winked the other Eye."

$32-36 **LOCK**

A Louis Wain postcard, by Davidson, "A Cat's Matrimony."

$38-42 **LOCK**

A Louis Wain postcard, by Faulkner, "Men were Deceivers ever."

$38-42 **LOCK**

A Louis Wain postcard, by Faulkner, "Wheelbarrow race."

$36-42 **LOCK**

A Louis Wain postcard, by Tuck, "CHEER UP! You can still post me for a halfpenny!"

$38-42 **LOCK**

"SCOTLAND BY 'THE NIGHT SCOTSMAN,'" by Robert Bartlett, lithographic poster, backed on linen, repaired tear from center of right-hand margin into image, further minor repaired tears.

This poster was sold in April 2019 alongside 14 others advertising Scotland by rail (all but one sold). The Art Deco image and Robert Bartlett are highly rated in the poster collecting/railroadiana worlds.

1932 *40¼in (102cm) high*

$19,000-26,000 **L&T**

"EDINBURGH," signed "BERRY 1951," lithograph, not backed.

1951 *40¼in (102cm) high*

$800-900 **L&T**

"LINLITHGOW PALACE," by Claude Buckle, lithograph, not backed.

ca. 1950 *40¼in (102cm) high*

$500-650 **L&T**

"AIR FRANCE CORSE," desigend by Raoul Eric Castel (1915-97), printed by Havas, Paris, repaired tears.

1949 *38in (96.5cm) high*

$1,050-1,300 **SWA**

"AUSTRALIA THE WORLD'S LOVELIEST HARBOUR, SYDNEY," designed by Albert Collins (1883-1951), printed by The Moore Young Litho Co., Melbourne, losses, margins trimmed, restoration in margins and image.

1930 *39½in (100.5cm) high*

$1,600-2,100 **SWA**

A CLOSER LOOK AT AN ART DECO POSTER

Michel Bouchaud (1902-65) is a well-known Art Deco poster artist. He was also a painter and illustrator and designed many album covers.

This is a highly stylized Art Deco image, from the woman's hair to the suggestion of waves in the water.

A fashionable couple flirts beneath a decorative trellis, at the confluence of the bay and a pool, with the beaches and town in the distance.

Bouchaud is known to have designed one other poster, for Val d'Esquieres, another waterside resort, but it is far less Art Deco than this scene.

"LA PLAGE DE MONTE CARLO," printed by Publicité Vox, Paris, framed, small stains in image.

1929 *46¼in (117.5cm) high*

$3,900-5,200 **SWA**

"DROITWICH THE BRINE BATHS SPA," designed by Leonard Campbell Taylor (1874-1969), printed by David Allen & Sons Ltd., London, extensive creases and abrasions in margins.

This poster depicts an elegant couple watching a car pass them on a driveway shrouded in shadows. The sophisticated Art Deco imagery combines a mixture of light and shadow with a contrast between the natural beauty and the architecture of this spa town. Taylor was a painter known for his portraits and interiors with figures. This is Taylor's only known poster.

1925 *39in (99cm) high*

$2,600-3,900 **SWA**

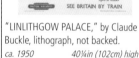

"CLEAR ROAD AHEAD," designed by Terence Cuneo, printed by Waterlow & Sons Ltd., lithograph, signed, some losses, fold marks, some staining.

39½in (100.5cm) high

$1,150-1,450 **SWO**

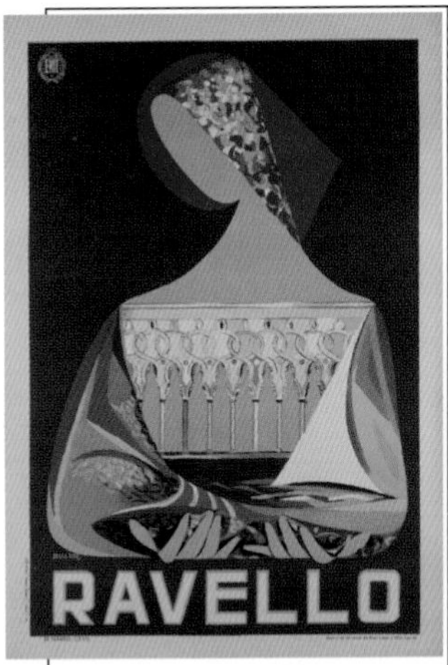

"RAVELLO," designed by Domenico (Mino) Delle Site (1914-96), printed by Di Mauro, Cava, restored losses.

1950 *39in (99cm) high*

$400-500 **SWA**

"WASHINGTON MANHATTAN UNITED STATES LINES," by R. Devignes, printed in France.

39in (99cm) high

$500-650 **DUK**

"GENÈVE ET LE MONT-BLANC," designed by Edouard Elzingre (1880-1966), printed by Atar, Geneva, repaired tears.

1925 *43¼in (110cm) high*

$950-1,250 **SWA**

"RODI," designed by Florestano Di Fausto (1890-1965), paper, printed by A. Marzi, Rome, minor tears and abrasions.

1927 *39½in (100.5cm) high*

$850-1,050 **SWA**

"San Francisco UNITED AIR LINES," by Stan Galli, minor creases and restoration at edges.

Born in San Francisco, Stan Galli (1912-2009) was a painter, illustrator, and printmaker. He was a member of the New York and California Society of Illustrators. Galli designed a series of posters for United Airlines in the 1950s and 60s.

40¼in (102cm) high

$650-800 **SWA**

"Travel by train CANADIAN PACIFIC RAILWAY LINES," by Norman Fraser, repaired tears, restored losses.

Although Norman Fraser was by far the most prolific artist commissioned by Canadian Pacific, he has remained an elusive figure. It is known that he lived in Montreal from 1930 to 1953 and that he was commissioned to design dozens of posters in that period.

1947 *36¾in (93.5cm) high*

$1,900-2,600 **SWA**

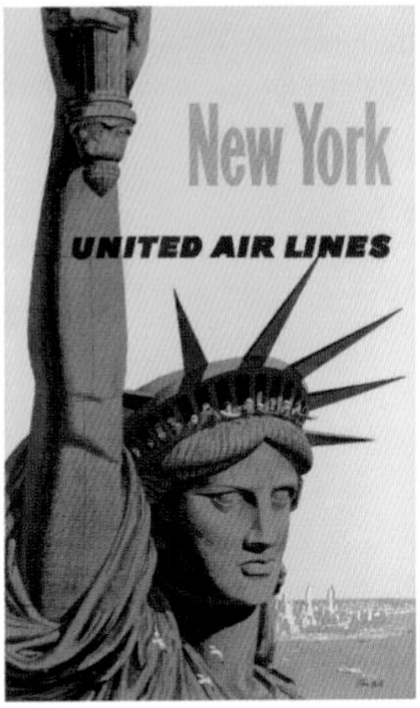

"New York UNITED AIR LINES," designed by Stan Galli, repaired tears, creases, and restoration on lower right edge.

ca. 1960 *40in (101.5cm) high*

$600-700 **SWA**

"CARLISLE THE GATEWAY TO SCOTLAND," by Maurice Greiffenhagen, for the London Midland and Scottish Regions, Japan backed.

ca. 1924

$1,300-1,900 **DUK**

"CHAMONIX-MONT BLANC," designed by Alo (Charles Hallo, 1884-1969), printed by Cornille & Serre, Paris, overpainting and airbrushing in margins.

In 1924, the eighth Olympic Games were held in Chamonix. One year later, "these successful Games were retrospectively recognized at the 'International Olympic Committee' Congress in Prague as the first Olympic Winter Games." The decision to hold these winter games came in 1921, and "triggered a period of frenzied construction as rail and road links and hotel development opened up the area to international tourism."

1924 *42½in (108cm) high*
$3,900-5,200 **SWA**

"LMS LONDON MIDLAND & SCOTTISH RAILWAY CONNEMARA 'IRELAND THIS YEAR,'" by Paul Henry, printed by S.C. Allen and Co., mounted on rice paper.

40in (101.5cm) high
$1,050-1,150 **WHYT**

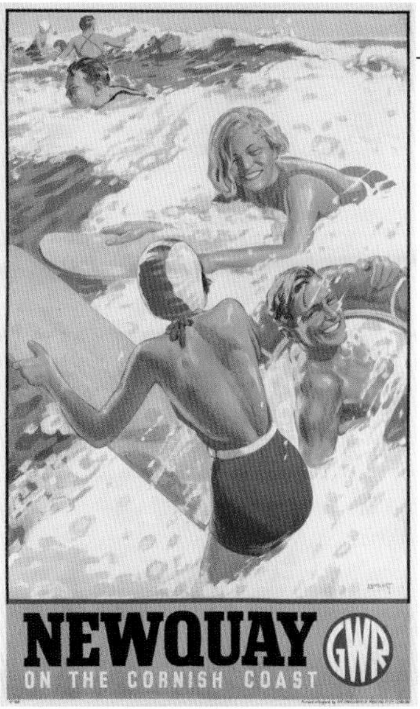

"NEWQUAY ON THE CORNISH COAST," designed by Alfred Lambart (1902-70), printed by The Dangerfield Printing Co. Ltd., London, repaired tears at edges.

1937 *40¼in (102cm) high*
$3,900-5,200 **SWA**

"CROSS THE CHANNEL FROM DOVER," by Lawrence, for the Southern Region.

ca. 1960 *39¾in (101cm) high*
$300-450 **DUK**

"MERANO," designed by Franz Lenhart (1898-1992), printed by Coen & Ci., Milan, light foxing on edges.

1934 *39¼in (99.5cm) high*
$2,600-3,200 **SWA**

"By Rail across GREAT SALT LAKE Overland route Southern Pacific," designed by Maurice Logan (1886-1977), printed on thick paper, flaking, and minor skinning in margins.

By the late 1920s, Logan had begun including a train in many of his designs. A particularly vivid image, of two Overland Limiteds passing as they cross the Great Salt Lake in opposite directions, summed up the campaign and the era, absorbing the drama of both the West and western railroading.

1928 *23in (58.5cm) high*
$800-900 **SWA**

"LOCH LOMOND," by Alasdair Macfarlane (1902-60), lithograph, not backed.

ca. 1950 *40¼in (102cm) high*
$800-900 **L&T**

"THE RIVER TWEED," by Jack Merriott (1901-68), lithograph, not backed.

ca. 1950 *40¼in (102cm) high*
$850-950 **L&T**

"Holland-America Line," designed by Franciscus J.E. Mettes (1909-84), minor repaired tears and abrasions, vertical lines in centered image.

1955 *37in (94cm) high*

$500-650 **SWA**

"YELLOWSTONE NATIONAL PARK-THRU GARDINER GATEWAY NORTHERN PACIFIC," designed by Louis Moen, printed on board, minor tears, creases, abrasions, and skinning in margins.

22in (56cm) high

$3,900-5,200 **SWA**

"FISHGUARD–ROSSLARE," by Arthur G. Muir, printed by Waterlow & Sons Ltd.

39½in (100.5cm) high

$600-700 **DUK**

"RAILROADS ON PARADE NEW YORK WORLD'S FAIR-1939," designed by Leslie Ragan (1897-1972), framed, minor creases and abrasions.

Among the exhibits at the 1939 New York World's Fair was the Court of Railways, "a sixteen-acre display of locomotives, trains, and the men who made them run. Twenty-seven principal railroads east of the Mississippi participated, and there were three and a half miles of track ... in the yards stood the British-built John Bull locomotive of 1831 alongside a modern 140-foot Pennsylvania streamlined giant that ran continuously at sixty miles an hour on a roller bed ... the highlight of the exhibit was Railroads on Parade ... a pageant about the 'romance of transport' from covered wagon days to the streamlined trains of 1939," *World of Tomorrow*, pp.101-102.

1939 *40¼in (102cm) high*

$1,150-1,450 **SWA**

"ROMA," designed by Virgilio Retrosi (1892-1975) printed by Novissima, Rome, mounted on paper, minor creases.

A student of the Accademia di Belle Arti in Rome, Retrosi was a painter, designer, and ceramicist.

ca. 1930 *37½in (95.5cm) high*

$450-600 **SWA**

"CONSTABLE'S COUNTRY," designed by Kenneth Slil, printed by Jarrold and Sons Ltd., Norwich, paper, tears and repaired tears at edges.

ca. 1950s *40in (101.5cm) high*

$600-700 **SWA**

"CULZEAN CASTLE PRESIDENT EISENHOWER'S SCOTTISH HOME," designed by Kenneth Slil, printed by Jarrold and Sons Ltd., Norwich, paper, small tears at edges, minor creases.

1955 *40¼in (102cm) high*

$650-800 **SWA**

"LE HAVRE TO NEW YORK FRANCE French Line," by Laura Smith, thick paper mounted onto board, minor creases and abrasions.

1979 *36in (91.5cm) high*

$1,050-1,300 **SWA**

"OVER THE SEA TO SKYE," by Kenneth Steel (1906-73), lithograph, not backed.

ca. 1950 *40¼in (102cm) high*

$700-850 **L&T**

"THE ROYAL MAIL LINE TO NEW YORK," designed by Horace Taylor (1881-1934), printed by The Baynard Press, London, minor staining, unobtrusive folds.

ca. 1925 *40in (101.5cm) high*

$1,600-2,100 **SWA**

"HOLLAND-AMERIKA LIJN," designed by Willem Frederik Ten Broek (1905-93), printed by Joh. Enschedé en Zonen, The Netherlands, margins trimmed off, airbrushing around lower text, abrasions and restoration in image.

1936 *36in (91.5cm) high*

$1,050-1,300 **SWA**

"DURHAM IT'S QUICKER BY RAIL," by Harry Tittensor, printed by Waterlow, published by London & N. Eastern Railway.

39¾in (101cm) high

$400-500 **PSA**

"KELSO ON THE BANKS OF THE TWEED IT'S QUICKER BY RAIL," by Harry Tittensor, printed by Jordison, published by London & Eastern Railway, dated, crease toward lower edge.

1941 *39¾in (101cm) high*

$400-500 **PSA**

"NOW FLY TO Bermuda by CLIPPER FROM BOSTON PAN AMERICAN WORLD AIRWAYS," by Adolph Treidler (1886-1981), overpainted margins, repaired tears.

Treidler worked on many advertising campaigns during his career. He designed propaganda posters during World War I, worked for the French and Furness Lines, and was employed by the Bermuda Board of Trade to help promote the island.

ca. 1955 *38in (96.5cm) high*

$400-500 **SWA**

"Fly to RIO by Clipper PAN AMERICAN WORLD AIRWAYS," designed by Mark von Arenburg, repaired tears and creases in margins, partial silkscreen.

ca. 1947 *42in (106.5cm) high*

$1,600-2,100 **SWA**

"PHILADELPHIA Go by Train PENNSYLVANIA RAILROAD," designed by Harley Wood, paper, minor abrasions in image.

40¼in (102cm) high

$400-500 **SWA**

"GEORGIAN MILITARY HIGHWAY," designed by Alexander Zhitomirsky (1907-93), printed by Intourist, USSR, replaced losses, repaired tears.

The Georgian Military Highway is a 125-mille (200-km) road leading from Tbilisi to Vladikavkaz in the Autonomous Republic of North Ossetia-Alania within the Russian Federation.

1939 *39in (99cm) high*

$2,600-3,200 **SWA**

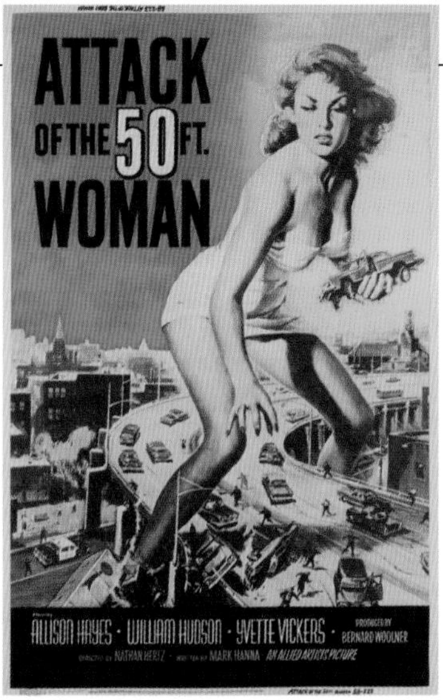

"ATTACK OF THE 50FT. WOMAN," partial silkscreen, mounted on thick paper, repaired tears, creases.

1958 *60¾in (154.5cm) high*

$3,200-3,900 **SWA**

"2001 lodyssee de lespace," Stanley Kubrick, printed by Cine Poster.

1968 *61in (155cm) high*

$650-800 **ROS**

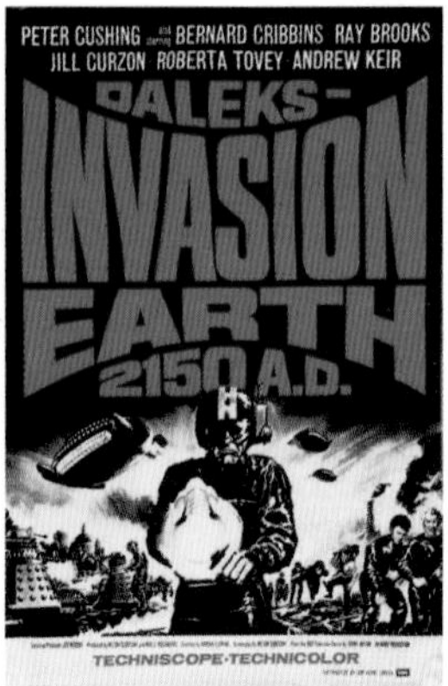

"DALEKS-INVASION EARTH 2150 A.D.," EMI Films, British one sheet rolled film poster.

The Daleks' fiendish plot in 2150 against Earth and its people is foiled when Doctor Who and friends arrive from the 20thC and figure it out. With Peter Cushing, Bernard Cribbins, and Ray Brooks.

1966 *40¼in (102cm) high*

$400-500 **SWO**

"JAMES BOND 007 CONTRE Dr. NO," French one sheet poster, the first James Bond film, centerfold, small hole in center, wear to edges.

1962 *63in (160cm) high*

$400-500 **WM**

"CHARLIE Chaplin," repaired tears on edges, some into image.

ca. 1930s *41in (104cm) high*

$1,250-1,450 **SWA**

"LE MANS," artwork completed by Tom Jung, printed by Lonsdale and Bartholomew.

Le Mans was made in 1971 and starred Steve McQueen as Michael Delaney, a racing driver competing in the Le Mans endurance race driving for the Porsche team. His character is haunted by the memory of an accident at the previous year's race, in which a competing driver was killed, and highlights the interaction between himself and the driver's widow, against the background of the race. The film was directed by Lee H. Katzin and features film recorded during the 1970 race.

1971 *40¼in (102cm) wide*

$1,300-1,600 **ROS**

"MOTHRA MIGHTIEST MONSTER IN ALL CREATION," small repaired tears and creases.

1962 *41in (104cm) high*

$400-500 **SWA**

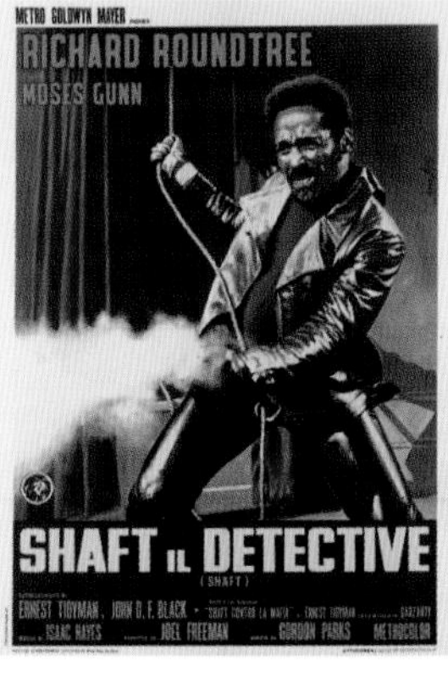

"SHAFT IL DETECTIVE," printed by Rotolitografica, Rome, repaired tears, creases, and restoration.

1971 *55¼in (140.5cm) high*

$1,050-1,150 **SWA**

"FRED ASTAIRE Ginger ROGERS SHALL WE DANCE," printed by Morgan Lith. Corp., Cleveland, repaired tears, creases, and restoration.

1937 *39¾in (101cm) high*

$1,600-2,600 **SWA**

"SNOW WHITE and the SEVEN DWARFS," US insert poster, framed.

Walt Disney had entertained the idea of producing a feature-length animated film for years, and when financial troubles began to brew, Disney knew he had to come up with something new to save his company. He invested $1,500,000 and three years of hard work, along with the combined talents of 570 artists, into the production of this animation classic. The film was a huge success, earning $8,500,000 Depression-era dollars, that not only saved the company financially, but also laid the foundation for the animation empire that was to follow. The film was such a significant screen innovation that it was given a special Oscar (and seven tiny oscars) in 1939.

1937 *35½in (90cm) high*

$2,300-2,900 GORL

"STAR WARS," British Quad film poster, artwork by Tim & Greg Hildebrandt, 20th Century Fox, minor nicks/bumps on edges.

This version of the British Quad poster was issued when the film was initially released in the UK. However, following the film's release it was discontinued in favor of Tom Chantrell's version, which portrayed the film's actors more accurately.

1977 *40in (101.5cm) wide*

$7,000-8,500 ECGW

"THE GHOST BREAKERS," Paramount Pictures, Morgan Litho Corp, US one-sheet, Paramount logo and 1940 copyright, numbered "18324 05-407/278," starring Bob Hope and Paulette Goddard, unframed.

1940 *41in (104cm) high*

$400-500 BELL

"THE MAN WITH THE GOLDEN GUN," Roger Moore, printed by Lonsdale and Bartholomew Ltd.

1974 *40in (101.5cm) wide*

$500-800 ROS

"THE PLAGUE OF THE ZOMBIES," British Quad film poster, Hammer Film Production, folded, grubby marks, general creasing, and handling marks.

1966 *40in (101.5cm) wide*

$3,900-5,200 ECGW

"THE TERROR OF THE TONGS," rare British quad film poster of 1910 Hong Kong-based Hammer Horror film, starring Christopher Lee, pin holes in corners, small tears.

1961 *40in (101.5cm) wide*

$1,050-1,400 SWO

"SEAN CONNERY 'THUNDERBALL,'" no.65/372, by United Artist Corporation.

1965 *59¾in (152cm) high*

$300-400 FLD

"THUNDERBIRDS are GO," printed in England by Leonard Ripley and Co. Ltd. London.

1966 *40¼in (102cm) wide*

$450-600 ROS

"YOU ONLY LIVE TWICE," designed by Robert McGinnis and Frank McCarthy, printed by Lonsdale and Bartholomew, England, framed and glazed.

1967 *39¼in (100cm) wide*

$1,600-2,100 ROS

"travel? adventure? answer - Join the Marines!," designed by James Montgomery Flagg (1870-1960), minor expertly repaired tears.

ca. 1918 *40in (101.5cm) high*

$6,000-7,000 SWA

"SEE THE WORLD AND GET PAID FOR DOING IT," designed by Alfred Leete (1882-1933), paper, small tears, unobtrusive folds.

1919 *30¼in (77cm) high*

$3,200-4,500 SWA

QUICK REFERENCE—CLARENCE COLES PHILLIPS

- **In what is perhaps the most "artistic" of the American World War I posters, Phillips unites the bold, direct elements of German object posters by top artists, such as Lucien Bernhard, with the intricate swirls and patterns of American Art Nouveau in the style of William Bradley. Interestingly, while it may echo the work of European artists, the poster represents a divergence from Phillips' usual style. He was nationally known for his "fadeaway girls," which graced the covers of *Life Magazine* from 1908 onward. In these images, which stylistically borrowed from both the Beggarstaff Brothers and Ludwig Hohlwein, Phillips features attractive young women whose clothing is the same color as the background, forcing the viewers to complete the image with their imagination.**

"LIGHT CONSUMES COAL SAVE LIGHT SAVE COAL," designed by Clarence Coles Phillips (1880-1927), printed by Edwards Deutsch & Litho Co. Chicago, repaired tears and losses.

ca. 1918 *27¼in (69cm) high*

$3,200-3,900 SWA

"POST OFFICE SAVINGS BANK SAVE for DEFENCE," by Frank Newbound, printed in England.

19¾in (50cm) high

$300-400 DUK

"WAR SAVINGS ARE WARSHIPS," by Norman Wilkinson, printed by J. Weiner Ltd, for HM Stationery Office.

29½in (75cm) high

$260-390 DUK

"Another call MORE MEN AND STILL MORE UNTIL THE ENEMY IS CRUSHED," printed by Hill, Sifflken and Co. London, published by the Parliamentary Recruiting Committee.

28¾in (73cm) high

$160-230 FLD

"CINÉMA Pathé Tous y mènent leurs enfants!," by Adrian Barrère (1877-1931), printed by Robert & Cie., Paris, repaired tears, minor creases, and restoration.

This early film poster shows the royal families of Europe bringing their children to the cinema to watch themselves on film. This political parody/celebrity endorsement is intended to promote the cinema as good family entertainment for all. Present at this screening are Alphonse XII of Spain and his son; Edward VII (the Prince of Wales); Leopold II of Belgium; French President Fallieres; Victor Emmanuel of Italy with his son Umberto and his daughter Yolande; and Czar Nicolas II of Russia with his wife Alexandra and their son Alexis.

ca. 1909 *46½in (118cm) high*

$9,000-10,500 SWA

"QUINQUINA DUHOMARD," designed by Dorfi (Albert Dorfinant, 1881-1976), printed by Affiches Camis, Paris, minor staining.

ca. 1935 *46¾in (118.5cm) high*

$2,600-3,900 SWA

"CASINO DE PARIS MISTINGUETT," designed by Louis (Zig) Gaudin (1882-1936), printed by Central Publicité, Paris, matted and framed.

1930 *23in (58.5cm) high*

$1,900-2,600 SWA

A Southern Railway "POOLE" enamel target sign, from the former London and South Western Railway station between Bournemouth and Wimborne.

$1,600-2,100 **GWRA**

A Southern Railway "CREDITON" lamp tablet, from the former London and South Western Railway station between Exeter and Okehampton, china glass with original wooden frame.

18in (45.5cm) wide

$300-350 **GWRA**

An LNWR "DOWN MAIN TO SEACOMBE" cast iron signal lever plate.

5½in (14cm) wide

$160-210 **GWRA**

A "GREAT EASTERN RAILWAY TRESPASSERS WILL BE PROSECUTED" cast iron sign, appears repainted.

21in (53.5cm) wide

$130-180 **LSK**

An early 20thC London, Midland and Scottish Railway "LMS 158" cast iron bridge plaque.

$60-100 **LOC**

A British Railways Southern Region buffer stop lamp, single aspect, with red warning ring around the red lens.

$130-180 **W&W**

An Adlake "Non Sweating" lamp, single aspect for TSR Advance Warning Board, with applied label "Lamp Manufacturing & Railway Supplies Ltd., Dorking, England.

$90-100 **W&W**

A pair of Great Western Railway locomotive whistles, top nuts stamped "GWR" and in polished condition.

largest 10in (25.5cm) high

$400-500 **GWRA**

A Great Western Railway mahogany cased single line block instrument.

1947 *12in (30.5cm) tall*

$300-400 **GWRA**

A Great Western Railway ship's clock, with an 8in (20.5cm) painted dial, cast brass bezel, brass case, and English lever movement, with GWR ivorine number plate "GWR 3612," in working condition complete with key.

$1,300-1,800 **GWRA**

A "LOVE ME DO" 7in single, by The Beatles, Parlophone, signed on the A side in blue ink by Paul McCartney, John Lennon, Ringo Starr, and George Harrison, bearing dead wax matrix number "7XCE 17144-1N," "ZT" tax code stamp.

1962 *11¼in (28.5cm) square*

$3,900-5,200 **WHYT**

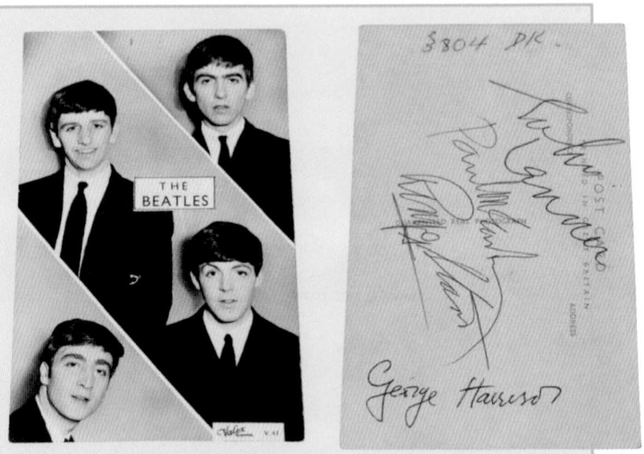

An autographed postcard, signed by the four members of The Beatles, John Lennon, Ringo Starr, George Harrison, and Paul McCartney, on reverse.

The signatures were acquired by the vendor's boyfriend on his summer vacation in July 1963. The vendor believes they were signed on either July 17 or 19, 1963, when the band were playing at the Rhyl Ritz Ballroom in North Wales.

$6,000-6,500 **AST**

An original set of psychedelic posters of The Beatles, three inscribed "Photographed by Richard Avedon for The Daily Express, Copyright by NEMS Enterprises Ltd... Limited First Edition," framed and glazed.

1971 *26¾in (68cm) high*

$260-320 **APAR**

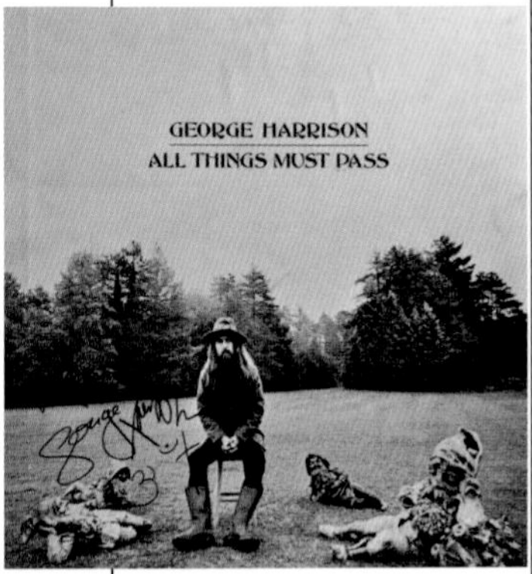

An album cover "GEORGE HARRISON, ALL THINGS MUST PASS," signed by George Harrison lower left, with certificate of authenticity verso, framed and glazed.

12in (30.5cm) square

$160-210 **APAR**

A photograph of John Lennon, by Robert Whitaker, an outtake from the infamous "Butcher" cover of *Yesterday and Today*, Capitol Records USA release, with annotation to back "John Studio 1964," printed notation for Uniphoto Press Inc., mounted.

The image of John Lennon was photographed and printed in 1966 by Robert Whitaker (1939-2011). Whitaker accompanied The Beatles to Tokyo in 1966.

6¾in (17cm) wide

$450-500 **ROS**

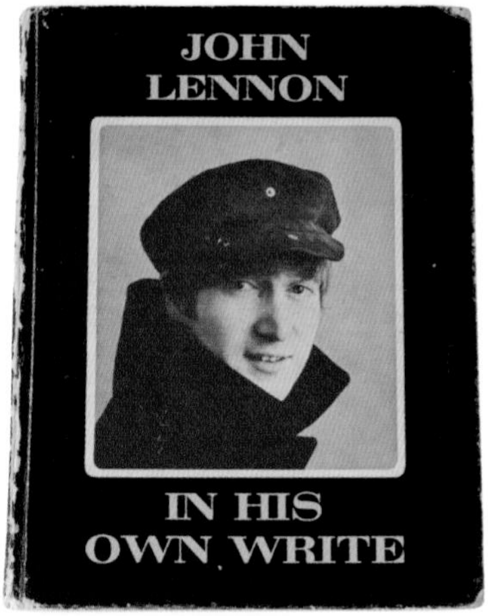

Lennon, John, *In His Own Write*, early edition, published by Jonathan Cape, London, signed by John Lennon to the opening page in blue ink, also inscribed in another hand "Foyles Luncheon, Dorchester Hotel 23rd April 1964."

This whimsical book of surrealist poems, drawings, and short stories was the first solo endeavor by any of The Beatles. Originally published in March 1964, it was a huge success, reportedly selling 50,000 copies on the first day of its release in England. To celebrate the book's success, Lennon was invited to a literary luncheon hosted by Foyle's at the Dorchester Hotel in London, for which he took a break from filming *A Hard Day's Night*. Unfortunately, Lennon was not aware that he was expected to make a speech and, according to his wife Cynthia, they were both painfully hungover. When the moment arrived, with the press and attendees waiting with bated breath to hear from the "intelligent" Beatle, Lennon stood and said "Er, thank you all very much, and God bless you."

1964

$3,200-3,900 **LSK**

A Live Aid gelatin silver print, by David Bailey, of Bob Geldof and Paula Yates, signed in pen by David Bailey, and signed on reverse by Bob Geldof and Paula Yates, stamped "ARCHIVAL DAVID BAILEY" and pencil initials "DB3/3," framed.

Five photographs were taken by David Bailey backstage at the Live Aid concert during the summer of 1985 for a benefit auction hosted by Sotheby's later that year. Each print is signed by the photographer and the majority are signed on the reverse by the subject. Only three of each image were printed for the auction. Live Aid was a dual-venue benefit concert held on July 13, 1985, and an ongoing music-based fundraising initiative. The original event was organized by Bob Geldof and Midge Ure to raise funds for relief of the ongoing Ethiopian famine. The event was held simultaneously at Wembley Stadium in London and John F. Kennedy Stadium in Philadelphia. On the same day, concerts inspired by the initiative happened in other countries, such as the Soviet Union, Canada, Japan, Yugoslavia, Austria, Australia, and West Germany. It was one of the largest-scale satellite linkups and television broadcasts of all time; an estimated global audience of 1.5 billion across 140 nations watched the live broadcast. This was nearly 40 percent of the world population at the time.

1985 *20in (51cm) high*

$1,900-2,600 **SWO**

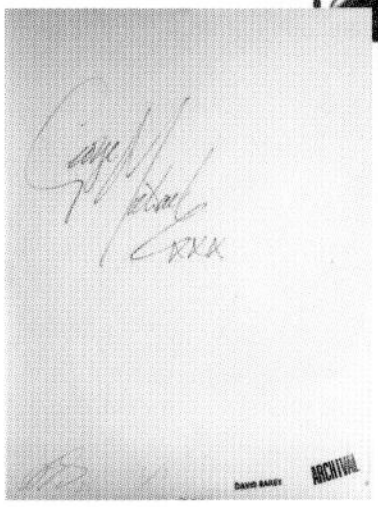

A Live Aid gelatin silver print, by David Bailey, of George Michael, signed by David Bailey, and signed on reverse by George Michael, stamped "ARCHIVAL DAVID BAILEY" and pencil initials "DB 85 3/3," framed.

During the Live Aid concert, Michael sang "Don't Let the Sun Go Down on Me" with Elton John on piano for the first time. The song found further success in 1991 as a duet between Elton John and George Michael, which reached No. 1 in the UK and US charts.

1985 *20in (51cm) high*

$7,000-8,000 **SWO**

A Live Aid gelatin silver print, by David Bailey, of Status Quo, signed in pen by David Bailey, and signed on reverse by Rick Parfitt and Francis Rossi, stamped "ARCHIVAL DAVID BAILEY" and pencil initials "DB 85 2/3," framed.

1985 *19¾in (50cm) high*

$3,200-3,900 **SWO**

A Live Aid gelatin silver print, by David Bailey, of Spandau Ballet, signed in pen by David Bailey, and signed on reverse by Gary Kemp, Martin Kemp, Tony Hadley, Steve Norman, and John Keeble, stamped "ARCHIVAL DAVID BAILEY" and pencil initials "DB 85 2/3," framed.

1985 *20in (51cm) high*

$2,600-3,200 **SWO**

QUICK REFERENCE—KEITH FLINT

- **Keith Flint (1969-2019) was born in Redbridge, London. After being expelled from school, Flint worked as a roofer and then traveled, working for a while in Israel, before returning to the UK.**
- **In the late 1980s, along with Leeroy Thornhill, Liam Howlett, Sharky, and MC Maxim Reality, Flint formed The Prodigy. Flint became lead vocalist in 1996.**
- **In 2006, Flint married Mayumi Kai, a Japanese DJ. They divorced in 2018. Flint died in 2019.**
- **All items on this page were part of the Keith Flint Collection.**

A carved and polychrome painted wooden head study of Keith Flint.

33in (84cm) high

$4,500-5,200 **CHEF**

A Steve Liddard custom-built oak and steel bed, supported at each corner by entwined thorns and accessed via steps supported on the back of a crouching winged mythical beast, branded mark.

It is understood that Keith worked closely with Steve Liddard on the design of this bed.

125in (317.5cm) long

$14,000-18,000 **CHEF**

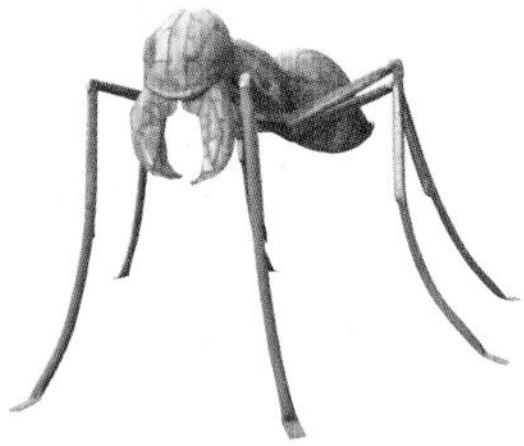

An Obediar Creations and Frailloop large welded aluminum and steel model ant, by Obediar Madziva and Gavin Darby, signed, dated.

When The Prodigy performed in Milton Keynes, UK, in 2010 at the Warriors Dance Festival, Frailloop were commissioned by the band's management to produce six large ant sculptures, based on the band's logo, to display at the venue. Each band member received one as a gift after the event.

2010 *99in (251.5cm) high*

$14,000-18,000 **CHEF**

A charcoal portrait of Keith Flint, by Kirk Andrews, framed, mounted with various inscriptions to the mount, commemorating Keith's 47th birthday in 2016.

This work was commissioned by The Prodigy Dirtchamber fan club and taken to the Leather Bottle, Keith's pub in Pleshey, where fans traveled from Europe to write messages to Keith on the mount.

22in (56cm) square

$4,500-5,800 **CHEF**

A pair of NME presentation awards to Keith Flint, one for Best Dance Act for The Prodigy in 1997, the other for Best Video for "Firestarter."

$13,000-16,000 **CHEF**

A Doug Murphy (PlasticGod) stretcher acrylic on canvas, Keith Flint signed and dated "Doug Murphy/4.25.03."

PlasticGod is the tag of Los Angeles-based artist, Doug Murphy (b.1973), also known as "The 21st Century Warhol." His paintings of pop icons from the world of music, art, fashion, films, theater, and celebrity have made PlasticGod a Pop icon in his own right.

4in (10cm) square

$2,600-3,900 **CHEF**

A Vivienne Westwood Anglomania Monty duffle coat, in branded suit carrier, with a Vivienne Westwood diamanté dress stud in the form of a bone.

$3,200-3,900 **CHEF**

A set of four MTV Music Television Awards, awarded to Keith Flint, comprising 1997 Award for Best Video, 1997 for Best Dance, 1997 Award for Best Alternative, and 1996 Award to The Prodigy for Best Dance, with a framed photograph of the band at the award ceremony.

$12,000-14,000 **CHEF**

"ABBA," signed by all four members in ink, some wear and staining, mounted on a board.

ca. 1977 *37¼in (94.5cm) high*

$450-500 **LOCK**

A *Dirty Deeds Done Dirt Cheap* sleeve of the international edition of AC/DC's third studio album, released in December 1976, signed in blue ballpoint by Bon Scott, Angus Young, Malcolm Young, Phil Rudd, and Cliff Williams, framed.

17¾in (45cm) square

$1,100-1,250 **WHYT**

An *ANDROMED*" record, RCA orange label, SF 8031.

$800-900 **LSK**

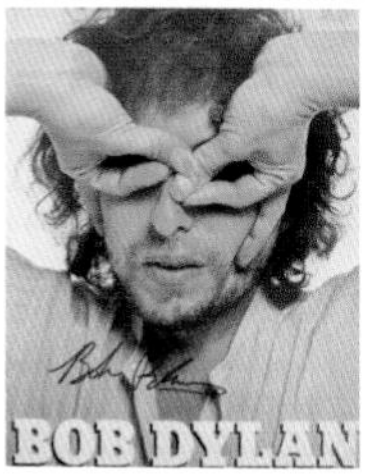

A Bob Dylan Earls Court, London, concert program, signed in black felt-tip pen on the front cover, mounted.

1978

$600-700 **WHYT**

A Bob Dylan magazine cutting, in blue ink, signed on the top right corner.

Acquired Albany Hotel, Birmingham, 1966.

9in (23cm) high

$260-390 **FLD**

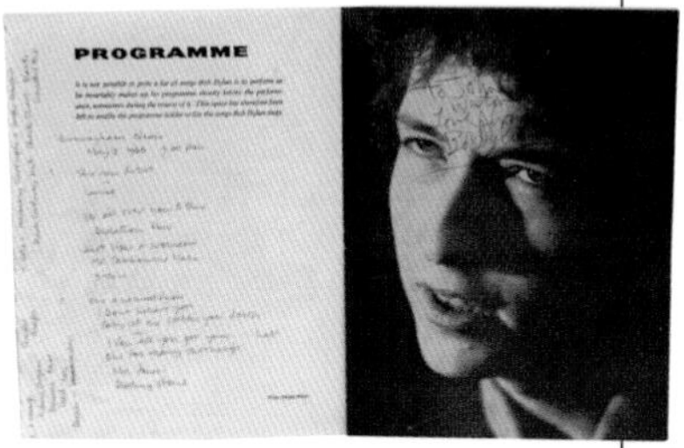

A Tito Burns presents signed Bob Dylan "66 (Highway Revisited) tour program, in black and white, signed on the fifth page "To John Weston, Bob Dylan."

Acquired from the Albany Hotel prior to the concert.

$2,300-2,900 **FLD**

A nude portrait of Marsha Hunt, by Patrick Lichfield, for the musical *Hair*, framed and glazed.

1969 *17½in (44.5cm) square*

$210-260 **BELL**

A Jimi Hendrix (1942-70) Polydor Records single sleeve, for "HEY JOE," signed Jimi Hendrix, mounted together with two press clippings from the *Musical Express*.

By repute this sleeve was signed by Hendrix at the Lauro Verde beach bar in Palma, Mallorca, on July 16, 1968. The bar owner had this record signed.

the mount 16½in (42cm) wide

$1,300-1,900 **ROS**

A *THIS WAS* album, by Jethro Tull, UK pressing, pink Island label, ILPS 9085 A.

$130-190 **LSK**

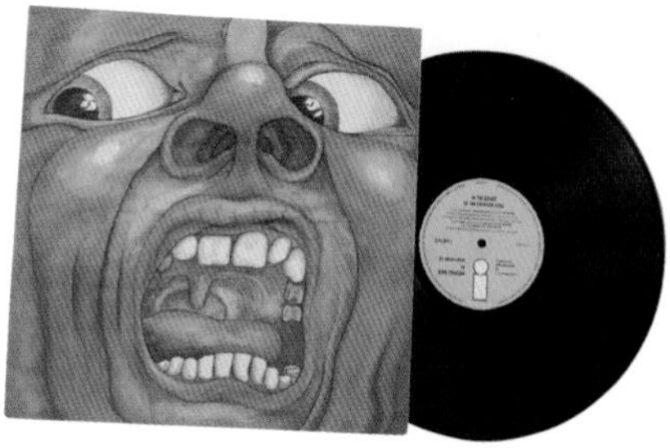

An *IN THE COURT OF THE CRIMSON KING* album, by King Crimson, UK first pressing, pink Island Records white "i" label ILPS-9111.

$190-260 **LSK**

A "SHE JUST SATISFIES, KEEP MOVING" 1st press Fontana 45 single, by Jimmy Page, TF 533, 267418 TF, Mono.

Jimmy Page's first solo single was not a favorite of Page himself, who was trying to move away from session music at the time (he later claimed that it was "better forgotten"). However, it is an interesting footnote in his career. Page undertook lead vocals and played all of the instruments except drums.

$800-900 **LSK**

An "Arnold Layne, Candy and a Current Bun" single, by The Pink Floyd, 7in original French release Columbia ESRF 1857, matrix M3 252951 7TCA 10350 21.

This 1967 debut single from The Pink Floyd was apparently about a transvestite knicker thief called Arnold Layne (B side "Candy and a Current Bun"). Despite charting, the unusual subject matter shocked some radio station personnel and the song was eventually removed from airplay.

$300-400 **LSK**

A *THE PIPER AT THE GATES OF DAWN* album, by Pink Floyd, Columbia blue/black label SX 6157, Matrix XAX 3420 1/ XAX 3420 2, file under POPULAR sleeve, "ROG 15.12.68" in pen to back cover.

$400-450 **LSK**

A signed *Sticky Fingers* LP album, by the Rolling stones, COC 59100, in zipper sleeve designed by Andy Warhol, printed inside with his signature, signed in red felt-tip pen by Mick Jagger, Keith Richards, Mick Taylor, and Charlie Watts.

$3,500-3,900 **WHYT**

A Rolling Stones black-and-white postcard, signed in black ink by Keith Richards, Brian Jones, Mick Jagger, Charlie Watts, and Bill Wyman, on the reverse signed in black ink, "Best Wishes to John from the Rolling Stones," with a Yamaha Soloist no.10 a.440 Harmonica reputedly given to the owner by Mick Jagger.

Acquired in person by the current owner at the Plaza Hansworth, 1963.

$3,200-3,900 **FLD**

A "Tommy" official souvenir brochure, signed by Paul Nicholas, Robert Powell, Pete Townshend, Tina Turner, Eric Clapton, and Arthur Brown.

$190-260 **FLD**

A *Led Zeppelin I*, by Led Zeppelin, UK first pressing Atlantic 588171, red/maroon label with Superhype, jewel credits, 588171 A//1 118, B//1 184.

This 1969 UK first pressing of the self-titled Led Zeppelin album depicts the Hindenburg air disaster on the cover with turquoise lettering and red/maroon Superhype/Jewel label. Within weeks of its release, the cover was replaced with the orange lettering version—which was considered more rock 'n' roll than turquoise.

$1,900-2,600 **LSK**

A Chris Ruocco pirate print shirt, worn by George Michael in Wham's American Tour in 1985, labeled "Tailored by Chris Ruocco."

Chris Ruocco tailors in Kentish Town, North London, dressed Bananarama, Spandau Ballet, and Wham in the 1980s. This shirt comes with the address packaging it was sent in from Andrew Ridgley.

$650-800 **SWO**

A *THE WHO LIVE AT LEEDS* album and cover, signed by Roger Daltrey, Peter Townshend, and John Entwhistle, with a poster for The Who in concert, at the Rainbow (formerly the Astoria Theatre), Finsbury Park, November 4, 5, and 6, 1971.

$1,900-2,600 **ROS**

A 19thC silver-gilt and glass scent bottle/vinaigrette, by S. Mordan and Co., the glazed front opens to reveal a silver-gilt grille, the reverse with a hinged compartment, with a chain and finger ring, the glass body is cracked.

Sampson Mordan (1790-1843) was a British silversmith. He went into business with John Isaac Hawkins in 1822 and together they invented the mechanical pencil, but Mordan later bought Hawkins out. Mordan then went into partnership with stationer Gabriel Riddle, but the partnership dissolved in 1837, and Mordan continued under the trading name of S. Mordan and Co. until his death in 1843, when the company passed to his sons. The company manufactured a wide variety of products, including scent bottles, pencils, locks, whistles, boxes, and inkwells. S. Mordan and Co. became a limited liability company in 1898. The company stopped trading in 1941.

3¼in (8.5cm) long

$600-650 WW

A 19thC silver scent bottle, by S. Mordan & Co., with bright-cut engraving.

2in (5cm) long

$500-650 JN

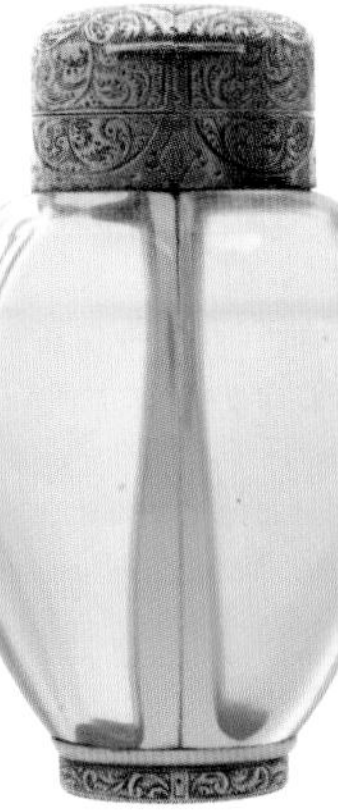

A 19thC silver-gilt mounted double scent bottle/vinaigrette, with foliate engraved split hinged covers, conforming silver-gilt heel, stamped on the underside "S. Mordan & Co. Makers," with diamond registration mark for September 1, 1858.

1858

$650-800 FLD

A 19thC S. Mordan & Co. double-ended cut glass scent bottle, with silver-gilt mounts, London.

1876. 5in (12.5cm) long

$260-390 JN

A 19thC engraved silver scent bottle and stopper, by S. Mordan & Co., London.

1881 2in (5cm) long

$300-400 JN

A 19thC silver scent bottle, by S. Mordan & Co., with engraved Kate Greenaway decoration, hinged cover.

1883 2¼in (5.5cm) high

$500-650 WW

A 19thC silver-mounted "fish" glass scent bottle, by S. Mordan & Co., the green glass body with gilded scales and details, red glass eyes.

1884 6¼in (16cm) long

$2,300-2,900 WW

A Thomas Webb three-layer cameo glass scent bottle, with a silver screw-fitted cap, hallmarks for S. Mordan & Co., London.

ca. 1887 4in (10cm) high

$1,100-1,250 WW

A cut glass scent bottle, by S. Mordan & Co., with screw-off silver cap, marked in leather case "H. W. BEDFORD, 67 REGENT STREET."

11in (28cm) long

$400-500 JN

QUICK REFERENCE—SCENT BOTTLES

- **Until the 19thC, the design of scent bottles was determined by the volatility and expense of scent. The bottles had to be airtight and impervious to light and were made to reflect the cost of the scent.**
- **Although glass had been used for scent bottles from Roman times, it became the most popular material for scent bottles from the end of the 18thC, with precious metals and hardstones often used previously.**
- **By the 20thC, perfume makers had begun to sell bottled perfume, leading collectors to generally focus on one parfumier or fashion house. Prior to this, perfume was sold to be mixed and decanted into scent bottles.**

A George III silver scent bottle, by Joseph Willmore, checkerboard decoration, screw-off cover with a ring attachment.

1805 *1½in (4cm) long*

$400-450 **WW**

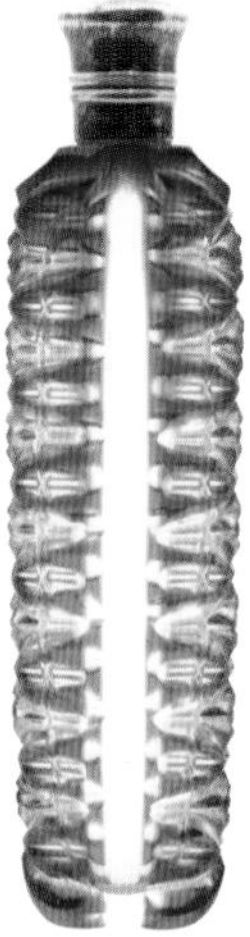

A 19thC red flash-cut lay scent bottle, with a hinged white metal cap.

4in (10cm) long

$160-230 **FLD**

An early-19thC silver "horn" vinaigrette/scent bottle, by Nathaniel Mills, with a pierced foliate grille, engraved decoration, with a chain and screw-off scent bottle cover set with an agate cabochon.

Vinaigrettes were small hinged boxes containing a perfume-soaked sponge behind a pierced grille. Some vinaigrettes had a small ring on the exterior allowing them to be worn around the neck. In the early 1800s, vinaigrette designs became increasingly elaborate and the boxes grew in size.

1828 *4in (10cm) long*

$950-1,100 **WW**

A 19thC double-ended glass scent bottle, with silver caps.

5½in (14cm) long

$120-140 **JN**

A 19thC ruby glass scent bottle, with silver cap.

3¼in (8.5cm) long

$70-80 **JN**

A 19thC double-ended glass scent bottle, with engraved silver caps, initialled.

5¼in (13.5cm) long

$120-140 **JN**

A 19thC tinted glass scent bottle, with engraved silver cap.

3½in (9cm) long

$160-210 **JN**

A 19thC ruby facet-cut glass scent bottle, with repoussé silver cap.

3¾in (9.5cm) long

$130-190 **JN**

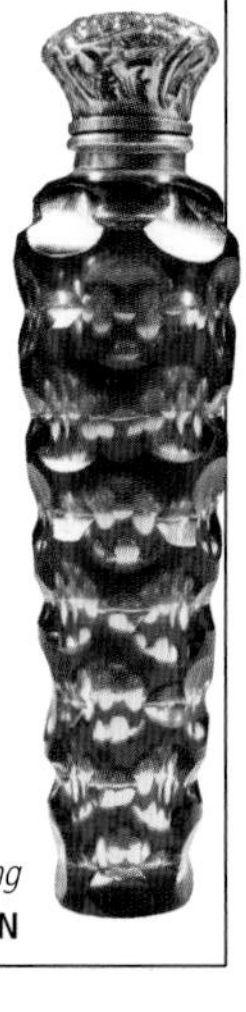

A 19thC blue tinted glass scent bottle, with repoussé silver cap and frosted glass stopper.

4¼in (11cm) long

$160-210 **JN**

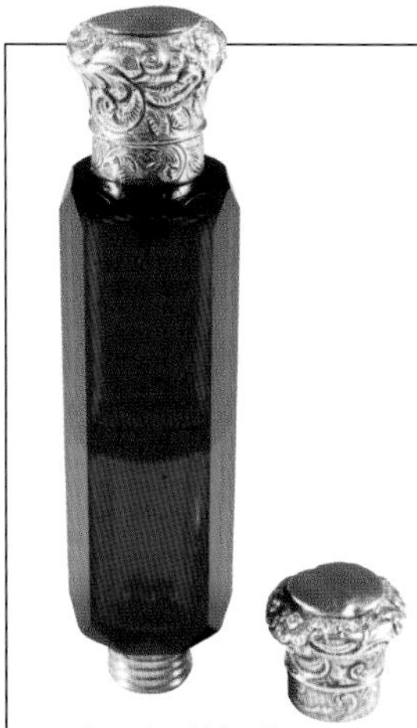

A 19thC Bristol blue facet-cut double-ended glass scent bottle, with repoussé silver caps.

5¼in (13.5cm) long

$120-140 **JN**

A 19thC ruby tinted facet-cut glass scent bottle, with repoussé silver cap.

1½in (4cm) high

$90-100 **JN**

A 19thC cut glass scent bottle, with repoussé silver cap, glass stopper and chain.

3½in (9cm) long

$130-180 **JN**

A 19thC facet-cut double-ended glass scent bottle and vinaigrette.

3¼in (8.5cm) long

$100-110 **JN**

A 19thC hobnail-cut glass folding scent bottle and vinaigrette, with repoussé silver caps and silver-gilt vinaigrette.

5½in (14cm) long

$300-400 **JN**

A 19thC ruby facet-cut double-ended glass scent bottle, with silver-gilt repoussé caps.

4¾in (12cm) long

$130-180 **JN**

A 19thC ruby glass and gold-mounted scent bottle and stopper, with a "Mary Gregory" child.

3in (7.5cm) long

$500-650 **JN**

A 19thC tapering ruby glass scent bottle, with flowers and foliage in gilt, with screw-off silver cap and glass stopper.

7¾in (19.5cm) long

$300-400 **JN**

A 19thC silver-gilt mounted overlay scent bottle/vinaigrette, by Abraham Brownett, the cover with engraved decoration and a concealed photograph frame, inset with turquoise and pearl cabochons, the front engraved "Lally" and opens to reveal a foliate pierced silver-gilt grille, engraved "Registered P. & F. Schafer, 27 Piccadilly, 21st Aug 1866," the reverse with a hinged compartment and engraved "Xmas 1916."

1867 *3in (7.5cm) long*

$1,700-2,100 **WW**

A 19thC clear glass perfume bottle, with silver cap, painted with a Chinese figure and deer.

4in (10cm) high

$170-210 **JN**

A late-9thC Russian silver-gilt and enamel scent flask, by Pavel Ovchinnikov, assay master V. Savinsky, pull-out stopper.

1876 *8in (20.5cm) high*

$2,900-3,900 **WW**

A 19thC silver engraved scent bottle, with frosted glass stopper, maker "C.M."

1882 *2¼in (5.5cm) long*

$190-260 **JN**

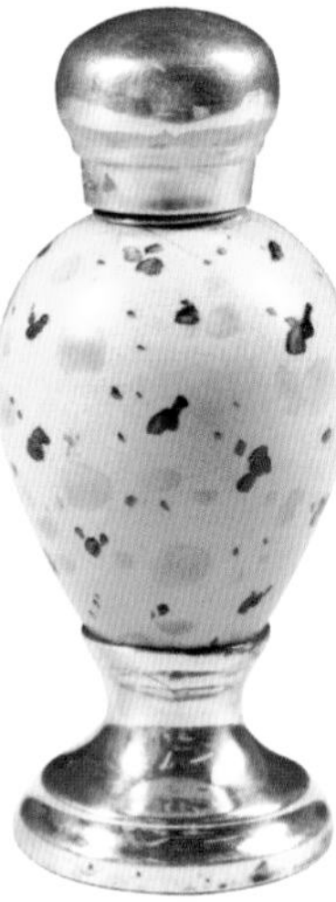

A 19thC silver-mounted egg-shaped scent bottle, made by F.S., Birmingham.

1885 *3in (7.5cm) high*

$400-450 **JN**

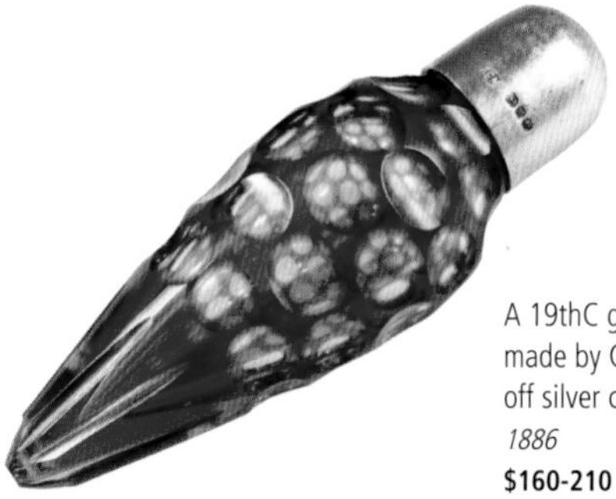

A 19thC glass scent bottle, made by C.M., with screw-off silver cap, Birmingham.

1886 *4in (10cm) long*

$160-210 **JN**

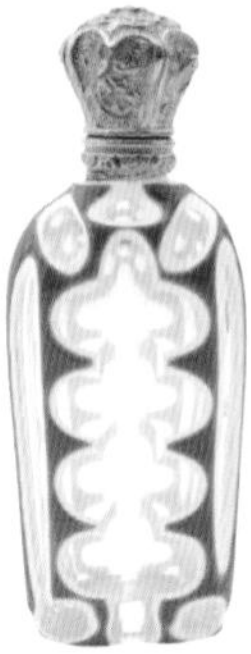

A 19thC scent bottle, the pink and white overlaid clear glass body below silver-gilt metal collar and hinged cover.

3½in (9cm) long

$300-350 **FLD**

A silver-mounted ceramic "egg" scent bottle, by Saunders and Shepherd, screw-off cover.

1885 *2½in (6.5cm) long*

$450-500 **WW**

A 19thC cameo glass scent bottle, with screw-off silver cap, Chester.

1890 *1½in (4cm) diam*

$450-500 **JN**

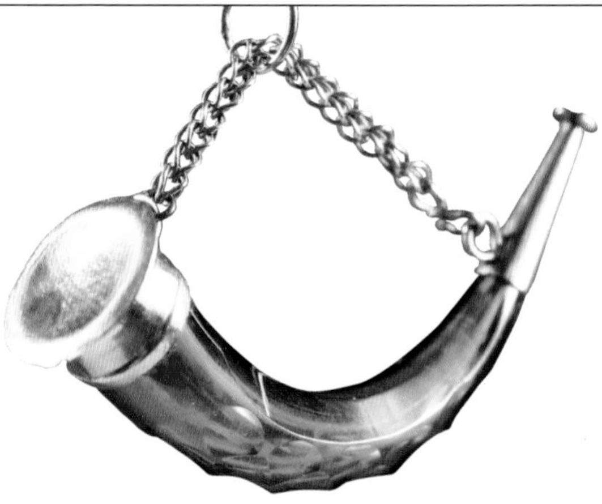

A 19thC facet-cut glass "horn" scent bottle.

1½in (4cm) long

$160-190 **JN**

A French novelty silver "owl" scent bottle and desk seal, the hinged cover set with glass eyes, with a glass stopper.

2¼in (5.5cm) high

$300-400 **WW**

A late-19thC Russian silver-gilt and enamel scent bottle, maker's mark worn, screw-off cover.

ca. 1890 *3in (7.5cm) long*

$650-800 **WW**

A Russian silver and enamel scent flask, by Ivan Saltykov, pull-out stopper, Moscow.

ca. 1890 *6in (15cm) high*

$1,600-2,100 **WW**

A Russian silver-mounted scent bottle, maker's mark possibly that of A.S. Bragin, with a stopper.

1896-1908 *5¾in (14.5cm) high*

$260-320 **WW**

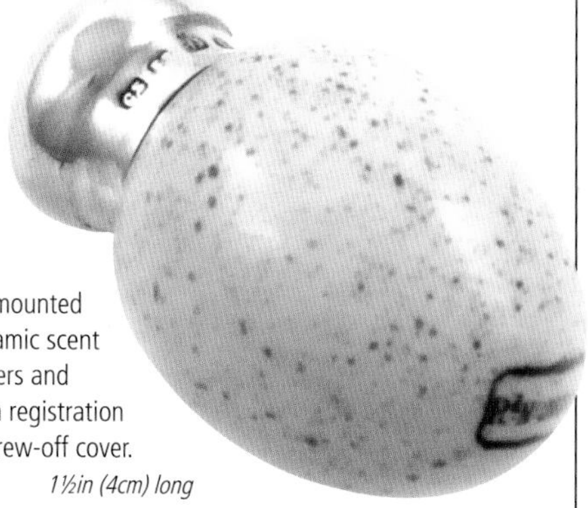

A novelty silver-mounted "bird's egg" ceramic scent bottle, by Saunders and Shepherd, with a registration number, plain screw-off cover.

1897 *1½in (4cm) long*

$190-260 **WW**

A 19thC glass and silver scent bottle, maker C.M., Birmingham.

1897 *1½in (4cm) long*

$90-100 **JN**

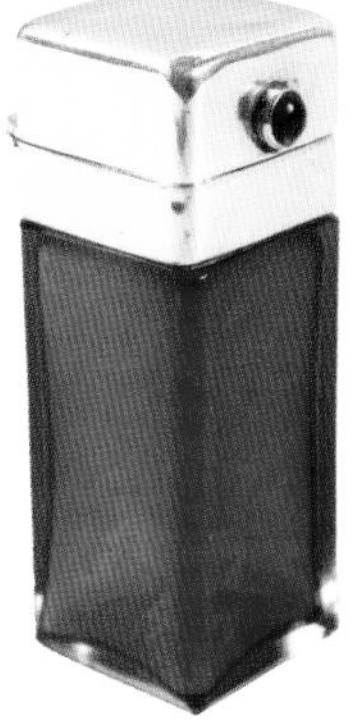

A 19thC glass scent bottle and stopper, made by C. & G., Birmingham, with plain silver cap.

1900 *2¾in (7cm) long*

$160-210 **JN**

A late-19thC Thomas Webb & Sons large cameo glass lay scent bottle, cut with flowering boughs on one side and peace lily and cow parsley verso, gilded silver mounts stamped "Gorham."

5¼in (13.5cm) long

$950-1,100 **FLD**

A Bristol blue glass facet-cut scent bottle, with silver cap.

1½in (4cm) long

$100-130 **JN**

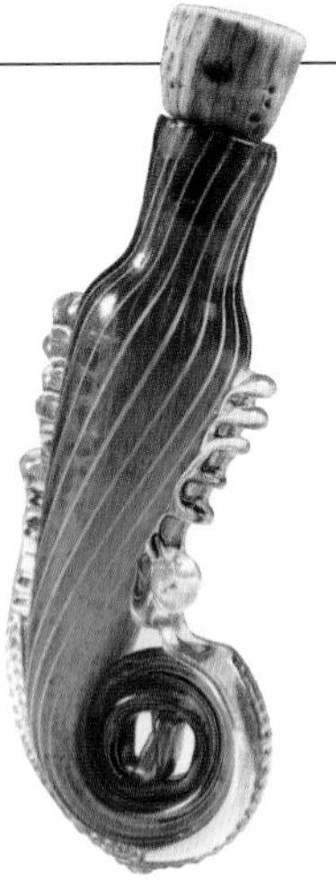

An Italian glass spiral-shaped scent bottle, with cork stopper.

3in (7.5cm) long

$80-100 **JN**

An early-20thC Continental silver finger scent bottle, with relief-molded flowers, with screw cap.

2½in (6.5cm) long

$120-140 **FLD**

A 20thC silver-plated glass faceted scent bottle.

5¼in (13.5cm) long

$60-70 **FLD**

An early-20thC glass scent bottle, overlaid with silver clover pattern, with a hinged silver lid, makers mark worn.

1907 *4in (10cm) high*

$230-290 **FLD**

A Webb's cameo glass scent bottle, with engraved silver cap, Birmingham.

1907 *1½in (4cm) high*

$400-500 **JN**

An early-19thC Levi & Salaman silver-framed and tortoiseshell egg-shaped scent bottle stand, the hinged body enclosing a pair of glass scent bottles.

1912 *4¼in (11cm) high*

$400-450 **APAR**

An Edward VII engraved silver scent bottle, made by D.M. & Co., with plain glass and frosted stopper, Birmingham.

1908 *2¼in (5.5cm) long*

$80-100 **JN**

A studio glass scent bottle, by Jonathan Harris, with gold leaf and mottled pastel-colored decoration, signed and dated on base, some abrasions on the bottom of the stopper.

2002 *4¼in (11cm) high*

$80-100 **APAR**

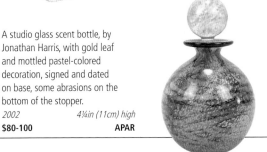

A late-19thC microscope magnifier, by R. and J. Beck Ltd., London, with fitted and adjustable side lens, chimney and colored slides over a clear glass reservoir, in mahogany case with slide box and funnel.

11¾in (30cm) high

$1,150-1,450 **FLD**

A late-19thC brass binocular microscope, by E.G. Wood, with accessories, including a brass bull's-eye lens and a brass adjustable night light, in a mahogany case, unsigned.

20in (51cm) high

$1,900-2,600 **BELL**

A brass binocular microscope, by John Browning, 63 Strand, London, no.823, in a mahogany case with a detachable part box of lenses.

John Browning (ca. 1831-1925) was an English inventor and maker of precision scientific instruments.

16½in (42cm) high

$700-800 **WHP**

A C. Reichert of Wien brass monocular microscope, numbered "21798."

$100-160 **APAR**

An E. Leitz Wetzlar brass and black lacquered monocular microscope, numbered "149146."

$50-60 **APAR**

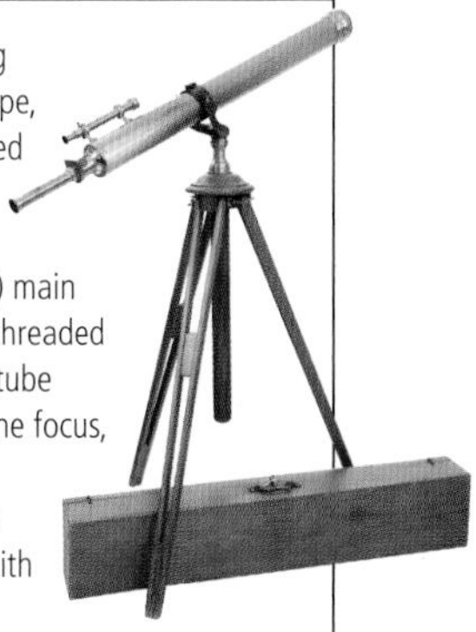

A 3½in (9cm) refracting lacquered brass telescope, by Secretan, Paris, signed on the backplate "Secretan, Epry SUCr, PARIS," 44½in (113cm) main tube with star spotter, threaded 11in (28cm) eye-piece tube with rack-and-pinion fine focus, in original case with maker's label and three eyepiece accessories, with original stand.

ca. 1880 *case 51¼in (130cm) wide*

$1,150-1,450 **CM**

A lacquered and oxidized brass theodolite, by Hildebrand & Schramm, Freiberg, the 10in (25.5cm) tube with rack-and-pinion fine focus and top sights secured to circular protractor with opposing vernier scales on a pillar with fine longitude adjustment, numbered "1558," in original case, with tripod stand.

ca. 1880 *18¼in (46.5cm) high*

$1,150-1,550 **CM**

A pair of German Schneider 25 x 105 field binoculars, with Zeiss lenses, chrome plated, on a wooden and chrome tripod stand.

1950s *52¾in (134cm) high*

$3,200-3,900 **DUK**

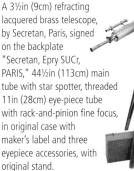

A late-9thC walnut stereoscopic viewer, the base with fitted drawer containing card stereoscope slides, including examples by the London Stereoscopic and Photographic Company of The International Exhibition of 1862.

15¾in (40cm) high

$1,700-2,100 **ROS**

A vernier octant, by Spencer, Browning & Rust, London, the scale divided to 95 degrees and stamped with "SBR" dividing letters, with brass index arm, pinhole sight, three shades and mirrors, with signed maker's plate.

ca. 1790 *13½in (34.5cm) radius*

$300-450 **CM**

A lean-pattern brass miner's dial, by Negretti & Zambra, 4¼in (11cm) silvered dial signed, with Diff of Hypo scale over with 7½in (19cm) sighting telescope, with rack-and-pinion fine focus top objective.

ca. 1880 *box 13½in (34.5cm) wide*

$500-650 **CM**

An 18thC tabletop 12in (30.5cm) terrestrial globe, by W. & S. Jones, London, 12 printed gores, labeled "THE NEW TWELVE INCH BRITISH Terrestrial Globe REPRESENTING THE ACCURATE POSITIONS OF THE PRINCIPAL KNOWN PLACES OF THE EARTH, FROM THE DISCOVERIES OF CAPTAIN COOK AND SUBSEQUENT CIRCUMNAVIGATORS TO THE PRESENT PERIOD," with a brass meridian ring, and horizon ring with calendar and zodiac markers, on an ebonized stand, dated.

1800

$3,900-4,500 **L&T**

A dry card binnacle compass, by Hooper & Son, Portsmouth, signed engraved, wax balancing, in painted brass bowl gimbal mounted within wooden binnacle with removable glass viewing panel, oil lamp, securing rings, top handle, and shaped lower edge.

ca. 1850 *13in (33cm) high*

$650-800 **CM**

A two-day marine chronometer, by Kelvin, White & Hutton, the silvered dial signed, evacuated from Singapore on HMS Bulan, impressed with Government broad arrow mark, blued steel hands, the Mercer movement, with Harrison's maintaining power, Earnshaw escapement, bimetallic standard balance with hellical balance spring, gimbal mounted within wooden box with ivorine maker's plate, Singapore adjuster's label inside lid for "Sept. 1940."

9½in (24cm) wide

$2,900-3,400 **CM**

A silver-mounted drawing set etui, by Benjamin Martin, the scissor protractor and folding rule signed, with a full set of instruments, in a silver-mounted shagreen case.

ca. 1760 *7in (18cm) high*

$5,200-6,500 **CM**

A solid silver miniature surveying quintant, by Cary, London, believed to have been owned by Isambard Kingdom Brunel, the 3in (7.5cm) radius T frame signed on the cross bar, with scale divided to 150 degrees, vernier with ebonized magnifier, pinhole sight, and index mirror with ebonized platform, with box of issue with brass plate inscribed "HM Brunel."

Isambard Kingdom Brunel's sons died childless, so his collection passed down the female line via his daughter Florence Coleridge née Brunel (b.1847), who, in turn, had daughters Celia and Lillian. Celia Brunel (1872-1962) made the principal donation of artifacts to Bristol University in 1950. However, it seems some items were retained, because her daughter, Lady Cynthia Noble Jebb (1898-1990), passed on this item as part of a group to one of her daughters, who had them evaluated when winding up her mother's estate.

ca. 1830 *box 4¾in (12cm) square*

$5,200-6,500 **CM**

A Negretti and Zambra brass pocket barometer, no.10772, the reverse a compass with locking button, in lined crocodile skin case.

$500-650 **FLD**

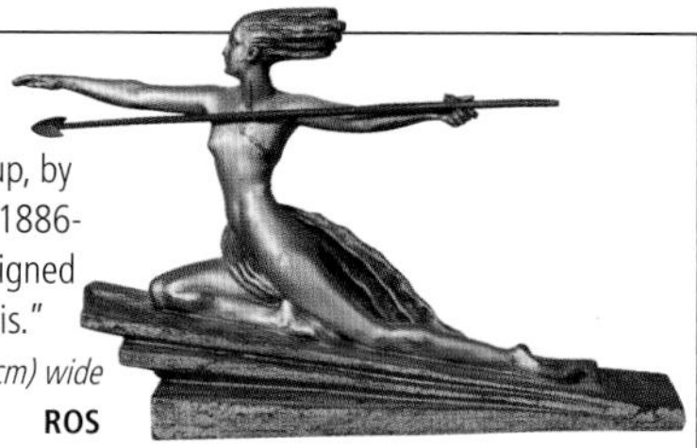

An Art Deco "Amazon" cold-painted bronze group, by Marcel-André Bouraine (1886-1948), on bronze base, signed "Bouraine and Etling Paris."

ca. 1930 *10in (25.5cm) wide*

$2,600-3,200 ROS

QUICK REFERENCE—DEMETRE H. CHIPARUS

- **Born in Romania, Demetre H. Chiparus (1880-1950) studied in France and worked predominantly with bronze and ivory.**
- **Most of Chiparus' work was handled by the Etling foundry. Models were made by Chiparus for Goldscheider and Les Neveux de J. Lehmann.**
- **Chiparus took inspiration from the theater, the Ballet Russes, and Egyptian culture. The tomb of Tutankhamen was opened in 1922, driving an interest in Ancient Egypt.**

An early-20thC French "La Danseuse Ayouta" ivory figurine, by Demetre H. Chiparus, patinated and cold-painted bronze figurine, on an onyx base, signed, light wear.

18¼in (46.5cm) high

$12,000-14,000 GORL

An Émile Carlier patinated spelter figurine of a dancer, on veined marble stepped base, signed.

20¾in (52.5cm) high

$400-450 WW

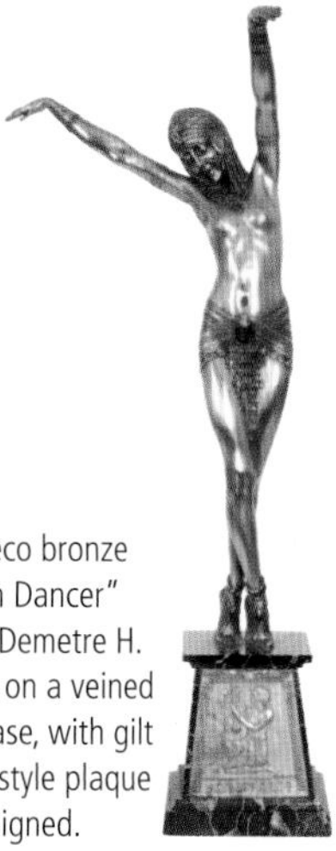

An Art Deco bronze "Egyptian Dancer" study, by Demetre H. Chiparus, on a veined marble base, with gilt Egyptian-style plaque to front, signed.

28¾in (73cm) high

$11,000-13,000 FLD

An Art Deco patinated bronze "Cleopatra" figurine, by Demetre H. Chiparus, on a variegated black marble base, signed.

$8,500-9,500 FLD

A gilt-bronze figurine of a girl balancing two balls, by Claire Jeanne Roberte Colinet (1880-1950), on a marble base.

10in (25.5cm) high

$650-800 JN

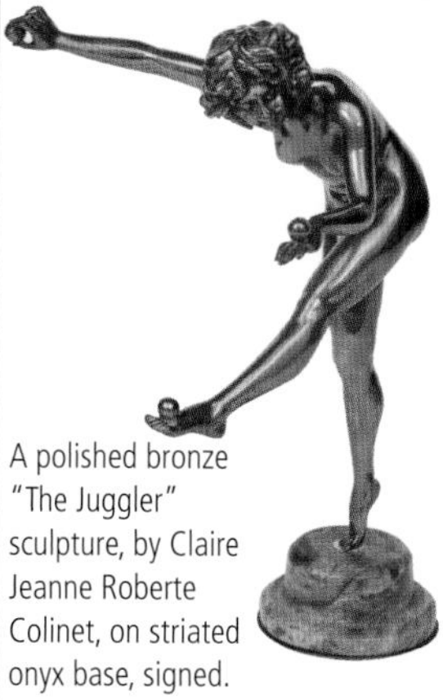

A polished bronze "The Juggler" sculpture, by Claire Jeanne Roberte Colinet, on striated onyx base, signed.

14½in (37cm) high

$850-950 WW

An Art Deco patinated spelter centerpiece of a girl and a borzoi, by A. Godard, on an onyx plinth.

23¼in (59cm) wide

$260-390 SWO

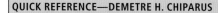

A cold-painted bronze and ivory figurine, by Josef Lorenzl, on onyx base, signed "LORENZL."

ca. 1925 *8¾in (22cm) high*

$2,900-3,600 TEN

QUICK REFERENCE—JOSEF LORENZL

- **Austrian sculptor and ceramicist Josef Lorenzl (1892-1950) trained and worked in Vienna.**
- **Lorenzl used bronze and ivory to sculpt figurines predominantly of slim female dancers with elongated limbs. The bronze figurines are usually cold-painted or silvered.**
- **The signature of "Crejo," the craftsman who enameled some of Lorenzl's figurines, appears on some of his work. Lorenzl also designed ceramic figurines for Goldscheider.**

An Art Deco bronze figurine of a nude dancer, by Josef Lorenzl, on onyx base, signed indistinctly to cast.

ca. 1925 *9¾in (25cm) high*

$700-850 HAN

An Art deco lacquered gilt-bronze nude figurine, by Josef Lorenzl, on onyx base, signed "R. Lor, Austria."

ca. 1930 *8in (20.5cm) high*

$900-1,050 ROS

A silvered bronze figurine of a dancer, by Josef Lorenzl, signed, on an onyx plinth.

10½in (26.5cm) high

$650-800 SWO

An Art Deco cold-painted bronze and ivory figurine of a woman, by Josef Lorenzl, modeled with a scarf hanging from each wrist, on onyx plinth, engraved "Lorenzl" on base.

ca. 1930 *8¾in (22.5cm) high*

$1,900-2,600 ROS

A bronzed figurine of a nude dancing girl, by Josef Lorenzl, signed, on onyx plinth, chips on base, some wear.

11in (28cm) high

$1,900-2,600 GORL

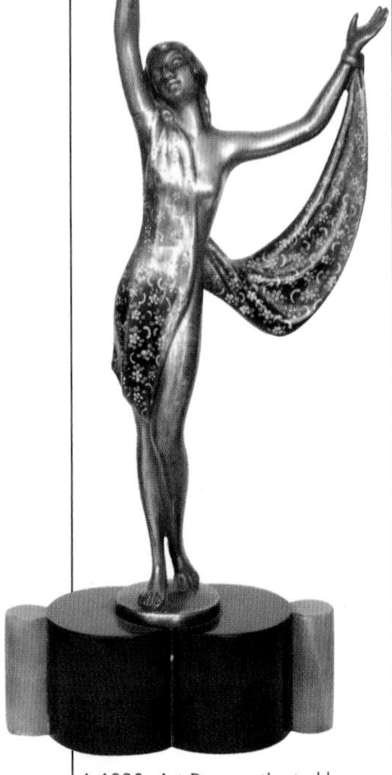

A 1920s Art Deco patinated bronze figurine of a semiclad female, by Josef Lorenzl, her robes enameled with floral sprays, signed, on an onyx base.

12¼in (31cm) high

$1,900-2,600 FLD

An Art Deco patinated gilt bronze dancer, by Josef Lorenzl, on onyx base, signed in the bronze, some surface wear.

12in (30.5cm) high

$1,600-2,100 CHEF

An Art Deco bronze figurine of a scarf dancer, by Josef Lorenzl, signed, on onyx plinth.

4¾in (12cm) high

$500-650 FLD

A 1920s French Art Deco spelter figurine, by Roland, Paris, of an exotic dancer in Egyptian revival-style costume, on a marble base.

14¼in (36cm) high

$260-320 FLD

A 1920s Vienna gilded and silvered painted bronze "Musette" figurine, on a marble base.

7½in (19cm) high

$650-800 QU

A 1930s Art Deco patinated bronze figurine of a female nude standing provocatively in a fur coat, by Bruno Zach, on a variegated black marble base, unsigned.

11½in (29cm) high

$2,600-3,200 FLD

A CLOSER LOOK AT A SPELTER FIGURINE

Although often thought of as much inferior to bronze, spelter figurines can be highly desirable.

The beauty of its finished patina (when spelter is cast it is produced without flaws) creates sculptural works that are perfect in form.

Spelter was first introduced to Europe from Asia by Dutch and Portuguese traders in the 17thC.

This figurine has all the movement and style that typifies Art Deco.

An Art Deco silvered spelter figurine of a female dancer, on a marble base, figurine loose on base, some rubbing to paint.

20in (50.5cm) high

$800-900 APAR

An untitled patinated bronze and copper sculpture, by Harry Bertoia, some oxidation.

Italian-born Harry Bertoia (1915-78) attended and taught at the Cranbrook Academy of Art in Michigan. Bertoia is known for his sculpture, prints, jewelry, and furniture. He died in 1978.

16in (40.5cm) high

$45,000-52,000 DRA

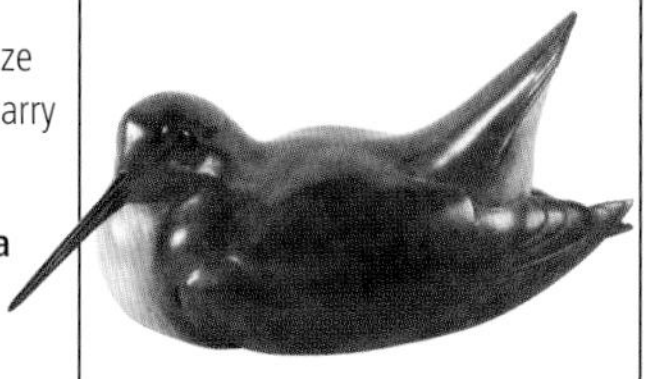

A patinated bronze figurine of a woodcock, by Nick Bibby (b.1960), Britain, limited edition no.11 of 12.

9in (23cm) long

$1,900-2,600 CHOR

A patinated bronze figurine of a partridge, by Geoffrey Dashwood (b.1947), Great Britain, limited edition no.12 of 12.

8½in (21.5cm) long

$2,600-3,200 CHOR

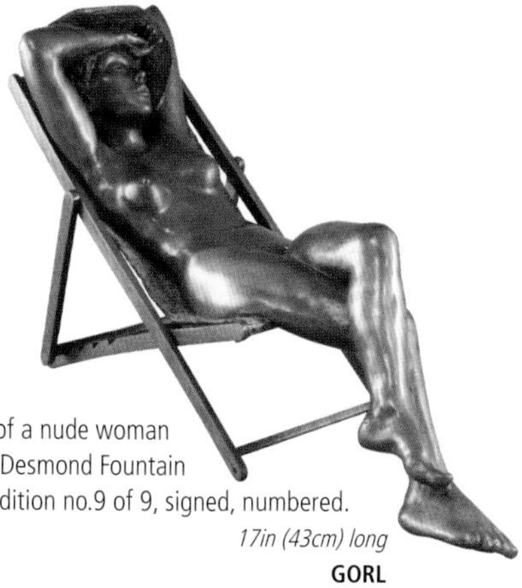

A bronze figurine of a nude woman in a deck chair, by Desmond Fountain (b.1946), limited edition no.9 of 9, signed, numbered.

17in (43cm) long

$3,900-5,200 GORL

A chrome-plated steel "Eight Elbows" sculpture, by William Pye, stamped "PYE" signature, dated, numbered "2/6" and "25," Redfern Gallery label on underside, light surface pitting.

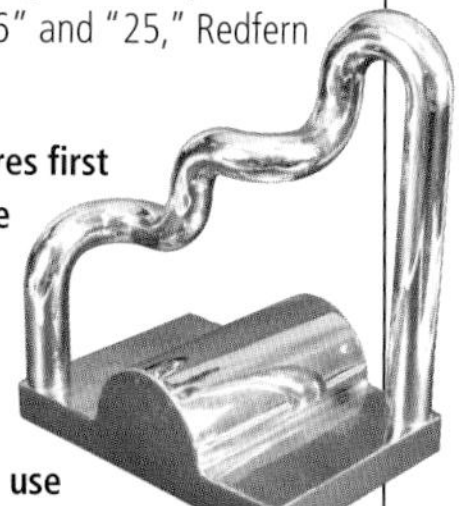

"Eight Elbows" was part of a series of sculptures first exhibited by Pye in his second solo show at the Redfern Gallery, London. Although an abstract composition, it was influenced by the rapidly evolving cultural production and industrial terrain of the 1960s. Consisting of eight 90-degree steel elbows welded together, Pye's use of "the tube" was a conscious departure from modeling in order to lower "immediate sensuality" and mask the effort involved in its production. See William Pye, Rupert Brown, and Oliver Brown, *William Pye, His Work and Words*, Brown & Brown (2010), pp.52-53.

1968 *13in (33cm) high*

$6,500-8,000 CHEF

QUICK REFERENCE—SEWING

- **Most sewing accessories available to collectors date from the 19thC and early 20thC. Items from the 18thC and earlier, before mass production made these items common, are especially prized.**
- **Collectors tend to focus on one type of sewing tool or accessory, such as thimbles, pincushions, or needle cases. Pincushions were very widely produced and remain popular with collectors, in part due to the aesthetic appeal of novelty pincushions.**
- **Sewing accessories and tools were made from a range of materials, including silver, gold, ivory, bone, mother-of-pearl, tortoiseshell, and wood. Silver pieces became increasingly common in the early-19thC period, because the price of silver dropped.**

An early-20th silver duck pincushion, by Abrahall & Bint, Birmingham.
1905 *4in (10cm) long*
$450-500 **WW**

An early-20thC silver gondola pincushion, by Adie & Lovekin Ltd., Birmingham, velvet cushion.
1906 *3¾in (9.5cm) long*
$230-290 **WW**

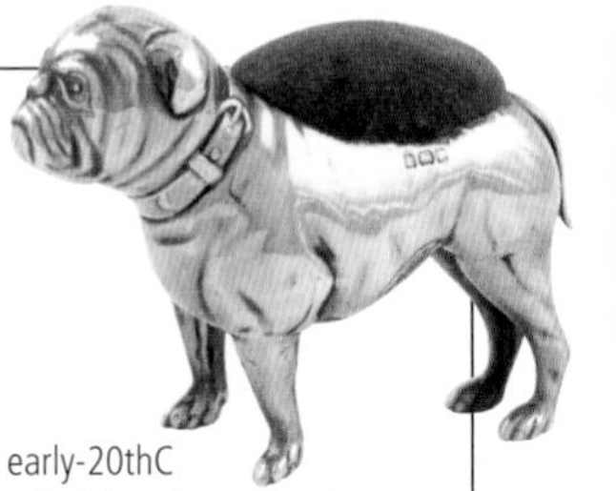

An early-20thC silver bulldog pincushion, by Adie & Lovekin Ltd., Birmingham, later cushion.

Adie & Lovekin was established in Birmingham in the latter half of the 19thC by Alfred Lovekin and James Adie. The company, which produced silver items, including pincushions, buckles, button hooks, and baby rattles, became Adie & Lovekin Ltd. in 1889. The company closed in the late 1920s.
1906 *2in (5cm) high*
$400-500 **WW**

An early-20thC silver camel and cart pincushion, by Adie & Lovekin Ltd., Birmingham, the camel pulling a mother-of-pearl cart, one wheel damaged.
1909 *5in (12.5cm) long*
$600-650 **WW**

An early-20thC silver goat pincushion, by Adie & Lovekin Ltd., Birmingham, one green glass eye.
1909 *1¾in (4.5cm) high*
$650-700 **WW**

An early-20thC silver swan pincushion, by Adie & Lovekin Ltd., Birmingham, set with glass eyes.
1909 *3in (7.5cm) long*
$400-450 **WW**

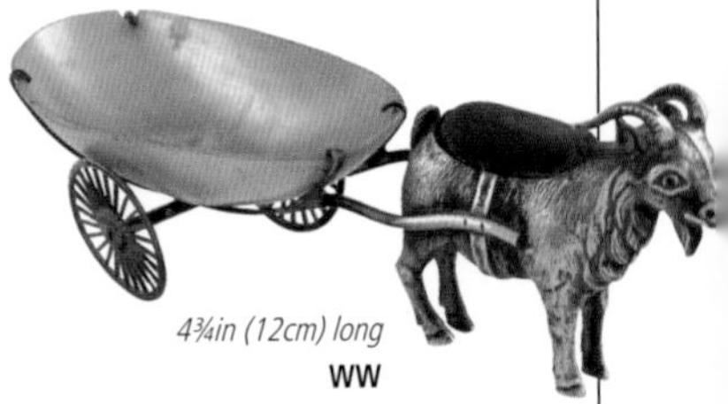

An early-20thC silver billy goat and cart pincushion, by Adie & Lovekin Ltd., Birmingham, the goat pulling a mother-of-pearl cart.
1909 *4¾in (12cm) long*
$900-1,050 **WW**

A silver Newfoundland dog pincushion, by Adie & Lovekin Ltd., Birmingham, with green glass eyes, date letter worn.
2¼in (5.5cm) long
$1,250-1,450 **WW**

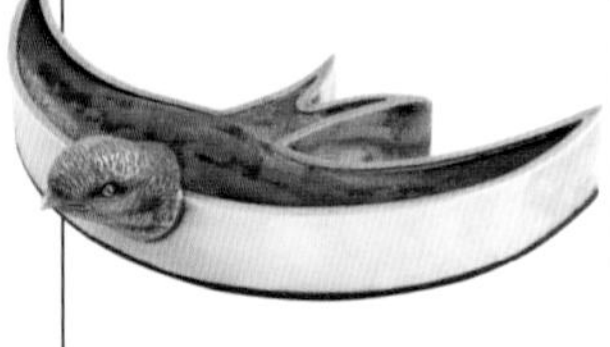

A late-19thC silver "flying swallow" pincushion, by James Samuel Bell & Louis Willmott, London.
1895 *5in (12.5cm) long*
$950-1,100 **WW**

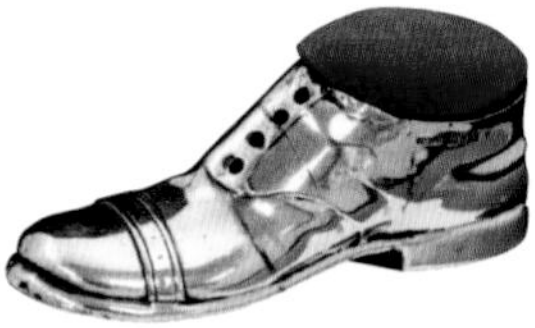

A early-20thC silver shoe pincushion, by S. Blanckensee & Son, Chester.

S. Blanckensee & Son was founded by Solomon Blanckensee in Bristol in the early 19thC. The firm went on to acquire silversmiths Nathan & Hayes, Albion Chain Co. and J.W. Tiptaft Ltd., among others.
1910
$180-230 **HAN**

A silver pincushion, by S. Blanckensee & Sons Ltd., Chester, modeled as the ship *Royal George*, with a rudder and propeller.
1910 *5¼in (13.5cm) long*
$600-700 **WW**

An early-20thC silver hare pincushion, by Boots Pure Drug Co., Birmingham.
1907 *2¼in (5.5cm) long*
$500-650 **WW**

A silver lizard pincushion, by Crisford & Norris Ltd., Birmingham, with red cabochon eyes.

1913 *4¼in (11cm) long*

$800-850 **WW**

A late-19thC silver moon pincushion, by Deakin and Sons, London, set with five stars, velvet cushion.

1894 *3in (7.5cm) long*

$300-400 **WW**

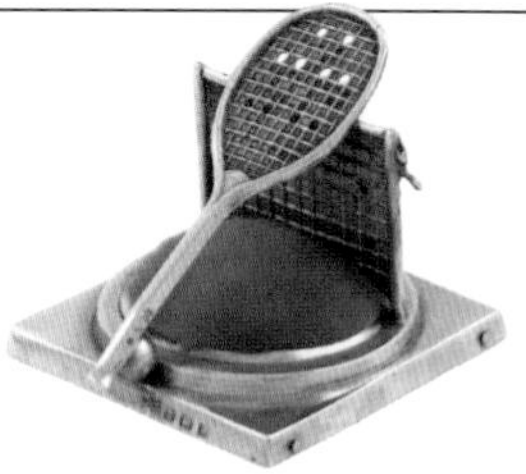

An early-20thC silver pincushion, by Jones & Crompton, Birmingham, modeled as a tennis racket leaning against a tennis net.

1909 *1½in (4cm) high*

$800-900 **WW**

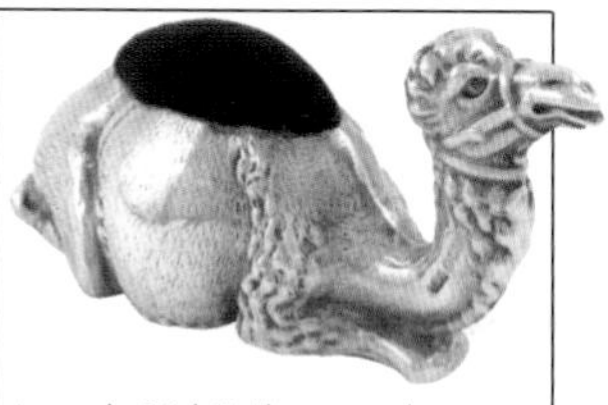

An early-20thC silver camel pincushion, by Levi & Salaman, Birmingham.

Levi & Salaman was founded in ca. 1870 in Birmingham by Phineas Harris Levi and Joseph Wolff Salaman. The company produced jewelry and silver items. In 1878, Levi & Salaman bought Potosi Silver, a manufacturer of silverplate cutlery. The company became Levi & Salaman Ltd. in 1910.

1903 *4in (10cm) long*

$900-1,050 **WW**

An early-20thC silver hedgehog pincushion, by Levi & Salaman, Birmingham.

1905 *1¾in (4.5cm) long*

$400-450 **WW**

An early-20thC silver bull pincushion, by Levi & Salaman, Birmingham.

1905 *2¼in (5.5cm) long*

$500-600 **WW**

A silver robin pincushion, by Levi & Salaman Ltd., Birmingham, modeled as a robin holding a golf club, with original red padded chest.

1910 *4in (10cm) high*

$900-1,050 **WW**

An early-20thC silver arched cat pincushion, by Levi & Salaman, Birmingham.

This is an unusual pincushion and also appeals to cat collectors.

1905 *2¼in (5.5cm) long*

$1,600-2,100 **WW**

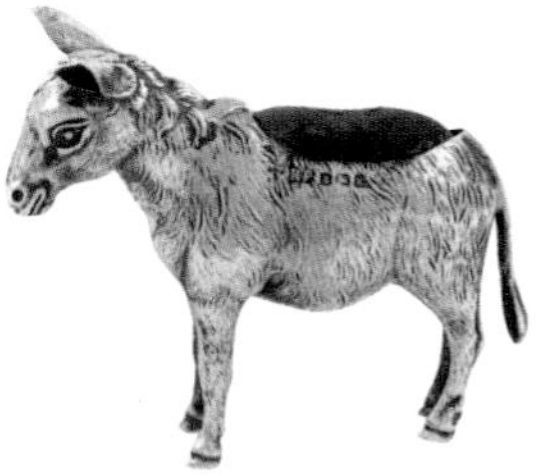

An early-20thC silver donkey pincushion, by Robert Pringle, Birmingham.

1909 *2½in (6.5cm) high*

$800-900 **WW**

A silver hatching chick pincushion, by S. Mordan & Co., Chester, dent on front, replaced fabric.

1907 *2½in (6.5cm) high*

$190-260 **DN**

An early-20thC silver-mounted leather boot pincushion, hallmarked Samuel M. Levi, Birmingham 1909, Rd 556959.

1909 *3in (7.5cm) long*

$160-210 **FELL**

An early-20thC silver tortoise pincushion, by Saunders and Shepherd, Birmingham.

1906 *2in (5cm) long*

$500-650 **WW**

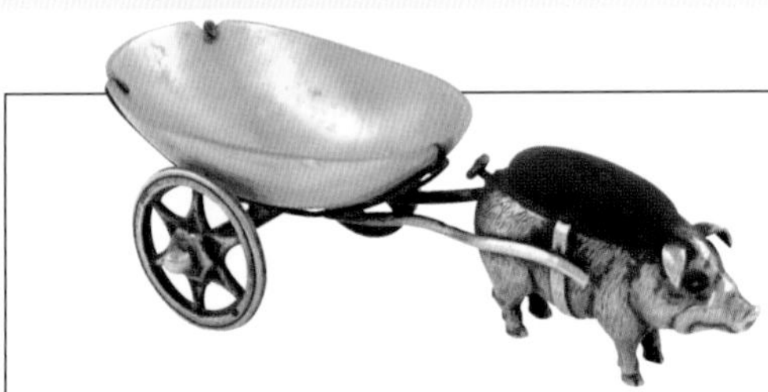

An early-20thC silver pig and cart pincushion, by Sydney & Co., Birmingham, the pig pulling a mother-of-pearl cart.
1909 *3¾in (9.5cm) long*
$600-700 **WW**

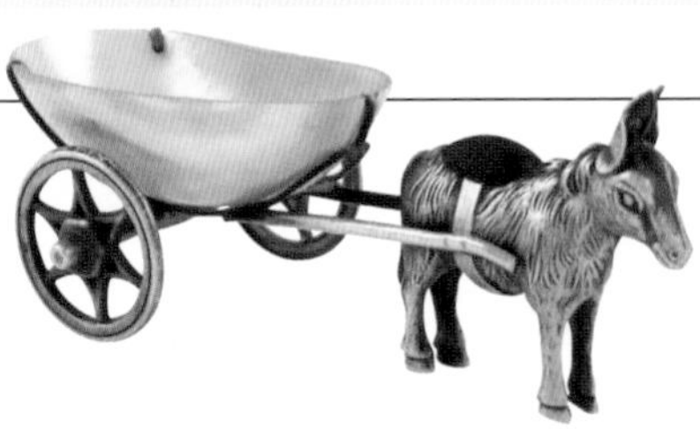

A silver donkey and cart pincushion, by Sydney & Co., Birmingham, the donkey pulling a mother-of-pearl cart.
1910 *3¼in (8.5cm) long*
$600-700 **WW**

An early-20thC silver fox pincushion, by Walker & Hall, Birmingham.
1906 *2½in (6.5cm) long*
$650-800 **WW**

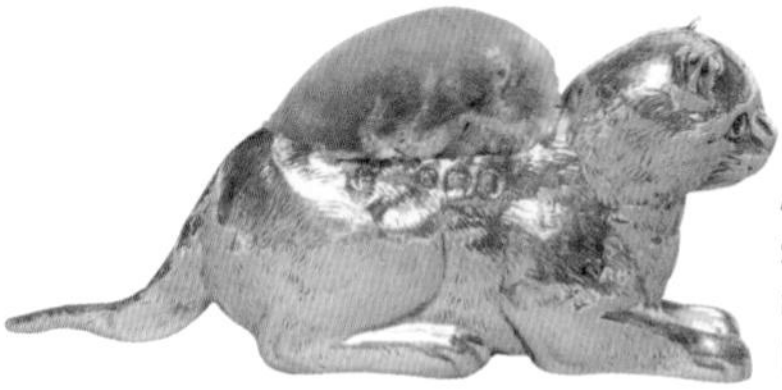

An early-20thC silver cat pincushion, maker probably W.J. Myatt & Co. Ltd.
1908 *1¼in (3cm) high*
$500-600 **HT**

A 19thC silver butterfly pincushion, with spread velvet wings, maker's mark worn.
1894 *5in (12.5cm) long*
$450-600 **WW**

An early-20thC silver chicken pincushion, importer's mark of S. Landeck, import marks for Chester.
1901 *4¼in (11cm) long*
$500-650 **WW**

An early-20thC silver porcupine pincushion, maker's mark worn.
1902 *2¾in (7cm) long*
$400-500 **WW**

A silver elephant pincushion, maker's mark "A. & L. LTD.," Birmingham.
1905 *2½in (6.5cm) long*
$260-320 **JN**

An early-20thC silver bulldog pincushion, no maker's mark.
1906 *2in (5cm) high*
$400-500 **WW**

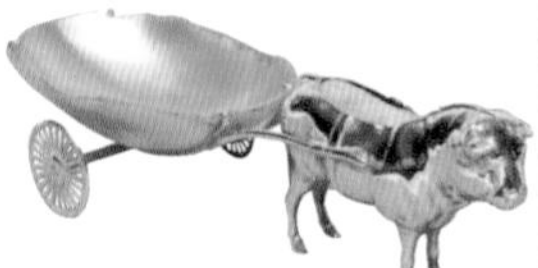

An early-20thC silver ox and cart pincushion, the ox pulling a polished shell cart on fixed wheel axle, maker's mark rubbed.
1909 *6in (15cm) long*
$400-500 **HT**

A 19thC silver sewing egg, the gilded interior with holes for pins, a centered column for cotton reels, maker's mark worn, and a later thimble.
1891 *2¼in (5.5cm) long*
$400-500 **WW**

A 19thC sewing machine, designed by Elias Howe, serial no.1401266.
$45-60 **LOCK**

A Singer "222k Featherweight" electric sewing machine, with original instructions, in original case.
$650-800 **LOCK**

A "Shakespear 19thC" sewing machine, with plaque that reads "Not for an Age, But for All Time, The Royal Sewing Machine Co. Birmingham."
ca. 1870
$170-230 **LOCK**

A possibly American folding enamel thimble, with floral decoration.
$80-90 **LOCK**

A 19thC 15-carat gold thimble, maker's mark partly worn, Birmingham 1899, in a later case.
0.15oz
$260-320 **WW**

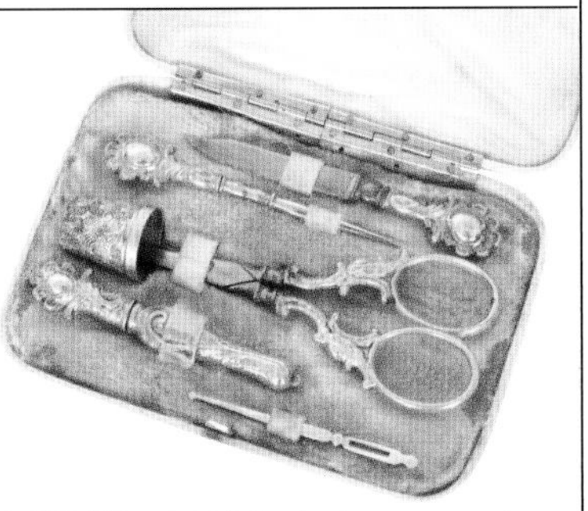

A 19thC French etui, the ivorine case opening to interior with six silver sewing implements, with a matched thimble.
$260-320 **FLD**

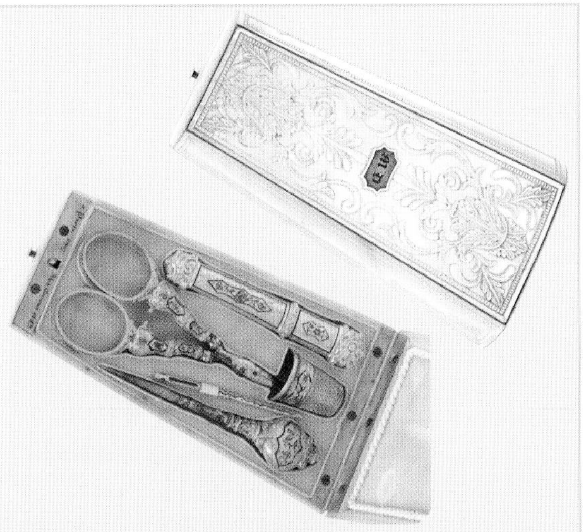

A 19thC French etui, the mother-of-pearl case opening to fitted interior, with five sewing implements with enamel highlights, case engraved "Paris Chez Alph Giroux et Cie."
$900-1,050 **FLD**

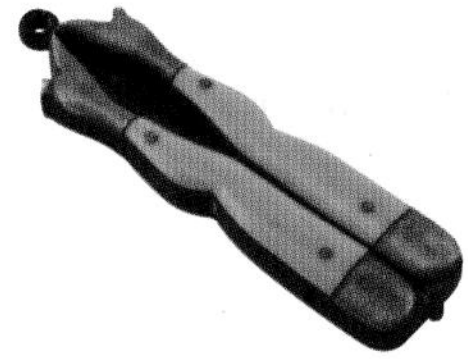

A pair of scissors, in the shape of a lady's legs.
$80-90 **LOCK**

A 19thC William Francis Garrud silver chatelaine, with a tape measure case, Levi & Salaman, Birmingham 1888, a vesta case, George Unite, Birmingham 1875, a scent bottle, Edwin Culver, London 1876, and a notepad case, Heinrich Levinger, Birmingham 1900.
12½in (32cm) long 7½oz
$160-230 **APAR**

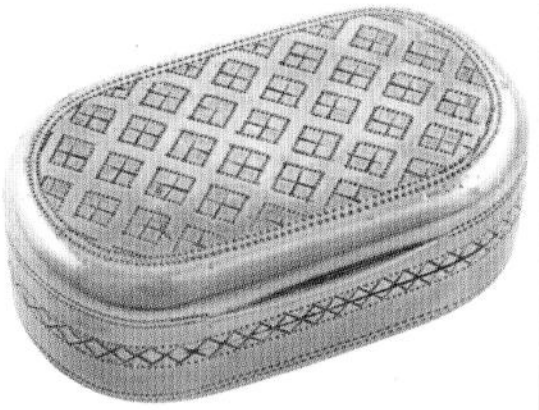

A late-18thC silver-gilt vinaigrette, probably by John Bough, London.
1803 *1¾in (4.5cm) long 0.7oz*
$400-500 **WW**

A late-18thC silver-gilt vinaigrette, possibly by William Thompson II, London, maker's mark "WT."
1804
$300-400 **FLD**

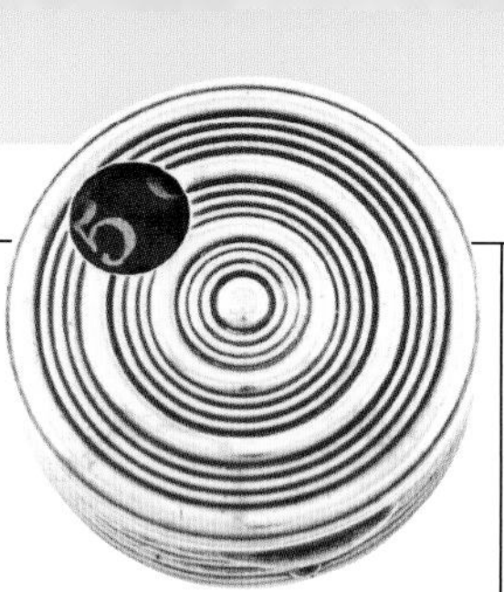

A late-18thC silver vinaigrette/whist marker, by Matthew Linwood, Birmingham, the hinged cover with a turning wheel and numbered 1-10, lacking pin.
1805 *1¼in (3cm) diam 0.8oz*
$800-900 **WW**

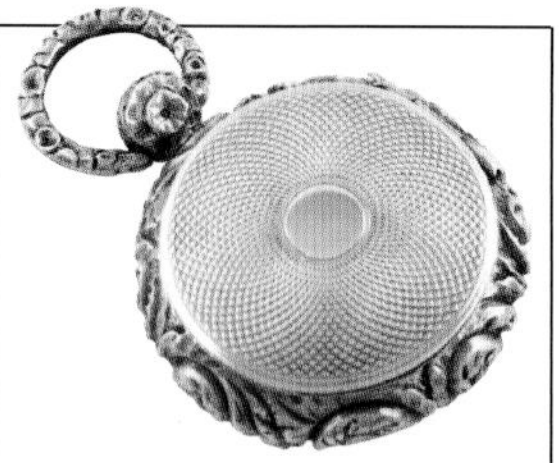

A late-18thC silver-gilt pocket watch vinaigrette, by Samuel Pemberton, Birmingham, the reverse a glass locket compartment.
1816 *1¼in (3cm) diam 0.8oz*
$650-800 **WW**

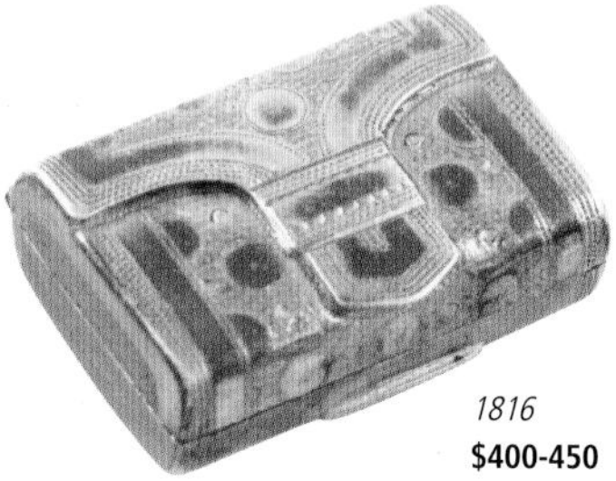

A late-18thC silver-gilt purse vinaigrette, by Joseph Willmore, Birmingham.
1816 *1¼in (3cm) long 0.4oz*
$400-450 **WW**

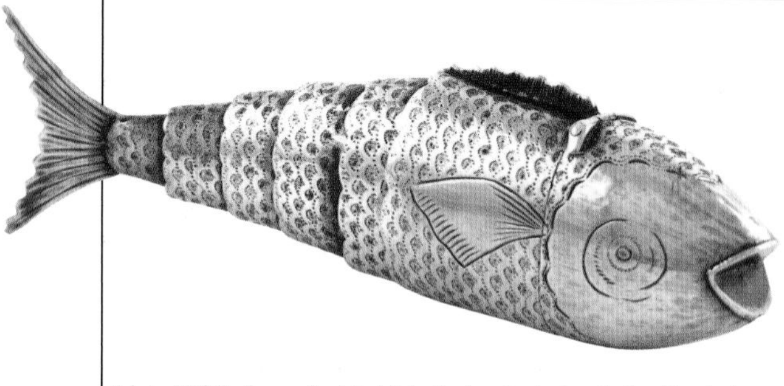

A late-18thC silver reticulated fish vinaigrette, by Lea & Co., Birmingham.
1817 *3¼in (8.5cm) long 0.6oz*
$1,600-1,900 **WW**

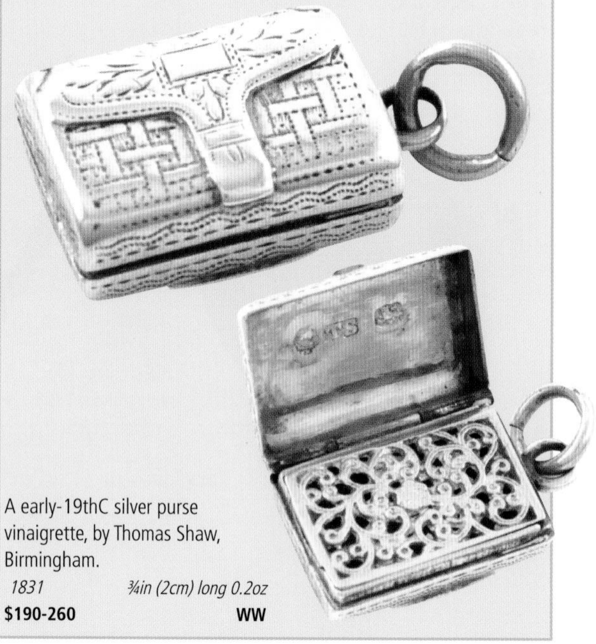

A early-19thC silver purse vinaigrette, by Thomas Shaw, Birmingham.
1831 *¾in (2cm) long 0.2oz*
$190-260 **WW**

A 19thC silver "castle-top" vinaigrette, by Nathaniel Mills, Birmingham, of Kenilworth Castle.
1837 *1½in (4cm) long 0.7oz*
$800-850 **WW**

A silver vinaigrette, by Nathaniel Mills, Birmingham.
1841 *1¾in (4.5cm) long 0.6oz*
$260-320 **WW**

A silver "castle-top" vinaigrette, by Nathaniel Mills, of Abbotsford House.
1848 *1½in (4cm) long*
$850-950 **FLD**

A 19thC New Zealand silver tobacco/vesta box, by Stewart Dawson and Co., Dunedin and Wellington.

See p. 338 for other vesta cases.

2¾in (7cm) long 1.1oz

$300-400 **WW**

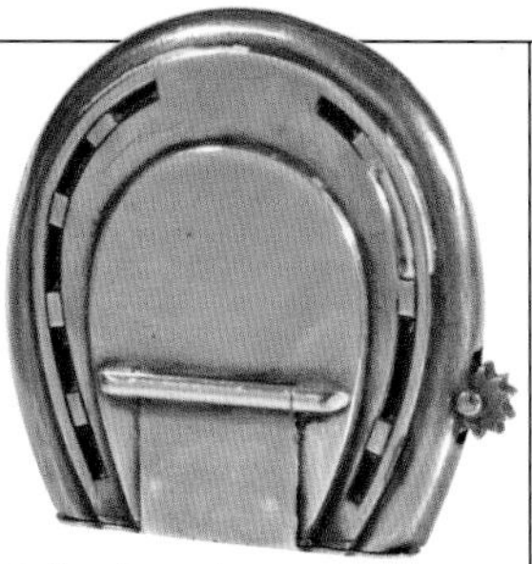

A silver horseshoe vesta case, with base metal striking plate, the side to be threaded with a wick operated by a spoked wheel, maker's mark misstruck, Birmingham.

1871 *2in (5cm) long*

$160-190 **DN**

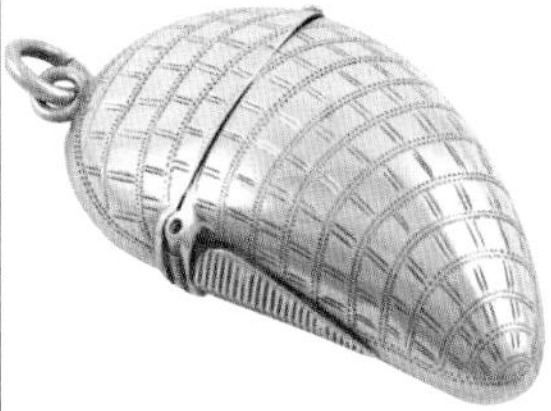

A silver mussel shell vesta case, by Hilliard and Thomason, Birmingham.

1888 *2¼in (5.5cm) long 0.5oz*

$650-800 **WW**

An Art Nouveau silver vesta case, by Charles Lyster & Son, Chester, with an embossed portrait of Queen Victoria, inscribed with "RD274173."

1900 *2in (5cm) high 1oz*

$400-450 **MART**

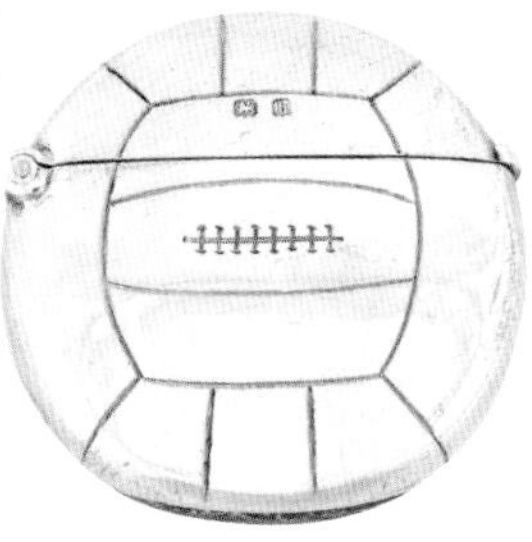

A silver football vesta case, maker possibly J.H. Hillcox, retailed by George Maurice & Co., Birmingham.

1907 *0.81oz*

$500-600 **BELL**

A silver sovereign/vesta case, by H. Matthews, Birmingham, lid with striker.

1911 *3in (7.5cm) long 1oz*

$190-260 **WW**

A silver dog and kennel table vesta case, by L. Emmanuel, Birmingham, back with a striker.

1917 *2in (5cm) long 2.5oz*

$600-650 **WW**

A silver card case, by Nathaniel Mills, Birmingham, with figure leaning on a lyre, some damages.

1846 *4in (10cm) long*

$400-450 **FLD**

A silver "castle-top" card case, by Nathaniel Mills, Birmingham, of The Scott Memorial.

1848 *4in (10cm) long 2.5oz*

$1,150-1,450 **WW**

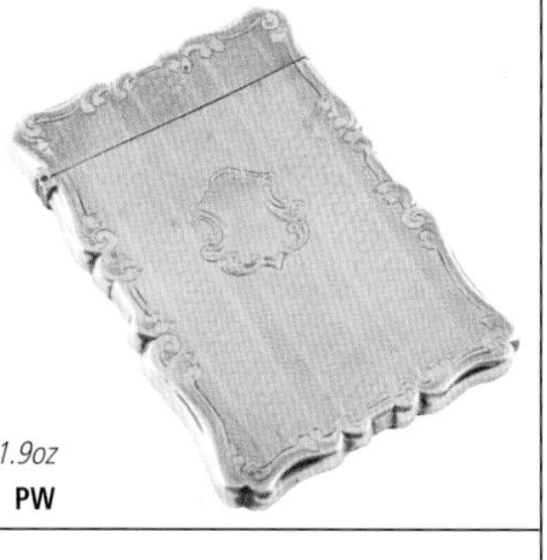

A silver card case, by Owen & Boon, Birmingham.

1856 *4in (10cm) high 1.9oz*

$140-190 **PW**

An early-19thC silver "castle-top" card case, of Battle Abbey, Sussex, maker's mark "T&W," possibly for Birmingham maker Tongue & Walker.

3¾in (9.5cm) long

$300-350 **DN**

A mid-18thC silver and agate snuff box.
ca. 1750 *3¼in (8.5cm) long*
$230-290 **WW**

A late-18thC silver and parcel-gilt Neoclassical snuff box, maker "TP ER," London.
1810 *3¾in (9.5cm) long*
$400-450 **WHP**

A late-18thC silver-gilt snuff box, by Robert Mitchell & Co., Birmingham.
1811 *2in (5cm) long 0.7oz*
$500-600 **WW**

A late-18thC silver snuff box, by Thomas Shaw, Birmingham, the cover with men around a table with a harp player.
1828 *2¾in (7cm) long 3.4oz*
$400-450 **WW**

An early-19thC silver and mother-of-pearl snuff box.
2¼in (5.5cm) long
$260-320 **WW**

A early-19thC silver snuff box, by Nathaniel Mills, Birmingham, with two coats of arms with mottos, rubbing on marks.
1831 *6oz*
$1,050-1,150 **ECGW**

A Russian silver and niello snuff box, by Ivan Kaltikov, Moscow, 84 zolotniki, engraved with the Bronze Horseman statue of Peter the Great in the Senate Square, Saint Petersburg.
1836 *3¼in (8.5cm) long 3.2oz*
$190-260 **DN**

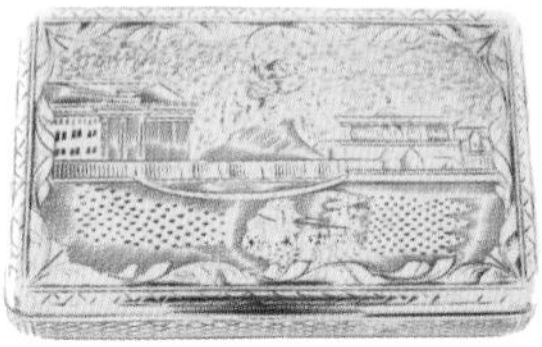

An early-19thC "castle-top" snuff box, by Edward Smith, Birmingham, of Abbotsford House, the underside engraved "Elma."
3in (7.5cm) wide 2.6oz
$500-600 **CHEF**

A snuff box, by Nathaniel Mills, Birmingham.
1843 *2½in (6.5cm) wide 1.8oz*
$450-500 **PSA**

A silver-mounted snuff mull, the horn body carved as a stylized horse's head, with a plaque inscribed "Mrs J. Gourlay, 1852."
ca. 1850 *3½in (9cm) long*
$650-700 **WW**

A silver naval snuff box, by Asprey and Co. Ltd., London, engraved with a battleship, interior engraved with the badge of the Women's Royal Navy Service and inscribed "14 Oct. 42," and "Evelyn."
1940 *3in (7.5cm) long 2.7oz*
$260-320 **WW**

A silver owl pepperette, by George Fox, London, with glass eyes and stylised foliate piercing.
1863 *3¼in (8.5cm) high 2oz*
$600-650 **FELL**

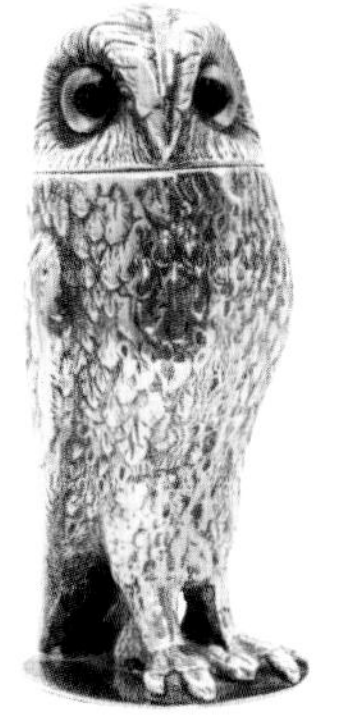

A silver owl pepperette, by Hawksworth, Eyre & Co., with glass eyes.
1867 *3¼in (8.5cm) high 2oz*
$600-650 **FLD**

Two pairs of matching 19thC silver owl casters, by Richards & Brown, London, with glass eyes, stamped "7433," "7432, "6939," "6938," some denting.
1871 *3¼in (8.5cm) high 5.6oz*
$1,150-1,300 **CHEF**

A pair of silver owl salt and pepper pots, by Francis Higgins and Sons Ltd., London.
1938 *2¾in (7cm) high 6oz*
$900-1,050 **WW**

QUICK REFERENCE—ROYAL CONNECTIONS

- **Queen Charlotte, of Mecklenburg-Strelitz, was the queen consort of the late 18thC. Between 1789 and 1805, the royal family visited Weymouth. Sea bathing was thought to benefit the king's health. In 1789, the family stayed with the king's brother, the Duke of Gloucester, at Gloucester Lodge (later called Royal Lodge). They visited regularly until 1805, when the king's deteriorating health prevented them from traveling.**
- **The initials "RH" are reputed to have been those of the daughter of the king's physician, Sir William Heberden junior. He was the queen's personal doctor and probably visited Dorset with the family.**

A late-18thC silver mustard pot, by Robert Hennell I, London, with a blue glass liner, engraved "The Gift of the Queen, Weymouth 1796" and "RH," with an old English salt spoon, by Thomas Wallace, London 1794.
1795 *2½in (6.5cm) high 3.65oz*
$950-1,100 **DN**

An Austrian silver elephant salt pot, by Georg Adam Scheid, blue stone eyes, later resin tusks, stamped "Ges Gesch."
3in (7.5cm) high 1.7oz
$700-800 **WW**

A late-18thC silver mustard pot, by Hester Bateman, London, engraved with a crest, with a glass liner.

The crest is that of Mortlock, for John George Mortlock, of Melbourn and Meldreth, Cambridgeshire.
1787 *4in (10cm) long 2.4oz*
$500-600 **WW**

A late-18thC silver barrel mustard pot, maker's mark worn, with a blue glass liner and a spoon, London.
1800
$190-260 **WW**

A early-19thC silver mustard pot, by William Bateman, London, engraved with a crest.
1835 *4in (10cm) 6.2oz*
$800-850 **WW**

A silver drum mustard pot, by Samuel Whitford, London, with a later blue glass liner.
1867 *3in (7.5cm) high 5.5oz*
$300-400 **WW**

A silver mouse box, by Thomas Johnson, London.
1885 *3in (7.5cm) long 2oz*
$850-900 **WW**

A silver duck cream boat, by George Fox, London.
1869 *4in (10cm) long 2.6oz*
$1,050-1,150 **WW**

An electroplated silver bee honeypot, by Mappin and Webb, screw-out glass body.
6¼in (16cm) long
$500-650 **WW**

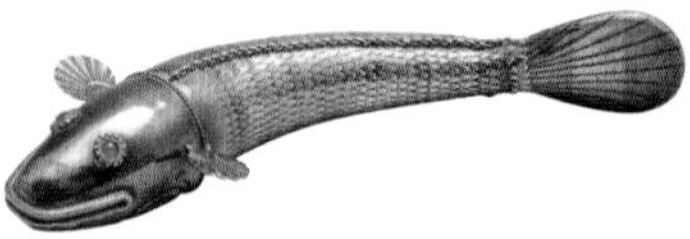

A silver koi carp, with inset red paste eyes, unmarked.
7in (18cm) long 2.9oz
$450-500 **FELL**

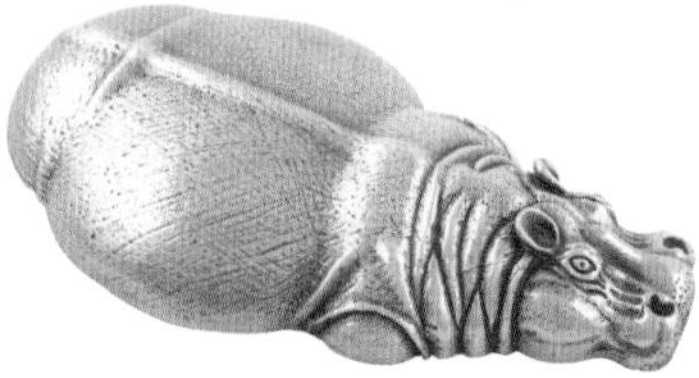

A Zimbabwean silver model of a hippo, by Patrick Mavros, signed, and Zimbabwean hallmarks.
5¼in (13.5cm) long 7.7oz
$1,050-1,150 **WW**

A silver-gilt cookie jar, by Atkin Brothers, Sheffield, engraved "1881-1931, 16th Feb from C.M.B.," some wear.
1928 *7¼in (18.5cm) long 24.1oz*
$850-950 **DN**

A late-18thC silver filigree toothpick box, cover with a wheatsheaf under glass.
ca. 1790 *3¼in (8.5cm) long 1oz*
$500-600 **WW**

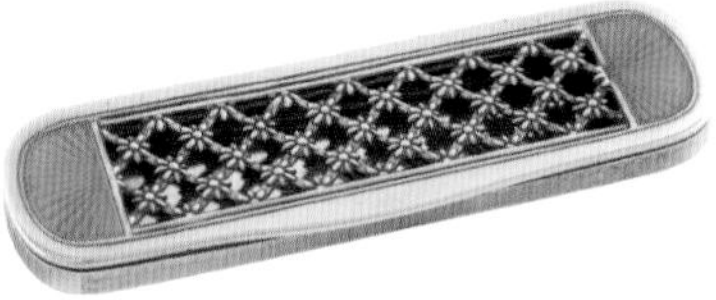

A French silver and pink enamel toothpick box, retailed by E. Dreyfous, Paris.
3¼in (8.5cm) long 1.1oz
$260-320 **WW**

A silver box, sponsor's mark David Bridge, London import marks.
1896 *6¼in (16cm) wide 4.3oz*
$160-210 **CHEF**

A Portuguese silver toothpick holder, maker's mark "IM."
6¾in (17cm) high
$260-320 **WW**

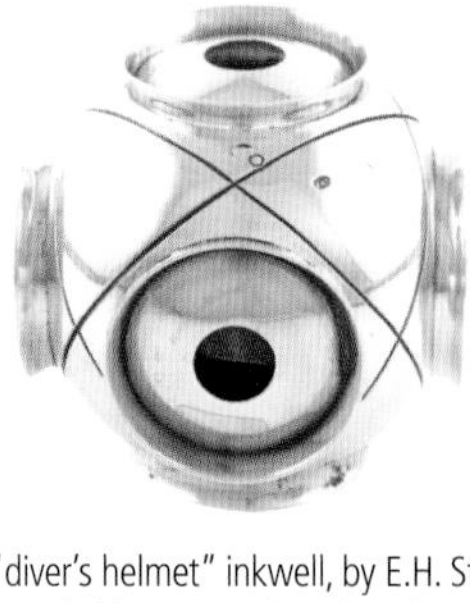

A silver "diver's helmet" inkwell, by E.H. Stockwell, London, retailed by Percy Edwards and Co.
1890 *2¾in (7cm) high*
$700-800 **WW**

A 19thC silver-mounted aide mémoire, by William & Edward Turnpenny, Birmingham, of Emmanuel College on one side and King's College on the other.
1844 *3¼in (8cm) long*
$850-900 **BELL**

A pair of early-20thC silver napkin rings, by S. Glass, Birmingham, embossed with the bust of Shakespeare.

1903 *1.7oz*

$190-260 **WW**

An early-20thC silver Arts and Crafts enamel decorated napkin ring, with stylized floral decoration, maker's mark "L.C. & C.LD.," some wear.

2in (5cm) diam 1.25oz

$260-320 **APAR**

An early-20thC Arts and Crafts silver napkin ring, by Ramsden and Carr, London.

1909 *2¼in (5.5cm) diam 1.1oz*

$300-400 **WW**

An Arts and Crafts silver napkin ring, by Amy Sandheim, London, with centered pink cabouchon flanked by Celtic knot motifs.

1930 *1.39oz*

$300-400 **HAN**

A silver duck napkin ring, by Crisford and Norris, Birmingham.

1913 *3¼in (8.5cm) long*

$260-320 **WW**

A late-18thC silver jockey cap caddy spoon, by Joseph Taylor, Birmingham.

1800 *2in (5cm) long 0.3oz*

$850-900 **WW**

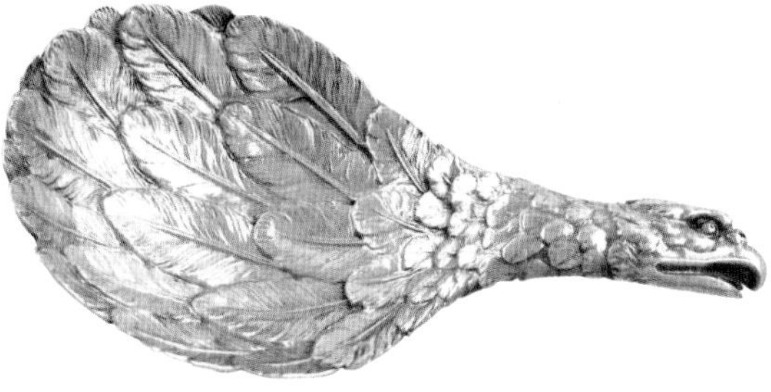

A late-18thC silver eagle's wing caddy spoon, by Joseph Willmore, Birmingham.

1814 *3in (7.5cm) 0.2oz*

$2,600-3,200 **WW**

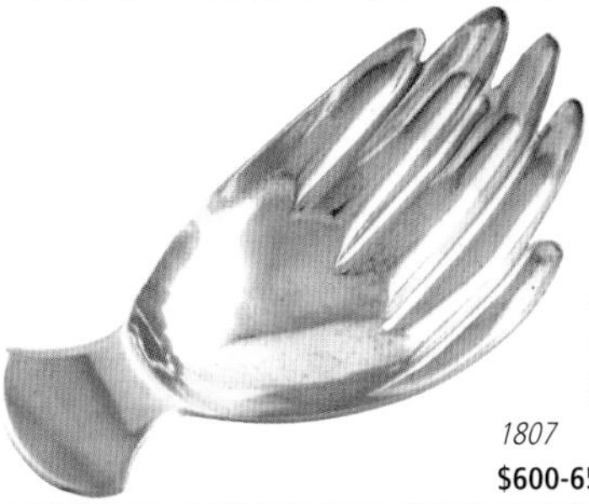

A late-18thC silver caddy spoon, by Josiah Snatt, London.

1807 *2¾in (7cm) long 0.2oz*

$600-650 **WW**

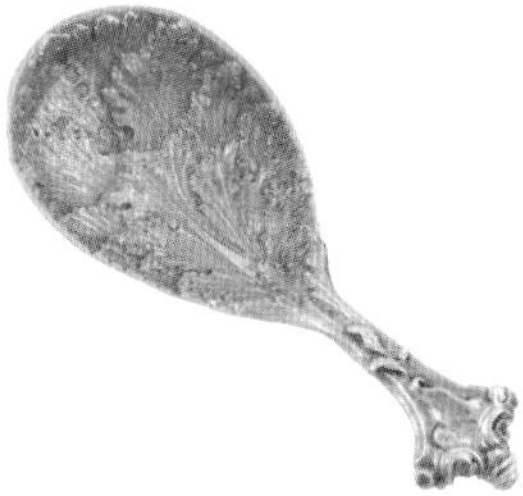

A cast silver caddy spoon, by George Adams, London, initialed.

1848 *3¼in (8.5cm) long 0.6oz*

$600-650 **WW**

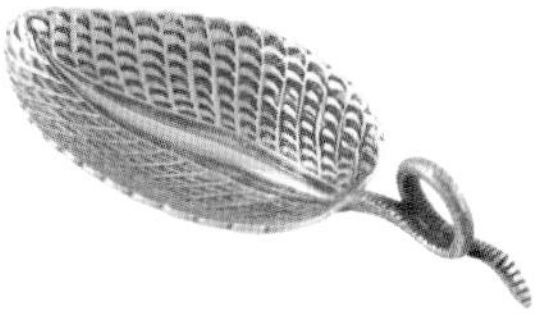

A cast silver caddy spoon, by George Adams, London.

1862 *3in (7.5cm) long 0.5oz*

$600-650 **WW**

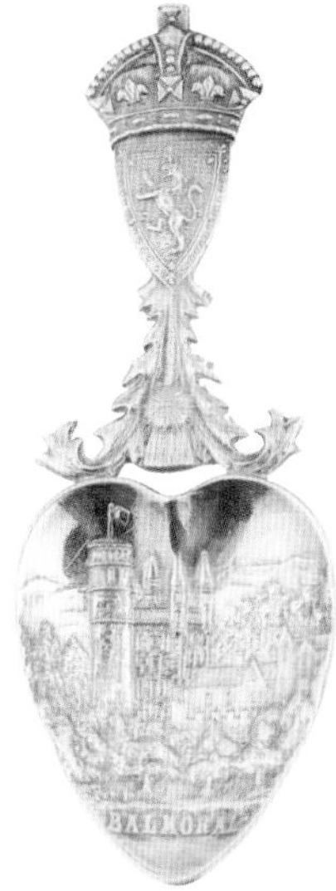

A Scottish Provincial caddy spoon, by William Robb, Ballater, Edinburgh, of Balmoral Castle.

1905 *3½in (9cm) long 0.74oz*

$500-650 **L&T**

A parcel-gilt silver and enamel commemorative caddy spoon, by Stuart Devlin, London, limited edition no.38, celebrating the birth of Prince William, in case.

1982 *2¾in (7cm) long 0.9oz*

$260-320 **WW**

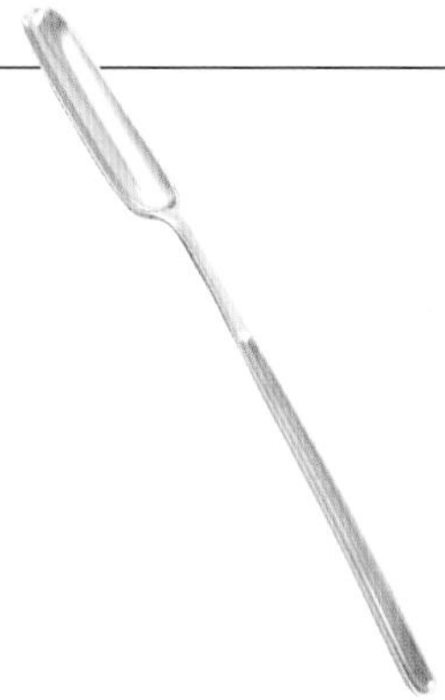

A late-18thC silver marrow scoop, by Peter and Ann Bateman, London.

1799 *9in (23cm) long 1.2oz*

$130-190 **WW**

A Liberty & Co. Cymric silver and enamel coronation spoon, by Archibald Knox, inscribed "Anno Coron ERVII," stamped marks, Birmingham, repaired.

1901 *8in (20.5cm) long*

$950-1,100 **WW**

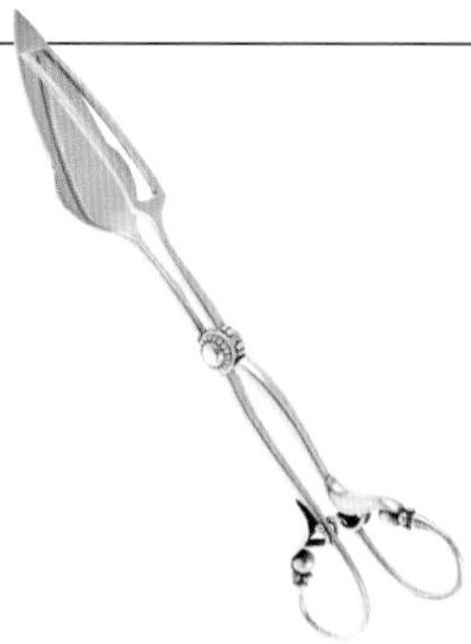

A pair of sandwich tongs, by Georg Jensen, no.141, with berry and leaf motif grips, maker's mark.

8¼in (21cm) long 3.73oz

$300-400 **FELL**

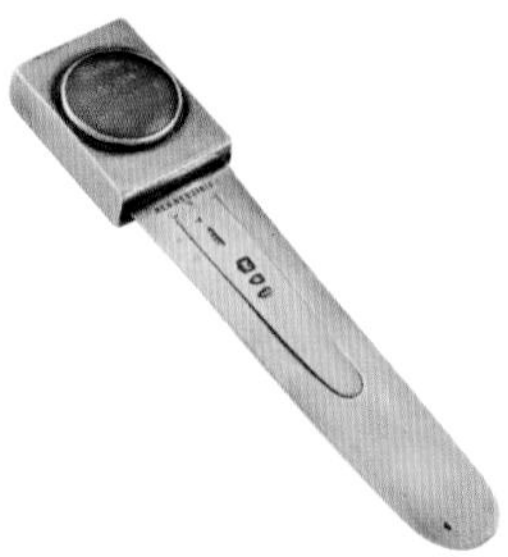

A silver page marker, by S. Mordan and Co., London, the terminal with a magnifying glass and a miniature copy of *The English Dictionary*.

1894 *8in (20.5cm) long*

$300-400 **WW**

A silver paper knife, by Sebastian Garrard, London, inscribed "Presented by H.R.H. Prince and Princess of Wales A.C. Bully Esq. HMS Renown Indian 1905-6."

On October 19, 1905, Prince George and his wife set out on a tour to India. There they traveled to Genoa, where they boarded HMS *Renown* to Bombay. They spent four months in India and often slept on a special train.

1905 *9½in (24cm) long 3.8oz*

$2,100-2,900 **WW**

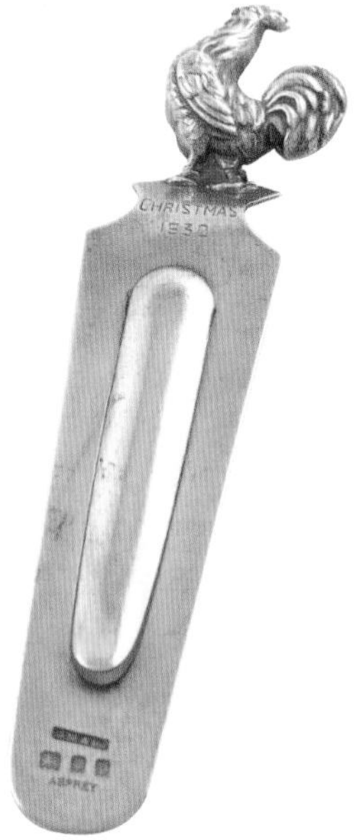

A silver cockerel page marker, by S. Mordan and Co., retailed by Asprey, London.

1930 *3¼in (8.5cm) long 0.4oz*

$260-320 **WW**

A silver mermaid ruler, by William Hutton and Sons, Sheffield.

1923 *12in (30.5cm) long 9.4oz*

$800-850 **WW**

An English silver bridge card suit marker.

1946 *3¼in (8.5cm) high*

$130-190 **FLD**

A 19thC Russian silver spice tower, impressed assay marks for St. Petersburg, with an assay master mark "O.C." over "1888."

12¼in (31cm) high 10oz

$1,700-2,100 **FELL**

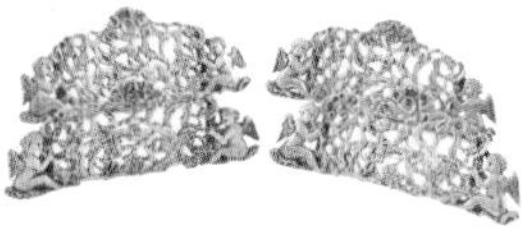

A matched set of four silver menu card holders, two by Brook & Son, Edinburgh, two unmarked, inscribed.

1891 *3¼in (8.5cm) long 3.6oz*

$400-450 **WW**

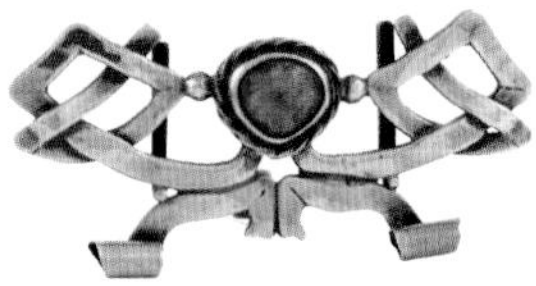

An Edwardian silver and enamel menu card holder, by Ramsden and Carr, London.

1907 *3¼in (8.5cm) long 1.2oz*

$500-600 **WW**

A silver pin stand, by Cornelius Desormeaux Saunders & James Francis Hollings (Frank) Shepherd.
1904 *5½in (14cm) high*
$70-80 **WHP**

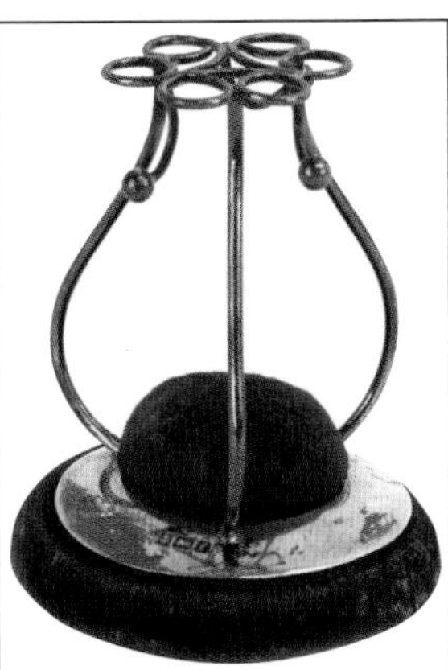

A silver hatpin stand.
1905 *2½in (6.5cm) high*
$60-80 **WHP**

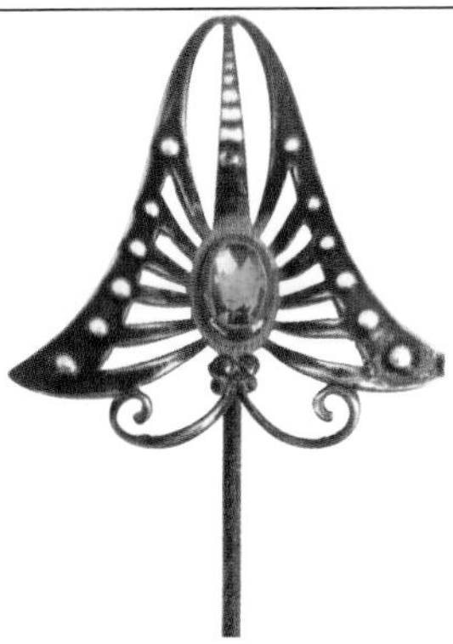

A silver butterfly hatpin, by Charles Horner, with glass inset.
1913 *8¼in (21cm) long*
$120-140 **WHP**

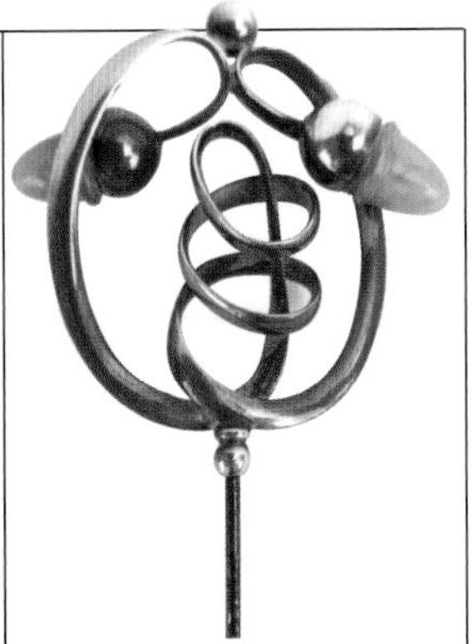

A silver hatpin, by Charles Horner, set two cabochon green beads.
1923 11½in (29cm) long
$160-210 **WHP**

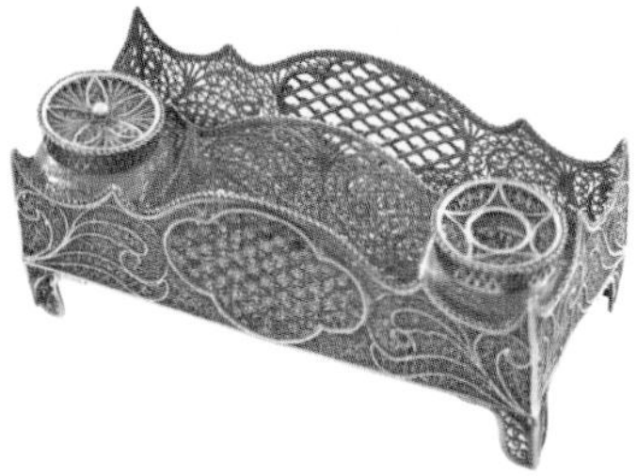

An early-19thC filigree silver inkstand, probably made in Birmingham, with two silver-mounted glass inkwells.
3¼in (8.5cm) long
$400-450 **WW**

An Atkin Brothers silver toast rack, the divisions spelling "TOAST," retailed by Thornhill & Co., Bond St.
1889 *5¼in (13.5cm) high 7oz*
$400-450 **DUK**

A miniature spinning jenny, with articulated wheel and foot pedal, possible Hanau pseudo marks and Austria-Hungary import marks.
ca. 1891-1901 *2¼in (5.5cm) high 0.75oz*
$170-210 **FELL**

An early-20thC silver import miniature steam engine train, by Singleton, Benda & Co Ltd., London, with Foreign mark, and Hanau psuedo marks for Karl Kurz.
1903 *6½in (16.5cm) long 2.82oz*
$500-600 **FELL**

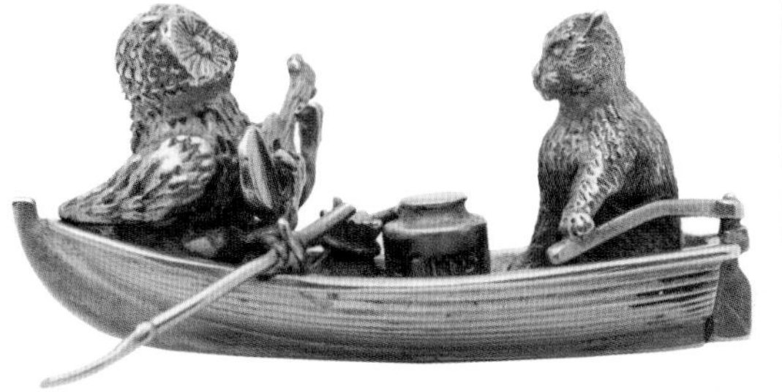

A silver miniature "Owl and The Pussy Cat," by Sarah Jones, London.
1981 *2¼in (5.5cm) long 1.38oz*
$700-800 **BE**

A late-19thC Austro-Hungarian silver and enamel Moor hatpin, in later Cartier box.
$600-650 **WW**

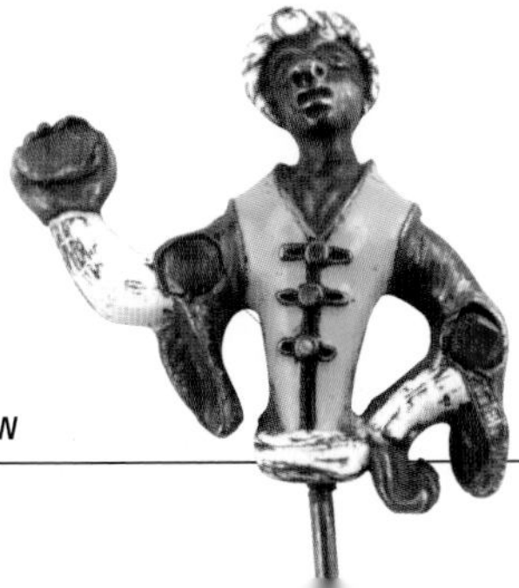

A pair of thistle hatpins, with set polished stone.
9in (23cm) long
$100-110 **WHP**

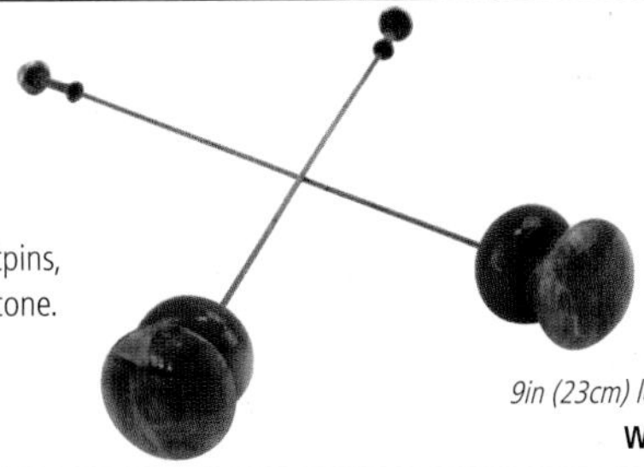

A set of 12 beakers, by Stuart Devlin, London.

Born in Gelong, Australia, Stuart Devlin (1931-2018) studied goldsmithing and silversmithing at the Royal Melbourne Technical College, before studying at the Royal College of Art, London, and Columbia University, New York. In 1965, Devlin set up a goldsmithing and silversmithing workshop, the first of seven, in London. Devlin was granted a royal warrant in 1982, and between 1996 and 1997 he worked as prime warden for the Goldsmith's Company.

1969-72 *4¼in (11cm) high 3oz*

$8,500-9,500 **L&T**

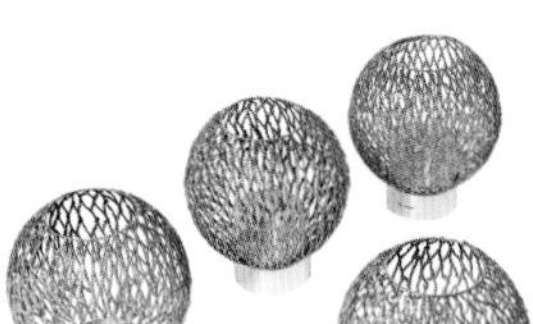

A set of four parcel-gilt-silver candle holders, by Stuart Devlin, with three glass liners and four detachable pierced wirework spherical shades.

1970 *5½in (14cm) high 41oz*

$7,000-8,500 **SOU**

A Bristol "600" silver goblet, by Stuart Devlin, with gilt-washed interior, stamped to underside and numbered "12/600," London.

1973 *6in (15cm) high 13¼oz*

$400-500 **LSK**

A parcel-gilt silver rose bowl centerpiece, by Stuart Devlin, the pierced silver-gilt wirework cover with six holders, mounted with bark effect finial inset with an amethyst crystal, London.

1975 *6¼in (16cm) high 19oz*

$3,900-4,500 **SOU**

A matched set of seven Elizabeth II silver and gilt champagne flutes, by Stuart Devlin, London, with gilded stems.

1977-81 *8¾in (22.5cm) high 46¼oz*

$2,900-3,600 **BE**

A silver-gilt "Surprise" easter egg, by Stuart Devlin, the exterior reveals five enameled flowers.

1978 *2¾in (7cm) high 2¾oz*

$650-800 **DUK**

A silver-gilt "Surprise" egg, by Stuart Devlin, no.279, opening to reveal a turtle with enamel decoration, London.

1979 *3in (7.5cm) high*

$300-400 **WW**

A silver candlestick, by Stuart Devlin, with pierced stem raised on a conical foot, maker's marks "SD," hallmarked London.

1980 *9in (23cm) high 0.17oz*

$500-650 **L&T**

A gold ring, by Stuart Devlin, London, set with tourmalines, aquamarines, and sapphires within cornucopia design and a cherub.

1981 *size O*

$3,200-3,900 **WW**

A silver cigarette box, by Stuart Devlin, London, with gilt highlighted raised mosaic-shaped lined top, with a stained wooden interior.

1989 *6¾in (17cm) wide 29oz*

$1,300-1,900 **GYM**

A 19thC four-sectional silver cigar case, with engraved floral decoration, Birmingham.

1901

$260-320 **FLD**

A Continental silver and enamel cigarette case, depicting a seminude female, hallmarked "Birmingham import 1904," with "925" standard mark, maker's mark worn, with scratches and wear.

3½in (9cm) long

$450-600 **FELL**

A CLOSER LOOK AT A CIGARETTE CASE

This an unusual and desirable subject in exceptional condition.

It has dual function—that of a cigarette case and snuff box.

The hinged cover enameled with a cartoon of a man on bended knee with a woman in Islamic dress, with a man peeping round a corner.

It has import marks for London 1930, importer's mark of H.C. Freeman, with Irish import marks for 1940.

A silver and enamel box, signed "H.M. Bateman, Copyright."

3in (7.5cm) long

$1,700-2,100 **WW**

A silver and enamel cigarette case, with an enamel panel landscape scene, hallmarked "London import 1929," sponsor's mark "FBR," probably F.B. Reynolds, and "925," with wear and tarnishing.

3½in (9cm) long

$500-650 **FELL**

A mid-20thC hallmarked silver and guilloche enamel cigarette case, by Henry Clifford Davies, Birmingham.

1950 *3¼in (8.5cm) high*

$500-600 **WM**

An Austrian silver and enamel cigarette case, maker's mark possibly "CD," with a panel of a lady in hunting dress.

3¼in (8.5cm) long

$650-800 **WW**

A Persian metalware and enamel cigarette box, with buildings in a landscape.

7¼in (18.5cm) long

$300-450 **WW**

A Russian silver-gilt and enamel cigarette case.

1896-1908 *4in (10cm) long*

$1,150-1,450 **WW**

A novelty oak smokers' compendium, modeled as a Great Western Railway coal truck, slight damage.

This appeals to railroadiana collectors as well as those interested in smoking memorabilia.

13in (33cm) long

$400-500 **FLD**

A 19thC silver and enamel vesta case, by S. Mordan and Co., London, retailed by Percy Edwards and Co., with a huntsman being thrown from his horse, the reverse initialed "J.W.D."

1885 *1¾in (4.5cm) long*

$1,300-1,800 WW

A 19thC enamel vesta case, with foxes, a lady and hound, and wild bird.

2in (5cm) high

$800-850 BELL

A French late-19thC gold-mounted vesta case, enameled with a lady and gentleman, the sides with "Allumettes - Chimiques" and "Paris 15c," some damage.

2in (5cm) long

$450-500 FLD

A Continental silver and enamel vesta case, with a naked lady, the hinged lid stamped "935" to reverse.

Match cases, commonly called vesta cases, were popular from the late 1830s until the 1920s, when pocket lighters had begun to replace matches. Early matches could ignite accidentally when they rubbed against each other, so they were placed in a small box, usually made of metal. Vesta cases often contained a textured surface on which to strike matches.

2¼in (5.5cm) high

$850-950 FELL

A late-19thC Russian silver-gilt and enamel cigarette and vesta case, maker's mark "K.A.," St. Petersburg.

ca. 1890 *3¾in (9.5cm) long*

$1,700-2,300 WW

A silver-gilt and shagreen cigarette/vesta case, by Thomas Callow and Sons Ltd., London, inscribed "With Best Love From Tones, Xmas 1918."

1918 *3¾in (9.5cm) long*

$260-390 WW

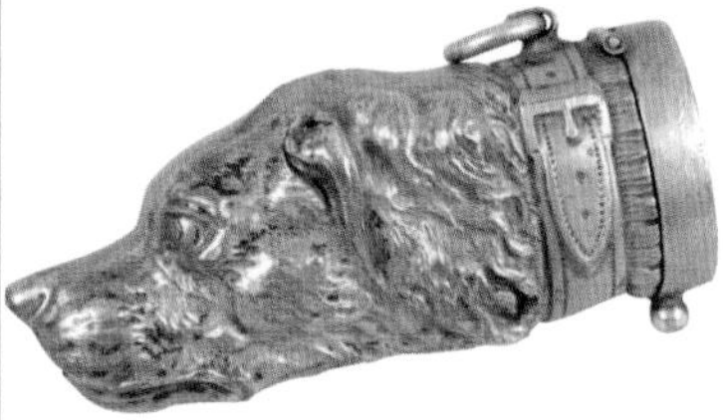

A 20thC silver-plated dog vesta case, wear and tarnishing.

2¾in (7cm) long

$130-190 FELL

A 19thC silver fish bowl table vesta holder, "London 1891," retailed by Asprey.

2in (5cm) high

$400-450 WW

A Henry Howell & Co. "YZ" rabbit vesta case, with phenolic resin ears and feet, with glass eyes, on Macassar ebony tray, impressed marks.

4in (10cm) high

$140-190 WW

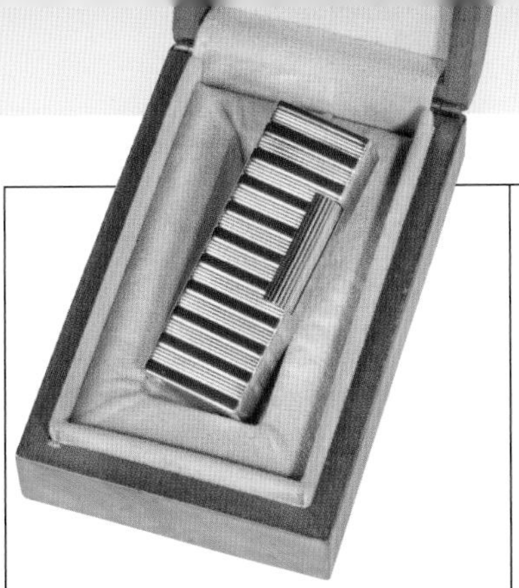

A Dunhill 18ct yellow gold cigarette lighter, no.340, stamped marks, in original wooden case.

Dunhill was formed in London in 1893 when Alfred Dunhill took over his father's saddler business, changing its focus to luxury car accessories. Dunhill's 1905 "Windshield Pipe" proved popular and the company moved into the tobacco business, producing pipes and smoking accessories. Dunhill was bought by Richemont in the 1990s.

2½in (6.5cm) long

$1,250-1,450 DUK

A Dunhill silver unique golf ball table lighter, limited edition no.332, in fitted case, and a hand-signed copy of "Golf Studios, Harold Riley at Dunhill, Publ. Alfred Dunhill Limited, 2001."

$1,900-2,600 DUK

A Dunhill "Longitude" stainless steel and chrome-plated table lighter, inset with a clock, impressed marks, in fitted case.

2¾in (7cm) high

$450-500 DUK

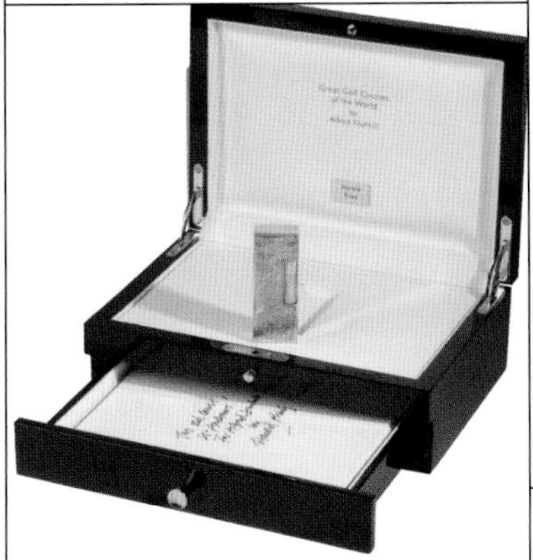

A Dunhill "Great Golf Courses of the World" silver lighter, designed by Harold Riley, limited edition no.271 of 288, with original case, outer sleeve, and booklets.

ca. 1999 *2¾in (7cm) high*

$1,150-1,450 DUK

A Dunhill silver and wood grain-effect Rollagas lighter, the base stamped "US24163 Patented, Made in Switzerland, Dunhill," with import hallmarks, boxed with paperwork.

2½in (6.5cm) high

$650-800 APAR

A Dunhill "The Aldunil" silver and rose gold-plated lighter, stamped "Dunhill Paris," with import marks.

2½in (6.5cm) high

$450-500 APAR

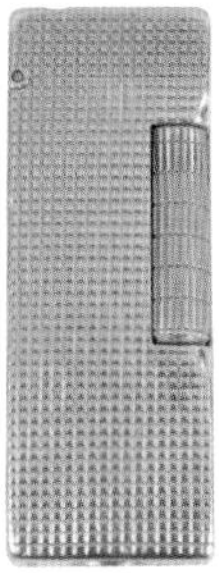

A Dunhill 9ct gold-cased cigarette lighter, marked "9 375," surface scratches, wear.

2½in (6.5cm) high

$650-800 FELL

A Dunhill 9ct gold-cased cigarette lighter, marked "9 375 AD," surface scratches, wear.

2½in (6.5cm) high

$600-700 FELL

A Dunhill 9ct gold-cased cigarette lighter, marked "9 375," with scratches and wear.

2½in (6.5cm) high

$1,050-1,150 FELL

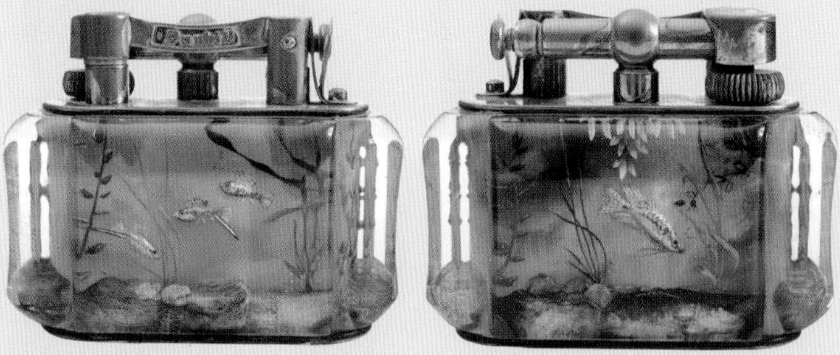

A Dunhill Aquarium table lighter, each side with reverse-painted intaglio fish and rock decoration on lucite panels, silver-plated mounts, registration no.737418, signed on arm.

4in (10cm) long

$4,500-5,200 **BE**

A mid-20thC pilot's Dunhill silver-plated "Goliath" table lighter, inscription "To W.H. Fell 1953" and signatures from other test pilots, including Brian Trubshaw.

$850-950 **SWO**

A Dunhill silver-plated "foot rule" table lighter, engraved with inches and centimeters, no.0001, impressed marks, in a fitted box.

13in (33cm) long

$650-800 **DUK**

A Cartier gold-plated cigarette lighter, no. E89285, 20 microns, in fitted case.

$300-450 **DUK**

A Colibri Monogas 9ct gold-cased cigarette lighter, marked "9 375," surface scratches, wear.

1¾in (4.5cm) high

$400-500 **FELL**

An S.T. Dupont gold-plated cigarette lighter, no.9039B, 20 microns, in fitted case.

1¾in (4.5cm) long

$290-320 **DUK**

A novelty terrier lighter, some damage and wear.

5¼in (13.5cm) high

$60-80 **LOCK**

A 9ct gold lighter, with engine-turned body, hallmarked "London 1929 by GS*FS."

0.63oz

$500-650 **LOCK**

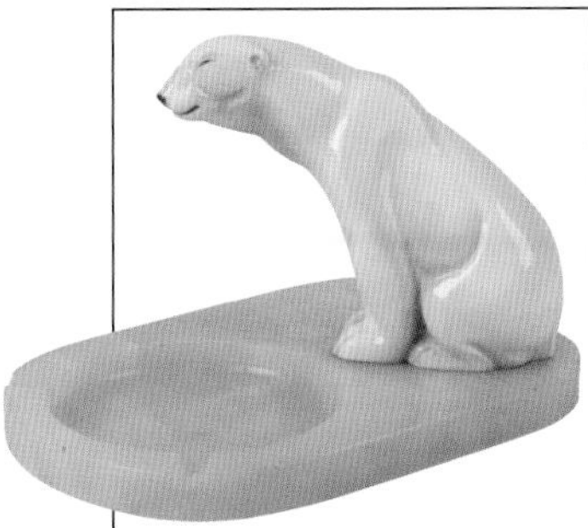

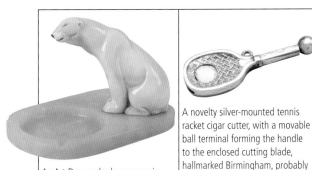

An Art Deco polar bear ceramic ashtray, with painted features, on a marble base, stamped "Made in England," with serial number.

5¾in (14.5cm) high

$190-260 **DUK**

A novelty silver-mounted tennis racket cigar cutter, with a movable ball terminal forming the handle to the enclosed cutting blade, hallmarked Birmingham, probably William Oliver.

1887 *2½in (6.5cm) long*

$260-320 **FELL**

A CLOSER LOOK AT AN ASHTRAY

An ashtray in the popular Art Deco style.

The circular green onyx tray has an asymmetric dished center.

It is surmounted to the edge with six various cold-painted bronze dogs in very good condition.

They include an Airedale, Scottie, and Irish Setter.

An onyx ashtray, with bronze dog figurines.

tray 7¾in (19.5cm) diam

$1,300-1,600 **HT**

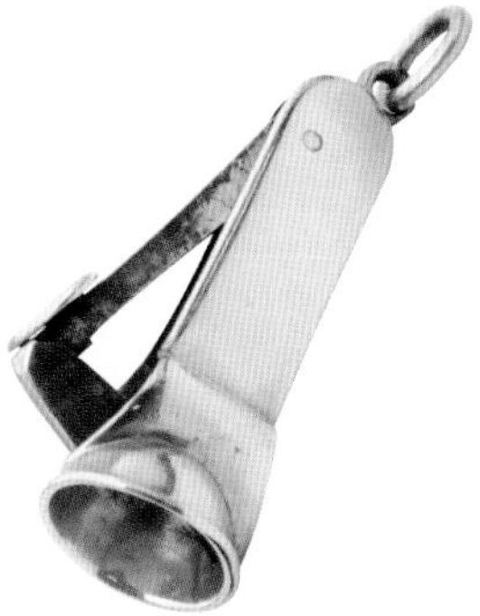

A 9ct gold cigar cutter, with suspension loop.

$160-230 **FLD**

An early-20thC German match striker, the base marked "Gesetzl. Geschutzt."

6¼in (16cm) high

$60-80 **LOC**

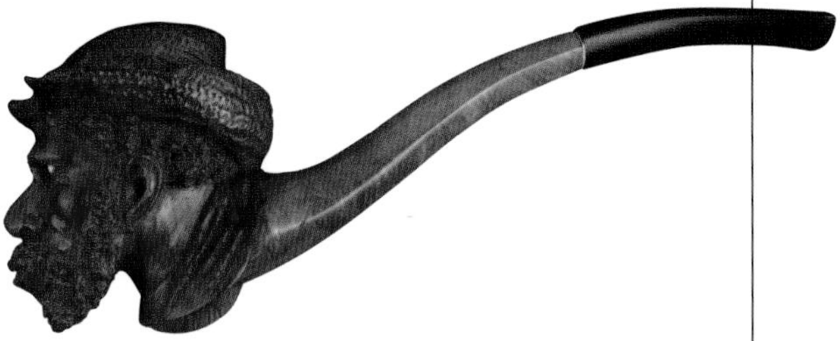

An early-20thC briar pipe, carved as a man's head wearing a straw hat, with inset two-color glass eyes, with a vulcanite mouthpiece.

8in (20.5cm) long

$400-500 **DN**

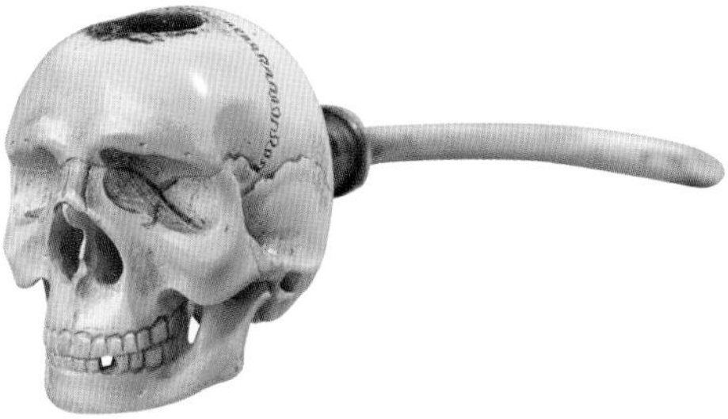

A 19thC meerschaum pipe, the bowl carved as a human skull, with animal horn mouthpiece, with case.

1½in (4cm) high

$260-320 **BELL**

A 19thC large carved meerschaum pipe, of a lady with plumed hair, engraved gold band, and amber stem, some damage, cased.

$100-130 **FLD**

A 19thC treen snuff box, with a dog carrying a dead rabbit, titled "To Be delivered immediately," wear and rubbing, foil lining missing to interior.

3in (7.5cm) wide

$100-130 **FELL**

A Black Forest carved tobacco jar, in the form of a standing bear holding a bough and a brass bowl, inset glass eyes, some damage.

11¾in (30cm) high

$300-400 **FLD**

A Frank Roberts England international soccer (UK football) shirt, season 1924-25, woollen button-up neck, with embroidered FA three lions badge.

Frank Roberts (1894-1961), an English professional soccer player, played from the 1910s to 1928.

$3,500-3,900 **GBA**

A white England no.4 international jersey, worn by Bobby Robson in the England vs. Wales match at Ninian Park October 14, 1961, by Bukta, with a signed handwritten card "THIS IS THE SHIRT THAT I WORE AGAINST WALES AT NINIAN PARK IN CARDIFF ON OCTOBER 14th 1961 WE DREW 1-1, BOBBY ROBSON."

$3,900-4,500 **GBA**

A Pelé match-worn jersey and boots, the jersey a signed white Santos no.10 jersey worn in the match vs. Roma March 3, 1972, with a letter of authenticity from the son of Nocaute Jack, the Brazil team masseur 1970-94, and two dealer issued certificates of authenticity from JSA and Jersey14, with a pair of match-worn black and white Puma Pelé Santos boots, with a certificate of authenticity from BidAMI Auctions, together with Pelé memorabilia comprising a Pelé featured rosette issued for the Santos vs. Fulham game December 3, 1973, an Original Pelé Match Flyer Advertising Santos FC vs. Washington Darts 1970, and a NY Cosmos Official Pelé Farewell Program October 1, 1977, Cosmos vs. Santos.

$9,500-11,000 **GBA**

A rare 1966 England World Cup winners replica shirt, signed by ten players, mounted with Bobby Moore signature on card in frame with two photos.

1966

$650-800 **LOCK**

A match-worn Santos no.10 match jersey, signed by Pelé on the reverse no.10 as "Edson Pelé," the signature is certified by a PSA/DNA sticker.

$2,600-3,200 **GBA**

A Lionel Messi blue-and-white striped Argentina vs. Colombia international jersey, from November 15, 2016, FIFA Russia 2018 qualifiers and Fair Play sleeve badges, the reverse lettered "MESSI," with a certificate of authenticity issued by BidAMI Auctions.

$2,600-3,900 **GBA**

A photograph montage, signed by Ian Wright, Arsenal and England striker.

12in (30.5cm) wide

$50-60 **LOCK**

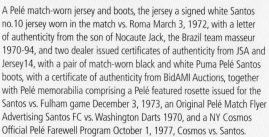

A Manchester United black-and-white photograph, signed by George Best and Dennis Law.

8in (20.5cm) wide

$80-90 **LOCK**

A 1966 World Cup winners image, signed by Geoff Hurst, Roger Hunt, Martin Peters, Ray Wilson, and George Cohen.

1966

$60-80 LOCK

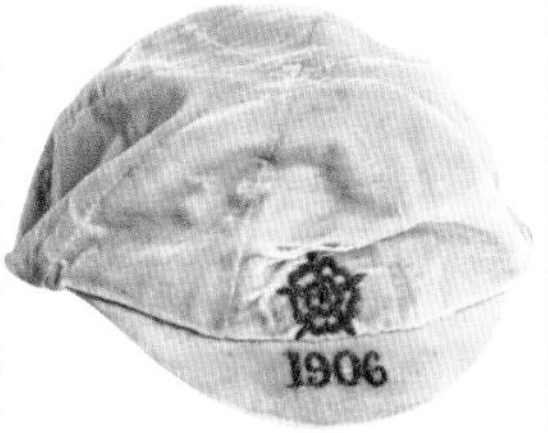

A Jimmy Ashcroft debut England vs. Ireland international 1905-06 cap, with gold wire rose, tear above rose, dated.

This match was played at the Solitude Ground, Belfast, February 17, 1906. England won 5-0.

1906

$2,600-3,200 GBA

A Frank Roberts England international debut cap, England vs. Belgium, orange and purple quartered, dated.

This match was played at West Bromwich Albion's Hawthorns ground, December 8, 1924. England won 4-0.

1924

$1,400-1,900 GBA

A soccer ball, signed by Brazilian footballer Pelé.

$160-210 LOCK

A UEFA Super Cup Competition silver-plated replica trophy, with UEFA inset logo, on a marble base with "SUPER COMPETITION" band.

The UEFA Super Cup is an annual super cup soccer (UK football) match organized by UEFA and contested by the reigning champions of the two main European club competitions, the UEFA Champions League and the UEFA Europa League.

pre-2006 *18in (45.5cm) high*

$2,600-3,200 GBA

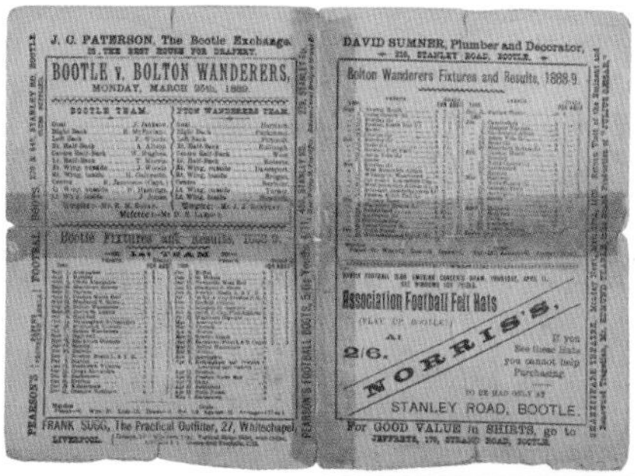

A UK football program, published for Bootle vs. Bolton Wanderers March 25, 1889, taped repairs.

This is the earliest known Bootle program.

1889

$950-1,100 GBA

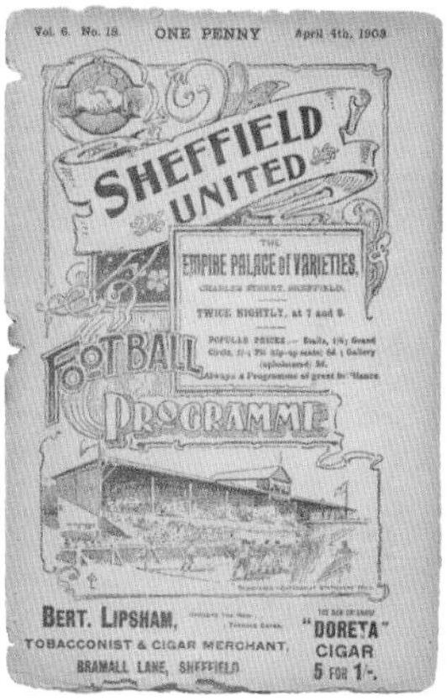

An England vs. Scotland international program, played at Sheffield United April 4, 1903, some paper loss.

$1,900-2,600 GBA

A souvenir program for the Everton vs. Newcastle United FA Cup Final, played at Crystal Palace April 21, 1906, eight-pager published by the *London Evening News*.

$2,300-2,900 GBA

An English Southampton vs. Watford program FA Cup tie, January 12, 1907, in the form of a bifold match card.

1907

$850-950 GBA

An FA Cup Final Replay program, Barnsley vs. Newcastle United played at Goodison Park, Everton, on Thursday April 28, 1910, Everton and Liverpool Official Program, vol.6 no.54, 16 pages, typo in the team lineups heading reading "BARNSLEY v NEWCANTLE UNITED," with illustrations.

The program is in good, stable condition, which is uncommon as the paper from these period Everton/Liverpool issues is often in a fragile state.

1910

$11,000-13,000 GBA

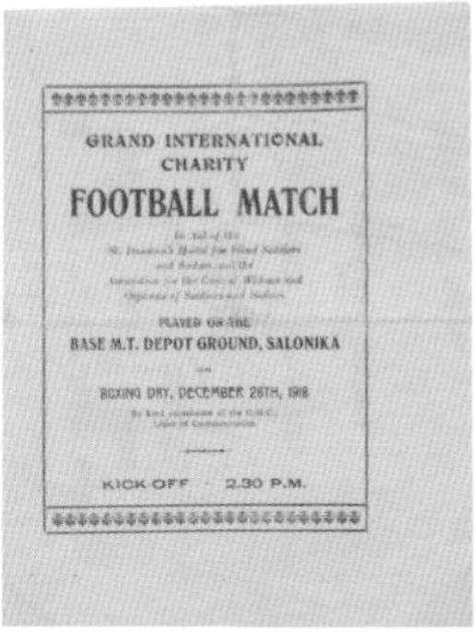

A World War I period English football program, for the England and Wales vs. Scotland and Ireland grand international charity soccer match, played in Salonika, December 26, 1918.

1918

$300-450 **GBA**

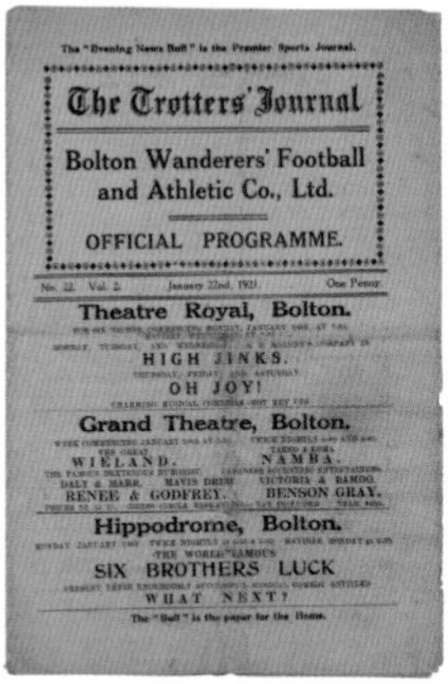

An English football program, Bolton Wanderers vs. Oldham Athletic, Div. 1, January 22, 1921.

$300-400 **LOCK**

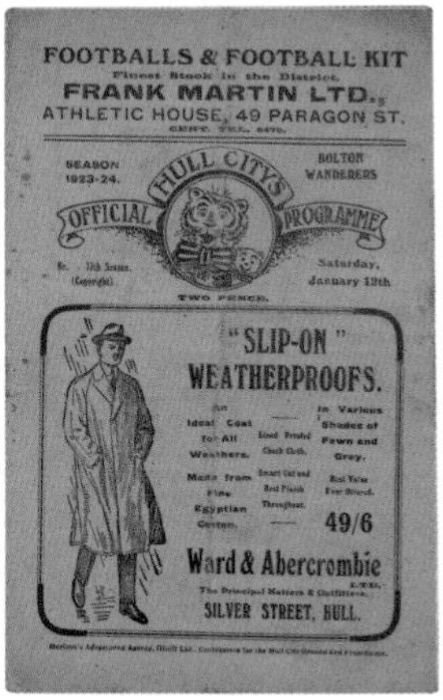

An FA Cup English football program, Hull City vs. Bolton Wanderers, January 12, 1924.

$260-320 **LOCK**

A UK football program, Scotland vs. England, April 2, 1927, at Hampden Park.

$400-500 **LOCK**

An FA Cup final program, Birmingham vs. West Bromwich Albion, April 25, 1931.

$450-600 **LOCK**

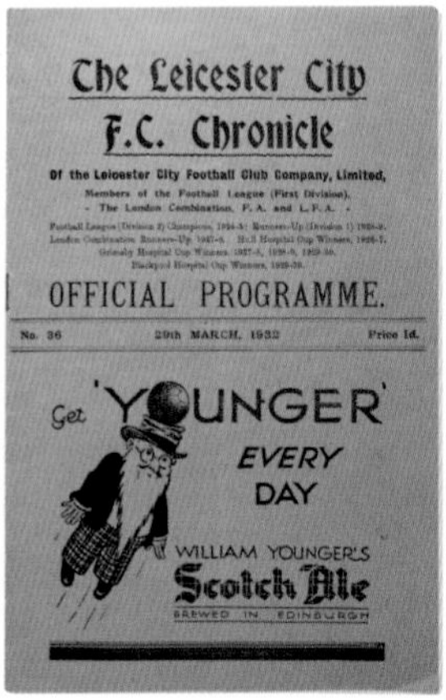

A UK football program, Leicester City vs. Newcastle, March 29, 1932.

$260-320 **LOCK**

An FA Cup final program, Everton vs. Manchester City, April 29, 1933.

1933

$450-500 **LOCK**

An official program for the first European Cup Final, Real Madrid vs. Reims, on June 13, 1956 at Parc des Princes, the 27-page program with center page of the team sheets of Real Madrid and Reims.

The European Cup, now known as the UEFA Champions League, was played at the Parc des Princes in Paris in front of 38,000 people on June 13, 1956, resulting in Real Madrid beating Reims 4-3.

1956

$3,900-5,200 **GBA**

A football program, England vs. Scotland, Wembley, April 14, 1934.

1934

$190-260 **LOCK**

An Irish Football Association Cup gold medal, awarded to William Gouk in 1882 QIFC, boxed.

Queen's Island FC won 1-0 against Cliftonville on May 13, 1882 at Prospect (Ballynagagh).

1in (2.5cm) wide

$1,050-1,550 **GBA**

A 9ct. gold England Football League vs. Scottish Football League victory match representative medal, awarded to Frank Womack, inscribed "VICTORY MATCH, ENGLAND v SCOTLAND, THE FOOTBALL LEAGUE, St ANDREWS, BIRMINGHAM, FEBRUARY 22nd 1919, F. WOMACK."

Frank Womack (1888-1968) represented the England Football League in the match vs. the Scottish F.L. in 1918-19. The England Football League won 3-1.

1918-19

$400-500 **GBA**

QUICK REFERENCE—JIMMY ASHCROFT

- **James (Jimmy) Ashcroft (1878-1943) was an English soccer goalkeeper and Arsenal's first England international soccer player. Ashcroft signed as a professional soccer player in June 1900 for Woolwich Arsenal; his debut match was on September 15, 1900, against Burton Swifts. With Woolwich Arsenal, he made 303 appearances in eight seasons until 1908. Ashcroft was the first Arsenal player to be capped for England, winning three caps in the British Home Nations Championship matches of 1906. In 1908, Ashcroft moved to Blackburn Rovers, leaving in 1913 on a free transfer and signing for Tranmere Rovers. He played one season before World War I halted first-class soccer.**

A 9ct. gold FA Cup runners-up medal, awarded to a Manchester City player, with fitted case, recipient unknown, dated.

The Bolton Wanderers defeated Manchester City 1-0.

1926

$2,600-3,900 **GBA**

A Woolwich Arsenal 9ct. gold medal, awarded to goalkeeper Jimmy Ashcroft, during which Ashcroft kept a club record 20 clean sheets, inscribed "WOOLWICH ARSENAL FOOTBALL CLUB, TO COMMEMORATE PROMOTION TO FIRST LEAGUE, PRESENTED TO J. ASHCROFT, 1903-4."

$2,600-3,900 **GBA**

A England Football League Division One Championship silver-gilt medal, awarded to Allenby Chilton of Manchester United in season 1951-52, inscribed "THE FOOTBALL LEAGUE, CHAMPIONS DIVISION 1, SEASON 1951-52, MANCHESTER UNITED FC, A. CHILTON," in original case.

Allenby Chilton (1918-96), played briefly for Liverpool and then Manchester United from 1938 to 1955. Chilton served with the Durham Light Infantry. Postwar he was center half for Matt Busby's team and was a key member in the 1951/52 league championship. In 1955, he went on to become player/manager for Grimsby Town, then manager for both Wigan Athletic and Hartlepool United.

$35,000-39,000 **GBA**

A bronze 1968 UEFA European Football Championship third-place medal, belonging to Roger Hunt, reverse inscribed "UEFA CHAMPIONNAT D'EUROPE 1968 IIIe RANG," in original Huguenin fitted case.

1968

$3,900-4,500 **GBA**

A Tommy Docherty 1967 FA Cup runners-up medal, official FA retrospective presentation in 2010 to pre-1996 FA Cup Final managers, the medal in 9ct. gold by Toye, Kenning & Spencer Ltd., hallmarked Birmingham 2010, inscribed "THE FOOTBALL ASSOCIATION, CHALLENGE CUP, RUNNERS-UP," the edge inscribed "1966-67," cased in 2010.

Following a campaign by Lawrie McMenemy, the FA agreed to honor the managers who took their clubs to an FA Cup final but at the time did not receive a medal. From 1996, managers joined the players and received medals on the day.

$4,500-5,200 **GBA**

A Fulham 1975 FA Cup Final runners-up 9ct. gold medal, belonging to John Mitchell, inscribed "THE FOOTBALL ASSOCIATION, CHALLENGE CUP, RUNNERS-UP," the edge inscribed "1974-75," in original fitted case, with a 1975 FA Cup Final program and ticket stub.

$6,000-6,500 **GBA**

A 1994 FIFA World Cup winners 14ct. gold medal, with "FIFA WORLD CUP USA 1994" reverse, hallmarks and maker's mark Huguenin, recipient unknown.

This medal would have been awarded to a member of Brazil backroom staff, not a player.

1994 *2in (5cm) diam*

$18,000-26,000 **GBA**

"The INCOMPARABLE PRIZE FIGHT, JACK JOHNSON vs JIM JEFFRIES," framed, signs of watermarks in places.

Jeffries, "The White Hope," was persuaded out of retirement to restore pride to the white race. He was, however, outclassed and defeated by the superior opponent.

1910 *16½in (42cm) high*

$950-1,150 **MM**

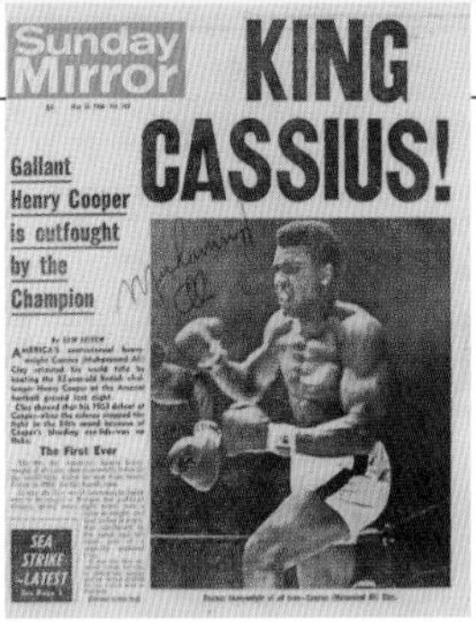

A *Sunday Mirror* newspaper, edition of May 22, 1966, signed in pen by Muhammad Ali the day after his defeat of Henry Cooper at Arsenal FC's Highbury Ground.

The seller of this lot obtained this autograph of Muhammad Ali on May 22, 1966, when he encountered Ali taking a Sunday stroll in St James's Park, London.

1966

$400-500 **GBA**

A Muhammad Ali and Joe Frazier double signed poster, for their 1971 World Heavyweight Championship fight, poster has been rolled and has a series of creases.

$700-850 **GBA**

An autographed Muhammad Ali training leather boxing glove, original yellow lace, signed in gold "Muhammad Ali 19-78," with two letters of authenticity, dated.

This glove was signed by Muhammad Ali at his training camp at Deer Lake, Pennsylvania, during preparation for his fight against Leon Spinks. It was signed for Pete Morkovin, who visited the training camp during this time with his father. Subsequently sold to Craig Hamilton of JO Sports Inc. by Pete Morkovin. Includes two letters of authenticity from Pete Morkovin and Craig Hamilton.

1978 *12in (30.5cm) long*

$3,900-5,200 **GBA**

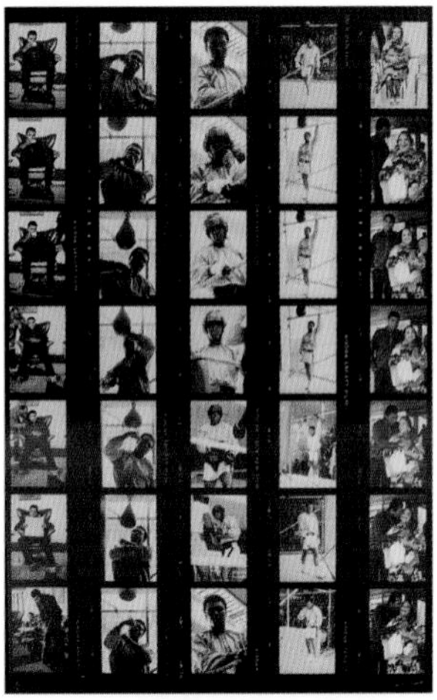

A contact sheet, by Terry O'Neill CBE (b.1938), of Muhammad Ali preparing for his fight with Alvin Lewis in Dublin, 1972, printed later, signed, and numbered "7/50," framed with Plexiglass.

sheet 48in (122cm) high

$2,600-3,900 **ROS**

A pair of Rocky Marciano leather boxing gloves, by Goldsmith of Cincinnati, with a wooden display plaque, with gilt titling from The National Sporting Club.

These gloves were in the Roland Dakin Collection. They were acquired from Mickey Duff via The National Sporting Club. Roland Dakin was a British Boxing Board of Control referee for 38 years and presided over 40 World Fight titles. He was an avid collector of boxing memorabilia and his professional capacity gave him wonderful access to leading boxing personalities.

$2,300-2,900 **GBA**

A boxing glove, signed by Evander Holyfield and Mike Tyson, in dome frame, mounted with replica fight poster behind.

$260-390 **LOCK**

A former five weight World Boxing Champion Sugar Ray Leonard signed glove, in a dome frame.

$160-230 **LOCK**

A World Boxing Champion Floyd Mayweather signed glove, in a box frame, with action image behind.

$230-290 **LOCK**

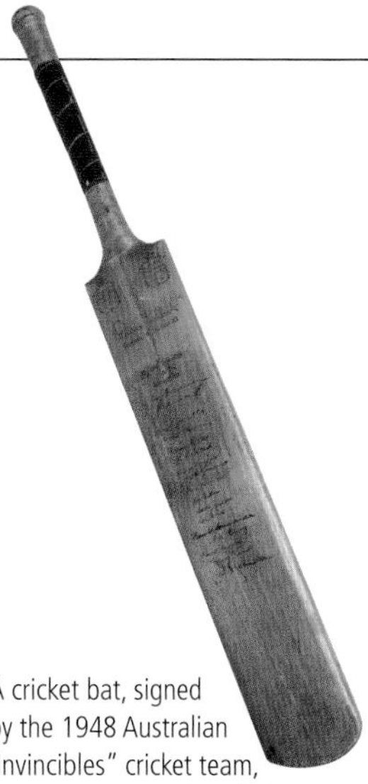

A cricket bat, signed by the 1948 Australian 'Invincibles" cricket team, 17 signatures in ink, including Bradman, Morris, Hassett, Harvey, Barnes, Lindwall, Miller, and Johnston.

$900-1,050 GBA

A cricket bat, signed by Packer Rebels, the face signed in ink by the World Team, the reverse signed by the West Indies and Australian teams of 1977.

$400-500 GBA

A 19thC silver-plated inkwell, modeled as a cricket ball, stamped "EPNS."

3¼in (8.5cm) diam

$230-290 GBA

A Gillette Cup Final cricket ball, set with a silvered shield inscribed "GILLETTE CUP FINAL, 1973, GLOS. V SUSSEX, GLOS. 248-8. M.S. PROCTOR 94, A.S. BROWN 77 N.O."

1973

$260-320 GBA

A John Hampshire's Yorkshire County Cricket Club 1965 Gillette Cup Final winner's medal, silvered, in original case.

1965

$500-600 GBA

An 18ct. gold Rothmans World Cup XI 1966 champions medallion, presented to the winners at Lord's September 1966, hallmarked, in a fitted Gregory & Nicholas Ltd. box.

2in (5cm) diam

$3,200-3,900 GBA

A signed photograph of the Australian 2001 Ashes series winning cricket team, with 20 signatures, including Fleming, Warne, Slater, the Waugh brothers, Langer, Gilchrist, Ponting, Katich, Gillespie, Hayden, McGrath, and Martyn, framed, glazed.

2001

$160-230 GBA

A team-signed India ODI cricket shirt, from the 2006 Tour of Sri Lanka, 15 signatures including Dravid, Tendulkar, Sehwag, Yuvraj Singh, Kaif, Dhoni, Pathan, Agarkar, Harbhajan Singh, Powar, and Patel.

2006

$210-260 GBA

A 19thC Staffordshire pottery figure,of the cricketer George Parr.

This figure was produced in 1861 to commemorate the first England trip to Australia.

13¾in (35cm) high

$850-950 CAN

A terracotta figure of Dr. W.G. Grace, after Edwin Roscoe Mullins (1849-1907), signed, dated.

1885 32in (81.5cm) high

$17,000-21,000 CAN

A set of vintage racing silks, in the colors of Ada L. Rice.

These colors are associated with the 1940s and the racehorse Model Cadet, who won the 1949 Washington Futurity, ridden by Anthony Skoronski and trained by Seabiscuit's trainer Tom Smith.

$700-850 **GBA**

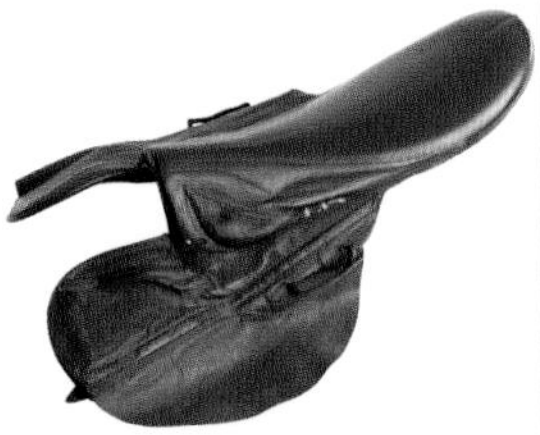

A Walter Swinburn horse racing saddle, with Bates Saddlery Perth label, signed.

19¾oz

$1,150-1,450 **GBA**

A racing plate worn by Seabiscuit in the Massachusetts Handicap July 8, 1937, mounted on a sterling silver hoof-shaped ashtray, engraved with "JACK MCDONALD FROM C.S. HOWARD 1937," with sterling mark.

The US champion Seabiscuit (1933-47) recorded his seventh consecutive stakes victory in the 1937 Massachusetts Handicap in a track record time of 1 minute 49 seconds. The winner's purse money of $51,780 was the highest amount he had won to date.

5in (12.5cm) long

$5,200-6,500 **GBA**

A silver cigar box, mounted with a racing plate worn by Mill Reef, hallmarked Birmingham 1968 by Padgett & Braham Ltd.

Mill Reef (1968-86) was bred in Virginia by his owner Mr. Paul Mellon but was sent to be trained by Ian Balding at Kingsclere. In a career lasting three years, he raced 14 times, ridden exclusively by Geoff Lewis, winning 12 of his races.

1968 *7in (18cm) wide*

$6,000-6,500 **GBA**

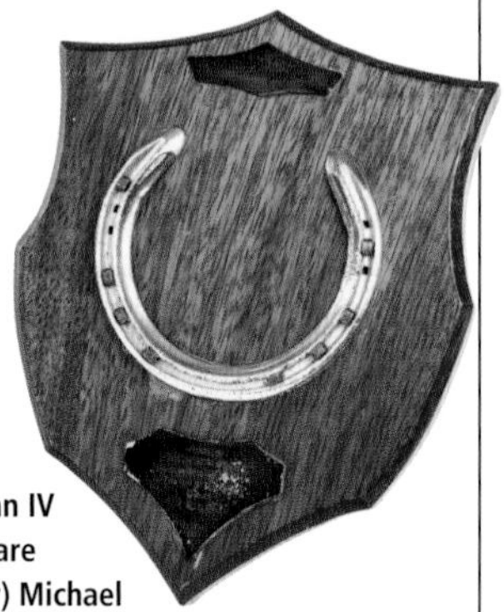

A racing plate, on a mahogany shield, set with plaques inscribed "Shergar" and "WINNER, 1981 EPSOM DERBYRIDDEN BY WALTER SWINBURN, TRAINER MR STOUTE, OWNER THE AGA KHAN."

Shergar (1978-ca. 1983), a bay colt, was bred by HH The Aga Khan IV at his private stud in County Kildare and trained at Newmarket by (Sir) Michael Stoute. Shergar won his first race in September 1980 ridden by Lester Piggott. He was retired to Ballymany Stud in October 1981. Shergar had won six of his eight races. He was sydincated for £10 million ($13 million) at £250,000 ($320,000) for each of 40 shares, with a covering fee of £60,000-80,000 ($80,000-100,000). In 1983, Shergar was kidnapped and a ransom demanded. When this was refused, Shergar ended up dead. It is widely believed that the horse was killed by men inexperienced in handling stallions, yet speculation still surrounds his death.

1981 *10in (25.5cm) long*

$6,000-6,500 **GBA**

A photograph of the stallion Nearco, by equestrian photographer Anscomb, signed, inscribed "Nearco," mounted, framed and glazed.

Nearco (1935-57) was bred by Federico Tesio and retired undefeated after 14 races, with his crowning glory being his facile win in the Grand Prix de Paris in 1938. He was bought by British bookmaker Martin Benson for £60,000 ($80,000) and sent to the Beech House Stud at Newmarket. He was thought so valuable that his own underground bomb shelter was constructed at Beech House.

1941 *8in (20.5cm) wide*

$500-650 **GBA**

A Royal Worcester porcelain figurine of Arkle, by Doris Lindner, factory marks, limited edition 447 of 500, with a framed certificate.

ca. 1967 *10¾in (27.5cm) high*

$500-650 **GBA**

A sterling silver sculpture of Desert Orchid with Simon Sherwood up, modeled by Edwina Emery, hallmarked London 1990 by Garrard & Co. Ltd., agate and wooden base, facsimile signature of Edwina Emery, with a limited edition certificate no.2 of 9 in a leather frame.

$12,000-14,000 **GBA**

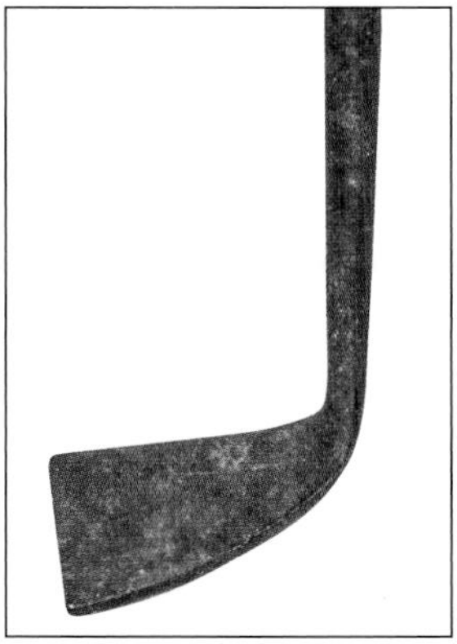

A rare square-toe blacksmith's general iron, with curved cutoff blade and heavy ash shaft, with a nail and sawteeth nicking.

ca. 1700 *41¼in (105cm) long*

$13,000-16,000 **GBA**

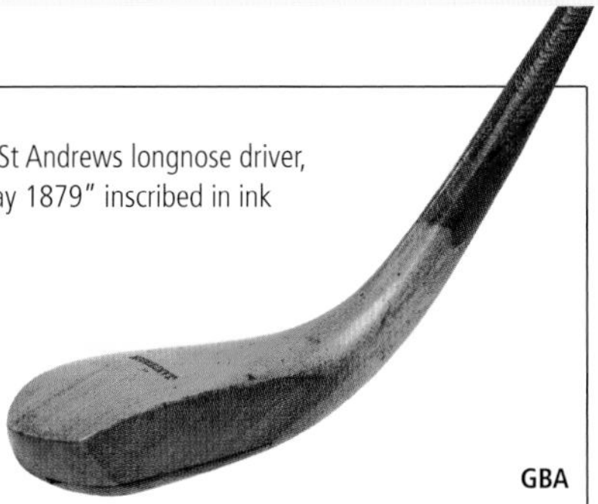

A James Anderson of St Andrews longnose driver, beech head, with "May 1879" inscribed in ink on the sole.

ca. 1879

$900-1,150 **GBA**

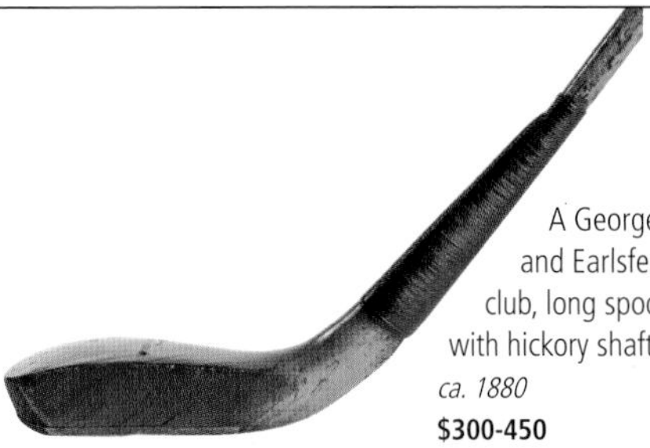

A George Forrester, Elie and Earlsferry longnose club, long spoon, beach head, with hickory shaft.

ca. 1880

$300-450 **GBA**

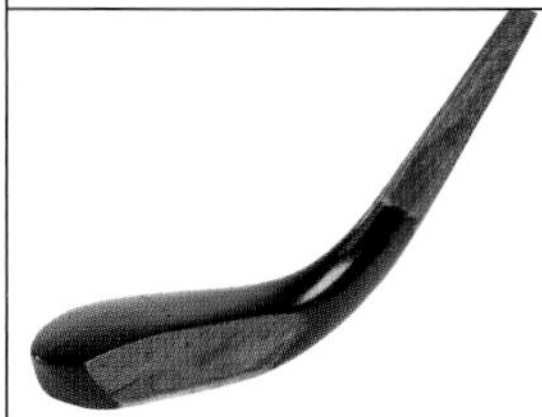

A Tom Morris St Andrews longnose driver head, the sole with ink signature of J. Anderson, dated.

1889

$3,200-3,900 **GBA**

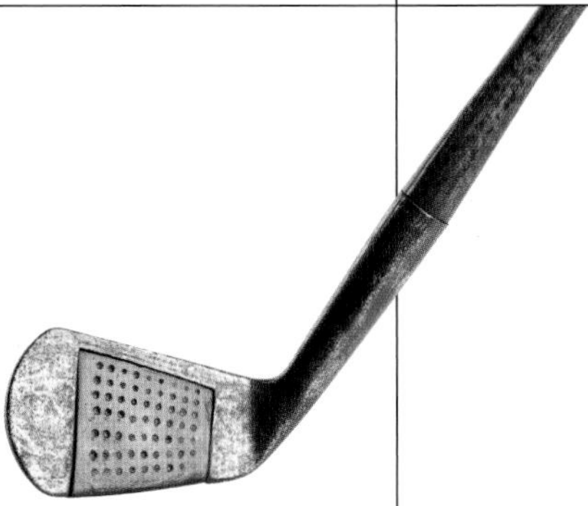

A Jacobs Patent iron, by James Gourlay of Carnoustie, with vulcanite insert to face.

ca. 1912

$400-450 **GBA**

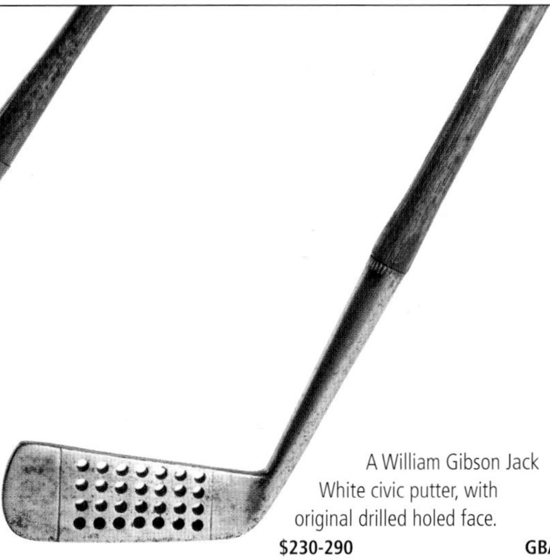

A William Gibson Jack White civic putter, with original drilled holed face.

$230-290 **GBA**

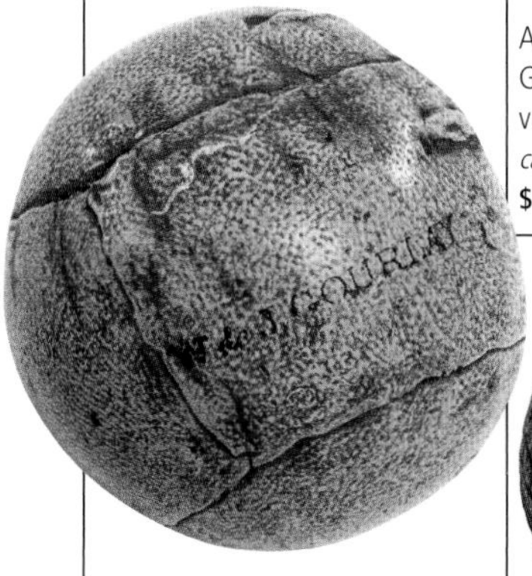

A William & John Gourlay of Musselburgh feather golf ball, stamped with maker's name "W. & J. GOURLAY" and inscribed in ink "31."

ca. 1840

$6,000-6,500 **GBA**

A red gutta-percha hand-hammered golf ball.

ca. 1860

$500-650 **GBA**

A Tom Morris black rubber core bramble pattern golf ball.

$300-400 **GBA**

A Thornton Patent "27½" gutta-percha square mesh golf ball.

ca. 1896

$230-290 **GBA**

A Taylor-Tunnicliffe pottery golfing tobacco jar and cover, with patent nondetachable fitting to airtight cover, the base stamped "A.F.C. PATENT 17870."

ca. 1900 *6¼in (16cm) high*

$300-400 **GBA**

A Royal Doulton Kingsware golfing jug, designed by Crombie.

9in (23cm) high

$300-400 **GBA**

An early-20thC soft-paste porcelain teapot, decorated with golfing scenes, marked "4271."

5¼in (13.5cm) high

$260-320 **GBA**

A solid bronze golfer car mascot, by Louis Lejeune Ltd. of London.

ca. 1935 *6½in (16.5cm) high*

$130-190 **GBA**

A rare Professional Golfers' Association medal for the Victory Tournament played at St Andrews in 1919, unhallmarked but probably silver gilt, the obverse inscribed "PROFESSIONAL GOLFERS ASSOCIATION, VICTORY TOURNAMENT 1919, PEACE BY VICTORY."

Harry Vardon had been the last winner of an Open Championship in 1914 before it was suspended and not competed for again until after the hostilities in 1920. However, in 1919 the PGA organized the St Andrews Tournament, which was sponsored by the *Daily Mail* newspaper, and played over 36 holes per day on 25 and 26 May on the Old Course. As there had not been time to organise the usual qualifiers associated with an Open Championship, the field was restricted to 60 professionals. Despite this, it was referred to as the Victory Open. It was deemed to have resulted in a tie between George Duncan and Abe Mitchell, both with 312 strokes. There was no playoff.

$1,800-2,300 **GBA**

An Augusta score card photographic display, with a color photograph of Tiger Woods, mounted next to an Augusta scorecard reverse mounted and signed by Woods, the reverse taped with a certificate of authenticity issued by ASA Accugrade Inc., limited edition numbered "18/25," framed and glazed.

29½in (75cm) wide

$190-260 **GBA**

A color photograph, signed by Seve Ballesteros, mounted, framed, and glazed.

$130-180 **GBA**

A pin flag from the 143rd Open Championship, signed in black permanent marker by the winning golfer Rory McIlroy, with certificate of authenticity and photo proof of golfer signing the flag.

2014

$230-290 **GBA**

A pin flag from the 147th Open Championship, signed in black permanent marker by the winning golfer Francesco Molinari, with certificate of authenticity and photo proof of golfer signing the flag.

2018

$190-260 **GBA**

A signed Michael Schumacher Ferrari Fila shirt, with Vodafone and Shell sponsors badges.

large (US)

$300-400 **APAR**

A Mercedes 2014 F1 World Championship season mini helmet, signed by Lewis Hamilton on the crown in black marker pen, with a photo proof dealer's certificate of authenticity.

$400-450 **GBA**

A print, signed by auto racing's Jack Brabham, chief Brabham designer Ron Tauranac, and artist Randall Wilson, limited edition no.192/850, rolled.

$50-60 **LOCK**

A 2000 West McLaren-Mercedes Formula 1 racesuit, worn by David Coulthard, his name and Scottish Saltire stitched above the waistband.

Coulthard finished second behind his team mate, Mika Häkkinen, in that year's Spanish Grand Prix at Barcelona on May 7.

$4,500-5,200 **GBA**

A Mercedes AMS Petronas 2012 F1 season 1:2 scale helmet, signed by Michael Schumacher in gold marker pen, with a photo proof dealer's certificate of authenticity.

$700-850 **GBA**

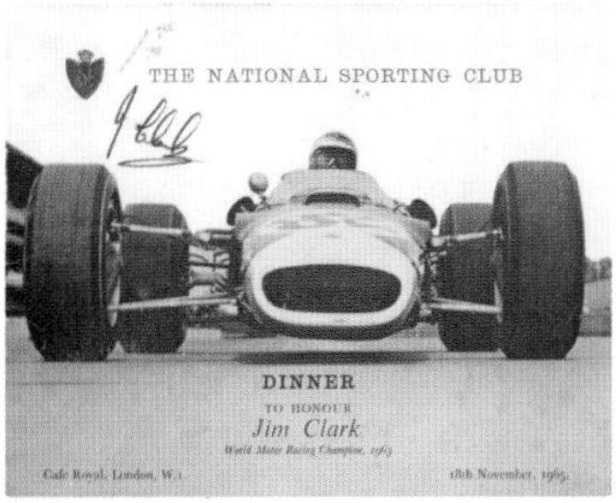

A 1965 National Sporting Club menu, signed by Jim Clark on the front cover above his Indianapolis 500 winning Lotus, for the dinner at the Cafe Royal on November 18, the eight-page menu including a two-page celebration of his achievements, with a copy of "Jim Clark At The Wheel."

The 1965 World Champion and first Formula 1 driver to win the "Indy 500," Jim Clark signed this for club member Derrick Richard Hornby, who sat on an adjacent table to him throughout the dinner.

$700-850 **GBA**

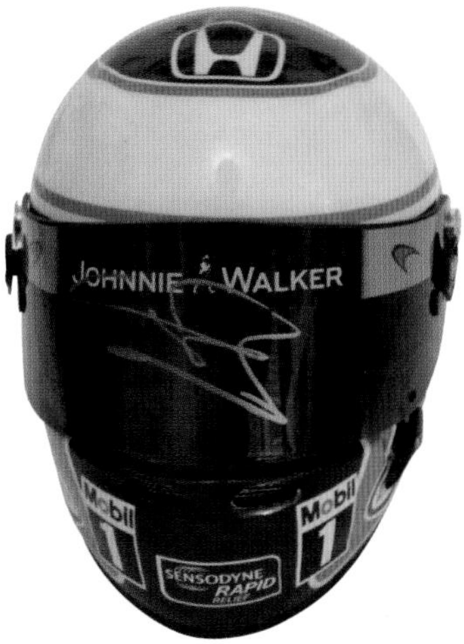

A McLaren Honda Japanese GP mini helmet, signed by Jenson Button on the visor in gold marker pen, sold with a photo proof dealer's certificate of authenticity.

$230-290 **GBA**

A photograph, signed in gold marker pen by Ayrton Senna, mounted in the colors of the Brazilian National Flag, in a wooden frame under glass, with a certificate of authenticity.

22½in (57cm) wide

$900-1,050 **GBA**

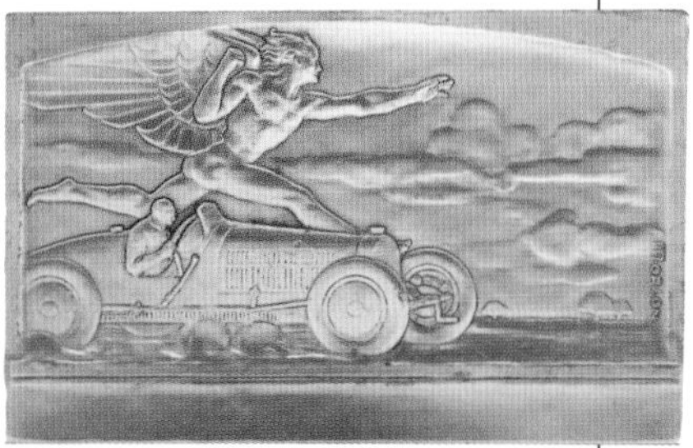

A French silver-plated automotive plaque, by A. Morlon, of a racing car and Hermes on a landscape setting.

3¼in (8.5cm) long

$450-500 **FLD**

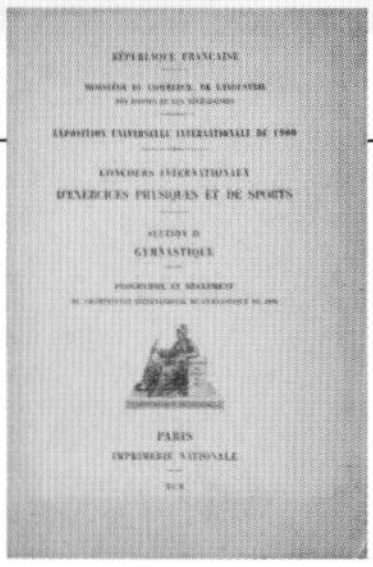

A rare Paris 1900 Olympic Games program for gymnastics, the booklet program in French, "CONCOURS INTERNATIONAUX, D'EXERCICES PHYSIQUES ET DE SPORTS, SECTION II, GYMNASTIQUES, Program ET RÈGLEMENT."
1900
$2,600-3,200 GBA

An Antwerp 1920 Olympic Games Football [Soccer] Prize Trophy, in the form of a bronze urn, by Henri Fugere, with a flying winged nude female figure of Victory holding Olympic rings.

This is the first time the Olympic rings were shown at the Games.

15¾in (40cm) high
$2,600-3,200 GBA

A London 1948 Olympic Games football (soccer) official's badge, silvered, with Olympic Rings, Big Ben, and the Houses of Parliament, ribbon stamped gilt "FOOTBALL."
1948
$400-500 GBA

A vest worn by Great Britain's Terry Spinks when winning the flyweight boxing division gold medal at the Melbourne 1956 Olympic Games, the white Ampro tank top with Union Jack cloth badge inscribed "OLYMPIC GAMES 1956, GREAT BRITAIN," framed and glazed.

Terence (Terry) George Spinks MBE (1938-2012), a Great British featherweight boxer, won the gold medal in the flyweight division at the 1956 Melbourne Summer Olympics. Spinks had two hundred amateur bouts and was the 1956 ABA flyweight champion, turning professional in April 1957 with a bout against Jim Loughrey at Harringay Arena, North London, which he won on a stoppage for a cut eye. He won his last bout against Johnny Mantle in December 1962 and became a trainer and coach on retirement, going on to coach the South Korean team in the 1972 Munich Summer Olympics.

1956 *28¼in (72cm) long*
$1,700-2,100 GBA

A Jamaica athletics running shirt, signed in black marker pen by Usain Bolt, a replica of his Rio 2016 Olympic Games Vest, sold with a certificate of authenticity.
2016
$650-800 GBA

A CLOSER LOOK AT AN OLYMPIC TORCH

This is a rare example of a Rome 1960 Olympic Games bronzed aluminum bearer's torch

The design is based on drawings of torches on ancient Etruscan ceramics.

It was designed by Professor Maiure and his team from the National Museum of Archeology in Naples.

Unusually, it is still complete with its original burner.

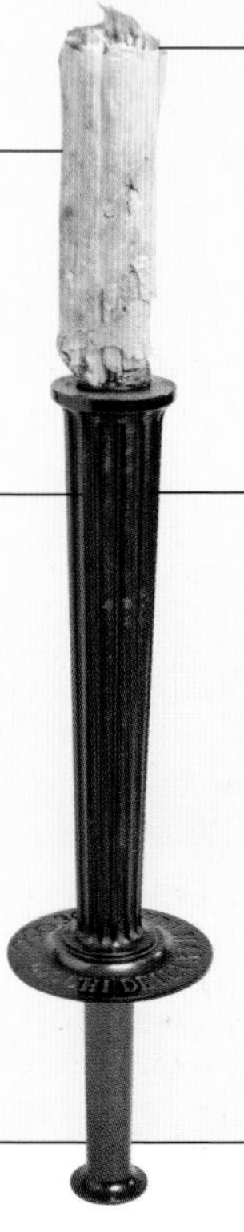

A bronzed aluminum bearer's torch.
1960 *15½in (39.5cm) high*
$6,500-8,000 GBA

A British Olympic Asscociation car grille badge, chrome metal and enamel, inscribed "BRITISH OLYMPIC ASSOCIATION."
$260-320 GBA

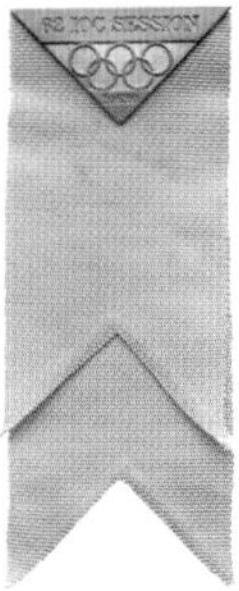

A badge for the International Olympic Committee 62nd Session, inscribed "62 IOC SESSION, TOKYO," double white ribbon suspension. *1964*
$1,900-2,600 GBA

A Tokyo 1964 Olympic Games stainless steel bearer's torch, blackened aluminum alloy bowl inscribed "XVIII OLYMPIAD TOKYO 1964."

1964 *25½in (65cm) high*

$8,000-9,000 **GBA**

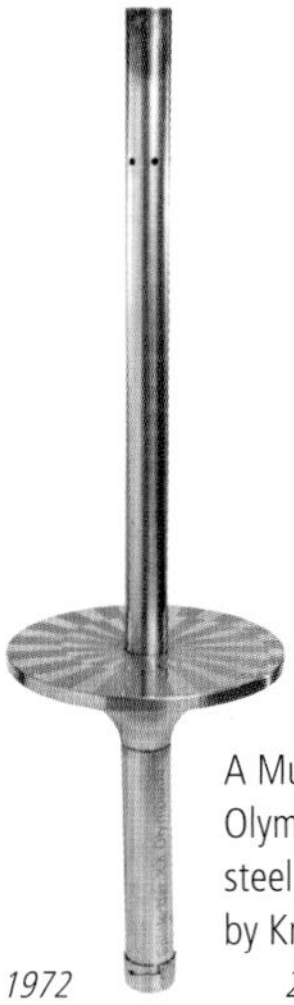

A Munich 1972 Olympic Games steel bearer's torch, by Krupp.

1972 *28¾in (73cm) high*

$1,900-2,600 **GBA**

A Moscow 1980 Olympic Games aluminum alloy bearer's torch, designed by Boris Tuchin, Moscow Games logo and legend in red.

1980 *22in (56cm) high*

$1,100-1,250 **GBA**

An Atlanta 1996 Olympic Games official bearer's torch, designed by Peter Mastrogiannis, in aluminum and Georgia pecan wood, with 22 reeds representing the cities where Olympic Games had taken place since 1896.

1996 *31½in (80cm) high*

$1,900-2,600 **GBA**

A silver "B" winner's prize medal for the 2nd National Greek Olympic Games ("Zappas Olympics") held in Athens in 1870, struck by Paris Mint, designed by Barre, stamped "ARGENT" on edge, obverse with head of King George I, reverse with Greek legend.

These Games were made possible through the sponsorship of the Greek businessman Evangelis Zappas. The first Games had been held in 1859. As such, the Zappas Olympics were among the first revivals of the ancient Games, the other notable example being the Wenlock Olympian Games, organized by William Penny Brookes in England from 1850.

$1,900-2,600 **GBA**

An 1896 Olympic Games participation gilt-bronze medal, designed by N. Lytras, struck by Honto-Poulus.

1896

$800-900 **GBA**

A London 1908 Olympic Games Committee member's silvered bronze badge, by Vaughton of Birmingham, with inscribed blue enamel band.

$1,600-2,100 **GBA**

A London 1908 Olympic Games unawarded second prize bronze medal for the 7-meter yacht race, designed by Bertram Mackennal, the rim inscribed "SECOND PRIZE 7 METRE YACHT RACE."

Only two boats entered the competition, both with British crews. The race was in the Solent from the Royal Victoria Yacht Club, Ryde, Isle of Wight, England. However, only one boat, *Heroine*, made the start line and the gold medal was awarded by a "sail-over." The second boat, which did not make the start, was *Mignonette*.

$3,900-4,500 **GBA**

A Helsinki 1952 Olympic Games participant's bronze medal, designed by K. Rasanen, in original paper box.

1952

$190-260 **GBA**

A Westmorland County Rugby Football Union cap, gold cap, dated "1895-6-7-8."

1895-1898

$190-260 GBA

A North of Scotland RFU representative cap, awarded to William Gladstone Falconer of Dollar Academy, Aberdeen Nomads and North of Scotland, embroidered dates for 1897-8-9, 1899-1900, and 1900-1901, pinned name tag in interior.

Falconer later became a Scotland RFU administrator.

$350-400 GBA

A Bath Rugby Football Club cap, dated.

1903

$260-320 GBA

A Neath Rugby Football Club cap, awarded to Gryff Bevan in season 1931-32, named to interior.

Gryff Bevan was a versatile player (center, wing, outside half) who played for Neath between 1929-30 and 1932-33. Bevan scored a total of 15 tries and was occasionally a goalkicker.

$190-260 GBA

A G.H. "Mick" Exley England Rugby League International cap, rose emblem, inscribed in ink on the label inside "G.H. EXLEY," dated.

Wakefield Trinity's Mick Exley played three times for England between 1932 and 1939.

1932-33

$260-320 GBA

A Northampton Rugby Football Club cap.

1933-37

$300-350 GBA

A Wales retro rugby jersey, signed by Gareth Edwards, J.P.R. Williams, Barry John, John Dawes, and Phil Bennett.

$190-260 GBA

A rare Ireland vs. South Africa rugby union program, played at Lansdowne Road, Dublin, November 30, 1912.

This was the second ever international between Ireland and South Africa and the first to be played in the south. The tourists won the game 38-0.

1912

$2,600-3,200 GBA

A Rugby League Challenge Cup Final program, Dewsbury vs. Wigan played at Wembley Stadium May 4, 1929.

1929

$300-400 GBA

A Rugby League Challenge Cup Final program, York vs. Halifax played at Wembley Stadium May 2, 1931, covers restored.

1931

$260-320 GBA

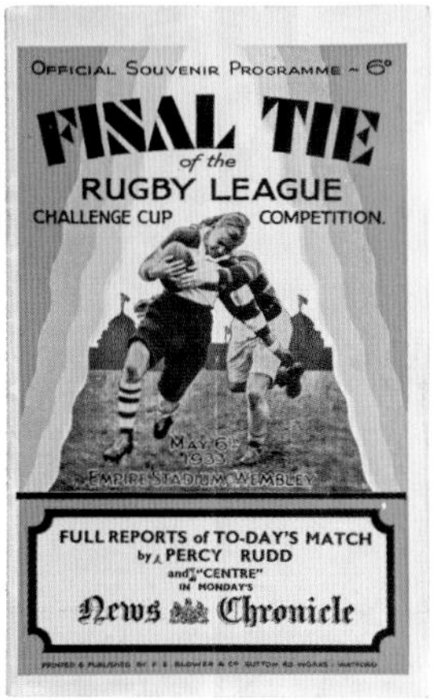

A Rugby League Challenge Cup Final program, Huddersfield vs. Warrington played at Wembley Stadium May 6, 1933.

1933

$190-260 GBA

A rare Feltham's Climax tennis racket, stamped R. Whitty, 14 Tythebarn St Liverpool and H. Faulkner on the wedge and frame, the frame is also stamped with a registered number "49148," dating it to 1886, breaks to the original string.

This innovative frame is special because it has a very early laminated hoop with ash on the outside and cane on the inside.

ca. 1886

$400-450 **GBA**

A "Birmal" tennis racket, aluminum frame, wire stringing and leather/whipped handle, patents stamped on frame by the Birmingham Aluminium Company.

ca. 1923

$600-700 **GBA**

A Wilson "Indestruts" tennis racket, made in steel by Dayton, Ohio, with original steel stringing.

ca. 1928

$300-350 **GBA**

An oversize tennis racket, by Greaves & Thomas, in the style of an early-20thC convex wedge racket ironically named "Extra Light."

It has faithfully reproduced features, such as shoulder reinforcement, grooved handle, and stringing pattern.

ca. 1980s *55½in (141cm) long*

$600-700 **GBA**

A tennis shirt worn by Andy Murray when winning his second Wimbledon men's singles title in the match against Milos Raonic July 10, 2016, in a frame, with a certificate of authenticity signed by Matt Gentry, managing director of Murray's management company, a photograph of Murray hugging the trophy on Centre Court, and a title plaque.

Sir Andrew (Andy) Barron Murray OBE (b.1987) British Tennis Professional Player and former World Tennis No.1, represented Great Britain in the 2012 and 2016 Olympics, wining gold medals for the singles titles, and was on the winning Davis Cup Team in 2015. He became the first British player to win a Grand Slam Singles title since 1977 in the 2012 US Open Final, and the first British man since 1936 to win a Grand Slam singles title. In 2016, Murray became the first British man to win two Wimbledon singles titles since Fred Perry, and the first Scot to win a Wimbledon singles title since Harold Mahony in 1896. Murray's management company confirmed by letter that Andy wore two shirts on court during the 2016 final, this being one of them. The other shirt was donated by Murray to the Wimbledon Lawn Tennis Museum.

$12,000-14,000 **GBA**

An Andre Agassi and John McEnroe double-signed Nike Air Challenge Court windbreaker jacket.

1990s

$190-260 **GBA**

A Kayzerzinn silver-plated tennis figurine, by W. Zwick.

13in (33cm) high

$500-650 **GBA**

A Karl Ens Volkstedt porcelain lady tennis figurine, model no.3031 2, "KVE" mark on base.

ca. 1910 *11½in (29cm) high*

$650-800 **GBA**

A 19thC silver tennis racket bangle.

ca. 1880

$300-400 **GBA**

A chrome eight-day, tennis racket-shaped desk clock, by C.M. Depose.

ca. 1930s *9in (23cm) long*

$650-800 **GBA**

A taxidermy cased Pike (Esox), with W. Howlett Newmarket label, reed, and gravel base in glazed bow front case.

42in (106.5cm) wide

$300-400 **CHEF**

A taxidermy brace of perch (*Perca*) and a rudd (*Scardinius erythrophthalmus*), W.B. Griggs, London, label and another label, "Perch and Rudd, caught by Aldborough, M. Bourne at Stamford Waters, Norfolk August 1928."

31½in (80cm) wide

$1,600-1,900 **CHEF**

A set of three F.W. Anstiss stuffed roach, trade label in interior and handwritten detail on rear.

ca. 1908 *35in (89cm) wide*

$1,150-1,450 **BELL**

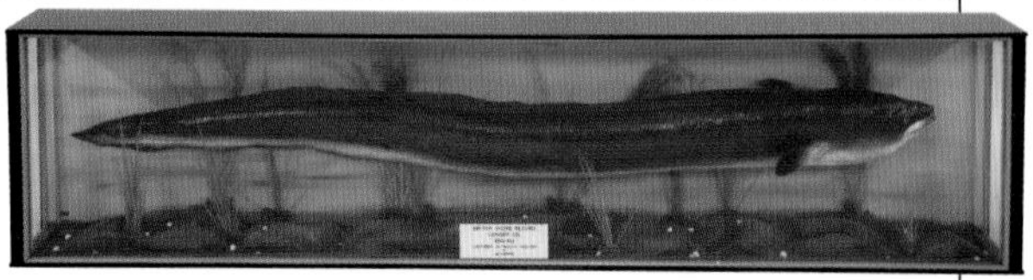

A British record conger eel, plaque states "British Shore Record Conger Eel 68lb 8oz, captured Plymouth - Nov 1991 by M. Larkin."

94½in (240cm) wide

$2,600-3,200 **SWO**

A late-19thC full-mount brown bear, grasping a tree branch and trunk frame, previously a stick stand.

75½in (192cm) high

$1,900-2,600 **L&T**

A late-19thC preserved Indian sun, or sloth, bear head mount, by James Gardner, the verso with a printed paper trade label.

16¼in (41.5cm) high

$1,050-1,150 **WW**

An early-20thC tiger head mount, attributed to Theobald Bros, from Mysore, India.

As this tiger's head mount dates from earlier than 1947, it needs no certification for sale in this country.
May be subject to CITES regulations if exported.

30¾in (78cm) high

$2,600-3,200 **SWO**

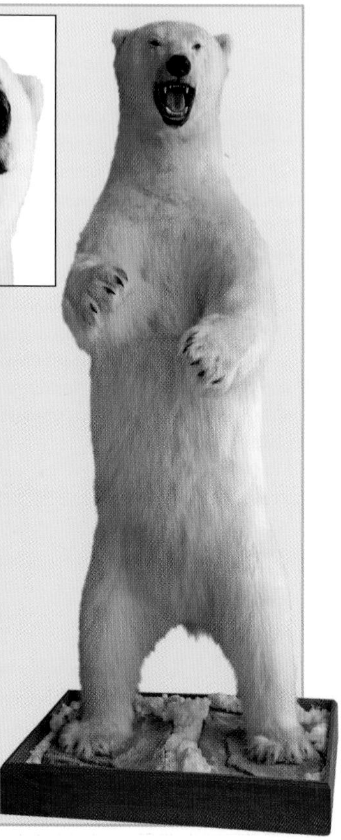

A late-20thC full-mount Canadian Polar bear (*Ursus maritimus*).

Of the 19 subpopulations of polar bear, 13 live in Canada. Adult males measure up to 10 feet (3 meters) in length and adult females up to 8 feet (2.4 meters). Their diet consists mainly of seals and their life expectancy is around 25 years.

90½in (230cm) high

$32,000-39,000 **SWO**

QUICK REFERENCE—TYPEWRITERS

- **In the 19thC, there were various bids to develop writing machines, but it was Christopher Latham Sholes' 1867 model that is considered the first practical typewriter. Sholes patented his second typewriter model in 1868. After design improvements, in 1873, E. Remington and Sons began manufacture of the typewriter. The machine was called the Remington.**
- **In 1872, the first electrically operated typewriter was invented by Thomas A. Edison.**
- **Portable typewriters were sold from the late 19thC, but those considered truly portable did not appear until 1909. Portable electric typewriters appeared in 1956. Following the invention of the modern computer, the need for typewriters declined.**

A German Frolio no.5 typewriter, 41007, cased.
ca. 1929
$70-80 WHP

A German Gundka Junior Model 3 tinplate typewriter, with roller inking, cased.
ca. 1920
$60-80 WHP

An American Blickensderfer no.7 typewriter, 93606, cased.
ca. 1899
$260-320 WHP

An Imperial B typewriter, no.22795.
ca. 1915
$260-320 WHP

An Oliver no.5 typewriter, no.322588.
ca. 1908
$90-100 WHP

An American Remington Portable, serial no.NL 56808.
ca. 1925
$70-80 WHP

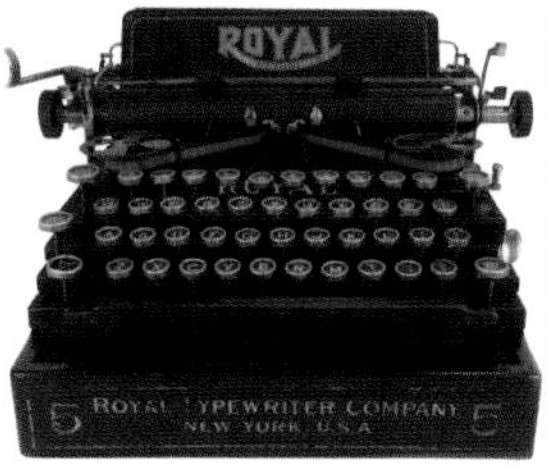

An American Royal Standard no.5 typewriter, no.275306.
ca. 1912
$120-140 WHP

A German Triumph Weke Perfekt typewriter, no.2190.
ca. 1928
$100-110 WHP

A Canadian "The Empire" typewriter, no.8812, cased.
ca. 1917
$190-260 WHP

A Yost "Light Running" no.10 typewriter, no.107563.
ca. 1903
$190-260 WHP

An early-20thC refurbished "Skeleton" telephone, by L.M. Ericsson & Co., no.16, for the UK market, signed, numbered on the ebonite insulation stage "No.16," with original silk-covered cable to handset and wall.

11½in (29cm) high

$1,300-1,900 **CM**

An ebonized cradle telephone.

1940s

$120-140 **FLD**

A cream GPO model 300 Bakelite telephone, numbered on handset underside "164 57," later converted, slight damage.

1950s

$160-210 **FLD**

A Bush DAC 90A valve radio in ivory Bakelite.

1950s *12in (30.5cm) long*

$60-80 **FLD**

An E.K. Cole Ltd. "Ekco" all-electric model SH25 radio, in Bakelite case, with a fret "Willow Tree" design on the speaker, slight damage.

1932 *18¼in (46.5cm) high*

$300-400 **FLD**

An Ekco model M23 radio, in a Bakelite case, medium-wave/long-wave meters, slight damage.

1931 *15¾in (40cm) high*

$90-100 **FLD**

A Perspex-cased television, of globular translucent "Sputnik" form, on a circular chrome foot.

1970s(?) *18¼in (46.5cm) high*

$500-650 **BELL**

A prewar RCA unidirectional type KU-3A ribbon microphone, with metal bracket.

Property of the late Ray Merrin film rerecording sound mixer, part of the Oscar-winning Best Sound team for *The Last Emperor* (1987) and recipient of the Bafta Lifetime Achievement Award for outstanding contribution to sound design. Merrin's filmography includes *A Clockwork Orange, The Shining, Tommy, Alien, The Killing Fields, Little Voice, Hilary & Jack, Trainspotting,* and the two first *Harry Potter* films.

$1,800-2,300 **BELL**

An AKG D25 dynamic microphone, with metal boom bracket.

Property of the late Ray Merrin.

ca. 1960

$500-650 **BELL**

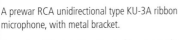

A Metropolitan-Vickers desk fan.

17¼in (44cm) high

$350-400 **SWO**

QUICK REFERENCE—STEIFF BEARS

- **Steiff was founded by Margarete Steiff (1847-1909) in Giengen, Germany, in 1880.**
- **Margarete's nephew Richard Steiff (1877-1939) joined the company in 1897.**
- **In 1902, he designed his "Steiff Bär 55PB," the first soft-toy bear with jointed arms and legs. More than 3,000 bears were sold at the first trade fair and Steiff's new "Teddy" bear was an international success. The name "Teddy" supposedly comes from an incident on a 1902 hunting trip, where president Theodore "Teddy" Roosevelt refused to kill an injured bear tied to a tree.**
- **Margarete's nephews took over the business following her death in 1909.**
- **Materials, color, form, and labels can all be used to identify and accurately date bears. Check for the distinctive "Button-in-Ear" trademark, which Steiff used from 1904 to distinguish its bears from those of its rivals.**
- **Damaged bears can usually be restored by professionals, but tears, stains, replaced pads, or worn fur can all reduce value.**

A very rare Steiff 35PB rod-jointed bear, with black boot-button eyes, replacement gutta-percha nose, swivel head with seam from ear to ear across top of head, five claws in thick wool, hump, firm stuffing, and rare elephant button with S-shaped trunk, about 10 percent of the plush has been rewoven, small patched hole in tip of muzzle, and slight repair to pads.

1904 *19in (48.5cm) high*

$8,000-9,000 **SAS**

A CLOSER LOOK AT AN EARLY STEIFF BEAR

The Steiff 35PB and 28PB are the earliest bears available to buy, made in 1904, the second model after the original 55PB. The 35 is the height in centimeters in a sitting position and the P is for plush and the B is for beweglich (jointed). These bears are before the name Teddy, so just called bears.

This is an extremely rare, shaggy white mohair Steiff 35PB rod joint bear, with black boot-button eyes.

He has a pronounced muzzle and extremely rare original gutta-percha nose.

He has a swivel head with a seam from ear to ear across the top of his head and rod-jointed elongated limbs.

A Steiff bear, excellently replaced felt pads, five claws in thick wool, hump, and firm stuffing, neat repair on right wrist, small patch on tip of right toe, and slight general wear and thinning.

1904 *21in (53.5cm) high*

$10,500-13,000 **SAS**

An early Steiff cinnamon center-seam teddy bear, with black boot-button eyes, swivel head, jointed elongated limbs with felt pads, hump, working large side-squeezed squeaker, soft stuffing, and FF button.

1908 *20in (51cm) high*

$6,000-7,000 **SAS**

An early Steiff white center-seam teddy bear, with black boot-button eyes, swivel head, jointed elongated limbs with felt pads, hump, inoperative growler, soft stuffing, and FF button.

1908 *20in (51cm) high*

$6,000-7,000 **SAS**

An early Steiff teddy bear, with black boot-button eyes, swivel head, jointed elongated limbs with felt pads, hump, inoperative growler, and FF button, some slight thinning and damage to pads.

ca. 1909 *20in (51cm) high*

$7,000-8,500 **SAS**

An early Steiff teddy bear, with blonde mohair, black boot-button eyes, swivel head, jointed elongated limbs with felt pads, inoperative growler, and FF button, slight general wear and thinning.

This bear is known as "Irene" from the Wendy Jaques Collection.

ca. 1909 *13½in (34.5cm) high*

$2,900-3,600 **SAS**

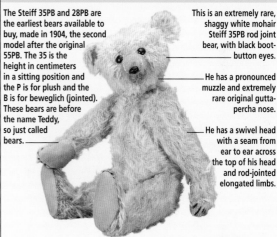

A Steiff blonde mohair teddy bear, straw stuffed, some sparse areas, feet pads replaced, lacks button.

ca. 1909 *10¼ (26cm) high*

$600-700 **C&T**

An early-20thC Steiff dachshund on wheels, brown velveteen with black boot-button eyes and four cast spoked wheels, well loved.

11¾in (30cm) long

$700-850 **FLD**

A Steiff bear, with movable head, collar, and plush fur, on metal spoked wheels.

ca. 1909 *13¾in (35cm) high*

$800-900 **CHOR**

A Steiff dark blonde plush straw-filled teddy bear, with swivel joints, brown button eyes, and cloth pads.

ca. 1910 *13½in (34.5cm) high*

$700-850 **HT**

A Steiff large plush teddy bear.

ca. 1910 *29¼in (74.5cm) high*

$4,500-5,200 **ROS**

An early-20thC teddy bear, probably Steiff, with dark golden brown mohair, black boot-button eyes, swivel head, jointed elongated limbs, hump, and inoperative growler, slight damage.

ca. 1910 *15¾in (40cm) high*

$2,300-2,900 **FLD**

A Steiff World War I substitute plush teddy bear, with unusual fine blonde corduroy material body, black boot-button eyes, swivel head, jointed elongated limbs, woven paper plush (or nettle) fabric feet pads, inoperative side squeaker, missing most of left and half of right feet pads, some general wear.

Because resources ran out during the war, Steiff came up with some unusual substitute plush to continue production, including a paper-plush material made from nettles. Stylistically, this is a typical Steiff 8/9in teddy bear with a side squeaker and no hand pads, but this is the first time seen in this, possibly unique, corduroy.

8½in (21.5cm) high

$2,600-3,900 **SAS**

An early-20thC Steiff "Bully" dog, swiveling head with velveteen forehead and muzzle with airbrushed detail, glass eyes, retains button in ear and label.

8in (20.5cm) high

$650-800 **FLD**

A Steiff white mohair teddy bear, with clear and black glass eyes with brown backs, swivel head, jointed elongated limbs with felt pads, hump, inoperative growler and FF button with remains of red tag, slight wear.

1920s *20in (51cm) high*

$2,600-3,900 **SAS**

A Steiff golden mohair teddy bear, with glass eyes, stitched nose and claws, a pronounced hump, Steiff underlined F button, both ears requiring restitching.

16in (40.5cm) high

$800-900 BER

A Steiff teddy bear, with golden mohair, brown and black glass eyes, swivel head, jointed elongated limbs, hump, growler, and small FF button, replaced pads, slight thinning, and a little faded.

1920s *25in (63.5cm) high*

$3,200-3,900 SAS

A rare Steiff cinnamon mohair "Treff" dog, with brown and black glass eyes inserted into heavy eyelids, swivel head, inoperative squeaker, and FF button, slight thinning and general wear.

1920s *10½in (26.5cm) high*

$450-600 SAS

A Steiff "Young Riding Bear" on wheels, with brown and black glass eyes, inoperative pull growler, on metal frame, pull cord, some wear and fading.

1960s *39in (99cm) long*

$500-650 SAS

A Steiff African elephant, limited edition no.846 of 1,500, with tag certificate.

1998 *17in (43cm) long*

$170-230 SAS

A Steiff Netherlands Exclusive "Tomato Teddy Bear," limited edition no.848 of 1,500, in original window box with certificate.

2000

$260-390 SAS

A Steiff "Millennium Musical Band," limited edition no.793 of 2,000, in original box with certificate, the bears' heads could do with a firm brush, box flattened and worn.

2000

$450-600 SAS

A Steiff "Harley Davidson 100th Anniversary Bear," limited edition no.3,424 of 5,000, in original box with certificate, some scuffing to box.

2003

$160-230 SAS

A Steiff large teddy bear 1906 replica, limited edition no.549 of 1,906, in original box with certificate, a slight musty odor.

2005

$300-450 SAS

A rare BMC large teddy bear, orange and black glass eyes, swivel head, jointed elongated limbs with felt pads, large rounded hump, inoperative squeaker, and remains of black and gold woven label on foot pad, very minimal thinning.

The Bruin Manufacturing Company (BMC), based in New York, produced bears from 1907 to 1909. It is believed that this is the first time this bear has appeared in such a large size.

1907 *28in (71cm) high*
$3,200-4,500 SAS

A rare British United Toy Manufacturing Co. Ltd World War I "Highlander Soldier" teddy bear, with clear and black oily glass eyes with brown painted backs, swivel head, jointed limbs with felt pads, original khaki jacket with brass buttons and leather Sam Brown belt, felt Glengarry bonnet, wool tartan kilt, loss of mohair from moth attack.

This is the only known example of this bear, probably dating from around World War I and very similar to Harwin's example. This bear was found with a fair amount of moth damage, but whatever the material used in the jacket, fortunately it was not attractive to the moth.

14½in (37cm) high
$1,700-2,100 SAS

A Chad Valley teddy, with orange and black glass eyes, swivel head, jointed limbs, inoperative squeaker, celluloid covered metal button in ear, and woven red and white label on foot, some thinning, some wear.

This bear is known as "Bradman," because the vendor was told that he was originally presented as a prize after a cricket match.

1920s *26in (66cm) high*
$450-600 SAS

A Chad Valley clown teddy bear, with orange and black glass eyes, swivel head, jointed limbs, HM Queen and woven blue and white label on feet pads, inoperative squeaker, one ear split to make two ears with new halves, replaced pompons.

1930s *16in (40.5cm) high*
$260-320 SAS

QUICK REFERENCE—CHILTERN BEARS

- **The Chiltern Toy Works was founded in 1908 in Buckinghamshire by Josef Eisenmann and Leon Rees. Originally called Eisenmann & Co., it traded under the name Einco.**
- **The first teddy bear, "Master Teddy," was produced in 1915. The "Hugmee" bear was produced in 1923, becoming the company's most popular bear.**
- **Registered in 1924, the Chiltern Toys trademark was formed from a collaboration between Rees and founder of H.G. Stone & Co. Ltd., Harry Stone (previously of J.K. Farnell).**
- **Pam Howells worked for Chiltern between 1957 and 1967, designing the sitting, unjointed bear.**
- **The company was taken over by Chad Valley in 1967.**

A Chad Valley "Navy Week Bulldog," for HMS *Revenge*, of cream velvet, orange and black glass eyes, oilcloth collar, sailor's hat with HMS *Revenge* hat band, unusual label "CHAD VALLEY PRODUCTS BRITISH SELLICKS, PLYMOUTH," celluloid covered blue button and card tag, slight discoloration.

8in (20.5cm) long
$260-320 SAS

A large plush teddy bear, probably Chad Valley, with interior bells in the ears, vacant patch for label on foot.

25¼in (64cm) high
$190-260 ROS

A Chiltern large "Hugmee" teddy bear, with orange and black glass eyes, swivel head, jointed limbs, rounded hump, and inoperative squeaker, known as "Honey Bear," pads recovered, some slight thinning.

1930s *26in (66cm) high*
$450-600 SAS

A Chiltern sheepskin "Hugmee" teddy bear, with orange and black glass eyes, swivel head, jointed limbs with leather pads, label in side seam "Chiltern Hugmee Toys Real Sheep Skin Made in England," some slight wear.

1940s *13½in (34.5cm) high*
$130-190 SAS

A rare Chiltern "Home Guard" teddy bear, with orange and black glass eyes, khaki velvet integral uniform with stripes on arms, black velvet feet, and replacement felt helmet, some thinning to mohair.

This is believed to be the second known example of this bear, the other is in the Teddy Bears of Witney Collection and was later replicated by Merrythought.

1940s *13in (33cm) high*

$2,600-3,200 SAS

An early FADAP teddy bear, with clear and black glass eyes, swivel head, jointed elongated limbs with felt pads, slight hump, and inoperative growler, worn, faded, and slight damage on pads.

This actual bear appears on page 55 of Eric Petit's book on FADAP and was the childhood toy of a lady from Divonne-les-Bains who later worked at the FADAP factory. This bear is known as "Pradalet" from the Eric Petit Collection.

French company Fabrication Artistique d'Animaux en Peluche (FADAP) began producing teddy bears in 1925. Early FADAP bears had a metal button in one ear, embossed with "FADAP" and "France." The bears were chubby, with thick paws. They typically had a seam under the chin and an upturned nose. FADAP closed in 1978.

1926/27 *15½in (39.5cm) high*

$260-390 SAS

An early FADAP teddy bear, with black boot-button eyes, swivel head, jointed limbs with cloth pads, small hump, and growler, fairly worn.

This actual bear appears on pag 57 of Eric Petit's book on FADAP and is known as "Theuyis" from the Eric Petit Collection.

1928/29 *23in (58.5cm) high*

$300-400 SAS

An early FADAP teddy bear, with clear and black glass eyes, swivel head, jointed elongated limbs with felt pads.

1926/27 *16½in (42cm) high*

$260-320 SAS

An early FADAP teddy bear, with black boot-button eyes, swivel head, jointed limbs with cloth pads, hump, inoperative squeaker, and original ribbon on chest.

This bear is known as "Mazuc" from the Eric Petit Collection.

1930 *22½in (57cm) high*

$260-320 SAS

A Farnell teddy bear, with orange and black glass eyes, swivel head, jointed limbs with felt pads, hump and inoperative growler, stitched repairs on feet pads.

This bear is known as "Maurice" from the Wendy Jaques Collection.

1920s *21½in (54.5cm) high*

$1,600-2,100 SAS

A Farnell teddy bear, with orange and black glass eyes, swivel head, jointed limbs with cloth pads, hump and inoperative growler, balding on face and ear, general wear.

1920s *16½in (42cm) high*

$300-400 SAS

A Farnell teddy bear, with orange and black glass eyes, swivel head, jointed limbs with painted cloth pads, rounded hump, inoperative growler, blue and white woven label on foot, known as "Edward," slight wear.

1930s *28in (71cm) high*

$650-800 SAS

A rare MAP purple wool plush teddy bear, with clear and black glass eyes, swivel head, jointed limbs with plush pads, hump, and inoperative growler, slight wear.

This bear is known as "Esquine" from the Eric Petit Collection.

1950/55 *23½in (59.5cm) high*

$260-390 SAS

A MAP large teddy bear, with clear and black glass eyes with brown backs, swivel head, jointed limbs with velvet pads, rounded hump and inoperative growler, very minor wear.

Manufacture D'animaux en Peluche (MAP) was a Parisian company run by Emile Lang. This bear is known as "Peyreret" from the Eric Petit Collection.

31½in (80cm) high

$650-800 SAS

A large Merrythought "Cheeky" teddy bear, with unusual cinnamon dralon plush, orange and black plastic eyes, ears with bells, swivel head, jointed limbs, and printed yellow label on foot, some aging.

1960s *26in (66cm) high*

$120-140 SAS

A rare Omega walking teddy bear, with clear and black glass eyes with brown painted backs, swivel head, jointed arms, hinged legs with knees, felt pads with a leather toe, and inoperative growler, general wear and thinning.

When you hold the bear and walk him along, the weight of his feet gives him a walking motion.

1920s *14¾in (37.5cm) high*

$1,300-1,800 SAS

A Peacock large teddy bear, orange and black glass eyes, swivel head, jointed limbs, slight rounded hump, squeaker and red and white label on foot, known as "Percy," general thinning and wear.

1920s *29in (73.5cm) high*

$300-400 SAS

A Pintel teddy bear, clear and black glass eyes, swivel head, chunky body, jointed arms and inoperative growler, fairly worn.

Pintel bears look very like FADAP bears at this time. This bear is known as "Esquinle" from the Eric Petit Collection.

1930/35 *23in (58.5cm) high*

$190-260 SAS

An early-20thC Gebruder Sussenguth "Peter" teddy bear, with swiveling black and white eyes and open mouth with teeth and moving tongue, jointed limbs, his neck with original ribbon and metal rimmed card tag "Peter Ges. gesch. Nr.895257," within an original part box.

14in (35.5cm) high

$1,600-2,300 ROS

A plush teddy bear, in the Steiff style, with elongated arms and legs.

14½in (37cm) high

$190-260 ROS

An Arnold tinplate "KLM Flying Dutchman," friction-powered airplane, boxed.

ca. 1950 *18½in (47cm) long*

$300-400 **BELL**

An early-20thC tinplate and clockwork limousine, by Karl Bub, no.788, number plate on both front and rear reads "KB-788," fitted with a single fixed key and with battery compartment for front light operation.

15½in (39.5cm) long

$900-1,050 **LSK**

A Carette tinplate clockwork limousine, interior with fold-down seats and a roof rack, sporadic paint wear, lacking carriage lamps.

16in (40.5cm) long

$16,000-21,000 **POOK**

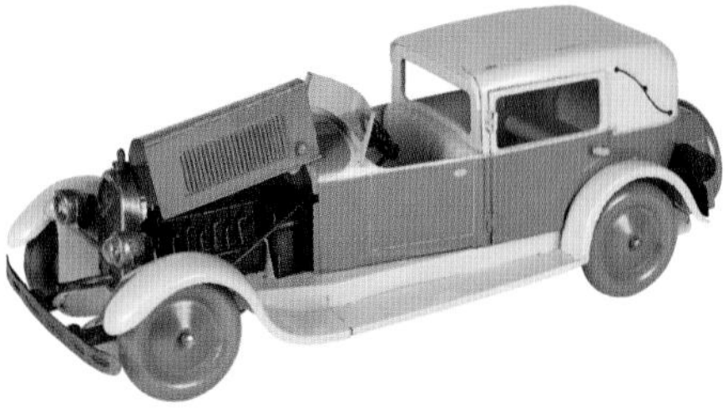

A Jep Darrack painted tinplate clockwork Talbot coupé, with operable headlights, opening doors and hood that reveals engine, restored.

17¼in (44cm) long

$1,600-2,100 **POOK**

A Japanese tinplate "BATTERY OPERATED Fire Tricycle," made by T.N. (Nomura), in original box.

ca. 1960s

$300-350 **LOCK**

A Japanese tinplate "INTERPLANETARY SPACE FIGHTER," made by T.N. (Nomura), in original box, play worn.

ca. 1960s

$650-800 **LOCK**

An Alps Television Spaceman tinplate robot.

ca. 1960s

$260-320 **PSA**

A Cragstan SSS Tokyo tinplate battery-powered Cadillac "Cragstan SSS," boxed.

17in (43cm) long

$400-450 **BELL**

A Japanese Shasta tinplate Bandai "Rambler" travel trailer, no.523.

ca. 1960 *11in (28cm) long*

$210-260 **BELL**

A Yoshiya tinplate "Planet Robot," in need of attention.

ca. 1960s

$80-100 **PSA**

A Lehmann tinplate "St. Vincent 672" clockwork battleship, not in working order.

13¼in (33.5cm) long

$170-230 **LOCK**

A Marx tinplate "Flying Fortress 2095" clockwork military airplane, boxed.

ca. 1940 *13¼in (34cm) long*

$180-230 **BELL**

A Schuco "Examico 4001" tinplate clockwork car, boxed with instructions, slight damage.

$130-180 **FLD**

A Schuco "ELEKTRO-PHANOMENAL" 5503 Mercedes 190SL tinplate, with opening trunk, chrome fittings, black tonneau, and Mercedes badges, boxed, with instructions, lacking control and accessories.

8¼in (21cm) long

$130-190 **FLD**

A Spot-On "Austin Prime Mover with Articulated Flat Float," no.106A/OC, in original box.

$450-500 **LOCK**

A painted tin paddle wheel clockwork steamboat, attributed to The Stevens & Brown Mfg. Co., Cromwell, Connecticut, stenciled "COLUMBIA," with key.

ca. 1870-80 *15in (38cm) long*

$3,200-3,900 **NA**

A tinplate and clockwork fire brigade engine, tires read "CONTINENTAL-BALLOON CORD 895 x 135."

11½in (29cm) long

$100-110 **LOCK**

QUICK REFERENCE—CORGI

- **In 1956, the Mettoy company launched a range of die-cast models, partly inspired by the success of Dinky Supertoys. Die-cast toys are made from a metal alloy that can be cast in a mold, also known as a die.**
- **Corgi cars were more realistic than Dinky cars, with clear windows, detailed interiors, "Glidamatic" spring suspension, and opening doors and hoods. The earliest cars produced were modeled after contemporary British-built sedan cars.**
- **In the 1960s and 1970s, Corgi produced models inspired by TV shows and films, including cars used by James Bond and Batman. These are often highly sought-after by collectors.**
- **Unusual colors increase the value, as do unusual combinations of wheel, interior, and body colors. Condition is important for collectors of Corgi cars. Mint boxed examples tend to fetch the highest prices.**
- **Today, Corgi produces most of its cars and trucks as one-shot limited-edition pieces.**

A near-mint Corgi Toys "JAMES BOND 007 TOYOTA 2000GT," no.336, in the original all-card sliding tray box with packing piece, packing ring, lapel badge, secret instructions, with eight various missiles.
$230-290 **LSK**

A mint Corgi "MORRIS MINI MINOR WHIZZWHEELS," no.204, boxed.
$180-230 **W&W**

A near-mint Corgi Toys "JAMES BOND'S ASTON MARTIN DB5," no.261, with James Bond figure and bandit figure, in original all-card sliding tray box with secret instructions envelope, secret instructions leaflet, and a spare bandit figure, pencil "9/11D" on box, base slightly collapsed.
$300-350 **LSK**

A near-mint Corgi Toys "CHRYSLER IMPERIAL," no.246, with two figures, with golf trolley in trunk, in original all-card box.
$160-210 **LSK**

A Corgi "FORD CONSUL CORTINA SUPER ESTATE CAR," no.440, boxed, with inner display and inner card packaging.
$230-290 **WM**

A Corgi "THE GREEN HORNET 'BLACK BEAUTY' CRIME FIGHTING CAR," no.268, with two interior figures and accessories, in picture card box, with display stand.
$300-350 **WM**

A near-mint Corgi Toys "251 HILLMAN IMP," in original all-card box, with luggage piece, with Corgi Model Club leaflet.
$120-140 **LSK**

A Corgi Toys "TRIUMPH HERALD COUPE," no.231, in original all-card box with Model Club leaflet.
$100-120 **LSK**

A near-mint Corgi Toys "THE "SAINT'S" CAR VOLVO P.1800," no.258, in original all-card box.
$300-400 **LSK**

A near-mint Corgi Toys "'E' TYPE JAGUAR WITH DETACHABLE HARD TOP," no.307, in the original all-card box.
$300-350 **LSK**

A Corgi Toys "Chitty Chitty Bang Bang," no.266, in original box, some damage.
$100-120 **LOCK**

A Corgi Toys "Charlie's Angels Custom Van," no.434, in the original window box with header card.
$50-60 **LSK**

A Corgi Toys, "MORRIS MINI COOPER," no.227, competition model.
$170-210 **LSK**

A Corgi Toys, Triumph TR3 Sports Car, no.305, in original all-card box, with leaflet.
$80-90 **LSK**

A near-mint Corgi Toys "NEVILLE CEMENT MIXER," no.460 ERF, in original all-card box.
$70-80 **LSK**

A Corgi Toys "HEINKEL ECONOMY CAR," no.233, in original all-card box.
$90-100 **LSK**

A Corgi "CIRCUS GIRAFFE TRANSPORTER WITH GIRAFFES," no.503, boxed, with original inner card packaging.
$160-210 **WM**

A Corgi Major Toys Gift set, no.27, in original box, loss to polystyrene.
$90-100 **LOCK**

A Corgi "COMMER "WALLS" REFRIGERATOR VAN," no.453, boxed.
$90-100 **BELL**

A near-mint Corgi Toys "ECURIE ECOSSE RACING CAR TRANSPORTER," no.1126, in original lift-off lid all-card box, with three packing pieces, with Corgi Model Club leaflets.
$170-210 **LSK**

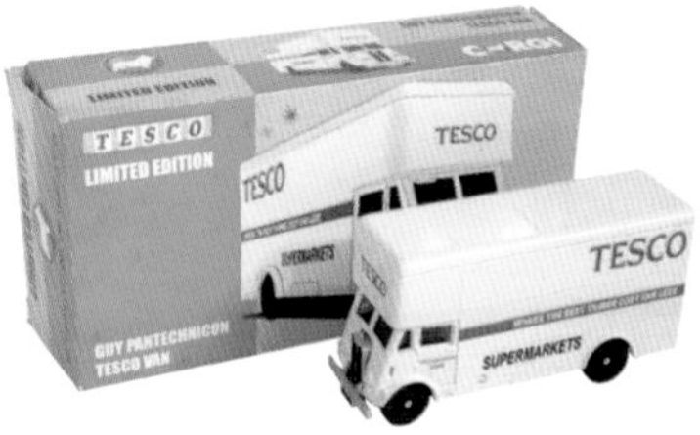

A Corgi Toys 1:76 scale "GUY PANTECHNICON TESCO VAN," in original plastic packed box, limited edition with certificate no.0839/2000 released.

$25-30 LSK

A near-mint Corgi Toys "BATBOAT AND TRAILER," no.107, boat with tinplate fin, in original all-card box.

$300-400 LSK

A Corgi "DOLPHIN 20 CRUISER" boat, no.104, in card picture box.

$80-100 WM

A Corgi Major Toys "Bristol BLOODHOUND GUIDED MISSILE WITH LAUNCHING RAMP," no.1108, in original box, some wear.

$45-50 LOCK

A Corgi Major Toys "MASSEY FERGUSON '780' COMBINE HARVESTER," no.1111, in original box, hole in lid.

$58-60 LOCK

A near-mint Corgi Toys "FORD 5000 SUPER MAJOR TRACTOR," no.67, in original all-card box, with original packing piece and model club leaflet.

$140-190 LSK

A Corgi Toys "CHIPPERFIELDS CIRCUS CRANE TRUCK," no.1126, in original all-card box, with original hook.

$80-100 LSK

A Corgi Toys Gift Set, no.24, Constructor Set GS/24, complete, in original box.

$60-80 LOCK

A Corgi Toys "The Beatles Yellow Submarine," no.803, with two red hatches, boxed.

$450-500 WM

A Corgi "Magic Roundabout" carousel, no.852, with Swiss musical movement, boxed.

$300-400 WM

QUICK REFERENCE—DINKY

- **Starting out as Model Miniatures in 1931, Dinky toys were designed to accompany the Hornby railroad sets. The majority of models were produced in a scale of 1:48.**
- **The first car, no.23a, was produced in 1934. In the same year, the range was renamed Dinky.**
- **After World War II, Dinky expanded its ranges, introducing Supertoys. This range of trucks was modeled to the standard Dinky scale of 1:48. Supertoys were typically sold in blue and white horizontally striped boxes. They were marketed separately from Hornby's railroads. To many die-cast collectors, these are the most desirable Dinkys. Rare variations and models fetch high prices. Production at Dinky's Binns Road factory stopped in the 1970s.**

A near-mint Dinky Toys "VOLKSWAGEN KARMANN GHIA COUPE," no.187, in original panel box.

$100-120 **LSK**

A Dinky Toys "VOLKSWAGEN SALOON" (sedan), no.181, in original correct color spot all-card box, with unusual "MY" decal on passenger side door.

$90-100 **LSK**

A near-mint Dinky Toys "M.G. MIDGET SPORTS" car, no.102, in original correct color spot all-card box.

$500-600 **LSK**

A Dinky Toys "MORRIS MINI TRAVELLER," no.197, in original box.

$50-60 **LOCK**

A near-mint Dinky Toys "VAUXHALL VIVA," no.136, in original all-card box.

$70-80 **LSK**

A Dinky Toys "VAUXHALL VICTOR" station wagon (estate car), no.141, in original all-card picture sided box.

$60-80 **LSK**

A Dinky Toys "FORD "FORDOR" SEDAN" trade box, no.139A, in original all-card trade box, split on one end.

$70-80 **LSK**

A Dinky Toys "ROLLS-ROYCE SILVER WRAITH," no.150, in original all-card box, one end flap missing.

$45-60 **LSK**

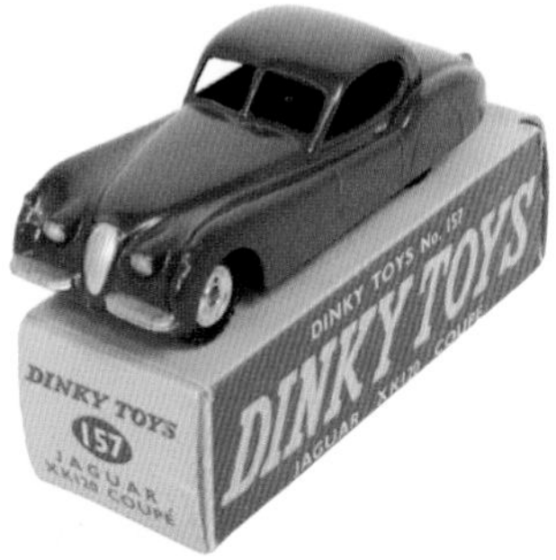

A near-mint Dinky Toys "JAGUAR XK120 COUPÉ," no.157, in original all-card box, missing one end flap.

$160-210 **LSK**

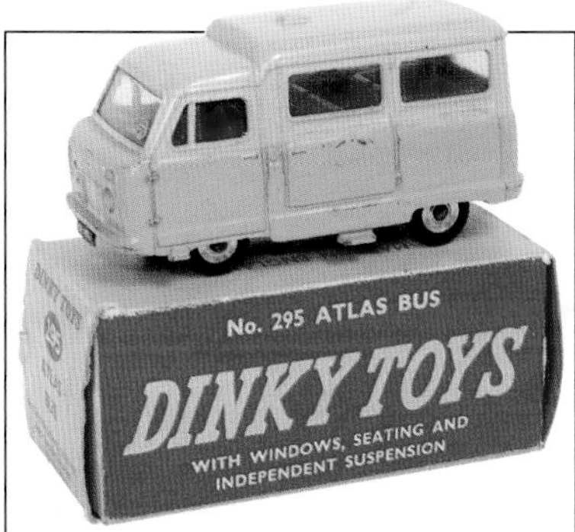

A Dinky Toys "ATLAS BUS," no.295, in original all-card box.
$40-50 LSK

A Dinky Toys "CADILLAC TOURER," no.131, with driver, in original all-card spot box.
$70-80 LSK

A Dinky Junior "2 CV CITROËN," no.105, original chassis mounting with game.
This car is one of the rarest in the series.
1961
$1,700-2,100 IVN

A prewar Dinky "Trade Box (A1009)," no.28/2, with six "Type 2 Delivery Vans," including; no. 28D "OXO," "OXO BEEF IN BRIEF" on side; no.28G "Kodak Film," "Use Kodak Film To Be Sure" on both sides; no.28H "Dunlop Tyres," "DUNLOP TYRES" on both sides; no.28K "Marsh's Sausages," "Marsh's Sausages" on both sides; no.28M "Wakefield Castol," "Wakefield Castol Motor Oil" on both sides; no.28P "Crawford's," "CRAWFORD'S BISCUITS" on both sides, minor crazing and minimal paint loss throughout, contained in trade box with dividers.
ca. 1935
$18,000-23,000 M&M

A near-mint Dinky Toys "FERRARI RACING CAR," no.234, with racing number "5," in original all-card box.
$480-500 LSK

A Dinky Toys "AUSTIN-HEALEY "100" SPORTS," no.109, with racing number "23," in original correct color spot all-card box.
$120-140 LSK

A Dinky Toys "ASTON MARTIN DB3 SPORTS" car, no.110, racing number "20," with driver, in original all-card box.
$160-210 LSK

A Dinky Toys "SUNBEAM ALPINE SPORTS" car, no.107, with driver and racing number "34," in original all-card box.
$100-130 LSK

A Dinky Toys "TRIUMPH TR2 SPORTS" car, no.111, with driver and racing number "25," in original all-card box.
$160-210 LSK

A Dinky Toys "CONNAUGHT RACING CAR," no.236, with driver and racing number "32," in original all-card box.

$100-110 **LSK**

A Dinky Toys prewar "Mobiloil" gas tank wagon, no.25D, some playwear.

$300-350 **LSK**

A Dinky Toys "SPRATT'S GUY VAN," no.917, in original box.

$90-100 **LOCK**

A Dinky Toys "GUY FLAT TRUCK," no.512, in original box.

$80-90 **LOCK**

A near-mint Dinky Toys, "FODEN 14-TON TANKER 'MOBILGAS,'" no.504, in original all-card box.

$935-1,050 **LSK**

A Dinky Toys "TANK TRANSPORTER," no.660, in original lift-off lid, all-card box, with one packing piece.

$90-100 **LSK**

A near-mint Dinky Toys "SHELL B.P. FUEL TANER," no.944, with windows version, in original pictorial all-card box.

$300-350 **LSK**

A Dinky Toys "BEDFORD 10 CWT. Van Kodak," no.480, in original box.

$80-100 **LOCK**

A Dinky Toys "BEDFORD END TIPPER" trade box and contents, no.25M, in original all-card trade box.

$90-100 **LSK**

A near-mint Dinky Toys "AUSTIN COVERED WAGON" trade box, no.30S.

$80-90 **LSK**

A near-mint Dinky Toys Trojan delivery van, no.454, with "CYDRAX" livery.

$120-140 **LSK**

A Dinky Toys 00 "AUSTIN LORRY," no.064, playworn, in original all-card box.

$25-40 **LSK**

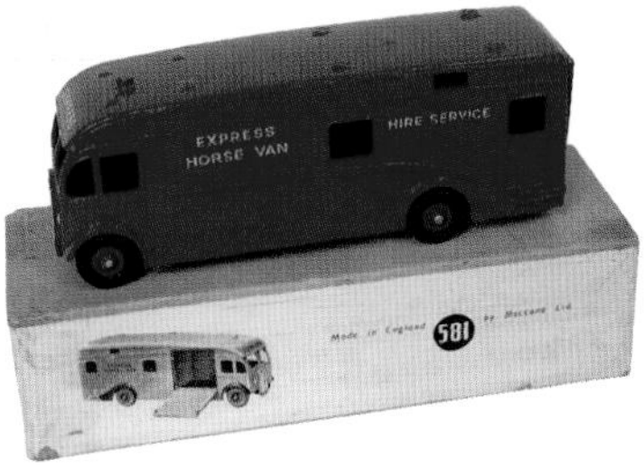

A Dinky Toys "EXPRESS HORSE VAN," no.581, US export version, in original Hudson Dobson labeled box, with packing pieces, box lid faded.

$170-230 **LSK**

A Dublo Dinky Toys "LANSING BAGNALL TRACTOR & TRAILER," no.076.

$70-80 **LSK**

A near-mint Dinky Toys "Souvenir Set London Scene," no.300, with "London Taxi" and "London Bus," in original polystyrene sliding tray pictorial box.

$30-45 **LSK**

QUICK REFERENCE—FRENCH DINKY

- **French Dinky began in Bobigny, Paris, in the early 1930s. At first, model trains and cars were produced in line with its British parent company, but French Dinky's range became increasingly different, focusing on commercial vehicles, aircraft, and cars by French makers. It continued production into the 1970s, after Dinky had declined in England. Production was transferred to the Pilen factory in Spain in 1977, and the company closed in 1981.**

A near-mint French Dinky Toys 33AN "DÉMÉNAGEUR SIMCA 'CARGO'" truck, in original all-card box.

$260-320 **LSK**

A Dinky Toys "Blaw Knox" bulldozer, no.561, in rare blue with tan driver and original tracks, play worn.

$60-70 **LSK**

A French Dinky Toys "MASERATI SPORT 2000," no.22A, in original all-card box.

$120-160 **LSK**

A French Dinky Toys "ALFA ROMEO 1900 SUPER SPRINT" coupé, no.24J, in original all-card box.

$60-80 **LSK**

A French Dinky toys single-axle covered trailer, no.25T, with tinplate draw bar and rear hook.

$20-25 **LSK**

A French Dinky Toys "C'EST UNE FABRICATION MECCANO" Unic Articulated BP tanker, no.887, with five hoses for filling tank, with electrical lights operated by spare wheel, in original Supertoys box.
$260-320 LSK

A mint French Dinky Toys "AUTOBUS PARISIEN OU URBAIN," no.889, in original pictorial lift-off lid Supertoys box.
$210-260 LSK

A Dinky Toys "FODEN 14-TON TANKER," no.504, in original Supertoys box.
$120-140 LOCK

A near-mint Dinky Supertoys "BIG BEDFORD VAN "HEINZ"" delivery van, no.923, in original Supertoys all-card box.
$210-260 LSK

A Dinky Toys "Weetabix GUY VAN," no.514, yellow Supertoys hubs, in original pictorial labeled all-card box.
$2,100-2,600 LSK

A near-mint Dinky Toys "GUY FLAT TRUCK WITH TAILBOARD," no.513, in original Supertoys all-card box.
$180-230 LSK

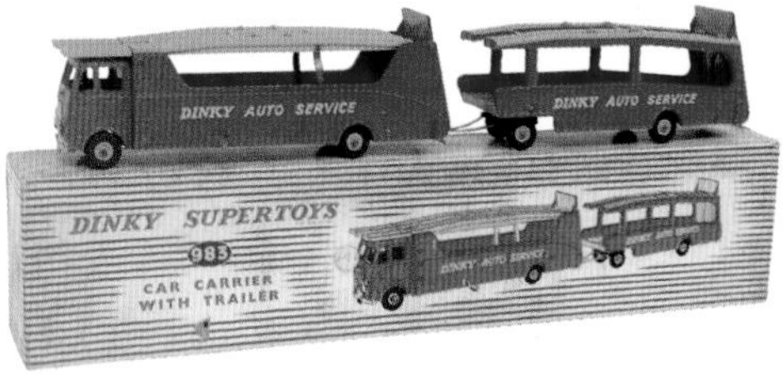

A Dinky Supertoys "CAR CARRIER WITH TRAILER," no.983, with matching trailer and Dinky Auto Service livery, in original Supertoys all-card box.
$260-390 LSK

A Dinky Supertoys "LEYLAND OCTOPUS WAGON," no.934, in original Supertoys box.
$190-260 LSK

A Dinky Toys "PULLMORE CAR TRANSPORTER WITH FOUR CARS" gift set, no.990, with four cars, no.582 Pullmore Transporter, with a Hillman Minx no.154, repainted no.161 Austin Somerset, a Rover 75, and a Ford Zephyr, in original all-card box with packing piece and upper deck ramp.
$1,400-1,800 LSK

A Bandai "Rolls-Royce SILVER CLOUD Sedan," no.767, friction drive, boxed.

ca. 1960 *10½in (26.5cm) long*

$190-260 **BELL**

A Bing painted tin fire pumper, with composition driver, copper boiler, battery-operated headlights.

19½in (49.5cm) long

$600-700 **POOK**

A near-mint Brian Norman Farm Miniatures 1/32 scale model of a David Brown Cropmaster tractor, no.FM05, in original all-card labeled box.

$160-210 **LSK**

A Buddy L pressed steel "WRIGLEY'S SPEARMINT CHEWING GUM RAILWAY EXPRESS AGENCY" tractor trailer, with battery-operated headlights, minor paint loss.

23in (58.5cm) long

$650-800 **POOK**

A Buddy L yellow pressed steel Coca-Cola delivery truck, no.5426, with trays of bottles and two carts, in original box.

ca. 1960s

$230-290 **LOCK**

A Bura & Hardwick stop-frame animation prison truck and driver, the 1920s style G.A.D. truck with prison bars back and a foam rubber articulated man wearing denim dungarees, some perishing.

38in (96.5cm) long

$400-450 **SAS**

A Chestnut Miniatures "MASSEY FERGUSON 510 COMBINE," 1:32 scale, with driver, limited edition no.11/500, in original foam-packed box, as issued with specification leaflet and certificate.

$800-900 **LSK**

A CIJ of France Renault Autobus, no.3/40, in original all-card box.

$70-80 **LSK**

A Citroën friction-powered tinplate four-door sedan, on the base faintly marked "Jouet a Propulsion Andre Citroen Made-In-France," minor paint loss.

1930s

$260-320 **W&W**

A CMC M-098 "Mercedes-Benz W154" die-cast model, 1:18 scale, boxed.

1938

$190-260 **FLD**

A Japanese Cragstan "RAMBLER CLASSIC STATION WAGON," boxed.

ca. 1960

$100-110 BELL

A mint Exoto Porsche 934 RSR racing car, 1:18 scale, with Jägermeister livery and racing no.24, in original polystyrene packed box.

$260-320 LSK

A rare Exoto 1966 Ford GT 40 Mk2, 1:10 scale, with racing no.2 and silver racing stripes with gold hubs, as driven by Amon/Maclaren, limited edition no.573, with dedication plaque addressing the men and women of the Ford Motor Company as signed by the President of Exoto Incorporated, in original polystyrene packed all-card box, with envelope with return response card to Exoto, Moor Park, California.

$2,300-2,900 LSK

A JRD Miniatures refuse truck, no.131, in original all-card box, play worn.

$80-90 LSK

A Lehmann Spielzeug "Gnom" tinplate open-back truck, no.813, an Opel Blitz-style vehicle, with some rusting, boxed, some wear, one outer end flap missing.

1930s

$160-210 W&W

A near-mint Matchbox 1/75 series "Morris J2 pickup," no.60, in the original type B all-card box.

$95-100 LSK

A near-mint Matchbox 1/75 Series Bedford tipper (dump truck), no.40, in the original B2 all-card box.

$58-60 LSK

A near-mint Matchbox 1/75 series Foden "CEMENT LORRY" (cement mixer truck), no.26, in original type D all-card box.

$60-70 LSK

A Meccano prewar constructor kit no.2 model car and driver, play worn with chips on paintwork, rear left wheel loose, some bolts missing.

13in (33cm) long

$850-950 APAR

A Mercury Models "KEHRLI & OELER BERNE" Saurer advertising van, no.88, made for a company in Switzerland, TIR decal under headlight, some wear on decals, boxed.

Founded in 1932, Mercury manufactured machine parts. After World War II, the company made 1:43 scale die-cast models. Mercury closed in 1978.

$1,300-1,900 BTA

A Taylor & Barratt "AIR MAIL" van, in RAF blue, with silver livery, with some minor play wear.

$130-180 LSK

A Tipp Co. Steamlined Racing Car, no.959, with driver, fitted with fixed key mechanism, number plate reads "TC 959," missing rear spare wheel.

14¼in (36cm) long

$1,250-1,450 LSK

A Tonka Toys large pressed-steel Aerial Ladder Fire Engine/Truck, no.1348, in original box.

ca. 1960s

$180-230 LOCK

A Tri-ang Spot-On models 1/42 scale model of an ERF 68G, no.109/3B, with nine plastic barrels, in original box with packing piece, box lid reinforced.

$400-450 LSK

A Tri-ang Spot-On models Aston Martin DB3, no.113, in original all-card box.

$300-400 LSK

A Tri-ang pressed-steel London Transport double-decker bus, no. 93, with working bell, number plate reads "LIB 4242."

12in (30.5cm) high

$210-260 LOCK

Judith Picks

I do love a toy with a story! And this racing car is also in excellent condition. This model was made to celebrate the record breaking MG Magic Midget, which was the first baby car to do over 100 mph, and the first to do over 120 mph, driven by Captain G.E. Eyston. Eyston's photo appears on the side of the box. It is tinplate with rubber tires and wind-up mechanism, and it comes with the original box and key. The winding and spinning mechanism still works well. No wonder it made almost three times the estimate price.

A Tri-ang "MAGIC MIDGET" record-breaking car,

ca. 1933

$3,900-5,200 GIL

An early-20thC Tri-ang large pressed-steel and metal pedal car, number plate reads "LIB.4242," with original steering wheel and windshield with original glazing, requires extensive restoration.

$1,250-1,450 LSK

An Ugo Fadini handbuilt 1954 Cooper MkV record car, 1:43 scale, limited edition no.43 of 150, in original card box.

$190-260 LSK

A CIJ Alfa Romeo P2 Clockwork Racing Car, pressed-steel body, racing no.2, original pneumatic tires with tread, with CIJ manufacturer's mark on base, with original key, missing fuel and radiator caps.

CIJ (Compagnie Industrielle Du Jouet) produced this Alfa Romeo P2. It was based on the Grand Prix racing car designed by Vittorio Jano that raced between 1924 and 1930. Three of these Alfa Romeo P2s sold in the UK in March 2019.

1930s *21in (53.5cm) long*

$7,000-8,000 **C&T**

A CIJ Alfa Romeo P2 tinplate clockwork racing car.

21in (53.5cm) long

$8,000-9,000 **BRI**

A CLOSER LOOK AT A CIJ RACING CAR

This is a scarce example of an iconic toy car with a pressed-steel body.

It has a working clockwork motor, driving the rear wheels and later issue original Michelin pneumatic tires.

It has spoked wheels, knock-off hub caps, with drum brakes, rack and pinion steering, hand brake, starter handle, fuel and radiator caps.

Although it is missing the key and has some paint flaking, it's rarity still commands a strong price.

A CIJ Alfa Romeo P2 racing car, racing no.2.

1930s *21in (53.5cm) long*

$8,500-9,500 **C&T**

A Märklin construction set limousine, no.1101, with clockwork motor.

ca. 1930 *15½in (39.5cm) long*

$500-650 **BELL**

A Meccano Constructors Car, no.1, with key and fixed clockwork mechanism.

$650-800 **LSK**

A Shackleton Toy "Foden F.G." clockwork flatbed Lorry, in original box, one front wheel detached.

$600-650 **LOCK**

A Tri-ang "MINIC" tinplate and clockwork model of a traction engine, in original line drawing all-card box.

$30-45 **LSK**

A Gunthermann tin clockwork fire ladder truck, with hand-crank ladder, tin lithograph driver and two sitting firemen, missing one fireman, old resolder to fender, clicker tab on one gear is replaced.

14in (35.5cm) long

$1,050-1,300 **POOK**

A rare Märklin rear-entry clockwork limousine, with glass windshield, nickel headlamps, clockwork motor, and worm-gear steering system, restored.

11in (28cm) long

$9,500-11,000 **BER**

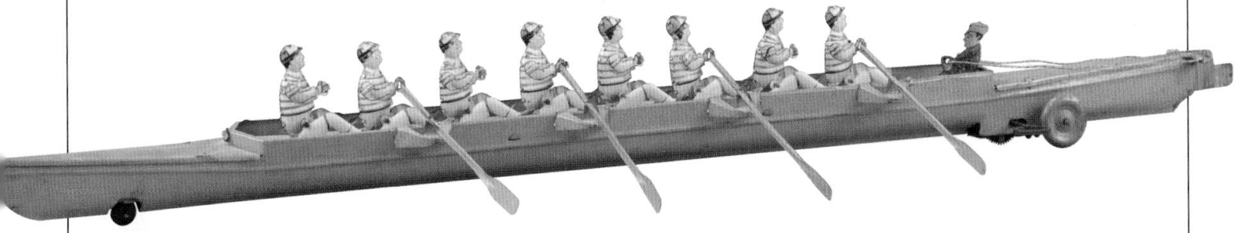

A Gunthermann eight-man scull, clockwork driven with synchronised rowing action like an actual racing skull.

29in (73.5cm) long

$18,000-21,000 **BER**

A Kuramochi celluloid clockwork "Circus Elephant," holding bell and "WELCOME! SEE OUR CIRCUS" sign, the mechanism causing the elephant to move his head and arms, damage on shoulder of one arm.

10in (25.5cm) high

$260-320 **SAS**

A Roullet & Decamps clockwork tiger, the fabric-covered tiger balances on a wood ball with applied paper stars, age crack in ball.

12¼in (31cm) high

$16,000-18,000 **POOK**

A Schuco clockwork monkey, no.985, with dancing baby mouse, some damage.

$90-100 **LSK**

A Schuco clockwork mouse, swinging a baby mouse, key present.

4¼in (11cm) high

$90-100 **LOCK**

An early English Perry & Co. "Dancing Scotsman" automaton, dancing on a paper-covered wooden box housing the clockwork mechanism, with maker's labels, slight wear.

1860-70s *10¼in (26cm) high*

$800-900 **SAS**

A Mohr and Krauss, Nuremburg, clockwork motorcycle, with driver, reproduces a twin-cylinder, lithographed blue flywheel engine operated by a crank launching.

1900 *5½in (14cm) high*

$6,000-6,500 **IVN**

An Ives clockwork butter churner, appears to be original outfit, some paint loss on face and losses on back of bonnet, currently working.

10½in (26.5cm) high

$1,150-1,450 **POOK**

A scarce American clockwork ball and mallet player, possibly Ives, remains of original label on underside, one of three examples extant, working, figure is redressed.

18¾in (47.5cm) long

$9,500-11,000 **POOK**

QUICK REFERENCE—BRITAINS

- **The William Britain Company manufactured lead mechanical toys from 1845. In 1893, William Britain Jr. developed a method of hollow casting lead die-cast toys, decreasing the production costs of toy soldiers. By 1900, the company had produced more than 100 different sets of toy lead figures.**
- **Britains also made toy cars and die-cast military trucks. After World War I, it made civilian figures, including soccer players and Disney characters, and began its "Home Farm" series.**
- **In the late 1950s, Britains launched its plastic "Swoppet" series and its production of lead hollow-cast figures ceased in 1966. The company was bought by The Dobson Park Group in 1984 and the name was changed to Britain Petite Ltd. After a series of acquisitions, the company was bought by The Good Soldier LLC company in 2016.**

A Britains Fordson "TRACTOR & REAR DUMP," no.9630, with original shovel, rear fitting and puppet steering control attachments with string, in original box.

$1,900-2,600 **LSK**

A near-mint Britains Model Farm 128F "Fordson Major TRACTOR," with driver, in original box, with Britains complaints leaflet and packing piece.

$300-400 **LSK**

A Britains "FORD SUPER MAJOR 5000 DIESEL TRACTOR," no.9527, air filter and exhaust attachment and jeweled headlights, in original sliding tray all-card box, some wear.

$140-180 **LSK**

A Britains "Home Farm" series farm wagon, no.5F, in original labeled all-card box.

$60-70 **LSK**

A Britains "Premier" series Thornycroft AA truck with service detachment, created by Charles Biggs, no.8926, in original foam packed all-card box.

$100-130 **LSK**

A near-mint Britains "ARMY LORRY" (truck), no.1334, with tilting action, with driver, in original all-card box.

$210-260 **LSK**

A Britains Military 155mm field gun, no.2064, in original labeled all-card box, with missiles and packing pieces.

$120-140 **LSK**

A Britains height finder, no.1729, with operator figure.

$40-50 **LSK**

A Britains Military "BEETLE LORRY" (truck), no.1877, with driver, in original picture sided all-card box, with complaints leaflet.

$130-190 **LSK**

A scarce Britains "CIVILIANS" set, no.168, in red box with gray-green Fred Whisstock picture label showing street scene, some wear.

1920s

$650-800 W&W

A scarce Britains "POLICE" set, no.319, in red box with purple Fred Whisstock picture label showing the three types of figures, minor wear and tape repair on one end of lid, "428" stamped on label suggesting the box was possibly intended for the US Police set.

1920s

$800-900 W&W

A Britains "COMPLETE RAILWAY STATION SET," no.158, with 13 figures and 12 accessories, retied into green box with picture label and inner card, some wear.

$600-650 W&W

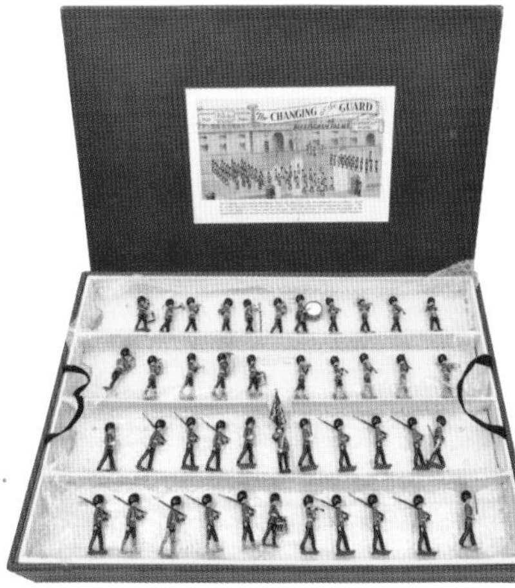

A scarce set of Britains "The CHANGING of the GUARD at BUCKINGHAM PALACE," no.1555, contains 84 guards, with two sentry boxes complete with sentries, in a presentation display case, minor wear.

$800-900 W&W

A rare "TIMPO STATION FIGURES" Railway Series set, no.850, with 15 figures and five accessories, retied into blue-green box with picture label and inner card, some wear and tape repair to all corners of the lid.

1950s

$450-500 W&W

A Britains first issue "Soldiers of the British Empire" Madras Native Infantry, no.67, in original replacement Infantry in Steel Helmets, no.1794 box.

These examples have the very early oval bases.

ca. 1900

$130-190 LSK

A Britains British Soldiers "DRUMS AND BUGLES of the LINE" set, no.30, comprising eight figures, boxed, minor wear.

$160-210 W&W

A Britains "TYPES of the WORLD'S ARMIES" Seaforth Highlanders set, no.88, boxed, with insert, minor wear, contents in mint condition, unused and still tied in.

$170-220 W&W

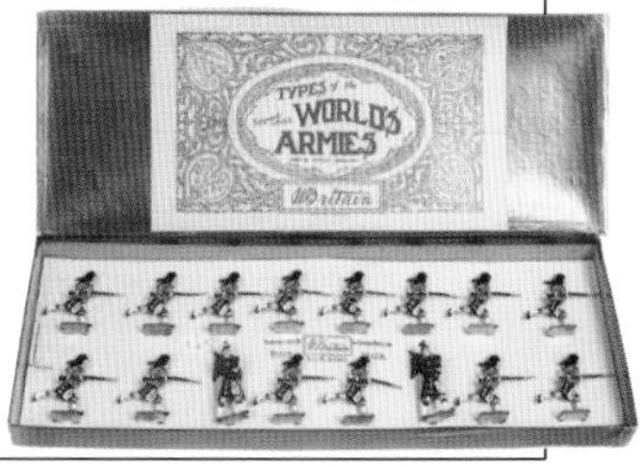

A French 19thC rocking horse, made by the Auguste Reidmeister Studio, carved wood with metal head and fittings, with a removable handlebar and wheels that drop down to make a pull-along toy.

42¼in (107.5cm) wide

$1,150-1,450 **SWO**

An early-20thC Baby Carriages of Liverpool pine rocking horse, painted dapple gray, with original saddle, bears "BCL Rambler Liverpool" label on the base.

40¼in (102cm) wide

$800-900 **FLD**

A White Horses "Linford-Christmas 1994" twin-pillar rocking horse.

48¾in (124cm) high

$500-650 **WHP**

A 19thC carved wood and painted rocking horse.

$1,300-1,900 **JN**

An early-20thC rocking horse, with horse hair mane and tail, mounted on a frame.

36¼in (92cm) long

$160-260 **LOCK**

An early-20thC dapple-gray rocking horse, with horse hair mane and tail, leather bridle and reins, on a wood trestle base with painted iron hardware.

59in (150cm) long

$1,050-1,150 **L&T**

An original wooden Lines Juvenile fairground "Jake" merry-go-round horse, a hole where the pole would have been fitted.

ca. 1900 *27½in (70cm) high*

$1,050-1,550 **LSK**

An original wooden Lines Juvenile fairground "Fizz" merry-go-round horse, a hole where the pole would have been fitted.

ca. 1900 *27½in (70cm) high*

$1,700-2,100 **LSK**

A Phalibois trio of performing composition clowns musical automaton, under a glass dome, with clowns dressed in fanciful outfits, performing a balancing act, one twirling a chair on his nose, another with a bass drum and cymbals, with a small poodle and monkey, working, glass repair on side of dome.

26in (66cm) high

$7,000-8,500 **POOK**

A possibly French mid-19thC HMS *Franklin* papier mâché automaton, depicting the HMS *Franklin* trapped on an iceberg, with a sailor on deck swinging an ax at a polar bear, as a second sailor climbs the rigging while a second polar bear chases after him, as they disappear in the iceberg they reappear to resume the chase, with a Plexiglass display case.

This scene was inspired by the Arctic Expedition of Sir John Franklin who sailed ships to the Arctic in 1845 and mysteriously disappeared.

19½in (49.5cm) high

$5,200-6,500 **POOK**

A scarce Hubley cast iron Beach Patrol surfer boy pull toy.

7½in (19cm) high

$3,900-5,200 **POOK**

A Lehmann painted tin windup figurine of Heavy Swell, with the original cane and key, working.

8¾in (22cm) high

$1,600-2,100 **POOK**

A rare early G. & J. Lines pedal car, "L.457" number plate, pedal, and chain driven, original finish, general wear, and rusting on grille.

ca. 1912 *36¾in (93.5cm) long*

$2,600-3,200 **SAS**

A Märklin central station, for the English market, with real glass windows, missing one lead finial and bell.

18in (45.5cm) wide

$1,600-1,900 **BER**

A Martin "Le Cherif Arab on camel," with lead feet, with wheels and rubber band mechanism, feet possibly replaced.

7¾in (20cm) high

$9,500-11,000 **BER**

A Meccano prewar wooden constructor car garage, left door not shutting, some loss on decal, wear to paintwork.

14¼in (36cm) long

$450-500 **APAR**

A prewar Meccano Outfit no.10, complete, in an original green enameled wooden cabinet, with a correct set of manuals, numbers 6, 7/8, and 9/10, plus an edition of "How to Use Meccano Parts."

1937-41

$2,300-2,900 **LSK**

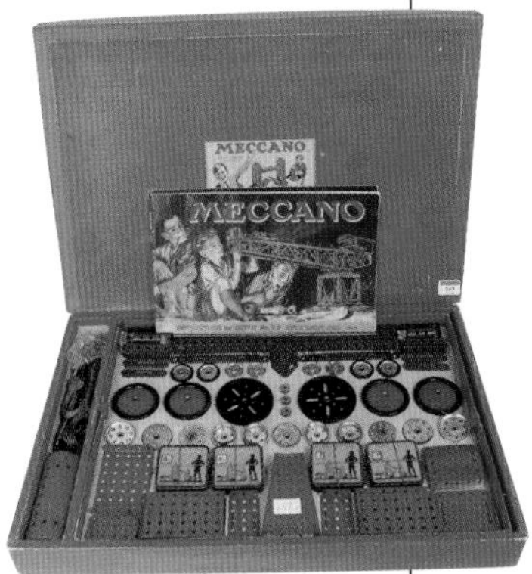

A postwar Meccano no.8 set, restrung on original cards.

ca. 1949-53

$400-450 **LSK**

A Marx plastic battery-operated "BIG LOO GIANT MOON ROBOT," with original box and instruction sheet, to include two rockets, four balls, four darts, a syringe, and a moon grenade, with a hand crank that operates the voice.

38in (96.5cm) high

$1,600-2,100 **POOK**

An early-20thC carved and painted wood fox hunting group, attributed to Frank Whittington of Forest Toys, comprising six horses and riders, seven hound dogs, and a fox.

Frank Whittington (1876-1973) established a toy company at the end of World War I in the New Forest, England, making carved animals and people. Whittington began production from his home, but, in 1922, as demand increased, he built a factory on the edge of the New Forest. Queen Mary ordered two dozen of Whittington's Noah's Arks after seeing them at the British Industries Fairs during the interwar period.

highest 9in (23cm) high

$1,300-1,800 **WW**

A prewar Taylor & Barrett "ZOO SERIES VISITORS AT TEA," set 30, of hollow-cast figurines, in plain card box, with illustrated label.

$700-850 **FLD**

A painted Noah's Ark, with 83 carved and painted whimsical animals, some paint and paper losses on the ark.

ark 17in (43cm) long

$950-1,100 **POOK**

An early-20thC German wooden Noah's Ark, polychrome painted with "bluebird" to the roof, 40 pairs of original painted wooden animals.

24¾in (63cm) wide

$1,400-1,800 **BELL**

A German large painted wood Noah's Ark, the interior with six stalls and an aviary under the lift lid, with 18 large-scale carved and painted animals, minor wear.

1987 16¾in (42.5cm) high

$1,900-2,600 **POOK**

A German composition "Walking Santa," with rabbit-fur beard, some flaking of boot paint.

13in (33cm) high

$2,900-3,600 **BER**

A Zero-X Thunderbirds space toy, by Century 21 Toys Ltd., Hong Kong, (China), battery operated, boxed.

$700-850 **FLD**

QUICK REFERENCE—VENTRILOQUISM

- **While evidence of forms of ventriloquism, at the time a ritual or religious practice, have been found in Egyptian and Hebrew archaeology, the first known ventriloquist was Louis Brabant, valet to King Francis I of France, in the 16thC.**
- **The term comes from the Latin *venter* and *loqui* to mean "belly speaking." To create the illusion of the speaker's voice coming from somewhere else, the speaker opens their mouth as little as possible, releases their breath slowly and withdraws the tongue, reducing its movement. Today, ventriloquism is used for popular entertainment.**

A Bob Bura's "Mr Punch" marionette, probably by Gordon Murray, a papier-mâché large stage puppet with moving lower jaw, jointed wooden limbs, papier mâché torso, and original costume, and a photographic montage, including an image of Bob Bura with Mr. Punch and David Jacobs.

Bob Bura (1924-2018) was a London-born animator and puppeteer. In the 1930s, he worked as a ventriloquist and entertainer in London's West End. Bura went on to work on children's TV programs including *Camberwick Green, Captain Pugwash,* and *Chigley* with Alan Hardwick.

38in (96.5cm) high

$400-450 SAS

A ventriloquist puppet, "Cassy" (William Casanova) from Whirligig, made by Francis Coudrill, a composition or papier-mâché head with fixed blue striated glass eyes, articulated jaw revealing front teeth, the ears converted to alien points, a jointed body, and some old and some new clothing, some wear.

With a letter from Joanna Coudrill, on Francis Coudrill headed paper, dated July 13, 1990, stating, "received the sum of £1,000 (cheque) from Bob Bura for one ventriloquial puppet 'William.'"

30in (76cm) high

$1,100-1,250 SAS

An early 20thC ventriloquist dummy of a girl, papier-mâché head with glass eyes and mouth, was used professionally.

35in (89cm) long

$180-260 LOCK

An old lady character ventriloquist dummy, with papier-mâché head, articulated jaw with single tooth and wart on chin, carved wooden hands, wooden jointed legs, knitted sweater, felt skirt, shopping bag, and papier mâché bottle of stout, some wear.

A video available online shows Bob Bura entertaining a young girl with this character, calling the girl a "silly sausage."

28in (71cm) high

$550-650 SAS

An Effanbee Charlie McCarthy ventriloquist doll, with button, monocle, and original outfit, in original box.

19¾in (50cm) high

$190-260 POOK

A Hooray Henry-type character ventriloquist dummy, with papier-mâché head, articulate jaw, large Roman nose, protruding two top teeth, the right eyebrow raised and eye shaped possibly for a monocle, hair moustache and side parted hair, wooden articulated body, foam stuffing, some wear.

36in (91.5cm) high

$450-600 SAS

An unusual Insull ventriloquist character jug, papier mâché or composition, hand painted with levers to operate eyes, top lip, and bottom lip.

8in (20.5cm) high

$900-1,050 SAS

A magician's two-tiered stand, inscribed "STROMBOLI Presents THE VICTORIAN CABINET of CURIOSITIES."

36¼in (92cm) high

$450-600 APAR

A set of early-20thC French Grand Etteilla tarot reader's cards, numbered 1-78 with two blank cards, in used condition.

$500-650 **SWO**

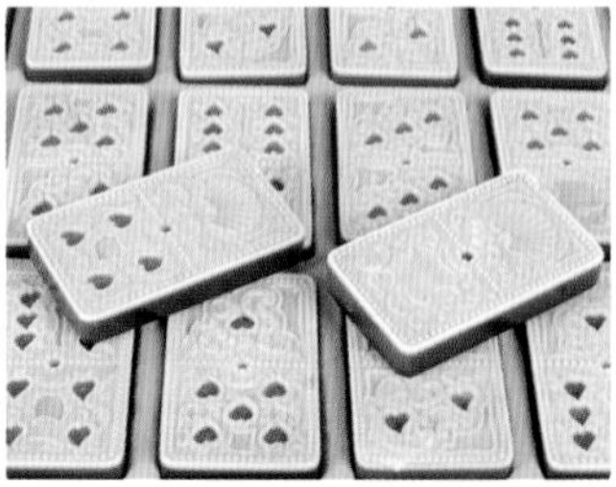

A 19thC set of carved agate dominoes, probably Italian, in a leather case.

1¾in (4.5cm) wide

$300-450 **WW**

A scarce McLoughlin Bros. "BULLS AND BEARS The GREAT WALL ST. GAME," patented 1883, with a lithograph box lid of a dressed bull and bear standing on Wall Street, a spinning board, play money, and contracts, as well as the original instruction booklet.

1883 *box 15¼in (38.5cm) wide*

$23,000-29,000 **POOK**

A Milton Bradley "Whirligig of Life" animated praxinoscope, with 9 full-color strips and 18 larger strips.

7in (18cm) high

$600-700 **POOK**

A Jaques solitaire board game, the mahogany board with 16 recesses and corresponding numbered white glazed pottery marbles, impressed maker's marks "JAQUES LONDON."

ca. 1858 *7in (18cm) diam*

$900-1,050 **L&T**

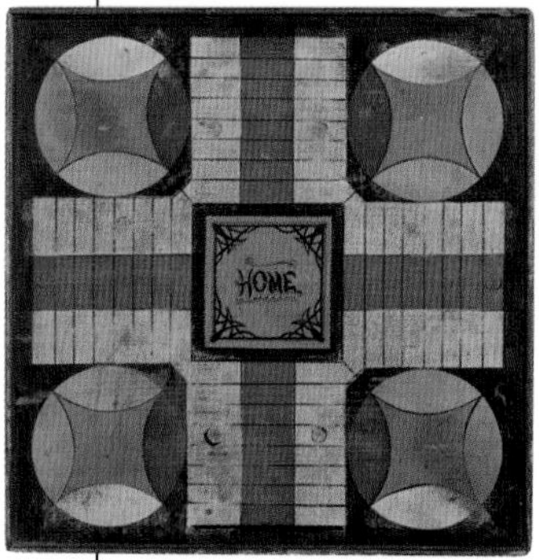

A 19thC painted pine Parcheesi game board, with polychromed blocks centering a "HOME" block on blue background.

21in (53.5cm) square

$3,200-3,900 **POOK**

A Renzo Romagnoli black leather and gilt-metal games box, of modern manufacture.

18½in (47cm) wide

$500-650 **ROS**

A mahogany games compendium, with a set of boxwood and hardwood chess pieces, dominoes, cribbage, and bezique scorers, checkers counters, die-cast horses, dice and shakers, and a "Rules Booklet" by J.W. Spear and Sons.

13.5in (34cm) wide

$130-190 **DA&H**

A French Jeu De Course horse race game, with interior and exterior rows of painted lead horses, lacking box lid.

14¾in (37.5cm) wide

$300-450 **POOK**

A Bing gauge I LNER green 4-4-2 c/w Precursor tank loco, top section of coal rail detached, with a key.

Founded by Ignatz and Adolf Bing in 1863, wholesalers Gebrüder Bing began producing its own toys in 1879. The company produced toy boats, cars, trains, train tracks, and railroad buildings. Bing also manufactured for Bassett-Lowke. In 1933, Bing was taken over by Karl Bub.

$650-800 LSK

A Bing 0-4-0 "APOLLO" c/w loco and six-wheel LMS red tender, tender no.513, crazing in paintwork.

$190-260 LSK

A Bing 0-4-0 live steam loco, spirit-fired single cylinder.

$190-260 LSK

A Bing 0-6-0 loco 12v DC three-rail, fitted with Bonds Motor, with an earlier Bing tender, loco has been repainted.

$140-190 LSK

A Bing for Bassett-Lowke 4-4-0 "GEORGE THE FIFTH" c/w loco and LMS tender no.5320, crazing in paintwork, drop links missing from couplings, box faded, water stained, and without labels.

$230-290 LSK

A Bing for Bassett-Lowke GNR 4-4-0 Atlantic loco, with tender 4-6v DC original mechanism, repainted in LNER livery no.3274, with coal added to tender.

$450-500 LSK

A Bing for Bassett-Lowke LNER D class 4-4-0 loco and tender no.504 12v DC three-rail, fitted with Leeds Model Co. mechanism.

$300-350 LSK

A Bing gauge 1 Br/3rd corridor bogie coach, no.1921.

$350-400 LSK

A Bing teak LNER bogie coach, no.2568, with repainted hinged roof and set of tables and chairs.

$70-80 LSK

A near-mint Bassett-Lowke postwar LMS Standard Compound 4-4-0 12v DC, no.1036, with six-wheel LMS tender.

$400-500 LSK

A Bassett-Lowke 4-4-0 c/w "GEORGE THE FIFTH" loco and six-wheel tender, no.2663.

$210-260 LSK

A Bassett-Lowke gauge I 0-4-0 c/w loco, L&NER renumbered no.114, crazing in paintwork, corrosion on one coupling rod, not a Bassett-Lowke key.

$300-400 LSK

A Märklin clockwork LNER 0-6-0 tank loco, with "TM1020" on rear of bunker, with speed control.

$400-500 LSK

A Märklin DB green crocodile electric loco.

$230-290 LSK

A Bassett-Lowke L&NWR "GEORGE THE FIFTH" 4-4-0 c/w loco, cab roof distorted, corrosion to rods, handrails, and couplings.

$100-130 LSK

A Bassett-Lowke compound 4-4-0 loco and tender, LMS no.1108 red, base marked "12v DC," not Bassett-Lowke pickup fitted.

$140-180 LSK

A Bassett-Lowke lithographed LMS Royal Scot class 4-6-0 8v DC, no.6100, with a six-wheel Fowler LMS tender, with Permag instructions.

$650-800 LSK

A Märklin 0-4-2 loco and tender gauge 1, "1021D" on cab sides, six-wheel tender, key fits but is not Märklin.

$190-260 LSK

A Märklin for Gamages gauge 1 "NE 2883" meat van.

$140-190 LSK

QUICK REFERENCE—HORNBY

- **Hornby began in 1901, when Frank Hornby (1863-1936) applied for a patent for "Improvements in Toy or Educational Devices for Children and Young People." He went on to found Meccano Ltd. in 1907.**
- **Meccano produced toy trains from 1920. These Hornby trains were made of metal and were 0 gauge in size. They were powered first with a clockwork motor, then joined by an electric range in 1925.**
- **Hornby Dublo, of 00 gauge, was launched in 1938. These models were often decorated in the liveries of the then largest rail companies in Great Britain, such as London and North Eastern Railway and Great Western Railway.**
- **In 1964, Hornby was bought by Lines Bros., the parent company of Tri-ang. Trains were produced as Tri-ang Hornby, then Hornby Railways in 1972, after the Tri-ang Group was disbanded.**
- **In 1980, the company, then known as Hornby Hobbies Ltd., became independent. In 1986, it became a public company. Hornby, as the company is now known, moved its manufacturing to China in 1995.**

A Hornby LNER no.1 Special Tank loco 0-4-0, no.8123, eight boiler bands, link missing from front coupling, corrosion on rods.
1929-30
$140-180 LSK

A Hornby LNER green 0-4-0 clockwork loco, no.623, chips on front buffers, box in poor condition, heavily taped.
1926-27
$90-100 LSK

A Hornby green LNER E220 20v AC 4-4-0 "THE BRAMHAM MOOR," no.201, with six-wheel LNER tender, scratches on cab roof.
1935-36
$650-800 LSK

A Hornby 1929-39 Metropolitan 6v AC, with repainted roof.
1929-39
$400-500 LSK

A Hornby 1929-30 "UNITED DAIRIES MILK TANK" wagon, chips and scratches.
1929-30
$120-160 LSK

A Hornby "MECCANO" coal wagon, minute chips, boxed.
1931-32
$80-90 LSK

A Hornby "CARR'S Biscuits" van, black standard base, sliding door, revised transfers, roof and box in poor condition.
1934-41
$100-110 LSK

A Hornby E2E engine shed, fold in one door.
1935-41
$230-300 LSK

A Hornby "WINDSOR" station, no.2E, some chips on platform, one lamp bracket broken.
1933-34
$140-190 LSK

A near-mint Wrenn W2416 BR lined green streamlined "BIGGIN HILL" Bulleid Pacific loco, no.34057, limited edition no.21 of 250, with instructions, certificate, and wooden display plinth and track, packer no.2, box reference 90936 on box base.

G. & R. Wrenn was founded by George and Richard Wrenn in 1950 in South London. It specialized in producing track for model railroads. In 1955, the company moved to Basildon, Essex. Wrenn began producing 00-guage model railroad and later two-rail track for TT-gauge models. In 1965, Lines Brothers Ltd. bought shares in Wrenn and the company began producing Hornby Dublo models and Tri-ang's TT line, under the name Tri-ang Wrenn. Dapol bought Wrenn in 1992. Production ceased in 2001.

$800-900 **LSK**

A Wrenn W2219 LMS standard class 2-6-4 tank engine, no.2679, boxed.

$100-110 **LSK**

A near-mint Wrenn Railways W2217 LNER green 0-6-2 tank engine, with instructions, packer no.3 on box base.

$80-100 **LSK**

A Wrenn W2269 rebuilt BR green "Golden Arrow," "SIR KEITH PARK."

$350-400 **LSK**

A Wrenn W2212 LNER blue "Sir Nigel Gresley" engine and tender, packer no.3 on box base.

$70-80 **LSK**

A Wrenn Railways W2228 BR "City of Birmingham" engine and tender, packer no.3 on box base, with instructions.

$120-160 **LSK**

A Wrenn Railways W2268 BR streamlined "Bulleid Pacific," no.34004, "Yeovil" packer no.3, ref.05320 on box base, with instructions, c230 made.

$500-650 **LSK**

A Wrenn Railways W2226 BR "City of London" engine and tender, with box.

$100-130 **LSK**

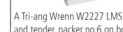

A Tri-ang Wrenn W2227 LMS post-war "City of Stoke on Trent" engine and tender, packer no.6 on box base.

$100-120 **LSK**

An Ace Trains maroon LMS freelance 4-4-4 tank loco E/1 standard 20v AC/DC, with test tag and operating instructions.

1996

$300-400 **LSK**

An Aster GI live steam black Japanese 4-6-2 VR 0276, no. C575, on cab sides with bogie eight-wheel tender, VR0276T.

$2,900-3,900 **LSK**

A mint Aster gauge one American outline two-rail electric tender New York Central System 4-6-4 "COMMODORE VANDERBILT" streamlined loco, with its 12-wheeled bogie tender with "NEW YORK CENTRAL" on sides, boxed with instruction manual.

$1,900-2,600 **W&W**

An Aster gauge 1 live steam GWR 0-6-0 Pannier Tank loco, serial no.0232, with instructions, in original box.

12¼in (31cm) long

$2,300-2,900 **LOCK**

A mint Aster Hobby Co. gauge 1 live steam loco and tender LNWR "Jumbo" Hardwicke, no.16 of 220, appears unsteamed, with small amount of G1 track.

$2,300-2,900 **LSK**

A Bachmann OO-gauge "MIDLAND PULLMAN" six-car DMU set 31-255DC, with two powered driving cars, two kitchen/dining cars and two dining cars, boxed, minor wear.

$300-400 **W&W**

A near-mint Fine Art Models PRR T1 engine and tender, in Plexiglas and wood display case.

51¼in (130cm) long

$6,500-8,000 **MORP**

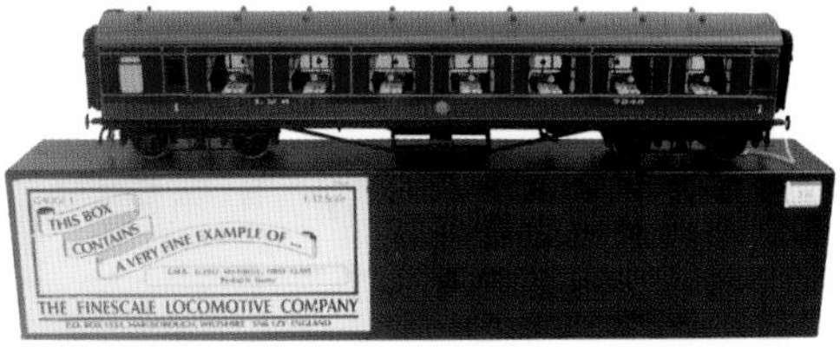

A near-mint Finescale Locomotive Co. gauge 1 coach LMS D1917 vestibule, first class period II livery.

$650-800 **LSK**

An American Flyer Lines "Shasta" 0-4-0 Standard GI blue/green electric loco, no. 4637.

$500-650 **LSK**

A near-mint Keith Murray green SR 4-4-2 12v DC electric tank loco, no.2025, O-gauge fine scale, two spoon pickup, not a skate.

$450-500 **LSK**

A Kit/Scratch built fine-scale maroon LMS 4-6-2 "DUCHESS OF DEVONSHIRE" streamlined loco, no.6227, with six-wheel LMS tender.

$300-400 LSK

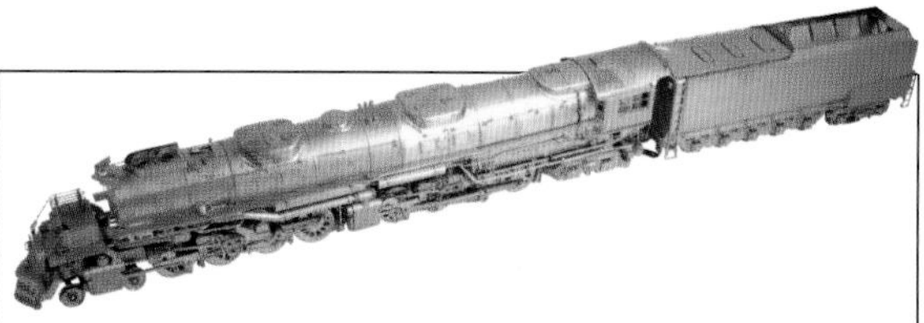

A mint KTM ready-to-run unpainted brass Pacific "Big Boy" 4-8-8-4 engine and tender, Japanese made for Westside Model Company.

$950-1,100 LSK

A Lionel no.42 black "Locomotive Outfit," missing one step and both couplers, no track, in early box.

The Lionel Manufacturing Company was founded by Joshua Lionel Cowen (1877-1965) in 1900 in New York city. In 1915, Lionel's O-gauge trains and track were launched. The company was renamed The Lionel Corporation in 1918. In 1970, Lionel opened a new plant in Michigan. The Lionel factory was briefly moved to Mexico in 1982, but after this proved unsuccessful, production was resumed in Michigan. Lionel moved its headquarters to Concord, North Carolina, in 2014.

15in (38cm) long

$1,150-1,450 BER

A near-mint Lionel three-rail Southern Pacific "Daylight" 4-8-4 engine, ref 6-8307, with electronic steam sound, in near-mint box.

$170-210 LSK

A Lionel black cast steam outline 4-6-4 electric Hudson-type 700E, no.5344, with a bogie Pennsylvania tender.

$700-850 LSK

A Lionel Lines 0-gauge dark/light umber 0-4-4-0 electric loco, no.256, motors turn freely.

$400-450 LSK

A Lionel Lines Standard "BILD-A-LOCO" GI 2-4-2 green electric outline loco, no.9E.

$300-350 LSK

A McCoy wide-gauge "SAN FRANCISCO MUNICIPAL RAILWAY" no.8 street car, with electric motor.

$260-320 LSK

An MTH Legionnaire passenger set, with 10-186E locomotive and 4380, 4381 and 4382 passenger cars.

$600-650 LSK

A Sunset models "CANADIAN PACIFIC" brass 2-10-4 Selkirk-type engine and tender, no.5931.

$600-700 LSK

A Suydam Japanese painted "PACIFIC ELECTRIC EXPRESS" Portland combine car, no.1872, motorized, with box.

$130-180 **LSK**

A Suydam Japanese unpainted brass powered Portland combine car, no decals, with box.

$120-140 **LSK**

A classic GI green/red steam outline 4-6-0, no.1108, fitted with electric can motor, with a bogie Southern tender.

$160-230 **LSK**

An exhibition-quality model of a 5in-gauge Great Western Railway Castle Class 4-6-0 "G.J. CHURCHWARD" loco and tender no.7017, built by Gold medal-winning builder Mr. Graham Hawkins of Bristol, England, built mainly in stainless steel, with name plates, numbers, and beading cut from brass plate by hand.

Castle Class no.7017 was never fitted with a double chimney.
Boiler History: Kingswood Boilers Bristol. Boiler Identity no.KB93003. Original boiler test Certificate and confirmation of copper materials. Southern Federation of Model Engineering Societies Boiler Test Record SF109076. Hydraulic test expired August 24, 2012. Test pressure 150 psi. Steam test expired July 2, 2011. Test pressure 100 psi.

$26,000-32,000 **DN**

A handmade wooden model of the Flying Dutchman Pullman Parlor Car, carpeted and wallpapered interior, in a glass display case, with a section of track.

Pullman, who was more famous for sleeping cars, produced parlor cars from the 1880s through the 1960s. This model exemplifies their production from the Gilded Age.

30½in (77.5cm) long

$6,000-7,000 **POOK**

A detailed 0-gauge two-rail electric BR rebuilt Battle of Britain Class 4-6-2 tender loco, Lord Dowding, RN 34052.

$1,150-1,450 **W&W**

A live steam 3½in-gauge 2-6-2 loco and tender LNER 3401 "BANTAM COCK."

$2,600-3,200 **LSK**

A 7¼in-gauge 0-6-0 tender loco, no.904, Great Eastern Railway (Stratford Works 1891).

$11,000-12,000 **LSK**

A 5in-gauge model of Great Western Railway King Class 4-6-0 tender loco "KING GEORGE V" no.6000, built by Mr. W.E. Wilks of Bourton, with a copper superheated boiler, with transportation case.

Boiler History: Western Steam Boiler no. WSME 073.03.2000. Test pressure 160 psi. Working pressure 80 psi. Southern Federation of Model Engineering Societies Boiler Test Certificate no.8911 Crawley ME. Hydraulic Test 160 psi expired August 5, 2002. Steam test 80 psi expired August 6, 2000.

72¾in (185cm) long

$11,000-12,000 **DN**

A Bing hand-painted Furst Bismarck Battleship, with cannons and guns, the two masts flying British flags, professionally restored.

32in (81.5cm) long

$19,000-21,000 **BER**

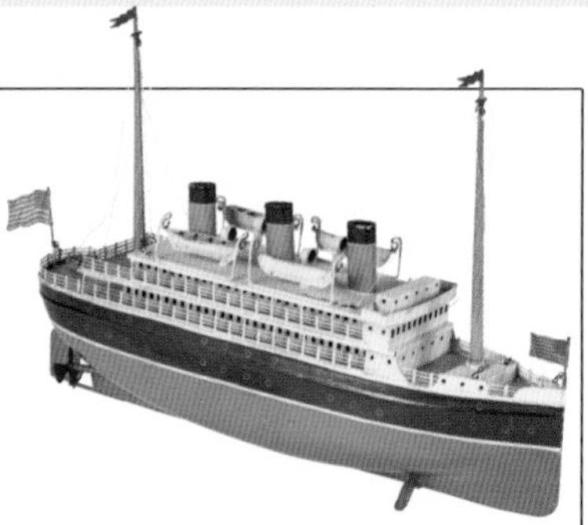

A Bing painted tin clockwork ocean liner, four lifeboats and twin screws, with fore and aft 42-star American flags, restoration of paint, working, rigging replaced.

16½in (42cm) long

$1,050-1,300 **POOK**

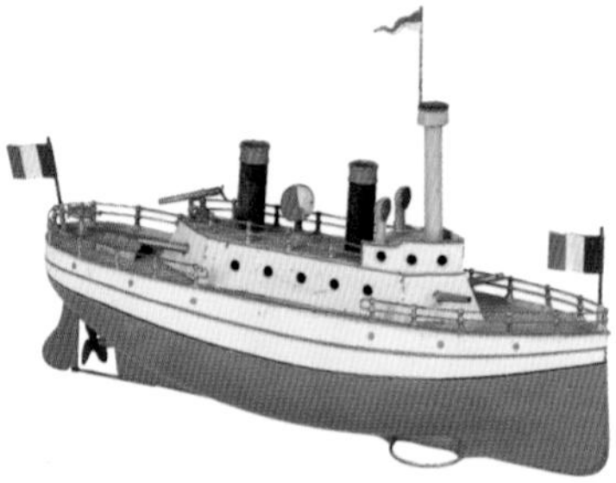

A Carette painted tin clockwork gunboat, with four cannons and swivel gun, with fore and aft French flags, restored, working.

13in (33cm) long

$600-700 **POOK**

A Märklin battleship *BALTIMORE*, with ornamental castings on bow, with two masts and various cannons, professionally restored.

34in (86.5cm) long

$23,000-26,000 **BER**

A steam-power model boat, with teak deck.

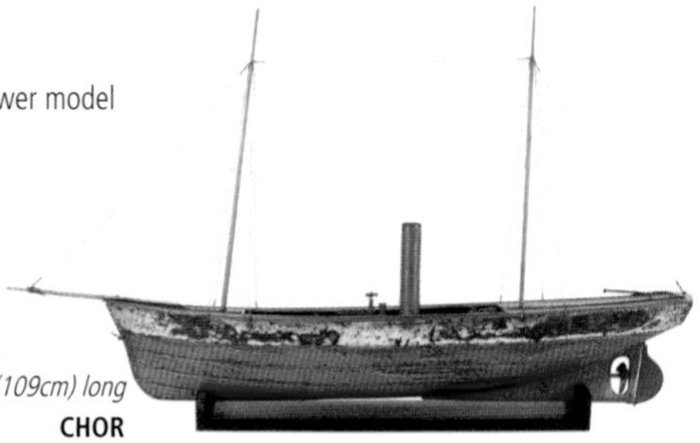

hull 43in (109cm) long

$800-900 **CHOR**

An early-20thC scale-model wooden steam ship, with an internal "Stuart" steam-power engine and boiler.

37¾in (96cm) long

$450-600 **BELL**

A cased model of the seven-masted schooner *Thomas W. Lawson*, carved and painted, with cloth sails, base inscribed "1902 – Collier – Thomas W. Lawson – Lost 1907."

case 28¾in (73cm) long

$1,400-1,800 **NA**

A 1:5 scale Royal Navy cadet training model, for a sailing and pulling cutter gig, constructed in pine and oak.

ca. 1890 *35½in (90cm) high*

$5,200-6,500 **CM**

A 20thC wooden pond yacht, fully rigged over a planked deck, on a wooden stand.

77½in (197cm) high

$650-800 **BELL**

A large pond yacht, with canvas sails and clinker built hull, brass mounts, on a carved wooden stand.

67¾in (172cm) long

$400-500 **DUK**

A medium pond yacht, with canvas sails and clinker built hull, brass mounts, on a carved wooden stand.

40½in (103cm) long

$300-400 **DUK**

A Kyosho Fairwind plastic hulled racing yacht, radio control fitted for steering and sail, with Bermuda rigging, on purpose-built model stand, with an Apex R. radio control hand unit.

64½in (164cm) high

$100-120 **LSK**

A possible Vindex/Hubley prototype airplane toy, inscribed "AMERICA" and "Fokker," with pilots and sitting passengers.

17in (43cm) wide

$2,300-2,900 **BER**

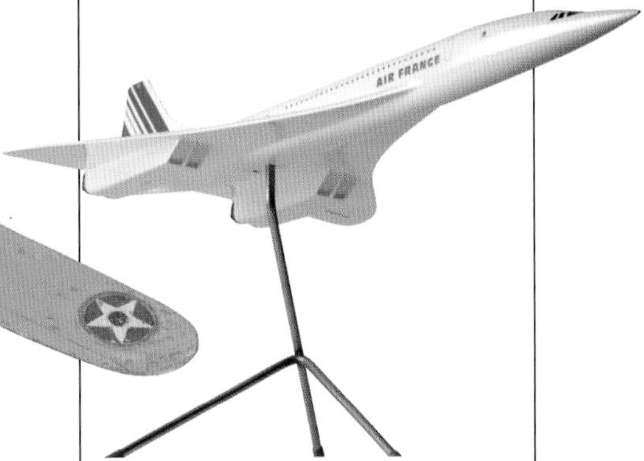

A Concorde scale model, in Air France livery, with accompanying certificate to certify that "Madame et Monsieur Winch broke the sound barrier aboard Concorde on 12th May 1997," signed by the Captain Monsieur Contresty.

33in (84cm) long

$700-850 **DUK**

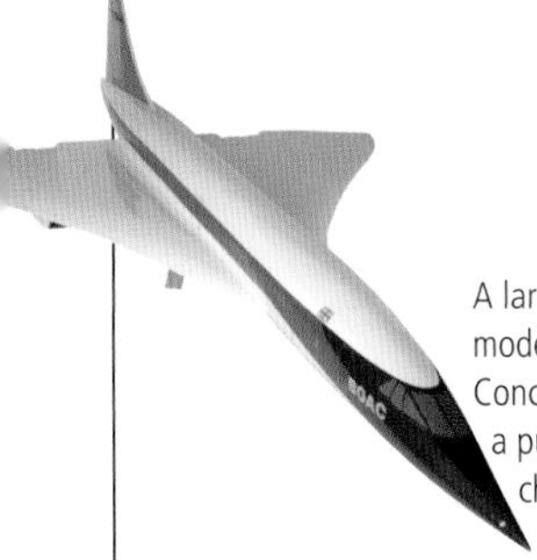

A large composite model of the BOAC Concorde G-BOAC, on a purpose-made chrome-plated tripod stand.

96½in (245cm) long

$3,200-3,900 **DUK**

An early model of a Curtiss Jenny airplane.

32in (81.5cm) long

$950-1,100 **CHOR**

A model Martin B-26 Marauder airplane.

34¼in (87cm) long

$450-500 **CHOR**

A Becker painted tin windmill steam toy accessory, no.257, with a gentleman prodding a lithograph tin mule.

9¾in (24.5cm) high

$450-500 **POOK**

An unusual German painted tin merry-go-round steam toy accessory, attributed to Bing, with three hanging dirigibles and four two-passenger seats, light wear.

12in (30.5cm) high

$1,900-2,600 **POOK**

A Bing tin lithograph enclosed tailor and shoe repair shop steam toy accessory, probably an early prototype, one window lacking pane.

ca. 1900 *8¼in (21cm) wide*

$950-1,250 **POOK**

A Bing painted tin weaving loom steam toy accessory, on a wood base, with complex action that simulates weaving, minor wear.

ca. 1890 *8¼in (21cm) high*

$650-800 **POOK**

A Bing painted tin deluxe roller coaster steam toy accessory, no.9956/336, with two four-passenger cars and a ticket gate, some wear.

16in (40.5cm) high

$6,000-7,000 **POOK**

QUICK REFERENCE—THE FERRIS WHEEL

- **The Ferris wheel was invented by George Washington Gale Ferris Jr., an engineer from Pittsburgh, Pennsylvania. Despite skepticism that the wheel was too tall and fragile, Ferris built a 250ft-diameter wheel for the 1893 World's Fair in Chicago, Illinois. It had 36 cars, which could each hold 60 people. The wheel proved a success at the fair, with 1.4 million people riding it.**
- **However, following the fair, Ferris struggled financially. He died from typhoid fever in 1896. The Ferris wheel was sold to the 1904 Louisiana Purchase Exposition in Missouri, before being scrapped.**
- **Ferris wheels have since cropped up all over Europe, as well as being copied in toy form.**

A Doll & Cie painted and embossed tin Ferris wheel steam toy accessory, no.729/2, with six gondolas, with painted composition riders, some older repaint.

15in (38cm) high

$1,600-2,100 **POOK**

A Bowman "SWALLOW" steamboat, boxed.

1930s

$210-260 **PSA**

A Doll & Cie painted and embossed tin lighthouse steam toy accessory, no.711, with a reservoir and two composition Native American figures in sailboats, during operation the top of the lighthouse rotates and the boats pitch back and forth, flags replaced.

14½in (37cm) high

$5,200-6,500 **POOK**

A CLOSER LOOK AT A STEAM TOY ACCESSORY

Ernst Plank & Company started out in 1866 in Nüremberg Germany as a toy-repair shop. Named after the company founder, they made magic lanterns, steam engines, die-cast metal planes, boats, cars, steamboats, and sewing machines produced from pressed tin plate.

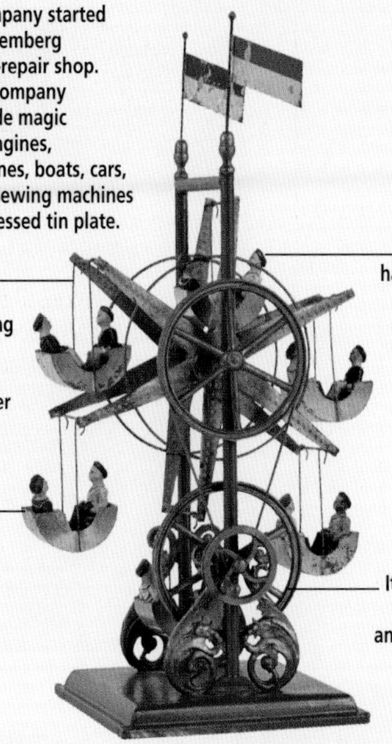

Plank's toys were notable for their quality, often being ornate in design and more finely finished than other manufacturers of that era.

This very topical toy Ferris wheel has six gondolas.

Each gondola has two painted composition dressed sailors and two flags.

It has a stepped platform base, and a hand crank on flywheel.

An Ernst Plank painted tin Ferris wheel steam toy accessory, platform overpainted.

16in (40.5cm) high

$1,900-2,600 POOK

An Eberl painted and lithographed tin Indian elephant steam toy accessory, with plink-plank-plunk music box.

9in (23cm) wide

$1,900-2,600 POOK

A Märklin painted tin and metal oval water fountain steam toy accessory, with six fish and dolphin spouts, paint loss.

7in (18cm) high

$800-1,050 POOK

A Mohr & Krauss painted tin ice-skating rink steam toy accessory, with skaters that twirl about a mica-flecked rink, the sign inscribed "Eislauf Bahn."

12in (30.5cm) wide

$3,200-3,900 POOK

A Schoenner painted tin horse merry-go-round steam toy accessory, no.11/2, in original condition, some paint loss, a horse's leg is bent.

ca. 1875 *12in (30.5cm) high*

$3,200-3,900 POOK

A German dolls" trestle-style Ferris wheel, with elaborate suspended gondolas, hand-crank or steam-power engine, professionally restored.

18in (45.5cm) high

$1,900-2,600 BER

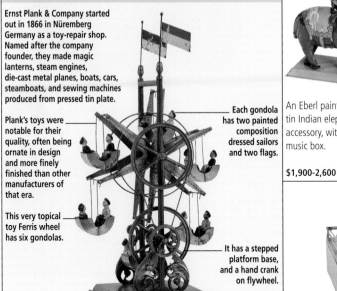

A painted and embossed tin wheelwright shop steam toy accessory, with three figures working, sporadic paint loss.

11in (28cm) wide

$850-950 POOK

QUICK REFERENCE—TREEN

- **The term "treen" refers to small items made from turned wood, usually beech, elm, or chestnut. They were designed to be used around the home, on a farm, or in a workshop. Common items include snuff and spice boxes, drinking vessels, spoons, measures, salts, bowls, and utensils.**
- **The earliest pieces available to collectors today date from the 17thC and the most desirable pieces date from ca. 1720 to ca. 1800. Many of the pieces on the market now date from the 19thC; because there are many of them and they are often ignored by collectors, values tend to be lower.**
- **As the 19thC progressed, fewer items were made from wood, because advances in technology meant they could be made more quickly and economically from pottery or metal.**
- **When buying treen, look carefully at the quality of the carving, the type of wood, and the age of the item. The more decorative the piece, the more desirable it will probably be. A warm, rich patina, built up over years of use, will add value.**

An early-19thC French carved coquilla nut snuff box, carved with two female missionaries, one holding a cross, the other the Bible.

3in (7.5cm) wide

$230-290 **WW**

A 19thC Tyrolean carved boxwood snuff box, carved with a girl feeding cattle, full length wooden hinge.

3¾in (9.5cm) wide

$260-320 **BLEA**

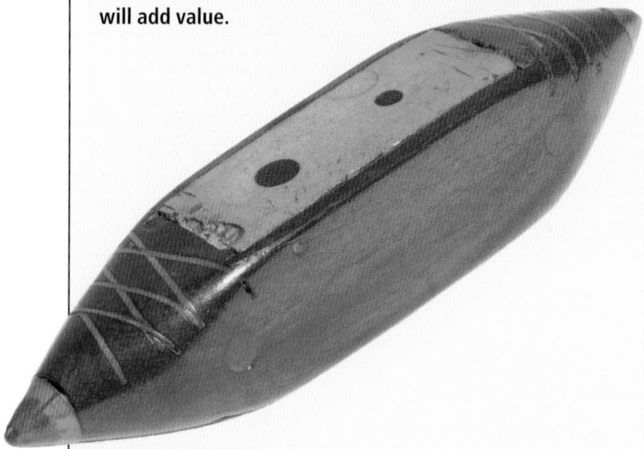

A 19thC treen snuff box, in the form of a sewing shuttle, with inlaid decoration and a hinged lid.

4½in (11.5cm) long

$190-260 **WW**

A 19thC pressed treen snuff box, the cover with Masonic symbolism that includes a Temple and emblems, tortoiseshell simulated interior, inventory label no.583.

3¼in (8.5cm) diam

$400-450 **HAN**

A 19thC French carved coquilla nut snuff box, in the form of a basket, carved with a wheelbarrow filled with baskets of flowers and fruit and a watering can.

3in (7.5cm) wide

$230-290 **WW**

A carved treen "Tam-o'Shanter" blind man's snuff box, the lid with relief carved scene of Tam being chased by a Nellie the witch, the sides carved with animals.

6¾in (17cm) wide

$600-650 **BE**

A Scottish "blind man" wooden snuff box, the lid with two male figures (Tam and Souter) centered by a woman with child, sides and front carved with dogs and sheep, base branded "W. Ward," chip on hat of one figure.

6¼in (16cm) long

$600-700 **BLEA**

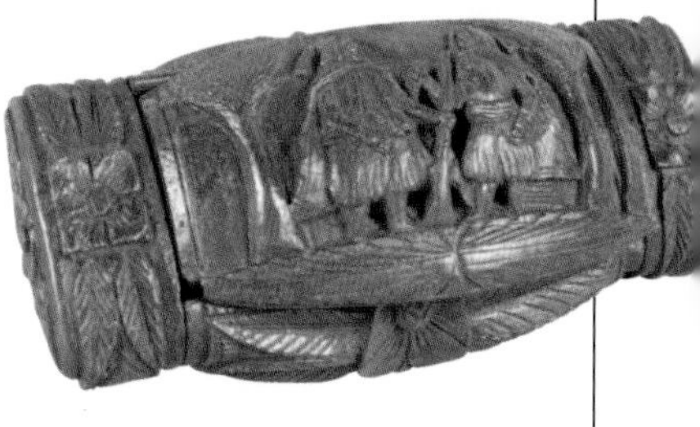

A coquilla nut snuff box, carved with motifs and figures.

3¼in (8.5cm) long

$300-350 **JN**

A near pair of early-19thC treen snuff shoes, with brass tack inlay, each with a sliding cover and vacant plaque.

6½in (16.5cm) long

$1,600-1,900 **WW**

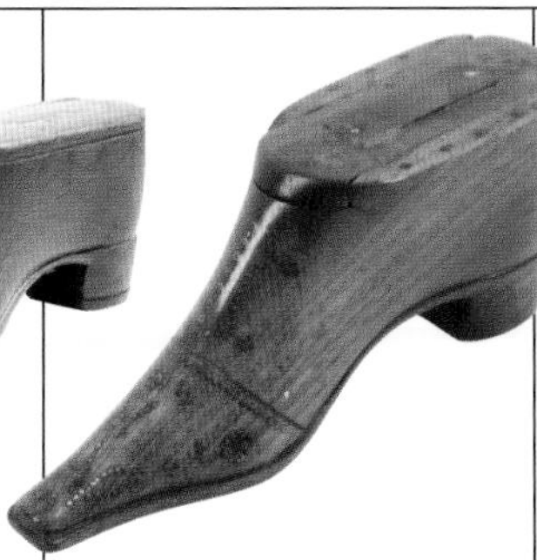

An early-19thC mahogany table shoe snuff box, decorated in brass tacks, the toe with a thistle, the sliding lid with soft metal plaque.

5¾in (14.5cm) long

$400-450 **BLEA**

A rare 19thC large treen fruitwood table snuff shoe, with brass laces and tack decoration and inlaid with ivory and mother-of-pearl rondels.

This item may be subject to CITES regulations when exported.

10¼in (26cm) long

$5,200-6,500 **WW**

A late-19thC lacquered floral painted snuff box, modeled as a shoe.

3¼in (8.5cm) long

$80-100 **MART**

A 19thC treen snuff shoe, with pewter stringing and tack inlay, the hinged lid inset with a carved bone portrait medallion.

4¾in (12cm) long

$450-500 **WW**

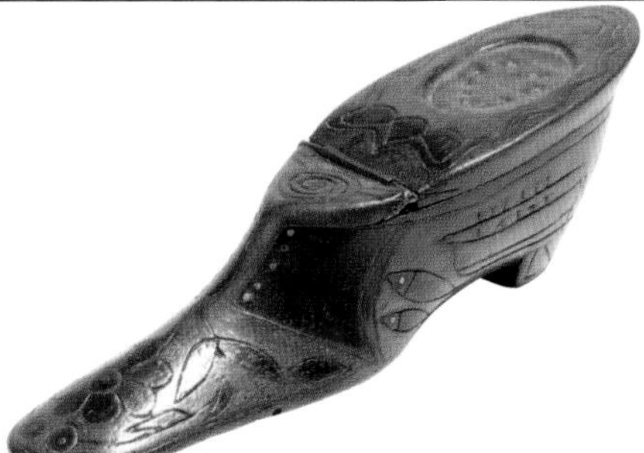

A 19thC treen sailor's valentine snuff shoe, with brass tack inlay, the hinged lid with an inset pewter panel decorated with a love heart, the body with ships, fish, and an anchor.

5¼in (13.5cm) long

$650-800 **WW**

An early-19thC pressed horn lidded snuff box, the cover with Masonic symbolism that includes a beehive and swarm, inventory label no.602, some damage.

3¼in (8.5cm) diam

$400-500 **HAN**

A 19thC four-tier spice tower, each section labeled "Mace," "Cloves," "Cinnamon," and "Nutmegs," large split on top and wear and tear.

8in (20.5cm) high

$230-290 **APAR**

An early-19thC treen urn, the cover decorated with bands of leaves, above a pineapple-shaped body.

7in (18cm) high

$650-800 **WW**

An early-19thC Scottish Mauchline ware sycamore and penwork snuffbox, decorated with a scene of lovers on a garden bench, inscribed "PRESENTED To M.J.R. Williams late of the Theatre Royal by several young Gentlemen of ABERDEEN as a mark of respect for his private character and admiration of his Theatrical Talents."

3in (7.5cm) wide

$1,600-2,100 **WW**

An early-19thC Mauchline ware sycamore and penwork snuff box, with a scene of returning Highland soldier greeting his loved one, the body decorated with thistles.

3in (7.5cm) wide

$500-650 **WW**

An early-19thC Scottish Mauchline ware small sycamore and penwork snuff box, by George Sliman of Catrine, the foil-lined interior stamped "G. SLIMAN CATRINE."

2in (5cm) wide

$300-400 **WW**

An early-19thC Scottish Mauchline ware sycamore and penwork snuff box, with a tavern scene.

3in (7.5cm) wide

$260-390 **WW**

A late-19thC Mauchline tartanware snuff box, the top with a bird, the body in Davidson tartan, stamped maker's marks for Smith, Mauchline.

The success of "Mauchline ware" is due, in part, to the Smiths of Mauchline—it being initially manufactured by Andrew and William Smith, who produced wares from the 1820s. It became an industry that was to dominate the market for wooden souvenirs during most of the 19thC era. During the course of the 19thC, the factory developed new pieces, shapes, sizes, and finishes. The company responded to the new 19thC taste for vacations and souvenirs, as commercial railroads were developed and visits to the seashore became increasingly popular. Their wares were despatched to all parts of the British Isles, Europe, North and South America, South Africa, Australia, and New Zealand. The Smiths' innovations earned them the Royal Warrant, enabling them to dominate the "fancy goods" market. The business rejuvenated the local economy in Mauchline and inspired many other makers of similar wares in Scotland. It closed in the 1930s.

1½in (4cm) wide

$600-650 **L&T**

A late-19thC Mauchline ware penwork snuff box, the lid with hand-painted scene of a curling match.

5¼in (13.5cm) wide

$1,250-1,450 **L&T**

A Mauchline tartanware photograph album, the boards in Stuart tartan, with a portrait of Mary, Queen of Scots, the interior with gilt-edged pages having blank apertures for photographs.

ca. 1890 *12in (30.5cm) high*

$650-800 **L&T**

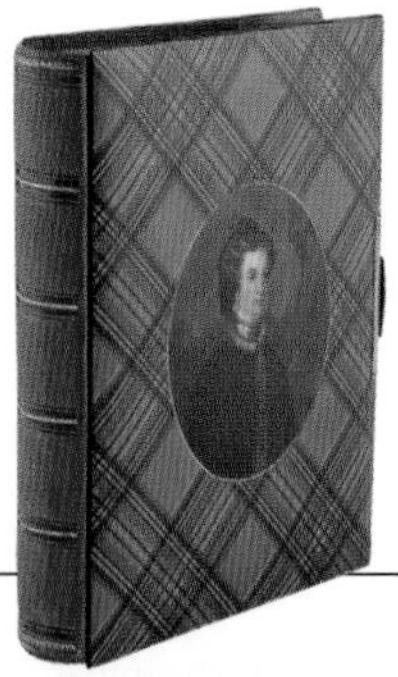

A late-19thC Mauchline tartanware necklace, with eleven links on a later thread.

19¼in (49cm) long

$400-500 **L&T**

Judith Picks

As with all Black Forest carvings, this begging dog is full of character, and I do have a soft spot for dogs! "Black Forest" carvings were once thought to have been made in the Black Forest region of Bavaria, Germany, hence the name. In fact, most were produced in Brienz, Switzerland, over the course of the 19thC. These carvings were a key part of the town's economy and were highly popular with tourists.

The craftsmen of Brienz carved figures, furniture, boxes, and clock cases from tree trunks, often linden or walnut. The most popular subjects were bears. Many carved bear figures were depicted engaging in human activities, including playing musical instruments, socializing, or hiking. Dogs are rarer.

A 19thC Black Forest begging dog stick stand.

36¼in (92cm) high

$5,200-6,500 **HANN**

A Black Forest linden wood tobacco or match holder, carved as a dog in Tyrolean dress and holding an Alpine horn.

ca. 1860 *8¼in (21cm) high*

$1,300-1,900 **L&T**

A late 19thC Black Forest carved wood table wine coaster, with three Bacchanalian cherubs, on serpent spoke wheels and bone casters.

18¼in (46.5cm) wide

$2,600-3,200 **WW**

A late-19thC Black Forest table gong, in the form of a standing bear, with a brass gong and a beater.

12½in (32cm) high

$800-900 **WW**

An early-20thC Black Forest carved wooden bear, with glass eyes, on a later separate wooden plinth.

15½in (39.5cm) wide

$600-650 **BELL**

A pair of late-19th/early-20thC Black Forest carved spill vases, with carved figures of a bull and cows.

11¾in (30cm) high

$1,050-1,150 **L&T**

A near pair of late-19thC Black Forest carved wood epergnes, each with a glass vase, one with remains of a printed paper trade label "A.M. ... FABRIC. Grand-..."

14¾in (37.5cm) high

$260-390 **WW**

A late-19thC Black Forest carved and painted wood royal stag head mount, applied with a set of real 13-point antlers.

48¾in (124cm) high

$1,300-1,900 **WW**

A late-19thC/early-20thC treen screw-action nutcracker, in the form of a squirrel eating a nut.

6¾in (17cm) high

$450-500 **WW**

A 19thC carved treen nutcracker, in the form of Mr. Punch, with a tapered and faceted screw handle, slight damage.

7¾in (19.5cm) long

$160-210 **FLD**

An early-20thC carved walnut nutcracker, in the form of a Breton-style smiling character wearing a hat.

7in (18cm) high

$100-130 **FLD**

A 19thC treen dairy bowl.

23in (58.5cm) diam

$450-500 **WW**

A painted wood dummy board, in the form of a Hussar soldier.

60¾in (154.5cm) high

$500-650 **WW**

An early-20thC French wooden merry-go-round fighting bull, with carved ornamental saddle, sword, and banderillas.

27¼in (69cm) high

$1,700-2,300 **SWO**

A 19thC Tunbridge ware cottage money box, of painted white wood.

5in (12.5cm) high

$400-450 **WW**

A 19thC Tunbridge ware box, the cover with a scene of a castle.

10¾in (27.5cm) wide

$190-260 **L&T**

A 19thC Tunbridge ware and rosewood sewing box.

7¼in (18.5cm) wide

$300-400 **WW**

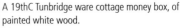

A 19thC Tunbridge ware rosewood table cabinet, the top panel inset with a castellated building.

12in (30.5cm) wide

$900-1,050 **L&T**

QUICK REFERENCE—TRIBAL ART

- **The term "tribal art" is used to describe the cultural, ritual, and functional items produced by the indigenous peoples of Africa, Oceania, South East Asia, and the Americas. Many of these items were originally functional rather than decorative. Today, pieces are collected both for their historic and ethnographic interest and for their visual impact and appeal. Many collectors choose to focus on one tribe or region or one type of item.**
- **Interest in tribal pieces began in the Western world in the 18thC and 19thC as explorers reached new places and cultures. This interest grew in the 20thC due to the influence tribal art had on European artists, such as Pablo Picasso.**
- **Pieces from the 19thC and before with verifiable history tend to be the most valuable. Look for signs of use and age, such as wear or patina, but examine carefully, because patina can be easily faked. From the early 20thC, some tribes made large quantities of items purely for export or to sell as souvenirs. These pieces can be variable in quality and tend to be less valuable.**
- **In the past 20 years, the value of tribal art has been steadily increasing. Older pieces with clear provenances are often only accessible to wealthy collectors or museums.**

A Bamana carved wood door lock, with stylized head finial and long ears, mounted.

18in (45.5cm) high

$1,150-1,450 L&T

A 20thC cast Benin-style bronze leopard's head, with five clearly defined whiskers.

15in (38cm) high

$850-950 DUK

A Dan mask, Ivory Coast, with a beak and applied metal strips.

13in (33cm) high

$300-400 WW

A Jokwe carved wood dancing mask, Central Congo, with scarification marks carved on cheeks, the crown with trade beads and braided grass hair.

Collected between 1898 and ca. 1920 by Major Ian Kelsey.

11in (28cm) high

$650-800 WHYT

A Nigerian Yoruba Ibeji figure, with a tiered coiffure, facial scarifications, with a bead and shell necklace, with brass bangles.

10in (25.5cm) high

$3,900-4,500 WW

A wooden mancala gaming board, possibly Mbala, Republic of Congo, a sitting figure supporting the board.

26in (66cm) long

$600-700 DUK

A Nigerian Mama masked dancer figure, with a stylized bird mask with abrus seed eyes.

22in (56cm) high

$2,300-2,900 WW

A Songye kifwebe mask, pronounced disk coiffure, on stand.

23½in (60cm) high

$700-850 MOR

A Songye mask, Congo, with protruding, lozenge-shaped lips, incised crosshatched design on brow and cheeks, with woven cowl.

Collected between 1898 and ca. 1920 by Major Ian Kelsey.

15in (38cm) high

$800-900 WHYT

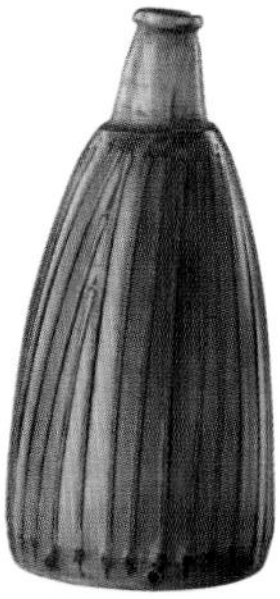

A Zulu carved and wired horn snuff bottle, with delicate neck and rounded lip.

3¼in (8.5cm) high

$1,250-1,450 L&T

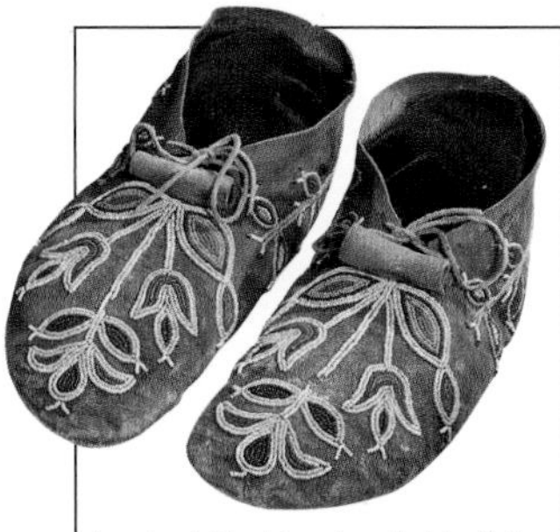

A pair of Blackfeet beaded buffalo hide moccasins, the soft-sole forms with multicolored floral designs, traces of cloth at the ankle, minor bead loss.

1870s *10½in (26.5cm) long*

$1,050-1,150 **SK**

A pair of Blackfeet beaded hide moccasins.

ca. 1890 *10½in (26.5cm) long*

$2,300-2,900 **SK**

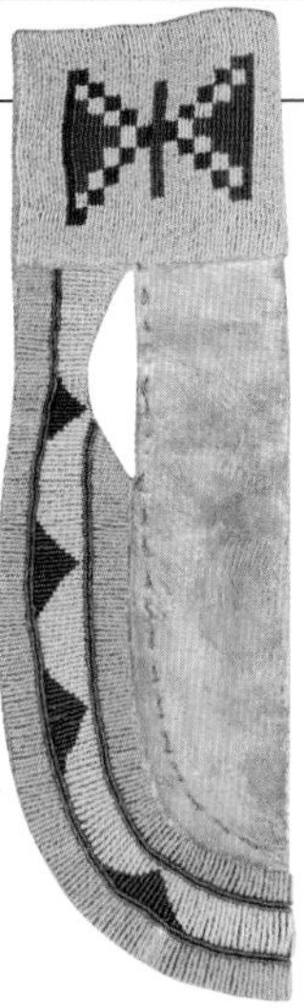

A Blackfoot part-beaded knife sheath rawhide, brass wire, colored glass beads, and paint.

15½in (39.5cm) long

$1,700-2,100 **WW**

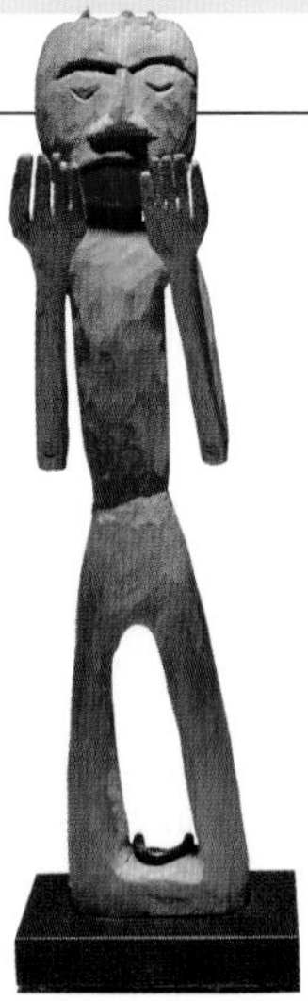

A Kwakiutl puppet figure, British Columbia, with remains of fiber on the head, on a stand.

9in (23cm) high

$1,900-2,600 **WW**

A late-19thC Crow beaded buffalo hide pouch, beaded with classic crow designs.

8½in (21.5cm) wide

$3,200-3,900 **SK**

A late-19thC Lakota beaded buffalo hide knife sheath, beaded with long loom-beaded strap and drop, tin cone danglers, some bead loss.

10½in (26.5cm) long

$1,700-2,100 **SK**

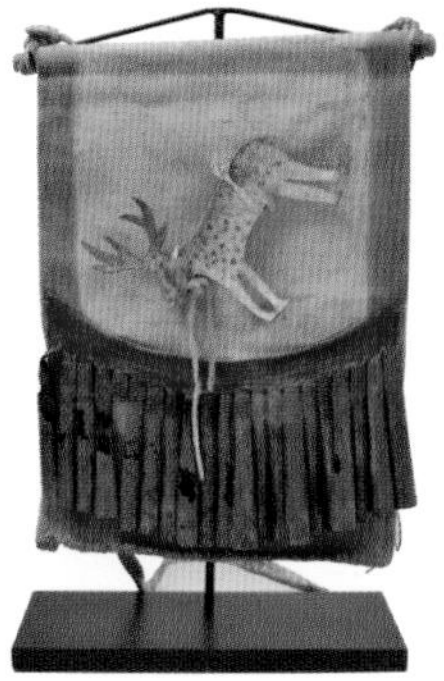

An early-20thC Navajo canvas apron, Southern North America, with an applied leather cut-out stag with a red glass bead, hung with tin cones.

10¼in (26cm) high

$260-320 **WW**

A North American roach spreaderbone, carved with two bears and nine tines, with sinew and metal wire.

6¼in (16cm) long

$500-600 **WW**

A Zuni carved stone bear fetish, Southwest, with a band of glass beads, shell, quill, and a carved stone hare.

3¼in (8.5cm) high

$850-950 **WW**

A pair of Southern Cheyenne buckskin leggings, Southern Plains, with a border of colored glass beads.

25½in (65cm) long

$1,050-1,150 **WW**

A Sioux feather dance bustle, Plains, cloth, rawhide, and ribbon.

48½in (123cm) high

$400-500 **WW**

A Costa Rica metate grinding stone, Central America, with a jaguar head terminal, raised on three legs, with an oblong pestle.

Collected by a charity worker in Honduras in the 1950s.

14in (35.5cm) long

$400-500 **WW**

A set of four 20thC Peruvian dolls, with AD 1000-1400 textile fragments.

10¼in (26cm) wide

$160-210 **WW**

A pair of Chancay pottery male and female figures, Peru.

1100-1400 *largest 11¾in (30cm) high*

$400-500 **WW**

A Chimu weaving shuttle, Peru, with a carved figure finial and a tapering blade.

1100-1400 *14½in (37cm) long*

$260-390 **WW**

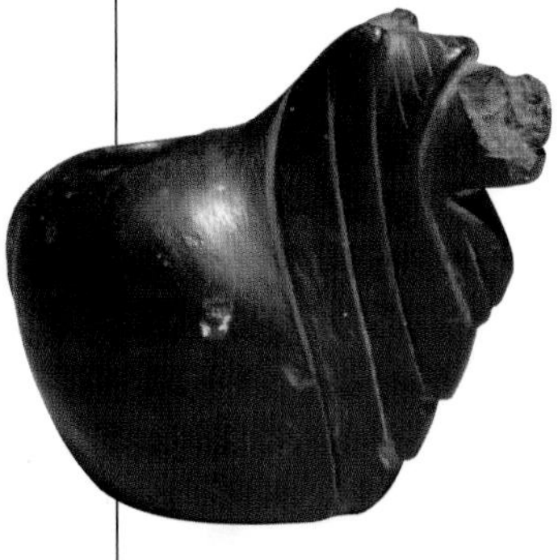

A probably 15thC/16thC Inca effigy container stone conopa, Peru, in the form of an alpaca, with a layered mane, mouth, snout, and ear, with a chevron tail.

2½in (6.5cm) high

$120-160 **WW**

An Inca-style pottery vessel, Peru, decorated with four standing figures.

Provenance: Mr. and Mrs. John Pert, Lima, Peru, 1965-75.

8in (20.5cm) high

$260-320 **WW**

A Pima coiled basketry plaque, with squash blossom design.

11in (29cm) diam

$700-850 **SK**

QUICK REFERENCE—INUIT ART

- **Much of what is considered to be "Inuit art" today has been made since the 1950s, when the work of Alaskan and North Canadian artists and sculptors was promoted by a young Canadian artist called James Houston. In the last few decades, the market has dramatically increased in size.**
- **Many sculptures are carved in local soapstone, then embellished with whalebone, ivory, antler, sinew, and other materials.**
- **It is chiefly the artist that brings value to a work of Inuit art, although the visual appeal also plays a key role. Sculptures tend to be signed on the base, sometimes in Roman letters or syllabics, but often with a combination of numbers and letters assigned to the artist as an identifier, because there is no tribal tradition of written language.**

A "Polar Bear" stone figurine, by Henry Evaluardjuk (1923-2007), Frobisher Bay/Iqaluit.

2in (5cm) high

$400-500 WAD

A "Kneeling Man" stone figurine, by Joanasie Lyta (b.1921), Lake Harbour/Kimmirut, signed in syllabics, dated.

1976 7¾in (19.5cm) high

$120-160 WAD

A "Musk Ox" stone figurine, by Barnabus Arnasungaaq (1924-2017), E2-213, Baker Lake/Qamani'tuaq, signed syllabics.

2011 16in (40.5cm) long

$2,600-3,900 WAD

A "Polar Bear Swimming with Cubs" stone figurine, by Bill Nasogaluak (b.1953), Yellowknife, signed in Roman, dated.

2007 9in (23cm) long

$800-900 WAD

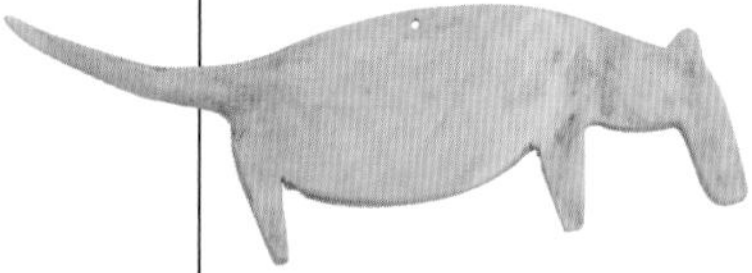

A "Dog" antler figurine, by Andy Miki (1918-83), Eskimo Point/Arviat.

9½in (24cm) long

$650-800 WAD

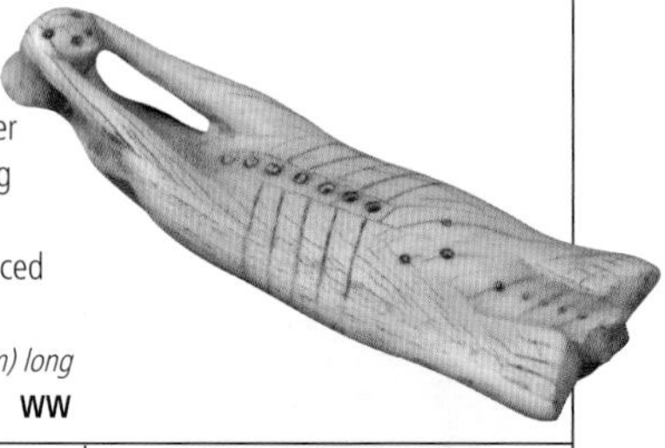

A 19thC Alaskan Inuit sea otter marine ivory amulet, in feeding posture, with incised ribs and spine with inlay, with two pierced attachment holes.

3¼in (8.5cm) long

$12,000-14,000 WW

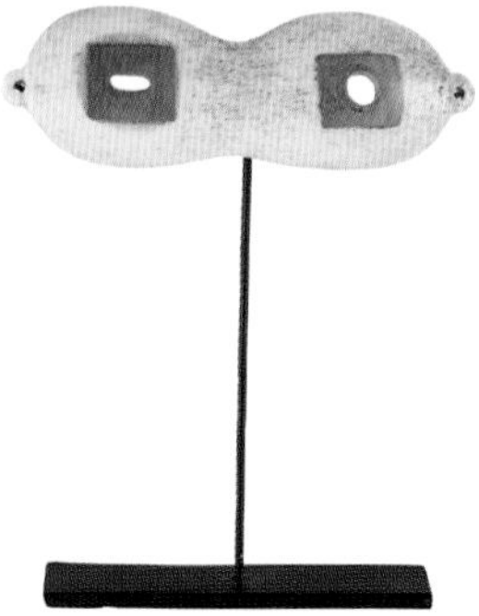

An Alaskan Inuit carved whalebone snow goggle, with asymmetrical encrusted wooden panels over each eye, mounted.

5½in (14cm) wide

$1,300-1,900 L&T

A lidded woven basket with bear knop, by John Harrow, Point Barrow, Alaska, of grass, baleen, and ivory, signed in Roman.

5in (12.5cm) diam

$600-700 WAD

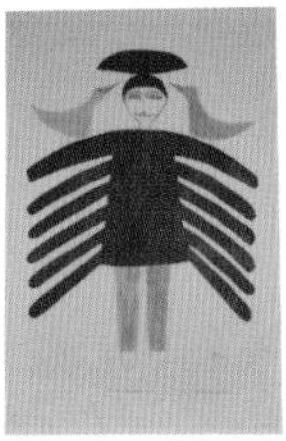

A "Two Birds Guard Sleeping Kiviiuk" linocut and stencil, by Jessie Oonark O.C. R.C.A. (1906-85), Baker Lake/Qamani'tuaq, no.35/50.

1981 37in (94cm) high

$900-1,150 WAD

A "Small Tundra Bird" stencil, by Kenojuak Ashevak C.C. R.C.A. (1927-2013), Cape Dorset/Kinngait, no.37/50.

1996 23in (58.5cm) high

$1,900-2,600 WAD

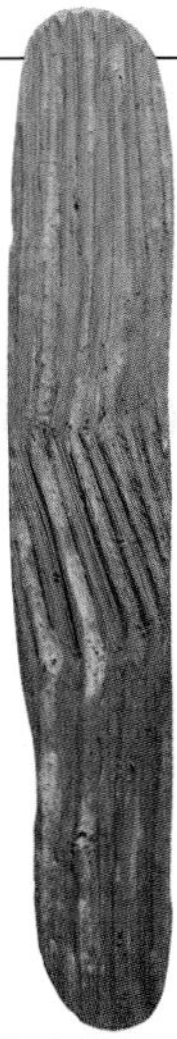

An Aboriginal wunda shield, Western Australia, the back with linear carved decoration and an integral handle.

35in (89cm) long

$1,600-2,100 WW

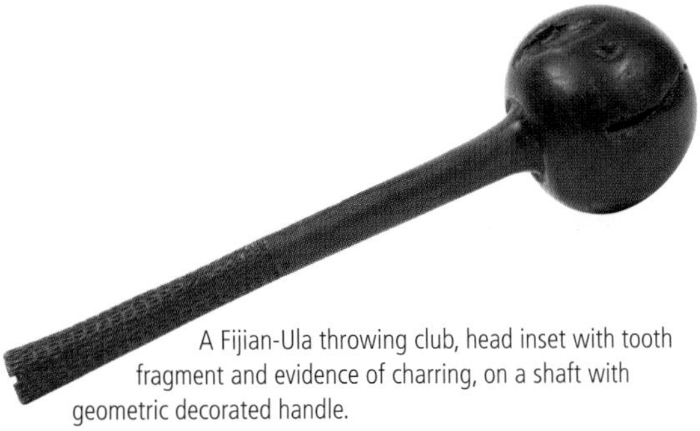

A Fijian-Ula throwing club, head inset with tooth fragment and evidence of charring, on a shaft with geometric decorated handle.

After battle, a victim's tooth was hammered into the head of the club and it was then hung in a priest hut and used for ritualistic purposes.

15¾in (40cm) long

$650-800 BE

A 19thC Fijian ula or throwing club, with lobe carved head and zigzag carved grip section.

15in (38cm) long

$1,050-1,150 HT

A Fiji trumpet davui, Melanesia, shell and coconut fiber sennit, the shell with a pierced mouthpiece, with handwritten sticker "Major Douglas-Jones, High Salvington Mill, Worthing, Sx."

Provenance: Admiral Sir Crawford Caffin (1812-83); Major Douglas-Jones, Sussex, UK; James T. Hooper, Arundel, UK, acquired in 1956.

15¾in (40cm) long

$4,500-5,200 WW

A Batak medicine horn, Indonesia, buffalo horn with carved wood finials of mounted ancestor figures.

20½in (52cm) wide

$130-190 WW

A Dayak baby carrier, Indonesia, fiber, colored wire and fabric, hung with strands of teeth, glass beads, figural amulets, and metal bells, with beaded and teeth-mounted straps.

11½in (29cm) high

$650-800 WW

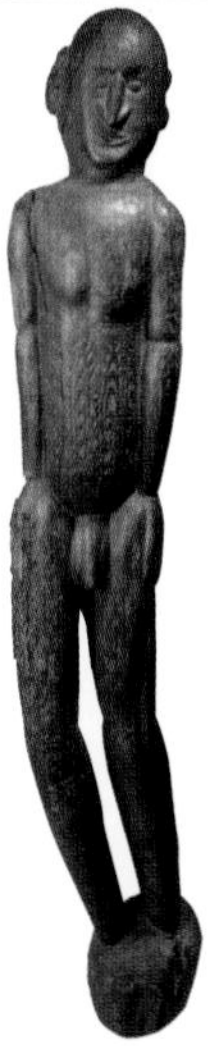

A Lake Sentani male figure, Irian Jaya, Indonesia, with carved motifs to the abdomen.

65½in (166.5cm) high

$1,300-1,900 WW

A Humboldt Bay figure, Irian Jaya.

18in (45.5cm) high

$400-450 WW

A Kanak bamboo flute, New Caledonia, with incised and stained pictorial decoration of a chief's house and two smaller houses with figural roof finial, with a figure hunting with bow and arrow, with three figures below, three two-masted ships, a large turtle, linear geometric decoration, and a band of animals, with seven pierced holes.

28¼in (72cm) long

$2,600-3,200 WW

An early-19thC Maori hei-tiki, green nephrite.

5in (12.5cm) high

$9,500-11,000 **JN**

A Maori hei-tiki nephrite pendant, New Zealand, with a sticking out tongue and suspension hole.

2¾in (7cm) high

$5,200-6,500 **WW**

A Maori bowl, New Zealand, with all-over carved linear and notched decoration, with end figural handles, the eyes and rim inlaid with haliotis shell.

15¼in (38.5cm) wide

$3,200-3,900 **WW**

A Papua New Guinea mask, Melanesia, with pigment decoration.

16¾in (42.5cm) high

$450-500 **WW**

A Ramu River ancestor mask, Papua New Guinea, with gum and hair and with painted decoration.

19½in (49.5cm) high

$450-500 **WW**

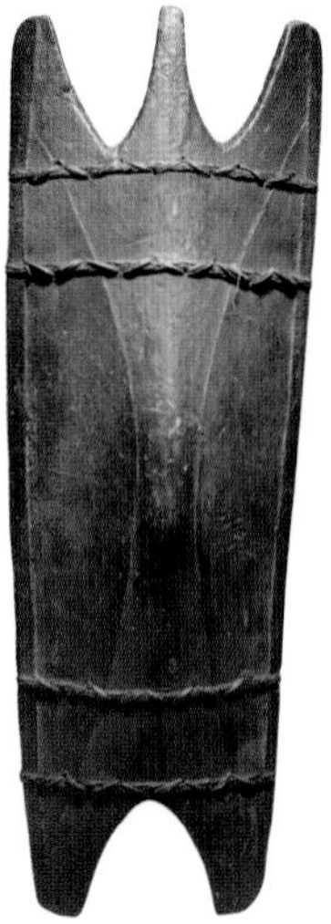

A Bontoc shield, Luzon Island, Philippines, with an integral handle and fiber binding.

34in (86.5cm) high

$600-700 **WW**

A Cook Islands ceremonial adze, Mangaia Island, Polynesia, with a faceted stone blade sennit.

31¾in (80.5cm) long

$1,600-2,100 **WW**

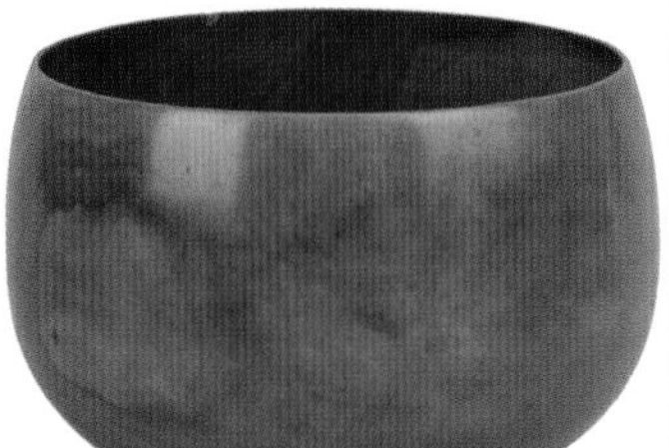

A Hawaii kou wood bowl, Polynesia.

9in (23cm) diam

$1,800-2,300 **WW**

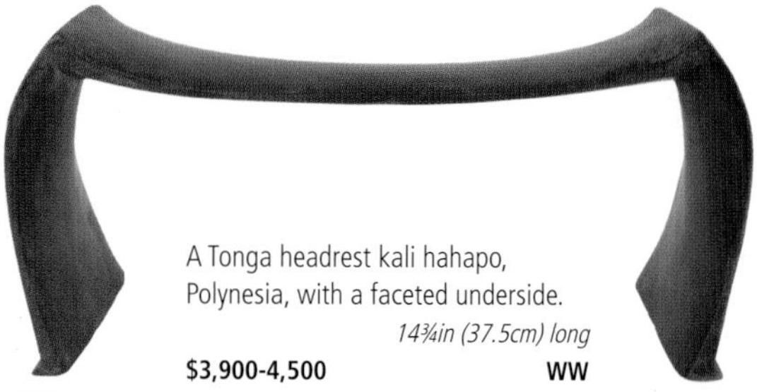

A Tonga headrest kali hahapo, Polynesia, with a faceted underside.

14¾in (37.5cm) long

$3,900-4,500 **WW**

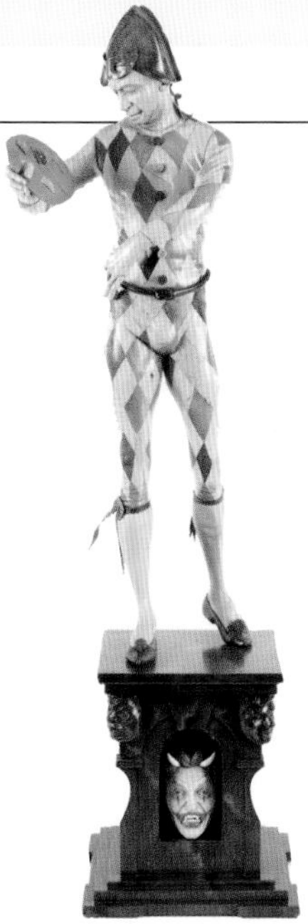

A standing "Harlequin - The Politician" figurine of Tony Blair, by Ian Norbury, supported by four gargoyles depicting Peter Mandelson, Gordon Brown, John Prescott, and Cherie Blair, limewood, walnut, bog oak, and other woods, each side set with a carved face representing the artist's interpretation of Blair's different characteristics.

39¾in (101cm) high

$4,500-5,800 **CHOR**

An aluminum scale model of the Stautue of Liberty, after the original designed by Frédéric Auguste Bartholdi (1834-1904), fitted for electricity.

90½in (230cm) high

$6,500-8,000 **DUK**

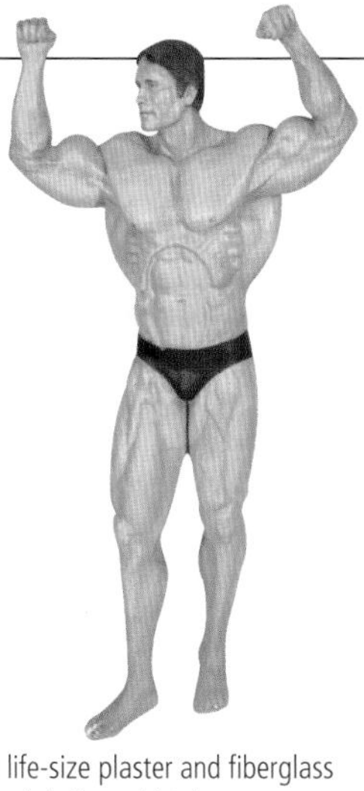

A life-size plaster and fiberglass model of Arnold Schwarzenegger.

74in (188cm) high

$650-800 **DUK**

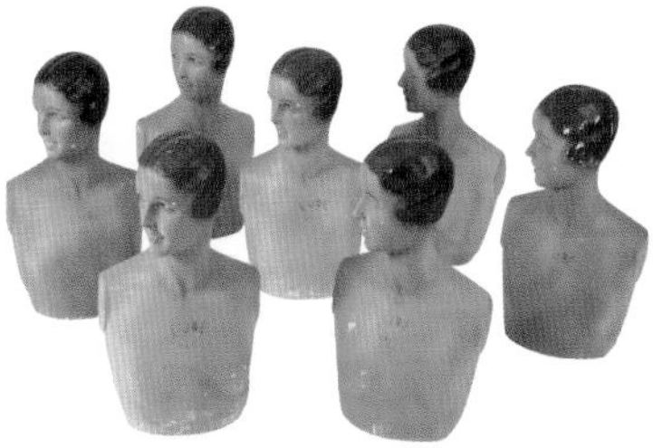

A collection of seven Lube Paris shop display mannequins, painted features, and painted marks.

24in (61cm) high

$900-1,050 **DUK**

A life-size fiberglass emperor penguin, painted in polychrome.

34¾in (88.5cm) high

$300-350 **DUK**

A large vintage fiberglass and painted "Flying Dumbo," painted in polychrome.

95¼in (242cm) long

$1,600-2,100 **DUK**

A 20thC large painted "Shamu" whale shop advertising mascot.

98½in (250cm) long

$1,400-1,800 **DUK**

A rare mid-20thC privately owned cast iron Guernsey Post pillar-shaped mailbox, with "GR" cypher on front, manufactured by the Carron Company, Stirlingshire, with Chubb lock with key and interior cage and chute fitments.

66in (167.5cm) high

$39,000-45,000 **MART**

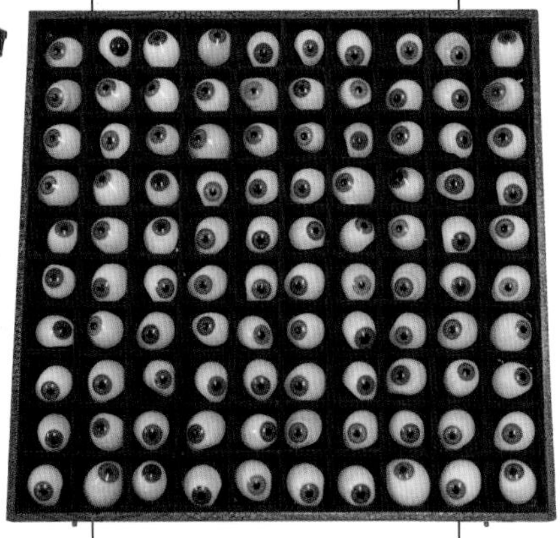

An early-20thC collection of one hundred prosthetic glass eyes, from the Jackson Cox Practice in Cambridge, shell gray, cased.

$2,600-3,200 **HAN**

QUICK REFERENCE—WINE LABELS

- **Produced in silver from ca. 1740, wine labels were hung around the neck of a bottle on a chain or wire hoop, replacing parchment labels.**
- **After the Licensing Act of 1860 required wine merchants to label individual bottles prior to selling them, very few wine labels were made.**
- **Wine labels from the 18thC and 19thC are usually made of silver or silver plate. However, enamel, pottery, porcelain, ivory, bone, and mother-of-pearl were also used.**

A silver wine label, by Hester Bateman, London, incised "SHERRY."
ca. 1780 *3in (7.5cm) long 0.3oz*
$400-450 **WW**

A silver wine label, by Hester Bateman, London, incised and blackened "RUM."
ca. 1780 *2¼in (5.5cm) long 0.3oz*
$700-850 **WW**

A silver wine label, by George Adams, London, modeled as an heraldic Talbot, engraved decoration, incised, and blackened "PORT."
1866 *1¾in (4.5cm) long 0.4oz*
$800-900 **WW**

A Scottish provincial silver wine label, by James Erskine, Aberdeen, incised "BRANDY."
ca. 1795 *1¾in (4.5cm) long 0.3oz*
$650-800 **WW**

A silver-gilt armorial wine label, by Robert Garrard, London, incised "CLARET."
1864 *2in (5cm) long 0.8oz*
$650-800 **WW**

A silver wine label, by Robert and Samuel Hennell, London, incised "PORT."
1806 *1½in (4cm) long 0.9oz*
$650-800 **WW**

An early-19thC Maltese silver wine label, by Gioacchino Lebrun, incised "SHERRY."
ca. 1805 *2¼in (5.5cm) long 0.2oz*
$950-1,100 **WW**

A silver wine label, by Matthew Linwood, Birmingham, incised "SHERRY."
1810 *1½in (4cm) long 0.4oz*
$400-450 **WW**

A silver wine label, by Stephen Noad, London, incised "W.PORT."
1826 *2¾in (7cm) long 0.5oz*
$400-450 **WW**

A silver wine label, by Phipps and Robinson, London, with an armorial mythical fish, incised "PORT."
1799 *2in (5cm) long 0.5oz*
$1,300-1,800 **WW**

A silver armorial wine label, by Phipps, Robinson and Phipps, London, modeled as an eagle's head with spread wings, pierced "MADEIRA."

1812 *1¾in (4.5cm) long 0.8oz*

$700-800 **WW**

A silver wine label, by Charles Rawlings, London, with bacchanalian putti, pierced "L.CHRISTIE."

1818 *2¼in (5.5cm) long 0.8oz*

$450-500 **WW**

A silver-gilt "Lady Bountiful" wine label, by Charles Rawlings, London, pierced "BURGUNDY," with a heavy chain.

1822 *2¾in (7cm) long 1.2oz*

$800-850 **WW**

A silver-gilt wine label, by Paul Storr, London, with bacchanalian cherubs, incised "ZERRY."

1824 *2¼in (5.5cm) long 0.7oz*

$850-950 **WW**

A silver wine label, by Paul Storr, London, incised "BRANDY."

1827 *2½in (6.5cm) long 0.6oz*

$500-600 **WW**

A silver armorial wine label, by John Terrey, London, modeled as a dragon head, incised "MADEIRA."

1828 *1¾in (4.5cm) long 0.6oz*

$900-950 **WW**

A pair of silver wine labels, by George Unite, Birmingham, incised "THE DUKE 1812" and "RIOTORTO "1820."

1844 *2¼in (5.5cm) long 5.4oz*

$500-650 **WW**

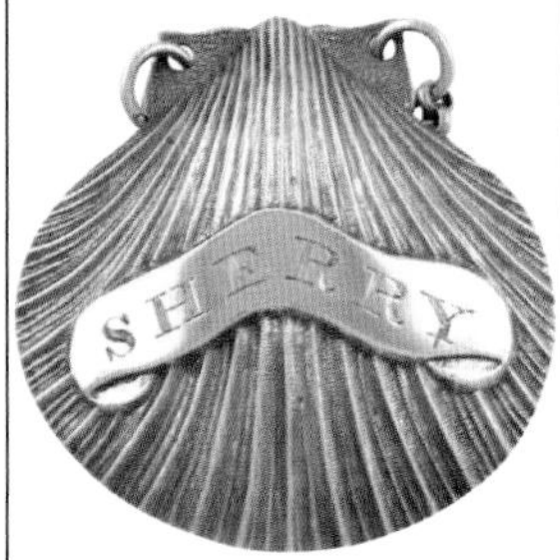

A silver wine label, by Joseph Willmore, Birmingham, incised "SHERRY."

1825 *1½in (4cm) diam 0.3oz*

$300-400 **WW**

A silver armorial wine label, unmarked, modeled as two demi-greyhounds, pierced "MADEIRA."
The crest is that of Bratt, Lysons and Atkins.

1½in (4cm) long

$800-900 **WW**

A silver armorial wine label, unmarked, modeled as a mythical dolphin, incised "PORT."

ca. 1800 *2in (5cm) long 2oz*

$800-900 **WW**

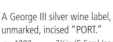

A George III silver wine label, unmarked, incised "PORT."

ca. 1800 *2¼in (5.5cm) long 0.5oz*

$800-900 **WW**

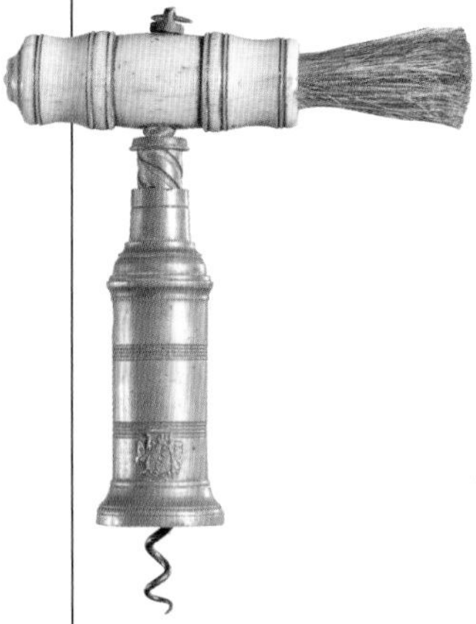

A mid-19thC Thomason-type brass barrel corkscrew, with turned bone handle and brush, badge marked "Patent."

$190-260 **BELL**

A mid-19thC twin-pillar open rack corkscrew, with turned bone handle and brush.

$400-500 **BELL**

A 19thC brass Cope and Cutler rack corkscrew, with turned bone handles, with an applied plaque.

7½in (19cm) long

$400-500 **WW**

A Lund's Queen's Patent corkscrew, with a King's screw, the rosewood handle originally with a brush, the plaque, inscribed "LUND'S PATENT 57 CORNHILL," the triple bottle grips stamped with three crowns and "THE QUEENS PATENT GRANTED TO T. LUND LONDON."

7¼in (18.5cm) long

$3,900-4,500 **WW**

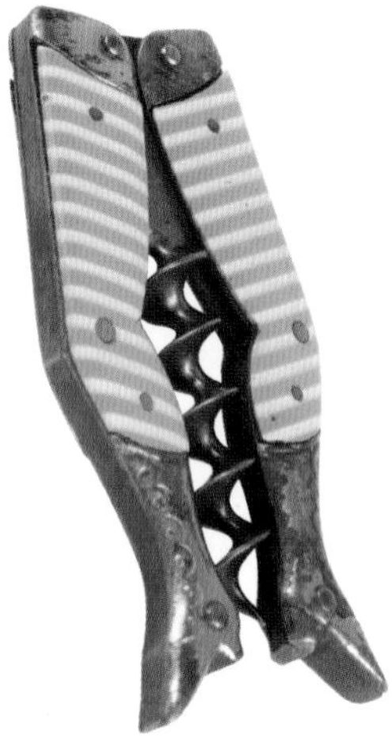

A German corkscrew, depicting a pair of female legs.

ca. 1930s *2½in (6.5cm) long*

$260-320 **LOCK**

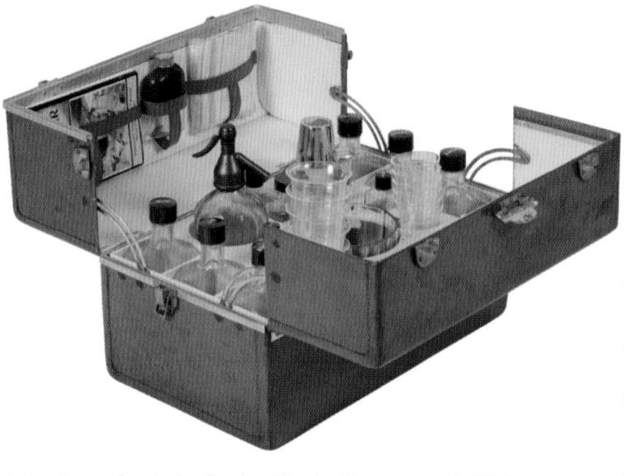

A Pendragon "porta-bar" set, with a leather case, with 12 glasses, a soda siphon, silver-plated cocktail shaker, ice bucket, 5-quart bottles for liquors, and 2 bottles for flavorings and essences.

18½in (47cm) long

$2,300-2,900 **DUK**

A barside cocktail "shaker" recipe menu, with a flick menu of 35 recipes, stamped patent number "186582."

5½in (14cm) high

$260-390 **SWO**

An American "Price-O-Mat" bartender's icemaker.

9½in (24cm) high

$130-190 **SWO**

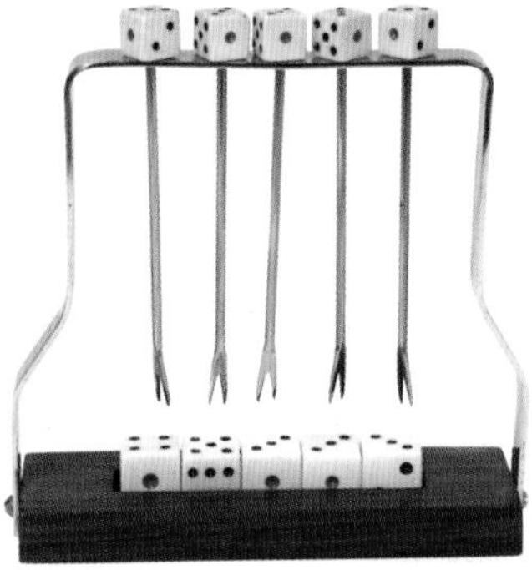

A pair of five novelty dice cocktail picks, with five further dice on the plinth.

5in (12.5cm) wide

$260-390 **SWO**

QUICK REFERENCE—WRISTWATCHES

- **Over the last two decades, interest in wristwatches has grown. The trend has been prompted in part by men's magazines and the popularization of formal appearance and retro looks in men's fashion. Watches can be status symbols as well as investment pieces. The style, maker, complexity of the movement, date of manufacture, and condition affect value.**
- **The first wristwatch, the Santos, was developed by Cartier in ca. 1904 and is still produced today. Prior to this, pocket watches were adapted into wristwatches using a leather pocket and strap or wire strap "lugs" soldered onto the case.**
- **Wristwatches became popular shortly after World War I, during which some (such as the Trench watch, identifiable by the protective grille over the glass dial cover) were issued to servicemen.**
- **Wristwatches can be dated from the case, hands, numbers, and general design.**
- **After 1920, the range of case shapes developed to include rectangular, octagonal, oval, and square wristwatches, having previously been predominantly circular. By the 1930s, wristwatches had nearly replaced pocket watches. In the 1940s, the cocktail watch was developed, influenced by fashions of the time. Simple circular styles with pared down dials were popular in the 1950s. Bulkier, more sculptural and futuristic watches are often from the late 1960s and 1970s.**

A gentleman's Audemars Piguet wristwatch, no.10462.

$4,500-5,200 JN

A mid-size Blancpain "Villeret" chronograph wristwatch, 18ct yellow gold case, numbered "107," signed automatic movement with quick date set, signed crocodile strap, stamped "750."

12½in (32cm) diam

$3,900-4,500 FELL

A gentleman's Breitling "Navitimer Chrono-Matic" chronograph steel wristwatch, Breitling monogrammed crown, steel bracelet strap.

1970s dial 1¾in (4.5cm) diam

$2,300-2,900 HAN

A gentleman's steel Breitling "Chrono Superocean" wristwatch, integral steel bracelet, ref. A1334011, serial no.2012053, boxed with paperwork and certificate.

ca. 2005 1½in (4cm) diam

$2,600-3,200 HAN

A Cartier 18ct yellow gold diamond-faced "Pasha" wristwatch, stamped "18K 1035 CC715855," in original box.

$6,500-8,000 JN

A Cartier "Santos" 18ct yellow gold wristwatch, in original box, with papers.

$5,200-6,500 JN

A Cartier "Ronde Solo" wristwatch, ref.2934, serial no.740069PX, signed quartz caliber 115A with quick date set, stainless steel case, with signed alligator strap.

1½in (4cm) wide

$1,700-2,100 FELL

A Cartier "Quadrant" wristwatch, stamped "750" with poincon, numbered "A100772."

1in (2.5cm) diam

$1,600-2,100 FELL

A Cartier "Must De Cartier Ronde" wristwatch, ref.1810, serial no.006400, signed quartz caliber 01401/1.

1¼in (3cm) wide

$700-800 FELL

A gentleman's Chopard "Mille Miglia Competitor Edition 2017" chronograph wristwatch, ref.8585, serial no.2014064, signed automatic caliber 109558 stainless steel case with tachymeter bezel, on a signed rubber strap with stainless steel pin buckle.

1¾in (4.5cm) wide

$2,600-3,200 **FELL**

A Corum "Admirals Cup" wristwatch, ref.285.630.20, no.797310, automatic chronograph movement, 30-minute and 12-hour recording, date aperture at 6 o'clock, rotating bezel with enameled signal flags for the numerals and degrees in-between, stainless steel, dial and movement signed, on a Corum black rubber strap.

ca. 2005 *1¾in (4.5cm) diam*

$1,800-2,300 **DN**

A Dubois gentleman's chronograph wristwatch, gold-plated case with stainless steel case back, numbered "0194/1499," automatic movement with quick date set, subsidiary recorder dials at 6, 9, and 12, day and date aperture at 3, outer tachymeter track, on an unsigned leather strap.

1½in (4cm) diam

$650-800 **FELL**

A gentleman's Roger Dubuis "Acqua Mare Just For Friends" wristwatch, limited edition no.25 of 888, signed automatic caliber 4565, stainless steel case, on a signed black rubber strap with stainless steel pin buckle.

1½in (4cm) wide

$3,900-4,500 **FELL**

A Girard-Perregaux "Traveller" 21ct gold wristwatch, ref.4980 OJNO394, with leather strap.

$8,000-9,000 **JN**

A gentlemans's Hamilton "Khaki" Automatic T2 wristwatch, series no.H775450, the 21 jewel movement with exhibition case back, crowns at 2, 4, and 9 positions, on original rubber strap, cased and boxed with instruction manual and warranty, dated.

2010

$500-650 **HT**

A lady's Hermès "Cape Cod Deux Zones" wristwatch, ref.CC3-210, serial no.1739837, signed movements, stainless steel case, on a signed green lizard strap with stainless steel pin buckle.

¾in (2cm) wide

$1,300-1,800 **FELL**

A gentleman's Tag Heuer "Carrera Caliber 1887" chronograph wristwatch, ref.CAR2110-3, serial no.EKQ8238, signed automatic caliber 1887 with quick date set, stainless steel case with exhibition case back, on a signed leather strap with stainless steel deployant clasp, box and papers.

1½in (4cm) wide

$2,300-2,900 **FELL**

An International Watch Co. stainless steel mark "II Military" gun camera watch, marked on back case "10AF/807 N.I 064."

1½in (4cm) diam

$1,900-2,600 **LOCK**

A gentleman's Jacob & Co. "Five Time Zone" wristwatch, stainless steel factory diamond set bezel, on a signed crocodile strap with stainless steel deployant clasp, with box and papers, some scratches.

1¾in (4.5cm) diam

$2,300-2,900 **FELL**

A gentleman's 9ct gold Swiss Jaeger-LeCoultre wristwatch, jewelled movement detailed "Jaeger-le Coultre Swiss 119321," retailed by Cartier, on an associated 9ct gold oval link bracelet, with a foldover clasp, Birmingham 1961, case maker W.T. & Co., London.
1956
$1,300-1,800 BELL

A British military issue Jaeger-LeCoultre stainless steel cased wristwatch, stamped on case with broad arrow "6b/346 2278/48."
$8,000-9,000 LOCK

A gentleman's Jaeger-LeCoultre stainless steel "Grandsport Reverso" wristwatch, original strap, inner and outer box, booklets, and certificate from purchase, scratches.
1999
$2,300-2,900 APAR

A gentleman's Romain Jerome "Octopus Titanic-DNA" wristwatch, ref.RJTAUDI003, serial no.5005578, limited edition no.002 of 888, stainless steel case with oxidized bezel containing trace metal from the *Titanic*, on a signed rubber strap with stainless steel pin buckle.
2in (5cm) wide
$4,500-5,200 FELL

A gentleman's Maurice Lacroix "Pontos Décentrique GMT" wristwatch, ref.PT6118, serial no.AO54888, signed automatic caliber ML121 with quick date set, stainless steel case on a signed black crocodile strap with stainless steel deployant clasp.
1¾in (4.5cm) wide
$1,150-1,550 FELL

A gentleman's Longines "Evidenza" automatic wristwatch, model no.L2.670.4, leather strap, with box and papers.
$700-850 FLD

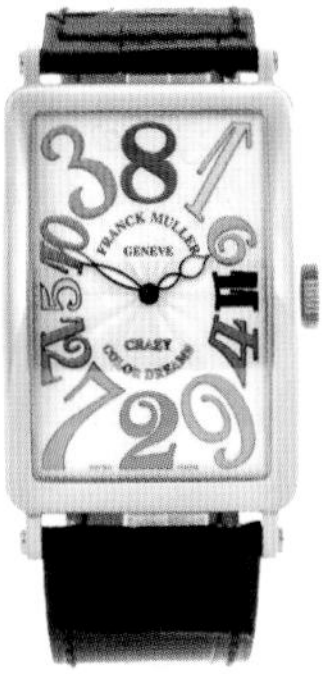

A gentleman's Franck Muller "Crazy Hours Colour Dreams" wristwatch, ref.1200 CH, numbered "255," signed automatic caliber 2800 V, stainless steel case, on a signed alligator strap with stainless steel pin buckle.
1¼in (3cm) wide
$4,500-5,200 FELL

An Omega "Speedmaster Automatic Michael Schumacher" wristwatch, limited edition no.4,563 of 11,111, with original boxes and papers, dated.
2003
$2,300-2,900 AST

A gentleman's Omega "Speedmaster Professional" steel bracelet wristwatch, no.861, the caseback detailed "First watch worn on the moon, flight-qualify by Nasa, for all manned space missions," slight wear on clasp, case back key missing.
dial 1½in (4cm) diam
$3,900-5,200 BELL

A gentleman's Omega "Speedmaster Co-Axial" chronometer wristwatch, with stainless steel case, visible rear movement, original strap, both inner and outer box, tags, booklet, international warranty card, chronometer certificate card, and pictogram card, minor surface scratches.
$2,900-3,600 APAR

An Omega "Seamaster" wristwatch, ref.105.005-65, manual wind chronograph movement, 17 jewels, cal.321, no.24012161, stainless steel, screw-down back, case, dial and movement signed, on an unsigned leather strap.

ca. 1965 *1½in (4cm) diam*

$2,600-3,200 **DN**

A gentleman's Omega wristwatch, ref.2643S.C, serial no.11162322, stamped 0.750 with poinçon, yellow metal case, on an unsigned crocodile strap with gold-plated pin buckle.

1¼in (3cm) wide

$850-950 **FELL**

A gentleman's Omega "Seamaster 300 M" stainless steel bracelet watch, with automatic movement, on Omega bracelet, in original box and outer box.

$2,300-2,900 **DUK**

An Omega "Speedmaster Professional" MKII stainless steel bracelet wristwatch, tachymeter, Omega crown, on Omega "Speedmaster" bracelet.

ca. 1970s *1½in (4cm) diam*

$3,200-3,900 **DUK**

A gentleman's Omega stainless steel cased wristwatch, serial no.8998565.

ca. 1930s

$300-400 **LOCK**

A gentleman's Omega wristwatch, 9ct gold case, hallmarked Birmingham, numbered "224432," signed bumper automatic caliber 28.10RA, numbered "11306393," on an unsigned leather strap with gold-plated pin buckle, some scratches.

1948 *1¼in (3cm) diam*

$800-900 **FELL**

A lady's Patek Philippe wristwatch, strap stamped "Patek Philippe Geneve," with a signed maroon leather case, with certificate of origin confirming date of purchase.

1997

$3,900-4,500 **BE**

A World War II military issue Vertex wristwatch, "Dirty Dozen" type, inscribed on the back "^w.w.w A 8082 3520998."

$1,050-1,150 **LOCK**

A gentleman's Raymond Weil "Maestro" wristwatch, reference 2827, serial no.VI36309, signed automatic movement, stainless steel case with exhibition case back, on an unsigned leather strap.

1½in (4cm) diam

$600-650 **FELL**

A gentleman's Zenith Defy Xtreme El Primero chronograph bracelet wristwatch, numbered "96.0525.4000," automatic movement on a signed titanium bracelet with double folding clasp, with box and papers.

1¾in (4.5cm) diam

$3,900-4,500 **FELL**

QUICK REFERENCE—ROLEX

- **In 1905, Hans Wilsdorf founded a company in London that focused on the distribution of timepieces. The company then began producing wristwatches, using pieces manufactured in Bienne, Switzerland. In 1908, Wilsdorf came up with the name "Rolex."**
- **A Rolex watch was awarded the Swiss Certificate of Chronometric Precision, in 1910. In 1914, Kew Observatory, UK, awarded a Rolex wristwatch a class A precision certificate. This certificate had previously only been awarded to marine chronometers. In 1919, Wilsdorf moved the company to Geneva, Switzerland. The company was renamed Rolex Watch Co. Ltd. in 1915, before becoming Montres Rolex S.A. in 1920.**
- **The company went on to develop the first waterproof watch in 1926 and, in 1931 it patented the world's first self-winding mechanism with a perpetual rotor. By 1978, Rolex had developed a wristwatch that was waterproof to a depth of 1,220 meters. In 2012, the "Oyster Perpetual Rolex Deepsea Challenge" wristwatch, waterproof to a depth of more than 10,000 meters, was launched.**
- **Wilsdorf died in 1960, leaving the company to his charitable trust. From the early 2000s, Rolex began laser etching its trademark crown on its wristwatch crystals in an attempt to reduce counterfeiting.**

A gentleman's Rolex "Oyster Perpetual" bracelet watch, reference 6582, serial no.329565, signed automatic caliber 1030, silvered "Zephyr" dial, on a signed bimetal Jubilee bracelet with Oysterclasp, movement worn, marks and scratches on dial.

ca. 1957 *1½in (4cm) diam*

$1,900-2,600 FELL

A lady's Rolex "Precision" wristwatch, with a 1401 caliber 13-jewel movement, the case back marked inside "RW co," on a tricolored textured bracelet, in 9ct hallmarked London 1966, with box.

1966

$1,300-1,800 ECGW

A gentleman's Rolex "Oyster Perpetual" chronometer bubble-back steel wristwatch, later strap, case with light wear.

1950s

$1,600-2,100 HAN

A gentleman's Rolex "Oyster Perpetual Air King" stainless steel wristwatch, integral steel bracelet, serial number.

1967

$1,900-2,600 HAN

A gentleman's Police 18ct Rolex "Oyster Perpetual" day-date wristwatch, serial no.7397902, fitted "President" bracelet and after-market diamond set dial and bracelet.

ca. 1982-83

$6,500-7,000 AST

A lady's stainless steel Rolex "Datejust" wristwatch, serial no.L478430, with jubilee bracelet and aftermarket diamond dial and bezel.

ca. 1989-90

$2,300-2,900 AST

A gentleman's Rolex "Oyster Perpetual Date Explorer II" bracelet watch, ref.16570, serial no.Y998359, signed automatic caliber 3185, stainless steel case, replacement dial, on a signed stainless steel Oyster bracelet with Oysterlock clasp.

ca. 2002 *1½in (4cm) diam*

$4,500-5,200 FELL

A gentleman's 18ct yellow gold Rolex day-date chronometer, with dial set with diamonds, in a Rolex box.

$10,500-12,000 JN

A lady's 18ct gold Rolex wristwatch, "President" bracelet stamped "Rolex," with Rolex box, guarantee pamphlet and spare link.

2oz

$4,500-5,200 BE

Every item illustrated has a letter code that identifies the dealer, auction house, or private collector that owns or sold it.

AB
ALDRIDGES OF BATH
www.aldridgesofbath.com

AJ&S
ARTHUR JOHNSON AND SONS
www.arthurjohnson.co.uk

APAR
ADAM PARTRIDGE
www.adampartridge.co.uk

AST
ASTON'S AUCTIONEERS AND VALUERS
www.astonsauctioneers.co.uk

BBR
BBR AUCTIONS
www.onlinebbr.com

BE
BEARNES HAMPTON & LITTLEWOOD
www.bhandl.co.uk

BELL
BELLMANS
www.bellmans.co.uk

BER
BERTOIA AUCTIONS
www.bertoiaauctions.com

BLEA
BLEASDALES LTD.
www.bleasdalesltd.co.uk

BLO
BLOOMSBURY
(now part of Dreweatts 1759)
www.bloomsburyauctions.com

BMN
AUKTIONSHAUS BERGMANN
www.auction-bergmann.de

BOL
BOLDON AUCTION GALLERIES
www.boldonauctions.co.uk

BRI
BRIGHTWELLS
www.brightwells.com

BTA
BRITISH TOY AUCTIONS
www.britishtoyauctions.co.uk

C&T
C&T AUCTIONEERS AND VALUERS
www.candtauctions.co.uk

CAN
THE CANTERBURY AUCTION GALLERIES
www.thecanterburyauctiongalleries.com

CHEF
CHEFFINS
www.cheffins.co.uk

CHOR
CHORLEY'S
www.chorleys.com

CHT
CHARTERHOUSE AUCTIONEERS & VALUERS
www.charterhouse-auction.com

CLAR
CLARS
www.clars.com

CM
CHARLES MILLER LTD.
www.charlesmillerltd.com

CUTW
CUTTLESTONES AUCTIONEERS & VALUERS
www.cuttlestones.co.uk

DA&H
DEE ATKINSON & HARRISON
www.dee-atkinson-harrison.co.uk

DAWS
DAWSONS AUCTIONEERS & VALUERS
www.dawsonsauctions.co.uk

DN
DREWEATTS 1759
www.dreweatts.com

DRA
RAGO AUCTIONS
www.ragoarts.com

DUK
DUKE'S
www.dukes-auctions.com

ECGW
EWBANK'S
www.ewbankauctions.co.uk

FELL
FELLOWS
www.fellows.co.uk

FIS
AUKTIONHAUS DR FISCHER
www.auctions-fischer.de

FLD
FIELDINGS AUCTIONEERS LTD.
www.fieldingsauctioneers.co.uk

FOM
FONSIE MEALY AUCTIONEERS
www.fonsiemealy.ie

FRE
FREEMAN'S
www.freemansauction.com

GHOU
GARDINER HOULGATE
www.gardinerhoulgate.co.uk

GBA
GRAHAM BUDD AUCTIONS
www.grahambuddauctions.co.uk

GIL
GILDINGS AUCTIONEERS
www.gildings.co.uk

GORL
GORRINGE'S
www.gorringes.co.uk

GRV
GEMMA REDMOND VINTAGE
www.gemmaredmondvintage.co.uk

GWA
GREAT WESTERN AUCTIONS LTD.
www.greatwesternauctions.com

GWRA
GW RAILROADIANA AUCTIONS
www.gwra.co.uk

GYM
GOLDING YOUNG & MAWER
www.goldingyoung.com

HALL
HALLS
www.fineart.hallsgb.com

HAN
HANSONS AUCTIONEERS AND VALUERS LTD.
www.hansonsauctioneers.co.uk

HANN
HANNAM'S
www.hannamsauctioneers.com

HT
HARTLEYS AUCTIONEERS AND VALUERS
www.hartleysauctions.co.uk

HUTC
HUTCHINSON-SCOTT AUCTIONEERS
www.hutchinsonscott.co.uk

IVN
IVOIRE NIMES
www.ivoire-nimes.fr

JDJ
JAMES D JULIA INC.
(now part of Morphy Auctions)
www.morphyauctions.com

JN
JOHN NICHOLSON'S FINE ART AUCTIONEERS & VALUERS
www.johnnicholsons.com

JNEW
JOHN NEWTON ANTIQUES
www.johnnewtonantiques.com

K&O
KINGHAM & ORME AUCTIONEERS VALUERS
www.kinghamandorme.com

KEY
KEYS AUCTIONEERS AND VALUERS
www.keysauctions.co.uk

KT
KERRY TAYLOR AUCTIONS
www.kerrytaylorauctions.com

L&T
LYON & TURNBULL
www.lyonandturnbull.com

LC
LAWRENCES AUCTIONEERS
www.lawrences.co.uk

LOC
LOCKE & ENGLAND
www.leauction.co.uk

LOCK
LOCKDALES AUCTIONEERS & VALUERS
www.lockdales.com

LPA
LEITZ PHOTOGRAPHICA AUCTION
www.leitz-auction.com

LSK
LACY SCOTT & KNIGHT
www.lsk.co.uk

LYN
LYNWAYS
www.lynways.com

M&DM
M&D MOIR
www.manddmoir.co.uk

M&K
MELLORS & KIRK
www.mellorsandkirk.com

M&M
M&M AUCTIONS
www.mm-auctions.com

MAB
MATTHEW BARTON LTD.
www.matthewbartonltd.com

MART
MARTEL MAIDES AUCTIONS
www.martelmaidesauctions.com

MM
MULLOCK'S
www.mullocksauctions.co.uk

MOR
MORPHETS
www.morphets.co.uk

MORP
MORPHY AUCTIONS
www.morphyauctions.com

NA
NORTHEAST AUCTIONS
northeastauctions.com

PC
PRIVATE COLLECTION

POOK
POOK & POOK INC.
www.pookandpook.com

PSA
POTTERIES AUCTIONS
www.potteriesauctions.com

PW
PETER WILSON FINE ART AUCTIONEERS
www.peterwilson.co.uk

QU
QUITTENBAUM
www.quittenbaum.de

ROS
ROSEBERY'S
www.roseberys.co.uk

SAS
SPECIAL AUCTION SERVICES
www.specialauctionservices.com

SK
SKINNER
www.skinnerinc.com

SOU
CATHERINE SOUTHON AUCTIONEERS & VALUERS LTD.
www.catherinesouthon.co.uk

SWA
SWANN AUCTION GALLERIES
www.swanngalleries.com

SWO
SWORDERS FINE ART AUCTIONEERS
www.sworder.co.uk

T&F
TAYLER & FLETCHER
www.taylerandfletcher.co.uk

TDM
THOMAS DEL MAR LTD.
www.thomasdelmar.com

TEN
TENNANTS AUCTIONEERS
www.tennants.co.uk

THER
THERIAULT'S
www.theriaults.com

TRI
TRING MARKET AUCTIONS
www.tringmarketauctions.co.uk

VEC
VECTIS
www.vectis.co.uk

W&W
WALLIS & WALLIS
www.wallisandwallis.co.uk

WAD
WADDINGTON'S
www.waddingtons.ca

WES
WESCHLER'S AUCTIONEERS & APPRAISERS
www.weschlers.com

WHP
W&H PEACOCK
www.peacockauction.co.uk

WHYT
WHYTE'S
www.whytes.ie

WM
WRIGHT MARSHALL
www.wrightmarshall.co.uk

WW
WOOLLEY & WALLIS
www.woolleyandwallis.co.uk

The following list of general antiques and collectibles centers, markets, and stores has been organized by region. Any owner who would like to be listed in our next edition, space permitting, or who wishes to update their contact information, should email publisher@octopusbooks.co.uk

USA

ALABAMA
Antique Attic
www.antiqueatticdothan.com

ALASKA
Duane's Antique Market
www.duanesantiquemarket.com

The Pack Rat Antiques
Tel: +1 907 522 5272

ARIZONA
American Antique Antiques
www.americanantiquemall.com

Brass Armadillo
www.brassarmadillo.com

ARKANSAS
Midtown Vintage Market
www.midtownvintagemarket.com

CALIFORNIA
Ocean Beach Antique Mall
www.antiquesinsandiego.com

COLORADO
A. & J. Antiques Mall
www.ajantiques.com

Brass Armadillo
www.brassarmadillo.com

CONNECTICUT
The Antique and Artisan Gallery
www.theantiqueandartisangallery.com

DELAWARE
Lewes Mercantile Antiques
www.antiqueslewes.com

FLORIDA
Avonlea Antiques & Interiors
www.avonleamall.com

Wildwood Antique Malls
wildwoodantiquemalls.com

GEORGIA
Kudzu Antiques + Modern
www.kudzuantiques.com

HAWAII
Antique Alley
www.portaloha.com/antiquealley

IDAHO
Antique World Mall
www.antiqueworldmall.com

ILLINOIS
Second Time Around Antique Market
www.2xaroundantiques.com

INDIANA
Exit 76 Antique Mall
www.exit76antiques.com

Manor House Antique Mall
Tel: +1 317 888 8887

IOWA
Brass Armadillo
www.brassarmadillo.com

KANSAS
Flying Moose Antique Mall
www.flying-moose.com

Paramount Antique Mall
www.paramountantiquemall.com

KENTUCKY
Preservation Station
www.visitpreservationstation.com

LOUISIANA
Magazine Antique Mall
www.magazinestreet.com/merchant/magazine-antique-mall

MAINE
Cornish Trading Company
www.cornishtrading.com

MARYLAND
The Antique Center
www.antiquecentersavage.com

MICHIGAN
Collette's
www.collettesvintage.com

Michiana Antique Mall
www.michianaantiquemall.com

MINNESOTA
Staples Mill Antiques
www.staplesmillantiques.com

MISSISSIPPI
Flowoods Antique Flea Market
www.flowoodantiquefleamarket.com

MISSOURI
Relics Antiques Mall
www.relicsantiquemall.com

River Market Antiques
rivermarketantiquemall.com

MONTANA
Montana Antique Mall
www.montanaantiquemall.com

NEBRASKA
Platte Valley Antique Mall
www.plattevalleyantiquemall.com

NEVADA
Cheshire Antiques
www.cheshireantiques.com

NEW HAMPSHIRE
Antiques at Colony Mill Marketplace
www.facebook.com/colonymillantiques

NEW JERSEY
Lafayette Mill Antiques Center
www.millantiques.com

Somerville Center Antiques
www.somervilleantiques.net

The Yellow Garage Antiques Marketplace
www.yellowgarageantiques.com

NEW MEXICO
Antique Connection Mall
www.antiqueconnectionmall.com

NEW YORK
L.W. Emporium Co-op
www.lwemporium.com

The Manhattan Art and Antiques Center
www.the-maac.com

Showplace
www.nyshowplace.com

NORTH CAROLINA
Fifteen Ten Antiques
www.1510-antiques.com

Granddaddy's Antique Mall
www.granddaddys.com

Sleepy Poet Antique Malls
sleepypoetstuff.com

NORTH DAKOTA
Plain and Fancy Antique Mall
www.facebook.com/PlainandFancyAntiqueMall

Grand Antique Mall
www.grandantiquemall.com

Hartville Market Place and Flea Market
www.hartvillemarketplace.com

Heart of Ohio Antique Center
www.heartofohioantiques.com

OKLAHOMA
Antique Co-op
www.antiquecoopokc.com

OREGON
Old Town Antique Mall
www.grantspassantiques.com

PENNSYLVANIA
Antiques Showcase & German Trading Post
Tel: +1 717 336 8447

RHODE ISLAND
Rhode Island Antiques Mall
www.riantiquesmall.com

SOUTH CAROLINA
The Old Mill Antique Mall
www.oldmillantiquemall.com

SOUTH DAKOTA
4 Seasons Flea Market
www.4seasonsfleamarket.com

TENNESSEE
Goodlettsville Antique Mall
www.goodlettsvilleantiquemall.net

TEXAS
Antique Pavilion
www.antique-pavilion.com

Forestwood Antiques Mall
www.forestwoodantiquemall.com

Montgomery Street Antiques
www.montgomerystreetantiques.com

Snider Plaza Antique Shop
www.sniderplazaantiques.net

Uncommon Objects
www.uncommonobjects.com

UTAH
Capital City Antique Mall
www.capitalcityantiquemall.com

VERMONT
The Vermont Antique Mall
www.vermontantiquemall.com

VIRGINIA
Antique Village
www.antiquevillageva.com

Factory Antique Mall
factoryantiquemall.com

WASHINGTON
Seattle Antiques Market
www.seattleantiquesmarket.com

Thorp Fruit and Antique Mall
www.thorpfruit.com/antiques

WEST VIRGINIA
South Charleston Antique Mall
www.southcharlestonantique.com

WISCONSIN
Red Shed Antiques
www.redshed.biz

WYOMING
Antiques Central
www.antiquescentralonline.com

CANADA
Antique Market
www.antiquesdirect.ca

Finnegan's Market
finnegans-market.hudson-village.com

Green Spot Antiques
www.greenspotantiques.com

Post Office Antique Mall
www.postofficeantiquemall.com

Old Strathcona Antique Mall
www.oldstrathconamall.com

One-of-a-Kind Antique Mall
www.oneofakindantiquemall.com

Toronto Antiques on King
www.torontoantiquesonking.com

Vanity Fair Antique & Collectables Mall
vanityfairantiques.ca

If you would like to have any item valued, it is advisable to contact the dealer or specialist in advance to check that they will carry out this service and whether there is a charge. While most dealers will be happy to help you with an enquiry, do remember that they are busy people with businesses to run. Telephone valuations are not possible. Please mention the Miller's Collectibles & Antiques Handbook & Price Guide by Judith Miller when making an enquiry.

ADVERTISING

Junktion Antiques Ltd.
www.junktionantiques.co.uk

Awsum Auctionz LLC
awsumauctionzllc.com

ANTIQUITIES

Frank & Barbara Pollack
Email: barbarapollack@comcast.net

AUSTRIAN BRONZES

European Bronze
www.europeanbronze.com

ASIAN

Hellios Auctions
www.heliosauctions.com

Polly Latham Asian Art
pollylatham.com

Marc Matz Antiques
www.marcmatz.com

Mellin's Antiques
www.mellinsantiques.com

AUTOMOBILIA

Automobilia Auctions
automobiliaauctions.com

Dunbar's Gallery
www.dunbarsgallery.com

BOOKS

Abebooks
www.abebooks.com

Aleph-Bet Books
www.alephbet.com

Bauman Rare Books
www.baumanrarebooks.com

CAMERAS

Brooklyn Film Camera
www.brooklynfilmcamera.com

Houston Camera Exchange
hcehouston.com

CANES

Tradewinds Antiques
tradewindsantiques.com

CERAMICS

Charles & Barbara Adams
Email: adams2430@gmail.com

Mark & Marjorie Allen Antiques
www.antiquedelft.com

HL Chalfant Antiques
www.hlchalfant.com

British Collectibles
www.britishcollectibles.net

Jill Fenichell
jillfenichellinc.com

Cynthia Findlay
www.torontoantiquesonking.com

Pam Ferrazzutti Antiques
www.pamferrazzuttiantiques.com

Samuel Herrup Antiques
www.samuelherrup.com

Mellin's Antiques
www.mellinsantiques.com

Pascoe & Company
www.pascoeandcompany.com

Rago Arts
www.ragoarts.com

Philip Suval, Inc
Email: jphilipsuval@aol.com

TOJ Gallery
www.tojgallery.com

CLOCKS

Kirtland H. Crump
www.kirtlandcrumpclocks.com

RO Schmitt Fine Art
www.roschmittfinearts.com

COMICS

Carl Bonasera
Tel: +1 708 425 7555

Comic Connect
www.comicconnect.com

Comic Gallery Collectibles
www.ebay.com/str/comicgallerycollectibles/

Heritage Auctions
comics.ha.com

Metropolis Collectibles
www.metropoliscomics.com

DOLLS

All Dolled Up
www.alldolledup.ca

Sara Bernstein Dolls
www.rubylane.com/shop/sarabernsteindolls

Theriault's
www.theriaults.com

FASHION

Lofty Vintage
www.loftyvintage.com

Vintage Swank
www.vintageswank.com

FILM & TV

Wonderful World of Animation
www.wonderfulworldofanimation.com

The Prop Store
propstore.com

Julien's Auctions
www.juliensauctions.com

GLASS

Brookside Art Glass
www.wpitt.com

The End of History
www.theendofhistoryshop.blogspot.com

Cynthia Findlay
www.torontoantiquesonking.com

Holsten Galleries
www.holstengalleries.com

Lillian Nassau
www.lilliannassau.com

Jeffrey F. Purtell
www.steubenpurtell.com

Paul Reichwein
Tel: +1 717 569 7637

Retro Art Glass
www.retroartglass.com

Paul Stamati Gallery
www.stamati.com

GUITARS

Norman's Rare Guitars
www.normansrareguitars.com

JEWELRY

Ark Antiques
arkantiques.org

Deco Jewels Inc.
Tel: +1 212 253 1222

Fraleigh Jewellers
www.fraleigh.ca

Leah Gordon Antiques
www.leahgordon.com

Jeweldiva
www.jeweldiva.com

Fiona Kenny Antiques
www.fionakennyantiques.com

Macklowe Gallery
www.macklowegallery.com

Melody Rodgers LLC
www.melodyrodgers.com

LIGHTING

Chameleon Fine Lighting
www.chameleon59.com

Lillian Nassau
www.lilliannassau.com

MECHANICAL MUSIC

Mechantiques
www.mechantiques.com

The Music Box Shop
www.themusicboxshop.com

METALWARE

Wayne & Phyllis Hilt
www.hiltpewter.com

MILITARIA

Faganarms
www.faganarms.com

International Military Antiques
www.ima-usa.com

PAPERWEIGHTS

L.H. Selman Ltd.
www.theglassgallery.com

The Dunlop Collection
Tel: +1 800 227 1996

PENS & WRITING EQUIPMENT

Fountain Pen Hospital
www.fountainpenhospital.com

Go Pens
www.gopens.com

David Nishimura
www.vintagepens.com

Pendemonium
www.pendemonium.com

POSTCARDS

Vintage Postcards
www.vintagepostcards.com

POSTERS

Chisholm Larsson Gallery
www.chisholm-poster.com

Poster Connection Inc.
www.posterconnection.com

Posteritati
www.posteritati.com

Vintage Poster Works
www.vintageposterworks.com

ROCK & POP

Hein's Rare Collectibles
www.beatles4me.com

Julien's Auctions
www.juliensauctions.com

SCIENTIFIC INSTRUMENTS

Barometer Fair
www.barometerfair.com

George Glazer Gallery
www.georgeglazer.com

This Olde Office
www.branfordhouseantiques.com

Tesseract
www.etesseract.com

SCULPTURE

Valerio Art Deco
www.valerioartdeco.com

Olde Hope Antiques
www.oldehope.com

SILVER

Chicago Silver
www.chicagosilver.com

Richard Flensted-Holder
By appointment only, 416 961 3414

Imperial Half Bushel
www.imperialhalfbushel.com

Louis Wine Ltd.
www.louiswine.com

SMOKING

Vintage Lighters NJ
vintagelightersnj.net

Elegant Lighters
www.elegantlighters.com

SPORTING

Larry Fritsch Cards LLC.
www.fritschcards.com

Golf For All Ages
www.golfforallages.com

Hall's Nostalgia
stores.ebay.com/Halls-Nostalgia

Ingrid O'Neil Sports & Olympic Memorabilia
www.ioneil.com

TECHNOLOGY

Harry Poster
www.harryposter.com

TEDDY BEARS

The Calico Teddy
www.calicoteddy.com

TOYS & GAMES

Bertoia
www.bertoiaauctions.com

The Old Toy Soldier Home
oldtoysoldierauctions.com

Trains & Things Hobbies
www.traversehobbies.com

TREEN

Steven S. Powers
www.stevenspowers.com

TRIBAL ART

Arte Primitivo
www.arteprimitivo.com

Marcy Burns American Indian Arts
www.marcyburns.com

Morning Star Gallery
www.morningstargallery.com

Elliott & Grace Snyder
www.elliottandgracesnyder.com

Steven S. Powers
www.stevenspowers.com

Trotta-Bono American Indian Art
www.trottabono.com

Waddington's
www.waddingtons.ca

WATCHES

Matthew Bain Inc.
www.matthewbaininc.com

The Antique Watch Co.
www.antiquewatchco.com

WINE & DRINKING

Donald A. Bull
www.bullworks.net

Steve Visakay Cocktail Shakers
www.visakay.com

The following list of auctioneers who conduct regular sales by auction is organized by region. Any auctioneer who would like to be listed in our next edition, space permitting, or to update their contact information, should email publisher@octopusbooks.co.uk

USA

ALABAMA

Buddy's Antique Auction
www.buddysantiqueauction.com

High as the Sky Auction Company
www.highasthesky auctioncompany.com

Tucker Auctions
tuckerauctions.com

ALASKA

Alaska Auction Co.
www.alaskaauction.com

ARIZONA

Altermann Galleries & Auctioneers
www.altermann.com

The Stein Auction Company
www.garykirsnerauctions.com

Brian Lebel's Old West Show & Auction
www.oldwestevents.com

Old World Mail Auctions
www.oldworldauctions.com

ARKANSAS

Ponders Auctions
www.pondersauctions.com

CALIFORNIA

Bonhams
www.bonhams.com

Goldberg
www.goldbergcoins.com

I.M. Chait Gallery/Auctioneers
www.chait.com

Clark's Fine Art Gallery & Auctioneers
www.estateauctionservice.com

Clars Auction Gallery
www.clars.com

D.G.W. Auctioneers
www.dgwauctioneers.com

Heritage Auctions
www.ha.com

Julien's Auctions
www.juliensauctions.com

Michaan's Auctions
www.michaans.com

John Moran
www.johnmoran.com

L.H. Selman Ltd.
www.paperweight.com

Ingrid O'Neil Sports & Olympic Memorabilia
www.ioneil.com

P.B.A. Galleries
www.pbagalleries.com

Poster Connection Inc.
www.posterconnection.com

Profiles in History
www.profilesinhistory.com

Nate D. Sanders
www.natedsanders.com

San Rafael Auction Gallery
www.sanrafael-auction.com

Robert Slawinski Auctioneers
www.slawinski.com

Stacks Bowers Galleries
www.stacksbowers.com

Treasureseeker Auctions
www.treasureseekerauction.com

COLORADO

Pacific Auction Companies
www.pacificauction.com

CONNECTICUT

ATypicalFind
www.atypicalfind.com

Automobilia Auctions
automobiliaauctions.com

Greenwich Auction
www.greenwichauction.net

Heckler
www.hecklerauction.com

Litchfield County Auctions
litchfieldcountyauctions.com

Lloyd Ralston Gallery
www.lloydralstontoys.com

Shannon's Fine Art Auctioneers
www.shannons.com

Winter Associates Inc.
www.auctionsappraisers.com

DELAWARE

Angola Auction Services
auctionangola.nova-antiques.com

Reagan-Watson Auctions
www.reagan-watsonauctions.com

FLORIDA

Auctions Neapolitan
www.auctionsneapolitan.com

Burchard Galleries
www.burchardgalleries.com

Fine Art Auctions Miami
www.faamiami.com

Leslie Hindman
hindmanauctions.com

Kincaid Auction Company
www.kincaid.com

Kodner
www.kodner.com

A.B. Levy's
www.ablevys.com

Palm Beach Modern Auctions
www.modernauctions.com

TreasureQuest Auction Galleries Inc.
www.tqag.com

Turkey Creek Auctions
www.antiqueauctionsfl.com

GEORGIA

Ahlers & Ogletree Auctions
www.aandoauctions.com

Great Gatsby's
www.greatgatsbys.com

Red Baron's Antiques
www.rbantiques.com

HAWAII

Malama Auctions
www.malamaauctions.com

IDAHO

The Coeur d'Alene Art Auction
www.cdaartauction.com

ILLINOIS

Aspire Auctions
www.aspireauctions.com

Bunte Auction Services
www.bunteauction.com

Hack's Auction Center
www.hacksauction.com

Heritage Chicago
www.ha.com

Leslie Hindman
hindmanauctions.com

Rock Island Auction Company
www.rockislandauction.com

Susanin's Auctions
www.susanins.com

Toomey & Co. Auctioneers
toomeyco.com

Wright
www.wright20.com

INDIANA

Antique Helper & Ripley Auctions
www.antiquehelper.com

Schrader Auction
www.schraderauction.com

Stout Auctions
www.stoutauctions.com

Strawser Auctions
www.strawserauctions.com

IOWA

Jackson's
www.jacksonsauction.com

Tom Harris Auctions
www.tomharrisauctions.com

Tubaugh Auctions
www.tubaughauctions.com

KANSAS
Woody Auction
www.woodyauction.com

KENTUCKY
Hays & Associates
www.haysauction.com

The Sporting Art Auction
www.thesportingartauction.com

LOUISIANA
Crescent City Auction Gallery
www.crescentcityauctiongallery.com

Neal Auction Company
www.nealauction.com

New Orleans Auction Galleries
www.neworleansauction.com

MAINE
Thomaston Place Auction Galleries
www.thomastonauction.com

MARYLAND
Alexander Historical Auctions
www.alexautographs.com

Guyette & Deeter
www.guyetteanddeeter.com

Hantman's Auctioneers & Appraisers
www.hantmans.com

Richard Opfer Auctioneering
www.opferauction.com

Sloans & Kenyon
www.sloansandkenyon.com

Theriault's
www.theriaults.com

MASSACHUSETTS
James R. Bakker Antiques
www.bakkerproject.com

Douglas Auctioneers
www.douglasauctioneers.com

Eldred's
www.eldreds.com

Fontaine's Auction Gallery
fontainesauction.com

Grogan & Company
www.groganco.com

Willis Henry Auctions
www.willishenry.com

Kaminski
www.kaminskiauctions.com

Marion Antiques
www.marionantiqueauctions.com

Rafael Osona
www.rafaelosonaauction.com

Simond & Oakes
www.simondoakes.com

Skinner Inc.
www.skinnerinc.com

Tremont Auctions
www.tremontauctions.com

White's Auctions
www.whitesauctions.com

Willis Henry Auctions Inc.
www.willishenry.com

MICHIGAN
American Auctions
www.americanaauctions.com

Chamberlain's Auction Gallery
www.chamberlainsgallery.com

DuMouchelles
www.dumouchelles.com

MINNESOTA
Luther Auctions
www.lutherauctions.com

MISSISSIPPI
Edens
www.edensauctions.com

European Antique Auction Gallery
www.europeanauctiongallery.com

Stevens Auction Company
www.stevensauction.com

MISSOURI
Link Auction Galleries
www.linkauctiongalleries.com

Regency Superior
www.regencystamps.com

Selkirk Auctioneers & Appraisers
www.selkirkauctions.com

Simmons & Company Auctioneers
www.simmonsauction.com

Soülis Auctions
dirksoulisauctions.com

MONTANA
Allard Auctions Inc.
www.allardauctions.com

NEBRASKA
The Auction Mill
www.theauctionmill.com

Omaha Auction Center Ltd.
omahaauctioncenter.com

Wasner Auction Service
wanserauction.com

NEVADA
Auctions Imperial
auctionsimperial.com

Lightning Auctions, Inc.
www.lightningauctions.com

NEW HAMPSHIRE
Amoskeag Auction Company
www.amoskeagauction.com

The Cobbs
www.thecobbs.com

Gallery at Knotty Pine
www.knottypineantiques.com

Paul McInnis Inc. Auction Gallery
www.paulmcinnis.com

Northeast Auctions
www.northeastauctions.com

William A. Smith
www.wsmithauction.com

Withington Auction
www.withingtonauction.com

NEW JERSEY
Bertoia
www.bertoiaauctions.com

Bodnar's Auction
www.bodnarsauction.com

Dennis Auction Service
www.dennisauction.com

Nye & Co.
nyeandcompany.com

Rago Arts
www.ragoarts.com

Time and Again Auction Gallery
www.timeandagaingalleries.com

Waterford's
www.waterfordsauction.com

NEW MEXICO
Altermann Galleries & Auctioneers
www.altermann.com

Manitou Galleries
www.manitougalleries.com

NEW YORK
Antiquorum
www.antiquorum.com

Auctionata
auctionata.com

Bonhams
www.bonhams.com

Carlsen Gallery
www.carlsengallery.com

Christie's
www.christies.com

Clarke
www.clarkeny.com

Comic Connect
www.comicconnect.com

Copake Auctions
www.copakeauction.com

Cottone Auctions
www.cottoneauctions.com

Doyle New York
www.doylenewyork.com

Guernsey's Auctions
www.guernseys.com

Heritage Auctions
www.ha.com

Hellios Auctions
www.heliosauctions.com

Hesse Galleries
www.hessegalleries.com

William J. Jenack Auctioneers
www.jenack.com

Keno Auctions
www.kenoauctions.com

Kestenbaum & Company
www.kestenbaum.net

Mapes Auction Gallery
www.mapesauction.com

Phillips
www.phillips.com

Roland Antiques
www.rolandsantiques.com

Shapiro Auctions
www.shapiroauctions.com

Sotheby's
www.sothebys.com

Stair Galleries
www.stairgalleries.com

Swann Galleries
www.swanngalleries.com

Philip Weiss Auctions
www.weissauctions.com

NORTH CAROLINA

Brunk Auctions
www.brunkauctions.com

Leland Little
www.lelandlittle.com

Raynor's Historical Collectible Auctions
www.hcaauctions.com

NORTH DAKOTA

Curt D. Johnson Auction Company
www.curtdjohnson.com

Haugland's Action Auction
hauglandsactionauction.com

OHIO

Apple Tree Auction Center
www.appletreeauction.com

Aspire Auctions
www.aspireauctions.com

Cincinnati Art Galleries LLC
www.cincinnatiartgalleries.com

The Cobbs Auctioneers LLC
www.thecobbs.com

Cowan's Historic Americana Auctions
www.cowanauctions.com

Rachel Davis Fine Arts
www.racheldavisfinearts.com

Early Auction Company
www.earlyauctionco.com

Garth's Auctions
www.garths.com

Gray's Autioneers
www.graysauctioneers.com

Treadway Toomey Auctions
www.treadwaygallery.com

OKLAHOMA

Buffalo Bay Auction Co.
www.buffalobayauction.com

OREGON

Antique & Auction Company of Southern Oregon
www.oregonauctionhouse.com

O'Gallerie
www.ogallerie.com

PENNSYLVANIA

Alderfer Auction
www.alderferauction.com

Aspire Auctions
www.aspireauctions.com

Noel Barrett
www.noelbarrett.com

Briggs Auction, Inc.
www.briggsauction.com

William H. Bunch Auctions
www.bunchauctions.com

Concept Art Gallery
www.conceptgallery.com

Cordier Auctions & Appraisals
www.cordierauction.com

Dargate Auction Galleries
www.dargate.com

Freeman's
www.freemansauction.com

Hunt Auctions
www.huntauctions.com

James D. Julia Auctioneers
(now part of Morphy Auctions)
www.morphyauctions.com

Kamelot Auctions
www.kamelotauctions.com

Morphy Auctions
www.morphyauctions.com

Pook & Pook Inc.
www.pookandpook.com

Stephenson's
www.stephensonsauction.com

Witman Auctioneers
www.witmanauctioneers.com

RHODE ISLAND

Bruneau & Co. Auctioneers
bruneauandco.com

Web Wilson
www.webwilson.com

SOUTH CAROLINA

Charlton Hall
www.charltonhallauctions.com

Wooten & Wooten
www.wootenandwooten.com

SOUTH DAKOTA

Charles J. Fischer Agency
www.fischerauction.com

Girard Auction & Land Brokers, Inc.
www.girardauction.com

TENNESSEE

Berenice Denton Estate Sales and Appraisals
www.berenicedenton.com

Case Antiques
caseantiques.com

Kimball M. Sterling Inc.
www.sterlingsold.com

TEXAS

Altermann Galleries & Auctioneers
www.altermann.com

Austin Auction Gallery
www.austinauction.com

Dallas Auction Gallery
www.dallasauctiongallery.com

Gallery Auctions Inc.
www.galleryauctions.com

Houston Auction Company
www.houstonauctionco.com

Simpson Galleries
www.simpsongalleries.com

Heritage Auctions
www.ha.com

UTAH

Silcox Auctions
www.silcoxauction.com

VERMONT

Townsend Auction Gallery
townshendauctions.com

VIRGINIA

Bremo Auctions
bremoauctions.com

Jeffrey S. Evans & Associates
www.jeffreysevans.com

Ken Farmer & Associates
www.kfauctions.com

Freeman's
www.freemansauction.com

Green Valley Auctions & Moving Inc.
www.greenvalleyauctions.com

Old World Auctions
www.oldworldauctions.com

Phoebus Auction Gallery
www.phoebusauction.com

Quinn's Auction Galleries
www.quinnsauction.com

WASHINGTON

Mroczek Brothers
www.mbaauction.com

Pacific Galleries Auction House
www.pacgal.com

WASHINGTON DC

Seattle Auction House
www.seattleauctionhouse.com

Weschler's
www.weschlers.com

WEST VIRGINIA

Adkins Auctions
www.adkinsauction.com

Cozart Auction Service
cozartauctions.com

WISCONSIN

Leslie Hindman
hindmanauctions.com

Krueger's Auctions
www.kruegersauctions.com

WYOMING

Auction in Santa Fe
www.auctioninsantafe.com

CANADA

ALBERTA

Hall's Auction Services Ltd.
www.hallsauction.com

Hodgins Art Auctions Ltd.
www.hodginsauction.com

Lando Art Auctions
www.landoartauctions.com

BRITISH COLUMBIA

Augeo Gallery
augeogallery.com

Bolylin Auction
www.bolylin.com

Gosby Antiques
gosby.ca

Heffel Fine Art Auction House
www.heffel.com

Kilshaw's Auctioneers
www.kilshaws.com

Maynards Fine Art Auction House
www.maynards.com

Waddington's
www.waddingtons.ca

Westbridge Fine Art
www.westbridge-fineart.com

ONTARIO

888 Auctions
www.888auctions.com

A Touch of Class
www.atouchofclassauctions.com

Auction Network
auctionnetwork.ca

Dupuis
dupuis.ca

Eins Auction
einsauction.com

Empire Auctions
www.toronto.empireauctions.com

The Great Estate Sale
www.thegreatestatesale.com

Heffel Fine Art Auction House
www.heffel.com

Ritchies
www.rbauction.com

Sotheby's
www.sothebys.com

Waddington's
www.waddingtons.ca

Walker's
www.walkersauctions.com

A.H. Wilkens
ahwilkens.com

QUEBEC

Empire Auctions
www.montreal.empireauctions.com

Enchères Champagne
champagneauctions.ca

Iegor - Hôtel des Encans
www.iegor.net

Kavanagh Auctions
kavanaghauctions.com

Montréal Auction House
pages.videotron.com/encans

Valeona Gallery Inc.
valeona.com

AUCTIONEERS

INTERNET RESOURCES

Miller's Antiques & Collectables
www.millersguides.com

@millersantiques

1stdibs
www.1stdibs.com

ADA
www.adadealers.com

Antique Trail
www.antiquetrail.com

The Antiques Trade Gazette
www.antiquestradegazette.com

Auction.fr
www.auction.fr

BADA
www.bada.org

Barnebys
www.barnebys.co.uk

Bidsquare
www.bidsquare.com

Collectors Weekly
www.collectorsweekly.com

eBay
www.ebay.com

Go Antiques
www.goantiques.com

La Gazette du Drouot
www.drouot.com

LAPADA
www.lapada.org

Live Auctioneers
www.liveauctioneers.com

Maine Antique Digest
www.maineantiquedigest.com

Rubylane
www.rubylane.com

Rubylux
www.rubylux.com

The Saleroom
www.the-saleroom.com

WorthPoint
www.worthpoint.com

The following list is organized by the type of collectible. If you would like your club, society, or organization to appear in our next edition, or would like to update your details, please contact us at publisher@octopusbooks.co.uk

GENERAL
The North American Collectibles Association
www.nacacollectors.com

ADVERTISING
Antique Advertising Association of America
www.pastimes.org

Coca-Cola Collectors Club
www.cocacolaclub.org

ANTIQUITIES
Association of Dealers & Collectors of Ancient & Ethnographic Art
adcaea.wildapricot.org

BOOKS
Antiquarian Booksellers' Association of America
www.abaa.org

CAMERAS
The American Society of Camera Collectors
cameracollectors.wordpress.com

The Ohio Camera Collector's Society
historiccamera.com

CANES
International Association of Antique Umbrella and Cane Collectors
www.antiquecaneworld.com

CERAMICS
American Art Pottery Association
www.aapa.info

American Ceramic Circle
www.americanceramiccircle.org

Tansferware Collectors Club
www.transcollectorsclub.org

Homer Laughlin China Collectors' Association
www.hlcca.org

M.I. Hummel Club
www.hummelgifts.com

National Shelley China Club
www.shelleychinaclub.com

Southern Folk Potter Collectors Society
www.southernfolkpotterysociety.com

CLOCKS
National Association of Watch & Clock Collectors
www.nawcc.org

COMICS & ANNUALS
CGC Collectors Society
comics.www.collectors-society.com

DOLLS
Annalee Doll Society
www.annalee.com

National Antique Doll Dealers Association
www.nadda.org

United Federation of Doll Clubs
ufdc.org

FANS
Fan Association of North America
fanassociation.org

FASHION
The Costume Society of America
www.costumesocietyamerica.com

International Organization of Lace
www.internationalorganizationoflace.org

FILM & TV MEMORABILIA
Disneyana Fan Club
www.disneyanafanclub.org

GLASS
American Carnival Glass Association
www.myacga.com

National Imperial Glass Collectors' Society
www.imperialglass.org

JEWELRY
The American Hatpin Society
www.americanhatpinsociety.com

Costume Jewely Collectors International
www.costumejewelrycollectors.com

Jewelcollect
www.jewelcollect.org

LIGHTING
Historical Lighting Society of Canada
www.historical-lighting.org

National Association of Aladdin Lamp Collectors Inc.
www.aladdincollectors.org

MECHANICAL BANKS
Mechanical Bank Collectors of America
www.mechanicalbanks.org

MECHANICAL MUSIC
The Musical Box Society International
www.mbsi.org

The Automatic Musical Instrument Collectors' Association
www.amica.org

MILITARIA
Association of American Military Uniform Collectors
www.aamuc.org

Medal Collectors of America
www.medalcollectors.org

The Society of American Bayonet Collectors
bayonetcollectors.org

PAPERWEIGHTS
Paperweight Collectors Association Inc.
www.paperweight.org

PENS & WRITING
The American Pencil Collectors Society
www.pencilcollector.org

Pen Collectors of America
pencollectorsofamerica.org

The Society of Inkwell Collectors
soicmember.com

POSTCARDS
San Francisco Bay Area Post Card Club
www.postcard.org

POSTERS
The International Vintage Poster Dealers Association
www.ivpda.com

SCENT BOTTLES
International Perfume Bottle Association
www.perfumebottles.org

SEWING
Thimble Collectors International
thimblecollectors.com

SILVER
International Association of Silver Art Collectors
thesilverbugle.com

SMOKING
The North American Society of Pipe Collectors
www.naspc.org

SPORTING
Golf Collectors' Society
www.golfcollectors.com

National Fishing Lure Collectors' Club
www.nflcc.com

Society for American Baseball Research
www.sabr.org

Tennis Collectors of America
tenniscollectors.org

TECHNOLOGY
Antique Wireless Association
www.antiquewireless.org

TEDDY BEARS
The Steiff Club
www.steiffusa.com

TOYS & GAMES
Antique Toy Collectors of America
www.atca-club.org

Canadian Toy Collectors Society
www.ctcs.org

Chess Collectors' International
chesscollectormagazine.sharepoint.com

Lionel Collectors Club of America
www.lionelcollectors.org

Miniature Figure Collectors of America
www.mfcashow.com

National Model Railroad Association
www.nmra.org

The Train Collectors Association
www.traincollectors.org

TRIBAL ART
Antique Tribal Art Dealers Association
www.atada.org

WATCHES
Early American Watch Club
www.nawcc-ch149.com

National Association of Watch & Clock Collectors
www.nawcc.org

WINE & DRINKING
International Correspondence of Corkscrew Addicts
the-icca.net